MATHEMATICS OF
AUTONOMY
Mathematical Methods for
Cyber-Physical-Cognitive Systems

T0350197

MATHEMATICS OF
AUTONOMY
Mathematical Methods for
Cyber-Physical-Cognitive Systems

Vladimir G Ivancevic

Darryn J Reid

Michael J Pilling

Defence Science & Technology Group, Australia

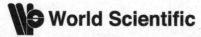 **World Scientific**

NEW JERSEY · LONDON · SINGAPORE · BEIJING · SHANGHAI · HONG KONG · TAIPEI · CHENNAI · TOKYO

Published by

World Scientific Publishing Co. Pte. Ltd.

5 Toh Tuck Link, Singapore 596224

USA office: 27 Warren Street, Suite 401-402, Hackensack, NJ 07601

UK office: 57 Shelton Street, Covent Garden, London WC2H 9HE

Library of Congress Cataloging-in-Publication Data

Names: Ivancevic, Vladimir G., author. | Reid, Darryn J., author. | Pilling, M. J., author.
Title: Mathematics of autonomy : mathematical methods for cyber-physical-cognitive systems /
   by Vladimir G. Ivancevic (Defence Science & Technology Group, Australia),
   Darryn J. Reid (Defence Science & Technology Group, Australia),
   Michael J. Pilling (Defence Science & Technology Group, Australia).
Description: [Hackensack] New Jersey : World Scientific, [2017] |
   Includes bibliographical references and index.
Identifiers: LCCN 2017039522 | ISBN 9789813230385 (hardcover : alk. paper)
Subjects: LCSH: Intelligent control systems--Mathematics. | Self-organizing systems--
   Mathematical models. | Cooperating objects (Computer systems)
Classification: LCC TJ217.5 .I93 2017 | DDC 003/.7--dc23
LC record available at https://lccn.loc.gov/2017039522

British Library Cataloguing-in-Publication Data
A catalogue record for this book is available from the British Library.

Printed in Singapore

Preface

Mathematics of Autonomy is a graduate-level monographic textbook, intended to be a novel and rigorous contribution to modern theory of *trusted autonomous systems*.

Mathematics of Autonomy contains nine Chapters and two Appendices. Chapter 1 gives: (i) a comprehensive introduction to trusted autonomy, (ii) introduces the more specific concept of *cyber-physical-cognitive* (CPC) autonomy that can be rigorously analyzed, and (iii) gives the necessary technical preliminaries for competent reading of the monograph. Chapter 2 presents the physics of interconnected autonomous systems in the form of Port-Hamiltonian network dynamics and its categorical abstraction. Chapter 3 gives the first CPC-application: autonomous supervisor for a swarm of robots based on the Nobel-awarded hippocampus path integration system. Chapter 4 deals with micro-cognitive autonomy in the form of entangled quantum-computational tensor networks. Chapter 5 presents cyber-cognitive autonomous systems: TensorFlow and other deep neural networks. Chapter 6 reviews cognitive control in autonomous systems, in the form of perceptual control theory and its alternatives. Chapter 7 gives the second CPC-application: using a controlled wind turbulence as a soft attrition model against a team of autonomous vehicles. Chapter 8 presents recursive Bayesian techniques for cognitive estimation in autonomous systems and FastSLAM algorithms. Chapter 9 presents the general super-dynamics formalism for a universal, large-scale, autonomous operation. Appendix 1 gives a review of tensor methodology and Appendix 2 gives a review of classical neural networks and artificial intelligence in general.

Primary target readership for *Mathematics of Autonomy* are all experts and students of autonomous systems, both in industry and in academia.

The book would also be interesting for both undergraduate and graduate-level students of mechatronics, robotics, electrical and mechanical engineering, signal processing, computer science and AI, psychology, physics and applied mathematics.

As a textbook, *Mathematics of Autonomy* is designed for a one-semester course in mathematical methods for autonomous systems, at either last-year undergraduate level or first-year graduate level.

Adelaide, 1st March, 2017   Authors

Vladimir.Ivancevic@dst.defence.gov.au
Darryn.Reid@dst.defence.gov.au
Michael.Pilling@dst.defence.gov.au

Joint and Operations Analysis Division
Defence Science & Technology Group

Acknowledgments

The authors are very grateful to the Joint and Operations Analysis Division, Defence Science and Technology Group, Australia, and in particular to Dr. Jason Scholz, Research Leader, Trusted Autonomous Systems and Dr. Sharon Boswell, Ag Group Leader, Behaviour and Control, as well as Dr. Jennifer Palmer, Aerospace Division — for their valuable support.

We also express our gratitude to *World Scientific Publishing Company*, and especially to the Editor, Ms. Lai Fun KWONG.

Glossary of Acronyms

Adaptive Autonomy A mode in which the autonomous computing agent has exclusive control of the system, and allocates tasks to the human operator as it sees fit.

Adjustable Autonomy A mode in which the human has exclusive control of the system, deciding which tasks to delegate to autonomous computing subsystems.

AI Artificial Intelligence.

ATC Air Traffic Control.

Autonomic System A system with capacity to measure its own capacity, health and performance and either report its "health" or preferably reconfigure itself as appropriate (see subsection 1.2.3).

Authorised Entity An individual [human] operator or [machine] control element authorized to direct or control system functions or mission.

AUAS Autonomous UAS.

AUV Autonomous Underwater Vehicle.

CPC Autonomy Cyber-Physical-Cognitive autonomy (see section 1.4).

DARPA Defense Advanced Research Projects Agency (US).

Drone Any remotely piloted vehicle.

DSS Decision Support System. A system designed to aid humans reaching decisions.

Firing Autonomy The ability of an automated system to commence firing / engagement without recourse to a human.

Full Autonomy Firing Autonomy + Target Selection Autonomy.

GCS Ground Control Station.

GPS Global Positioning System, a space-based satellite navigation system that provides location and time information in all weather conditions, anywhere on or near the Earth where there is an unobstructed line of sight to four or more GPS satellites.[1]

---

[1] See Wikipedia: Global Positioning System, (2016).

Heterachical System One in which no entity in the system exerts a permanently dominant influence on the system elements.

HFT High Frequency Trader. A trader that uses algorithms to move in and out of positions is seconds or fractions of a second.

HMI Human Machine Interface. The physical or software tools and processes by which the human and machine communicate.

ICRC International Committee of the Red Cross. The part of the Red Cross movement that deals specifically with the Geneva Conventions.

IHL International Humanitarian Law.

IHRL International Human Rights Law.

ILS Instrument Landing System: A ground-based instrument approach system that provides precision guidance to an aircraft approaching and landing on a runway, using a combination of radio signals and, in many cases, high-intensity lighting arrays to enable a safe landing during instrument meteorological conditions, such as low ceilings or reduced visibility due to fog, rain, or blowing snow.[2]

In-the-loop Refers to the sense-think-act loop used by automations. "In" refers to a human, inserted into this repeatedly executed sequence to approve significant actions, usually decisions to target, engage or fire.

IoT Internet of Things.[3]

IW Information Warfare.

LAR see Lethal Autonomous Robots.

Lethal Autonomous Robots A term used by the UN defined as a weapons system that, once activated, can select and engage targets without further human intervention.

Lidar Light detection and ranging: A remote sensing technology that measures distance by illuminating a target with a laser and analyzing the reflected light.

LOA Level of Automation.

LOAC Law of Armed Conflict. Includes IHR and IHRL.

MAS Multi-Agent System(s).

Mixed Initiative A system mode in which the human and autonomous computing agent share responsibility for allocating tasks between the computing system and the human. Each may request the other to perform a function it finds difficult to perform alone.

Network Centric Warfare (NCW) The linking of sensors, engagement systems and decision-makers [across multiple platforms] into an effective and responsive whole.

NGO Non-government organization. A community group, often a charity or not-for-profit organization. For example, the Red Cross.

---

[2] See Wikipedia: Instrument Landing System, (2016).

[3] See Wikipedia: Internet of Things, (2016).

On-the-loop A human approval is not needed to action decisions, but it is intended a human will intervene and countermand any inappropriate decision. See in-the-loop.

Operator A human in command of some aspect of a system.

Out-of-the-loop No human is in-the-loop and the system can action its decisions without oversight: see in-the-loop.

Outside-the-loop See Out-of-the-loop.

Remote Operation Systems which allow the pilot or operator of a system to be physically distant from the actual hardware or weapon, operating it by a communications link which provides sensor information and the ability to command the system from a remote location.

ROE Rules of Engagement.

Semi Autonomous A system which can make some autonomous decisions within a highly constrained range of choices prescribed by a human, often with respect to the low-risk or mundane parts of a mission such as navigating automatically to a human defined destination but not choosing that destination.

Shared Situation Awareness Situation Awareness in which the overall perception of elements is distributed among multiple human or automated entities. The overall awareness is formed by the union of each entities awareness. Each entity's awareness may overlap with those of others but should not conflict with them. Ideally, each entity should have enough awareness of the environment being managed by other entities they are directly working with to be able to quickly recover full local awareness should any entity fail or leave.

Situation Awareness There are several definitions, but a commonly accepted one is: The perception of elements in the environment within a volume of time and space, the comprehension of their meaning, and the projection of their status in the near future.

Supervised Autonomy An autonomous system with a human outside-the-loop monitoring it with view to overriding its decisions.

T & E Test and Evaluation.

Target Selection Autonomy A system where the automation is free to select targets based on its own assessment of their relative military value.

Temporary Autonomy The ability of a system to continue to perform some useful functions autonomously in between operator commands.

Test and Evaluation The process by which a system or components are compared against requirements and specifications through testing. The results are evaluated to assess progress of design, performance, supportability, etc. Developmental test and evaluation is an engineering tool used to reduce risk throughout the defense acquisition cycle.

Threat Evaluation The process of determining if an entity intends to inflict evil, injury or damage to our forces or their interests, along with ranking these entities according to their level of threat.

UAS Uninhabited Air System. A UAV including its support systems such as the remote pilot, maintenance staff, landing area, remote computing support, network connectivity etc.

UAV Uninhabited Air Vehicle.

UCAV Uninhabited Combat Air Vehicle. A UAV that is armed.

UGV Uninhabited Ground Vehicle.

V & V Verification and Validation.

Verification and Validation Independent procedures that are used together for checking that a product, service, or system meets requirements and specifications and that it fulfills its intended purpose.

Weapons Allocation The assignment of weapon systems to engage or counter identified threats.

Glossary of Symbols

General Conventions

– 'iff' means 'if and only if';
– DOF(s) means degree(s)-of-freedom;
– AI means artificial intelligence;
– ODE(s) means ordinary differential equation(s), PDE(s) means partial differential equation(s) and DAE(s) means differential-algebraic equation(s);
– TNT means tensor network theory; TFT means topological field theory;
– *Einstein's summation convention over repeated indices* (not necessarily one up and one down) *is assumed always,* unless explicitly stated otherwise; e.g., $-J_{ij}\sigma_i\sigma_j = -\sum_i^n \sum_j^n J_{ij}\sigma_i\sigma_j$ is the Ising spin Hamiltonian;
– nD system (space, group) means n−dimensional system (space, group), for $n \in \mathbb{N}$; e.g., 2D means two-dimensional, etc.

Sets

$\mathbb{N}$ – natural numbers;
$\mathbb{Z}$ – integers;
$\mathbb{R}$ – real numbers;
$\mathbb{C}$ – complex numbers.

Maps

$f : A \to B$ – a function, (or map) between sets $A \equiv \mathrm{Dom}\, f$ and $B \equiv \mathrm{Cod}\, f$;

$$\mathrm{Ker}\, f = f^{-1}(e_B) - \text{a kernel of } f;$$

$$\mathrm{Im}\, f = f(A) - \text{an image of } f;$$

$$\mathrm{Coker}\, f = \mathrm{Cod}\, f / \mathrm{Im}\, f - \text{a cokernel of } f;$$

$$\mathrm{Coim}\, f = \mathrm{Dom}\, f / \mathrm{Ker}\, f - \text{a coimage of } f;$$

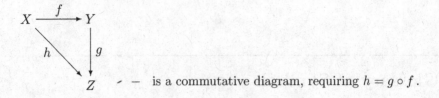

$-$ $-$ is a commutative diagram, requiring $h = g \circ f$.

Derivatives

$C^\infty(A, B)$ – set of *smooth* functions between sets A to B;
$C^0(A, B)$ – set of *continuous* functions between sets A to B;
$f'(x) = \frac{df(x)}{dx}$ – derivative of f with respect to x;
$\dot{x}$ – total time derivative of x;
$\partial_t \equiv \frac{\partial}{\partial t}$ – partial time derivative;
$\partial_{x^i} \equiv \partial_i \equiv \frac{\partial}{\partial x^i}$ – partial coordinate derivative;
$\dot{f} = \partial_t f + \partial_{x^i} f \, \dot{x}^i$ – total time derivative of the scalar field $f = f(t, x^i)$;
$u_t \equiv \partial_t u$, $u_x \equiv \partial_x u$, $u_{xx} \equiv \partial_{x^2} u$ – only in partial differential equations;
$L_{x^i} \equiv \partial_{x^i} L$, $L_{\dot{x}^i} \equiv \partial_{\dot{x}^i} L$ – coordinate and velocity partial derivatives of the Lagrangian function;
d – exterior derivative;
d^n – coboundary operator;
∂_n – boundary operator;
$\nabla = \nabla(g)$ – affine Levi–Civita connection on a smooth manifold M with Riemannian metric tensor $g = g_{ij}$;
Γ^i_{jk} – Christoffel symbols of the affine connection ∇;
$\nabla_X T$ – covariant derivative of the tensor–field T with respect to the vector–field X, defined by means of Γ^i_{jk};
$T_{;x^i} \equiv T_{|x^i}$ – covariant derivative of the tensor–field T with respect to the coordinate basis $\{x^i\}$;
$\mathcal{L}_X T$ – Lie derivative of the tensor–field T in direction of the vector–field X;
$[X, Y]$ – Lie bracket (commutator) of two vector–fields X and Y;
$\{F, G\}$ – Poisson bracket of two functions F and G.

Manifolds and Bundles

Unless otherwise specified, all *manifolds* $M, N, \ldots$ are assumed C^∞–smooth, real, compact, finite–dimensional, Hausdorff, connected and without boundary,[4] while all maps are assumed smooth (C^∞). We use the symbols $\otimes$, $\vee$, $\wedge$ and $\oplus$ for the tensor, symmetrized and exterior products, as well as the Whitney sum,[5] respectively, while $\rfloor$ denotes the interior product (contraction) of

---

[4] The only 1D manifolds obeying these conditions are the real line $\mathbb{R}$ and the circle S^1.
[5] *Whitney sum* $\oplus$ is an analog of the direct (Cartesian) product for vector bundles. Given two vector bundles Y and Y' over the same base X, their Cartesian product

(multi)vectors and p–forms.

TM – tangent bundle of the manifold M;

$\pi_M : TM \to M$ – natural projection;

T^*M – cotangent bundle of the manifold M;

$\pi : Y \to X$ – fibre bundle;

(E, π, M) – vector bundle with total space E, base M and projection π.

Lie and (Co)Homology Groups

$GL(n)$ – general linear group with real coefficients in dimension n;

$SO(n)$ – group of rotations in dimension n;

T^n – toral (Abelian) group in dimension n;

$T(n)$ – group of translations in dimension n;

$SE(n)$ – Euclidean group in dimension n;

$H_n(M) = \operatorname{Ker} \partial_n / \operatorname{Im} \partial_{n-1}$ – nth homology group of the manifold M;

$H^n(M) = \operatorname{Ker} d^n / \operatorname{Im} d^{n+1}$ – nth cohomology group of the manifold M.

Other Spaces and Operators

$i \equiv \sqrt{-1}$ – imaginary unit;

$C^\infty(M)$ – space of k–differentiable functions on the manifold M;

$\Omega^k(M)$ – space of k–forms on the manifold M;

$\mathfrak{g}$ – Lie algebra of a Lie group G, i.e., the tangent space of G at its identity element;

$Ad(g)$ – adjoint endomorphism; recall that *adjoint representation* of a Lie group G is the linearized version of the action of G on itself by conjugation, i.e., for each $g \in G$, the inner automorphism $x \mapsto gxg^{-1}$ gives a linear transformation $Ad(g) : \mathfrak{g} \to \mathfrak{g}$, from the Lie algebra $\mathfrak{g}$ of G to itself;

$\triangleright$ – semidirect (noncommutative) product; e.g., $SE(3) = SO(3) \triangleright \mathbb{R}^3$;

$\psi(x, t)$ – complex-valued spatiotemporal wave function, whose absolute square $|\psi(x, t)|^2$ represents the probability density function (PDF) of a quantum-mechanical system defined by the Schrödinger wave equation;

$\oint$ – Feynman path integral symbol, denoting integration over continuous spectrum of smooth paths and summation over discrete spectrum of Markov chains; e.g., $\oint \mathcal{D}[x]\, e^{iS[x]}$ denotes the sum over all possible paths $x^i = x^i(t)$ defined by the action: $S[x] = \frac{1}{2} \int_{t_0}^{t_1} g_{ij}\, \dot{x}^i \dot{x}^j \, dt$.

---

is a vector bundle over $X \times X$. The *diagonal map* induces a vector bundle over X called the Whitney sum of these vector bundles and denoted by $Y \oplus Y'$.

Contents

1

Introduction

In this Chapter we firstly introduce the concept of *trusted autonomous systems*. Then we define a rigorous model of trusted autonomy in the form of *cyber-physical-cognitive* (CPC) autonomy. Finally, we provide the necessary technical preliminaries for comprehensive reading of the monograph.

1.1 Autonomous Systems

Autonomous Systems are the fast building new wave of computing research and without judicious management of their development and deployment including understanding of the trust issues that pervade their use, one critical failure could destroy the social licence for their development and deployment.[1]

This book focuses on *artificial autonomy* — artificial systems that exhibit autonomous behavior — and trust issues surrounding artificial autonomy.

Artificial Autonomy offers many potential benefits for humanity, this introduction broadly examines uses, issues and technologies of artificial autonomy with a view to how they might be built or engineered to reliably produce trustworthy systems. While potential and deployed artificial autonomy applications span a wide gamet including decision making, classification, market trading, space exploration, vehicle guidance and defence applications; much research pertaining to artificial autonomy has been performed on robotics platforms which can inform more general artificial autonomy issues including legalities, ethics and maintaining a social licence. This book does not examine questions of human autonomy, except with respect to how humans interact with artificial autonomy, and it is generally left up to the reader to recognise when the autonomy referred to is human or artificial.

Autonomous systems are intended for use in dangerous, tedious, exacting and often safety critical applications such as warfighting, mining, extreme

---

[1] Experience shows it only take one mishap during early operations or research experiments to turn public opinion against whole areas of research [MW09].

environments, self driving cars, invalid care and even surgery. For instance, P. W. Singer [Sin09b] describes the robotics revolution as the next major revolution in military affairs, akin to gunpowder and nuclear weapons. According to Singer [Sin09a], as of 2009 44 countries were developing robotic weapons systems including the UK, France, Russia, China, Israel, Iran and the UAE. As such the notion of trust becomes absolutely critical in delivering systems that can safely perform their required function without exposing humans to unacceptable risk and, therefore, will be adopted and used.

The military have been at the forefront of investigating autonomous systems due to the immense benefits on offer:

> The over-riding motivation for moving to unmanned systems is a desire to deliver new or enhanced capability by embracing new technology while reducing costs and the threat to personnel [MoD11].

There are huge potential military advantages in deploying autonomous systems [Hey13]: they offer higher force projection and force multiplication and can do the dirty, dangerous and dull work. They offer the possibility of using less than lethal force, and to provide a digital trail of their decision making in a way that would enhance accountability. Their reaction time may be far superior to that of humans and the increasing tempo of warfare can leave humans as the weakest link. Their strengths such as lack of fatigue, fast reaction time, ability to process huge amounts of data, and to find the most unexpected correlations can potentially complement the best human characteristics such as "intuition", fine judgement and compassion. They can also continue to operate, in a perhaps degraded manner, when communication with the command structure is unavailable.

Ideally, and as we shall see, in a sense unavoidably autonomous systems will be implemented and deployed in a way that forms "teams" which take full advantage of the complementary strengths of humans and automations. Teamwork requires trust, but before we tackle trust, lets consider what is autonomy.

1.1.1 What is an Autonomous System?

We note that the Oxford dictionary defines a *system* to include "a set of things working together as parts of a mechanism or an interconnecting network; a complex whole" and "a set of principles or procedures according to which something is done; an organized scheme or method". It defines *autonomy* as "the right or condition of self-government" and also notes "(in Kantian moral philosophy) the capacity of an agent to act in accordance with objective morality rather than under the influence of desires".

While philosophical discussions of what autonomy is in human terms are both interesting and useful in their own right; just as understanding the way tailors stitched together garments was not particularly helpful in developing effective sewing machines, understanding human autonomy does not appear to overly inform building useful Autonomous Systems so we do not cover such arguments here.

There is no single, generally accepted definition of autonomy and autonomous systems in the literature. Worse still, the discourse on autonomy in general is confounded by the conflation of several types of systems that operate with minimal human intervention. However, it is clear that a spectrum of increasing environmental uncertainty and hence system complexity and adaptability exists between Automatic Systems, Automation and Autonomous Systems. We now propose working definitions of these places along that spectrum:

Automatic Systems are rigid and operate with limited or negligible human intervention. They have very limited inputs, both in terms of number of dimensions and in having defined ranges or a small number of discrete values. The only way they embody a history of their interactions is through which of a limited number of system states is current. The output for each combination of inputs and system state is predefined and is a deterministic simple function of that combination.

Automatic systems are the simplest class of system in the spectrum of automation complexity and are typically rigid in their operation. They are often direct implementations of mundane human physical or cognitive work into a machine. Examples include: the simplest type of traffic lights which operate either on a timed loop, or respond to simple inputs such as pedestrian request buttons and under road car sensors which may accelerate the next signal change in the absence of conflicting inputs; simpler building elevator control systems; simple railway signals that transmit stop and caution signals down the line in the presence of a train; simple automatic transmissions that set the gear based purely on the current speed of the car. Many alarms and fail-safe mechanisms are implemented with automatic systems, in part because such simple systems have fewer failure modes.

Automations are more complex systems dealing with more complex inputs that exhibit considerable complexity and may have a large volume of data or many different types of input. Nevertheless, these inputs and their values are well defined and bounded and their meaning is well understood by the system designer. Moreover the environment or context of an automation is tightly constrained and presents risks to the system that can be quantified by stochastic risk analysis. The outputs of automations may be a simple or complex function of the current inputs and the history of inputs and system state but is well defined and understood *a priori* by the system's designers. Automation outputs are deterministic functions of inputs unless deliberately randomized to achieve optimization, fairness or secrecy.

The generally deterministic or specifically random nature of automations mean they can be tested by input elaboration, at least if one had infinite time. Alternatively, a formal proof of correctness may be possible. When automation inputs fall outside of their design expectations, a common response is for the automation to shutdown and return control to its operators or to fail-safe. For example an autopilot will disengage and return control to the human pilot, or a nuclear reactor control system will perform an emergency shutdown.

Automations represent an intermediate area on the spectrum of automation complexity. Examples of automations include: networked traffic lights or train control that include aspects of scheduling, system optimization or adapting to recent or repeated historic demands; process control systems for manufacturing; sophisticated automatic gearboxes that learn the driving patterns of their users to optimism future gear choices; Roomba type vacuum cleaners lie somewhere in the spectrum between automatic systems and automations depending on the sophistication of their programming; Autopilots; and the Traffic Collision Avoidance System (TCAS). Although TCAS is clearly giving directions autonomously, and it could be argued to be an autonomous system, we believe it is simple enough to be considered just an automated system because the mapping between well defined input data and outputs is clearly elaboratable at design time. It is also convenient for us to reserve the definition of autonomous systems to ones which we find particularly challenging to design and build. In this way our definition of autonomous systems will focus our attention on precisely those systems that we wish to build, but currently lack sufficient understanding of, to reliably engineer on demand.

Autonomous Systems operate in highly complex environments where the inputs to the system can include values or dimensions unforeseen at design time. The data environment is often infinite in potential range and dimensions requiring data reduction by selection, filtering and interpretation (i.e. several conclusions may be drawn from the data and it is important that the machine's deal with the appropriate ones while ignoring those that are irrelevant). Alternatively, the meaning of the data can be contextually dependent on a highly variable or even chaotic system. Such environments exhibit unquantifiable uncertainty. The outputs generated by such inputs can not be fully predicted at design time and the system designers may use methods such as heuristics or machine learning to limit outputs to "acceptable" as opposed to singularly correct ones.[2] They are autonomous in the sense that their decisions or actions are not totally foreseeable at design time, but may generate unexpected novel solutions. The system's decision criteria or decision algorithms are often emergent properties of the system's history of inputs and its interactions with its environment over time. In this sense they are self governing. Once commanded by their operator, most autonomous systems operate for significant periods or over significant volumes of data without seeking or requiring further human guidance even when unexpected inputs arise. Unlike lower level systems, such commands tend to be strategic or at least operational.

---

[2] The problems faced by Autonomous Systems are too complex to assume a single correct solution exists, or that the system will have time to find an optimal result. Herbert A. Simon coined term "satisficing" [Sat09, Sat14] expresses this idea of searching for a solution that meets minimum criteria, however unlike his postulated "Administrative Man" Autonomous Systems should perform affordable partial optimization.

The range, dimensions and highly variable nature of data input to autonomous systems preclude system testing solely by elaboration of input cases, and preclude complete formal proofs of correctness. Autonomous Systems are generally goal directed, executing multiple steps to achieve their goal(s), and many Autonomous Systems must engage in some level of multi-step forward planning in order to fulfil their mission. Larger autonomous systems also need to actively manage their own operation, which requires various levels of autonomic capability[3] (see section 1.2.3).

Autonomous systems represent the most complex area in the spectrum of automation. Examples of autonomous systems include proposed deep space vehicle control systems that reconfigure themselves from software component libraries [SA09], data mining systems that develop new correlations from masses of input data and control systems that learn from being exposed repeatedly to their environment and modify their behavior.

It is immediately clear from our definition of Autonomous Systems the prime role that trust plays in their effective use and hence effective development. Given that unlike other lower level systems on the autonomy spectrum we can not rigourously test them, nor prove them correct, we must find ways of establishing sufficient trust in them to allow their use. This has implications for their development because we must not only develop them to work but also to demonstrate their trustworthiness in ways that are convincing but not misleading.

These three definitions represent exemplars on the spectrum of automation, however it is important to note that systems representing more complex levels of automation may contain subsystems lower in the spectrum of automation complexity. It makes perfect sense for autonomous systems to contain some automatic systems, just as animals relegate some responses to reflexes rather than engaging the brain. Many systems will not fall entirely under one of the definitions given above but lie somewhere between automatic and automated systems, or somewhere between automated and autonomous systems.

Despite our definitions, it is awkward to avoid the venacular usages of "automation" so throughout this book we use "automation" in lower case as a noun to refer to this entire spectrum, and as a verb to refer to the process of increasing the complexity or level of automation; and refer to our definitions using capitals.

Given the above discussion, we can now define autonomy as it applies to systems or machines:

The *autonomy* is the ability of a system or machine to operate for a significant period of time, or over significant volumes of data, without further external human direction while progressing socially agreed or directed goals even when faced with unexpected situations.

---

[3] The capacity to self monitor and to self regulate.

We note that this definition could equally be applied to human systems such as corporations or public service departments provided we distinguish between external directions and those originating from within the organization. It is appropriate that this definition spans both human and non-human systems because being autonomous does not imply operating as a sole agent but operating within a social context. Clearly a system that operated randomly or purely to its own ends would exhibit a form of autonomy, however in this paper we are only interested in systems which are useful to build. Moreover, humans exhibiting such extreme random or purely selfish behavior, as opposed to socialized autonomy, are labeled insane or criminal. Acceptable autonomy always occurs within a social construction, even if that construction occurs at design time, and effective autonomous agents operate as part of a team. Interestingly such a definition of autonomy was not one we had foreseen when commencing this work but rather one that emerged when the paradox of autonomy became apparent: being usefully autonomous requires interdependence. This leads us nicely into our discussion of trust.

1.2 What is Trust and Why Do We Need It?

Intuitively, we know that trust makes the world go round. The world and its problems are too large for a single person or organization to tackle in isolation for any problem of significant size. Trust enables a party to delegate work, especially work they do not does not specialism in, to other parties to perform. With Autonomous Systems, we are generally not talking about trust in the emotional or intimate sense, but just in the sense of being able to organdie to work together for a socially agreed goal. Nevertheless, we will see that the calculus of human trust can inform which factors we choose to include in machine trust. Parties that delegate need to have confidence in the outcome of their delegation so we adopt the working hypothesis that:

Trust is the expectation of a trusting party of sufficient predictability in another trusted party that:

1. The trusted party will do what they say they do
2. The trusted party will inform you in a timely manner if they can't (because circumstances change)
3. In the worst case, the trusting party will be able to live with the outcome if the trusted party fails to live up to their promises

and refine this as we discuss approaches in the literature.

Consider the trust that is needed to work in teams with Autonomous Systems: clearly the humans must trust the Autonomous Systems, but larger systems are not monolithic either and each subsystem must trust those it delegates to, likewise the humans involved must trust each other, and in some cases the Autonomous System may need to delegate tasks to humans. Therefore, in the most general case we conceptually have the *trusts* relation drawn from:

$$\{\mathbb{H} \; trusts \; \mathbb{A}, \mathbb{A} \; trusts \; \mathbb{A}, \mathbb{H} \; trusts \; \mathbb{H}, \mathbb{A} \; trusts \; \mathbb{H}\} \qquad (1.1)$$

Where $\mathbb{H}$ is the set of all humans and $\mathbb{A}$ the set of all Autonomous Systems. In actual systems, the *trusts* relation will be consist of specific pairs or trust relationships such as *John trusts Autopilot*. In this introduction, we will discuss multiple ways of calculating or populating it.

1.2.1 Inter Human Trust $\mathbb{H}$ *trusts* $\mathbb{H}$

Unsurprisingly, the study of trust began in the social sciences including business, law, medicine and psychology.

Rempel *et al.* [RHZ85] distinguish between predictability, dependability and faith as components contributing to human trust and emphasis that trust is born from successful experiences with interpersonal risk while noting that trust while taking a long time to build can be rapidly destroyed. Delgado *et al.* [DFP05] showed that *a priori* reporting or assessment that a partner was "good" could induce a bias overriding feedback providing evidence to the contrary. This opens the possibility of Autonomous Systems being better judges of trust than humans. Deutsch saw trust as arising from cooperation [Deu62] and notes [Deu77] that trust is a function of the qualities of the individual, those of the situation and of whether trusting the will further or hinder one's own goals. This element of self interest is important and recurs when we discuss multi-agent systems. Luhmann as translated by Davis *et al.* [LHD84] considers the temporal horizon of trust regarding trust as an assessment of the near future that is informed and stabilized by the past. Kipnis [Kip95] states that trusting others introduces "unwanted uncertainty" in our lives. So trust management must, in part, be a process of limiting this uncertainty to acceptable levels.

In a business context, Wells [Wel01] could not find evidence for her prediction that managers would trust diverse subordinates less than self similar ones. She did find that subordinates did have less trust in managers of a different race. She found no relationship between the length of time managers knew their subordinates and their level of trust but did find that both managers' and subordinates' impressions that the other was a "gossip" were given as a reason for less trust in that individual and that men and women focused on different reasons for distrust. Wells and Kipnis [WK01] found that less trust in the intra-organizational context was associated with more attempts to influence subordinates on the managers part but also less dependency on them, while subordinates who distrusted their managers reduced their interaction with them but still adopted stronger tactics to influence them. Whitener *et al.* [WBK98] give common elements of many researchers' definitions of interpersonal trust:

1. Trust in another party reflects an expectation or belief that the other party will act benevolently.

2. The truster cannot control or force the trustee to fulfill this expectation. Trust necessarily involves a risk that the other party won't fulfil that expectation and a willingness to be vulnerable.
3. Trust involves some level of dependence on the other party so that the outcomes of one individual are influenced by the actions of another.

They conclude that managers and organization must actively establish trust by designing organization in ways that encourage managers to initiate trusting relationships and thereby allowing and encouraging manages to exhibit the five factors that influence employees' perceptions of managerial trustworthiness namely:

- behavioral consistency
- behavioral integrity
- sharing and delegating of control
- communication including accuracy, explanations, openness
- demonstration of concern (acting in the employees' interests and not exploiting them)

McKnight *et al.* [MCC98] argue that an individuals trusting stance (propensity to trust) would have an affect on initial trust formation Spector and Jones [SJ04] found this was true empirically but found no change in trust based on organizational affiliation nor hierarchial relationship. They also found men more likely to trust men than women but women to be gender neutral with respect to trust.

How does this inform Trust in the context of Artificial Autonomy? Artificially Autonomous systems need to model trust and form trust judgements about other entities protect themselves from risk. While they can make judgements based on observed behavior over time they will still have to form an initial judgement. This initial judgement may be informed by organisational stance towards the other entity, or some other recommendation by another trusted entity. This recommendation may simply be the knowledge that the other system is provided by a business or coalition partner. However the Artificially Autonomous System forming the judgement may discount any recommendations based on its evaluation of the recommender's trustworthiness and over time, unlike humans, this recommendation should not be allowed to overdue direct observations as they accumulate. In many ways the most important trust judgements will be those made without any prior direct observation because these will be the riskiest interactions yet there is a requirement to form relationships with as yet unknown entities in order to make progress. The level of trust given to any entity in an interaction should also ideally take into account the context of that interaction including the value, risk and situational context of that interaction or delegation. So we can say that trust in an entity e will be some function

$$trust(e) =$$
$$f(ownRiskStance, goals, situation, task, timeframe, reports, history)$$

1.2.2 Inter Machine Trust A *trusts* A

Marsh [Mar94b] is one of the earliest to formally model trust and he does so in the context of Distributed Artificial Intelligence, now covered by the term *Multi-Agent Systems*. These are systems that consist of many distinct programs or agents, each with its own goals and perhaps its own loyalties (ownership or programming by various parties each with their own interests). He provides a heuristic of trust including several measures spanning the interval $[-1, 1]$: *basic trust* (effectively McKnight's trusting stance), *general trust* in specific agents (overall trustworthiness) and *situated trust* (trust in an agent's ability to perform a specific task). He distinguishes between *distrust* (negative values) and *no trust* being disinterest or zero information. He also uses measures in the interval $[-1, 1]$ of *utility* being the quantifiable value of an outcome and *importance* the agents subjective desire for that outcome or if negative the desire for that outcome not to occur. Although recognizing the temporal aspects of trust, Marsh does not specifically code this into his heuristic formulation seeing it only a timestamp or index over calculations performed at particular times. Marsh also covers concepts of agent optimism and pessimism [Mar94b, Mar94a] in which the agent favors the most positive or negative information it has obtained, while Jonker and Treur [JT99] extend this to a six point spectrum of optimism and pessimism. Marsh finally arrives at the following formula for situated trust

$$T_x(y, \alpha) = U_x(\alpha) \times I_x(\alpha) \times \widehat{T_x(y)} \qquad (1.2)$$

calculated as the trust agent x has in agent y's ability to perform task α, the product of the utility of α, the importance of α to x and the general trust x has in y. The criteria for utilizing or cooperating with a trusted party is given as

$$T_x(y, \alpha) > CooperationThreshold_x(\alpha) \rightarrow WillCooperate(x, y, \alpha) \qquad (1.3)$$

where

$$CooperationThreshold_x(\alpha) = \frac{PerceivedRisk_x(\alpha)}{PerceivedCompetence_x(y, \alpha) + \widehat{T_x(y)}} \times I_x(\alpha) \qquad (1.4)$$

Burnett *et al.* [BNS11] use trust to explicitly decide whether to delegate tasks. Griffiths and Luck [GL99] use a simpler model based on the interval $[0, 1]$ representing total distrust to complete trust they integrate this into planning architectures to achieve option-tree node and thus plan selection. Abdul-Rahman and Hailes [ARH00] simplify the trust model by evaluating four discrete trust levels: very trustworthy, trustworthy, untrustworthy and very untrustworthy and they distinguish between direct observations and recommendations which are discounted according to how indirect the recommendation is. Upon a final evaluation of each discrete trust level, the one with the highest support is acted upon. Likewise Josang [Jos99] evaluates the concepts of belief, disbelief and uncertainty, while Cahill *et al.* [CGS03] combines risk and trust into a probability density function. The TRAVOS system [TPJ06] ignores situated trust in favor of scoring each transaction with another party as either 1 for complete contract fulfilment or 0 otherwise. These results are fed into Bayesian equations to derive a probability density function. Several systems [ZL04, Lev09, Jos99, MMS05] use flow models that start with a distinguished trust seed to calculate trust for each node by following long chains of trust relationships. Still others [Gri06, AT14] utilize *Fuzzy Sets* to calculate and characterize the level of trust in each agent. Trust Region methods [Yua15, CGT00] use optimization theory to generate a mathematical region that approximates the objective function of trust, expanding the region when it corresponds to the objective function and reducing it otherwise. Others models use particle swarms to solve the trust problem have been implemented [XXT12, HDLT13] or proposed [MM09]. Approaches such as those of Zacharia [Zac99] and others [XL04, HWZ08, ZCY09] emphasise calculating the *reputation* of agents by collecting observations from the entire network as opposed to relying on more local measures.

A theory and calculus of *Promises* is offered by Bergstra and Burgess [BB14] as a way of tracking and reasoning about the commitments agents make to each other. Their calculus allows for both broken and renegotiated promises.

Several researchers incorporate cheating and malicious intent into their models, particularly if they wish to use agents in highly competitive industries in a society of agents of different "loyalties". For instance [JMT05, HJM06, HJV09, FSB05] deal with deception in trading environments while Das *et al.* [DIS11] deals with deception and malicious behavior on computer networks.

Many other systems for assessing trust have been devised, reviewed and classified: [YSL13] covers areas such as cognitive or game theoretical (numerical) assessment, information sources: direct experience vs. witness reports vs sociological information (inferred from role, qualifications, provider), visibility: pubic or private, granularity of information i.e. how many contexts, cheating: considered impossible, accidental or deliberate, boolean or continuous measures, is a reliability placed on the trust measure or not [SS05]. Others consider the context of highly contested peer to peer networks where some peers are trying to game the system and may attempt to defect (cheat on) a transaction. They may build a good reputation to gain privileges before becoming a traitor, cooperate with malicious accomplices in order to improve their reputation or leave and reenter the system in order to whitewash their reputation; they may also engage in denial of service attacks. Their capacity to do this is affected by whether system identities are effectively anonymous, spoof resistant, or to unforgeable and whether reputations are maintained in a trusted global repository such as a trust chain [MGM06]. Josang *et al.* [JIB07] distinguish between summation or averaging of ratings and using *Bayesian probability* density functions which few humans can interpret. They also mention the use of *Fuzzy measures* for human comprehension. Pinyol and Sabater-Mir [PSM08] provide the *LRep Language* for communicating and arguing about reputation. It uses formal description logic and ontologies to communicate images that may be used by parties to form reputations. It detects some information contradictory to the world state and excludes such information from affecting reputations. Koster *et al.* [KSM13] extend this to formal arguments about trust and show how to integrate trust models into the *BDI architectures* (Beliefs, Desires and Intentions) that drive many autonomous agents [KSS13]. Other researchers [JJ06, Tai10] have also used BDI archetichtures to explore trust models. When Pinyol and Sabater-Mir [PSM13] revisit Sabater and Sierra's 2005 review, they include extra distinctions such as whether there is an external objective rating agency and whether initial trust or other bootstrap criteria are described in their literature. Fullam *et al.* [FKM05] evaluate the performance of various trust schemes using a simulation testbed.

Fan *et al.* [FOM08] see reliability as only contributing to trust whereas many researchers equate the two. Abbas *et al.* [ALM16] argue that trust contains many factors and that simple reliability is only the first stop on a continuum including privacy, security and safety. They argue that merely performing a delegated task does not make them trustworthy, and that shared data must not be misused for other purposes (privacy), maintain security [AG15] to prevent theft or tampering with the data which could give incorrect results or cause reputational damage. Similarly in some instances such as air traffic control [HCH12] the safety of the trusting party is of paramount importance. Leu and Abbass [LA16] propose a "Trust Bus" to manage the collection and distribution of trust information within BDI type architectures.

1.2.3 Human Trust of Machines $\mathbb{H}$ *trusts* $\mathbb{A}$

Human trust in Autonomic Systems is critical for their adoption because without such trust, they will simply be rejected and not used or more active forms of rejection may even occur.

The relationship between humans and machines has been explored in science fiction, arguably before serious scientific study. The tall order of expectations imposed on machines fitting into human society is perhaps well summed up by author Robert A. Heinlein [Hei73]:

> "A human being should be able to change a diaper, plan an invasion, butcher a hog, conn a ship, design a building, write a sonnet, balance accounts, build a wall, set a bone, comfort the dying, take orders, give orders, cooperate, act alone, solve equations, analyze a new problem, pitch manure, program a computer, cook a tasty meal, fight efficiently, die gallantly. Specialization is for insects."

However in the more constrained world of human interaction with Autonomous Systems one can immediately see that the normal cues for building trust are not automatically present in and systems must be designed to allow humans to trust them.

It is perhaps opportune to introduce the concepts of embodiment and autonomic capacity in autonomous systems as they well be relevant both for this issue and later in the book.

Embodied Agents

An *embodied agent* is one which can sense its environment, and control actuators or other leverage points that directly or indirectly alter the state of the agent's environment. Embodiment does not have to be a physical body, it is about sensing, altering its environment and being affected by its environment in a generative feedback loop. While for a robot agent embodiment means physically interacting with and sensing its environment; for a software system optimization agent embodiment would entail being able to measure and sense attributes of the software environment such as system load, available memory and being able to alter them by changing say process priorities, scheduling policies and enforcing process migration.

While Tweedale states "At present machines can solve problems or achieve human-like functionality; however they are not intelligent, they are merely making smart decisions" [Twe12], a significant number of researchers have come to the view that embodiment is a necessary but not sufficient condition for real intelligence. For instance Brooks [Bro90] produced the Subsumption Architecture to "tightly connect perception to action, embedding robots concretely in the world." Likewise, Sporns [Spo09] argues strongly that true intelligence is situated and a result of embodied systems that affect and interact with their environment, "We found that coordinated and dynamically coupled sensorimotor activity induced quantifiable changes in sensory information, including decreased entropy, increased mutual information, integration, and complexity within specific regions of sensory space." In other words the quality of information to learn from is enhanced by information exchanges between coupled systems.

Autonomic Systems

An *autonomic system*, first introduced by Horn [Hor01], mimics the anatomy of living animals. It consists of sensors and other measures to assess the state of the system, and a control system to regulate the state and behavior of the system itself. Its objective of providing both system stability/optimisation and reconfiguration for mode changes mimic homeostasis and diurnal rhythms in animals. While currently relatively rare at the application level, in some industries such as civil aviation invest considerable resources into system health monitoring — allowing airlines through telemetry to become aware of in-flight faults in real-time so that repairs can be expedited once the plane has landed. Autonomic systems should not be considered to be limited only to physically sensing the system, they may include or be entirely composed of sensing the software state. Murch [Mur04] defines an autonomic system as:

> "[The] ability to manage your computing enterprize through hardware and software that automatically and dynamically responds to the requirements of your business. This means self-healing, self-configuring, self-optimizing, and self-protecting hardware and software that behaves in accordance with defined service levels and policies. Just like the nervous system in the body, the autonomic computing system responds to the needs of business."

An Autonomic System 'is a special case of an Embodied Agent in which the environment may be purely virtual or consist of the system itself rather than being physical and external.

Muir [Mui87] claims that "The more specific expectation of technically competent role performance is at the heart of the trust between humans and machines." She also points out that there is also and expectation of fiduciary responsibility: that the machine will act in the human's best interests. It is natural given the absence of non-verbal cues humans rely on in assessing others that the human's comprehension of what the autonomous system is doing, and why, become even more important. Muir explains that the human will make trust decisions based on the perceived intent of the system's questions of the user and actions it takes. To the extent that the systems decision criteria are not obvious from observed behavior, the system must be able to explain in a human terms the reasons for its behavior. This calls on an autonomic capacity of the system to be self reflective and explain its steps. Muir notes the difficulty that an autonomous system is often provided to perform roles that the human is incapable of, making it even more difficult for the human to assess its competency. She suggests four ways to improve the human's trust assessment:

1. Improving the perception of trustworthiness. For example through training the user on how the system works, providing data on its predictability and increasing observability or the machines actions and internal logic.
2. Modifying the criterion of trustworthiness. For example demonstrating the difference in overall performance with or without the decision aid.
3. Enhancing the user's ability to allocate functions. Allowing the user to determine which areas the system takes on gives them the opportunity to maximize the cooperative relationship rather than accepting the designer's assumptions of work behavior.
4. Identifying and selectively manipulating the source(s) of poor calibration.

1.2.4 Machines Trusting Humans A *trusts* ℍ

Abbass *et. al.* [APM16] note that adaptive automation was invented to prevent the rapid decline in human performance when they are monitoring static automation — humans quickly get bored and cannot maintain attention. They require the human to perform small manual tasks from time to time. *Cognitive Cyber Symbiosis* goes far further, envisaging a cloud computing network where many of the computing nodes are humans tasked by other humans but more often machines to perform the tasks machines are poor at. They propose an architecture based on virtual nodes or cookies each dedicated to managing the interaction of one pair of agents being any combination of computer or human. They go on to discuss several new technologies that a system could use to monitor the capacity of a human in terms of sensing brain function, heart rate and other physiological attributes [Emo16a, Emo16b, Koh, Beu16, Com16, Com16].

1.3 Motivations from Uncertainty

The basic position underpinning this book is that autonomous systems of the past have suffered from limited ability to operate successfully outside relatively narrow domains where the environment manifests benign statistical properties. This constraint shows up as the well-known brittleness of artificial intelligence methods, as compared with the flexibility and robustness — but not optimality — of human decision-making performance. This fundamental weakness shows up in both artificial intelligence and in economics [Smi16]; in both cases research has also been largely tied to statistical and Bayesian methods and hence to the perhaps surprisingly strong limitations incumbent in their assumptions [GPS04].

Wishful mnemonics refers to the tendency for humans to apply biological labels to algorithmic constructions for autonomous systems in the absence of defensible cases for drawing the comparison [McD76]. This tendency was heavily implicated during earlier phases of hype surrounding artificial intelligence for its effect of masking the strength of the customary assumptions driving much of the research, and more recent work [Smi16] maintains that this effect is still prominent today. In particular, the assumptions most responsible for the brittleness of most current artificial intelligence methods lies in their inability to handle non-stochastic uncertainty, or what is sometimes known in economics as ontological uncertainty [Dav10, Key73, LM05, Smi16, Ter10].

Autonomous systems will be bound to tightly controlled environments — or environments where it is possible to cost-effectively impose such tight control — until they improve in generalization ability and their ability to handle environments where future states are unpredictable to the agent, because they are the consequences of the complex interactions of the elements of the overall environment, which includes the agent itself. Such environments are also of high interest in economics, because real economic environments display exactly this kind of uncertainty because any economic system worthy of the title is intrinsically a highly complex environment involving many interacting agents.

The connection of economic qualitative notions of non-stochastic uncertainty to mathematics has been established [Dav12, Ter10], in which ontological uncertainty equates to phenomena arising as a consequence of non-ergodicity. An ergodic system [Gra09, Hal13] is one for which the phase-space average is the same as the infinite time average, for all Lebesgue-integrable functions almost everywhere (meaning except possibly in sets of measure zero). In other words, an ergodic system conveniently evolves towards a limiting form that is independent of its initial state, and thus more sampling will yield more information about the system. So ergodicity delineates circumstances under which obtaining additional data provides additional information. The statistical properties of such systems are stationary and satisfy some regularity conditions. Ergodicity effectively means that an agent can reason about its world in a detached manner, building up an increasingly accurate model of it against a predefined and fixed notion of optimal performance.

Like real economic systems, the kinds of environments in which we should like to have autonomous systems operating are inherently non-ergodic: such environments are not regular nor stationary and consequently they will not converge to equilibrium distributions, and so they cannot be amenable to reliable forecast as a result. Economics' ontological uncertainty pertains to the behavior of such non-ergodic processes; this stands also in contrast to the other economic notion of non-stochastic uncertainty, known as epistemological uncertainty, which still presumes the presence of ergodic processes [Dav12, Ter10]. In the latter case, the surprising outcome simply lies far out on the tail of a nonetheless fixed and otherwise reasonably well-behaved distribution, with the surprise of given by the exorbitant sampling time for its expected occurrence. Epistemological uncertainty mostly appears in the artificial intelligence literature as decision-making under various models of partial observability.

Non-ergodic processes may be categorized into distinctly different types. The ergodic hierarchy [Gra09, Hal13] is the recognised classification scheme for deterministic dynamical Hamiltonian systems, distinguishing classes of systems by their relative unpredictability. Note that the trajectories of non-linear dynamic systems may be encoded as infinite sequences by dividing the state space of the system up into cells and tracing state space trajectories through these cells, to produce a computational view of the system dynamics. Any such trajectory is said to be random when there exists some partitioning of the state space into cells such that the encoding of the trajectory is algorithmically random, in the Kolmogorov complexity sense. In this computationally oriented view of system dynamics, the complexity of the system is defined as the size of the smallest effective procedure, with respect to some reference machine model, that reproduces the data observed from that system [LV08]. The remarkable fact is that this complexity is asymptotically independent of the particular machine model, up to additive constants. The conditional complexity of a sequence with respect to some information is the smallest effective procedure that takes the information as an input and produces the sequence as an output. A sequence is then said to be incompressible when the smallest size effective procedure is asymptotically comparable to the size of the sequence. For infinite sequences, the complexity is the limit, as the length of the sample of the sequence approaches infinity, of the size of the smallest effective procedure that reproduces the sample, divided by the length of the sample; if the complexity in the limit is non-zero then the sequence is incompressible, which means that it represents a random mathematical object in the sense of it being indistinguishable from the flips of a coin by any kind of statistical test.

Ontological uncertainty in dynamical systems takes the form of questions about the long-term behavior of the system to which there are no answers shorter than merely waiting to see what happens. In algorithmic information theory terms, these phenomena are formally incompressible; the predictability that autonomous decision-making methods may rely upon is equivalent to asserting that we have a compression — in terms of some effective procedure — for anticipating the outcomes of the system in advance, within some finite error tolerance associated with the granularity of the state space division into cells. For questions about the long-term behavior of systems higher in the ergodic hierarchy, there are simply not enough finite compressions to go around.

Ergodic systems lie at the bottom of the ergodic hierarchy, manifesting only the familiar stochastic uncertainty addressed by most available artificial intelligence methods. Above them are weak and strong mixings, then K-systems, whose behavior is already very strongly unpredictable. The topmost classification currently recognised are Bernoulli systems, whose behavior is the most strongly unpredictable in the hierarchy, in terms of the sets of problems that are unsolvable for these systems. The relationships between classes is quite complex, and an area of active research: entropy is not sufficient to classify K-systems, meaning that there are uncountably many K-systems with the same entropy but that are not isomorphic, so Ornstein's isomorphism theorem does not work for K-systems. All K-systems are also Bernoulli systems, but not vice versa, meaning that Bernoulli systems potentially manifest greater unpredictability. Yet oddly Ornstein Theory is sufficient to classify Bernoulli systems. It is worth noting that the criteria for strong mixings have been convincingly proposed as the demarcation of what is commonly regarded as deterministic chaos [Werndl2009]. There are also interesting systems that straddle between K-systems and Bernoulli systems, known variously as C-systems or Anosov systems; the details of their relationships to other members of the ergodic hierarchy are quite complex.

Note that non-ergodic systems do not undergo arbitrary change at any moment. Ontological uncertainty does not require or imply a situation of total disorder: systems that are non-ergodic display unique transient state behavior (apparently this is a formal basis for the punctuated equilibria of social theory and evolutionary biology), whereby they manifest periods of apparent stability marked by sudden transitions. Even irreducibly random sequences contain sequences of length that is of logarithmic order that appear to be regular and stationary [LV08]. The failures of ergodic models in non-ergodic systems cannot be ergodic, meaning that they will also manifest the unpredictability of non-ergodic systems.

The potential of complex systems to produce surprisingly long sequences of apparent predictability is highly seductive: the formation of self-reinforcing beliefs about predictability of future states of the market is a highly visible and widely recognised example of this from economics [Tim93]. The precision risk models that are heavily implicated in the securities bubble and subsequent Global Financial Crisis of 2007–2008 provide a highly topical example of the cascading system-wide failure of ergodic models in environments that are actually uncertain in a non-stochastic sense. Anecdotes about brittleness of artificial intelligence methods may be seen in much the same light. Yet real people clearly can and do manage to successfully operate under non-ergodic conditions, so it would be just as unreasonable to assert that our agents cannot ever do so as it is to expect that methods assuming ergodicity will be able to succeed adequately under such conditions.

Lurking underneath this picture of non-stochastic uncertainty manifest in complex real-world systems is the fact that questions on which we might typically build our autonomous methods concerning future system behavior might be paradoxical when taken in non-ergodic environments. The broad range of phenomena that economics knows as ontological uncertainty is built into the very foundations of mathematics and computer science: the Halting Problem for Turing Machines is unsolvable, every formal axiomatic system that contains basic arithmetic (either explicitly or implicitly) is incomplete, and there are recursively inseparable sets. All of these limitations occur because the questions involve formal paradoxes, though the lack of obvious self-reference means that their paradoxical nature is hidden from view. Ontological uncertainty amounts to the fact that problems of determining future outcomes in non-ergodic economic systems are paradoxical, because in reasoning about such systems we have to allow the possibility of self-reference, though the self-reference need not be obvious.

Formal axiomatic systems are mathematical languages supporting reasoning about phenomena in which we are interested — in pure mathematics this is often the behavior of other axiomatic systems — and such systems lie at the basis of automated reasoning methods for autonomy. Any such system of reasoning is comprised of a set of primitive terms, including contradiction which is false in all interpretations of the theory, and a set of axioms that describe what conclusions we can draw from combinations of statements in the theory. It allows us to formally state propositions, some of which might be provably true in the sense of being logically entailed by the axioms, and some of which might be provably false in the sense of reducing to contradiction. An axiomatic system in which the axioms themselves logically entail contradiction is said to be inconsistent, and it does not represent a viable basis for reasoning because in such a system it is possible to conclude that any proposition expressible in the language is both true and false. An axiomatic system is complete if we can determine, from within that system, the truth or falsity of every possible proposition. It turns out that any non-trivial consistent axiomatic system, cannot be complete, so there will also be expressible propositions that cannot be proven either true or false from within the theory. The most famous instance of this is given by the incompleteness theorems of Gödel [God92], who proved that the most basic question about whether we have a viable axiomatic system is not determinable from with the system, in general.

Gödel constructed a numbering of all of the propositions in Peano Arithmetic, and on this basis, selected out a statement that says something about its own corresponding number, and hence about itself: this Gödel sentence amounts to the statement "this statement is not provable". The theorems — to the effect that there can be no effectively axiomatizable system containing basic arithmetic that is both consistent and complete — are basically the fixed-point solution to this statement that eliminate the direct self-reference. Church's proof on the unsolvability of the Entscheidungsproblem, Tarski's theorem on the undefinability of truth, and Turing's unsolvability proof of the Halting problem all followed soon after. The theorem Gödel presented was effectively replaced by an improved theorem (known as the Gödel-Rosser theorem) a few years later by Rosser that removes the assumption of ω-consistency, by replacing the Gödel sentence with the Rosser sentence, which essentially states "If this statement is provable then its logical negation has a smaller proof" (where "smaller" is in the sense of having a smaller Gödel number).

Models of computation that really set the ultimate basis for machine intelligence such as Turing machines [Nie12, Soa16] are non-trivial formal axiomatic systems, and consequently suffer from the limitations of incompleteness. In this setting, incompleteness shows up as the unsolvability of problems, and, in the more modern setting of Algorithmic Information Theory, as the incompressibility of sequences. We are bound to compute solutions from within the absolute limitations incumbent in general models of computation, all of which are all known to be equivalent, and which are unsurpassable under the terms of the Church-Turing thesis.

The reason that questions such as those about future system behavior may be paradoxical but not obviously so is that direct self-referential expression is not as primitive a notion as it might appear. numerous systems of logic come with various kinds of implicit function theorem by which self-referential statements can be turned into equivalent statements, called "fixed-points", that lack obvious self-referentiality. Gödel effectively did this in his original proofs, but it is possible to reproduce his results and arbitrary generalizations of it using a separate logic to reason about the power of any logic containing Peano Arithmetic. Turing's proof of the unsolvability of the Halting Problem for Turing Machines, by the Cantor Diagonalization Argument [Nie12, Soa16], further reveals the detailed nature of logical paradoxes, and hence of the irreducible nature of uncertainty: they are kind of folded-up infinite regresses.

The proof in question is essentially just an infinite successive unfolding of the Halting Problem paradox in which each step never becomes simpler.

Gödel's Incompleteness Theorems [God92] and subsequent stronger results tell us that any system that allows for the possibility of self-reference — and perhaps surprisingly basic arithmetic will do — will give rise to paradoxes, and this will manifest as uncertainty in the form of the presence of problems we might like to solve but to which there can be no solution from within the system. A bigger system might be able to provide a solution, but we don't in general have the luxury of stepping out to it and peering into the phenomena with which we are concerned from the outside.

This is the backdrop behind the methods that are presented in this book: the variety of approaches to particular autonomous systems problems reflects our position that there will be can be no complete solution to autonomy, and that the success of any approach depends on carefully understanding the complexity of the intended environment and deciding what will constitute an acceptable solution within limits we understand. We have deliberately embraced hybrid approaches that bring together different technical methods, have attempted to represent important results in neuroscience by formalizing them to turn them into computational systems for robots, and have explored the potential for quantum computation to extend the types of uncertainty that our autonomous systems may handle.

1.4 Cyber-Physical-Cognitive (CPC) Autonomy: A Rigorous Model of Trusted Autonomy

We feel that not all of currently existing *"trusted autonomous systems"* satisfy necessary mathematical requirements to be included in the book entitled *Mathematics of Autonomy*. So, in the rest of the book, we will focus on a rigorous subset of trusted autonomy that we call *cyber-physical-cognitive autonomy* (CPC-autonomy, for short), which comprises of the following three broad categories of autonomous systems:

- Those using *physical autonomy*, including various autonomous robots;
- Those using *cyber-autonomy*, including various agents acting on computer-networks like the *internet of things* (IoT, see [Wik16f]), Google, Facebook, etc., as well as *cyber-physical autonomy* (see [Wik16o] and the references therein); and
- Those using *cognitive autonomy*, including *cyber-cognition* and *embodied-cognition* (see [Wik16r] and the references therein).

In particular, being the most vital part of the CPC-autonomy, the cognitive autonomy is studied from the following four different points of view:

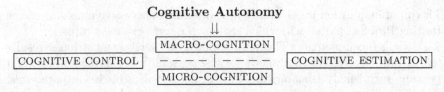

where MACRO-COGNITION is studied from the *deep-learning tensor neural networks* point of view, MICRO-COGNITION is studied from the *quantum information and computation* point of view,[4] COGNITIVE CONTROL is studied from the *perceptual control theory* and *fuzzy-logic control* point of view and COGNITIVE ESTIMATION is studied from the recursive *Bayesian filters* and *FastSLAM algorithms* point of view.

For example, in a recent paper [IY16] we have proposed an affine Hamiltonian formalism for global control of joint swarms of unmanned aerial and ground vehicles (UAVs and UGVs, respectively). This global control formalism is based on the concept of *swarm configuration manifold*, (see Figure 1.1) which includes all degrees-of-freedom (DOFs) of a system of N unmanned vehicles, physically representing Newtonian rigid bodies, each with 6 DOFs.

1.5 Technical Preliminaries

As a necessary background for comprehensive reading of the rest of the book, we give here various technical preliminaries.

1.5.1 Linear Control Preliminaries

For the later reference, we give here the basic elements of linear control theory. The standard elements of a cybernetic control diagram are given in Figure 1.2.

A single linear control block has input $U(s)$, output $Y(s)$ and the transfer function $G(s)$ between them (see Figure 1.3). Its transfer function is:

$$Y(s) = G(s)U(s).$$

Series connection of two linear control blocks (see Figure 1.4) has the transfer function:

$$Y(s) = G_1(s)G_2(s)U(s).$$

The set of all basic control elements is given in Figure 1.5.

---

[4] Quantum-mechanical information flow and computation of the MICRO-COGNITION is based on the fact that human concentrated thoughts can be seen as quantum wave-packets of energy and can be modeled via Schrödinger's wave ψ-functions (see [IA07, II08b, II09, Nit16] and the references therein).

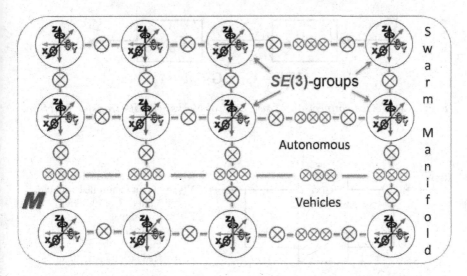

Fig. 1.1. *A 6N-dimensional swarm manifold M defined as a matrix of tensor products* $M = \bigotimes\limits_{i=1}^{m} \bigotimes\limits_{k=1}^{n} SE(3)_{ik}$ *of all (N = m × n) autonomous vehicles included in the swarm, where each vehicle is represented by the Euclidean group SE(3) of rigid motions (including three Cartesian translations and three Euler rotations; see [IY16] for technical details).*

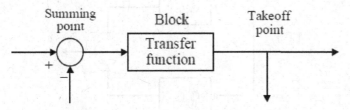

Fig. 1.2. *Basic elements of a cybernetic control diagram.*

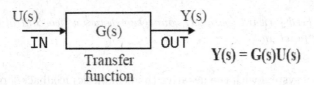

Fig. 1.3. *A single control block with its transfer function.*

Parallel (or, feed-forward) connection between two control blocks (see Figure 1.6) has the transfer function:

$$Y(s) = [G_1(s) + G_2(s)]U(s).$$

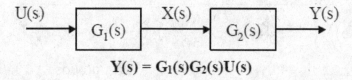

$$Y(s) = G_1(s)G_2(s)U(s)$$

Fig. 1.4. *Series connection of two control blocks with its transfer function.*

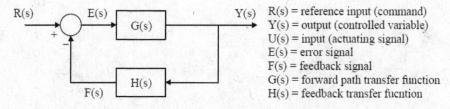

R(s) = reference input (command)
Y(s) = output (controlled variable)
U(s) = input (actuating signal)
E(s) = error signal
F(s) = feedback signal
G(s) = forward path transfer function
H(s) = feedback transfer fucntion

Fig. 1.5. *Standard terminology for control block diagrams (U(s) is shown in previous Figures).*

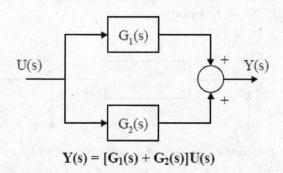

$$Y(s) = [G_1(s) + G_2(s)]U(s)$$

Fig. 1.6. *Feed-forward (parallel) connection between two control blocks with its transfer function.*

A control system with the negative (homeokinetic) feedback-loop (see Figure 1.7) has the transfer function:

$$Y(s)/R(s) = G(s)/[1 + G(s)].$$

Full closed-loop control diagram with the negative feedback is given in Figure 1.8.

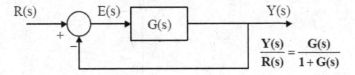

Fig. 1.7. *Negative feedback-loop system with its transfer function.*

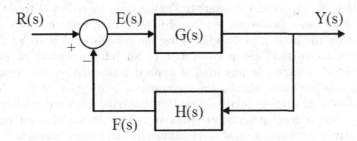

Fig. 1.8. *Full closed-loop cybernetic control diagram.*

1.5.2 Pictorial Reasoning

Recall that *composing functions* (or, maps, paths, arrows, processes, signals, systems, transformations, etc.)[5] is like following directed paths from one object to another (e.g., from one set/space to some other set/space). Formally, a *commutative diagram*:[6]

---

[5] Recall that a function (or, a map) f is a *rule* that assigns to each element x in a set/space A exactly one element, called $f(x)$, in a set B. A function could be also thought of as an *input-output system* $[[f]]$ with $x-$input (the *domain* of f is the set of all possible inputs) and $f(x)-$output (the *range* of f is the set/space of all possible outputs):

$$x \rightarrow [[f]] \rightarrow f(x).$$

Let $f : A \rightarrow B$ be a map between two sets/spaces: $A \equiv \mathrm{Dom}\, f$ and $B \equiv \mathrm{Cod}\, f$. Then:

$$\mathrm{Ker}\, f = f^{-1}(e_B) - \text{is a kernel of } f;$$
$$\mathrm{Im}\, f = f(A) - \text{is an image of } f;$$
$$\mathrm{Coker}\, f = \mathrm{Cod}\, f / \mathrm{Im}\, f - \text{is a cokernel of } f;$$
$$\mathrm{Coim}\, f = \mathrm{Dom}\, f / \mathrm{Ker}\, f - \text{is a coimage of } f;$$

[6] We remark that the word 'commutative' in this context *does not* mean that $g \circ f = f \circ g$, because we are dealing here with maps (or, directed paths), not scalars (numbers).

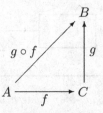

means, that is, 'expresses the semantics', that from an object A to an object B we can go either indirectly via an object C using first the path[7] f and subsequently the path g, or directly, using the *composition*[8] path $g \circ f$.[9]

From mathematical perspective, out of an infinite variety of possible action-control diagrams in any area of applied mathematics, *only commutative diagrams are automatically valid:* commutative diagrams define the general process of *functional composition*, thus implying both the existence and uniqueness of the corresponding algebraic equations. In modern mathematics, commutative diagrams are used as visual means for rigorous theorem proving. They are both illustratively appealing and formally valid (for more technical details, see, e.g. [II06b] and the references therein).

For example, consider the following commutative diagram representing a 'street directory' and the path $\overrightarrow{\mathbf{AB}}$ on it:

$$g \circ e = h \circ f$$
$$= k \circ c \circ a \circ i$$
$$= k \circ d \circ b \circ i$$
$$= k \circ c \circ j \circ e$$
$$= k \circ d \circ l \circ f$$

---

[7] Let $f : A \to B$ and $g : A \to B$ be two paths/maps from A and B. Then the paths/maps $f + g$, $f - g$, fg, and f/g are defined as follows (see, e.g. [II06b])

$$
\begin{aligned}
(f + g)(x) &= f(x) + g(x) & \text{domain} &= A \cap B, \\
(f - g)(x) &= f(x) - g(x) & \text{domain} &= A \cap B, \\
(fg)(x) &= f(x)\,g(x) & \text{domain} &= A \cap B, \\
\left(\frac{f}{g}\right)(x) &= \frac{f(x)}{g(x)} & \text{domain} &= \{x \in A \cap B : g(x) \neq 0\}.
\end{aligned}
$$

[8] Given two maps f and g, the composite map $f \circ g$, called the *composition* of f and g, is defined by
$$(f \circ g)(x) = f(g(x)).$$
The $(f \circ g)$−machine is composed of the g−machine (first) and then the f−machine:
$$x \to [[g]] \to g(x) \to [[f]] \to f(g(x)).$$

[9] In this book, we will consistently follow the classical notation of mathematical analysis, where the composition $f(g(x))$ of two functions, $f(x)$ and $g(x)$ is denoted as: $g \circ f = g \circ f(x)$.

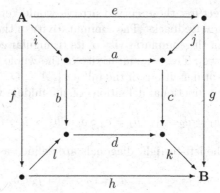

More generally, a *complex architecture* is commutative iff any two paths along arrows that start at the same point and finish at the same point are mutually equivalent. Commutativity of the whole diagram follows from commutativity of its triangular components.

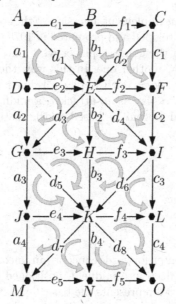

Fig. 1.9. *A four-story commutative architecture (see text for explanation).*

For example, the four-story commutative architecture in Figure 1.9 includes the set of objects (vertices): $\{A, B, C, ..., M, N, O\}$ and the set of functions (maps, or edges, or arrows) between the objects: $\{a_1, ..., a_4, b_1, ..., b_4, c_1, ..., c_4, d_1, ..., d_8, e_1, ..., e_5, f_1, ..., f_5\}$. In case of a PCT-architecture representing say a part of the human visual cortex cerebri, these arrows would represent nonlinear neural feedbacks. In addition, the curved arrows denote the commutative flow within the triangular components. In case of the above

PCT-architecture, these curved arrows would represent functional compositions of neural feedbacks. The commutativity of the whole architecture follows directly from the commutativity of its triangular components (denoted by the curved arrows). The commutativity of the whole architecture implies any of the equivalent definitions of the full path $A \rightrightarrows O$. It also implies, for instance, the following functional definitions of the middle vertical pilar:

$$b_1 = d_2 \circ f_1; \quad b_2 = e_3 \circ d_3; \quad b_3 = d_6 \circ f_3; \quad b_4 = e_5 \circ d_7.$$

Similarly, the left-to-right diagonals are defined as:

$$d_1 = b_1 \circ e_1 = e_2 \circ a_1; \quad d_4 = c_2 \circ f_2 = f_3 \circ b_2; \quad d_5 = b_3 \circ e_3 = e_4 \circ a_3;$$

$$d_8 = c_4 \circ f_4 = f_5 \circ b_4.$$

Optimal Tactics for Robot Soccer

The best RoboCup teams implement a version of the so-called 'total football', a soccer-game tactics developed and promoted in 1970s by Dutch player Johan Cruyff. In the tactics of the game, a player who moves out of his position is immediately replaced by another one. In this way, the team's organizational structure is preserved, while no outfield player is fixed in a nominal role: every player needs to be able to play as an attacker, a midfielder and a defender.

More precisely, 'total football' is based on the tactics called *Cruyff's Diamond (4-3-3) formation*:

```
* * * * ⇓
    *
  *   *
    *
  *   *
```

and utilizes the 'false center-forward' concept (an unconventional, withdrawn, lone striker, who drops deep into midfield, positioned behind two wide strikers).[10] The formation 4-3-3 represents the basic team structure which is maintained throughout the game. Its quick, short-term variation is 4-2-4, where another attacker is temporarily added to the attack formation, for the purpose of penetrating the opponent's defense. As soon as the attack is executed (either successfully or unsuccessfully), the team is responsible for returning to its basic 4-3-3 formation. Any player, be they attacker, mid-fielder, or defender, has a chance to briefly become the fourth attacker (within the quick

---

[10] In recent years, Lionel Messi has been the world's best 'false center-forward' in much the same way that Cruyff was in the 1970s. The whole game of FC Barcelona today is arranged around this 'false no. 9', in much the same way that it was arranged around Cruyff in FC Ajax Amsterdam in 1970s.

4-2-4 formation), as long as they still hold the full responsibility of fulfilling their own defense task (see [IGG14] for more details).

Technically speaking, Cruyff's Diamond is an example of a *tensor* (see next section).

1.5.3 Tensors

Our CPC-autonomy will be largely formalized using *tensor machinery*[11] (for technical details, see Chapter 10, Appendix 1 and also [IR15]). In particular, the *core* concept of *tensor networks* (TNs) has both its microscopic (quantum) and macroscopic (neural) meaning. TNs are elaborated firstly, in the micro-context of quantum computation/information in Chapter 4, and secondly, in the macro-context of deep learning neural networks in Chapter 5. In an ideal scenario (which is slightly futuristic at the moment), the majority of CPC-autonomy would be based on deep learning tensor networks (e.g., deep convolutional nets), in which the main computations are realized using entangled quantum tensor networks.

In this section, we start with several motivations for general tensor machinery that provides a unique computational framework, both algebraic and geometric, useful for rigorous predictive modeling in traditionally "soft" socio-politico-economic sciences.

Tensorial Modeling in Social Sciences

Our first motivation is a basic geometric interpretation of De Mesquita's 'social game' decision model based on *expected utility theory* (see [SCS11] and references therein).

From the analysis of Figure 1.10, we give here the following geometric interpretation of De Mesquita's 'social game' decision dynamics:

1. The action of each *actor* in the 'social game' represents a *cognitive decision vector*, so that a game of N actors can be seen as dynamics in an N-dimensional (ND, for short) linear *decision vector space* (which can be based either on Lewinian 'field theory in social science' [Lew47, Lew51, Lew97, Gol99, IA07], or on 'perceptual control theory' [Pow73a, Pow73b, IRS14]) that is spanned by all actors' vectors.

2. Dr. Jason Scholz (Research Leader for Trusted Autonomous Systems, from JOAD, DST Group, Australia) has conjectured the existence of some form of *chaotic behavior* (or, highly-nonlinear behavior)[12] of hypothetical actors

---

[11] Recall that a *tensor* is an array of (real or complex) scalars (numbers or functions). It is an n-dimensional generalization of a *matrix*, a linear in-out machine, computed as a list of lists ... of lists, a "black box" that takes an array of numbers/functions as an input and transforms it into another array of numbers/functions as an output.

[12] For this purpose, we propose the following computational approach:

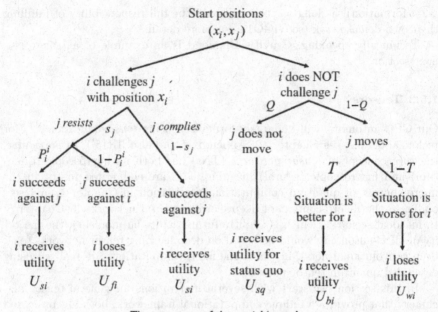

The structure of the social 'game'.

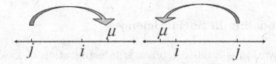

Case 3A: i between j and μ – i gets better as a result of j moving.

Fig. 1.10. *The basic structure of De Mesquita's 'social game' (adapted from [SCS11]).*

a) To start, we calculate the MaxLyapunov exponent, just to see if it is positive in De Mesquita's 'social game', which would indicate chaotic behavior in the Game (a preferred tool for this single task would be the R-package for Nonlinear Time Series analysis);

b) If the MaxLyapunov exponent is positive, then we suggest some deeper analysis, using the open-source TISEAN (v.3.x) package, to calculate:
   (i) the whole Lyapunov spectrum;
   (ii) the Kolmogorov-Sinai entropy (associated to the Lyapunov spectrum); and
   (iii) the Kaplan-Yorke information dimension (associated to the Kolmogorov-Sinai entropy). This would be a thorough analysis of the chaotic behavior in De Mesquita's 'social game';

c) Otherwise, if the MaxLyapunov exponent is negative (but we still anticipate some nonlinearity in De Mesquita's 'social game'), then we could try testing for its overall nonlinearity, using the following TISEAN methods:

in the social game, which implies that the above hypothetical model of linear decision vectors acting in a linear decision vector space is not quite correct; it should be generalized to a similar but nonlinear vector structure.

3. With a 'nonlinear/chaotic social game' we are dealing with some form of complicated dynamics of nonlinear decision vectors (or, rank-1 tensors) acting within some form of a nonlinear decision vector space, which is a nonlinear deformation of the above linear decision vector space. This nonlinear deformation is performed in such a way that at any local point of the new nonlinear geometric structure (around each individual actor) still looks like the above linear decision vector space, but as a whole (globally) it is quite different, in fact so different that it becomes 'sensitive to initial conditions'.

4. A modern geometric solution to the problem of a nonlinear vector is the *tangent vector* that is defined as an infinitesimal arrow at a single point in a nonlinear/curved space as a *directional derivative* at that point, while the whole nonlinear space consisting of (or, spanned by) all tangent vectors is called the *configuration manifold* (the set of all possible game configurations[13]). In the case of social game, we can call it the *decision configuration manifold*, or decision N-manifold.[14]

    (i) General constrained randomization; and
    (ii) Measures of weak nonlinearities.

d) Once we really know the degree of nonlinearity/chaos in De Mesquita's 'social game', then it would justify further geometric/topological modeling along the following lines:

    (i) defining the overall system's configuration-manifold dynamics and dividing it into several possible phases/states;

    (ii) postulate that the above numerically discovered chaotic behaviors in the system are related to the phase transitions occurring in the configuration-manifold dynamics, including (a) strong/non-smooth phase transitions and (b) weak/smooth phase transitions;

    (iii) model the strong/non-smooth phase transitions as caused by topological changes in the configuration manifold dynamics; and

    (iv) model the weak/smooth phase transitions as caused by geometric changes in the configuration manifold dynamics.

---

[13] In particular, Lewinian group manifold represents a 'landscape' in which any kind of aggregate attractor dynamics of N human agents flows.

[14] Here we give three examples of simple configuration manifolds, used later in the text:
(i) A single agent's 3D configuration manifold $M = SO(2) \times \mathbb{R}$, coordinated by $\mathbf{x} = \{x, y, \theta\}$;
(ii) A 4D configuration manifold of a car: $M \equiv SO(2) \times \mathbb{R}^2$, coordinated by $\mathbf{x} = \{x, y, \theta, \phi\}$, where $SO(N)$ is the N-parameter group of rotations; and
(iii) A humanoid robot's configuration N-manifold is the set of all movable joints angles, topologically defined as the Cartesian product $\prod_i SO(3)^i$ of $(i = 1, ..., N)$ rotational $SO(3)$-groups for all robot joints.

5. In this way, we derive a hypothetical geometric model for a nonlinear social game as a *decision N-manifold*, in which each actor is represented by a tangent vector defined as a directional derivative at a point in the manifold. The manifold concept allows for representation of the general multivariate dynamics, formulated as *tensor flows on manifolds* (see Chapter 10, Appendix 1 and also [IR15]).

6. Nonlinear and chaotic social behaviors of actors are now represented in the following way:

   (i) Individual actors' decision-movements are defined as motions along the *geodesics* (shortest, straightest lines) in the curved decision N-manifold;

   (ii) Chaotic sensitivity to initial conditions is modeled by the *geodesic deviation equation* in the decision N-manifold (that defines a *divergence* between individual geodesics).

"Everything Is a Tensor" in *Mathematica*®

In Wolfram's computer algebra system *Mathematica*®, one of the basic concepts is that any kind of symbolic computational expression is internally represented as a tensor, computed as a list of lists of lists ...

So, if we combine the above two concepts, we almost arrive at a "zoo" of various tensors on smooth configuration manifolds. However, at a first glance, it seems that by restricting our computational framework to smooth geometric objects (tensors) living in smooth configuration spaces (manifolds) — we are completely missing discrete computational structures like graphs, networks and decision trees.

A quick answer to this apparent insufficiency of our proposed approach is: if we make a street-like network of 'tramlines' on a flat surface (which is a flat 2D manifold) we get a planar graph, which is easily generalized to non-flat and higher-dimensional manifolds. In other words, every graph or a network is simply a geometric constraint on a manifold, that is a tensor. That is, from computational perspective, 'everything is a tensor'.

A more technical answer to the same apparent insufficiency of our tensorial approach is given in the next (and last) motivational subsection.

Topological Decision Chain Model

Informally, 'topology is rubber-sheet geometry'.[15] As our final motivation for this section, we propose a *topological decision system* (TDS) model: $\mathcal{T} = (V, E, \Phi) \equiv (X_0, X_1, X_2)$, defined as a dynamical planar digraph given by the following three sets:

---

[15] This popular dictum is based on the fact that in 2D topology, there is no difference between a circle and a square and a triangle — they are all topological circles (closed lines). Likewise, for computational purposes, they are all combinatorial triangles, or simplices (a plural of a simplex). This fact is heavily used in graph and network theory, where shape is not important, only the connections matter.

1. A set $V \equiv X_0 = \{v_1, v_2, ...\}$ of *vertices*, or decision processing units, geometrically represented by points v_i, $(i \in \dim V)$ in the plane $\mathbb{R}^2 \simeq \mathbb{C}$;
2. A set $E \equiv X_1 = \{e_1, e_2, ...\}$ of *edges*, or decision processing channels, given by oriented connecting links $e_j : v_{src} \rightarrow v_{trg}$, $(j \in \dim E)$, each connecting two vertices (source and target, which are its boundaries ∂e_j); and
3. A set $\Phi \equiv X_2 = \{\phi_1, \phi_2, ...\}$ of *faces*, or decision processing media $\phi_k : e_{src} \rightarrow e_{trg}$, $(k \in \dim \Phi)$, given by oriented 2D surfaces whose boundaries $\partial \phi_k$ consist of two edges (source and target).

More specifically, the TDS model $\mathcal{T}$ is instantiated by the following planar digraph, (called the *2-cell* in the language of n-categories):

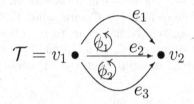

with the boundaries:

$$\{\partial e_1 = v_2 - v_1, \quad \partial e_2 = v_2 - v_1, \quad \partial e_3 = v_2 - v_1\}$$
$$\{\partial \phi_1 = e_1 - e_2, \quad \partial \phi_2 = e_2 - e_3\} \tag{1.5}$$

The sets of vertices $V \equiv X_0$, edges $E \equiv X_1$ and faces $\Phi \equiv X_2$ can be lifted-up to following free Abelian groups with integer coefficients:

$$C_0 \cong \mathbb{Z}^V, \qquad C_1 \cong \mathbb{Z}^E, \qquad C_2 \cong \mathbb{Z}^\Phi, \qquad \text{with respective} \tag{1.6}$$

ordered bases $V \equiv X_0, E \equiv X_1, \Phi \equiv X_2$, and boundaries:

$$\partial e_j: C_1 \rightarrow C_0 = \{\partial e_1 = v_2 - v_1, \quad \partial e_2 = v_2 - v_1, \quad \partial e_3 = v_2 - v_1\},$$
$$\partial \phi_k: C_1 \rightarrow C_0 = \{\partial \phi_1 = e_1 - e_2, \quad \partial \phi_2 = e_2 - e_3\}.$$

The boundary maps $\partial e_j \equiv \partial_1$ and $\partial \phi_k \equiv \partial_2$ can be presented in tensor form, relative to the ordered bases $\{v_1, v_2\} \subset X_0$ for C_0, $\{e_1, e_2, e_3\} \subset X_1$ for C_1, and $\{\phi_1, \phi_2\} \subset X_2$ for C_2, by the matrices:

$$\partial e_j \equiv \partial_1 = \begin{bmatrix} -1 - 1 - 1 \\ 111 \end{bmatrix}, \qquad \partial \phi_k \equiv \partial_2 = \begin{bmatrix} 10 \\ -11 \\ 0 - 1 \end{bmatrix},$$

$$\text{so that} \quad : \quad \partial_1 \partial_2 = \begin{bmatrix} 00 \\ 00 \end{bmatrix} \Leftrightarrow \text{BBZ},$$

thus reflecting J. Wheeler's core topological concept [MTW73, CW95]: 'The boundary of a boundary is zero' (BBZ), with many applications to physics (ranging from Kirchoff's laws in electrical circuits, across the topological foundation of Maxwell's equations, to the Bianchi identities in general relativity (see [Wis06] for a review).

More generally, a generic decision system can be formulated as a topological *cell complex,* $\mathbf{X} = (X, \partial)$, which consists of a list of sets, $X = \{X_0, X_1, X_2 \ldots, X_k\}$ and the corresponding list of boundaries between them $\partial = \{\partial_0, \partial_1, \ldots, \partial_{k-1}\}$. Each individual set $X_k = X_k(\mathbf{X})$ is called the set of k-cells in $\mathbf{X}$, so that the corresponding boundary ∂_k of a k-cell is an 'algebraic sum' of $(k-1)$-cells.

More formally, for each k, let $C_k(\mathbf{X}) = \mathbb{Z}^X$ be the free Abelian group defined on the set X_k, as we did before in the (1.6), so that $C_k = C_k(\mathbf{X})$ consists of all formal linear combinations of k-cells with integer coefficients. In algebraic topology, the elements of C_k are called the k-*chains* in the cell complex $\mathbf{X}$. The corresponding boundary maps $\partial_k \colon C_k \to C_{k-1}$ are required to be linear over the set of integers $\mathbb{Z}$. In addition, if $\partial_0 \colon C_0 \to 0$ is the unique map from C_0 to the trivial group 0, then the nD decision chain is given by [Wis06, II07b, IR10b]:

$$0 \xleftarrow{\partial_0} C_0 \xleftarrow{\partial_1} C_1 \xleftarrow{\partial_2} C_2 \xleftarrow{\partial_3} \cdots \xleftarrow{\partial_n} C_n \,, \tag{1.7}$$

so that Wheeler's BBZ principle can be simply stated:

$$\partial_{k-1} \partial_k c = 0, \qquad \text{for every chain } c \in C_k, \qquad (k = 1, \ldots, n),$$
$$\text{or, formally:} \quad \partial \partial = \partial^2 = 0 \quad \Leftrightarrow \text{BBZ}.$$

In algebraic topology, such a sequence of maps $\partial \colon C_k \to C_{k-1}$ satisfying $\partial \partial = 0$ is called a *chain n-complex* (see, e.g., [II07b, IR10b]). Therefore, a generic decision chain is formally represented by a chain n-complex $\mathbf{X}$ defined by relation (1.7) of free Abelian groups $C_k(\mathbf{X})$, each with its own graph-basis $X_k(\mathbf{X})$, and the corresponding boundary maps $\partial \colon C_k \to C_{k-1}$ satisfying the BBZ principle: $\partial \partial = 0$.

Dual to the topological chain n-complex (1.7) is the following physical cochain n-complex, obtained by taking the coboundary, or exterior derivative d_k, as a formal adjoint to each boundary map ∂_k [Wis06, II07b, IR10b]:

$$C^0 \xrightarrow{d_0} C^1 \xrightarrow{d_1} C^2 \xrightarrow{d_2} \cdots \xrightarrow{d_{n-1}} C^n \xrightarrow{d_n} 0 \,,$$

i.e., given a cochain tensor $\omega_k \in C^k$, called the *decision field potential,* we define its derivative $d_k \omega \in C^{k+1}$, the *decision field strength,* as: $d_k \omega(x) = \omega(\partial_{k+1} x)$ ... which are both governed by Maxwell-like electrodynamics equations [MTW73, CW95] — which brings us to the field of exterior differential forms, which are special kind of tensors (completely antisymmetric, covariant p-tensors, see subsection 10.5 in the Appendix 1). In this way, any graphs or networks (electrical, neural, small worlds, biokinetic, etc.) can be described by tensors.

Tensorial Chains and Lattices

Since all *distributed CPC-autonomous systems* are represented by various kinds of networks, the next three Chapters of the monograph are devoted to *complex networks*, from the following three perspectives: (i) classical dynamics and control, (ii) quantum[16] information and computation,[17] and (iii) deep learning neural networks. Our physical background for complex networks comprises of various models of lattices evolving in discrete time and chains evolving in continuous time. All models presented in this section are integrable Hamiltonian systems.

Classical Lattice-Spin Models

Ising Spin Model

The development of lattice models in physics started with the classical *Ising spin-glass model*, defined by the Hamiltonian energy function $H : \mathbb{R}^n \to \mathbb{R}$ (given here in its simplest dot-product form, see [Wik16g] and the references therein):

$$H_{\text{Ising}} = -J_{ij}\sigma_i\sigma_j\,, \tag{1.8}$$

where summing over $\langle ij \rangle \in \mathbb{N}$ (the nearest-neighbor interaction on the lattice) is assumed, $\sigma_i \in \{+1, -1\}$ are discrete spin-up and spin-down states (or, more generally, Pauli spin matrices), while J_{ij} is the *interaction tensor* (or, *interaction matrix*) with synaptic weights. Later (in the 1980s), the Ising Hamiltonian (1.8) was used in *Hopfield neural networks* [Hop82], as well as in *Markov random fields/networks* [KS80].

Heisenberg Spin Model

The classical *Heisenberg spin model* is an n-dimensional generalization of the Ising model (1.8) with the interaction tensor J_{ij}, defined by the following dot-product Hamiltonian function $H : \mathbb{R}^n \to \mathbb{R}$ (see [Wik16e] and the references therein):

$$H_{\text{Heis}} = -J_{ij}\,\boldsymbol{\sigma}_i \cdot \boldsymbol{\sigma}_j, \qquad (\text{with } \boldsymbol{\sigma}_i \in \mathbb{R}^n),$$

(where summing over $\langle ij \rangle \in \mathbb{N}$ is assumed), is used to describe *classical ferromagnetism*. Its important two-dimensional case (with $\boldsymbol{\sigma}_i \in \mathbb{R}^2$) is called the XY-model.

---

[16] For the necessary background on quantum mechanics (including: Hilbert spaces, Shcrödinger's wave functions, Dirac's "bra-ket" vectors and Feynman's probability amplitudes expressed as path integrals) as well as the basis of quantum information, see [IR15] and the references therein.

[17] For additional background in quantum computation and neural networks, see [II09] and the references therein.

Quantum Lattice-Spin Models

Fermionic Hubbard Model

The (original) *fermionic Hubbard Hamiltonian* operator usually takes the following form:

$$\hat{H}_{\text{Hub}} = -t \sum_{\langle ij \rangle \sigma} \left(c_{i\sigma}^\dagger c_{j\sigma} + c_{j\sigma}^\dagger c_{i\sigma} \right) + U \sum_i n_{i\uparrow} n_{i\downarrow},$$

where $c_i^\dagger, c_i$ denote the creation and annihilation operators of an electron (or, any other fermion[18]) on a localized orbital on site i, such that $n_i = c_i^\dagger c_i$ gives the number of fermions on site i. The first sum is called the *hopping integral* with the kinetic energy t of electrons hopping between atoms. The second sum is the *on-site repulsion* with the potential energy U arising from the charges on the electrons. The on-site interaction U can be attractive ($U < 0$) or repulsive ($U > 0$).

Bosonic Hubbard Model

The *bosonic Hubbard Hamiltonian* operator (with chemical potential μ) usually takes the following form:

$$\hat{H}_{\text{BH}} = -t \sum_{\langle ij \rangle} b_i^\dagger b_j + \frac{U}{2} \sum_i n_i \left(n_i - 1 \right) - \mu \sum_i n_i,$$

where $b_i^\dagger$ and b_i denote the creation and annihilation operators of a photon (or, any other boson[19]) with $n_i = b_i^\dagger b_i$. Both Hubbard models are used to study *quantum ferromagnetism*.

Continuous-Time Soliton Chains

The following three continuous-time chains are integrable spatiotemporal Hamiltonian systems. Their solutions are discrete-space solitons, kinks and breathers (see [II13] and the references therein).

---

[18] Fermions are matter particles that follow Fermi-Dirac statistics and obey the Pauli exclusion principle: only one fermion can occupy a particular quantum state at any given time and space.

[19] Bosons are elementary particles that follow Bose-Einstein statistics; they are force carriers, and several of them can occupy the same place in space.

Sine-Gordon Chain

The *Sine-Gordon chain* of harmonically coupled atoms in a spatially-periodic potential is usually represented as:[20]

$$\ddot{\phi}_n = \phi_{n+1} - 2\phi_n + \phi_{n-1} - \sin\phi_n, \qquad (1.9)$$

where ϕ_n denotes the position of the nth atom in the chain. The system (1.9) also represents a chain of torsionally-coupled pendula, where ϕ_n is the angle which the nth pendulum makes with the vertical. This set of differential-difference equations is obtained by spatial discretization of the (1+1) *Sine-Gordon equation*:

$$\phi_{tt} = \phi_{xx} - \sin\phi, \qquad (\phi_{zz} = \partial^2\phi/\partial z^2),$$

which is a nonlinear extension of the linear wave equation: $\phi_{tt} = \phi_{xx}$ for the real-valued wave function $\phi(t,x)$ (see, e.g. [IR14] and the references therein).

NLS Chain

The *NLS chain*, also called the discreet NLS (DNLS, see e.g. [OB07] and the references therein):

$$i\dot{\psi}_n + \psi_{n+1} - 2\psi_n + \psi_{n-1} = \gamma|\psi|^2\psi,$$

is obtained by spatial discretization of the (1+1) *nonlinear Schrödinger equation* (NLS):

$$i\psi_t + \psi_{xx} = \gamma|\psi|^2\psi,$$

for the complex-valued wave function $\psi(t,x)$ with the cubic potential well $\gamma|\psi|^2\psi$ (see, e.g. [IR12] and the references therein).

Toda Chain

The *Toda chain* (or, Toda lattice, see [Tod89]) is the following spatially-discrete Hamiltonian dynamical system:

$$\dot{q}(n,t) = p(n,t), \qquad \dot{p} = e^{-[q(n,t)-q(n-1,t)]} - e^{-(q(n+1,t)-q(n,t))},$$

where $[q(n,t), p(n,t)]$ are the displacements and momenta of the nth particle from its equilibrium position.

---

[20] This is the so-called *Frenkel-Kontorova chain* (see [BS98]).

1.5.4 Mechanics of Autonomous Vehicles

From mechanical perspective, all *unmanned autonomous vehicles*, including aerial vehicles (UAVs), ground vehicles (UGVs), sea vehicles (USVs) and underwater vehicles (UUVs), represent Newtonian rigid bodies, moving either in a 2D plane (UGVs and USVs), or in 3D space (UAVs and UUVs). Specifically, the motion of each ground vehicle defines a 3-parameter *Euclidean group* $SE(2)$ of rigid motions in a plane,[21] including two translations and one rotation, while each air vehicle defines a 6-parameter Euclidean group $SE(3)$ of rigid motions in 3D space,[22] including three coupled Euler rotations (roll, pitch and yaw), and three Cartesian translations. Properly described dynamics of each autonomous vehicle, defining both translational (or, 'linear') and rotational (or, 'angular') positions, velocities, accelerations and jerks, is defined as the *Newton-Euler dynamics* on the corresponding Euclidean group, with three active DOFs in the case of $SE(2)$ and six active DOFs in the case of $SE(3)$:

---

[21] Recall that the Euclidean $SE(2)$-group of rigid body motions in the plane, technically $SE(2) \equiv SO(2) \times \mathbb{R}$, is a set of all $3 \times 3-$matrices of the form (see [II13] and the references therein):

$$\begin{bmatrix} \cos\theta & \sin\theta & q \\ -\sin\theta & \cos\theta & p \\ 0 & 0 & 1 \end{bmatrix}, \qquad \theta = \arctan\left(\frac{p}{q}\right),$$

including both rigid translations [i.e., Cartesian $(x, y) \equiv (q, p)-$coordinates] and rotation matrix $\begin{bmatrix} \cos\theta & \sin\theta \\ -\sin\theta & \cos\theta \end{bmatrix}$ in the Euclidean plane $\mathbb{R}^2$. In particular, every ground vehicle (or boat) is a rigid body in a plane, thus it can be formally represented by the $SE(2)$-group.

[22] Briefly, the (special) Euclidean group is defined as a semidirect (noncommutative) product of 3D rotations and 3D translations, $SE(3) := SO(3) \rhd \mathbb{R}^3$. $SE(3)$ is the Lie group consisting of isometries of the Euclidean 3D space $\mathbb{R}^3$. Its most important subgroups are the following (see [II13] and the references therein):

Subgroup	Definition
$SO(3)$, group of rotations in 3D (a spherical joint)	Set of all proper orthogonal $3 \times 3 -$ rotational matrices
$SE(2)$, special Euclidean group in 2D (all planar motions)	Set of all $3 \times 3 -$ matrices: $\begin{bmatrix} \cos\theta & \sin\theta & r_x \\ -\sin\theta & \cos\theta & r_y \\ 0 & 0 & 1 \end{bmatrix}$
$SO(2)$, group of rotations in 2D subgroup of $SE(2)-$group (a revolute joint)	Set of all proper orthogonal $2 \times 2 -$ rotational matrices included in $SE(2) -$ group
$\mathbb{R}^3$, group of translations in 3D (all spatial displacements)	Euclidean 3D vector space

$$\text{Newton}: \begin{cases} \dot{p}_1 = F_1 - m_3 v_3 \omega_2 + m_2 v_2 \omega_3 \\ \dot{p}_2 = F_2 + m_3 v_3 \omega_1 - m_1 v_1 \omega_3 \ , \\ \dot{p}_3 = F_3 - m_2 v_2 \omega_1 + m_1 v_1 \omega_2 \end{cases} \qquad (1.10)$$

$$\text{Euler}: \begin{cases} \dot{\pi}_1 = T_1 + (m_2 - m_3) v_2 v_3 + (I_2 - I_3)\ \omega_2 \omega_3 \\ \dot{\pi}_2 = T_2 + (m_3 - m_1) v_1 v_3 + (I_3 - I_1)\ \omega_1 \omega_3 \ , \\ \dot{\pi}_3 = T_3 + (m_1 - m_2) v_1 v_2 + (I_1 - I_2)\ \omega_1 \omega_2 \end{cases}$$

where $\mathbf{v} = [v_1, v_2, v_3]^T$ and $\boldsymbol{\omega} = [\omega_1, \omega_2, \omega_3]^T$ are linear and angular velocity vectors; $\mathbf{p} = [p_1, p_2, p_3]^T$ and $\boldsymbol{\pi} = [\pi_1, \pi_2, \pi_3]^T$ are linear and angular momenta, while $\mathbf{F} = [F_1, F_2, F_3]^T$ and $\mathbf{T} = [T_1, T_2, T_3]^T$ are all active forces and torques, respectively. Numerical integration of the set of Newton-Euler equations of motion (1.10), for chosen initial conditions, gives the time evolution for both linear and angular displacements, velocities and accelerations, while their simple analytical differentiation gives both linear and angular jerks (see [II13] and the references therein).

A swarm of such $SE(3)$-vehicles can be represented by the *swarm manifold* M (as depicted in Figure 1.1) with the cotangent bundle T^*M called the *swarm phase space*. The swarm dynamics is governed by the following set of forced and dissipative Hamiltonian equations of motion [IY16]:

$$\dot{q}^i = \partial_{p_i} H - \partial_{p_i} R, \qquad (1.11)$$
$$\dot{p}_i = F_i - \partial_{q^i} H + \partial_{q^i} R,$$

where q^i (for $i = 1, ..., n$) are the generalized coordinates associated with all active DOFs within each swarm, p_i are their corresponding momenta (both linear and angular), $H : T^*M \rightarrow \mathbb{R} = H(q, p)$ is swarm's Hamiltonian, representing the total (kinetic and potential) energy function of the swarm, $F_i = F_i(t, q, p)$ are the generalized driving forces (including both translational forces $\mathbf{F}_i$ and torques $\mathbf{T}_i$), while $R = R(q, p) = \frac{1}{2} p_i^2 q_i^2$ denotes the Rayleigh dissipative function. This idea is further elaborated in the next Chapter.

1.5.5 Quantum Entanglement: $ER = EPR$

Our CPC-autonomy is underpinned by the fundamental physical concept of *quantum entanglement*[23] (see, e.g. [Wik16d] and the references therein), which provides quantum-computational representation of the holistic information flow and energy exchange occurring in trusted autonomous systems (this fundamental idea is further elaborated in Chapter 4).

---

[23] The term "entanglement" was coined by E. Schrödinger in a letter to A. Einstein, with a meaning "to describe the correlations between two particles that interact and then separate, as in the famous *EPR experiment*" [Wik16d]. The two particles remain connected regardless of how far apart they are (even over cosmologically large distances) with the same velocity/momentum and opposite (mirrored) spin [Nit16] and actions performed on one particle have an effect on the other" [Sta15].

Today it is well known that entanglement is a 'hidden' phenomenon that underpins the whole of nature,[24] as well as all highly-effective communication, information and computation systems. Entanglement is a complex process that consists of a large number of mutually-interacting sub-processes or subsystems with quantum origin but manifesting wherever a 'holistic' system behavior is observed at the macroscopic 'real-life' scale. It includes all natural particles (photons, electrons, neutrinos, etc.), as well as more complex systems (e.g., harmonic and anharmonic oscillators) and quantum-computational units (qubits and multiqubits). In particular, according to [Lan14]: "Entanglement lies at the core of quantum algorithms designed to solve problems that are intractable by classical approaches" — where the wave function for the quantum-state of each included subsystem cannot be described independently, but only as a joint system as a whole.

The motivation for placing the entanglement at the very foundation of the CPC-autonomy is "*The second Einstein equation*" (coined by L. Susskind from Stanford and J. Maldacena from Princeton):

$$ER = EPR \; \Leftrightarrow \; Wormhole = Entanglement$$

(see [Cow15] and the references therein), which relates two Einstein's papers from 1935:[25]

- *ER*, referring to the *Einstein-Rosen Bridge* [ER35] (or, a *wormhole* that connects two distant parts of the space-time continuum, as depicted in the movie *Interstellar* (2014)); and
- *EPR*, referring to the *EPR paradox* (the Einstein, Podolsky and Rosen paradox [EPR35] where entanglement was born, though not wanted by Einstein).

The concept of entanglement subsumes such fundamental scientific keywords as *correlation*, *causality* and *function*. It has become the cornerstone of 21st Century physics. For example, according to J. Preskill from Caltech,

---

[24] Although it is an essentially microscopic phenomenon, the effects of entanglement are seen in any macroscopic system/process that cannot be properly reduced to its components, but only for a joint system as a whole. In particular, entanglement provides arguably the only rigorous method to describe holistic swarming behaviors of bees, birds, bats, etc., as well as their navigation (e.g., in case of a bird navigation, their retina detects spin of photons affected by Earth's magnetic field and acts like a compass).

[25] Einstein did not believe in physical reality of quantum entanglement, which he called "spooky action at a distance". Ironically, the recent developments in theoretical physics (see [Cow15] and the references therein), show that entanglement is not only the foundation of quantum physics, but according to the $ER = EPR$ equation, it is also the foundation of Einstein's own general relativity theory — which makes it the most plausible pathway to the *quantum gravity*, the "Holy Grail" of modern physics.)

the essence of entanglement can be described as: "When we talk about information being encoded, [we mean that] we can split a system into parts and there is some *correlation* among the parts so we can learn something about one part by observing another part."

Our comment on this well-known fact from physics community is the following threefold interpretation:

1. We start with the '*statistical magic formula*':

$$\text{CORRELATION} = \text{ENTANGLEMENT}$$

   Therefore, any multivariate statistics, which are all based on the concept of (Pearson's) correlation, can be quantum-mechanically founded on the concept of entanglement, much like the *Bayesian probability* can be founded on the more fundamental *quantum probability* (see [IR15]).

2. Next, as a stronger particular case of correlation, any causal relation is an instance of entanglement, which gives us the '*philosophical magic formula*':

$$\text{CAUSALITY} = \text{STRONGER ENTANGLEMENT}$$

3. Finally, as a stronger particular case of causality, any functional relation is an instance of entanglement, so we have the '*mathematical magic formula*':

$$\text{FUNCTION} = the \text{ STRONGEST ENTANGLEMENT}$$

where we have assumed the following subset structure:

$$\text{CORRELATION} \supseteq \text{CAUSALITY} \supseteq \text{FUNCTION}$$

with the corresponding implication structure:

$$\text{FUNCTION} \Longrightarrow \text{CAUSALITY} \Longrightarrow \text{CORRELATION}$$

[Recall that Schrödinger's *wave-function* ψ is characterized by its absolute square $P = |\psi|^2$ that is the *probability density function* (PDF). ψ-wave is a complex-valued function of real space variables $\mathbf{x} = (x_1, x_2, ..., x_n) \in \mathbb{R}^n$, formally $\psi(\mathbf{x}) : \mathbb{R}^n \to \mathbb{C}$. For example, the one–dimensional *stationary plane wave* with wave number k is defined as: $\psi(x) = e^{ikx}$, (for $x \in \mathbb{R}$), where the real number k describes the wavelength, $\lambda = 2\pi/k$. In n dimensions, this becomes: $\psi(x) = e^{i\mathbf{p}\cdot\mathbf{x}}$, where the momentum vector $\mathbf{p} = \mathbf{k}$ is the vector of the wave numbers $\mathbf{k}$ in natural units (in which $\hbar = m = 1$).

More generally, ψ-wave function is also time dependent, $\psi = \psi(\mathbf{x}, \mathbf{t})$. The time-dependent plane wave is defined by:

$$\psi(\mathbf{x}, \mathbf{t}) = e^{i\mathbf{p}\cdot\mathbf{x} - ip^2 t/2}. \tag{1.12}$$

In general, $\psi(\mathbf{x}, \mathbf{t})$ is governed by the Schrödinger equation [Tha05, II08b] (in natural units $\hbar = m = 0$):

$$i\frac{\partial}{\partial t}\psi(\mathbf{x},t) = -\frac{1}{2}\Delta\psi(\mathbf{x},t), \tag{1.13}$$

where Δ is the n-dimensional Laplacian. The solution of (1.13) is given by the integral of the time–dependent plane wave (1.12):

$$\psi(\mathbf{x},t) = \frac{1}{(2\pi)^{n/2}}\int_{\mathbb{R}^n} e^{i\mathbf{p}\cdot\mathbf{x}-ip^2 t/2}\hat{\psi}_0(\mathbf{p})d^n p,$$

which means that $\psi(\mathbf{x},t)$ is the inverse Fourier transform of the function:

$$\hat{\psi}(\mathbf{p},t) = e^{-ip^2 t/2}\hat{\psi}_0(\mathbf{p}),$$

where $\hat{\psi}_0(\mathbf{p})$ has to be calculated for each initial wave-function. For example, if the initial wave-function is Gaussian:

$$f(x) = \exp(-a\frac{x^2}{2}), \quad \text{with the Fourier transform:} \quad \hat{f}(p) = \frac{1}{\sqrt{a}}\exp(-\frac{p^2}{2a}).$$

$$\text{then} \quad \hat{\psi}_0(p) = \frac{1}{\sqrt{a}}\exp(-\frac{p^2}{2a}).$$

]

The concept of ENTANGLEMENT is further expanded by B. Swingle from Stanford [Oue15]: "Entanglement is the thread that binds the system together, that makes the collective properties different from the individual properties. But to really see the interesting collective behavior, you need to understand how entanglement is distributed." A mathematical theory that defines the distribution of entanglement in any complex system is the *tensor network theory* (described in Chapter 4). Any system in this world, including the space-time continuum,[26] represents a complex network consisting of a huge number of interlinked nodes, all glued together via entanglement[27] that encodes the information between the interacting nodes in the system. The *principle of*

---

[26] The smooth space-time continuum emerges from discrete bits of quantum information.

[27] Swingle states: "Entanglement is the fabric of space-time." He argues that the macroscopic *gravitational universality*, that everything falls at the same rate, can be properly understood only in terms of the more fundamental microscopic *quantum universality*, entanglement, which is a transferable universal force between photons, electrons, neutrinos, or any other kind of particles, as well as tensor networks glued by entanglement. So, to continue in the same fashion, it can be argued that the four fundamental forces of nature (gravitational, electromagnetic, strong nuclear and weak nuclear) all emerge from entanglement, the real origin, the universal glue that connects everything. Therefore, notwithstanding the efforts of the superstring community to produce a mathematically consistent "theory of everything," we argue that we already know "the core" of any plausible future theory of everything: it is *quantum entanglement*.

locality[28] greatly simplifies this grand picture by the following discretization: any particle interacts only with its nearest neighboring particles. The nodes of the network are formally represented by *tensors*,[29] which are produced by entangling each particle with its neighbors. A tensor network is made up of many interlinked tensor nodes, which can be contracted[30] to simplify the analysis.

Representing the foundation of the physical universe, we argue that entanglement realized through tensor networks should also become the foundation of a CPC-autonomy. In the remainder of this subsection we briefly outline this new concept.

Informally and briefly, assuming that all the basic information of our hypothetical CPC-autonomous system, consisting of a number of simple (microscopic) ingredients, is contained in its wave function $|\Psi(t)\rangle$, a development of desired autonomous qualities can be described in terms of a *recursive tensor-network evolution*, as follows. We start with the initial wave function $|\Psi(t_{\text{init}})\rangle$ of a simple microscopic system containing only non-interacting particles (or, micro-ingredients), all in their lowest energy states. Then, we recursively apply a certain tensor network to this evolving system — until we obtain the final wave function $|\Psi(t_{\text{fin}})\rangle$ for a large and highly complex autonomous system, with many completely new macroscopic qualities and a full spectrum of energy states for each or them. In this way, the simple information contained in the initial wave function has evolved into a highly complex information contained in the final wave function. Therefore, by recursively applying a tensor network to any initial microscopic system, we can control its evolution into a complex macroscopic CPC-autonomous system.

Formally, this recursive tensor-network evolution can be defined by the following transition amplitude:

---

[28] A. Einstein formulated the principle of locality in general relativity before the advent of Bohr-Heisenberg's quantum mechanics. He says: "Physics is simple only locally," because locally (at any point) the surface of an apple looks flat (so, we can ignore the curvature of space-time). In geometric terminology, this is expressed as: a smooth n-manifold is an nD space which can be locally (at any point) approximated by the Euclidean space $\mathbb{R}^n$. This *topological equivalence* enables both local physics and geometry on manifolds: (i) performing local measurements, and (ii) using the $\mathbb{R}^n$-tools of calculus and linear algebra.

[29] Note that we will also use tensors in different contexts, e.g. "Tensor Flow"in *deep learning* and *tensor neural networks*, presented later in the book.

[30] The so-called *tensor contraction* (or, *tensor inner product*) reduces the dimensionality of a tensor (e.g., a contraction of the second-order metric tensor $\boldsymbol{g} = g_{ij}$) that can be represented by a square matrix $[g_{ij}]$ gives the scalar, its trace $g = \text{Tr}(\boldsymbol{g}) = \text{Tr}(g_{ij})$. Similarly, the fourth-order Riemannian curvature tensor $\boldsymbol{R}^4 = R^i_{jkl}$ can be contracted into the Ricci curvature tensor $\boldsymbol{R}^2 = R_{kl}$, which can further contracted into the scalar Gaussian curvature $\boldsymbol{R}^1 = R$ (see [IR15] and Chapter 10, Appendix 1). In a similar way, complex tensor networks can be contracted to give simpler and simpler tensor networks, while still retaining its entanglement essence.

$$\underset{\text{Tensor Network}}{\langle \text{Out}(t_{\text{fin}}) \mid \text{In}(t_{\text{init}}) \rangle} \Leftrightarrow |\Psi(t)\rangle : \underset{\text{Tensor Network}}{|\Psi(t_{\text{init}})\rangle \rightarrow |\Psi(t_{\text{fin}})\rangle}.$$

The objective of this section is to develop this fundamental structure to a certain level of completeness and consistency, so that it becomes applicable to CPC-autonomy.

1.5.6 Second-Quantization Formalism

Here we give a brief on the second-quantization formalism that is used in the Chapter 4.

Bosonic Second Quantization

Recall that the quantum harmonic oscillator is defined by the *Hamiltonian operator*:

$$\hat{H} = \left(\hat{p}^2/m + m\omega^2 \hat{x}^2 \right)/2, \tag{1.14}$$

where m and ω are oscillator's mass and frequency, while $\hat{x}$ and $\hat{p} = -i\partial/\partial x$ (assuming: $\hbar = 1$) are the *position and momentum operators*, which satisfy the *canonical commutation relation*:[31]

$$[\hat{x}, \hat{p}] = i. \tag{1.15}$$

In addition, the second-quantization treatment of the harmonic oscillator (1.14) requires also the (mutually 'dual') *creation and annihilation operators*, $\hat{a}^\dagger$ and $\hat{a}$, respectively defined by:

$$\hat{a} = (m\omega/2)^{1/2}\, \hat{x} + i\,(m\omega/2)^{-1/2}\, \hat{p}, \qquad \hat{a}^\dagger = (m\omega/2)^{1/2}\, \hat{x} - i\,(m\omega/2)^{-1/2}\, \hat{p},$$

and obeying the commutation relation:

$$[\hat{a}, \hat{a}^\dagger] = 1,$$

which follows directly from (1.15). Besides, the product of the creation and annihilation operators defines the *number operator*: $\hat{n} = \hat{a}^\dagger \hat{a}$. Using the second-quantization operators $\hat{a}^\dagger, \hat{a}$ and $\hat{n}$, the Hamiltonian (1.14) becomes:

---

[31] Recall that the *commutator* $[\hat{A}, \hat{B}]$ of two quantum-mechanical operators $\hat{A}$ and $\hat{B}$ is defined as: $[\hat{A}, \hat{B}] = \hat{A}\hat{B} - \hat{B}\hat{A}$. Note that an analogous relation in classical (Hamiltonian) mechanics is obtained by replacing the commutator with the *Poisson bracket* $[A, B]_{PB}$ multiplied by $i\hbar$; e.g., in case of position x and momentum p, their Poisson bracket is $[x, p]_{PB} = 1$. This correspondence is the basis of Dirac's quantization, also called

$$\text{canonical quantization} : [A, B]_{PB} \Rightarrow i\hbar[\hat{A}, \hat{B}].$$

$$\hat{H} = \omega(\hat{a}^\dagger \hat{a} + 1/2) = \omega(\hat{n} + 1/2). \tag{1.16}$$

An obvious particular case of (1.16) is a simplified oscillator with the Hamiltonian:

$$\hat{H} = \omega \hat{a}^\dagger \hat{a} = \omega \hat{n}. \tag{1.17}$$

The *ground state* $|0\rangle$ of the oscillator (1.14)–(1.16) has the following properties:

$$\hat{a}|0\rangle = 0, \qquad \hat{H}|0\rangle = \frac{\omega}{2}|0\rangle.$$

For example, in the *position representation* (i.e., in the basis of eigenstates of the $\hat{p}$-operator), the ground state $|0\rangle$,

with components: $\psi_0(x) = \langle x|0\rangle = e^{m\omega\hat{x}^2/2}$, satisfies: $\hat{a}|0\rangle = 0$.

The *excited states* of the oscillator are built-up by applying the creation operator $\hat{a}^\dagger$ repeatedly to the ground state $|0\rangle$:

$$\hat{a}^\dagger |n\rangle = \sqrt{n+1}\,|n+1\rangle,$$

where $|n\rangle$ denotes the vector of *occupation number states* and obeys the relation:

$$\hat{H}|n\rangle = \omega(\hat{n} + 1/2)|n\rangle. \tag{1.18}$$

To express the standard *partition function* for an arbitrary quantum-mechanical system (see, e.g. [ST99]):

$$Z = \text{Tr}[\exp(-\beta\hat{H})], \qquad (\text{with } \beta = 1/t)$$

(where t is the temperature, while the common trace operation 'Tr[·]' is the sum of the diagonal elements), one chooses any *complete set of states* $|a\rangle$ so that: $Z = \text{tr}(e^{-\beta\hat{H}}) = \sum_a \langle a|e^{-\beta\hat{H}}|a\rangle$.

It can be shown (by using (1.18) and $|n\rangle$ as the complete set of states) that the partition function of the harmonic oscillator (1.14)–(1.16) is:

$$Z = \sum_n \langle n\,|\exp\left[-\beta\omega\left(\hat{n}+1/2\right)\right]|\,n\rangle = e^{-\beta\omega/2}(1 - e^{-\beta\omega})^{-1}.$$

In particular, for the simplified oscillator (1.17), the partition function is: $Z = \left(1 - e^{-\beta\omega}\right)^{-1}$.

Given the partition function Z, the (finite-temperature) *expectation value* $\langle \hat{A} \rangle$ of an arbitrary quantum-mechanical operator $\hat{A}$ is given by:

$$\langle \hat{A} \rangle = Z^{-1}\text{Tr}[\hat{A}\exp(-\beta\hat{H})]. \tag{1.19}$$

In case of the oscillator (1.14), the relation (1.19) reduces to the expectation value of the number operator:

$$\langle \hat{n} \rangle = 1/\left(e^{-\beta\omega} - 1\right),$$

which is the *Bose-Einstein distribution* function.[32]

---

[32] Recall that the *spin* of a particle is its intrinsic angular momentum. The *spin-statistics theorem* classifies particles according to their spin into one of the two

Fermionic Second Quantization

The Hubbard model is usually written in terms of *fermion creation and anni-hilation operators*,[33] which differ in several aspects from the bosonic operators $\hat{a}^\dagger$ and $\hat{a}$. Firstly, the fermion operators in the Hubbard model are not introduced in terms of position and momentum operators, but they are rather independent operators. Secondly, instead of just one creation and one annihilation operator, in the Hubbard model there is a set of such operators, which are usually distinguished by indices $\mathbf{k}, \mathbf{j}$ (that label the spatial lattice sites) and σ (that labels the electron spin, up $|\uparrow\rangle$ or down $|\downarrow\rangle$), so that one usually writes $\hat{c}_{\mathbf{k}\sigma}^\dagger$ for the creation operator and $\hat{c}_{\mathbf{k}\sigma}$ for the annihilation operator. As a consequence, the occupation number states are no longer characterized by a single number n (as for a single harmonic oscillator) but instead by a collection of occupation numbers $n_{\mathbf{k}\sigma}$, with the states written by the ket: $|n_{1\sigma} \, n_{2\sigma} \, n_{3\sigma}...\rangle$.

To be able to describe fermions, these operators, by definition, obey the following *anticommutation relations*:[34]

$$\{\hat{c}_{\mathbf{k}\sigma}, \hat{c}_{\mathbf{j}\sigma}^\dagger\} = \delta_{\mathbf{k}\mathbf{j}}\delta_{\sigma\sigma'}, \qquad \{\hat{c}_{\mathbf{k}\sigma}^\dagger, \hat{c}_{\mathbf{j}\sigma'}^\dagger\} = 0, \qquad \{\hat{c}_{\mathbf{k}\sigma}, \hat{c}_{\mathbf{j}\sigma'}\} = 0. \qquad (1.20)$$

An immediate consequence of (1.20) is the *Pauli exclusion principle*,[35] which states that the maximum occupation number of a particular site with a given spin is 1.[36]

---

quantum statistics they obey:

(i) *bosons* are particles (such as four force-carrying gauge bosons of the Standard Model) with integer spin (1,2,3, etc.) and symmetric states (or, wave functions), obeying the *Bose-Einstein distribution*;

(ii) *fermions* are particles (such as electrons, quarks and leptons, which are the key building blocks of matter) with half-integer spin (1/2, 3/2, 5/2, etc.) and antisymmetric states, obeying the *Fermi-Dirac distribution*.

[33] As opposed to *boson creation and annihilation operators*, which we used so far in the second-quantization treatment of the harmonic oscillator (1.14).

[34] Recall that the *anticommutator* $\{\hat{A}, \hat{B}\}$ of two fermion operators $\hat{A}$ and $\hat{B}$ is defined as: $\{\hat{A}, \hat{B}\} = \hat{A}\hat{B} + \hat{B}\hat{A}$. Note here the use of the curly brackets for anticommutators, to distinguish them from the boson commutators $[\hat{A}, \hat{B}] = \hat{A}\hat{B} - \hat{B}\hat{A}$.

[35] The Pauli exclusion principle governs the behavior of all fermions, while bosons are not subject to it. A more rigorous statement states that the total wave function for two identical fermions is antisymmetric with respect to exchange of the particles, which means that the wave function changes its sign if the space and spin coordinates of any two particles are interchanged.

[36] Because of the anticommutation relation (1.20) one needs to specify a convention for the relation between a state like $|1 \, 0 \, 1 \, 0 \, 0 \, ...\rangle$ and the *vacuum state*: $|vac\rangle = |0 \, 0 \, 0 \, 0 \, 0 \, ...\rangle$. The following two possibilities:

$$|1 \, 0 \, 1 \, 0 \, 0 \, ...\rangle = \hat{c}_1^\dagger \hat{c}_3^\dagger \, |vac\rangle \quad \text{and} \quad |1 \, 0 \, 1 \, 0 \, 0 \, ...\rangle = \hat{c}_3^\dagger \hat{c}_1^\dagger \, |vac\rangle$$

— differ by a sign, yet they are both correct (provided the chosen one is used consistently).

Notational change: From now on (as we are consistently using the second-quantization formalism) for the sake of simplicity, we will drop all the 'hats'. So, we define $c_{\mathbf{j}\sigma}^{\dagger}$ to be the operator which creates an electron of spin σ on a lattice site $\mathbf{j}$; similarly, $c_{\mathbf{j}\sigma}$ is the destruction operator, and $n_{\mathbf{j}\sigma} = c_{\mathbf{j}\sigma}^{\dagger} c_{\mathbf{j}\sigma}$ is the occupation number operator.

As the most trivial 1DOF example, analogous to the *boson Hamiltonian* (1.17), there is the following *fermion Hamiltonian*:

$$H = \varepsilon c^{\dagger} c, \quad \text{with partition function:} \quad Z = \left(1 + e^{-\beta \varepsilon}\right), \tag{1.21}$$

that describes a simplified fermion oscillator with frequency ε, which represents a single fermion site without spin. Its basis states are: $\{|k\rangle\} = \{|0\rangle, |1\rangle\}$, in which $|0\rangle$ represents an unoccupied site, while $|1\rangle = c^{\dagger}|0\rangle$ is an occupied site. The corresponding (stationary) Schrödinger equation is: $H|k\rangle = E_k|k\rangle$, with $E_0 = 0$ and $E_1 = \varepsilon$. Its Hamiltonian matrix is given by:

$$\{H_{jk}\} = \begin{pmatrix} 0 & 0 \\ 0 & \varepsilon \end{pmatrix}, \quad \text{where} \quad H_{jk} = \langle k|H|j\rangle.$$

The 1DOF system (1.21) can be easily generalized to following (no-spin, no-hopping, no-interraction) model with M sites:

$$H = \varepsilon_k c_k^{\dagger} c_k, \tag{1.22}$$

which has the basis $\{|0\rangle_k, |1\rangle_k\}$ for each k-th site, which all comprise the many-particle basis of 2^M states:

$$\{|0\rangle_1, |1\rangle_1\} \otimes \{|0\rangle_2, |1\rangle_2\} \otimes \{|0\rangle_3, |1\rangle_3\} \otimes \ldots \otimes \{|0\rangle_M, |1\rangle_M\}$$
$$= |n_1\rangle_1 |n_2\rangle_2 |n_3\rangle_3 \ldots |n_M\rangle_M = |n_1\, n_2\, n_3...n_M\rangle.$$

We label basis states by occupation numbers:

$$\hat{n}_k |l\rangle \equiv \hat{n}_k |n_1\, n_2\, n_3...n_M\rangle = n_k |l\rangle.$$

The Hamiltonian (1.22) conserves separately the occupation of each site:

$$H|l\rangle = \varepsilon_k \hat{n}_k |l\rangle, \quad \text{such that} \quad [H, \hat{n}_k] = 0.$$

n_k is a good quantum number: the basis states $|l\rangle$ are eigenstates, that is, Hamiltonian matrix is again diagonal in this basis. The many-particle energy follows trivially:

$$E_l = \langle l|H|l\rangle = \langle n_1\, n_2\, n_3...n_M| \varepsilon_k \hat{n}_k |n_1\, n_2\, n_3...n_M\rangle = \varepsilon_k n_k.$$

For more technical details on the fermionic operators, see [Que12].

Physics of the CPC-Autonomy: Port-Hamiltonian Dynamics and Control of Multi-Physical Networks

2.1 Introduction to Port-Hamiltonian Modeling of Multi-Physical Networks

Port-Hamiltonian network modeling represents rigorous Hamiltonian generalization of classical *bond-graph* modeling (see Figure 2.1), in which interaction between ideal system components is modeled by *power-ports* representing the energy exchange between the components. The father of *port-Hamiltonian control systems* (PHS) evolving on dynamical networks is Arjan van der Schaft from the University of Twente (see [Sch06, SM13] and the references therein). Schaft's recipe for dealing with complex nonlinear multi-physical networks is: *"Modularity can beat complexity."*[1]

PHS constitute (a post-year 2000) second-generation of Hamiltonian control systems derived from the first-generation *affine Lagrangian and Hamiltonian control systems* (ACS), developed (in 1990) jointly by Henk Nijmeijer and Schaft [NS90]. ACS provide a unification of:

1. Modern Lagrangian and Hamiltonian mechanics of Arnold [Arn78] and Abraham-Marsden [AM78], with
2. Isidori's nonlinear generalization [Isi89] of Kalman's linear state-space MIMO control systems [KFA69],

   — to Lagrangian and Hamiltonian nonlinear MIMO control systems.

2.1.1 PHS Background

As a background to port-Hamiltonian control systems, we give here a brief review of the following classical systems and networks:

---

[1] We remark that this slogan is also the foundation of software engineering, pioneered by Niclaus Wirth, the father of the Pascal language.

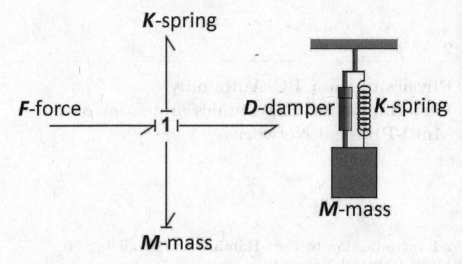

Fig. 2.1. *A bond graph model (left) of a standard mass-spring-damper system (right).*

RLC-circuit: A series *RLC-circuit* (see Figure 2.2) with voltage-input $u(t)$, resistance R, inductance L, capacitance C and current $i(t)$ is governed by:

$$L\frac{di(t)}{dt} + R\,i(t) + C^{-1}\int_0^t i(t)\,dt = u(t),$$

or, in Laplace transform notation:

$$Ls\,I(s) + R\,I(s) + (Cs)^{-1}\,I(s) = U(s),$$

which gives the circuit impedance:

$$Z(s) = \frac{U(s)}{I(s)} = Ls + R + (Cs)^{-1}.$$

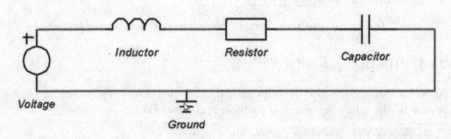

Fig. 2.2. *Diagram of a series RLC circuit.*

PID-controller: A conventional *PID-controller* of the error $e(t)$, with proportional (K_p), integral (K_i), and derivative (K_d) gains, is governed by:

$$K_d \frac{de(t)}{dt} + K_p e(t) + K_i \int_0^t e(t)\, dt = u(t),$$

or, in Laplace transform notation:

$$K_d s\, E(s) + K_p\, E(s) + (K_i/s)\, E(s) = U(s),$$

which gives the controller impedance:

$$Z(s) = \frac{U(s)}{E(s)} = K_d s + K_p + \frac{K_i}{s}.$$

Mass-spring-damper system: A *translational mass-spring-damper* system with force-input $f(t)$, mass M, damper B, spring K and velocity $v(t)$, is governed by:

$$M \frac{dv(t)}{dt} + B\, v(t) + K \int_0^t v(t)\, dt = f(t), \qquad (2.1)$$

or, in Laplace transform notation:

$$M s\, V(s) + B\, V(s) + (K/s)\, V(s) = F(s),$$

which gives the translational mechanical impedance:

$$Z(s) = \frac{F(s)}{V(s)} = M s + B + \frac{K}{s}.$$

Rotational mass-spring-damper: A *rotational mass-spring-damper* system with torque-input $\tau(t)$, inertia moment J, angular damper B, angular spring κ and angular velocity $w(t)$, is governed by:

$$J \frac{dw(t)}{dt} + D\, w(t) + \kappa \int_0^t w(t)\, dt = \tau(t),$$

or, in Laplace transform notation:

$$J s\, W(s) + D\, W(s) + (\kappa/s)\, W(s) = T(s),$$

which gives the rotational mechanical impedance:

$$Z(s) = \frac{T(s)}{W(s)} = J s + D + \frac{\kappa}{s}.$$

Generalization to linear networks: A *network of RLC-circuits* (see Figure 2.3) is governed by the matrix/tensor equation:

$$z_{11}i_1 + z_{12}i_2 + ... + z_{1n}i_n = u_1(t)$$
$$z_{21}i_1 + z_{22}i_2 + ... + z_{2n}i_n = u_2(t)$$
$$... \quad ... \quad ... \quad ... \quad ...$$
$$z_{n1}i_1 + z_{n2}i_2 + ... + z_{nn}i_n = u_n(t),$$

with integro-differential operators:

$$z_{jk}i_k = L_{jk}\frac{di_k(t)}{dt} + R_{jk}\,i_k(t) + C_{jk}^{-1}\int_0^t i_k(t)\,dt.$$

In Laplace transform notation this reads:

$$L_{jk}s\,I_k(s) + R_{jk}\,I_k(s) + (C_{jk}s)^{-1}\,I_k(s) = U_j(s),$$

which gives the network impedance:

$$Z_{jk}(s) = \frac{U_j(s)}{I_k(s)} = L_{jk}s + R_{jk} + (C_{jk}s)^{-1}.$$

The same equations (with the currents $i_k(t)$ replaced by the errors $e_k(t)$, or velocities $v_k(t)$, etc.) hold for and any other linear physical and control networks.

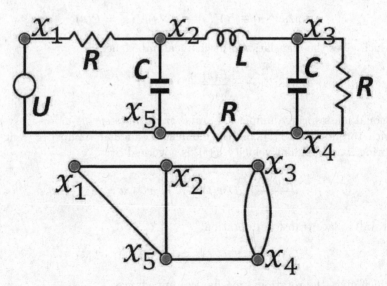

Fig. 2.3. *An RLC-network (top) and its graph (bottom) with five nodes* x_i $(i = 1, ..., 5)$.

Kalman's MIMO control systems: *Kalman's linear modular state-space* form [KFA69] (as implemented in *Matlab®*) for *continuous control systems* is governed by the following set of linear vector/matrix equations:

$$dx/dt = A(t)\,x(t) + B(t)\,u(t),$$
$$y(t) = C(t)\,x(t) + D(t)\,u(t),$$

and for *discrete control systems*:

$$x(n+1) = A(n)\,x(n) + B(n)\,u(n),$$
$$y(n) = C(n)\,x(n) + D(n)\,u(n).$$

These control systems become *Kalman filters* if Gaussian noise are added to the right-hand sides of all equations.

2.1.2 Informal PHS Description

PHS provide Hamiltonian generalization of classical *bond-graph* modeling. This generalization exploits various electro-mechanical (as well as thermal, hydraulic, etc.) analogies. The essence of PHS is the *interaction* between the system components, modeled by *power-ports* in which the energy exchange occurs between the components, where *power* P [in watts] equals the time-derivative of energy E [in joules]: $P = dE/dt \equiv \dot{E}$. Associated with every power-port there are conjugate pairs of variables, called *flows* f and *efforts* e (e.g., voltages [in volts] and currents [in amps], or forces [in N] and velocities [in m/s], or torques [in Nm] and angular velocities [in rad/s], etc.) — whose inner product is the power: $(e, f) = P$.

2.1.3 Gradient Operator and Gradient Descent

The *core* of PHS is the *gradient operator* $\nabla H(x)$ of the system *Hamiltonian energy function* $H : T^*M \to \mathbb{R}$ (see subsection 1.5.4), so the system evolves via *gradient descent*. The Hamiltonian $H(x) = H(q, p)$ is the *total system energy*, the sum of its potential and kinetic energies: $H(q, p) = E_{\text{pot}}(q) + E_{\text{kin}}(p)$. The *gradient operator* $\nabla \equiv \partial_x$ is the vector of partial derivatives with respect to the state variables $x = (q, p)$ consisting of generalized coordinates q and their conjugate momenta p. Geometrically, the Hamiltonian represents an n-dimensional *hypersurface* embedded in an $(n+1)$-dimensional Euclidean space $\mathbb{R}^{n+1}$ and the system evolves via gradient descent towards its *global minimum* — as a general direction.

2.1.4 PHS Definition

The formal PHS definition in vector-matrix form reads (see [IY16]):

$$\dot{x} = [J(x, v) - R(x, v)]\,\nabla H(x, v) + g(x, v)\,u,$$
$$y = g^T(x, v)\,\nabla H(x, v), \tag{2.2}$$

where (u, y) is the conjugate pair of input-output (or, flow-effort) variables and v is the vector of environmental variables;

$H(\boldsymbol{x}, \boldsymbol{v})$ is the Hamiltonian including environmental variables $\boldsymbol{v}$;
$\boldsymbol{J}(\boldsymbol{x}, \boldsymbol{v}) = -\boldsymbol{J}(\boldsymbol{x}, \boldsymbol{v})^T$ is the skew-symmetric matrix representing the power-conserving interconnection; $\boldsymbol{R}(\boldsymbol{x}, \boldsymbol{v}) = \boldsymbol{R}(\boldsymbol{x}, \boldsymbol{v})^T$ is the symmetric positive-definite matrix representing the dissipative structure; $\boldsymbol{g}(\boldsymbol{x}, \boldsymbol{v})$ is the input-output port function that modulates the inputs and defines the outputs.

For example, a swarm of general unmanned autonomous vehicles, defined by the forced and dissipative equations (1.11) can be easily generalized to the form (2.2).

2.1.5 First PHS Example: An LCL-Circuit

Consider an LCL-circuit with two inductors, L_1 and L_2, with magnetic energies, $H_1(\phi_1)$ and $H_2(\phi_2)$ (where ϕ_1 and ϕ_2 are the magnetic flux linkages), and a capacitor C with electric energy $H_3(q)$, (where q is the charge, see Figure 2.4). The first objective is to write this LCL-circuit as a *modular Hamiltonian system* (to be analyzed later).

We start with the *storage equations* for the circuit components (using shorthand notation: $\partial_x H = \partial H / \partial x$):

$$L_1 : \quad \begin{matrix} \dot{\phi}_1 = f_1 & \text{(voltage)} \\ \text{(current)} & e_1 = \partial_{\phi_1} H_1 \end{matrix} \; ,$$

$$L_2 : \quad \begin{matrix} \dot{\phi}_2 = f_2 & \text{(voltage)} \\ \text{(current)} & e_2 = \partial_{\phi_2} H_2 \end{matrix} \; , \qquad (2.3)$$

$$C : \quad \begin{matrix} \dot{q} = f_3 & \text{(current)} \\ \text{(voltage)} & e_3 = \partial_q H_3 \end{matrix} \; .$$

If the energy functions H_i ($i = 1, 2, 3$) are quadratic (e.g., $H_3(q) = q^2/2C$) then the elements are linear (e.g., voltage over capacitor $= \partial_q H_3 = q/C$, and similarly for the two inductors).

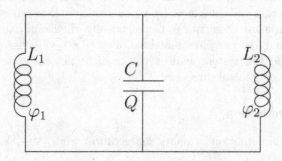

Fig. 2.4. *LCL-circuit (modified and adapted from A. Schaft's PHS presentations).*

Kirchhoff's voltage and current laws read:

$$\begin{pmatrix} -f_1 \\ -f_2 \\ -f_3 \end{pmatrix} = \begin{pmatrix} 0 & 0 & 1 \\ 0 & 0 & -1 \\ -1 & 1 & 0 \end{pmatrix} \begin{pmatrix} e_1 \\ e_2 \\ e_3 \end{pmatrix},$$

which, upon substitution of (2.3) gives the *modular Hamiltonian system*:

$$\begin{pmatrix} \dot{\phi}_1 \\ \dot{\phi}_2 \\ \dot{q} \end{pmatrix} = \begin{pmatrix} 0 & 0 & -1 \\ 0 & 0 & 1 \\ 1 & -1 & 0 \end{pmatrix} \begin{pmatrix} \partial_{\phi_1} H \\ \partial_{\phi_2} H \\ \partial_q H \end{pmatrix},$$

or $\dot{\boldsymbol{x}} = \boldsymbol{J}(\boldsymbol{x})\,\nabla H(\boldsymbol{x}),$ [with $\boldsymbol{J}(\boldsymbol{x}) = -\boldsymbol{J}^T(\boldsymbol{x})$],

where $H = H(\phi_1, \phi_2, q) = H_1(\phi_1) + H_2(\phi_2) + H_3(q)$ is the total circuit energy, while the skew-symmetric matrix $\boldsymbol{J}(\boldsymbol{x})$ is completely determined by the power-conserving interconnection structure of the system through which the components of the system exchange energy (in this case, Kirchhoff's current and voltage laws and Tellegen's theorem).

2.1.6 Poisson Structure

Recall that given the system's configuration manifold Q with the cotangent bundle T^*Q coordinated by n canonical coordinates (q_i, p_i), the canonical *Poisson bracket* $\{\cdot, \cdot\}$ on T^*Q is given by:

$$\{F, G\} = \sum_{i=1}^{n} \left(\partial_{q_i} F\, \partial_{p_i} G - \partial_{p_i} F\, \partial_{q_i} G \right), \tag{2.4}$$

so that classical Hamiltonian dynamics is defined by the Hamiltonian vector-field X_H given as:

$$X_H(F) = \{F, H\}, \qquad \text{for all } F : T^*Q \to \mathbb{R}. \tag{2.5}$$

In an arbitrary set of local coordinates $\mathbf{x}$ the Hamiltonian dynamics (2.5) takes the *closed Hamiltonian form*:

$$\dot{\mathbf{x}} = \mathbf{J}(\mathbf{x})\,\partial_\mathbf{x} H(\mathbf{x}), \tag{2.6}$$

where $\mathbf{J}(\mathbf{x}) = -\mathbf{J}^T(\mathbf{x})$ is the skew-symmetric structure matrix of the Poisson bracket (2.4) with elements: $J_{ik} = \{x_i, x_k\}$, (for $i, k = 1, ..., n$).

Even more general closed dynamical systems fall into this category. For example, Euler equations for the rigid body have the closed Hamiltonian form (2.6) of:

$$\begin{pmatrix} \dot{p}_x \\ \dot{p}_y \\ \dot{p}_z \end{pmatrix} = \begin{pmatrix} 0 & -p_z & p_y \\ p_z & 0 & -p_x \\ -p_y & p_x & 0 \end{pmatrix} \begin{pmatrix} \partial_x H \\ \partial_y H \\ \partial_z H \end{pmatrix},$$

where $\mathbf{p} = (p_x, p_y, p_z)$ is the body angular-momentum vector along the three principal axes with (principal) moments of inertia (I_x, I_y, I_z), and the kinetic energy is:

$$H(p) = \frac{1}{2} \left(p_x^2/I_x + p_y^2/I_y + p_z^2/I_z \right).$$

2.1.7 Open Port-Hamiltonian Systems

More generally, the closed Hamiltonian system (2.6) with the state-space $\mathcal{X}$ can be extended into open port-Hamiltonian systems:

$$\dot{\mathbf{x}} = \mathbf{J}(\mathbf{x})\,\partial_{\mathbf{x}}H(\mathbf{x}) + \mathbf{g}(\mathbf{x})\,\mathbf{f}, \qquad \mathbf{f} \in \mathbb{R}^m,$$
$$\mathbf{e} = \mathbf{g}^T(\mathbf{x})\,\partial_{\mathbf{x}}H(\mathbf{x}), \qquad \mathbf{e} \in \mathbb{R}^m, \quad \mathbf{x} \in \mathcal{X},$$

where the external ports defined by the matrix $\mathbf{g}(\mathbf{x})$, and $\mathbf{f} \in \mathbb{R}^m$, $\mathbf{e} \in \mathbb{R}^m$ are the power-variables at the external ports (open to interconnection to other systems). By skew-symmetry of $\mathbf{J}(\mathbf{x})$, we obtain for any $\mathbf{g}(\mathbf{x})$ the *energy-balance* relation:

$$\dot{H}[\mathbf{x}(t)] = \mathbf{e}^T(t)\,\mathbf{f}(t) : \text{power supplied to the system.} \tag{2.7}$$

2.1.8 Interconnection of Port-Hamiltonian Systems

Consider two open Hamiltonian systems:

$$\dot{\mathbf{x}}_i = \mathbf{J}_i(\mathbf{x}_i)\,\partial_{\mathbf{x}_i}H_i(\mathbf{x}_i) + \mathbf{g}_i(\mathbf{x}_i)\,\mathbf{f}_i, \tag{2.8}$$
$$\mathbf{e}_i = \mathbf{g}_i^T(\mathbf{x}_i)\,\partial_{\mathbf{x}_i}H(\mathbf{x}_i), \qquad \mathbf{x}_i \in \mathcal{X}_i, \quad (i = 1, 2).$$

Their feedback interconnection:

$$\mathbf{f}_1 = -\mathbf{e}_2, \qquad \mathbf{f}_2 = \mathbf{e}_1$$

(which is power-conserving since $\mathbf{f}_1\mathbf{e}_1 + \mathbf{f}_2\mathbf{e}_2 = 0$) yields the following port-Hamiltonian system:

$$\begin{pmatrix} \dot{\mathbf{x}}_1 \\ \dot{\mathbf{x}}_2 \end{pmatrix} = \overset{\mathbf{J}_{\text{inter}}(\mathbf{x}_1,\mathbf{x}_2)}{\begin{pmatrix} \mathbf{J}_1(\mathbf{x}_1) & -\mathbf{g}_1(\mathbf{x}_1)\mathbf{g}_2^T(\mathbf{x}_2) \\ \mathbf{g}_2(\mathbf{x}_2)\mathbf{g}_1^T(\mathbf{x}_1) & \mathbf{J}_2(\mathbf{x}_2) \end{pmatrix}} \begin{pmatrix} \partial_{\mathbf{x}_1}H(\mathbf{x}_1) \\ \partial_{\mathbf{x}_2}H(\mathbf{x}_2) \end{pmatrix},$$

with state space $\mathcal{X}_1 \times \mathcal{X}_2$, and total Hamiltonian $H_1(\mathbf{x}_1) + H_2(\mathbf{x}_2)$.

2.1.9 Including Dissipation

Energy-dissipation is included by terminating some of the ports by resistive elements:

$$\mathbf{f}_R = -F(\mathbf{e}_R),$$

where the mapping F is such that

$$\mathbf{e}_R^T F(\mathbf{e}_R) \geq 0 \qquad \text{for all } \mathbf{e}_R.$$

If $H \geq 0$ then the system stays passive[2] with respect to the remaining flows $\mathbf{f}$ and efforts $\mathbf{e}$; that is, the energy balance (2.7) is replaced by:

---

[2] A dynamical system is passive if it is not drawing energy from a supply.

$$\dot{H}[\mathbf{x}(t)] \leq \mathbf{e}^T(t)\,\mathbf{f}(t).$$

Hence, the system is *passive* if $H(\mathbf{x}) \geq 0$. Therefore, port-Hamiltonian systems extend passive systems in control theory [see subsection 2.1.13 on passive control systems].

A dissipative port-Hamiltonian system has the form:

$$\dot{\mathbf{x}} = [\mathbf{J}(\mathbf{x}) - \mathbf{R}(\mathbf{x})]\,\partial_{\mathbf{x}}H(\mathbf{x}) + \mathbf{g}(\mathbf{x})\,\mathbf{f}, \qquad \mathbf{f} \in \mathbb{R}^m,$$
$$\mathbf{e} = \mathbf{g}^T(\mathbf{x})\,\partial_{\mathbf{x}}H(\mathbf{x}), \qquad \mathbf{e} \in \mathbb{R}^m, \quad \mathbf{x} \in \mathcal{X}, \quad \mathbf{J}(\mathbf{x}) = -\mathbf{J}^T(\mathbf{x}), \qquad (2.9)$$

where the symmetric function $\mathbf{R}(\mathbf{x}) = \mathbf{R}^T(\mathbf{x}) \geq 0$ captures dissipative phenomena in the system.

2.1.10 Dirac Structure

A generalization of the Poisson structure $\mathbf{J}(\mathbf{x})$ for the port-Hamiltonian systems is the *Dirac structure* (see Figure 2.5), defined as follows.

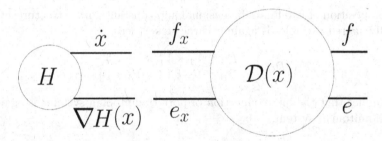

Fig. 2.5. *PHS defined by a Dirac structure (modified and adapted from A. Schaft's PHS presentations).*

In general, *power* is defined as the pairing (inner product):

$$P = \langle \mathbf{e}|\mathbf{f} \rangle := \mathbf{e}(\mathbf{f}), \qquad (\mathbf{f}, \mathbf{e}) \in \mathcal{V} \times \mathcal{V}^*,$$

where the linear space $\mathcal{V}$ is called the space of flows $\mathbf{f}$ (e.g., currents, velocities), and its dual space $\mathcal{V}^*$ is the space of efforts $\mathbf{e}$ (e.g., voltages, forces). The symmetrized form of power is the indefinite bilinear form $\langle\langle,\rangle\rangle$, on $\mathcal{V} \times \mathcal{V}^*$:

$$\langle\langle(\mathbf{f}^a, \mathbf{e}^a),(\mathbf{f}^b, \mathbf{e}^b)\rangle\rangle := \langle \mathbf{e}^a|\mathbf{f}^b \rangle + \langle \mathbf{e}^b|\mathbf{f}^a \rangle, \qquad (\mathbf{f}^a, \mathbf{e}^a),(\mathbf{f}^b, \mathbf{e}^b) \in \mathcal{V} \times \mathcal{V}^*.$$

A *constant Dirac structure* is a subspace: $\mathcal{D} \subset \mathcal{V} \times \mathcal{V}^*$, such that $\mathcal{D} = \mathcal{D}^\perp$, where $\perp$ denotes orthogonal complement with respect to the bilinear form $\langle\langle,\rangle\rangle$. For a finite-dimensional linear space $\mathcal{V}$ this is equivalent to:
  (i) $\langle \mathbf{e}|\mathbf{f} \rangle = 0$ for all $(\mathbf{f}, \mathbf{e}) \in \mathcal{D}$; and (ii) $\dim \mathcal{D} = \dim \mathcal{V}$.

Formally, if $\mathbf{J} : \mathcal{V}^* \to \mathcal{V}$ is a skew-symmetric mapping, then its graph:

$$\{(\mathbf{f}, \mathbf{e}) \in \mathcal{V} \times \mathcal{V}^* | \mathbf{f} = \mathbf{J}\mathbf{e}\}$$

is a Dirac structure.

For many systems, especially those with 3D mechanical components, the interconnection structure $\mathbf{J}$ will be modulated by the energy or geometric variables. This leads to the notion of *non-constant Dirac structure* on manifolds, defined as: A Dirac structure on a smooth configuration manifold Q with the tangent bundle TQ and the cotangent bundle T^*Q is a *vector subbundle* $\mathcal{D} \subset TQ \oplus T^*Q$ such that for every $\mathbf{x} \in Q$, the vector space $\mathcal{D}(\mathbf{x}) \subset T_{\mathbf{x}}Q \times T_{\mathbf{x}}^*Q$ is a constant Dirac structure.

Therefore, a port-Hamiltonian system is a dynamical system defined by the following DAEs:

$$[-\dot{\mathbf{x}}(t) = \mathbf{f}_{\mathbf{x}}(t), \, \partial_{\mathbf{x}}H[\mathbf{x}(t)] = \mathbf{e}_{\mathbf{x}}(t), \mathbf{f}(t), \mathbf{e}(t)\,] \in \mathcal{D}[\mathbf{x}(t)], \quad t \in \mathbb{R}.$$

2.1.11 Composition of Dirac Structures

The composition of two finite-dimensional and constant Dirac structures with partially shared variables is again a Dirac structure:

$$\mathcal{D}_A \| \mathcal{D}_B = \begin{cases} \mathcal{D}_A \subset \mathcal{V}_1 \times \mathcal{V}_1^* \times \mathcal{V}_2 \times \mathcal{V}_2^* \\ \mathcal{D}_B \subset \mathcal{V}_2 \times \mathcal{V}_2^* \times \mathcal{V}_3 \times \mathcal{V}_3^* \end{cases}.$$

This implies that the interconnection of port-Hamiltonian systems is again a port-Hamiltonian system.

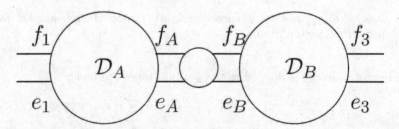

Fig. 2.6. *Interconnection of PH-systems defined by Composition of Dirac structures (modified and adapted from A. Schaft's PHS presentations).*

2.1.12 Control by Interconnection

We start control by connecting the given plant port-Hamiltonian system P (with energy H_P) to a to-be-designed controller port-Hamiltonian system C (with energy H_C). Interconnected system is again a port-Hamiltonian system with total energy $H_{\text{tot}} = H_P + H_C$, and composed Dirac structure $\mathcal{D}_{\text{comp}}$ is derived from $\mathcal{D}_P$ and $\mathcal{D}_C$.

Consider two port-Hamiltonian systems Σ_i in input-state-output (ISO) form (2.8), rewritten here in standard control notation:

$$\dot{\mathbf{x}}_i = \mathbf{J}_i(\mathbf{x}_i)\, \partial_{\mathbf{x}_i} H_i(\mathbf{x}_i) + \mathbf{g}_i(\mathbf{x}_i)\, \mathbf{u}_i,$$
$$\mathbf{y}_i = \mathbf{g}_i^T(\mathbf{x}_i)\, \partial_{\mathbf{x}_i} H(\mathbf{x}_i), \qquad (i = 1, 2).$$

Suppose we want to transfer the energy from the port-Hamiltonian system Σ_1 to the port-Hamiltonian system Σ_2, while keeping the total energy $H_{\text{tot}} = H_1 + H_2$ constant. This can be done, e.g., by the feedback:

$$\begin{pmatrix} \mathbf{u}_1 \\ \mathbf{u}_2 \end{pmatrix} = \begin{pmatrix} 0 & -\mathbf{y}_1\mathbf{y}_2^T \\ \mathbf{y}_2\mathbf{y}_1^T & 0 \end{pmatrix} \begin{pmatrix} \mathbf{y}_1 \\ \mathbf{y}_2 \end{pmatrix}.$$

By skew-symmetry of the matrix it follows the interconnected system is Hamiltonian, that is

$$\dot{H}_{\text{tot}} = \frac{d}{dt}\left(H_1 + H_2\right) = 0.$$

However, for the individual energies we have:

$$\dot{H}_1 = -\mathbf{y}_1^T \mathbf{y}_1 \mathbf{y}_2^T \mathbf{y}_2 = -\|\mathbf{y}_1\|^2 \|\mathbf{y}_2\|^2 \leq 0,$$

implying that H_1 is decreasing, while

$$\dot{H}_2 = \mathbf{y}_2^T \mathbf{y}_2 \mathbf{y}_1^T \mathbf{y}_1 = \|\mathbf{y}_2\|^2 \|\mathbf{y}_1\|^2 \geq 0,$$

implying that H_2 is increasing at the same rate.

2.1.13 Passive Control Systems

A general nonlinear control system with the coordinates $\mathbf{x} \in \mathbb{R}^n$ for an nD state space $\mathcal{X}$, given by:

$$\Sigma_{\text{nl}} : \begin{cases} \dot{\mathbf{x}} = \mathbf{f}(\mathbf{x}) + \mathbf{g}(\mathbf{x})\mathbf{u}, & \mathbf{u} \in \mathbb{R}^m \\ \mathbf{y} = \mathbf{h}(\mathbf{x}), & \mathbf{y} \in \mathbb{R}^m \end{cases},$$

is called *passive* if there exists a *storage function* $H : X \to \mathbb{R}$ with $H(\mathbf{x}) \geq 0$ for every $\mathbf{x}$, such that

$$H(\mathbf{x}(t_2)) - H(\mathbf{x}(t_1)) \leq \int_{t_1}^{t_2} \mathbf{u}^T(t)\mathbf{y}(t)dt, \qquad (2.10)$$

for all solutions $[\mathbf{u}(\cdot), \mathbf{x}(\cdot), \mathbf{y}(\cdot)]$ and times $t_1 \leq t_2$.

The system is called *lossless* if $\leq$ is replaced by $=$ in (2.10).

If the storage function H is *differentiable* then 'passive' is equivalent to:

$$\dot{H} \leq \mathbf{u}^T\mathbf{y},$$

while in the lossless case, $\leq$ is replaced by $=$.

In particular, the linear control system with the coordinates $\mathbf{x} \in \mathbb{R}^n$:

$$\Sigma_{\text{lin}} : \begin{cases} \dot{\mathbf{x}} = \mathbf{A}\mathbf{x} + \mathbf{B}\mathbf{u}, & \mathbf{u} \in \mathbb{R}^m \\ \mathbf{y} = \mathbf{C}\mathbf{x}, & \mathbf{y} \in \mathbb{R}^m \end{cases},$$

is passive if there exists a quadratic storage function

$$H(\mathbf{x}) = \frac{1}{2}\mathbf{x}^T\mathbf{Q}\mathbf{x},$$

where the symmetric matrix $\mathbf{Q} = \mathbf{Q}^T \geq 0$ satisfies the LMIs:

$$\mathbf{A}^T\mathbf{Q} + \mathbf{Q}\mathbf{A} \leq 0, \qquad \mathbf{C} = \mathbf{B}^T\mathbf{Q}.$$

Now, every linear passive system with storage function $H(\mathbf{x}) = \frac{1}{2}\mathbf{x}^T\mathbf{Q}\mathbf{x}$, satisfying: $\ker \mathbf{Q} \subset \ker \mathbf{A}$ can be rewritten as a linear port-Hamiltonian system:

$$\Sigma_{\text{lin}}^{\text{pH}} : \begin{cases} \dot{\mathbf{x}} = (\mathbf{J} - \mathbf{R})\,\mathbf{Q}\mathbf{x} + \mathbf{B}\mathbf{u}, & \mathbf{J} = -\mathbf{J}^T \\ \mathbf{y} = \mathbf{B}^T\mathbf{Q}\mathbf{x}, & \mathbf{R} = \mathbf{R}^T \geq 0 \end{cases},$$

in which case the storage function $H(\mathbf{x}) = \frac{1}{2}\mathbf{x}^T\mathbf{Q}\mathbf{x}$ is called the Hamiltonian.

Therefore, passive linear systems are port-Hamiltonian with non-negative Hamiltonian. Conversely every port-Hamiltonian system with non-negative Hamiltonian is passive.

More generally, 'most' nonlinear *passive* systems can be written in a control version of the port-Hamiltonian system (2.9), that is:

$$\dot{\mathbf{x}} = [\mathbf{J}(\mathbf{x}) - \mathbf{R}(\mathbf{x})]\,\partial_{\mathbf{x}}H(\mathbf{x}) + \mathbf{g}(\mathbf{x})\,\mathbf{u}, \quad (\mathbf{x} \in \mathcal{X}, \quad \mathbf{u} \in \mathbb{R}^m, \quad \mathbf{y} \in \mathbb{R}^m),$$
$$\mathbf{y} = \mathbf{g}^T(\mathbf{x})\,\partial_{\mathbf{x}}H(\mathbf{x}), \quad \text{with} \quad \mathbf{J}(\mathbf{x}) = -\mathbf{J}^T(\mathbf{x}), \quad \mathbf{R}(\mathbf{x}) = \mathbf{R}^T(\mathbf{x}) \geq 0,$$

where $\dot{\mathbf{x}} = [\mathbf{J}(\mathbf{x}) - \mathbf{R}(\mathbf{x})]\,\partial_{\mathbf{x}}H(\mathbf{x})$ is the internal dissipative physical dynamics with the Hamiltonian $H(\mathbf{x})$ representing the total (kinetic + potential) energy, such that

$$\dot{H}[\mathbf{x}(t)] = -\partial_{\mathbf{x}}H(\mathbf{x})\mathbf{R}(\mathbf{x})\partial_{\mathbf{x}}H(\mathbf{x}) + \mathbf{u}^T\mathbf{y} \leq \mathbf{u}^T\mathbf{y}.$$

In particular, most nonlinear *lossless* systems can be written in the port-Hamiltonian form as:

$$\dot{\mathbf{x}} = \mathbf{J}(\mathbf{x})\,\partial_{\mathbf{x}}H(\mathbf{x}) + \mathbf{g}(\mathbf{x})\,\mathbf{u}, \quad (\mathbf{x} \in \mathcal{X}, \quad \mathbf{u} \in \mathbb{R}^m, \quad \mathbf{y} \in \mathbb{R}^m),$$
$$\mathbf{y} = \mathbf{g}^T(\mathbf{x})\,\partial_{\mathbf{x}}H(\mathbf{x}), \quad \text{with} \quad \mathbf{J}(\mathbf{x}) = -\mathbf{J}^T(\mathbf{x}),$$

where the *closed Hamiltonian dynamics:* $\dot{\mathbf{x}} = \mathbf{J}(\mathbf{x})\,\partial_{\mathbf{x}}H(\mathbf{x})$ represents the internal conservative physical dynamics, which in classical mechanics is usually written as:

$$\dot{\mathbf{q}} = \partial_{\mathbf{p}}H(\mathbf{q}, \mathbf{p}), \qquad \dot{\mathbf{p}} = -\partial_{\mathbf{q}}H(\mathbf{q}, \mathbf{p}).$$

2.1.14 Second PHS Example: Mass-Spring-Damper System

Classical mass-spring-damper system (2.1) has two storage elements:

1. Spring Hamiltonian (potential energy):

$$H_s(q) = \frac{1}{2}kq^2, \qquad \text{which gives:}$$
$$\dot{q} = f_s : \text{velocity},$$
$$e_s = \partial_q H_s(q) = kq : \text{force},$$

and
2. Mass Hamiltonian (kinetic energy):

$$H_m(p) = \frac{1}{2m}p^2, \qquad \text{which gives:}$$
$$\dot{p} = f_m : \text{force},$$
$$e_m = \partial_p H_s(p) = \frac{p}{m} : \text{velocity}.$$

These two storage elements are interconnected by the following relations:

$$f_s = e_m = y, \qquad f_m = -e_s + u,$$

(these are power-conserving since $f_s e_s + f_m e_m = uy$), which gives the following *lossless* port-Hamiltonian system [with the total Hamiltonian $H(q,p) = H_s(q) + H_m(p)$]:

$$\begin{pmatrix} \dot{q} \\ \dot{p} \end{pmatrix} = \begin{pmatrix} 0 & 1 \\ -1 & 0 \end{pmatrix} \begin{pmatrix} \partial_q H(q,p) \\ \partial_p H(q,p) \end{pmatrix} + \begin{pmatrix} 0 \\ 1 \end{pmatrix} u,$$
$$y = \begin{pmatrix} 0 & 1 \end{pmatrix} \begin{pmatrix} \partial_q H(q,p) \\ \partial_p H(q,p) \end{pmatrix}.$$

Addition of the damper [including the Rayleigh dissipative function $R(f_d)$] gives:

$$e_d = \partial_{f_d} R(f_d) = cf_d, \qquad \text{with } R(f_d) = \frac{1}{2}cf_d^2,$$

which, via the extended interconnection:

$$f_s = e_m = f_d = y, \qquad f_m = e_s - e_d + u,$$

leads to the mass-spring-damper system in the *passive* port-Hamiltonian form:

$$\begin{pmatrix} \dot{q} \\ \dot{p} \end{pmatrix} = \left[\begin{pmatrix} 0 & 1 \\ -1 & 0 \end{pmatrix} - \begin{pmatrix} 0 & 0 \\ 0 & c \end{pmatrix} \right] \begin{pmatrix} \partial_q H(q,p) \\ \partial_p H(q,p) \end{pmatrix} + \begin{pmatrix} 0 \\ 1 \end{pmatrix} u,$$
$$y = \begin{pmatrix} 0 & 1 \end{pmatrix} \begin{pmatrix} \partial_q H(q,p) \\ \partial_p H(q,p) \end{pmatrix}.$$

2.2 Dirac Structures on Directed Graphs

2.2.1 Dirac Structures

Dirac structures generalize both the *Poisson bracket* from Hamiltonian mechanics and *Tellegen's theorem* in electrical circuit/network theory. They provide formal description of such interconnections of multiphysical elements which are both power-conserving and maximal-dimension. They can be formally defined in the following way. Consider the vector space $\mathcal{F}$ of *flow* variables, together with its dual vector space $\mathcal{F}^*$ of the *effort* variables and their Cartesian product $\mathcal{F} \times \mathcal{F}^*$. Dirac structure is a subspace $\mathcal{D} \subset \mathcal{F} \times \mathcal{F}^*$, such that it has the *power-conservation property*: $\langle e \mid f \rangle = 0$, $\forall (f, e) \in \mathcal{D}$ and maximal dimension with respect to this property: $\dim \mathcal{D} = \dim \mathcal{F}$ [DS99, Sch00].

Of a particular interest are the so-called *separable* Dirac structures, which generalize *Tellegen's theorem in circuit theory*: The product $\langle V_a \mid I_b \rangle = 0$ for any two vectors of voltages V_a and currents I_b satisfying Kirchhoff's laws. Formally, a Dirac structure $\mathcal{D} \subset \mathcal{F} \times \mathcal{F}^*$ is *separable* provided

$$\langle e_a \mid f_b \rangle = 0, \quad \forall (f_a, e_a), (f_b, e_b) \in \mathcal{D}. \tag{2.11}$$

We also recall the most important characteristic of Dirac structures: the *composition of Dirac structures is a Dirac structure* (much like the product of Gaussians is a Gaussian), this is not generally the case for symplectic or Poisson structures of Hamiltonian systems (see, e.g. [IR15]). The composition of Dirac structures can be defined in the following way. Consider two Dirac structures, $\mathcal{D}_A \subset \mathcal{F}_A \times \mathcal{F}_c \times \mathcal{F}_A^* \times \mathcal{F}_c^*$ and $\mathcal{D}_B \subset \mathcal{F}_B \times \mathcal{F}_c \times \mathcal{F}_B^* \times \mathcal{F}_c^*$, with a shared space of flow variables $\mathcal{F}_c$ and effort variables $\mathcal{F}_c^*$. Their composition is defined as:

$$\mathcal{D}_A \circ \mathcal{D}_B = \{(f_A, e_A, f_B, e_B) \in \mathcal{F}_A \times \mathcal{F}_B \times \mathcal{F}_A^* \times \mathcal{F}_B^* \mid \exists (f, e) \in \mathcal{F}_c \times \mathcal{F}_c^*$$

$$\text{such that } (f_A, e_A, f, e) \in \mathcal{D}_A, \quad (f_B, e_B, -f, e) \in \mathcal{D}_B\}, \tag{2.12}$$

which was shown in [Sch99, CS07] to be a Dirac structure.

In particular, if $\mathcal{D}_A \subset \mathcal{F}_A \times \mathcal{F}_c \times \mathcal{F}_A^* \times \mathcal{F}_c^*$ and $\mathcal{D}_B \subset \mathcal{F}_B \times \mathcal{F}_c \times \mathcal{F}_B^* \times \mathcal{F}_c^*$ are two separable Dirac structures:

$$\mathcal{D}_i = \mathcal{K}_i \times \mathcal{K}_i^\perp \quad \text{with} \quad \mathcal{K}_i \subset \mathcal{F}_i \times \mathcal{F}_c, \quad (\text{for } i = A, B),$$

then their composition $\mathcal{D}_A \circ \mathcal{D}_B$ is the separable Dirac structure (see [Sch99, CS07]):

$$\mathcal{D}_A \circ \mathcal{D}_B = (\mathcal{K}_A \circ \mathcal{K}_B) \times (\mathcal{K}_A \circ \mathcal{K}_B)^\perp, \quad \text{where}$$

$$\mathcal{K}_A \circ \mathcal{K}_B = \{(f_A, f_B) \in \mathcal{F}_A \times \mathcal{F}_B \mid \exists f \in \mathcal{F}_c$$

$$\text{such that } (f_A, f) \in \mathcal{K}_A, (f_B, -f) \in \mathcal{K}_B\}.$$

This propositional property of Dirac structures underpins the whole PHS-theory. It implies that the standard interconnection of PH-systems results in another PHS with Dirac structure defined as the *composition of the Dirac structures* of the component PH-systems, and Hamiltonian equal to the *sum of the Hamiltonians* of the component PH-systems [Sch99, CS07].

2.2.2 Directed Graphs or Digraphs

Recall that a *directed graph* (i.e., *digraph*) $\mathcal{G} = (\mathcal{V}, \mathcal{E})$ consists of a finite set $\mathcal{V}$ of *vertices* and a finite set $\mathcal{E}$ of directed *edges*, together with a map from $\mathcal{E}$ to the set of ordered pairs of $\mathcal{V}$ (without self-loops), such that to any edge $e \in \mathcal{E}$ there corresponds an ordered pair $(v, w) \in \mathcal{V} \times \mathcal{V}$ (with $v \neq w$, the tail vertex v and the head vertex w). A digraph can be fully specified by its *incidence* $N \times M$ *matrix* $\hat{B}$, where N is the number of vertices and M is the number of edges, with

$$(i,j)\text{-th element} = \begin{cases} -1, & \text{if the } j\text{th edge is an edge towards vertex } i, \\ +1, & \text{if the } j\text{th edge is an edge originating from vertex } i, \\ 0, & \text{otherwise.} \end{cases}$$

The *vertex space* $\Lambda_0 \equiv \mathbb{R}^N$ of a digraph is the vector space of all functions $\Lambda_0 : \mathcal{V} \to \mathbb{R}$, while its *edge space* $\Lambda_1 \equiv \mathbb{R}^M$ is the vector space of all functions $\Lambda_1 : \mathcal{E} \to \mathbb{R}$. Their respective dual spaces, Λ^0 and Λ^1, are defined by the following duality pairings between $f_0 \in \Lambda_0$ and $e_0 \in \Lambda^0$ and $f_1 \in \Lambda_1$ and $e_1 \in \Lambda^1$

$$\Lambda^0 : \langle f_0 \mid e_0 \rangle = \sum_{v \in \mathcal{V}} \langle f(v) \mid e(v) \rangle ,$$

$$\Lambda^1 : \langle f_0 \mid e_0 \rangle = \sum_{e \in \mathcal{E}} \langle f(v) \mid e(v) \rangle .$$

Following [SM13], we will borrow terminology from port-based and bondgraph modeling, and call the elements $f_0 \in \Lambda_0$ and $f_1 \in \Lambda_1$ as *flows*, and the elements of their dual spaces $e^0 \in \Lambda^0$ and $e^1 \in \Lambda^1$ as *efforts*.

An *open digraph* $\mathcal{G}_b$ is obtained from an ordinary digraph $\mathcal{G} = (\mathcal{V}, \mathcal{E})$ by identifying a subset $\mathcal{V}_b \subset \mathcal{V}$ of N_b *boundary vertices*, in which case $\mathcal{V}_b$ are the vertices that are open to interconnection with other open digraphs. The remaining subset $\mathcal{V}_i := \mathcal{V} - \mathcal{V}_b$ are the N_i *internal vertices* of $\mathcal{G}_b$. Also, the *boundary space* Λ_b and its dual space Λ^b are the linear spaces of all functions $\Lambda_b : \mathcal{V}_b \to \mathbb{R}$ and $\Lambda^b : \mathcal{V}^b \to \mathbb{R}$. The elements $f_b \in \Lambda_b$ and $e^b \in \Lambda^b$ are called the *boundary flows* and *boundary efforts*, respectively.

2.2.3 Dirac Structures on Digraphs

Consider an open digraph $\mathcal{G}_b = (\mathcal{V}_b, \mathcal{E}_b)$ with boundary spaces Λ_b, *incidence operator* $B : \Lambda_1 \to \Lambda_0$ and *boundary incidence operator* $B_b : \Lambda_1 \to \Lambda_b$. There exist two *separable Dirac structures* $\mathcal{D}(\mathcal{G}_b)$ on open digraphs [SM13]:

- The *flow-continuous* Dirac structure $\mathcal{D}_f(\mathcal{G}_b)$ is defined as:

$$\mathcal{D}_f(\mathcal{G}_b) = \{(f_1, e^1, f_{0i}, e^{0i}, f_b, e^b) \in \Lambda_1 \times \Lambda^1 \times \Lambda_{0i} \times \Lambda^{0i} \times \Lambda_b \times \Lambda^b \mid$$
$$B_i f_1 = f_{0i}, B_b f_1 = f_b, e^1 = -B_i^* e^{0i} - B_b^* e^b\}; \text{ and}$$

- The *effort-continuous* Dirac structure $\mathcal{D}_e(\mathcal{G}_b)$ is defined as:

$$\mathcal{D}_e(\mathcal{G}_b) = \{(f_1, e^1, f_0, e^0, f_b, e^b) \in \Lambda_1 \times \Lambda^1 \times \Lambda_0 \times \Lambda^0 \times \Lambda_b \times \Lambda^b \mid$$
$$B_i f_1 = f_{0i}, B_b f_1 = f_{0b} + f_b, e^1 = -B^* e^0, e^b = e^{0b}\}.$$

2.2.4 PHS with Dirac Structures on Digraphs

Consider the *effort-continuous* Dirac structure $\mathcal{D}_e(\mathcal{G}_b)$ involving the following flow and effort variables: $(f_1, e^1, f_0, e^0, f_b, e^b) \in \Lambda_1 \times \Lambda^1 \times \Lambda_0 \times \Lambda^0 \times \Lambda_b \times \Lambda^b$. A port-Hamiltonian system is specified by defining between all the *internal* conjugate flow and effort variables (f_1, e^1, f_0, e^0) either as an *energy-storing* relation, or a purely *dissipative* relation (see [SM13]). Dual energy-storing relations between a vector f of flow variables and a conjugate vector e of effort variables have the form:

$$\dot{x} = -f, \quad e = \frac{\partial H}{\partial x}(x) \qquad \text{and its dual} \qquad \dot{x} = e, \quad f = -\frac{\partial H}{\partial x}(x),$$

where x is a state vector of energy variables of the same dimension as f and e, and the Hamiltonian $H(x)$ is any function that represents the energy stored in the system. In addition, a dissipative relation between the flow and effort variables is any static relation: $R(f, e) = 0$, satisfying $\langle e \mid -f \rangle \geq 0$ for all (f, e).

For example, consider a mass-spring-damper system with two boundary masses and one inner mass. Firstly, the vertex flow f and effort e variables are related by the following energy-storing relations:

$$\dot{p} = f_0, \qquad e_0 = \frac{\partial K}{\partial p}(p),$$

where p are the momenta of the masses and $K(p)$ are their kinetic energies. Secondly, the flow f_{1s} and effort e^{1s} variables of the spring edges are related by the energy-storing relations

$$\dot{q} = e^{1s}, \qquad f_{1s} = -\frac{\partial V}{\partial q}(q),$$

where q are the spring elongations and $V(q)$ are their potential energies. Thirdly, the flow f_{1d} and effort e^{1d} variables of the damper edges are connected by energy-dissipating relations: $f_{1d} = -D(e^{1d})$, such that $(e^{1d})^T D(e^{1d}) \geq 0$.

To summarize, a PHS on a digraph is defined by the digraph Dirac structure and the *constitutive* relations between all the internal effort and flow variables, which are either of energy-storing or of a dissipative type.

2.3 Category-Theoretic Abstraction: Deductive Reasoning on Graphs .

In this section, we make a transition from PHS on graphs to *categorical logic*,[3] or more precisely, *graph-based deductive systems*, due to J. Lambek (see [LS86] and the references therein).

2.3.1 Digraphs as Deductive Systems

Slightly reformulated from before, a directed graph, or *digraph* Γ can be viewed as a mathematical structure that consists of two classes:
  (i) a class $\mathfrak{Arr}$ of *arrows* (or, oriented edges), and
  (ii) a class $\mathfrak{Obj}$ of *objects* (or, nodes, or vertices),
— together with a pair of maps (f, g) from $\mathfrak{Arr}$ to $\mathfrak{Obj}$ in Γ:

$$(f, g) : \mathfrak{Arr} \rightrightarrows \mathfrak{Obj} \subset \Gamma,$$

which are respectively called *source* and *target* (or, domain and codomain) and defined in Γ by:

$$\text{source}(f) = A, \quad \text{target}(f) = B, \quad \text{therefore } f : A \to B,$$
$$\text{source}(g) = B, \quad \text{target}(g) = C, \quad \text{therefore } g : B \to C.$$

A *deductive system* is a digraph Γ in which to each object $A \in \mathfrak{Obj}$ there is associated an *identity* arrow $1_A : A \to A \in \mathfrak{Arr}$ and to each pair of arrows, $f : A \to B$ and $g : B \to C$ in $\mathfrak{Arr}$, there is associated their *composition* $g \circ f : A \to C$ in $\mathfrak{Arr} \subset \Gamma$.

As pointed out by Lambek (see [LS86]), a logician may think of the *objects* $\mathfrak{Obj}$ as *formulas* and of the *arrows* $\mathfrak{Arr}$ as *deductions*, or *proofs*. In this way, from the above construction, we obtain the fundamental *rule of inference* in a digraph Γ:

$$\frac{f : A \to B, \qquad g : B \to C}{g \circ f : A \to C} \ \in \mathfrak{Arr} \subset \Gamma. \tag{2.13}$$

In particular, a deductive system Γ with the rule of inference (2.13) becomes a *category* $\mathcal{K}$, iff the following standard categorical equations also hold in $\mathfrak{Arr} \subset \mathcal{K}$:

for all $f : A \to B$, $g : B \to C$ and $h : C \to D$, we have:

$$f \circ 1_A = 1_B \circ f = f \quad \text{and} \quad h \circ (g \circ f) = (h \circ g) \circ f. \tag{2.14}$$

---

[3] For the basic introduction to *categories and functors* and their complex control applications, see [IR15] and the references therein.

2.3.2 Cartesian Closed Deductive Systems and Categories

A deductive system $\mathcal{K}$ has a *terminal object* T iff it has the special arrow: $k_A : A \to \mathsf{T}$ that satisfies the equation:

$$\text{for } f : A \to \mathsf{T}, \qquad f = k_A. \tag{2.15}$$

Furthermore, a binary operation $\times$ on arrows in $\mathfrak{Arr} \subset \mathcal{K}$ is called the Cartesian product and defined by the *projection arrows*:

$$\pi^1_{A,B} : A \times B \to A, \qquad \pi^2_{A,B} : A \times B \to B, \tag{2.16}$$

projecting onto the first and the second component of $A \times B$, respectively.

Finally, the *pairing operation* $\langle \, , \rangle$ on arrows is given by:

$$\frac{f : C \to A, \qquad g : C \to B}{\langle f, g \rangle : C \to A \times B} \;\; \in \mathfrak{Arr} \subset \mathcal{K}, \tag{2.17}$$

which can be derived from the inference rule (2.13).

A deductive system $\mathcal{K}$ with a terminal object T defined by (6.2), which is closed under projection arrows defined by (2.16) and the pairing operation $\langle \, , \rangle$ defined by (2.17) is called a *Cartesian closed deductive system* (or, CC-system for short). A CC-system which also satisfies the standard categorical equations (2.14) is a *Cartesian closed category* (CC-category) see [LS86] as well as Wikipedia articles based on [LS86]). In the case of a CC-category, the arrows must also satisfy the following set of *pairing equations* [DP01, DP04]:[4]

$$\pi^1_{A,B} \circ \langle f, g \rangle = f, \qquad \pi^2_{A,B} \circ \langle f, g \rangle = g,$$
$$\langle f, g \rangle \circ h = \langle f \circ h, g \circ h \rangle, \qquad \langle \pi^1_{A,B}, \pi^2_{A,B} \rangle = 1_{A \times B}.$$

Closely related to categorical logic is the so-called *topos theory*, a rigorous foundation for intuitionistic logic. In particular, all CC-categories are topoi.

2.3.3 Basics of Topos Theory and Intuitionistic Logic

Topos theory is a rich branch of mathematics, pioneered by fundamental topological studies of A. Grothendieck, which can be approached from a variety of different viewpoints (see, e.g. [BW05]), all based on category theory.[5]

---

[4] Note that usually, the closenes upon the implication $\Rightarrow$ is also requested for the CC-categories, as defined by a pair (ε, γ) of *implicational operations* on arrows in $\mathfrak{Arr} \subset \mathcal{K}$:

$$\varepsilon_{A,B} : A \times (A \Rightarrow B) \to B \quad \text{and} \quad \frac{f : A \times C \to B}{\gamma_{A,C} f : C \to A \Rightarrow B}.$$

[5] At the beginning of the 20th century, philosophers of mathematics were beginning to divide into various schools of thought, broadly distinguished by their pictures

In particular, there are logically interesting examples of topoi that are not Grothendieck's geometric topoi.[6] The current definition of topos goes back to 1963, when Bill Lawvere decided to formulate new foundations for mathematics, based on category theory (see [LS97]). His definition picks out the central role in topos theory of the *subobject classifier*. In the usual category of sets, this is the two-element set of Boolean truth-values, *true* and *false*. The subsets of a given set X are the same as the functions on X to any such given two-element set: fix the 'first' element and make a subset Y correspond to the function sending Y there and its complement in X to the other element. Lawvere formulated axioms for a topos that assumed a subobject classifier, and some limit conditions, to make a *Cartesian-closed category*. For a while this notion of topos was called *elementary topos*.

From Grothendieck's point of view, a topos is an abstraction of the category of sheaves over a topological space. From Lawvere's point of view, a topos is a category with certain properties characteristic of the category of sets, **Set**, a sort of a generalized set theory with some special constructions

---

of mathematical epistemology and ontology. Three schools: *formalism* (David Hilbert and his group of collaborators, including John von Neumann), *constructivism/intuitionism* (Henri Poincaré, Hermann Weyl and L.E.J. Brouwer), and *logicism* (Gottlob Frege and Bertrand Russell), emerged at this time, partly in response to the increasingly widespread worry that mathematics as it stood, and analysis in particular, did not live up to the standards of certainty and rigor that had been taken for granted. Each school addressed the issues that came to the fore at that time, either attempting to resolve them or claiming that mathematics is not entitled to its status as our most trusted knowledge. At the middle of the century, a new mathematical theory was created by Samuel Eilenberg and Saunders Mac Lane, known as *category theory*, and it became a new contender for the natural language of mathematical thinking. In our view, *topos theory* is a 'marriage' of constructivism and category theory.

[6] Historically, in the late 1950s Alexander Grothendieck chose the Greek word *topos* (which means "place") to define a mathematical object (usually denoted by τ) that would provide a general framework for his theory of *'etale cohomology* and other variants related to his algebraic geometry, philosophy of descent and Grothendieck topology. Two examples of a *Grothendieck topos* are [Ill04]:

1. The category of *sheaves* of sets on a topological space is a topos. In particular, the category of sets, **Set**, is a topos, for it is the category of sheaves of sets on the one point space. This topos, denoted $p\tau$, is called the *punctual topos*.
2. Let G be a *group*. The category BG of G-sets, i.e., sets equipped with a left action of G, is a topos. For $G = 1$, BG $= p\tau$.

What these categories have in common is that (i) they behave very much like the category **Set** of sets, and (ii) they possess a good notion of *localization*. In order to formalize (ii), Grothendieck conceived the idea of sheaf on a site, which generalizes the notion of sheaf on a topological space. That led him to the notion of topos, which encompasses (i) and (ii). The theory of a Grothendieck topos was a category of *sheaves*, where the word sheaf had acquired an extended meaning with respect to the idea of *Grothendieck topology*.

in **Set**. Briefly, a topos τ is a category which has the following two basic properties (see [Law75, Bel88, MM92]):

1. All limits taken over finite index categories exist.
2. Every object has a power object.

From these two basic properties, one can derive another four properties:
(a) All colimits taken over finite index categories exist.[7]
(b) The category τ has a subobject classifier.[8]
(c) Any two objects in the topos τ have an exponential object.[9]
(d) The category τ is Cartesian closed (as defined in the previous subsection).

As topos is a special type of category, it consists of objects, and arrows (or, *morphisms*) from one object to another, so that in certain critical respects it behaves like the category of sets, **Set**. In particular, the 'opposite' of a category C is a category, denoted C^{op}, whose objects are the same as those of C, and whose morphisms are defined to be the opposite of those of C; i.e., a morphism $f : A \to B$ in C^{op} is said to exist iff there is a morphism $f : B \to A$ in C. Also, an object 1 is said to be a terminal object in a category C if there is just one morphism from any other object in C to 1; it can be seen that any two terminal objects in C are isomorphic. In the category **Set**, a terminal object is any set $\{*\}$ with just a single element, so it is called a *singleton*. In this case a morphism is just a map, and hence a morphism $\{*\} \to X$ picks out a unique element of X.

For example, if C is a small category, then the associated *functor category* **Set**^{C} (consisting of all covariant functors from C to the category **Set**, with natural transformations as morphisms, see next section) is a topos. For instance, the category $Grph$ of graphs of the kind permitting multiple directed edges between two vertices is a topos. A graph consists of two sets, an edge set and a vertex set, and two functions s, t between those sets, assigning to every edge e its source $s(e)$ and target $t(e)$. The topos $Grph$ is thus equivalent to the functor category **Set**^{C}, where C is the category with two objects E and V and two morphisms $s, t : E \to V$ giving respectively the source and target of each

---

[7] This property (together with the property 1. above) means that in the topos τ there are: (i) an initial object (an object like the empty set); (ii) a terminal object (an object like a set with one element); (iii) binary coproducts (something like the disjoint union of two sets); (iv) binary products (something like the Cartesian product of two sets); (v) equalizers (something like the subset of X consisting of all elements x such that $f(x) = g(x)$, where $f, g : X \to Y$); and (vi) coequalizers (something like the quotient set of X, where two elements $f(y)$ and $g(y)$ are identified, where $f, g : X \to Y$).

[8] This means that in the topos τ there is an object Ω called the 'subobject classifier', which acts like $\{0,1\}$, in that functions from any set x into $\{0,1\}$ are 'secretly' the same as subsets of x. We can think of Ω as the replacement for the usual Boolean truth values 'true' and 'false'.

[9] For any objects x and y in τ, there is an object y^x, called an 'exponential', which acts like 'the set of functions from x to y'.

edge. More generally, the categories of finite sets, of finite G−sets (actions of a group G on a finite set), and of finite graphs are topoi. Another defining property for a category C to be a topos is that a product $A \times B$ exists for any pair of objects (A, B) in C. Yet another of the basic properties of a topos is that there is a $1-1$ correspondence between morphisms $f : A \times B \to \Omega$ and morphisms $\ulcorner f \urcorner : A \to PB := \Omega^B$, where is the so-called 'subobject classifier' (explained later). In general, $\ulcorner f \urcorner$ is called the *power transpose* of f. If $A \simeq 1$ then $\ulcorner f \urcorner$ is known as the *name* of the morphism $f : B \to \Omega$.

From logical perspective, topos-theoretic approach leads to a picture in which the 'truth values', or 'semantic values' of such contextual predictions are not just two-valued (i.e., 'true' and 'false') but instead lie in a larger logical algebra, the so-called *Heyting algebra*. Named after Dutch mathematician Arend Heyting (a student of L. Brouwer), the Heyting algebras are algebraic structures that play in relation to *intuitionistic logic* a role analogous to that played by *Boolean algebras* in relation to *classical logic*.[10] A Heyting algebra

---

[10] Recall that classical Aristotelian logic has only two truth-values, 'true' and 'false' (usually denoted by T, F, or 1,0), and includes five propositional truth functions: (1) negation, or logical *not*: ($\neg a$); (2) conjunction, or *logical and*: ($a \wedge b$); (3) disjunction, or *logical or*: ($a \vee b$); (4) material implication, or *logical if-then*: ($a \Rightarrow b$); and (5) material equivalence, or logical *if-and-only-if* (or, *iff*, for short): ($a \Leftrightarrow b$). In particular, both ($a \Rightarrow \neg\neg a$) and ($\neg\neg a \Rightarrow a$) are *theorems*, while conjunctions and disjunctions are combined into De Morgan's laws: ($\neg(a \vee b) = \neg a \wedge \neg b$); and ($\neg(a \wedge b) = \neg a \vee \neg b$). An expression is a *tautology* if it is true for all variable assignments. For example, the following expression is tautology: $t = (p \vee \neg r) \wedge s \Rightarrow (r \wedge s \Rightarrow (p \wedge q) \vee p)$. An expression is a *contradiction* if it is false for all variable assignments.

The basic *inference rules* of Aristotelian syllogistic logic are:

Modus ponens: $((a \Rightarrow b) \wedge a) \Rightarrow b$;

Modus tollens: $((a \Rightarrow b) \wedge \neg b) \Rightarrow (\neg a)$;

Modus tollendo ponens: $((a \vee b) \wedge \neg a) \Rightarrow b$;

Modus ponendo tollens: $(\neg(a \wedge b) \wedge a) \Rightarrow (\neg b)$; and

Reductio ad absurdum $((a \Rightarrow b) \wedge (a \Rightarrow (\neg b))) \Rightarrow (\neg a)$.

On the other hand, *intuitionistic logic*, or *constructive logic*, can be described as classical logic without the *Aristotelian law of excluded middle*: ($a \vee \neg a$) (since one can construct, via Gödel's *incompleteness theorems*, a mathematical statement that can be neither proven nor disproved); as well as without the *elimination of double negation*: ($\neg\neg a \Rightarrow a$); and without Peirce's law: ($(a \Rightarrow b) \Rightarrow a) \Rightarrow a$; but with the law of contradiction: ($\neg a \Rightarrow (a \Rightarrow b)$), and with Modus ponens as a main inference rule. Intuitionistic logic encompasses the principles of logical reasoning which were used by L.E.J. Brouwer in developing his intuitionistic mathematics, beginning in 1907. Philosophically, intuitionism differs from logicism by treating logic as a part of mathematics rather than as the foundation of mathematics; from finitism by allowing (constructive) reasoning about infinite collections; and from platonism by viewing mathematical objects as mental constructs with no independent ideal existence. A fundamental fact about intuitionistic logic is that it has the same consistency strength as classical logic. For propositional logic this

is a pseudocomplemented, distributive lattice[11] with zero element 0 and unit element 1, representing 'totally false' resp. 'totally true'. The pseudocomplement is denoted by ¬, and one has, for all elements α of a Heyting algebra H,

$$\alpha \vee \neg\alpha \leq 1,$$

in contrast to $\alpha \vee \neg\alpha = 1$ in a Boolean algebra. This means that the disjunction of a proposition α and its negation need not be (totally) true in a Heyting algebra. Equivalently, one has

$$\neg\neg\alpha \geq \alpha,$$

in contrast to $\neg\neg\alpha = \alpha$ in Boolean algebras. This shows that Boolean logic is a special case of intuitionistic logic.

Just as normal set theory is intimately associated with Boolean algebra (i.e., the 'Venn diagram' algebra of subsets of a set is Boolean), so a topos is associated with a more general Heyting algebra connected to the sub-objects of objects in the topos. In particular, *fuzzy set theory* (see, e.g. [II07a]) can be viewed as a sub-branch of topos theory.

For example, a general, formal-language-oriented, psycho-physical model of human crowds was proposed in [IR11], based on Doring-Isham (DI) physical topos theory [DI08a, DI08b, DI08c, DI08d], in such a way that DI's classical physics was translated into crowd mechanics, while DI's quantum physics was translated into crowd behavior. For many technical details of the topos theoretic formalism, see [IR11] and the references therein.

---

was first proved by Glivenko's Theorem 1929: An arbitrary propositional formula a is classically provable, iff $(\neg\neg a)$ is intuitionistically provable. Kurt Gödel proved in 1933 the *equiconsistency* of intuitionistic and classical theories [Sta09]. In particular, Gödel observed that intuitionistic propositional logic has the disjunction property: if $(a \vee b)$ is a theorem, then a is a theorem or b is a theorem. An embedding of classical first-order logic into intuitionistic logic is given by the Gödel–Gentzen *double-negation translation*.

[11] Lattice is meant in the algebraic sense: a partially ordered set L such that any two elements $a, b \in L$ have a minimum (greatest lower bound) $a \wedge b$ and a maximum (least upper bound) $a \vee b$ in L. A lattice L is distributive if and only if $a \vee (b \wedge c) = (a \vee b) \wedge (a \vee c)$ as well as $a \wedge (b \vee c) = (a \wedge b) \vee (a \wedge c)$ hold for all $a, b, c \in L$.

3

CPC-Application: Autonomous Brain-Like Supervisor for a Swarm of Robots

Recently, we have proposed in [IY16] a rigorous model for prediction and control of a large-scale joint swarm of *unmanned ground vehicles* (UGVs) and *unmanned aerial vehicles* (UAVs), performing an autonomous land-air operation. In that Chapter, we have also introduced a need for a *cognitive supervisor* for the high-dimensional distributed multi-robotic system. Its primary task is to have a bird's-eye view of the situation across the joint land-air operation, and based on the GPS locations of both the target and all included robots, to provide them with good 2D and 3D attractor fields so that they can reach the proximity of the target in the shortest possible time. The purpose of the present Chapter is to develop a rigorous model for this cognitive supervisor, based on recent discoveries in brain science that show us how humans navigate in 2D environments and how bats navigate in 3D environments, and to couple this with a meta-cognitive supervisor model that allows vehicles to reason about actions and construct simple plans.

The 2014 Nobel Prize in Physiology or Medicine was awarded jointly to John O'Keefe, May-Britt Moser and Edvard I. Moser "for their discoveries of cells that constitute a positioning system in the brain", in other words, for the *hippocampus path integration and navigation system*.

Briefly, there is a part of a mammal brain, called the *hippocampal formation*, which in humans is mostly developed in taxi drivers, grows in size with their experience and can be also trained (like a muscle) using fast-action video games. The hippocampal formation provides a *cognitive map* of a familiar environment which can be used to identify one's current location and to navigate from one place to another. This *mapping system* provides two independent strategies for locating places, one based on *environmental landmarks* and the other on a *path integration system* (see [MBJ06, MKM08] and the references therein), which uses information about distances traveled in particular directions. This brain navigation system exists in all mammals, while in humans it additionally provides the basis for the so-called *episodic memory* [OBD98]. For more technical details on the Nobel-awarded work of John

O'Keefe, May-Britt Moser and Edvard I. Moser, see the section 3.2 and the references therein.

Two main components of the hippocampal formation (discovered by O'Keefe) are: (i) hippocampal place cells, and (ii) grid cells from the entorhinal cortex (discovered by Mosers). In particular, according to Edvard Moser, "All network models for grid cells involve continuous attractors ..." — [which is similar to our attractor Hamiltonian dynamics of UGVs and UAVs, given by Eqs. (3.1)–(3.2) in the next section].

As inspired by this discovery in brain science, the present Chapter proposes a novel probabilistic spatio-temporal model for mammalian path integration and navigation, formulated as an *adaptive Hamiltonian path integral*. The model combines: (i) a cognitive map $p(t)$ performed by hippocampal place cells, (ii) an entorhinal map $q(t)$ performed by grid cells, (iii) a current of sensory (extra-hippocampal) stimuli $J(t)$, and (iv) Hebbian learning in hippocampal synaptic weights $w(t)$. This model represents an infinite-dimensional neural network, which can be simulated (using 10^6-10^7 neurons) on IBM's TrueNorth chip.

We also propose to couple this cognitive supervisor to a meta-cognitive supervisor, supporting dynamic mission planning, using on an established propositional multimodal logic framework. This approach gives robotic vehicles the ability to construct and execute simple plans on the fly against goals, given local sensor information, state information communicated locally between vehicles, and aspects of the state of the robot itself. The coupling to the cognitive supervisor and to the outside world is through the truth value of logical atoms and using multimodal actions.

3.1 Hamiltonian Control for a Robotic Swarm

The affine Hamiltonian control model with many degrees-of-freedom has been presented in the form of $2n$-dimensional (2ND) Langevin-type attractor matrix equations with nearest-neighbor couplings, which represent two recurrent neural networks:

UGV-swarm: (3.1)

$$\dot{q}_{jk} = \varphi^{2D} \left(q_A^{2D} - q_{jk} - \omega_{jk}\, q_{jk}^2 p_{jk} \right) - \sum_{j,k} \partial_{p_{jk}} H_{jk}\, u_{jk} + \eta_q(t),$$

$$\dot{p}_{jk} = \varphi^{2D} \left(p_A^{2D} - p_{jk} - \omega_{jk}\, p_{jk}^2 q_{jk} \right) + \sum_{j,k} \partial_{q_{jk}} H_{jk}\, u_{jk} + \eta_p(t).$$

UAV-swarm: $\hspace{8cm}$ (3.2)

$$\dot{q}_{jkl} = \varphi^{3D} \left(q_A^{3D} - q_{jkl} - \omega_{jkl}\, q_{jkl}^2 p_{jkl} \right) - \sum_{j,k,l} \partial_{p_{jkl}} H_{jkl}\, u_{jkl} + \eta_q(t),$$

$$\dot{p}_{jkl} = \varphi^{3D} \left(p_A^{3D} - p_{jkl} - \omega_{jkl}\, p_{jkl}^2 q_{jkl} \right) + \sum_{j,k,l} \partial_{q_{jkl}} H_{jkl}\, u_{jkl} + \eta_p(t).$$

The following terms are used in Eqs. (3.1)–(3.2): $q_{jk} = q_{jk}(t)$ and $p_{jk} = p_{jk}(t)$ are time-evolving matrices defining coordinates and momenta of the UGV-swarm, respectively, with initial conditions: $q_{jk}(0)$ and $p_{jk}(0)$. Similarly, $q_{jkl} = q_{jkl}(t)$ and $p_{jkl} = p_{jkl}(t)$ are time-evolving tensors defining coordinates and momenta of the UAV-swarm, respectively, with initial conditions: $q_{jkl}(0)$ and $p_{jkl}(0)$. q_A^{2D} and p_A^{2D} are the 2D attractors for the UGV swarm, while q_A^{3D} and p_A^{3D} are the 3D attractors for the UGV swarm. φ^{2D} and φ^{3D} are the attractor field strengths for the UGV and UAV swarms, respectively; ω_{jk} and ω_{jkl} are corresponding adaptive weights of both swarms which can be trained by Hebbian learning, (q_{jk}, p_{jk}) and (q_{jkl}, p_{jkl}) are the initial formations of both swarms, u_{jk} and u_{jkl} are Lie-derivative controllers for both swarms, H_{jk} and H_{jkl} are affine Hamiltonians of both swarms, while $\eta_q(t)$ and $\eta_p(t)$ are zero-mean, delta-correlated, Gaussian white noises added to q and p variables in both swarms. For more technical details on affine Hamiltonian (or, similar, *port-Hamiltonian*) control of large-scale dynamical systems, see [IY16] and the references therein.

The purpose of the cognitive supervisor is to provide the 2D and 3D inputs to the recurrent neural nets (3.1)–(3.2), or specifically, 2D attractors $\left(q_A^{2D}, p_A^{2D} \right)$ for the UGV-swarm and 3D attractors $\left(q_A^{3D}, p_A^{3D} \right)$ for the UAV-swarm (see, e.g. [MVB04]).

3.2 Nobel-Awarded Hippocampal Navigation System

We start with a brief history of *hippocampal navigation,* from O'Keefe's pioneering work to the discovery of grid cells by Mosers, which are all awarded with a 2014 Nobel Prize for Physiology.

While most of neural network theory (including the concepts of associative synaptic plasticity, cell assemblies and phase sequences) is founded on Hebb's seminal work [Heb49], and hippocampus as a spatial cognitive map was proposed in [OD71, ON78], the pioneering paper on hippocampal navigation was [O'Ke76], in which O'Keefe proposed a theoretical suggestion of a landmark-independent navigational system upstream of the hippocampus. A few years later, path integration in mammals was reported in [MM80], followed by a quantitative description of head direction-sensitive cells in the brain by [Ran85], a report of remapping in *hippocampal place cells* in [BMK91], and an early version of the *head-direction path-integrator model* in [MCM91], which formed the conceptual basis of subsequent continuous attractor models for path integration.

A landmark paper [WM93] introduced empirical understanding of *hippocampal neurodynamics*, by the ability to record simultaneously from many neurons in the freely behaving animal. The phase relationship between hippocampal place units and the EEG theta rhythm was shown in [OR93], and the *hippocampus as a path-integration system* was proposed in [McN96].

A series of continuous attractor papers started with [TS95], followed by an attractor model of head direction cell by angular velocity integration in [Zha96] and the introduction of the concept of *periodic boundaries* and an early introduction of *medial entorhinal grid cells* in mammals by [SM97].

Next two papers by O'Keefe, [OBD98, O'Ke99], consider human hippocampus place cells, which are signaling both spatial and non-spatial information.

The pioneering study [FMW04] reports that spatial position is represented accurately among ensembles of principal neurons in superficial layers of the *medial entorhinal cortex* (MEC), while the scale of representation increases along the MEC's dorsoventral axis. It is followed by [HFM05] that reports the discovery of *grid cells*, which are suggested as a foundation for a universal path integration-based neuronal map of the spatial environment. Spatial representation and the architecture of the entorhinal cortex was presented in [WM06].

Next, we give a current brief overview of *hippocampal formation: place cells and grid cells.*

The review paper [MBJ06] shows that the hippocampal formation is able to encode relative spatial location of mammals and humans (without any reference to external cues) by the integration of translational and rotational self-motion, which is called the *path integration.*

Both theoretical and empirical studies show that the synaptic matrix of the MEC-grid cells of young mammals perform heavy self-organizing path-integration computations, similar to Turing's symmetry-breaking operation,[1] while the scale at which space is represented increases systematically along the dorsoventral axis in both the hippocampus and the MEC. Spatially periodic inputs (at multiple scales) converging from the MEC-grid cells, result in non-periodic spatial firing of the *hippocampal place cells.*

The paper [MKM08] reviews how place cells and grid cells form the *entorhinal-hippocampal representations*, initially observed in [OB05] and mathematically modeled in [SME06, BBO07], for quantitative spatio-temporal representation of places, routes, and associated experiences during behavior and in memory.

It has been observed that place cells perform both *pattern completion* and *pattern separation*, while hippocampal representations cannot always be discontinuous as in a sequential Hopfield network [Hop82], but rather similar to the graded-response Hopfield network [Hop84].

---

[1] A landmark Turing's paper [Tur53] demonstrating that symmetry breaking can occur in the simple reaction-diffusion system, that results in spatially periodic structures can account for pattern formation in nature.

Finally, while all the research mentioned so far was dealing with 2D hippocampal path integration and navigation, which is relevant for our UGVs, in recent years this research has been generalized to 3D navigation of bats in [YU13, Yar13].

3.3 Adaptive Path Integral Model for the Hippocampal Navigation System

In his 2014 Nobel lecture, John O'Keefe referred to his pioneering 1976-paper [O'Ke76, ON78]), describing the function of the *hippocampal place cells* performing Tolman's *cognitive mapping:* "When an animal had located itself in an environment (using environmental stimuli) the hippocampus could calculate subsequent positions in that environment on the basis of how far and in what direction the animal had moved in the interim . . ." This quotation was accompanied by a *commutative diagram* depicting the *vector addition* and a suggestion that an *animal moves in a sequence of vectors.*

This extract from O'Keefe's lecture is the motivation for the present mathematical model. Basically, any two-dimensional (2D) vector is equivalent to a complex number: $z = x + iy$, where (x, y) are Cartesian coordinates and $i = \sqrt{-1}$. The same complex number z can be also given in the polar form as: $z = re^{i\theta}$, where r is the radius vector and θ is the heading. The sequence of N vectors is the sum of complex numbers:

$$\text{particle-like animal motion} = \sum_{k=1}^{N} z_k = \sum_{k=1}^{N} x_k + iy_k = \sum_{k=1}^{N} r_k e^{i\theta_k}. \quad (3.3)$$

In this way, we can describe a particle-like animal motion in the complex plane $\mathbb{C}$, from some *initial point A* to the *final point B*, performed in N steps, as an integral complex number (3.3). This basic idea describes an animal's motion in purely static and deterministic terms; it can be generalized into a more realistic, *probabilistic dynamics*, as follows.[2]

Now, instead of the complex plane $\mathbb{C}$, consider a particle-like animal motion in the *phase plane* (*p-q*), where $p = p(t, x)$ represents the action of the hippocampal place cells and $q = q(t, x)$ defines the action of the entorhinal grid cells. The animal moves from some initial point A given by canonical coordinates (q_0, p_0) at initial time t_0, to the final point B given by canonical coordinate (q_1, p_1) at final time t_1, via *all possible paths*, each path having an equal probability (so that the sum of all path-probabilities is $= 1$).

---

[2] For simplicity reasons, we are using the same Hamiltonian symbols, q and p, for the cognitive representation of robotic coordinates and momenta, to emphasize the one-to-one correspondence between the physical robotic level and the mental supervisor level. However, while at the physical robotic level, $q = q(t)$ and $p = p(t)$ are only temporal variables, at the cognitive level, $q = q(t, x)$ and $p = p(t, x)$ represent spatio-temporal wave functions.

This most general 2D motion is properly defined by the *transition amplitude*: $\langle B|A \rangle \equiv \langle q_1, p_1, t_1 | q_0, p_0, t_0 \rangle$ whose absolute square represents the *transition probability density* function: $PDF = |\langle B|A \rangle|^2 \equiv |\langle q_1, p_1, t_1 | q_0, p_0, t_0 \rangle|^2$.

The transition amplitude $\langle B|A \rangle$ can be calculated via the following *Hamiltonian path integral*[3]

$$\langle q_1, p_1, t_1 | q_0, p_0, t_0 \rangle = \int \mathcal{D}[q]\mathcal{D}[p] \exp\left\{ i \int_{t_0}^{t_1} [p(\tau)\dot{q}(\tau) - H(p,q)]\, d\tau \right\},$$

$$\text{with} \quad \int \mathcal{D}[q]\mathcal{D}[p] \equiv \frac{1}{2\pi} \int \prod_\tau dq(\tau) dp(\tau), \tag{3.4}$$

where the integration is performed over the $p(\tau)$ and $q(\tau)$ values at every time τ, with the time-step $d\tau \equiv t_j - t_{j-1}$ and the velocity $\dot{q}(\tau) \equiv \frac{q(t_j) - q(t_{j-1})}{t_j - t_{j-1}}$. For technical details of the derivation of the Hamiltonian path integral (3.4), see e.g. [II08, IR15] and the references therein.

Next, the *sources* from various extra-hippocampal stimuli can be incorporated into the basic transition amplitude (3.4) by adding some form of a bio-electric current J, as:

$$Z[J] = \int \mathcal{D}[q]\mathcal{D}[p] \exp\left\{ i \int_{t_0}^{t_1} [p(\tau)\dot{q}(\tau) - H(p,q) + J(\tau)q(\tau)]d\tau \right\}, \tag{3.5}$$

where $Z[J] = \langle q_1, p_1, t_1 | q_0, p_0, t_0 \rangle$ is the system's *partition function* dependent on the current J and obeying the *normalization condition:* $Z[J = 0] = 1$.

A generalization from a single particle Hamiltonian path integral (3.4) to the probabilistic dynamics of an N-particle system is straightforward. The phase-space functional integral that defines the transition amplitude $\langle q_1^1...q_1^N, p_1^1...p_N^1, t_1 | q_0^1...q_0^N, p_1^0...p_N^0, t_0 \rangle$, from the initial ND point $(q_0^1...q_0^N)$ at time t_0 to the final ND point $(q_1^1...q_1^N)$ at time t_1 is given by:

---

[3] The path integral $\int$ given by (3.4) was formulated by R. Feynman in [Fey51]. It has been widely appreciated that the phase-space (i.e., Hamiltonian) path integral is more generally applicable, or more robust, than the original, Lagrangian version of the path integral, introduced in Feynman's first paper [Fey65]. For example, the original Lagrangian path integral is satisfactory for Lagrangians of the form: $L(x) = \frac{1}{2} m\dot{x}^2 + A(x)\dot{x} - V(x)$, but it is unsuitable, e.g., for the case of a particle with the Lagrangian (in normal units): $L(x) = -m\,qrt1 - \dot{x}^2$. For such a system (as well as many more general expressions) the Hamiltonian path integral is more robust; e.g., the Hamiltonian path integral for the free particle: $\int \mathcal{D}[p]\mathcal{D}[q] \exp\{i \int [p\dot{q} - qrtp^2 + m^2]\, dt\}$ is readily evaluated.

$$\langle q_1^1...q_1^N, p_1^1...p_N^1, t_1 | q_0^1...q_0^N, p_1^0...p_N^0, t_0 \rangle$$

$$= \int \mathcal{D}[q]\mathcal{D}[p] \exp\left\{ i \int_{t_0}^{t_1} \left[\sum_{k=1}^{N} p_k(\tau)\dot{q}^k(\tau) - H(p_k, q^k) \right] d\tau \right\},$$

with $\displaystyle \int \mathcal{D}[q]\mathcal{D}[p] = \frac{1}{2\pi} \int \prod_{\tau} \prod_{k=1}^{N} dq^k dp_k$,

where we are allowing for the full Hamiltonian of the system $H(p_k, q^k)$ to depend upon all the N coordinates $q^k(\tau)$ and momenta $p_k(\tau)$ collectively.

Again, we can add various sources as incoming bio-currents J_k as a straightforward generalization of the single-particle partition function (3.5) to the system of N particles:

$$Z_N[J_k] = \int \mathcal{D}[p]\mathcal{D}[q] \exp\left\{ i \int_{t_0}^{t_1} \left[\sum_{k=1}^{N} p_k(\tau)\dot{q}^k(\tau) - H(p_k, q^k) + J_k(\tau)q^k(\tau) \right] d\tau \right\},$$

where $Z_N[J_k] = \langle q_1^1...q_1^N, p_1^1...p_N^1, t_1 | q_0^1...q_0^N, p_1^0...p_N^0, t_0 \rangle$ is the system's *partition function* dependent on all the incoming currents J_k and obeying the normalization condition: $Z_N[J_k = 0] = 1$, for $k = 1, ..., N$.

Our final step is to transform the N-particle partition function $Z_N[J_k]$ into an infinite-dimensional recurrent neural network (of a generalized Hopfield type) by including the hippocampal synaptic weights $w_k(\tau)$ into it (compare with [IRS14]), as:

$$Z_N[w_k, J_k] =$$

$$\int \mathcal{D}[w]\mathcal{D}[q]\mathcal{D}[p] \exp\left\{ i \int_{t_0}^{t_1} \left[\sum_{k=1}^{N} p_k(\tau)\dot{q}^k(\tau) - H(p_k, q^k) + J_k(\tau)q^k(\tau) \right] d\tau \right\},$$

with $\displaystyle \int \mathcal{D}[w]\mathcal{D}[q]\mathcal{D}[p] = \frac{1}{2\pi} \int \prod_{\tau} \prod_{k=1}^{N} dw_k dq^k dp_k$, (3.6)

where the weights $w_k(\tau)$ are adapted (in a discrete time) by Hebbian-type learning:

$$w_k(\tau + 1) = w_k(\tau) + \frac{q}{\eta} \left[w_k^D(\tau) - w_k^A(\tau) \right], (3.7)$$

where $q = q(\tau)$, $\eta = \eta(\tau)$ represent local *signal* and *noise* amplitudes, respectively, while superscripts D and A denote *desired* and *achieved* system states, respectively.

The system (3.6)–(3.7) defines the proposed adaptive Hamiltonian path integral model for a generic mammalian path integration and navigation. Both the sequential (Ising spin) Hopfield network [Hop82] with its Galuber dynamics and the graded-response Hopfield network [Hop84] with its Fokker–Planck dynamics can be considered as special cases of this general Hamiltonian neural system.

Direct computer simulations of the adaptive Hamiltonian path integral system (3.6)–(3.7) can be performed on the IBM TrueNorth chip (see [Ser14] and the references therein) as a *Markov-chain Monte Carlo simulation over a grid of Hopfield nets* (which are already implemented in the TrueNorth chip, using 10^6-10^7 artificial neurons).

In the next section we propose a more efficient approach to simulate the path integral system (3.6)–(3.7).

3.4 Coupled Nonlinear Schrödinger Equations

In this section, instead of the direct computer simulations on a supercomputer, we will present an indirect approach of simulating the path integral system (3.6)–(3.7) on an ordinary PC, represented as a pair of coupled nonlinear Schrödinger (NLS) equations. In his first paper [Fey65], Feynman showed that his Lagrangian q−path integral was equivalent to the standard linear Schrödinger equation from quantum mechanics, given here for the case of a free particle (in natural physical units: $\hbar = 1$, $m = 1$):

$$i\partial_t \psi(t, x) = -\frac{1}{2}\partial_{xx}\psi(t, x), \qquad (i = \sqrt{-1}; \quad \text{with } \partial_z \psi = \frac{\partial \psi}{\partial z}), \qquad (3.8)$$

which defines the complex-valued *microscopic wave function* $\psi = \psi(t, x)$, whose absolute square $|\psi(x, t)|^2$ defines the *probability density function* (PDF).

In the last decade it was shown (see [II09] and the references therein) that if the linear Schrödinger equation (3.8) is put into an adaptive (iterative) feedback loop, it adds a cubic nonlinearity with a potential field $V = V(x)$ and becomes the NLS equation:

$$i\partial_t \psi = -\frac{1}{2}\partial_{xx}\psi + V|\psi|^2\psi, \qquad (3.9)$$

which now defines the *macroscopic wave function* $\psi = \psi(t, x)$ whose absolute square $|\psi(x, t)|^2$ still defines the PDF [IR12].

Finally, to represent the Hamiltonian (q, p)−path integral, we can use the (q, p)−pair of NLS equations, as follows.

3.4.1 Special Case: Analytical Soliton

We start with a simple (q, p)−NLS pair representation for the path integral system (3.6)–(3.7), which admits the analytical closed-form solution, given by the so-called *Manakov system* (with the constant potential V):[4]

---

[4] The Manakov system has been used to describe the interaction between wave packets in dispersive conservative media, and also the interaction between orthogonally polarized components in nonlinear optical fibres (see, e.g. [HS94, Yan97] and the references therein).

$$i\partial_t q = -\frac{1}{2}\partial_{xx}q + V\left(|q|^2 + |p|^2\right)q, \tag{3.10}$$

$$i\partial_t p = -\frac{1}{2}\partial_{xx}p + V\left(|q|^2 + |p|^2\right)p, \tag{3.11}$$

which was proven in [Man74], using the *Lax pair representation* [Lax68], to be completely integrable Hamiltonian system, by the existence of infinite number of involutive integrals of motion.

The (q,p)−NLS pair (3.10)–(3.11) admits both 'bright' and 'dark' soliton as solutions, of which the simplest one is the so-called *Manakov bright 2-soliton* given by:

$$\begin{bmatrix} q(t,x) \\ p(t,x) \end{bmatrix} = 2b \begin{bmatrix} c_1 \\ c_2 \end{bmatrix} \text{sech}[2b(x+4at)]\, e^{-2i(2a^2t+ax-2b^2t)}, \tag{3.12}$$

where a and b are real-valued parameters and $|c_1|^2 + |c_2|^2 = 1$.

3.4.2 General Case: Numerical Simulation

Now that we have introduced the simple (q,p)−NLS pair, we can define our real representation for the path integral system (3.6)–(3.7), as the following more general (q,p)−NLS pair:

$$i\,\partial_t q(t,x) = -\frac{1}{2}\,w_k\,I(t,x)\,\partial_{xx}q(t,x) + V(t,x)\,|q(t,x)|^2\,p(t,x), \tag{3.13}$$

$$i\,\partial_t p(t,x) = -\frac{1}{2}\,w_k\,J(t,x)\,\partial_{xx}p(t,x) + U(t,x)\,|p(t,x)|^2\,q(t,x), \tag{3.14}$$

including the bell-shaped (sech) spatiotemporal potentials:

$$V(t,x) = \frac{1}{2}\,\text{sech}\left(a_1\,t\,x^3\right), \qquad U(t,x) = \frac{1}{2}\,\text{sech}\left(a_2\,t^3\,x\right),$$

and the soft-step shaped (tanh) spatiotemporal input currents:

$$I(t,x) = a_3 \tanh\left(a_4\,t^3\,x\right), \qquad J(t,x) = a_5 \tanh\left(a_6\,t\,x^3\right),$$

together with the common initial condition:

$$\chi(x) = \frac{1}{2}\exp(i\,x)\,\text{sech}\left(\frac{1}{2}x\right),$$

the set of parameters: ($i = \sqrt{-1}, a_1 = 0.4, a_2 = 0.6, a_3 = 0.3, a_4 = 0.8, a_5 = 0.7, a_6 = 0.2$) and the set of adaptive synaptic weights w_k.

The (q,p)−NLS pair (3.13)–(3.14) has been numerically simulated in *Mathematica*®, producing 3D plots of real and imaginary parts of the (q,p)−wave functions (see Figure 7.8) and density plots of attractor fields for robotic swarms (see Figure 3.2), using the following code:

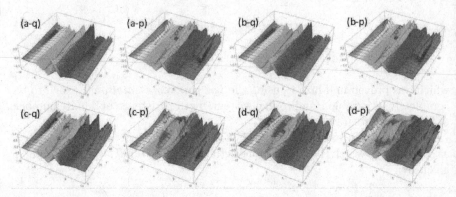

Fig. 3.1. *Simulation of the* $(q, p)-NLS$ *pair (3.13)–(3.14) in* $Mathematica^{\circledR}$*, showing the adaptation of the* $(q, p)-waves$ *with the change of the synaptic weights* $w_k \in [0, 1]$*. Each 3D plot shows the following two surfaces (real and imaginary values of the wave function): (a-q) is the* $q-wave$ *plot at* $w_1 = 0.1$*, (a-p) is the* $p-wave$ *plot at* $w_1 = 0.1$*; (b-q) is the* $q-wave$ *plot at* $w_2 = 0.3$*, (b-p) is the* $p-wave$ *plot at* $w_2 = 0.3$*; (c-q) is the* $q-wave$ *plot at* $w_3 = 0.5$*, (c-p) is the* $p-wave$ *plot at* $w_3 = 0.5$*; (d-q) is the* $q-wave$ *plot at* $w_4 = 0.7$*, (d-p) is the* $p-wave$ *plot at* $w_4 = 0.7$*.*

Defining potentials:
$V[t_-, x_-] := \frac{1}{2} \text{Sech} \left[0.4tx^3\right]$; $U[t_-, x_-] := \frac{1}{2} \text{Sech} \left[0.6t^3x\right]$;
$I[t_-, x_-] := 0.3\text{Tanh} \left[0.8t^3x\right]$; $J[t_-, x_-] := 0.7\text{Tanh} \left[0.2tx^3\right]$;
$IC[x_-] := \frac{1}{2}\text{Exp}[ix]\text{Sech} \left[\frac{1}{2}x\right]$; Tfin $= 50; L = 10; w = 0.9;$
Defining NLS-equations:
$NLS2 = \{i\partial_t q[t, x] == -\frac{w}{2}I[t, x]\partial_{x,x}q[t, x] + Vq[t, x]\text{Abs}[q[t, x]]^2 p[t, x],$
$\quad i\partial_t p[t, x] == -\frac{w}{2}J[t, x]\partial_{x,x}p[t, x] + Vp[t, x]\text{Abs}[p[t, x]]^2 q[t, x]\}$;
Numerical solution:
sol = NDSolve[{NLS2, $q[0, x]$ == IC[x], $q[t, -L]$ == $q[t, L]$,
$p[0, x]$ == IC[x], $p[t, -L]$ == $p[t, L]$}, {q, p}, {$t, 0, \text{Tfin}$}, {$x, -L, L$},
Method $\rightarrow$ { "MethodOfLines ", "SpatialDiscretization " $\rightarrow$
{ "TensorProductGrid", "DifferenceOrder" $\rightarrow$ "Pseudospectral"}}];
3D Plots:
Qplot = Plot3D[{Evaluate[Re[$q[t, x]$/.First[sol]]],
Evaluate[Im[$q[t, x]$/.First[sol]]]}, {$x, -L, L$}, {$t, 0, \text{Tfin}$}, PlotRange $\rightarrow$ All,
ColorFunction $\rightarrow$ (Hue[#]&), AxesLabel $\rightarrow$ { "x", "t", "Re/Im[q]"},
ImageSize $\rightarrow$ 400]
Pplot = Plot3D[{Evaluate[Re[$p[t, x]$/.First[sol]]],
Evaluate[Im[$p[t, x]$/.First[sol]]]}, {$x, -L, L$}, {$t, 0, \text{Tfin}$}, PlotRange $\rightarrow$ All,
ColorFunction $\rightarrow$ (Hue[#]&), AxesLabel $\rightarrow$ { "x", "t", "Re/Im[p]"},
ImageSize $\rightarrow$ 400]

The bidirectional associative memory, given by the NLS-pair (3.13)–(3.14) effectively performs quantum neural computation, by giving a spatiotemporal

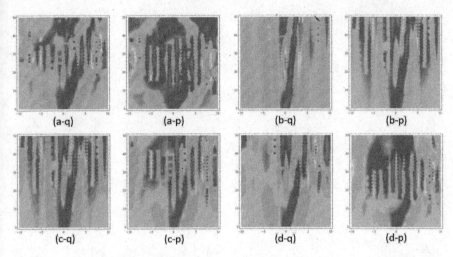

Fig. 3.2. Density plots corresponding to 3D plots in Figure 7.8, representing hypothetical attractor fields for robotic swarms.

generalization of Hopfield, Grossberg and Kosko BAM family of recurrent neural networks (see [II09] and the references therein). In addition, the shock-wave and solitary-wave nature of the coupled NLS equations may describe brain-like effects: propagation, reflection and collision of shock and solitary waves (see [HK99]).

4

Micro-Cognitive CPC-Autonomy: Quantum Computational Tensor Networks

In this Chapter we will propose a number of mathematical tools from *quantum information* and *quantum computation* adapted for modern theoretical autonomy. In particular, we will focus on quantum-mechanical tools suitable for analysis and design of the CPC-autonomy, based on the fundamental concept of *quantum entanglement*, expressed in the form of a certain composite wave function $|\Psi(t)\rangle$ equivalent to the composite transition (probability) amplitude $\langle \mathrm{Out}(t_{\mathrm{fin}}) \mid \mathrm{In}(t_{\mathrm{init}})\rangle$.

4.1 CPC-Autonomy in the Language of Quantum Information and Computation

In this section, we will develop a formal foundation of the CPC-autonomy, based on modern quantum information and quantum computation theory. The relevant autonomous system information will be stored in its composite wave function $|\Psi(t)\rangle$ with the following components:

- In a purely physical autonomy, this information will be stored in the wave function $|\Psi^{\mathrm{phys}}(t)\rangle$ with basic physical qualities of its micro-ingredients: mass, spin, electric charge, light-and-sound intensity, etc.
- In a cyber-physical world, we will add the wave function $|\Psi^{\mathrm{cyb}}(t)\rangle$ with some computer/internet measures (e.g., speed and capacity of internet servers, processing speed and memory capacity of various computer platforms, efficiency and complexity of different operating systems, etc.).
- In a cognitive-physical world, we will add the wave function $|\Psi^{\mathrm{cog}}(t)\rangle$ with the following cognitive measures (defined using correlation analysis and extracted using *factor analysis* (FA)):
  1. The *intelligence quotient* (IQ),
  2. The *emotional quotient* (EQ),
  3. The *personality factors* (PF).

- In a general CPC-system, we would have a general wave function:

$$|\Psi^{\text{gen}}(t)\rangle = w_1 \left|\Psi^{\text{phys}}(t)\right\rangle + w_2 \left|\Psi^{\text{cyb}}(t)\right\rangle + w_3 \left|\Psi^{\text{cog}}(t)\right\rangle,$$

comprising of (the weighted sum with the weights (w_1, w_2, w_3) of) all above qualities expressed as various energies, starting from their lowest energy states and evolving towards their full energy spectra (both discrete and continuous).

4.2 Entropy, the First Law of Entanglement and the Holographic Principle

It is clear that all interacting autonomous systems are entangled. However, even without a direct interaction, any two systems, A ("Alice") and B ("Bob"), can become indirectly entangled, as follows. Suppose that two other systems, C and D, are also in the game, such that A is directly entangled with C and B with D. Then, the joint measurement on C and D, with a subsequent unitary operation on A or B, produces *quantum teleportation* [BBC93], which is an example of *indirect entanglement*. Now, it is obvious that the directly-interacting systems have higher *degree of entanglement* than the systems without a direct interaction. This fundamental *entanglement measure* can be defined as follows.

We start with the basic, "black-and-white" entanglement rule, given by the following disjunction:

- A pure (ground) state of a quantum system[1] with the state vector Υ is called entangled, or *nonlocal state*, iff the state vector Υ cannot be expressed as a tensor product of pure states of its bipartite parts/subsistems:[2] $\Upsilon \neq \Upsilon_A \otimes \Upsilon_B$.
- Otherwise, iff the state vector Υ can be expressed as a tensor product of pure states of its bipartite parts, $\Upsilon = \Upsilon_A \otimes \Upsilon_B$, the system is not entangled (or, its entanglement is zero).

A finer rule, with various degrees of graded entanglement, can be defined using the *von-Neumann entropy* $S(\rho)$ (see [BBC93, BDS96]). Consider a *quantum lattice* in the pure ground state, defined by its density matrix $\rho = |\Upsilon\rangle\langle\Upsilon|$ and spatially distributed in the form of a *graph* $G = (\mathbf{V}, \mathbf{E})$, where $\mathbf{V}$ is the set of vertices and $\mathbf{E}$ is the set of edges. Being in a pure state, the von-Neumann entropy of the whole lattice is zero:

$$\varepsilon(\Upsilon) = S(\rho) = -\text{Tr}\left(\rho \ln \rho\right) = 0.$$

---

[1] We re-emphasize here that every entangled quantum system considered in this Chapter is an abstract quantum-computational representative of some fundamental, holistic, information flow and energy exchange occurring in trusted autonomous systems.

[2] The two subsystems, Alice and Bob, share the bipartite pure state Υ.

Now, let us select a subset of vertices: $A \subset \mathbf{V}$ with its complement: $B = \mathbf{V} \backslash A$. The subset A has the *reduced state* density matrix:

$$\rho_A = \mathrm{Tr}_B(\rho) = \mathrm{Tr}_B |\Upsilon\rangle\langle\Upsilon|,$$

given by tracing ρ over Bob's degrees-of-freedom. The von-Neumann entropy of the reduced states is:

$$S(\rho_A) = -\mathrm{Tr}(\rho_A \ln \rho_A), \qquad S(\rho_B) = -\mathrm{Tr}(\rho_B \ln \rho_B), \qquad (4.1)$$

and each of them defines the *entropy of entanglement* of a subsystem with respect to its complement [BBC93, BDS96]. The more entangled the subsystems A and B are, the larger are the entropies $S(\rho_A)$ and $S(\rho_B)$ in Eq. (4.1). If there is no entanglement between A and B (i.e., A and B are in a product state), then $S(\rho_A) = S(\rho_B) = 0$. The entropy $\varepsilon = \varepsilon(\Upsilon) = S(\rho)$ ranges from zero for a product state of pure states, $\varepsilon(\Upsilon) = \varepsilon(\Upsilon_A \otimes \Upsilon_B) = 0$, to $\varepsilon(\Upsilon) = \ln N$ for a maximally-entangled state of two N-state particles. The entanglement measure E is additive for independent systems and conserved under local unitary operations [BDS96].

Finally, consider an n-dimensional ball $B \in \mathbb{R}^{n+1}$, we define the entanglement entropy $\varepsilon(B)$ associated to this region as the von-Neumann entropy: $S_B = -\mathrm{Tr}(\rho_B \ln \rho_B)$. It was shown in [CHM11, BKH13] that the *variation* δS_B in this entanglement entropy is equal to the variation of a potential energy E_B of the region B, that is, $\delta S_B = \delta E_B$. This relation parallels the *first law of thermodynamics* and has been called in [SR14] the *first law of entanglement*.

Initially, different *measures of entanglement* (see, e.g. [XLS01, Sre93, LR08]) have enabled study of different regimes of *quantum matter*. More recently, [LH08] have showed that in case of a bi-partitioned many-body system (i.e., partitioned into two pieces), the *holographic principle* enables decoding of the information about the boundaries of the system, which is encoded in the so-called *entanglement spectrum*,[3] i.e., in the eigenvalues of the reduced density matrix of a bipartition: $\rho \propto e^{-H_E}$, where H_E is the so-called *entanglement Hamiltonian*. The authors claim that (at low energies) the Hamiltonian H_E describes the fundamental DOFs of the projection of the quantum state on a boundary; therefore, it is an entanglement realization of the holographic principle.

Tensor networks in general, and 2D PEPS [CPS11] in particular, represent a rich arena for analysis of entanglement Hamiltonians, which naturally emerge from entanglement via the *holographic projection* of a TN state on a "fake" boundary [Oru14].

---

[3] Specifically, [LH08] have showed that the eigenvalue-spectrum of the reduced density matrix ρ of a subsystem for the wave-function of the fractional quantum Hall effect was in 1-to-1 correspondence to the energy spectrum of a conformal field theory describing the boundary DOFs.

4.3 A Field-Theoretic Background

To give a fundamental field-theoretic background to our tensor networks, consider a *surface* Ξ, coordinated by 2D coordinates $x = \{x^\mu\}$, with a fermionic matter field on it, $\Phi = \Phi(x) \in \Xi$, and the background metric $g_{\mu\nu} = g_{\mu\nu}(x) \in \Xi$. The metric and field together give rise to the *action functional* $S_\Xi = S[\Phi, g_{\mu\nu}]$, such that the *least action principle*: $\delta S_\Xi = 0$ defines the Euler-Lagrange equations of motion on Ξ.

A 2D *topological field theory* (TFT) on the surface Ξ with the action S_Ξ can be defined by the *Euclidean path integral* (or, *partition function*):

$$ Z[g_{\mu\nu}] = \int \mathcal{D}_\Xi \, \Phi \, e^{-S_\Xi}, \tag{4.2} $$

where $\mathcal{D}_\Xi = \mathcal{D}[g_{\mu\nu}]$ is the *Feynman measure*[4] on the surface Ξ. The path integral (4.2) represents the sum over all quantum fluctuations of the metric $g_{\mu\nu}$ and fermionic field Φ.

Dynamics of the density and flux of energy and momentum on the surface Ξ are governed by the *stress-energy-momentum* (SEM) tensor $T_{\mu\nu} = T_{\mu\nu}(x) \in \Xi$, defined as (see [FHK94]):

$$ T_{\mu\nu} = -4\pi (g_{\mu\nu})^{-1/2} \frac{\delta}{\delta g^{\mu\nu}} \left\{ -\ln Z[g_{\mu\nu}] \right\}. $$

The required symmetry of the TFT can be imposed by the existence of fermionic conserved quantity Q_{BRST} that satisfies the *nilpotency condition*: $Q_{BRST}^2 = 0$. To make this field theory "topological," the partition function $Z[g_{\mu\nu}]$ has to be invariant under *local* changes of the metric $g_{\mu\nu}$:

$$ \frac{\delta Z[g_{\mu\nu}]}{\delta g^{\mu\nu}} \approx 0. $$

This can be achieved by restriction of the BRST-quantized fields[5] to the "physical" Hilbert space:

$$ \mathcal{H}_{phys} \equiv \{ \, |\text{phys}\rangle \, | Q_{BRST} \, |\text{phys}\rangle = 0 \, \}, $$

which implies that any BRST-invariant quantity calculated over $\mathcal{H}_{phys}$ is topological.

Next, to be really useful for TNT, our 2D TFT needs conversion into the 2D lattice. This is usually performed via the triangulation process, that is, by replacing the *sum over all quantum fluctuations of the metric* $g_{\mu\nu}$ by the *sum over all triangulations* T, formally:

$$ \int \mathcal{D}[g_{\mu\nu}] \ \leftrightarrow \ \sum_{T: \text{triang}}, $$

---

[4] For *Feynman's action-amplitude formalism*, see [IR15] and the references therein.
[5] For the BRST-quantization, see [Wik16b] and the references therein.

such that the partition function $Z[T]$ of the resulting 2D lattice is independent of the triangulation process (for further technical details, see [FHK94] and the references therein).

4.4 Tensor Product of Hilbert Spaces and the Logic of Entanglement

Recall that for any two quantum-mechanical systems with their respective Hilbert spaces $\mathcal{H}_1$ and $\mathcal{H}_2$, the compound system is described within their tensor product: $\mathcal{H}_1 \otimes \mathcal{H}_2$. According to [Coe04], the tensor product $\mathcal{H}_1 \otimes \mathcal{H}_2$ is related to a "virtual flow of information" in the *entanglement specification networks*, as:

$$\text{Entanglement} \equiv \text{Information Flow}$$

Coecke's approach allows quantum-mechanical reasoning about quantum information flow, without the explicit consideration of a classical information flow.

In case of a *bipartite entanglement*, consider two finite-dimensional complex Hilbert spaces, $\mathcal{H}_1$ (with a base $\{e_\alpha^{(1)}\}_\alpha$) and $\mathcal{H}_2$ (with a base $\{e_\alpha^{(1)}\}_\alpha$). The elements of the compound system $\mathcal{H}_1 \otimes \mathcal{H}_2$ are in bijective correspondence with: (i) the vector-space of *linear maps* $\mathcal{H}_1 \to \mathcal{H}_2$, as well as with the vector-space of *anti-linear maps* with $\mathcal{H}_1 \rightsquigarrow \mathcal{H}_2$ (both functional vector-spaces have domain $\mathcal{H}_1$ and codomain $\mathcal{H}_2$). Now we have the following correspondence of the bases [Coe04]:

$$m_{\alpha\beta} \langle e_\alpha^{(1)} \mid - \rangle \cdot e_\beta^{(2)} \simeq m_{\alpha\beta} \cdot e_\alpha^{(1)} \otimes e_\beta^{(2)},$$
$$m_{\alpha\beta} \langle - \mid e_\alpha^{(1)} \rangle \cdot e_\beta^{(2)} \simeq m_{\alpha\beta} \cdot e_\alpha^{(1)} \otimes e_\beta^{(2)},$$

where $\langle e_\alpha^{(1)} \mid - \rangle : \mathcal{H}_1 \to \mathcal{H}_2$, $\langle - \mid e_\alpha^{(1)} \rangle : \mathcal{H}_1 \rightsquigarrow \mathcal{H}_2$ are the linear and anti-linear duals to the vector $e_\alpha^{(1)}$, respectively, $m_{\alpha\beta}$ is the *tensor* of the functions in the bases $\{e_\alpha^{(1)}\}_\alpha$ and $\{e_\alpha^{(2)}\}_\beta$ and the summation is assumed over repeated indices.

Generalization to *multipartite entanglement* is straightforward (see [Coe04]), although it, in general, uses *higher order functions* and λ-calculus [Abr93, Bar94]. Due to associativity of the tensor product, a tripartite tensor admits interpretation as a function of a type within the union of two families of types: $\mathcal{H}_i \rightsquigarrow (\mathcal{H}_j \rightsquigarrow_k)$ and $(\mathcal{H}_i \rightsquigarrow_j) \rightsquigarrow_k$. Specifically, from the *tripartite tensor product*:

$$M_{\alpha\beta\gamma} \cdot e_\alpha^{(1)} \otimes e_\beta^{(2)} \otimes e_\gamma^{(3)} \in \mathcal{H}_1 \otimes \mathcal{H}_2 \otimes \mathcal{H}_3,$$

we obtain the corresponding functions:

$f_1 : \mathcal{H}_1 \rightsquigarrow (\mathcal{H}_2 \rightsquigarrow \mathcal{H}_3)$, given by:

$$\psi_\alpha \cdot e_\alpha^{(1)} \mapsto \left(\bar{\psi}_\alpha M_{\alpha\beta\gamma}\right) \langle - \mid e_\beta^{(2)} \rangle \cdot e_\gamma^{(3)}, \qquad \text{and}$$

$$f_2 : (\mathcal{H}_1 \rightsquigarrow \mathcal{H}_2) \rightsquigarrow \mathcal{H}_3, \text{ given by:}$$

$$m_{\alpha\beta} \langle - \mid e_\alpha^{(1)} \rangle \cdot e_\beta^{(2)} \mapsto \left(\bar{m}_{\alpha\beta} M_{\alpha\beta\gamma}\right) \cdot e_\gamma^{(3)},$$

where the complex conjugation of $\bar{\psi}_\alpha$ and $\bar{m}_{\alpha\beta}$ follows from the anti-linearity of the maps.

For more technical details on the logic of entanglement and teleportation, see [Coe04] and the references therein.

4.5 Introduction to Tensor Networks

Recent years have witnessed an explosive growth of *tensor network* (TN) theory, methods, techniques and algorithms in the physics (mainly condensed matter) community. TN methods offer efficient descriptions of quantum many-body states that are based on the entanglement content of the wave function. In TN techniques, the wave function of a complex system under consideration is defined by a *network of tensors connected by entanglement*. In other words, a TN is a *graph* $G = (\mathbf{T}, \mathbf{E})$ in which the nodes/vertices $\mathbf{T}$ are tensors and entanglement provides the links/edges $\mathbf{E}$, while the TN as a whole represents a decomposition of some complex wave function $\Psi(t)$. The fundamental building block of a quantum state Υ is the tensor $T \in \mathbf{T}$ (containing an array of parameters) and the wave function $\Psi(t)$ can be reconstructed from the tensor T by following a set of simple rules. This is a decomposition of the wave function $\Psi(t)$ in terms of LEGO-like pieces (tensors $\mathbf{T}$), glued together by entanglement $\varepsilon(\Upsilon)$ (see [Oru13] and the references therein).

TNs have become an essential tool for both theoretical and numerical study of quantum many-body systems (see, e.g. [XCY14] and the references therein), in particular in the simulation of strongly correlated systems (see, e.g. [ACL12] and the references therein). In TNs the structure and amount of entanglement is a consequence of the chosen network pattern and the parametric content of the tensors [Oru13].

Today, there is a whole "zoo" of (more-or-less) popular TNs, including [Oru13, Oru14]:

- Density Matrix Renormalization Group (DMRG) [Whi92a, Whi92b, PVC04, DKU04], which is a *de facto* standard in simulation of $1D$ quantum lattice systems;
- Tree Tensor Networks (TTN) [SDV06, TEV09, SVM10, MLN10];
- Time-Evolving Block Decimation (teb1) [Vid03, Vid04, Vid07a, OG08];
- Continuous Matrix Product States (CMPS) [VC10, HC10, HOV13] and Continuous Tensor Networks (CTN) [BHJ12];
- Projected Entangled Pair States (PEPS) [VC04];
- Entanglement Renormalization (ER) [Vid07b];

- Multiscale Entanglement Renormalization Ansatz (MERA) [Vid07b, Vid10] and Branching MERA [EV14a, EV14b];
- Folding Algorithms (FA) [BHV09];
- Tensor Renormalization Group (TRG) [LN07];
- Tensor-Entanglement Renormalization Group (TERG) [GLW08];
- Tensor Product Variational Approach (TPVA) [NHO01];
- Weighted Graph States (WGS) (see [HKH09] and the references therein);
- String-Bond States (SBS) [SWV08];
- Entangled-Plaquette States (EPS) [MSB09];
- Monte Carlo Matrix Product States (MCMPS) [SV07];
- Time-Dependent Variational Principle (TDVP) [HCO11];
- Second Renormalization Group (SRG) [XJC09, ZXC10]; and
- Higher Order Tensor Renormalization Group (HOTRG) [XCQ12],

— to mention the most well-known TNs only.

4.6 Formal Definition of Tensor Networks

In the TN-framework, a *rank-n tensor* is given by an nD array of complex numbers, which is written-down with n Greek-letter indices (e.g., a scalar c is a rank-0 tensor, i.e., a complex number; a vector v_α is a rank-1 tensor; a matrix $a_{\alpha\beta}$ is a rank-2 tensor, etc.).

4.6.1 Contraction of Tensor Networks

The basic TN-operation is an *index contraction* (see [Oru13, Oru14]), which is (much like in an ordinary tensor algebra and geometry) a generalized matrix product, defined by summing over all possible values of the repeated indices of all tensors involved in the product. This *inner tensor product* can be written with explicit sums or without them (using standard Einstein's convention over repeated indices). For example, for the following rank-2 tensor:

$$c_{\alpha\gamma} = \sum_{\beta=1}^{n} a_{\alpha\beta}b_{\beta\gamma} = a_{\alpha\beta}b_{\beta\gamma}, \tag{4.3}$$

we have the contraction of index β. More generally, for the following rank-4 tensor we have:

$$f_{\gamma\omega\rho\sigma} = \sum_{\alpha=1}^{n}\sum_{\beta=1}^{n}\sum_{\delta=1}^{n}\sum_{\nu=1}^{n}\sum_{\mu=1}^{n} a_{\alpha\beta\delta\sigma}b_{\beta\gamma\mu}c_{\delta\nu\mu\omega}e_{\nu\rho\alpha}$$

$$= \sum_{\alpha,\beta,\delta,\nu,\mu=1}^{n} a_{\alpha\beta\delta\sigma}b_{\beta\gamma\mu}c_{\delta\nu\mu\omega}e_{\nu\rho\alpha} = a_{\alpha\beta\delta\sigma}b_{\beta\gamma\mu}c_{\delta\nu\mu\omega}e_{\nu\rho\alpha},$$

where non-contracted indices (γ, ω, ρ and σ) are called *open indices*.

In general, the *TN-contraction* means contracting some (or, all) indices of a TN, which in the case of having some open indices produces another tensor. Otherwise, in the case of not having any open indices, the TN-contraction produces a scalar: e.g., a dot-product of two vectors gives a scalar complex number:

$$c = \sum_{\alpha=1}^{n} a_\alpha b_\alpha = a_\alpha b_\alpha.$$

More generally, if all indices of higher-order product are contracted, the result is again a scalar complex number:

$$c = \sum_{\alpha=1}^{n}\sum_{\beta=1}^{n}\sum_{\gamma=1}^{n}\sum_{\delta=1}^{n}\sum_{\omega=1}^{n}\sum_{\nu=1}^{n}\sum_{\mu=1}^{n} a_{\alpha\beta\delta\gamma} b_{\beta\gamma\mu} d_{\delta\nu\mu\omega} e_{\nu\omega\alpha}$$

$$= \sum_{\alpha,\beta,\gamma,\delta,\omega,\nu,\mu=1}^{n} a_{\alpha\beta\delta\gamma} b_{\beta\gamma\mu} d_{\delta\nu\mu\omega} e_{\nu\omega\alpha} = a_{\alpha\beta\delta\gamma} b_{\beta\gamma\mu} d_{\delta\nu\mu\omega} e_{\nu\omega\alpha}.$$

4.6.2 Wave Function of Quantum Many-Body States

Next, we give a TN representation of quantum many-body systems, following [Oru13, Oru14]. Consider a many-body system consisting of N quantum particles $r = 1, ..., N$. As each particles' DOFs can be described by p different states, we actually need to consider systems of N p-level particles. For example, the *spin-1/2 Heisenberg model* is a many-body system in which each particle is a 2-level system (or, a *qubit*), so that $p = 2$.

Physical properties of such a many-body system can be described by its wave function $|\Psi\rangle$. For this, we first need to choose an individual basis $|i_r\rangle$ for the states of each particle. Once the basis $|i_r\rangle$ is chosen, the system's wave function can be expressed as:

$$|\Psi\rangle = \sum_{i_1 i_2 ... i_N} c_{i_1 i_2 ... i_N} |i_1\rangle \otimes |i_2\rangle \otimes \cdots \otimes |i_N\rangle, \qquad (4.4)$$

where $\otimes$ is the standard *tensor product* of individual quantum states for each rth particle $i_r = 1, ..., p$ and the tensor indices $c_{i_1 i_2 ... i_N}$ are p^N (independent) complex numbers. For example, in the case of the spin-1/2 Heisenberg model, Eq. (4.4) reduces to:

$$|\Psi\rangle_{\text{Heis}} = \sum_{i_1 i_2} c_{i_1 i_2} |i_1\rangle \otimes |i_2\rangle.$$

Now we come to tensors. The p^N complex numbers $c_{i_1 i_2 ... i_N}$ in the definition of the wave function $|\Psi\rangle$ given by Eq. (4.4) are the coefficients of a tensor c with N indices $i_1 i_2 ... i_N$. As we are dealing with p-level quantum particles, each index i_r can take up to p different values: $i_r = 1, ..., p$. So, we are dealing with a rank-N tensor, with $O(p^N)$ coefficients. In other words, the system size, that is, the number of parameters that describe the wave function $|\Psi\rangle$ given by Eq. (4.4) is exponentially large. Therefore, to specify the exact values of the coefficients $c_{i_1 i_2 \ldots i_N}$ of a tensor $\mathbf{c}$ would be a computationally-inefficient description of the wave function $|\Psi\rangle$ of the quantum many-body system.

Now we come to tensor networks. TNs can provide an accurate description of the expected entanglement properties of the quantum state and therefore reduce the complexity in the representation of the wave function $|\Psi\rangle$. In other words, the tensor $\mathbf{c}$ with a big rank in (4.4) is replaced by a TN of tensors with smaller rank, by decomposing the "big" tensor $\mathbf{c}$ into its "fundamental DNA blocks," which are tensors of smaller rank. This is effectively a decomposition of the wave function $|\Psi\rangle$ given by Eq. (4.4) into small wave functions.

Such a TN-representation of the wave function $|\Psi\rangle$ depends, typically, on a polynomial number of parameters. This makes it a computationally-efficient description of the many-body system quantum state. Specifically, the total number of TN-parameters m_{tot} is defined as:

$$m_{\text{tot}} = \sum_{t=1}^{N_{\text{tens}}} m(t), \qquad (4.5)$$

where N_{tens} is the number of tensors t in a TN and $m(t)$ is the number of parameters for each tensor t. A TN is computationally-efficient if N_{tens} is sub-exponential in N: e.g., $N_{\text{tens}} = O(\text{poly}(N))$, or even better, $N_{\text{tens}} = O(1)$.

The number of parameters $m(t)$ in (4.5) is given by:

$$m(t) = O\left(N_t^{\text{rank}(t)}\right),$$

where N_t is the maximum of all the different possible values $N(a_t)$ of index a_t for a given tensor t, so that (4.5) can be expanded as:

$$m_{\text{tot}} = \sum_{t=1}^{N_{\text{tens}}} O\left(N_t^{\text{rank}(t)}\right) = O(\text{poly}(N)\text{poly}(N)),$$

where N is the maximal N_t of all the tensors t in the TN.

4.6.3 Matrix Product States TNs

The family of *Matrix Product States* (MPS, [FNW93]) is a 1D array of tensors (one tensor per site) which lays behind the *Density Matrix Renormalization Group* (DMRG, [Whi92a, Whi92b, PVC04, DKU04]) and some other efficient 1D many-body simulators. In MPS, the *bond indices* have $1, \ldots, N$ values and glue the tensors together, while the *open indices* have $1, \ldots, p$ values and represent physical DOFs of the local Hilbert spaces.

MPS tensor networks have the following basic properties (see [Oru13, Oru14]):

- *MPS translational invariance* (TI): while MPS itself is not TI (in general), the TI can be imposed if we take the thermodynamic limit of the MPS by choosing a fundamental *unit tensor cell*, which is infinitely repeated over the 1D lattice (e.g., if we have a 1-tensor unit cell, the MPS is TI over 1-site shifts; if we have a 2-tensor unit cell, the MPS is TI over 2-site shifts, etc.).

- *MPS density*: MPS can represent *all* possible Hilbert-space states of a quantum many-body system, if its size N is exponentially large. However, in the case of gapped local 1D Hamiltonians, low energy states can be approximated by a finite-N MPS [Whi92a].

- *1D area-law* scaling of the *entanglement entropy* for 1D systems:

$$S(L) = -\text{Tr}(\rho_L \log \rho_L) = O(\log N),$$

where ρ_L is the reduced density matrix of the MPS block. Such behavior is usually observed in ground states of gapped local 1D Hamiltonians for large block size L: $S(L) \sim$ constant for $L \gg 1$ [XLS01].

- *MPS correlation functions* always decay exponentially with the separation distance, thus their *correlation length* is always finite. The *two-body correlator* is given in terms of one-body operators O_i and O'_{i+r} at sites i and $i+r$ as:

$$C(r) \equiv \langle O_i O'_{i+r} \rangle - \langle O_i \rangle \langle O'_{i+r} \rangle$$

- *Exact expectation values*: the scalar product between two N-site MPS can be calculated exactly in a $O(Np\text{D}^3)$ time, while in case of infinite MPS, the calculation can be done in a $O(p\text{D}^3)$ time.[6]

- *MPS canonical form* [Vid03, Vid07a] represents a convenient choice of tensors for a given quantum state $|\Psi\rangle$ in terms of an MPS with open boundary conditions. In that case, each bond index α corresponds to the labeling of Schmidt vectors in the *Schmidt decomposition* of $|\Psi\rangle$:

$$|\Psi\rangle = \sum_{\alpha=1}^{N} \lambda_\alpha |\Phi_\alpha^L\rangle \otimes |\Phi_\alpha^R\rangle, \qquad (4.6)$$

where λ_α are Schmidt coefficients (with decreasing order: $\lambda_1 \geq \lambda_2 \geq \cdots \geq 0$) and Φ_α are the Schmidt vectors which are orthonormal: $\langle \Phi_\alpha^L | \Phi_{\alpha'}^L \rangle = \langle \Phi_\alpha^R | \Phi_{\alpha'}^R \rangle = \delta_{\alpha\alpha'}$.

In the case of a finite N-site system [Vid03], the Schmidt decomposition (4.6) corresponds to the decomposition of the wave-function coefficient C as:

$$C_{i_1 i_2 \ldots i_N} = \Gamma_{\alpha_1}^{[1]i_1} \lambda_{\alpha_1}^{[1]} \Gamma_{\alpha_1 \alpha_2}^{[2]i_2} \lambda_{\alpha_2}^{[2]} \Gamma_{\alpha_2 \alpha_3}^{[3]i_3} \lambda_{\alpha_3}^{[3]} \cdots \lambda_{\alpha_{N-1}}^{[N-1]} \Gamma_{\alpha_{N-1}}^{[N]i_N}, \qquad (4.7)$$

where λs are the Schmidt coefficients as before, while the Γ tensors represent the changes of basis between the different Schmidt basis and the spin basis.

---

[6] Using various tensor manipulations, similar calculations can be done for local observables.

The algorithm of successive Schmidt decompositions to obtain the canonical form in a finite MPS $|\Psi\rangle$ is defined in [Vid03] with a resulting quantum state:

$$|\Psi\rangle = \sum_{\{i\}} \sum_{\{\alpha\}} \left(\Gamma_{\alpha_1}^{[1]i_1} \lambda_{\alpha_1}^{[1]} \Gamma_{\alpha_1\alpha_2}^{[2]i_2} \lambda_{\alpha_2}^{[2]} \cdots \lambda_{\alpha_{N-1}}^{[N-1]} \Gamma_{\alpha_{N-1}}^{[N]i_N} \right) |i_1\rangle \otimes |i_2\rangle \otimes \cdots \otimes |i_N\rangle ,$$

(4.8)

where the $\{i\}$ and $\{\alpha\}$ sums run up to the allowed values of indices.

In the case of an infinite TI one-site MPS, the canonical form describes the whole state with a single tensor Γ and a single vector λ (see [Vid07a]).

4.7 Simple TN-Simulation in *TNTgo!*

Here we perform a simple ground state calculation of the $S = 1$ *Heisenberg chain* in *TNTgo!* [TNT14], while conserving the total spin. The ground state Hamiltonian with *ZZ-coupling*: $\hat{S}_j^z \hat{S}_{j+1}^z$ and *hopping*: $(\hat{S}_j^+ \hat{S}_{j+1}^- + h.c.)$ is given by:

$$H = \sum_{j=0}^{L-2} \{ f_1(j)\hat{S}_j^z \hat{S}_{j+1}^z + f_2(j)(\hat{S}_j^+ \hat{S}_{j+1}^- + h.c.) \}.$$

The initial state of the chain is given by: $|\Psi\rangle_{\text{start}} = \hat{O}_1 |\Psi\rangle_{\text{base}}$, with the product operator $\hat{O}_1$ defined as:

$$\hat{O}_1 = \prod_{j=0}^{L-1} (\hat{S}_j^+)^{f_1(j)} (\exp(\pi i \hat{S}_j^z))^{f_2(j)}.$$

Spatial function is given in the form of delta function: $A\delta(j - j_c)$.
Spin flip is used as: $\exp(\pi i \hat{S}_j^z)$.
Two-site expectation operators are used as: $\hat{S}_j^z \hat{S}_{j+1}^z$.

Time evolution calculation is performed in 500 steps, with the time-step size = 0.01, while 10 time-steps are used for expectation value evaluations. In the ground state calculation, ΔE_6 was 210^{-5}. The outputs are given in Figures 4.1, 4.2 and 4.3.

4.8 Fermionic Tensor Networks

The so-called *fermionisation procedure* of TNs is based on the following two rules:
(i) *using parity-2-symmetry (P2S) of tensors*[7] allows some important manipulations in the TN under consideration; and

---

[7] Note that *fermionic parity* (whether the total number of fermions is even or odd) is a $\mathbb{Z}_2$-symmetry for fermionic systems.

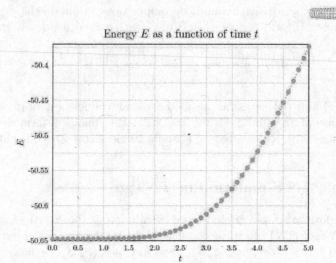

Fig. 4.1. *Time evolution of energy.*

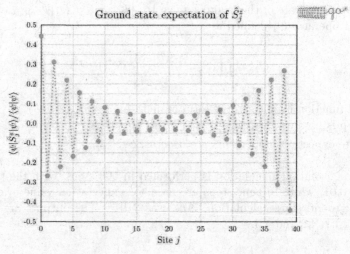

Mean value $\mu = 4.1633 \times 10^{-17}$; variance $= \frac{1}{L}\sum_j |\hat{S}_j^z - \mu|^2 = 2.8787 \times 10^{-2}$.

Fig. 4.2. *Ground state expectation.*

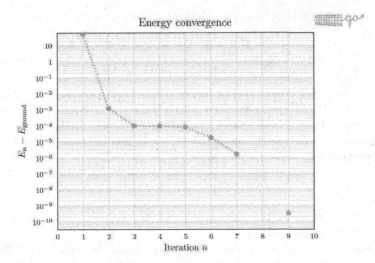

Converged energy density $E_{\text{ground}}/L = -1.3712844$.

Fig. 4.3. *Energy convergence.*

(ii) *replacing line crossings in the planar TN-representation by fermionic swap gates*,[8] which involves the fermionic statistics; this *fermionic swap* basically implies reading the *parity charge* of each index and multiplying the TN's wavefunction by -1 when an odd number of fermions (odd parity) swap their order with an odd number of fermions.

Recall that in the *second quantization* one must choose the *fermionic ordering* (that is, an ordering on how fermionic operators are applied to a fermionic vacuum). While 1D fermionic latices have a natural ordering, it is not so in nD (for $n \geq 2$) fermionic ones, which means that fermionic ordering is *not* a physical property.

It is well-known that the Hilbert space $\mathcal{H}$ (at a given physical site) decomposes into a direct sum $\bigoplus_c$ of the *irreducible representations* (irreps) of a global symmetry group G, which in our case is the P2S-group. The *fermionic operators* are properly defined by taking into account the P2S, because of which, states in the different local Hilbert spaces can be labeled as $|i\rangle \equiv |c, \eta_c\rangle$, where c is the irrep of the P2S: $c = 1$ for even, $c = -1$ for odd, and η_c is a degeneracy index (all irreps are 1D). Therefore, two types of fermionic operators can be identified: (i) *parity-preserving operators*: $c^\dagger_{(1,\eta_1)}$ which preserve the parity of a given state, and (ii) *parity-changing operators*: $c^\dagger_{(-1,\eta_{-1})}$ which change the given state (see [Oru14] and the references therein). For example,

---

[8] This planar replacement is physically interpreted so that every wire (or, line) in the TN diagram represents a fermionic DOF, which is either "physical" (physical indices) or "virtual" (bond indices).

for spin-1/2 fermions (like in the *Hubbard model*) we have:

$$c^\dagger_{(1,1)} = \qquad c^\dagger_{(1,2)} = b^\dagger_\uparrow b^\dagger_\downarrow$$
$$c^\dagger_{(-1,1)} = b^\dagger_\uparrow, \qquad c^\dagger_{(-1,2)} = b^\dagger_\downarrow,$$

where $b^\dagger_\uparrow$ and $b^\dagger_\downarrow$ are the operators which create fermions with spin up and down, respectively. These *generalized parity operators* can be written as $c^\dagger_i$, where index i represents the mode to be created, and they satisfy the following commutation relations:

$$c^\dagger_i c^\dagger_j = S(i,j) c^\dagger_j c^\dagger_i \qquad c^\dagger_i c_j = S(i,j) c_j c^\dagger_i, \tag{4.9}$$

where $S(i,j)$ denotes the *fermionic swap tensor*, whereas c_j and $c^\dagger_i$ are creation and annihilation operators.

Following [Oru14] we present here three examples of n-site MPS (for $n = 2, 3, 4$ fermions) of successively growing complexity, which illustrate how a fermionic quantum state in second quantization can be represented by a fermionic TN diagram using the above two rules.

The 2-site MPS for 2 fermions

Firstly, consider the following two parity-preserving fermionic operators:

$$\tau^{[1]}_{i_1\mu} c^\dagger_{i_1} c_\mu \quad \text{and} \quad \tau^{[2]}_{\mu i_2} c^\dagger_\mu c^\dagger_{i_2}, \tag{4.10}$$

where c_x and $c^\dagger_x$ denote creation and annihilation operators for mode x, index μ denotes a virtual mode, while indices i_1 and i_2 represent the fermionic DOFs of the physical fermions.

Secondly, the outer product π of the two parity-preserving operators in Eq. (4.10) reads:

$$\pi = \sum_\mu \tau^{[1]}_{i_1\mu} \tau^{[2]}_{\mu i_2} c^\dagger_{i_1} c_\mu c^\dagger_\mu c^\dagger_{i_2} = \sum_\mu \tau^{[1]}_{i_1\mu} \tau^{[2]}_{\mu i_2} c^\dagger_{i_1} c^\dagger_{i_2}.$$

Thirdly, the action of the product π on a *fermionic vacuum* $|\Omega\rangle$ gives a *two-site MPS quantum state*, with the wave-function:

$$|\Psi\rangle = \sum_{i_1 i_2} \left(\sum_\mu \tau^{[1]}_{i_1\mu} \tau^{[2]}_{\mu i_2} \right) c^\dagger_{i_1} c^\dagger_{i_2} |\Omega\rangle, \tag{4.11}$$

where the *bond dimension* of the MPS corresponds to a generalized parity DOF, which is traced out so that it can give the final quantum state.

Finally, swapping the position of the two physical fermions (using the $SWAP_{12}$ operator that swaps the physical fermions 1 and 2 in real space), gives the overall wave-function:

$$SWAP_{12}|\Psi\rangle = \sum_{i_1 i_2} \left(\sum_{\mu} \tau^{[1]}_{i_1 \mu} \tau^{[2]}_{\mu i_2} S(i_1, i_2) \right) c^\dagger_{i_2} c^\dagger_{i_1} |\Omega\rangle.$$

where the appearance of the fermionic swap tensor $S(i_1, i_2)$ is a consequence of the $SWAP_{12}$-operator action and the fermionic anti-commutation rules (4.9); see [Oru14] and the references therein.

The 3-site MPS for 3 fermions with periodic boundary conditions

Slightly more generally, consider the following three parity-preserving operators (using a normal ordering for sorting of the fermionic modes):

$$\tau^{[1]}_{i_1 \mu \nu} c^\dagger_{i_1} c_\mu c_\nu, \qquad \tau^{[2]}_{\nu i_2 \rho} c^\dagger_\nu c^\dagger_{i_2} c_\rho, \qquad \tau^{[3]}_{\rho \mu i_3} c^\dagger_\rho c^\dagger_\mu c^\dagger_{i_3}.$$

If we take a trace of the virtual DOFs (as before) and then apply the result to the vacuum $|\Omega\rangle$, we obtain the following quantum-state wave-function of the 3-site MPS with periodic boundary conditions:

$$|\Psi\rangle = \sum_{i_1 i_2 i_3} \left(\sum_{\mu \nu \rho} \tau^{[1]}_{i_1 \mu \nu} \tau^{[2]}_{\nu i_2 \rho} \tau^{[3]}_{\rho \mu i_3} \right) c^\dagger_{i_1} c_\mu c_\nu c^\dagger_\nu c^\dagger_{i_2} c_\rho c^\dagger_\rho c^\dagger_\mu c^\dagger_{i_3} |\Omega\rangle$$

$$= \sum_{i_1 i_2 i_3} \left(\sum_{\mu \nu \rho} \tau^{[1]}_{i_1 \mu \nu} \tau^{[2]}_{\nu i_2 \rho} \tau^{[3]}_{\rho \mu i_3} \right) c^\dagger_{i_1} c_\mu c^\dagger_{i_2} c^\dagger_\mu c^\dagger_{i_3} |\Omega\rangle$$

$$= \sum_{i_1 i_2 i_3} \left(\sum_{\mu \nu \rho} \tau^{[1]}_{i_1 \mu \nu} \tau^{[2]}_{\nu i_2 \rho} \tau^{[3]}_{\rho \mu i_3} S(i_2, \mu) \right) c^\dagger_{i_1} c^\dagger_{i_2} c^\dagger_{i_3} |\Omega\rangle,$$

where the appearance of the fermionic swap tensor $S(i_2, \mu)$ is a result of anti-commuted operators c_μ and $c^\dagger_{i_2}$; see [Oru14] and the references therein.

The 4-site MPS for 4 fermions with periodic boundary conditions

Even more generally, consider the following four parity-preserving operators (again using a normal ordering for sorting of the fermionic modes):

$$\tau^{[1]}_{i_1 \mu \omega} c^\dagger_{i_1} c_\mu c_\omega, \qquad \tau^{[2]}_{\mu i_2 \nu} c^\dagger_\mu c^\dagger_{i_2} c_\nu,$$

$$\tau^{[3]}_{\rho \nu i_3} c^\dagger_\rho c^\dagger_\nu c^\dagger_{i_3}, \qquad \tau^{[4]}_{\omega i_4 \rho} c^\dagger_\omega c^\dagger_{i_4} c_\rho.$$

Again, tracing out the virtual DOFs, we obtain the following quantum-state wave-function of the 4-site MPS with periodic boundary conditions:

$$|\Psi\rangle = \sum_{i_1 i_4 i_2 i_3} \left(\sum_{\mu\nu\rho\omega} \tau^{[1]}_{i_1\mu\omega} \tau^{[4]}_{\omega i_4\rho} \tau^{[2]}_{\mu i_2\nu} \tau^{[3]}_{\rho\nu i_3} \right) c^\dagger_{i_1} c_\mu c_\omega c^\dagger_\omega c^\dagger_{i_4} c_\rho c^\dagger_\mu c^\dagger_{i_2} c_\nu c^\dagger_\rho c^\dagger_\nu c^\dagger_{i_3} |\Omega\rangle$$

$$= \sum_{i_1 i_4 i_2 i_3} \left(\sum_{\mu\nu\rho\omega} \tau^{[1]}_{i_1\mu\omega} \tau^{[4]}_{\omega i_4\rho} \tau^{[2]}_{\mu i_2\nu} \tau^{[3]}_{\rho\nu i_3} \right) c^\dagger_{i_1} c_\mu c^\dagger_{i_4} c_\rho c^\dagger_\mu c^\dagger_{i_2} c_\nu c^\dagger_\rho c^\dagger_\nu c^\dagger_{i_3} |\Omega\rangle$$

$$= \sum_{i_1 i_4 i_2 i_3} \left(\sum_{\mu\nu\rho\omega} \tau^{[1]}_{i_1\mu\omega} \tau^{[4]}_{\omega i_4\rho} \tau^{[2]}_{\mu i_2\nu} \tau^{[3]}_{\rho\nu i_3} S(\mu,i_4) S(\rho,\mu) S(\rho,i_2) S(\rho,\nu) \right)$$
$$\otimes\, c^\dagger_{i_1} c^\dagger_{i_4} c^\dagger_{i_2} c^\dagger_{i_3} |\Omega\rangle$$

$$= \sum_{i_1 i_4 i_2 i_3} \left(\sum_{\mu\nu\rho\omega} \tau^{[1]}_{i_1\mu\omega} \tau^{[4]}_{\omega i_4\rho} \tau^{[2]}_{\mu i_2\nu} \tau^{[3]}_{\rho\nu i_3} S(\mu,i_4) \right) c^\dagger_{i_1} c^\dagger_{i_4} c^\dagger_{i_2} c^\dagger_{i_3} |\Omega\rangle, \qquad (4.12)$$

where we have used the fermionic anti-commutation relations (4.9) in the first three lines; in the fourth line, due to the parity symmetry of the $\tau^{[2]}$ operator we have: $S(\rho,\mu)S(\rho,i_2)S(\rho,\nu) = 1$, which makes a so-called *jump move* and gives the last line (4.12); see [Oru14] and the references therein.

4.9 CPC-Application: Entangled Quantum Computation for Swarm Intelligence

Continuous spatiotemporal probabilistic models have been proposed for *swarm robotics* [HW08], based on real-valued Langevin and Fokker-Planck (L-FP) equations, as well as for *turbulent crowd dynamics* [IR12], based on complex-valued nonlinear Schrödinger (NLS) equations. Also, decentralized temporal probabilistic models have been proposed for swarms of Brownian land robots [SHO14], based on L-FP equations, and for joint swarms of land and air robots [IY16], based on affine Hamiltonian control systems.

In this section we propose an abstract computational model for a general swarm intelligence, that is, AI of a swarm of unmanned vehicles (as depicted in Figure 1.1) — based on the concept of *entangled quantum computing*. [We remark that the associated technology of quantum sensing, chiefly promoted by DARPA [Gim15, Kum15], is not the subject of the present section.] The only class of algorithms in which quantum effects have so far been involved in swarm intelligence, to the best of our knowledge, has been the quantum-accelerated *particle swarm optimization* (QPSO, see [PKB07, RE12] and the references therein).

Recall that entanglement of interacting quantum systems (e.g., particles, harmonic oscillators, qubits and multiqubits) is a 'holistic' natural and communicational phenomenon, as well as a superior computational paradigm ["Entanglement lies at the core of quantum algorithms designed to solve problems that are intractable by classical approaches" [Lan14]] — in which the quantum-state wavefunction of each included system cannot be described independently (i.e., separately), but only for a joint system as a whole. In case of entanglement, the measurement of all included quantum observables (positions, momenta, spins, etc.) gives strong inter-correlations, caused by the collapse of the composite wavefunction (see, e.g. [Wik16s] and the references and links therein).

Although it is an essentially quantum phenomenon, the effects of entanglement are seen in any macroscopic system/process that cannot be properly reduced to its components. In particular, entanglement provides arguably the only rigorous method to describe holistic swarming behaviors of bees, birds and bats.

An "entangled swarm intelligence can be represented by a high-dimensional composite quantum-mechanical system that is naturally entangled (see, e.g. [II09]). An act of macroscopic measurement performed on its observables produces a high-dimensional set of strong inter-correlations, caused by the collapse of its high-dimensional entangled wavefunction. In other words, the distributed quantum brain model can be viewed from two perspectives:

Quantum : as a pure entangled quantum system, "one entangled whole" that cannot be reduced to its components; and

Classical : as a set of strong inter-correlations, caused by the act of macroscopic measurement which de-entangles a single composite high-dimensional wavefunction.

A technology suitable for building the distributed quantum brain model is called quantum computation, or quantum computing (see [Wik16bb, NC02] and the references therein; a brief is given in the next section), currently existing mainly in the form of mathematical models, software packages and specialized circuitry. However, scaling of these specialized architectures to build practical general-purpose processors with many millions to billions of qubits still proves challenging [Lan14].

The state-of-the-art in hardware-implemented quantum computing is a room-size machine called the *D-Wave* system [D-W16]. It is a mixed quantum-classical machine which demonstrates entanglement while implementing *quantum annealing* (QA), a generic optimization algorithm, based on the generalized Ising-spin Hamiltonian, designed to find the low-energy configurations of systems of interacting spins (see [Lan14] and the references therein).

Therefore, the quantum swarm intelligence (entangled swarm intelligence) model presented in this section can be currently only implemented in software on standard digital computers. However, near future will inevitably bring quantum computation in silicon chips ["Scientists and engineers from the Australian Research Council Centre of Excellence for Quantum Computation and Communication Technology (CQC2T), headquartered at UNSW, are leading the world in the race to develop a scalable quantum computer in silicon" [Gou15]] — that will enable fast-and-stable hardware implementations of the models presented herein.

The present section is a continuation of the autonomous robotic swarm development. It focuses on robotic swarm intelligence and proposes a new high-dimensional model of an entangled quantum-computational system, representing the swarm quantum brain. This parallelized, fully entangled computational structure is in one-to-one correspondence with the swarm manifold (Figure 1.1), where each vehicle has a dedicated quantum n-qubit (see next section), i.e., a qubit per DOF plus a few qubits for specific intelligent functions implemented on each robot.

4.9.1 Quantum-Computational Fusion

Recall that at the core of all quantum-computation protocols lies the basic unit of quantum information called *qubit* (see [BBC95, Wik16cc] and the references and links therein). Briefly, a qubit is a simple quantum-mechanical system, given by a pair of Dirac's ket-vectors (equivalent to Schrödinger's wave ψ-functions), $A_1 = \{|0\rangle, |1\rangle\}$. It is formally defined by a two-dimensional (2D) complex-valued Hilbert space of states, $\mathcal{H}_{A_1} = \mathbb{C}^2$, with the computational basis given by: $|0\rangle = \binom{1}{0}$ and $|1\rangle = \binom{0}{1}$, so that any pure qubit wave-state ψ represents the linear superposition: $|\psi\rangle = \binom{\alpha}{\beta} = \alpha|0\rangle + \beta|1\rangle$ of these basis states, conveniently visualized on the *Bloch sphere* (for more technical details see, e.g. [Sch95, Wik16cc] and the references therein). An arbitrary state like $\frac{1}{\sqrt{2}}|01\rangle - \frac{1}{\sqrt{2}}|10\rangle$ is called *entangled* if it cannot be described by the state of its individual qubits $\{|0\rangle, |1\rangle\}$ (see, e.g. [ABG13] and the references therein).

More generally, a multiqubit, or n-qubit circuit (also called a quantum network or a quantum gate array) consists of wires and various quantum logic gates (having the same number of inputs as outputs) so that an n-input gate carries a unitary operation of the group $U(2^n)$, that is a generalized rotation in a 2^nD Hilbert state-space [BBC95]. Standard n-qubits, including controlled-NOT gate (that operates on two qubits by changing the second bit only if the first bit is 1), Hadamard gate (based on the Walsh-Hadamard transform [Wik16v]), SWAP gate (that swaps input and output qubits), as well as more complex gates like Fredkin, Pauli, Toffoli, etc. can be represented by a $(2^n \times 2^n)$ unitary matrix (for technical details on n-qubit circuits, see e.g. [GS13, Sel13, Sel15] and the references therein). For instance, the *D-Wave* uses both two-qubit and eight-qubit unit cells, in such a way that the (ground state of the) system can be expressed as a *tensor product* (see below) of the (ground states of the) individual qubits [Lan14]: $\otimes_{k=1}^{N=2,8} (|\uparrow\rangle_k + |\downarrow\rangle_k)/\sqrt{2}$, where "$\uparrow, \downarrow$" denote spin-up and spin-down, respectively.

In general, the state-space of an n-qubit system, $A = A_1 \cdots A_n$, which can exist in any superposition of the 2^n basis states with the coefficients α_i $(i = 1, ..., n)$ such that $\sum_{i=0}^{2^n-1} |\alpha_i|^2 = 1$, is the 2^nD Hilbert space $\mathcal{H}_A = \mathbb{C}^2 \otimes \cdots \otimes \mathbb{C}^2$. Here, $\otimes$ denotes the (Kronecker) *tensor product*, a generalization of the vector/matrix outer product, as well as the Cartesian product $X \times Y = \{(x, y) \mid a \in X \text{ and } b \in Y\}$ of two sets/spaces X and Y. While Cartesian product "×" acts (element-wise) on sets/spaces only, the tensor product "⊗" acts also on the corresponding maps between these sets/spaces; therefore, it is a *functor*. A tensor-product space is a quotient space of the corresponding Cartesian-product space (with respect to certain equivalence classes; see, e.g. [Wik16ee] and the references and links therein).

For example, the 7th tensor power of a qubit template XX (to be replaced by any actual qubit) is given by:

$$(|XX_i\rangle)^{\otimes 7} = \otimes_{i=1}^{7} |XX_i\rangle = |XX_1\rangle \otimes |XX_2\rangle \otimes |XX_3\rangle \otimes |XX_4\rangle \otimes |XX_5\rangle \otimes |XX_6\rangle \otimes |XX_7\rangle = |XX_1, XX_2, XX_3, XX_4, XX_5, XX_6, XX_7\rangle.$$

This construction can be also applied to quantum gate circuits. For example, a triple controlled-NOT gate:

$$\otimes_{i=1}^{3} C^i [NOT_{i+1}] = C^1 [NOT_2] C^2 [NOT_3] C^3 [NOT_4]$$

can be expanded in the 4-digit computational basis as:

$|0000\rangle\langle 0000| + |0001\rangle\langle 0001| + |0011\rangle\langle 0010| + |0010\rangle\langle 0011| + |0110\rangle\langle 0100| + |0111\rangle\langle 0101| + |0101\rangle\langle 0110| + |0100\rangle\langle 0111| + |1100\rangle\langle 1000| + |1101\rangle\langle 1001| + |1111\rangle\langle 1010| + |1110\rangle\langle 1011| + |1010\rangle\langle 1100| + |1011\rangle\langle 1101| + |1001\rangle\langle 1110| + |1000\rangle\langle 1111|.$

All quantum-computational processes Q (including: quantum information-flow, entanglement swapping, teleportation and communication protocols, as well as quantum cryptography, games and gambling; see [NC02]), are naturally occurring between two quantum state-agents, traditionally called Alice (A) and Bob (B). They can all be represented by the causal maps from Alice to Bob, $Q : A \to B$, so that the Alice–Bob *compound quantum state* $|\psi\rangle_A \otimes |\psi\rangle_B$ lives in the composite Hilbert state-space $\mathcal{H}_A \otimes \mathcal{H}_B$, which is the tensor product of the component state-spaces $\mathcal{H}_A$ and $\mathcal{H}_B$. A generalization to any number of quantum state-agents is based on the bifunctorial tensor product methods as follows.

We approach the problem of parallel quantum-computational fusion from two angles, as follows. A categorical generalization of the Kronecker tensor product is the so-called *symmetric monoidal tensor product* (tensor, for short) $\otimes : \mathcal{K} \times \mathcal{K} \to \mathcal{K}$, valid for any category $\mathcal{K}$ (see [Coe06, Coe09, CP09]). From abstract computational perspective, to fuse two arbitrary n-qubit computational systems, A and B, into a parallel combined system, we can use their tensor $A \otimes B$, together with its compound operations: $A \otimes B \xrightarrow{f \otimes g} C \otimes D$. In this way, we can define a *symmetric monoidal category* $\mathcal{M}$ [Mac98] as a pair $(\text{Ob}(\mathcal{M}), \text{Mor}(\mathcal{M}))$ of generic objects: $A, B, \ldots \in \text{Ob}(\mathcal{M})$ and generic morphisms, $f : A \to B$, $g : C \to D, \ldots \in \text{Mor}(\mathcal{M})$, as:

$$\text{Ob}(\mathcal{M}) : \{A, B\} \mapsto A \otimes B, \tag{4.13}$$

$$\text{Mor}(\mathcal{M}) : \{A \xrightarrow{f} B, \ C \xrightarrow{g} D\} \mapsto A \otimes C \xrightarrow{f \otimes g} B \otimes D,$$

with the additional notion of commutative *bifunctoriality*: the order in which two n-qubit functions, f (applied to one n-qubit) and g (applied to another n-qubit), does not matter; i.e., the following symmetric square commutes:

$$
\begin{array}{ccc}
A_1 \otimes A_2 & \xrightarrow{\ f \otimes 1_{A_2}\ } & B_1 \otimes A_2 \\
\Big\downarrow{\scriptstyle 1_{A_1} \otimes g} & & \Big\downarrow{\scriptstyle 1_{B_1} \otimes g} \\
A_1 \otimes B_2 & \xrightarrow[\ f \otimes 1_{B_2}\ ]{} & B_1 \otimes B_2
\end{array}
$$

which shows that both paths yield the same result (for the proof of commutative bifunctoriality and more technical details, see [Coe06, CP09]). From (4.13), it follows that the *tensor* $\otimes$ represents a *bifunctor* that acts both on the objects $(A, B) \in \mathcal{M}$ and on the morphisms $(f, g) \in \mathcal{M}$. This implies that the monoidal category $\mathcal{M}$ is not an ordinary category, but rather Benabou's *bicategory* [Ben67], which also includes an identity object I and some natural isomorphisms obeying MacLane's coherence conditions [Mac98], including the "fancy pentagon" diagram. In the bicategory $\mathcal{M}$, the usual categorical composition '$\circ$' is naturally used to represent physical processes combined in *series*, while the *tensor* $\otimes$ represents physical processes combined in *parallel*. A class of quantum circuits that is closed under both $\otimes$ and '$\circ$' is the class of Clifford stabilizer circuits (see, e.g. [GS13, Sel13, Sel15, AG04]).

From quantum-mechanical perspective, the monoidal category $\mathcal{M}$ defined in (4.13) represents a bicategory $\mathcal{HILB}$ of Hilbert spaces, defined by:

$$
\mathrm{Ob}(\mathcal{Hilb}) \; : \; \{\mathcal{H}_A, \mathcal{H}_B\} \; \mapsto \; \mathcal{H}_A \otimes \mathcal{H}_B,
$$

$$
\mathrm{Mor}(\mathcal{Hilb}) \; : \; \{\mathcal{H}_A \xrightarrow{\ f\ } \mathcal{H}_B, \mathcal{H}_C \xrightarrow{\ g\ } \mathcal{H}_D\}
$$

$$
\mapsto \; \mathcal{H}_A \otimes \mathcal{H}_C \xrightarrow{\ f \otimes g\ } \mathcal{H}_B \otimes \mathcal{H}_D.
$$

Quantum-mechanical processes occurring in the *tensor* bicategory $\mathcal{HILB}$ are defined as follows. If $\{|k\rangle\}_k$ is a basis for the Hilbert space $\mathcal{H}_A$ and $\{|j\rangle\}_j$ is a basis for the Hilbert space $\mathcal{H}_B$, then their *tensor*, containing all composite states $|\psi\rangle_A \otimes |\psi\rangle_B$, is defined by the following comprehension set (see [Coe06, Coe09]):

$$
\mathcal{H}_A \otimes \mathcal{H}_B = \left\{ \sum_{k,j} \omega_{kj} \cdot |k\rangle_A \otimes |j\rangle_B : (\omega_{kj} \in \mathbb{C} \quad \text{for all } i, j) \right\}. \tag{4.14}
$$

Two such composite wave-state vectors, $|\psi\rangle = \sum_{k,j} \omega_{kj} \cdot |k\rangle \otimes |j\rangle$ and $|\psi'\rangle = \sum_{k,j} \omega'_{kj} \cdot |k\rangle \otimes |j\rangle$, are equal if and only if (*iff*) their complex weights ω_{kj} coincide for all k, j, that is, if their matrices $(\omega)_{kj}$ and $(\omega)'_{kj}$ are equal. As each matrix $(\omega)_{kj}$ is the matrix of some linear operator $\omega : \mathcal{H}_A \to \mathcal{H}_B$, namely the one for which we have $\omega(|j\rangle) = \sum_k \omega_{kj} \cdot |k\rangle$, this implies that there is a bijective correspondence between linear operators $\omega_{AB} : \mathcal{H}_A \to \mathcal{H}_B$ and the composite vectors $|\psi\rangle_{AB} \in \mathcal{H}_A \otimes \mathcal{H}_B$.

More specifically, the compound Alice–Bob quantum state $|\psi\rangle_{AB}$, defined as:

$$|\psi\rangle_A \otimes |\psi\rangle_B = \sum_{k,j} \omega_{kj} \cdot |k\rangle_A \otimes |j\rangle_B \in \mathcal{H}_A \otimes \mathcal{H}_B \qquad (4.15)$$

— is called *separable* in the compound Hilbert space $\mathcal{H}_A \otimes \mathcal{H}_B$ iff the weight matrix $(\omega)_{kj}$ can be decomposed as: $\omega_{kj} = \omega_k^A \omega_j^B$, which implies:

$$|\psi\rangle_A = \sum_k \omega_k^A \cdot |k\rangle_A \qquad \text{and} \qquad |\psi\rangle_B = \sum_j \omega_j^B \cdot |j\rangle_B .$$

Otherwise (when $\omega_{kj} \neq \omega_k^A \omega_j^B$), the compound Alice–Bob state $|\psi\rangle_{AB}$ given by (4.15) is called inseparable, or *entangled state*. Its extreme case, the maximally entangled state of two n-qubits is called the *Bell-state* (for technical details on multiqubit entanglement, see, e.g. [ZYZ13] and the references therein.)

4.9.2 Entangled Swarm Intelligence Model

Generalization of the compound quantum system (4.14)–(4.15) to a high-dimensional *quantum neural network* (see [II09]) is based on the following $(N \times N)$-matrix of Hilbert state-spaces in the *tensor bicategory* $\mathcal{HILB}$:

$$(\mathcal{H})_{NN} = \begin{bmatrix} \mathcal{H}_{11} & \otimes & \mathcal{H}_{12} & \otimes & \mathcal{H}_{13} & \otimes & \cdots & \otimes & \cdots & \mathcal{H}_{1N} \\ \otimes & \cdots & \otimes & \cdots & \otimes & \cdots\cdots & \cdots\cdots & \cdots & \otimes \\ \mathcal{H}_{21} & \otimes & \mathcal{H}_{22} & \otimes & \mathcal{H}_{23} & \otimes & \cdots & \otimes & \cdots & \mathcal{H}_{2N} \\ \otimes & \cdots & \otimes & \cdots & \otimes & \cdots\cdots & \cdots\cdots & \cdots & \otimes \\ \mathcal{H}_{31} & \otimes & \mathcal{H}_{32} & \otimes & \mathcal{H}_{33} & \otimes & \cdots & \otimes & \cdots & \mathcal{H}_{3N} \\ \cdots & \cdots & \cdots & \cdots & \cdots\cdots & \cdots\cdots & \cdots\cdots & \cdots & \\ \mathcal{H}_{N1} & \otimes & \mathcal{H}_{N2} & \otimes & \mathcal{H}_{N3} & \otimes & \cdots & \otimes & \cdots & \mathcal{H}_{NN} \end{bmatrix} \in \mathcal{HILB}, \qquad (4.16)$$

in which every element represents the Hilbert state-space of a single n-qubit circuit with its own quantum state: $|\psi\rangle_{kk} \in \mathcal{H}_{kk}$ (for $k = 1, ..., N$) so that all quantum states form the corresponding complex-valued $(N \times N)$-matrix:

$$(|\psi\rangle)_{NN} = \begin{bmatrix} |\psi\rangle_{11} & \otimes & |\psi\rangle_{12} & \otimes & |\psi\rangle_{13} & \otimes & \cdots & \otimes & \cdots & |\psi\rangle_{1N} \\ \otimes & \cdots & \otimes & \cdots & \otimes & \cdots\cdots & \cdots\cdots & \cdots & \otimes \\ |\psi\rangle_{21} & \otimes & |\psi\rangle_{22} & \otimes & |\psi\rangle_{23} & \otimes & \cdots & \otimes & \cdots & |\psi\rangle_{2N} \\ \otimes & \cdots & \otimes & \cdots & \otimes & \cdots\cdots & \cdots\cdots & \cdots & \otimes \\ |\psi\rangle_{31} & \otimes & |\psi\rangle_{32} & \otimes & |\psi\rangle_{33} & \otimes & \cdots & \otimes & \cdots & |\psi\rangle_{3N} \\ \cdots & \cdots & \cdots & \cdots & \cdots\cdots & \cdots\cdots & \cdots\cdots & \cdots & \\ |\psi\rangle_{N1} & \otimes & |\psi\rangle_{N2} & \otimes & |\psi\rangle_{N3} & \otimes & \cdots & \otimes & \cdots & |\psi\rangle_{NN} \end{bmatrix}, \qquad (4.17)$$

where every *tensor* product $\otimes_{kj} \in (|\psi\rangle)_{NN}$ has its associated weight matrix $(\omega)_{kj}$.

The matrix pair (4.16)–(4.17) is in one-to-one correspondence with the swarm configuration manifold (Figure 1.1), so that each n-qubit with its Hilbert state-space is associated to its own robot. For example, consider a swarm of UAVs, each equipped with the set of appropriate sensors (including GPS, IMU, altimeter, video camera, radar-in-a-chip, etc.), performing a search-and-rescue operation in an urban environment (as described in [IY16]). To start with, each UAV needs a stable flight and navigation based on its own collision avoidance system; these basic on-board functions can be performed by a single n-qubit. In addition, the same n-qubit can, using *quantum Monte Carlo* methods [Cep13], perform some higher navigation/search functions, like the particle-filter based *simultaneous localization and mapping* (SLAM) for GPS-denied environments (see [TMK04, SFG15] and the references therein), or the search for victims using the optic flow methods (see, e.g. [GC09]), etc.

The matrix pair (4.16)–(4.17) also defines an $(N \times N)$–dimensional *complex-valued neural network* (see, e.g. [II09]) with n-qubit processing units $|\psi(t)\rangle_{kj}$ representing artificial multineurons and obeying unitary quantum evolution defined by the Schrödinger equation (1.13) with the transition PDF given by $\||\psi(t)\rangle_{kj}|^2$. The network (4.16)–(4.17) has $(N \times N)$ layers, each given by the *tensor* $\otimes$, which itself has properties similar to the standard *convolution* operator '$*$', defined for two n-qubit functions, f and g by: $(f * g)(t) = \int_{-\infty}^{\infty} f(\tau) g(t-\tau) d\tau$ [e.g., a convolution of any n-qubit function $f(t)$ with any other function multiplied with Dirac-delta, $g(t)\delta(t)$, gives $f(\tau)$]. The convolution and $\otimes$ satisfy the interchange law: $(a \otimes b) * (c \otimes d) = (a * c) \otimes (b * d)$. Therefore, the matrix pair (4.16)–(4.17) represents the fully-entangled generalization of a *deep convolutional neural net* (DCNN, see [LBH15] and the references therein), in which every ψ-multineuron is inseparably connected to every other ψ-multineuron, and which could be trained by the *complex backpropagation* algorithm [Nit97]. This *tensor* $\otimes$-based DCNN represents a quantum-computational extension of the $TensorFlow^{TM}$ developed by the Google Brain Team [DM15].

Such a DCNN could be, in principle, implemented in *Mathematica* (using the above mentioned add-on for quantum computing [GM11]); however, its training would take days or even weeks, so it would be infeasible. [Although Wolfram's *Mathematica*® includes in its kernel a number of the state-of-the-art algorithms, like the superior integrators NIntegrate and NDSolve, still as a general-purpose interpreted language it is too slow for these kind of problems. What is needed in this case is a compiled language with a speed of both compilation and execution similar to the C-language (e.g., GCC, or Visual C/C++). Our language of choice for this problem is Haskell (by generalizing the basic quantum-computing code provided in [Sab03]), which can be optimized to match the speed of the C-language, while at the same time having higher-order functional abilities similar to *Mathematica*.]

Instead, we will focus on the related field of *quantum lambda calculus* (QLC; see, e.g. [Ton04, SV09] and the references therein) represents quantum computation in terms of higher-order functions. QLC has been used for implementation of such important algorithms as *quantum Fourier transform*, which is a variant of the FFT that operates on the amplitude of the quantum state as the map: $QFT : \sum_x f(x)|x\rangle \longrightarrow \sum_s F(s)|s\rangle$, where $F(s)$ is the FFT of

$f(x)$, while $0 \leq x, s \leq N-1$) based on the Hadamard gate: $H = \frac{1}{\sqrt{2}} \begin{pmatrix} 1 & 1 \\ 1 & -1 \end{pmatrix}$.

Other important algorithms implemented in QLC are: the *quantum Turing machine*, an abstract quantum computer proposed by D. Deutsch [Deu85] that allows formally expressing any quantum algorithm as its particular form; Deutsch-Jozsa algorithm (an abstract quantum-computing implementation of the map $f : \{0,1\}^n \to \{0,1\}$); *quantum teleportation protocol*, a quantum-computing process by which a qubit can be transmitted from one location to another without being transmitted through the intervening space (see, e.g. [FB12] and the references therein); as well as *Bell's inequalities* and the corresponding experiments, designed by J. Bell (starting with [Bel64]) to demonstrate the existence of macroscopic consequences of entanglement in the real world.

A plan for our immediate future work involves Haskell implementation of entangled swarm intelligence in the form of a complex, backprop-trained, deep convolutional net (4.16)–(4.17), expressed recursively using a fixed-point combinator in QLC.

As a summary, the proposed quantum system (4.16)–(4.17) represents the entangled swarm intelligence model that is fully scalable, parallel and fault tolerant (compare with [DB07]). In addition, it can serve as a quantum accelerator for both unsupervised and supervised learning (see [ABG13]). And, being fully entangled, it brings all the benefits of quantum entanglement to holistic brain modeling. Once a quantum chip with 100+ million qubits is available, the entangled system (4.16)–(4.17) can be used for the super-fast, distributed, quantum brain modeling.

The proper development of the entangled swarm intelligence, as a part of a holistic, high-dimensional quantum brain model, will require implementation of quantum circuitry in silicon chips with millions of qubits, which are almost becoming reality [Gou15]. The idea proposed in this section extends beyond the currently available quantum-computation technology. However, many computer scientists anticipate that the *future of artificial intelligence* will be based on quantum-computational circuitry embedded in silicon chips. This section is targeting that future.

Cyber-Cognitive CPC-Autonomy: TensorFlow and Deep Neural Tensor Networks

5.1 Modern Brain Models: Deep Learning Neural Networks

5.1.1 Introduction to Deep Learning

On the 23 November 2012, a front-page article at the New York Times [Mar12a] claimed that *deep learning* (DL), a sophisticated *machine learning* (ML) algorithm with unparalleled abilities to recognize syllables and images, is going to revolutionize the *artificial intelligence* (AI). Arguably, the most important DL-innovation is its capability to learn target categories incrementally, attempting to nail down lower-level categories (e.g. letters) before attempting to acquire higher-level categories (like words). However, while the Times reports that "advances in an artificial intelligence technology that can recognize patterns offer the possibility of machines that perform human activities like seeing, listening and thinking," the next-day article in New Yorker is somewhat skeptical about DL and asserts that "deep learning takes us, at best, only a small step toward the creation of truly intelligent machines" [Mar12b].

In its scepticism towards "the Deep Learning Wonder", the New Yorker article [Mar12b] recalls that it all started in the late 1950s, when Frank Rosenblatt from Cornell attempted to build a kind of mechanical brain called the *perceptron* [Ros58], technically the first generation of *artificial neural networks* (ANNs, see Chapter 11, Appendix 2) which was claimed to be "a machine which senses, recognizes, remembers, and responds like the human mind." The system was capable of categorizing (within certain limits) some basic shapes like triangles and squares. The New Yorker even suggested that this "remarkable machine was capable of what amounts to thought."

However, in 1969, Marvin Minsky[1] and Seymour Papert from MIT published a critical book *Perceptrons* [MP69] which demonstrated that

---

[1] Minsky was a co-founder of MIT's celebrated AI Lab.

Rosenblatt's original system was extremely limited, incapable of performing some simple logical functions like XOR, so, after a decade of excitement, the ANNs begun to fall out of favor.

The first renaissance of ANN-ideas happened in the mid 1980s, when Geoff Hinton from Carnegie-Mellon included a *hidden layer* of neurons that allowed a new generation of ANNs to learn more complicated functions (including the problematic XOR) and answer some of the Minsky-Papert questions, using the famous *backpropagation algorithm* (pioneered in 1974 by Paul Werbos [Wer74] from Harvard, and reinvented in 1986 by Rumelhart, Hinton, and Williams [RHW86]).

However, even the new NN-models had some serious problems (e.g., they learned very slowly and inefficiently, and they were not able to master even some of the basic things that children do, like learning the past tense of regular verbs [Mar12b]), so by the late 1990s, ANNs had again begun to fall out of favor.

The second (and current) renaissance of ANN-ideas happened in 2006, when Geoff Hinton invented a new technique that he dubbed "deep learning," by extending the ideas of Yann LeCun, the leading expert in the so-called convolutional ANNs from New York University (see [FCN13] and references therein), which are still in use at Google and Microsoft.

Here is a typical DL-setup for data-mining: a computer is confronted with a large set of data, and asked to sort/classify the elements of that data into categories, without specific instructions given (this is much like a child who is asked to sort a set of toys; they might sort them by color, by shape, by function, etc.). Machine learners try to do this on a grander scale, seeing, for example, millions of handwritten digits, and making guesses about which digit looks more like one another, *clustering them together* based on some kind of similarity [Mar12b]. In this way, DL learns data categories incrementally, from letters at the bottom level, to words at the top level.

Technically speaking, DL makes an effective use of stacks of ANNs to build extra-large NNs, the so-called *deep belief networks* (DBNs). Most often, the following three kinds of ANNs are used as DBN components: *recurrent neural nets* (RNNs), *restricted Boltzmann machines* (RBMs), and *convolutional neural nets* (CNNs) (for the recent overview, see [Sch14] and references therein).

In general, a *deep neural network* (DNN) is an ANN with multiple hidden layers of units between the input and output layers. Similar to shallow ANNs, DNNs can model complex non-linear relationships. DNN architectures, e.g., for object detection and parsing generate compositional models where the object is expressed as layered composition of image primitives. The extra layers enable composition of features from lower layers, giving the potential of modeling complex data with fewer units than a similarly performing shallow network (see [Wik16p] and the references therein).

A DNN can be discriminatively trained with the standard *backpropagation* algorithm. The weight updates can be done via *stochastic gradient descent*[2] using the following learning rule:

$$\Delta w_{ij}(t+1) = \Delta w_{ij}(t) + \eta \frac{\partial C}{\partial w_{ij}},$$

where η is the *learning rate*, and C is the *cost/objective function*. The choice of the cost function depends on factors such as the learning type (supervised, unsupervised, reinforcement, etc.) and the activation function. For example, when performing supervised learning on a multiclass classification problem, common choices for the activation function and cost function are the softmax function (defined as: $p_j = \frac{\exp(x_j)}{\sum_k \exp(x_k)}$, where p_j represents the class probability and x_j and x_k represent the total input to units j and k respectively) and cross entropy function (defined as: $C = -\sum_j d_j \log(p_j)$, where d_j represents the target probability for output unit j and p_j is the probability output for j after applying the activation function), respectively.

We wrap-up this DL-introduction by giving a brief timeline of the DL-history up to Hinton's milestone paper in 2006 (see [Sch13]):

1962: Neurobiological inspiration through simple and complex neural cells [HW62];
1974: Backpropagation learning [Wer74];
1979: Deep neocognitron, weight sharing and convolution [Fuk79];
1987: Autoencoder hierarchies [Bal87];
1989: Backpropagation for CNNs [LBD89];
1991: Deep hierarchy of RNNs [Sch91];
1997: Supervised deep learner with long short-term memory for RNNs [HS97];
2006: Deep belief networks [HS06] and BP-trained CNNs [RPC06].

5.1.2 Deep Belief Networks (DBNs) using Restricted Boltzmann Machines (RBMs)

Hinton's *deep belief networks* (DBNs) are probabilistic generative models that are composed of multiple layers of stochastic, latent variables. The latent variables typically have binary values and are often called hidden units or

---

[2] In stochastic gradient descent, the true gradient of $C(w)$ is approximated by a gradient at a single example:

$$w(t+1) = w(t) - \alpha \nabla C_i(w).$$

As the algorithm sweeps through the training set, it performs the above update for each training example. Several passes can be made over the training set until the algorithm converges. If this is done, the data can be shuffled for each pass to prevent cycles. Typical implementations may use an adaptive learning rate to ensure that the algorithm converges.

feature detectors. The top two layers have undirected, symmetric connections between them and form an associative memory. The lower layers receive top-down, directed connections from the layer above. The states of the units in the lowest layer represent a data vector (see [Hin09]).

The two most significant properties of deep belief nets are: (i) there is an efficient, layer-by-layer procedure for learning the top-down, generative weights that determine how the variables in one layer depend on the variables in the layer above; and (ii) after learning, the values of the latent variables in every layer can be inferred by a single, bottom-up pass that starts with an observed data vector in the bottom layer and uses the generative weights in the reverse direction.

Deep belief nets are learned one layer at a time by treating the values of the latent variables in one layer, when they are being inferred from data, as the data for training the next layer. This efficient, greedy learning can be followed by, or combined with, other learning procedures that fine-tune all of the weights to improve the generative or discriminative performance of the whole network.

Discriminative fine-tuning can be performed by adding a final layer of variables that represent the desired outputs and backpropagating error derivatives. When networks with many hidden layers are applied to highly-structured input data, such as images, backpropagation works much better if the feature detectors in the hidden layers are initialized by learning a deep belief net that models the structure in the input data (see [HS06]).

Now, recall that standard *Boltzmann machines* (BMs) are particular form of log-linear *Markov random fields* (MRF), for which the energy function is linear in its free parameters (see, e.g. [Hin07]). To make them powerful enough to represent complicated distributions, some of the variables are never observed and they are called hidden. By having more hidden variables (or, hidden units), the modeling capacity of the BM can be increased. Finally, the so-called *restricted Boltzmann machines* (RBMs) further restrict BMs to those ANNs without visible-visible and hidden-hidden connections (see, e.g. [Hin10]).

An RBM consists of a layer of visible units and a layer of hidden units with no visible-visible or hidden-hidden connections [Smo86]. With these restrictions, the hidden units are conditionally independent given a visible vector, so unbiased samples from $< s_i s_j >_{\text{data}}$ can be obtained in one parallel step. To sample from $< s_i s_j >_{\text{model}}$ still requires multiple iterations that alternate between updating all the hidden units in parallel and updating all of the visible units in parallel. However, learning still works well if $< s_i s_j >_{\text{model}}$ is replaced by $< s_i s_j >_{\text{reconstruction}}$, which is obtained in the following 3-step algorithm: (i) starting with a data vector on the visible units, update all of the hidden units in parallel; (ii) update all of the visible units in parallel to get a 'reconstruction; and (iii) update all of the hidden units again.

The energy function E of an RBM is defined as:

$$E(v, h) = -b'v - c'h - h'Wv$$

where W is the matrix of weights connecting hidden and visible units, while b, c are the offsets of the visible and hidden layers respectively.

The associated *free energy* is given by:

$$\mathcal{F}(v) = -b'v - \sum_i \log \sum_{h_i} e^{h_i(c_i + W_i v)}.$$

Because of the specific structure of RBMs, visible and hidden units are conditionally independent given one-another. Using this property, we can write (see [Hin10]):

$$p(h|v) = \prod_i p(h_i|v), \qquad p(v|h) = \prod_j p(v_j|h).$$

RBMs with Binary Units

In the commonly studied case of using binary units (where $v_j, h_i \in \{0, 1\}$), we obtain a probabilistic version of the usual neuron activation function:

$$P(h_i = 1|v) = \mathrm{sigm}(c_i + W_i v) \qquad P(v_j = 1|h) = \mathrm{sigm}(b_j + W'_j h)$$

The free energy of an RBM with binary units further simplifies to:

$$\mathcal{F}(v) = -b'v - \sum_i \log(1 + e^{(c_i + W_i v)}).$$

Update equations for RBMs with binary units read (see [Hin10]):

$$-\frac{\partial \log p(v)}{\partial W_{ij}} = E_v[p(h_i|v) \cdot v_j] - v_j^{(i)} \cdot \mathrm{sigm}(W_i \cdot v^{(i)} + c_i),$$

$$-\frac{\partial \log p(v)}{\partial c_i} = E_v[p(h_i|v)] - \mathrm{sigm}(W_i \cdot v^{(i)}),$$

$$-\frac{\partial \log p(v)}{\partial b_j} = E_v[p(v_j|h)] - v_j^{(i)}.$$

For more technical details on RMS in general, see [Hin10].

Learning DBNs by Composing RBMs

After learning one hidden layer, the activity vectors of the hidden units, when they are being driven by the real data, can be treated as 'data' for training another RBM. This can be repeated to learn as many hidden layers as desired. After learning multiple hidden layers in this way, the whole network can be viewed as a single, multilayer generative model and each additional hidden layer improves a lower bound on the probability that the multilayer model would generate the training data. Learning one hidden layer at a time is a very effective way to learn deep neural networks with many hidden layers and millions of weights. Even though the learning is unsupervised, the highest level features are typically much more useful for classification than the raw data vectors. These deep networks can be fine-tuned to be better at classification or dimensionality reduction using the backpropagation algorithm [HS06]. Alternatively, they can be fine-tuned to be better generative models using a version of the 'wake-sleep' algorithm (see [Hin07] and the references therein).

More technically, the key idea behind DBNs is that the weights, W, learned by a RBM define both $p(v|h, W)$ and the prior distribution over hidden vectors, $p(h|W)$, so the probability of generating a visible vector, v, can be written as:

$$p(v) = \sum_h p(h|W)p(v|h, W).$$

After learning W, we keep $p(v|h, W)$ but we replace $p(h|W)$ by a better model of the aggregated posterior distribution over hidden vectors (i.e. the non-factorial distribution produced by averaging the factorial posterior distributions produced by the individual data vectors). The better model is learned by treating the hidden activity vectors produced from the training data as the training data for the next learning module. This replacement, if performed in the right way, improves a variational lower bound on the probability of the training data under the composite model (see [Hin09]).

5.1.3 Recurrent Neural Nets (RNNs)

Recurrent neural networks (RNNs), originating in Grossberg–Hopfield–Kosko nets (see Chapter 11, Appendix 2) give a powerful model for sequential data processing. RNNs are inherently deep in time, since their hidden state is a function of all previous hidden states. End-to-end training methods such as Connectionist Temporal Classification make it possible to train RNNs for sequence labeling problems where the input-output alignment is unknown. The combination of these methods with the Long Short-term Memory RNN architecture has proved particularly fruitful, delivering state-of-the-art results in cursive handwriting recognition (see [GMH] and the references therein).

Formally, given an input sequence $x = (x_1, \ldots, x_T)$, a standard recurrent neural network (RNN) computes the hidden vector sequence $h = (h_1, \ldots, h_T)$ and output vector sequence $y = (y_1, \ldots, y_T)$ by iterating the following equations from $t = 1$ to T [GMH]:

$$h_t = \mathcal{H}\left(W_{xh}x_t + W_{hh}h_{t-1} + b_h\right) \tag{5.1}$$

$$y_t = W_{hy}h_t + b_y \tag{5.2}$$

where the W terms denote weight matrices (e.g., W_{xh} is the input-hidden weight matrix), the b terms denote bias vectors (e.g., b_h is hidden bias vector) and $\mathcal{H}$ is the hidden layer function, W_{xh} is the input-hidden weight matrix,

W_{hh} is the hidden-hidden weight matrix, b_h is the hidden bias vector and $\mathcal{H}$ is the hidden layer function.

5.1.4 Convolutional Neural Networks (ConvNets)

Since their introduction in the early 1990's by [LBD89] *convolutional neural networks* (ConvNets)[3] have demonstrated excellent performance at tasks such as hand-written digit classification and face detection.

A ConvNet is composed of one or more convolutional layers with fully connected layers (matching those in typical artificial neural networks) on top. It also uses tied weights and pooling layers. This architecture allows ConvNets to take advantage of the 2D structure of input data. In comparison with other deep architectures, convolutional neural networks are starting to show superior results in both image and speech applications. They can also be trained with standard backpropagation. ConvNets are easier to train than other regular, deep, feed-forward neural networks and have many fewer parameters to estimate, making them a highly attractive architecture to use.

ConvNets are usually trained by stochastic gradient descent and usually contain different types of layers, including (see [Wik16p] and the references therein):

1. The *convolutional layer*: Unlike a hand-coded *convolution kernel* (e.g., Sobel), in a convolutional neural net, the parameters of each convolution kernel is trained by the backpropagation algorithm. There are many convolution kernels in each layer, and each kernel is replicated over the entire image with the same parameters. The function of the convolution operators is to extract different features of the input. The capacity of a neural net varies, depending on the number of layers. The first convolution layers will obtain the low-level features, like edges, lines and corners. The more layers the network has, the higher-level features it will get.

2. The *ReLU layer* (of rectified linear units): This is a layer of neurons that use the non-saturating activation function $f(x) = max(0, x)$. It increases the nonlinear properties of the decision function and of the overall network without affecting the receptive fields of the convolution layer. Other functions are used to increase nonlinearity. For example the saturating hyperbolic tangent: $f(x) = tanh(x), f(x) = |tanh(x)|$, and the sigmoid function: $f(x) = (1 + e^{(-x)})^{(-1)}$. Compared to tanh units, the advantage of ReLU is that the neural network trains several times faster.

---

[3] The design of convolutional neural networks follows the discovery of visual mechanisms in living organisms. In particular the visual cortex in the brain contains large number of neural cells, which are responsible for detecting light in small, overlapping sub-regions of the visual field, called *receptive fields*. These cells act as local filters over the input space. The more complex cells have larger receptive fields. A *convolution operator* is created to perform the same function by all of these cells.

3. The *pooling layer*: In order to reduce variance, pooling layers compute the max or average value of a particular feature over a region of the image. This will ensure that the same result will be obtained, even when image features have small translations. This is an important operation for object classification and detection.

4. The *dropout layer*: Since a fully connected layer occupies most of the parameters, it is prone to overfitting. The dropout method is introduced to prevent overfitting. Dropout also significantly improves the speed of training. This makes model combination practical, even for deep neural nets. Dropout is performed randomly. In the input layer, the probability of dropping a neuron is between 0.5 and 1, while in the hidden layers, a probability of 0.5 is used. The neurons that are dropped out, will not contribute to the forward pass and back propagation. This is equivalent to decreasing the number of neurons. This will create neural networks with different architectures, but all of those networks will share the same weights.

5. The *loss layer*: It can use different loss functions for different tasks. Softmax loss is used for predicting a single class of K mutually exclusive classes. Sigmoid cross-entropy loss is used for predicting K independent probability values in [0,1]. Euclidean loss is used for regressing to real-valued labels $[-inf, inf]$.

In particular, *convolutional deep belief networks* (CDBNs) are structurally very similar to normal ConvNets. Therefore, like ConvNets they are also able to exploit the 2D structure of images combined with the advantage gained by pre-training in a DBN. They provide a generic structure which can be used in many image and signal processing tasks and can be trained in a way similar to that for DBNs. Recently, many benchmark results on standard image datasets like CIFAR have been obtained using CDBNs (see [Wik16p] and the references therein).

In the recent years, several papers have shown that ConvNets can also deliver outstanding performance on more challenging visual classification tasks. In particular, [CMS12] have demonstrated state-of-the-art performance on NORB and CIFAR-10 datasets, while [KSH12] have showed record beating performance on the ImageNet 2012 classification benchmark, with their ConvNet model achieving an error rate of 16.4%, compared to the 2nd place result of 26.1%. Several factors are responsible for this renewed interest in ConvNet models:

1. The availability of much larger training sets, with millions of labeled examples;

2. Powerful GPU implementations, making the training of very large models practical; and

3. Better model regularization strategies, such as Dropout (see [HSK12] and the references therein).

Despite this encouraging progress, there is still little insight into the internal operation and behavior of these complex models, or how they achieve such good performance. Recently, [ZF13] have introduced a novel visualization technique that gives insight into the function of intermediate feature layers and the operation of the classifier. The visualization technique that they propose uses a multi-layered *deconvolutional neural network* (DCNN) to project the feature activations back to the input pixel space. They also perform a sensitivity analysis of the classifier output by occluding portions of the input image, revealing which parts of the scene are important for classification. This is a form of supervised pre-training, which contrasts with the unsupervised pre-training methods popularized by [HOT06].

According to [ZF13], understanding the operation of a ConvNet requires interpreting the feature activity in intermediate layers. A DConvNet can be thought of as a ConvNet model that uses the same components (filtering, pooling) but in reverse, so instead of mapping pixels to features does the opposite.

5.2 TensorFlow: The State-of-the-Art in Machine Learning

It is well known that the last few years have witnessed the explosive growth of *machine learning* (ML) in various fields more-or-less related to *computer science* (CS, see [AKV15, BMK14, FCS13, GLM15, HDY12, HVS13, KTS14, LRM12, MHS14, MCC13, NSB15, SVL14, SLJ14, VKK14, ZRM13]). This huge success of modern AI can be generally attributed to:

- Invention of new highly sophisticated ML models [KSH12, MKS15],
- Availability of the *Big Data* (or, large datasets untractable by traditional data processing methods, see [Wik16c]) in conjunction with the *internet of things* (IoT, see [Wik16f]) for experimentation and research in these fields [CMS13, RDS15], and
- Development of new hardware-and-software platforms/computational resources that enable efficient training of these ML models on these large datasets [CSA14, DCM12].

TensorFlow (TF) is a state-of-the-art *machine learning and inference* system (MLI, see e.g., [MLI16]), developed and released by *Google* as an open-source package in November, 2015. TF is designed to be both an interface for expressing a wide variety of ML algorithms (with a strong support for training and inference of DNNs) and an implementation for executing such algorithms. TF operates at large scale and in heterogeneous environments, ranging from mobile devices (e.g., phones and tablets) up to *large-scale distributed systems* of hundreds of machines and thousands of computational devices, such as *graphics processing units* (GPUs). TF has been used employed for research and deploying ML systems in a number of CS-related fields, including *speech recognition* (SR) *computer vision* (CV) *natural language processing* (NLP) *robotics*, etc. (see [Aba16a, Aba16b] and the references therein).

TF has been developed by simplifying and generalizing of Google's previous system *DistBelief* (see [DCM12]), to be able to support both large-scale training and inference. Firstly, TF efficiently uses hundreds of powerful (GPU-enabled) servers for fast deep learning. Secondly, TF runs so trained models for inference in production on various platforms. Also, TF is flexible and general enough to support experimentation and research into new MLI models and system-level optimizations.

TensorFlow represents algorithmic computation and shared state on which the algorithm operates, as well as the operations that mutate that state, using *dataflow graphs*. TF maps the nodes of a dataflow graph across many machines in a cluster, as well as within a machine across multiple computational devices (including multicore CPUs, general-purpose GPUs and *tensor processing units* (TPUs, see [Aba16a, Aba16b])).

TF has been inspired by high-level programming models of *dataflow systems* [ALR16, DG04, ZCD12], as well as the low-level efficiency of *parameter servers* [CSA14, DCM12, LAP14].

While traditional dataflow systems use vertices of dataflow graphs to represent functional computation on *immutable data* only, TF allows vertices to represent computations that own/update mutable states as well. TF's edges carry multi-dimensional arrays (tensors) between nodes, so that TF transparently inserts appropriate communications between distributed subcomputations. In this way, by unifying the computation and state management in a single programming model, TF enables programmers to experiment with different parallelization schemes [Aba16a, Aba16b].

It is well known that ML algorithms generally perform better with bigger training data, which motivates a *data-parallel approach to training* (which eliminates the I/O bottleneck for input data and enables independent application of preprocessing operations on input records). The most prominent examples are recent breakthroughs in *image classification* models have benefited from the public *ImageNet dataset*, which contains 136 gigabytes of digital images [RDS15]; similarly, *language modeling* has benefited from efforts like the *One Billion Word benchmark* [CMS13]. Also, any distributed system for model training must use the network efficiently; e.g., many scalable algorithms train a model using *mini-batch gradient descent* algorithm (see [DCM12, LZC14]). TensorFlow uses distributed execution of ML algorithms, based on the fact that a cluster of powerful computers can solve many ML problems more efficiently than a single supercomputer, using more data and larger models. Recently, TF designers have built various *coordination protocols with synchronous replication* [CMB16, CZG16], which contradicts a common belief that asynchronous replication is required for scalable learning [CSA14, DCM12, LAP14].

TF fully supports *GPU-acceleration*, efficiently using modern general-purpose GPUs (with a large number of graphics cores that can operate on fast local RAMs); e.g., a single NVIDIA Titan X GPU card has 6 TFLOPS peak performance [Pow15]. While in 2012, best image classification results were achieved using 16,000 CPU cores for three days [LRM12] and using two GPUs for six days [KSH12], in 2014, NVIDIA's cuDNN library [CWV14] for GPU-based DNN training accelerates several popular image models by 2–4× by replacing version R2 with version R4 (see [Chi16] for technical details).

In addition to standard CPU/GPU based acceleration, TensorFlow uses the so-called *tensor processing unit* (TPU), designed by Google specifically for ML implementations, which achieves the full order-of-magnitude improvement in performance-per-watt compared to alternative state-of-the-art technology [Jou16]; e.g., the *Movidius Deep Learning Accelerator* uses a low-power Myriad-2 processor with custom vector processing units to accelerate many ML and CV algorithms [Mov16], significant performance of improvements and power savings for some *convolutional NNs* (CNNS) using *field programmable gate arrays* (FPGAs) [ORK15].

TF supports both training and inference models, acknowledging that scalable and high-performance *inference* is a requirement for using ML algorithms in production [CBG15]. Since inference can be computationally intensive (e.g., an image classification model might perform 5 billion FLOPS per image [SVI15]), it must be possible to accelerate it with GPUs, as it is designed in TF.

TF has high extensibility: single-machine ML frameworks [JSD14, ALR16, CBM02] have extensible programming models, such as *adversarial learning* (AL, see [GPM14]) and *deep reinforcement learning* (DRL, see [MKS15]).

A lot of recent ML research was carried on a single (often GPU-equipped) computer platform [Kri14, KSH12]. Several flexible single-machine frameworks have emerged within this scenario, including:

- *Caffe* [JSD14] (a high-performance framework for training declaratively specified CNNS that runs on multicore CPUs and GPUs);
- *Theano* [ALR16] designed as a *dataflow graph* that generates efficient compiled code for training that model); and
- *Torch* [CBM02] (which has an *imperative programming* model for scientific computations, including ML, that supports *fine-grained control* over the order of execution and memory utilization).

TF uses a distributed generalization of Theano-like dataflow graph model with tensorial edges.

Recall that the so-called *batch dataflow systems* have been initiated by *MapReduce* [DG04] and subsequently applied to many ML algorithms (see [CKL07]). Both expressivity and performance of MapReduce have been improved in the following three systems:

- *DryadLINQ* [IFB08] has added a high-level query language that supports more sophisticated algorithms;
- *Spark* [ZCD12] has added the ability to cache previously computed datasets in memory, so it is better suited to iterative ML algorithms (such as *k-means clustering* and *logistic regression*), provided the input data fits in memory;
- *Dandelion* has added support for generating code for GPUs [RYC13] and *field-programmable gate arrays* (FPGAs) [CDL13].

The main limitation of batch dataflow systems is that they require the immutable input data and only deterministic subcomputations, in order the system could re-execute subcomputations when some of machines in the cluster fail, which significantly slows-down updating/convergence of ML models [BCN12]; e.g., it takes 20 sec for the *SparkNet* (system for training DNNs on Spark) to broadcast weights and collect updates from five workers [MNS16]. TensorFlow generalizes batch dataflow systems by removing these two limits; as a result, TF can train larger models on larger clusters with much shorter step times (down to 2 sec).

Another popular kind of computation architectures are *parameter servers* (PS) which are designed for *scalable topic modeling* [SN10]. Google's system *DistBelief* (TF's mother system [DCM12], with a Caffe-like model definition format [JSD14]) demonstrated how a PS could be applied to DNN training. Similarly, project *Adam* [CSA14] showed an efficient PS-architecture for training CNNS, while the so-called Li's PS [LAP14] improved consistency of models, elastic rescaling and fault tolerance. Initially, it was thought that PS were compatible with GPU acceleration [CSA14], until *GeePS* (a GPU-based PS, see [CZG16]) demonstrated significant speedups on modest-sized clusters, while *flexible programming* system *MXNet* (with interfaces for many languages) [CLL15] supports GPU acceleration and uses a PS-architecture to scale training.

Being a simplification and generalization of DistBelief, TF has improved all these qualities. While TF's mutable states implemented by mimicking a PS-architecture are crucial when training very large models (to make in-place updates to very large parameters, and quickly propagate them to parallel training steps), TF has additional flexibility which makes it possible to execute arbitrary dataflow subgraphs using shared model parameters.

Using a dataflow graph structure, *TF-vertices* represent atomic computation units performing *computational operations*, while *TF-edges* represent the outputs from and/or inputs to the corresponding vertices. Data values that flow along the edges are referred to as *tensors* (i.e., dense nD arrays). In TF, all data are represented as dense tensors with each element being an `int32`, `float32`, or `string`. The reason for this is that tensors naturally represent the inputs to and results of the common mathematical operations in many ML algorithms: e.g., a matrix multiplication takes two 2D tensors and produces another 2D tensor; and a mini-batch 2D convolution takes two 4D tensors and produces a 4D tensor. Each *TF-operation* has a named "type" (e.g., `Const`, `AddN`, `MatMul`, or `Assign`); it takes $m \geq 0$ tensors as input, and produces $n \geq 0$ tensors as output.

Most ML algorithms train a set of parameters using a variant of *stochastic gradient descent* (SGD), which entails computing the *gradients of a cost function* with respect to those parameters, then updating the parameters based on those gradients. For this purpose, TF implements a user-level *automatic differentiation* (AD)[4] library, so that a user can define an NN (as a composition of layers and a loss function), and then using the AD library to derive the *backpropagation* algorithm [RHW88].

The standard AD-algorithm has been extended in TF to differentiate conditional and iterative subcomputations and also manage GPU memory when iterating/accumulating over long sequences in the input data, using the *GeePS* [CZG16] approach. TF has implemented optimizations like *batch normalization* [IS15] and *gradient clipping* [PMB13] to accelerate training and make it more robust.

TF implements a wide range of *optimization algorithms*, which update the parameters in each training step. For example, SGD is easy to implement in a PS-architecture, using the following update rule:

$$w' \leftarrow w - \alpha \times \partial L / \partial w,$$

for each parameter w, gradient $\partial L / \partial w$, and learning rate α. A PS can implement SGD by using `-=` as the write operation, and writing $\alpha \times \partial L / \partial w$ to each w after a training step. In addition, a number of optimization algorithms have been implemented by the users on top of TF, including Momentum, Adam, Adagrad, L-BFGS Adadelta, and RMSProp.

For more technical details on TensorFlow, see [Aba16a, Aba16b] and the references therein.

5.3 Tensor Decompositions for Deep Representation Learning

5.3.1 Multi-Task Representation Learning: Shallow and Deep

The so-called *multi-task learning* (MTL) approach to *machine learning* was formulated in late 1990s with classical (shallow) ANNs in the work of [Car97], with the purpose of mutual reusing the common knowledge obtained by simultaneous learning of multiple related tasks. In the new century reformulated into kernel machines and sparse linear models (see [EP04, AEP08, KD12] and the references therein). Recently, this important learning paradigm has

---

[4] The AD algorithm in TF performs breadth-first search to identify all of the backwards paths from the target operationto a set of parameters, and sums the partial gradients that each path contributes.

been generalized to *deep neural networks* (DNNs) in [YH16], using the *tensor factorization* method. Tensor factorization is used here to divide each set of model parameters, i.e., both fully-connected (FC) weight matrices, and convolutional kernel tensors, into task-specific and shared parts.

5.3.2 Basics of Tensor Factorization

Recall that a rank-N tensor $\omega = \omega_{d_1,d_2,\ldots,d_N}$ represents an ND array containing $\prod_{n=1}^{N} d_n$ elements, which can be defined as a *Cartesian product* of N vectors (columns): $d_1 \times d_2 \times \cdots d_N$, including rank-0 scalars, rank-1 vectors, rank-2 matrices and rank-3 tensors. If we fix all but the nth index in the tensor ω we obtain its *mode-n fibre*. If we concatenate all of the $\prod_{i\neg n} d_i$ mode-n fibres (along columns) we obtain the corresponding *mode-n flattening* $\omega_{(n)}$ of the tensor ω (which is the matrix of size $d_n \times \prod_{i\neg n} d_i$).

A natural extension of a matrix dot product is the dot product of two tensors: the tensor dot product $\alpha \bullet \beta$ of a tensor α of size $M_1 \times M_2 \times \cdots P$ and a tensor β of size $P \times N_1 \times N_2 \ldots$, is obtained by matrix dot product $\alpha_{(-1)}^\tau \beta_{(1)}$ and reshaping (see [YH16]). In general, the tensor dot product is usually performed along specified subscript-labeled axes: $\alpha \bullet_{(i,j)} \beta = \alpha_{(i)}^\tau \beta_{(j)}$ and reshaping. For example, if tensor α is of size $M_1 \times P \times M_3 \times \cdots M_I$ and tensor β is of size $N_1 \times N_2 \times P \times \cdots N_J$, then their tensor dot product $\alpha \bullet_{(2,3)} \beta$ is of size $M_1 \times M_3 \times \cdots M_I \times N_1 \times N_2 \times \cdots N_J$.

5.3.3 Knowledge Sharing Between the Tasks

Consider the case of having τ linear tasks (or, models) parameterized by dD weight vectors, which makes the collection of all models into the matrix ω of size $(d \times \tau)$. A frequently used MTL-approach is to factorize the matrix ω by placing a *structure constraint* on it, as $\omega = \lambda\sigma$, where the matrix $\lambda = \lambda_{d,\kappa}$ is called the *shared factor* and the matrix $\sigma = \sigma_{\kappa,\tau}$ is called the *task-specific factor* (see [KD12] and the references therein). In this arrangement, the columns of λ become latent basis tasks, so that the model $w^{(i)}$ for the ith task becomes the linear combination of λs with task-specific information $\sigma_{.,i}$:

$$w^{(i)} := \omega_{.,i} = \lambda\sigma_{.,i} = \sum_{k=1}^{\kappa} \lambda_{.,k}\sigma_{k,i}. \tag{5.3}$$

This SISO (single-input single-output) matrix-factorization can be extended to the MIMO case of multiple inputs and outputs, so that the model for each task becomes a $(d_1 \times d_2)$ matrix, for d_1 inputs and d_2 outputs. This whole collection constructs a $(d_1 \times d_2 \times \tau)$-tensor, by a straightforward extension of Eq. (5.3), as:

$$\omega^{(i)} := \omega_{.,.,i} = \sum_{k=1}^{\kappa} \lambda_{.,.,k}\sigma_{k,i}, \tag{5.4}$$

which means imposing the same structural constraint on $\left(\omega^{(i)}\right)^T$ and is called *transposed mode-3 flattening* $\omega_{(3)}$ of ω.

5.3.4 Tensor Decompositions

Following [YH16], we present two common tensor decompositions:

The *Tucker decomposition* (TD) applied to a rank-N tensor $\omega = \omega_{d_1,d_2,\ldots,d_N}$ outputs the *core tensor* $\sigma = \sigma_{k_1,k_2,\ldots,k_N}$ multiplied with N matrices $\nu^{(n)}_{d_n,k_n}$, according to the following prescription:

$$\omega_{d_1,d_2,\ldots,d_N} = \sum_{k_1=1}^{\kappa_1}\sum_{k_2=1}^{\kappa_2}\cdots\sum_{k_N=1}^{\kappa_N}\sigma_{k_1,k_2,\ldots,k_N}\nu^{(1)}_{d_1,k_1}\nu^{(2)}_{d_2,k_2}\cdots\nu^{(N)}_{d_N,k_N} \quad (5.5)$$

$$\omega = \sigma \bullet_{(1,2)} \nu^{(1)} \bullet_{(1,2)} \nu^{(2)} \cdots \bullet_{(1,2)} \nu^{(N)} \quad (5.6)$$

TD can be implemented either using *alternating least squares* (ALS, see [KB09]), or more efficiently, as a *higher-order singular value decomposition* (HOSVD, see [LMV00]): $\nu^{(n)}$ is exactly the ν matrix from the SVD of *mode-n flattening* $\omega_{(n)}$ of ω, while the core tensor σ is given as:

$$\sigma = \omega \bullet_{(1,1)} \nu^{(1)} \bullet_{(1,1)} \nu^{(2)} \cdots \bullet_{(1,1)} \nu^{(N)}. \quad (5.7)$$

The *tensor train decomposition* (TTD) applied to a rank-N tensor $\omega = \omega_{d_1,d_2,\ldots,d_N}$ outputs two matrices $\nu^{(1)}_{d_1,\kappa_1}$ and $\nu^{(N)}_{\kappa_{N-1},d_N}$ and $(N-2)$ rank-3 tensors $\nu^{(n)}_{\kappa_{n-1},d_n,\kappa_n}$, according to the following prescription:

$$\omega_{d_1,d_2,\ldots,d_N} = \sum_{k_1=1}^{\kappa_1}\sum_{k_2=1}^{\kappa_2}\cdots\sum_{k_{N-1}=1}^{\kappa_{N-1}}\nu^{(1)}_{d_1,k_1}\nu^{(2)}_{k_1,d_2,k_2}\nu^{(3)}_{k_2,d_3,k_3}\cdots\nu^{(N)}_{k_{N-1},d_N} \quad (5.8)$$

$$= \nu^{(1)}_{d_1,\cdot}\nu^{(2)}_{\cdot,d_2,\cdot}\nu^{(3)}_{\cdot,d_3,\cdot}\cdots\nu^{(d)}_{\cdot,d_N} \quad (5.9)$$

$$\omega = \nu^{(1)} \bullet \nu^{(2)} \cdots \bullet \nu^{(N)} \quad (5.10)$$

where $\nu^{(n)}_{\cdot,d_n,\cdot}$ represents the matrix $\nu^{(n)}_{\kappa_{n-1},\kappa_n}$ sliced from $\nu^{(n)}$ with the second axis fixed at d_n. TTD is most often implemented using the *recursive SVD method* (see [Ose11]).

In both decompositions, if $d_N = \tau$ then the last factor $\nu^{(N)}$ represents the task specific knowledge, while the other factors: $\nu^{(1)} \bullet \nu^{(2)} \cdots$ represent the shared knowledge.

5.3.5 Deep Multi-Task Representation Learning

The so-called *deep multi-task representation learning* (DMTRL) with τ linear tasks, can be realized by the system of τ DNNs (each with the same architecture), by training one DNN per-task, in such a way that the weight tensors of each layer are generated (i.e., constructed from smaller pieces) by one of the above knowledge sharing structures (i.e., Eqs. (5.4), (5.6) or (5.10); see [YH16]). All the weight tensors generated in this way are C^k-*differentiable*, which means that this DMTRL can be trained via standard backpropagation.

More specifically, in the backward pass over *fully-connected (FC) layers*, these methods learn either $\{\sigma, \nu_1, \nu_2, \nu_3\}$ (using TD, Eq. (5.6)), or $\{\nu_1, \nu_2, \nu_3\}$ (using TTD, Eq. (5.10)), or in the simplest case $\{\lambda, \sigma\}$ (using SVD, Eq. (5.4)), instead of direct learning of the rank-3 tensor ω.

Similarly, *convolutional DNN layers* most often contain *kernel filter parameters*, which are rank-3 tensors (of size $a \times b \times c$, with the height-a, width-b, and the number of input channels c) or rank-4 tensors (of size $a \times b \times c \times m$, the number of output channels, i.e., the number of filters in this layer: m. All the above methods naturally extend to convolutional layers, because convolution simply adds new axes, e.g., a tensor $\omega_{a,b,c,m,\tau}$ of shape $(a \times b \times c \times m \times \tau)$ is the collection of parameters from a given convolutional layer of τ *DNNs*.

5.4 Generalized Tensor Decompositions in ConvNets

5.4.1 Introducing ConvNets

While DNNs are continuously demonstrating their superiority over other ML algorithms (see [LBH15, GBC16]), the most successful DL architectures so far have been *convolutional neural networks* (*ConvNets*, [LB95]), which have extended their dominance from the field of *computer vision* to many other application domains as well (see, e.g. [SHG14, WDH15, CS14]). Recall that modern ConvNets are formed by stacking a number of layers, where each layer consists of a *linear convolutional operator* followed by the activation: $\alpha(z) = \max\{0, z\}$ of a *rectified linear unit* (*ReLU* [NH10]), followed either by max pooling: $\pi\{c_j\} = \max\{c_j\}$, or by average pooling: $\pi\{c_j\} = \text{mean}\{c_j\}$. These models represent the cutting edge of the ConvNet architecture ([SLJ15, SZ14]) and have been called *convolutional rectifier networks* (CRNs) in [CS16a, CS16b]. CRNs have been rigorously defined in [CS16b] using *generalized tensor decompositions* (see [Hac12, CSS15]), as follows.

5.4.2 Tensors in ConvNets

In this section, a *tensor* represents a multi-dimensional array: $\mathbf{T}_{d_1,\ldots,d_N}$ (living in the *tensor space* $\mathbb{R}^{M_1 \times \cdots \times M_N}$) with the rank defined by the number of *tensor modes* (or, indexing entries in the array), while *tensor dimension* is the number of values an index can take (in a particular mode). The core operator is the *tensor product* $\otimes$, which combines any two tensors $\mathbf{T} \in \mathbb{R}^{M_1 \times \cdots \times M_P}$ (of rank P) and $\mathbf{S} \in \mathbb{R}^{M_{P+1} \times \cdots \times M_{P+Q}}$ (of rank Q) into a product-tensor $\mathbf{T} \otimes \mathbf{S} \in \mathbb{R}^{M_1 \times \cdots \times M_{P+Q}}$ (of rank $P + Q$) defined by:

$$\left(\mathbf{T} \otimes \mathbf{S}\right)_{d_1,\ldots,d_{P+Q}} = \mathbf{T}_{d_1,\ldots,d_P} \cdot \mathbf{S}_{d_{P+1},\ldots,d_{P+Q}}. \qquad (5.11)$$

In the rank-1 case ($P = Q = 1$) the tensor product $\otimes$ is reduced to the vector outer product; e.g., the tensor product $\mathbf{u} \otimes \mathbf{v}$ of a vector $\mathbf{u} \in \mathbb{R}^{M_1}$ and a vector $\mathbf{v} \in \mathbb{R}^{M_2}$ is the rank-1 matrix

$$\mathbf{u} \otimes \mathbf{v} = \mathbf{u}\mathbf{v}^\top \in \mathbb{R}^{M_1 \times M_2}.$$

5.4.3 Generalized Tensor Decompositions

Recall from the previous section that *tensor decompositions* are general schemes for expressing tensors via tensor products and iterative weighted sums; e.g., a tensor $\mathbf{T} \in \mathbb{R}^{M_1 \times \cdots \times M_N}$ can be defined by the *Tucker decomposition* (TD) as:

$$\mathbf{T} = \sum_{j_1 \ldots j_N = 1}^{J} c_{j_1 \ldots j_N} \cdot \mathbf{w}^{j_1,1} \otimes \cdots \otimes \mathbf{w}^{j_N,N},$$

parameterized by the coefficients $\{c_{j_1 \ldots j_N} \in \mathbb{R}\}_{j_1 \ldots j_N \in [J]}$ and vectors $\{\mathbf{w}^{j,i} \in \mathbb{R}^{M_i}\}_{i \in [N], j \in [J]}$.

Generalization of the tensor product $\otimes$ given by Eq. (5.11) would produce the *generalized tensor decompositions*, as follows (see [CS16b] and the references therein). Consider a binary operator $\gamma : \mathbb{R} \times \mathbb{R} \to \mathbb{R}$ which is commutative: $\gamma(a,b) = \gamma(b,a)$ and associative: $\gamma(\gamma(a,b),c) = \gamma(a,\gamma(b,c))$ for any real constants (a,b,c). The *generalized tensor product* $\overset{G}{\otimes}$ combines any two tensors, $\mathbf{T} \in \mathbb{R}^{M_1 \times \cdots \times M_P}$ and $\mathbf{S} \in \mathbb{R}^{M_{P+1} \times \cdots \times M_{P+Q}}$, into a generalized product-tensor $\mathbf{T} \overset{G}{\otimes} \mathbf{S} \in \mathbb{R}^{M_1 \times \cdots \times M_{P+Q}}$, defined as:

$$\left(\mathbf{T} \overset{G}{\otimes} \mathbf{S}\right)_{d_1,\ldots,d_{P+Q}} = \gamma(\mathbf{T}_{d_1,\ldots,d_P}, \mathbf{S}_{d_{P+1},\ldots,d_{P+Q}}). \qquad (5.12)$$

If we replace the ordinary tensor product $\otimes$ given by Eq. (5.11) with the generalized tensor product $\overset{G}{\otimes}$ given by Eq. (5.12) we obtain the generalized tensor decompositions.

5.4.4 A Typical ConvNet Architecture

Now, following [CS16b], we consider a typical ConvNet architecture with the input X (composed of N *patches* $\mathbf{x}_1 \ldots \mathbf{x}_N \in \mathbb{R}^s$) and Λ hidden layers $\lambda = 0 \ldots \Lambda - 1$. As stated before, each locally-connected λ-layer [TYR14] begins with a (1×1)-*conv operator*, which is a 3D convolution[5] with r_λ channels and

---

[5] The convolutions are allowed to operate without weight sharing (the *unshared ConvNet* case of [CS16b], in contrast to the *shared ConvNet* case that gives rise to a standard (1×1)-convolution), with varying coefficients on the filters that generate feature maps.

receptive (1×1)-field followed by point-wise activation $\alpha(\cdot)$ and ends with the spatial pooling operator $\pi(\cdot)$ (e.g., max or average). ConvNet has the following three classes of trainable parameters (weights):

1. the *representation weights*: θ_d;
2. the *conv weights*: $\mathbf{w}^{\lambda,j,\gamma}$ for λ-layer, j-location and γ-channel (unshared case); $\mathbf{w}^{\lambda,\gamma}$ for λ-layer and γ-channel (shared case); and
3. the *output weights*: $\mathbf{w}^{\Lambda,1,y}$.

The ConvNet type is determined by the choice of activation and pooling operators as follows:

- linear activation $[\alpha(z) = z]$ and product pooling $[\pi\{c_j\} = \prod c_j]$ gives a convolutional arithmetic circuit (see [CSS15]);
- ReLU activation $(\alpha(z) = \max\{0, z\})$ and max pooling $[\pi\{c_j\} = \max\{c_j\}]$ or average pooling $[\pi\{c_j\} = \operatorname{mean}\{c_j\}]$ gives CRNs.

5.4.5 ConvNet Classification

Now, we consider the standard classification task in which the Y outputs of a ConvNet correspond to different categories, and prediction is determined by the estimated output $\hat{y} \in Y$ with the highest activation. Given the *ConvNet input-output map* $\eta_y(\cdot) : X \to Y$, representing the *score function* of a category y, the predicted output $\hat{y}$ for the instance $X = (\mathbf{x}_1, \ldots, \mathbf{x}_N) \in (\mathbb{R}^s)^N$ is given by the *argmax classification rule* [CS16b]:

$$\hat{y} = \arg\max_{y \in [Y]} \eta_y(X).$$

Score functions can be analyzed using *grid tensors* as follows. Given the set of M *ConvNet templates* (i.e., fixed vectors $\mathbf{x}^{(1)} \ldots \mathbf{x}^{(M)} \in \mathbb{R}^s$), the grid tensor $\mathbf{T}(\eta_y)$ of the score function η_y, is the rank-N tensor of dimension M defined as:

$$\mathbf{T}(\eta_y)_{d_1 \ldots d_N} = \eta_y(\mathbf{x}^{(d_1)}, \ldots, \mathbf{x}^{(d_N)}), \qquad (5.13)$$

and is therefore holding score values on the exponentially-large grid of instances

$$\{X_{d_1 \ldots d_N} := (\mathbf{x}^{(d_1)}, \ldots, \mathbf{x}^{(d_N)}) : d_1 \ldots d_N \in [M]\}.$$

Next, we define the matrix $\mathcal{M} \in \mathbb{R}^{M \times M}$ as:

$$\mathcal{M} := \begin{bmatrix} f_{\theta_1}(\mathbf{x}^{(1)}) & \cdots & f_{\theta_M}(\mathbf{x}^{(1)}) \\ \vdots & \ddots & \vdots \\ f_{\theta_1}(\mathbf{x}^{(M)}) & \cdots & f_{\theta_M}(\mathbf{x}^{(M)}) \end{bmatrix},$$

(to hold the values taken by the representation functions $f_{\theta_1} \ldots f_{\theta_M} : \mathbb{R}^s \to \mathbb{R}$ on the selected templates $\mathbf{x}^{(1)} \ldots \mathbf{x}^{(M)} \in \mathbb{R}^s$) and we also set the *activation-pooling operator* $\gamma : \mathbb{R} \times \mathbb{R} \to \mathbb{R}$ defined via ConvNet's activation functions

$\alpha(\cdot)$ and pooling functions $\pi(\cdot)$, as:[6]

$$\gamma(a,b) = \pi(\alpha(a), \alpha(b)).$$

5.4.6 Grid Tensors for Shallow and Deep ConvNets

Firstly, we define the grid tensor $\mathbf{T}$ (5.13) of the *shallow score function* $\eta_y^S(\cdot) : X \to Y$, generated by the *shallow ConvNet*, as the *generalized CP decomposition*:[7]

$$\mathbf{T}\left(\eta_y^S\right) = \sum_{z=1}^{Z} a_z^y \cdot (\mathcal{M}\mathbf{w}^{z,1}) \overset{G}{\otimes} \cdots \overset{G}{\otimes} (\mathcal{M}\mathbf{w}^{z,N}), \qquad (5.14)$$

where Z denotes the number of channels in the ConvNet's single hidden layer, $\mathbf{w}^y \in \mathbb{R}^Z$ denote the weights of output y and $\{\mathbf{w}^{z,i} \in \mathbb{R}^M\}_{z\in[Z],i\in[N]}$ represent the hidden convolution weights.

Secondly, we define the grid tensor $\mathbf{T}$ (5.13) of the *deep score function* $\eta_y^D(\cdot) : X \to Y$, generated by the *deep ConvNet* (with $\Lambda = \log_2 N$ hidden layers and 2 pooling windows), as the following hierarchical tensor decomposition called the *generalized HT decomposition*:[8]

$$\psi^{1,j,a} = \sum_{\alpha=1}^{r_0} a_\alpha^{1,j,a}(\mathcal{M}\mathbf{w}^{0,2j-1,\alpha}) \overset{G}{\otimes} (\mathcal{M}\mathbf{w}^{0,2j,\alpha}),$$

$$\cdots \qquad\qquad (5.15)$$

$$\psi^{\lambda,j,a} = \sum_{\alpha=1}^{r_{\lambda-1}} a_\alpha^{\lambda,j,a} \underbrace{\psi^{\lambda-1,2j-1,\alpha}}_{\text{rank } 2^{\lambda-1}} \overset{G}{\otimes} \underbrace{\psi^{\lambda-1,2j,\alpha}}_{\text{rank } 2^{\lambda-1}},$$

$$\cdots$$

$$\psi^{\Lambda-1,j,a} = \sum_{\alpha=1}^{r_{\Lambda-2}} a_\alpha^{\Lambda-1,j,a} \underbrace{\psi^{\Lambda-2,2j-1,\alpha}}_{\text{rank } \frac{N}{4}} \overset{G}{\otimes} \underbrace{\psi^{\Lambda-2,2j,\alpha}}_{\text{rank } \frac{N}{4}},$$

$$\mathbf{T}\left(\eta_y^D\right) = \sum_{\alpha=1}^{r_{\Lambda-1}} a_\alpha^{\Lambda,1,y} \underbrace{\psi^{\Lambda-1,1,\alpha}}_{\text{rank } \frac{N}{2}} \overset{G}{\otimes} \underbrace{\psi^{\Lambda-1,2,\alpha}}_{\text{rank } \frac{N}{2}},$$

---

[6] We remark that the activation-pooling operator $\gamma : \mathbb{R} \times \mathbb{R} \to \mathbb{R}$ is both associative and commutative under product-pooling with linear activation: $[\gamma(a,b) = a \cdot b]$ and under max-pooling with ReLU activation: $[\gamma(a,b) = \max\{a,b,0\}]$, see [CS16b].

[7] We remark that the factorization (5.14) is a generalization of the classic *candecomp/parafac decomposition* (CP decomposition, see [KB09] for a historic survey), so it is referred to as the generalized CP decomposition.

[8] We remark that the factorization (5.15) generalizes the *Hierarchical Tucker decomposition* (see [HK09]) so in [CS16b] it is called the generalized HT decomposition.

where $r_0 \ldots r_{\Lambda-1} \in \mathbb{N}$ denote the number of channels in the ConvNet's hidden λ-layers, $\mathbf{w}^{\Lambda,1,y} \in \mathbb{R}^{r_{\Lambda-1}}$ represent the weights of the output y, $\{\mathbf{w}^{0,j,\gamma} \in \mathbb{R}^M\}_{j\in[N],\gamma\in[r_0]}$ denote the weights in the first hidden convolution and $\{\mathbf{w}^{\lambda,j,\gamma} \in \mathbb{R}^{r_{\lambda-1}}\}_{\lambda\in[\Lambda-1],j\in[N/2^\lambda],\gamma\in[r_\lambda]}$ represent the weights in the subsequent hidden convolutions.

5.4.7 From Tensors to Matrices in ConvNets

From the computational perspective, it is often convenient to represent the above grid tensors in the form of matrices, using the following *matricization procedure* (see [CS16b]): an even rank N tensor $\mathbf{T}_{d_1,\ldots,d_N} \in \mathbb{R}^{M_1 \times \cdots \times M_N}$ is rearranged as a matrix $[\mathbf{T}_{d_1,\ldots,d_N}] \in \mathbb{R}^{(M_1 \cdot M_3 \cdot \ldots \cdot M_{N-1}) \times (M_2 \cdot M_4 \cdot \ldots \cdot M_N)}$, with rows corresponding to odd modes and columns corresponding to even modes, in such a way that $[\mathbf{T}_{d_1,\ldots,d_N}]$ has row index $1 + \sum_{i=1}^{\frac{N}{2}}(d_{2i-1}-1)\prod_{j=i+1}^{\frac{N}{2}} M_{2j-1}$ and column index $1 + \sum_{i=1}^{\frac{N}{2}}(d_{2i}-1)\prod_{j=i+1}^{\frac{N}{2}} M_{2j}$.

Nest, we use the *Kronecker product* $\odot$ as the matrix analogy of the tensor product $\otimes$ (5.11). Given two matrices, $A \in \mathbb{R}^{M_1 \times M_2}$ and $B \in \mathbb{R}^{N_1 \times N_2}$, their Kronecker product $A \odot B \in \mathbb{R}^{M_1 N_1 \times M_2 N_2}$ is the matrix $A_{ij}B_{kl}$ with row index $(i-1)N_1 + k$ and column index $(j-1)N_2 + \lambda$. More generally, for any two matricized tensors $\mathbf{T}$ and $\mathbf{S}$ of even rank, the relation

$$[\mathbf{T} \otimes \mathbf{S}] = [\mathbf{T}] \odot [\mathbf{S}] \tag{5.16}$$

shows that $\otimes$ and $\odot$ are completely analogous products (representing the same algebraic operation from two perspectives). So, the Kronecker product $\odot$ can be generalized in the same way as the tensor product was generalized in Eq. (5.12). Formally, given a binary operator $\gamma(\cdot,\cdot) : \mathbb{R} \times \mathbb{R} \to \mathbb{R}$ [which is both commutative: $\gamma(a,b) = \gamma(b,a)$ and associative: $\gamma(\gamma(a,b),c) = \gamma(a,\gamma(b,c))$], the *generalized Kronecker product* $\overset{G}{\odot}$, represents a generalized binary operator which makes a matrix $A \overset{G}{\odot} B \in \mathbb{R}^{M_1 N_1 \times M_2 N_2}$ out of two component matrices $A \in \mathbb{R}^{M_1 \times M_2}$ and $B \in \mathbb{R}^{N_1 \times N_2}$, in such a way that $\gamma(A_{ij}, B_{kl})$ has row index $(i-1)N_1 + k$ and column index $(j-1)N_2 + \lambda$. The generalization of the relation (5.16) is valid for arbitrary tensors $\mathbf{T}, \mathbf{S}$ of even rank:

$$[\mathbf{T} \overset{G}{\otimes} \mathbf{S}] = [\mathbf{T}] \overset{G}{\odot} [\mathbf{S}]. \tag{5.17}$$

Using the relation (5.17), we can translate the generalized HT decomposition (5.15) to the following matricized grid tensor (generated by the deep ConvNet), which is called the *matricized generalized HT decomposition* in [CS16b]:

$$\phi^{1,j,\gamma} = \sum_{\alpha=1}^{r_0} a_\alpha^{1,j,\gamma}(F\mathbf{w}^{0,2j-1,\alpha}) \overset{G}{\otimes} (F\mathbf{w}^{0,2j,\alpha}) \cdots \left[\phi^{l,j,\gamma}\right]$$

$$= \sum_{\alpha=1}^{r_{l-1}} a_\alpha^{l,j,\gamma} \underbrace{\left[\phi^{l-1,2j-1,\alpha}\right]}_{M^{2^{l-2}}\text{-by-}M^{2^{l-2}}} \overset{G}{\odot} \underbrace{\left[\phi^{l-1,2j,\alpha}\right]}_{M^{2^{l-2}}\text{-by-}M^{2^{l-2}}} \cdots \left[\phi^{L-1,j,\gamma}\right]$$

$$= \sum_{\alpha=1}^{r_{L-2}} a_\alpha^{L-1,j,\gamma} \underbrace{\left[\phi^{L-2,2j-1,\alpha}\right]}_{M^{\frac{N}{8}}\text{-by-}M^{\frac{N}{8}}} \overset{G}{\odot} \underbrace{\left[\phi^{L-2,2j,\alpha}\right]}_{M^{\frac{N}{8}}\text{-by-}M^{\frac{N}{8}}} \left[\mathbf{T}\left(\eta_y^D\right)\right]$$

$$= \sum_{\alpha=1}^{r_{L-1}} a_\alpha^{L,1,y} \underbrace{\left[\phi^{L-1,1,\alpha}\right]}_{M^{\frac{N}{4}}\text{-by-}M^{\frac{N}{4}}} \overset{G}{\odot} \underbrace{\left[\phi^{L-1,2,\alpha}\right]}_{M^{\frac{N}{4}}\text{-by-}M^{\frac{N}{4}}},$$

where the rank-2 tensors $\psi^{1,j,\gamma}$ are matrices, so they remain the same as in Eq. (5.15).

Similarly, to perform the matricization of the shallow ConvNet grid tensor, we translate the generalized CP decomposition (5.14) into the following *matricized generalized CP decomposition*:

$$\left[\mathbf{T}\left(\eta_y^S\right)\right] = \sum_{z=1}^{Z} \mathbf{w}_z^y \cdot \left[(\mathcal{M}\mathbf{w}^{z,1}) \overset{G}{\otimes} (\mathcal{M}\mathbf{w}^{z,3}) \overset{G}{\otimes} \cdots \overset{G}{\otimes} (\mathcal{M}\mathbf{w}^{z,N-1})\right]$$
$$\overset{G}{\otimes} \left[(\mathcal{M}\mathbf{w}^{z,2}) \overset{G}{\otimes} (\mathcal{M}\mathbf{w}^{z,4}) \overset{G}{\otimes} \cdots \overset{G}{\otimes} (\mathcal{M}\mathbf{w}^{z,N})\right]^\top.$$

For more technical details of the tensor analysis of ConvNets, see [CS16a, CS16b] and the references therein.

6

Cognitive Control in CPC-Autonomy:
Perceptual Control Theory and Its Alternatives

6.1 Brief Introduction to Perceptual Control Theory (PCT)

Perceptual Control Theory (PCT, for short), founded by engineer-psychologist Bill Powers in 1970s (see [Pow73a, Pow73b]), has been proposed as a general model of human and animal behaviors (see [Pow11, Pow05]) of the common *compositional form*:

$$\boxed{\text{Percept}} \xrightarrow{\ f\ } \boxed{\text{Control}} \xrightarrow{\ g\ } \boxed{\text{Act}} , \tag{6.1}$$

where f and g represent *negative feedbacks* of homeostatic nature (or, more appropriately, homekinetic nature, in terms of L. von Bertalanffy's homeokinesis; see, e.g. [Fra04]). Therefore, as a type of complex control theory, which is indirectly using many redundant degrees of freedom, PCT is founded on a series of negative homekinetic feedback loops,[1] popularized in late 1940s by the father of cybernetics, Norbert Wiener.[2]

---

[1] R. Ashby states in [Ash57] that *feedback* exists between two parts when each affects the other. In the contemporary parlance, this means that there is a feedback-loop between the two parts of a system. While negative feedbacks tend to stabilize the system they act on, positive feedbacks usually have catastrophic tendencies.

[2] Wiener defined cybernetics in [Wie48] as "the scientific study of control and communication in the animal and the machine". The word "cybernetics" has a Greek origin, initially meaning "government", and latter meaning to "steer," "navigate," or "govern". Contemporary cybernetics began as an interdisciplinary study connecting the fields of engineering control systems, electrical network theory, mechanical engineering, logic modeling, evolutionary biology, neuroscience, anthropology, and psychology in the 1940s. Among the fields of study which have been influenced by cybernetics, besides PCT, are also game theory, systems-and-signals theory, neuropsychology, cognitive psychology and organizational theory (see [Wik16i] and references therein, for more details on classical and modern cybernetics).

However, in contrast to standard engineering control theory approaches to control of simple technical mechanisms, PCT-actions are highly-redundant by their nature, so they are not explicitly controlled, but are rather varied, in order to be able to cancel, or, counteract, the uncertain effects of environmental disturbances, which are assumed to be unpredictable.[3]

The key PCT contribution, demonstrated in a number of simulation experiments, is that human or animal organism controls neither its own behavior, nor external environmental variables, but rather *its own perceptions* of those variables. PCT demonstrates *circular causation* in a negative feedback loop closed through the environment (which is similar to classical Bernstein's loop).

This complex and nonlinear feedback concept fundamentally contradicts the classical notion of linear causation of behavior by stimuli, in which environmental stimuli are thought to cause behavioral responses, mediated by intervening cognitive processes (see [Wik16h] and references therein, for more introductory details on PCT).

In terms of *commutative diagrams* (see section 1.5.2 in Chapter 1), the fundamental PCT relation (6.1) can be represented as:

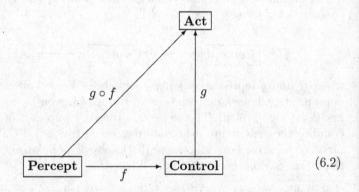

$$\tag{6.2}$$

where the time-dependent functions $f = f(t)$ and $g = g(t)$ correspond to nonlinear feedbacks, so that their composition: $g \circ f = g \circ f(t)$ is itself a nonlinear feedback. The diagram (6.2) both demonstrates the fundamental PCT-validity and shows the place of internal control in human behaviors.

---

[3] In its robustness/stability with respect to uncertain effects of environmental disturbances, the PCT approach to multi-valued control mimics adaptive fuzzy-logic controllers.

6.2 Predecessors of PCT: Wiener's Cybernetics, Beinstein's Neural Control and Gardner's Cognitive Control

6.2.1 Wiener's Cybernetics and Linear Control Theory

As, after all, PCT is a theory derived from cybernetic control theory, we start the broad PCT-related review with a brief exposé on the basic terminology of cybernetic control systems, as developed mainly by two leading mathematical engineers of the 20th Century: (i) the single-input single-output (or, transfer-function) approach of Norbert Wiener in late 1940s,[4] and (ii) the multi-input multi-output (or, state-space) approach of Rudolf Kalman in early 1960s (see, e.g. [Son99]).

6.2.2 Primary Control Example: Inverted Pendulum Balance

One of the first control models considered by Bill Powers in his PCT develop-ment, was the balance control system [Pow04] for the inverted pendulum (for an introduction to the inverted pendulum balance problem, see [Wik16j] and references therein). The model consists of an inverted pendulum, mounted (with a hinge joint) on a cart moving horizontally. The balance control objec-tive is to position the bob at its target (see Figure 6.1). Mechanically speak-ing, this control system has two degrees-of-freedom (DOF), one angular (φ) and one translational (x). The control objective of balancing the angle φ is achieved by appropriately adjusting the translational displacement x.

---

[4] One of the pillars of cybernetics was Claude Shannon's information theory [Sha48, SW49], originally developed to mathematically formalize the transmission of signals through a communication channel (the theory provides a quantitative measure of the amount of information, which depends only on the probabilistic structure of the communication channel under study). His key concept was an *entropy* H of a discrete random variable X defined as a measure of the amount of uncertainty associated with the value of X. If $\mathbf{X} = \{x_1, ..., x_n\}$ is the set of all messages that could be transmitted through a communication channel as variable X, and $p(x)$ is the probability of some $x \in \mathbf{X}$, then the entropy $H(X)$ is defined as:

$$H(X) = -\sum_{x \in \mathbb{X}} p(x) \log p(x).$$

Similarly, the *joint entropy* of two discrete random variables X and Y equals the entropy of their pairing: $H(X, Y) = -\sum_{x,y} p(x,y) \log p(x,y)$. Furthermore, the *mutual information* $I(X; Y)$ measures the amount of information that can be obtained about one random variable (X) by observing another variable (Y); it is defined as: $I(X; Y) = \sum_{x,y} p(x,y) \log \frac{p(x,y)}{p(x)\,p(y)} = H(X) - H(X|Y)$.

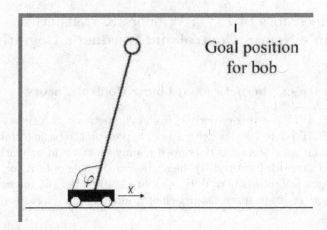

Fig. 6.1. *An inverted pendulum balance control problem (adapted from [Pow04]).*

A Simplified Inverted Pendulum Model

The basic inverted pendulum model with a single DOF is a nonlinear and unstable dynamical system, which consists of a beam of mass M, positioned vertically above the hinge joint that allows rotation for the angle $\varphi = \varphi(t)$, using a spring (that exerts a restoring torque $-k\varphi$) to prevent its falling. We consider two cases: (i) unloaded, in which there is no external loading to the beam, and (ii) loaded, in which a load P in $[N]$ is applied at the upper end of the beam and acts vertically down. The behavior of the pendulum is governed by the following 2nd-order *ordinary differential equation (ODE)*:

$$I\ddot{\varphi} + b\dot{\varphi} + k\varphi = \alpha \sin\varphi, \qquad (6.3)$$

where overdot denotes time derivative, $\alpha = \left(PL + \frac{1}{2}MgL\right)$, I in $[kgm^2]$ and L in $[m]$ are beam's moment of inertia and length, respectively, b in $[Nms]$ is the damping coefficient, k in $[Nm]$ is the torsion spring constant, while $g = 9.8$ in $[m/s^2]$ is the gravitation constant.

The pendulum system has been simulated in Fortran 95, implementing the 2nd-order Euler (or, leap-frog) integrator. In case of unloaded pendulum ($P = 0$), with the small initial disturbance from the vertical beam position, the time plot is given in Figure 6.2, while its phase-plot and 'signature' are given in Figure 6.3.

In case of loaded pendulum ($P = 2$), with the same initial disturbance, the time plot is given in Figure 6.4, while its phase-plot and 'signature' are given in Figure 6.5.

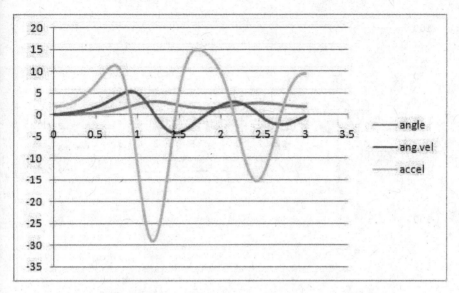

Fig. 6.2. *Time plot of an unloaded inverted pendulum.*

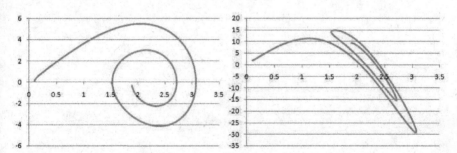

Fig. 6.3. *Phase plot (velocity vs. angle; left) and 'signature' (acceleration vs. angle; right) of an unloaded inverted pendulum.*

Here is the Fortran 90 code used for this simulation (in case of unloaded simulation, $P = 0$):

```fortran
! Basic Inverted Pendulum: 2nd-order Euler integrator
! ODE: I*x'' = a*sin(x) - k*x - c*x';  a = (P*L + M*g*L/2)
  implicit none   ! data declaration
real*8::t=0.,dt=0.001,tFin=3.,x0=0.1,v0=0.1,x1,v1
real*8::k=0.667,M=0.2,L=2.,P=2.,g=9.8,I,c,pi,f
! defining the forcing function = acceleration:
  f(x1,x0)=((P*L+M*g*L/2.)*sin(x1)-k*x1-c*(x1-x0)/dt)/I
  ! defining pi=3.14 and inertia:
  pi=4.*atan(1.);  I=M*L**2/12.;  c=I
  open(1,file='invPend.csv')  ! output file   ! header:
```

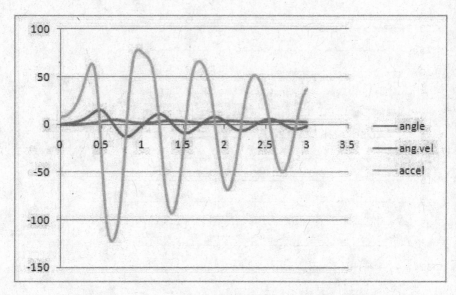

Fig. 6.4. *Time plot of an unloaded inverted pendulum.*

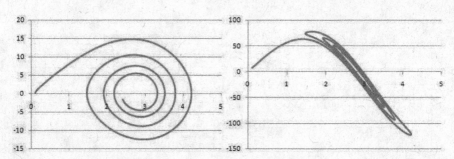

Fig. 6.5. *Phase plot (velocity vs. angle; left) and 'signature' (acceleration vs. angle; right) of a loaded inverted pendulum.*

```
   write(1,*) 'time',',','angle',',','ang.vel',',','accel'
do while(t<=tFin) ! ODEs of motion in Euler form
x1 = x0 + v0*dt
v1 = v0 + f(x1,x0)*dt    ! output:
write(1,*) t,',',x1,',',v1,',',f(x1,x0)
t=t+dt;   x0=x1;   v0=v1 ! time increment & new step
end do   ! end time-loop
close(1)  ! close file
END
```

Pendulum Balance via Linear Control Feedback

To start with, we formulate a classical linear control problem out of the pendulum balance. If we linearize the pendulum equation (6.3) around the stable vertical equilibrium position, we obtain the following simplified linear ODE:

$$\ddot{\varphi} - \varphi = u, \tag{6.4}$$

where $u = u(t)$ is the required control input for balancing the pendulum around the vertical equilibrium position. Although this is a highly simplified system, this type of "servo" problem illustrates what is done in common engineering practice (see, e.g. [Son99]). A naive first attempt at solving this balancing control problem can be stated in the form of the following two simple *heuristic IF–THEN rules*:

(i) If the pole is to the left of the vertical, then we have to move it to the right by applying a clockwise torque;

(ii) If the pole is to the right of the vertical, then we have to move it to the left by applying a counterclockwise torque.

While this kind of reasoning is fully elaborated within fuzzy logic control (see next section), here, within the linear control theory, it means that we apply a *proportional feedback*: $u = -k\varphi$, where k is the feedback gain, mechanically representing a spring. If we plug-in this proportional feedback input into the linear open-loop pendulum ODE (6.4), we obtain the closed-loop pendulum ODE:

$$\ddot{\varphi} + (k - 1)\varphi = 0.$$

However, the solutions of this 2nd-order ODE are either oscillatory (for $k > 0$), or diverge to infinity (for $k < 0$); only in case $k = 1$ the initial velocities are zero. Therefore, in neither case the system is guaranteed to approach the stable equilibrium.

In other words, we need to keep $k > 0$, but also to add damping b to prevent oscillations. In this way, we come to the *proportional-derivative* (PD) *feedback law*:

$$u = -k\varphi - b\dot{\varphi}, \qquad (\text{with } k > 1, b > 0). \tag{6.5}$$

If we plug-in the PD-regulator (6.5) into the linear open-loop pendulum ODE (6.4), we obtain the following closed-loop pendulum ODE:

$$\ddot{\varphi} + b\dot{\varphi} + (k - 1)\varphi = 0. \tag{6.6}$$

All the solutions of the 2nd-order ODE (6.6) converge to zero. This effectively means that the linearized pendulum system has been *stabilized* under feedback. An additional condition: $b^2 > 4(k - 1)$ would prevent the oscillations within the convergence, as the solutions would become combinations of decaying exponentials. This design will also work locally[5] (around the vertical equilibrium) for the original nonlinear inverted pendulum system (6.3).

We remark here that an alternative description of the open-loop pendulum ODE (6.4) is provided by R. Kalman's state-space formulation:

$$\dot{\mathbf{x}} = \mathbf{A}\mathbf{x} + \mathbf{B}\mathbf{u}, \tag{6.7}$$

where $\mathbf{x} = \mathbf{x}(t)$ is the column state vector $[\varphi, \dot{\varphi}]^T$, while $\mathbf{A}$ and $\mathbf{B}$ are the following matrices:

$$\mathbf{A} = \begin{pmatrix} 0 & 1 \\ 1 & 0 \end{pmatrix}, \qquad \mathbf{B} = \begin{pmatrix} 0 \\ 1 \end{pmatrix}.$$

In general, the vector state equation (6.7) represents an arbitrary linear and time-invariant (LTI) control system in continuous time. For example, *Matlab*® Control Systems Toolbox is mostly based on this state-space formulation (which is similarly used in new *Mathematica*®). This formalism will be consistently used in Chapter 3 for Kalman Filtering (KF) and KF-based Cognitive Control Theory.

Feedback Control Versus Precomputed Feedforward Control

We remark that the PD-regulator (6.5) gives a *feedback law* $u(t)$ which is calculated in terms of the current position and velocity of the pole, which are then "fed back" (after suitable weighings). This feedback law provides a *closed-loop control design* that is in contrast to an *open-loop control design*, in which the expression of the entire control function $u(\cdot)$ is given in terms of the initial conditions $[\varphi(0), \dot{\varphi}(0)]$, and one applies this function $u(\cdot)$ blindly thereafter, with no further observation of positions and velocities. In real systems there will be random perturbations that are not accounted for in the mathematical model. While a feedback law will tend to correct automatically for these, a precomputed control takes no account of them.

For example, suppose that we are only interested in controlling the linear pendulum (6.4), starting from the initial position $\varphi(0) = 1$ and velocity $\dot{\varphi}(0) = -2$. Using trial-and-error type guessing, we find the satisfactory control function: $u(t) = 3e^{-2t}$, which gives the exponentially-decaing solution (pendulum position): $\varphi(t) = e^{-2t}$ and velocity $\dot{\varphi}(t) = -2e^{-2t}$, which both quickly approach zero, that is the vertical equilibrium of the pendulum. This is the example of the *precomputed feedforward control*. However, if we made any mistakes in estimating the initial velocity $\dot{\varphi}(0)-$ the precomputed control law: $u(t) = 3e^{-2t}$ would no longer work.

Therefore, the feedback solution is not only more robust to errors, but it can also be simpler than the open-loop one, as the explicit form of the control

---

[5] We remark here that from an engineering point of view, local solutions to control problems are often enough; when they are not, *ad hoc methods* sometimes may be used in order to 'patch' together such local solutions, using the so-called *gain scheduling*; see [Son99].

function $u(t)$ need not be calculated. However, the cost of implementing the feedback controller is that the position and velocity need to be continuously observed/measured [Son99].

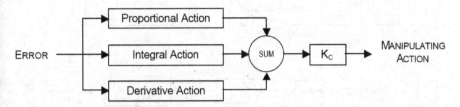

Fig. 6.6. *Combined feedback control action of the PID controller.*

Inverted Pendulum Balance via Linear PID Controller

To make our inverted pendulum balance problem more realistic, we suppose now that an unknown but constant disturbance e acts on the pendulum system (6.4), which is now described by the following linear 2nd-order ODE:

$$\ddot{\varphi} - \varphi = u + e. \tag{6.8}$$

We can still try to use the PD controller (6.5) to stabilize this system independently of disturbance e. Since stability should hold in particular when $e = 0$, we should have $(k > 1, b > 0)$ as before. However, although necessary, the PD controller is not sufficient, because the linear pendulum ODE now becomes:

$$\ddot{\varphi} + b\dot{\varphi} + (k - 1)\varphi = e,$$

and its solution converges too slowly (i.e., it takes a long time to stabilize a small disturbance from the vertical 0-equilibrium): $\varphi(t) \to 0$ as $t \to \infty$.

So, we need to extend the common linear PD controller (6.5) as:

$$u = -k\varphi - b\dot{\varphi} - c \int_0^t \varphi(\tau)d\varphi, \tag{6.9}$$

to ensure that both the position $\varphi(t)$ and the velocity $\dot{\varphi}(t)$ converge quickly to zero. The effect of the integral in the feedback law (6.9) is to offset a nonzero error e. The controller (6.9) is a PID, or proportional-integral-derivative feedback (see Figure 6.6), the control mechanism most widely used in linear control applications (see, e.g. [Son99]). A complete closed-loop responses of the inverted pendulum-on-a-cart system balanced via PID servo-controller are given in Figure 6.7.

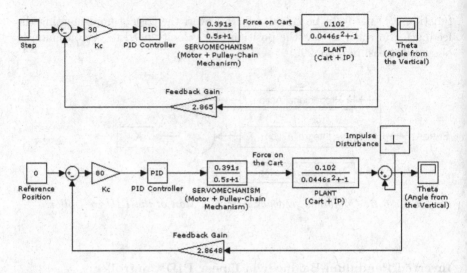

Fig. 6.7. *Simulink diagrams for the closed-loop responses of the inverted pendulum-on-a-cart system balanced via PID controller: step response (top) and impulse-disturbance response (bottom).*

Analog Circuitry Implementation of the PID Controller

A generic *operational amplifier circuit*, dedicated to linear feedback control applications (see Figure 6.8), has the transfer function: $V_2/V_1 = - - Z_2/Z_1$, where Z_1 and Z_2 are input and feedback impedances, while V_1 and V_2 are input and feedback voltages. PID implementation using this analog circuit is based on the following three gains:

Proportional Gain : $K_{pr} = R_f/R_i + C_i/C_f$;
Integral Gain : $K_{int} = 1/R_iC_f$; and
Derivative Gain : $K_{der} = R_fC_i$.

6.2.3 Bernstein's Neural Control and Motion Pattern Architecture

Nicolay Bernstein, Russian neurophysiologist, a contemporary of Norbert Wiener and a student of the Nobel Laureate Ivan P. Pavlov, replaced Pavlov's idea of human movement control based on the concept of an *open reflex arc*, with the idea of *closed somato-sensory feedbacks* (see [Ber47, Ber67, Ber96] and references therein). According to Bernstein, for the correct execution of any human movement, the brain sends an initial command to the muscles, and also receives from the peripheral senses signals about the achieved/executed movement and on that basis gives a new corrective command. Thus, the process of construction of movements, as interplay between the brain and the

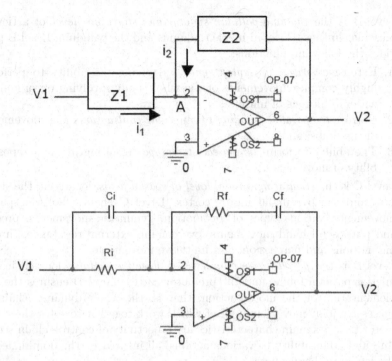

Fig. 6.8. *Basic operational amplifier circuit used for linear feedback control applications: impedance diagram (top) and R-C diagram (bottom). Here, Z_1 and Z_2 are input and feedback impedances (denoted by i and f indices, respectively), while V_1 and V_2 are input and feedback voltages.*

peripheral nervous system, includes not only feed-forward connections, but also nonlinear feedback loops, which are similar to Wiener's linear feedbacks but much more complex.

Bernstein's main hypothesis was that in the *formation of movement patterns* of varying complexity, or *development of motor skills*, the commands are given to and from the various hierarchical levels of the nervous system. At the beginning of learning of a new movement, the direction commands start from the highest level; as the movement becomes more automatic, this function is transferred to the lower level. More specifically, according to Bernstein, there are five hierarchical levels of the *neural motion-pattern architecture*, listed here bottom-up:

- Level-A is the lowest, *rubro-spinal level of paleodynamic tone regulations*, located both in the spinal cord and in the red nucleus group. This level completely determines the posture-related muscle tone of the trunk and neck, and is also responsible for excitability of the limbs' muscles.

- Level-B is the *thalamo-pallidar synergy-and-stereotype level* of articulo-muscular linkages, located in the thalamus and the pallidum. Level B provides the following functions:

  1. Extensive *spatial muscular synergies*, giving the ability to perform highly complex movements of the whole body involving an organized action of dozens of muscles;
  2. Correct *temporal sequencing of muscular contractions* and movements of the limbs; and
  3. The ability to form *dynamical stereotypes* resulting in exact repeatability of movements.

- Level-C is the *striatal-pyramidal level of spatial fields*, located in the striatum and the pyramidal motor cortex. Level C enables holistic spatial movements: various types of locomotion, gymnastic movements, precise and purposeful hand movements, overcoming external resistance, throwing motions and percussion, and imitative movements.

- Level-D is the *parieto-premotor level of objective actions*, located in the inferior parietal lobule and the premotor cortex. Level D ensures the implementation of the motor action, that is, the whole dynamic chain of successive joint movements, all of which work together to solve the given motor task. Its main characteristics are objectivity of control, chain structure and adaptability to various actions, all insured by the dominance of the left brain hemisphere.

- Level-E is the highest, distributed group of levels lying above the action level in the cortex of the D-level and defining symbolic and conceptual structures as well as *meta-cognitive coordinations*. This group provides higher symbolic actions (like speaking and writing) as well as a variety of abstract, goal-directed motor actions.

For more technical details on Bernstein's neural architecture, see [Ber47, Ber67, Ber96], as well as [IGG14].

6.2.4 Gardner's Cognitive Control: Cognitive Behavior and Adaptation

Cognitive control was an old psychological control theory developed by Riley Gardner of Harvard and his collaborators in 1950s [Gar53, GHK59] and 1960s [GJM60, Gar61, GL62a, GL62b, GS62, Gar62, Gar64]. For a more recent review, see [MSR12].

In particular, studies of individual consistencies in cognitive behavior, termed studies of *cognitive controls*, have emphasized the importance of differing characterological response dispositions, which also serve ego defensive functions as elaborated in psychopathology and mental disorders (see, e.g. [Sil64] and references therein).

It is well-known that thought, perception, and visual-motor organization are basic psychological functions from which many stable and persisting modes of adaptation evolve, including the defense mechanisms used in coping with internal conflict and external stress, various symptom formations, and the relatively conflict-free activities seen in interests and skills. Gardner's research on cognitive styles and cognitive control principles has offered some support for this formulation by demonstrating that there are consistent and preferred modes of cognition-perception which are utilized in relatively neutral, conflict-free situations as well as in the psychological defenses used to cope with internal and external conflict and stress. Thus, cognitive-perceptual processes appear to be an integral part of many aspects of personality organization (see [BAF69] and references therein).

A modern engineering incarnation of the old psychological cognitive control has been developed by Simon Haykin and his collaborators. In particular, a recent review [Hay12] addresses the many facets involved in the brain-like cognitive control of directed information flow in a generic dynamical system, culminating in the notion of information gap, defined as the difference between relevant information (useful part of what is extracted from the incoming measurements) and sufficient information representing the information needed for achieving minimal risk. The notion of information gap leads naturally to how cognitive control can itself be defined. Then, another important idea is described, namely the two-state model, in which one is the system's state and the other is the entropic state that provides an essential metric for quantifying the information gap. It is computed in the perceptual part (i.e., perceptor) of the dynamic system and sent to the controller directly as feedback information. This feedback information provides the cognitive controller the information needed about the environment and the system to bring reinforcement leaning into play; reinforcement learning (RL), incorporating planning as an integral part, is at the very heart of cognitive control.

6.3 PCT Fundamentals

As already stated in the Introduction, PCT actions are not directly/explicitly controlled, but are rather varied in order to cancel the effects of unpredictable environmental disturbances on controlled perceptions. The main PCT phrase is: "behavior is the control of perception" (not the other way around) [Wik16h].

PCT-perceptions are constructed and controlled in a hierarchy of levels, similar to those of Bernstein's motion pattern architecture (described in the Introduction).

6.3.1 Controlled Variables in Psychology

As already stated, PCT views behavior as the control of perception. The central explanatory concept in PCT is the controlled variable, which is a perceived aspect of the environment that is brought to and maintained in states specified by the organism. According to PCT, understanding behavior is a matter of discovering the variables that organisms control. But the possible existence of controlled variables has been largely ignored in the behavioral sciences. One notable exception occurs in the study of how baseball outfielders catch fly balls. In these studies it is taken for granted that the fielder gets to the ball by controlling some visual aspect of the ball's movement. This article describes the concept of a controlled variable in the context of research on fly ball catching behavior and shows how this concept can contribute to our understanding of behavior in general [Mar01].

PCT was developed to explain the purposeful behavior of organisms [Mar90]. Purposeful behavior involves producing consistent results in a world where unpredictable disturbances make such consistency highly unlikely (Old Faithful notwithstanding). For example, a person sipping tea is producing a consistent result-the sips-despite unpredictable disturbances, such as head movements, that change the relative location of cup and lips. Sipping tea is a purposeful behavior. PCT is based on the realization that purposeful behavior, like that of the tea drinker, is equivalent to the controlling done by artificial control systems, such as a thermostat. In both cases, a consistent result is produced despite unpredictable disturbances that should produce inconsistency. The thermostat produces a consistent room temperature despite unpredictable changes in outdoor air temperature; the tea drinker produces consistent sips despite unpredictable changes in the relative location of cup and lips. Control systems act to bring variable aspects of the environment to preselected states while protecting these variables from the effects of disturbance. This process is called control. The variable aspects of the environment that a system controls are called controlled variables; room temperature and distance from cup to lips are controlled variables. The purposeful behavior of a control system, whether it is living (like the tea drinker) or artificial (like the thermostat), is organized around controlled variables. Control theory explains how a control system acts to keep these variables under control. PCT is the application of control theory to understanding the purposeful behavior of control systems in general and living control systems in particular.

A very simple procedure, based on PCT, can be used to determine whether a variable that can be perceived by an observer corresponds to a variable that is being controlled by a control system (see [Mar01] and the references therein). The procedure, called the test for the controlled variable (TCV), involves applying a disturbance to a possible controlled variable and looking for lack of effect of the disturbance. For example, we can test whether a thermostat is controlling room temperature by applying a disturbance, such as a blast of cold air, and looking to see whether it has the expected effect: lowering the room temperature. If room temperature, which is perceived by the observer as the reading of a thermometer, is under control, the disturbance will have little or no effect; the room temperature reading stays about the same. The same type of test can be used to determine whether a tea drinker is controlling the distance from cup to lips. The test is done by applying a disturbance, such as a gentle push on the cup, and looking to see whether it has the expected effect: increasing the distance between cup and lips. If distance between cup and lips is under control, the disturbance will have little or no effect: The distance between cup and lips stays about the same. A properly conducted TCV involves applying many different disturbances, all of which would have an effect on the hypothetical controlled variable if that variable were not under control. Although it is impossible to prove that a variable is unquestionably under control, it is possible to conduct tests until one becomes very confident that the variable is under control. If every disturbance that should have an effect on the variable does not, then one can be almost certain that the variable is under control.

The PCT approach to understanding behavior, which is based on the TCV, is rarely seen in psychological research [Mar01]. A notable exception occurs in research aimed at determining how baseball outfielders catch fly balls. The behavior under study is quite familiar: When the ball is hit in the air, the outfielder runs to the spot where the ball will land and (usually) catches it. The conventional approach to understanding this behavior would be aimed at finding its causes; it would try to determine what variables guide the fielder to the spot where the ball lands. The PCT approach to understanding fly ball catching behavior is aimed at finding controlled variables; it tries to determine what variables, if controlled, would result in our seeing the fielder move to the spot where the ball lands.

What is needed is a way to choose which one of several different hypotheses about the controlled variable is the best representation of the variable under control. The most straightforward approach is systematically to produce disturbances that should affect one variable at a time and watch to see whether the disturbances affect each of the variables. For example, it may be possible to disturb optical velocity without disturbing optical acceleration or LOT. If the disturbance affects optical velocity, then that variable can be eliminated as a hypothetical controlled variable; if not, then optical velocity remains in the pool of possible controlled variables.

6.3.2 Marken's PCT Tracking Tests

A number of computer simulations of specific behavioral situations demonstrate the efficacy of PCT-methods with very high correlations to observational data (see, e.g. [Mar14] and local demos and references therein). Probably the best introduction to PCT could be provided with some of R. Marken's PCT tracking tests, reviewed in the next subsection.

Here, we give a brief review three tracking PCT tests designed by R. Marken.

Stimulus–Response vs. Control Task

The responses (e.g., mouse movements) that keep a stimulus (e.g., cursor position) under control in a tracking task occur in a closed feedback loop.

The stimulus in this loop (the controlled variable) is both a cause and an effect of responses. This means that Stimulus–Response (S-R) explanations of control will not work. An S-R interpretation of control says that something about the stimulus (such as how far the cursor is to the left or right of the target) causes one to respond in just the right way so that the cursor stays close to the target.

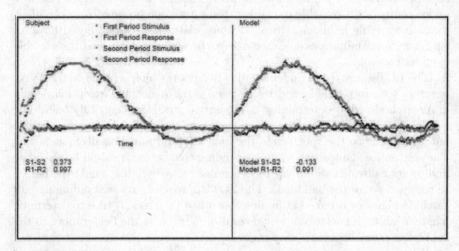

Fig. 6.9. *Stimulus–response vs. control tracking task. The left side of the graph shows the results for the human subject; the right side of the graph shows the results for a control model doing the same task. Note that variations in R during the first (black squares) and second (red squares) periods of the experiment are virtually identical for both subject and model. The R1-R2 correlation between response variations during these two periods is typically on the order of 0.99. Note that the variations in S during the first (black squares) and second (red squares) periods of the experiment are not identical for both subject or model. Indeed, the S1-S2 correlation between stimulus variations during these two periods is typically far lower than the correlation between response variations during the same periods. The S1-S2 correlation is typically close to 0.0 and rarely more than 0.3, certainly not high enough to account for the nearly perfect correlation between responses (typically > 0.99) on repeated trials.*

The results of this task are so surprising that some have suggested that the high correlation between R1 and R2 results from the fact that the subject is simply repeating the mouse movements made during the first part of the experiment from memory. This would presumably explain why there is a high correlation between R1 and R2 when there is a low correlation between S1 and S2. The subject is matching second phase mouse movements (R2) to those made in the first phase (R2) without even watching the cursor.

Nature of Control Task

The purpose of this second task is to develop and test a general tracking (with a mouse) ability. This disturbance-compensation task involves keeping the cursor, which is randomly jumping left-right, directly under the target. After several seconds of attempted tracking, the graph appears (see Figure 6.10), showing two signals/curves:

RMS Error that measures the average deviation (in pixels) of the controlled variable from a 0−reference value. The closer RMS Error is to 0.0, the better is the control of the cursor. RMS Error can be used to measure control when the reference value of the controlled variable is known.

Stability that measures the ratio of expected to observed variation of the controlled variable. Expected variation is the amount the controlled variable would have varied if you had done nothing to control it; observed variation is the actual amount of variation of the controlled variable. If expected and observed variation are the same, there is no control and Stability $= 1.0$. If expected is much larger than observed variation of the controlled variable then this variable is under control and Stability $\gg 1.0$. The greater the Stability measure, the better your control of the controlled variable. The Stability measure makes it possible to measure the reference value of the controlled variable is not known.

The Figure 6.10 shows temporal changes in the values of the variables in this control task; cursor position (C), mouse position (M) and disturbance value (D). Note that the trace of cursor position (C) is nearly a straight line when the cursor is under control. The traces of mouse (M) and disturbance (D) mirror one another, as they must if the cursor is to stay nearly constant (under control). The red trace shows the mouse movements made by a computer model doing this control task. This trace will be nearly identical to your own mouse movement trace when you have learned to control the cursor well. The correlation between your mouse movements (M) and mouse movements made by the model (Model) can be seen in the upper right of the display in red.

Levels of Control: Tracking Task with a Positive Feedback

This third tracking task is a continuation of the Nature of Control task. It shows that control systems operate in the context of other control systems. In this case, the cursor control system works in the context of another, higher-level 'quality' control system, which controls the quality of the controlling done by the cursor control system. When the quality of cursor control becomes poor (due to the sudden change in the polarity of the connection between mouse and cursor movements), the quality control system acts to return the quality of cursor control back to what it was before the polarity change. The quality control system does this by changing the way the cursor control system deals with error (the deviation of intended from actual cursor position). If, prior

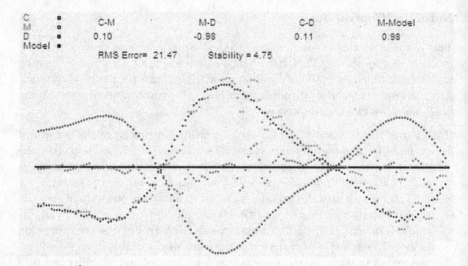

Fig. 6.10. *Nature of control: tracking task, showing RMS Error and Stability. Above the graphic display and RMS Error and Stability measures are the correlations between the variables in this control task. The number on the left is the correlation between cursor and mouse movements (C-M). The number in the center is the correlation between mouse and disturbance (M-D) movements. And the number on the right is the correlation between cursor and disturbance (C-D). Finally the number on the right is the correlation between your mouse movements (M) and the mouse movements made by a control model that performed the same tracking task.*

to the polarity shift, the cursor control system had moved the mouse in a direction that is opposite to the sign of the error, it now moves the mouse in a direction that is the same as the sign of the error. Similarly, if the cursor control system had moved the mouse in a direction that was the same as the sign of the error, it now moves the mouse in a direction opposite to the sign of the error (see Figure 6.11).

It is virtually impossible to avoid the brief 'runaway' period that occurs when the polarity of the connection between mouse and cursor changes. During this runaway period the volunteer is actually pushing the cursor away from the target in an exponentially accelerated manner. This happens because the change in polarity makes the sign of the cursor control loop positive. Therefore, the runaway represents a *positive feedback* in action. We recall the common fact that positive feedbacks usually have catastrophic tendencies, in the sense that the system exponentially diverges from its equilibrium.

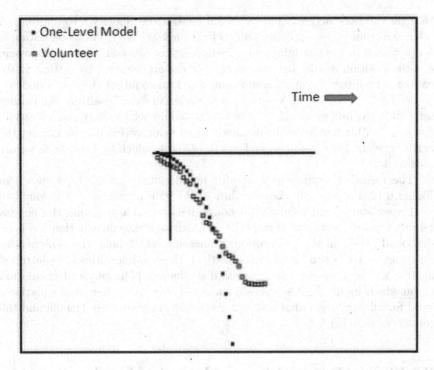

Fig. 6.11. *Levels of control: again, the objective is to keep the cursor directly under the target, by moving the mouse to compensate for the disturbances to the cursor. After some time the effect of the mouse on the cursor will suddenly reverse. The objective is to try to regain control as quickly as possible — which has failed in the shown graph.*

6.4 PCT Approach to Inverted Pendulum Balance

Consider the inverted pendulum problem with an 1D cart and the bob at the top, as designed by Powers. We will assume that the cart travels on a frictionless track, the rigid pendulum rod swivels freely at its base, and that there is an actuator which applies any specified horizontal force to the cart. To move the pendulum bob to a specified horizontal position by means of this actuator is a complicated task. Nevertheless, it can be achieved by breaking the matter down into simpler tasks, as follows (see [Ken99] and the references therein).

If we had an actuator that could set the bob immediately to any desired position, no control system would be necessary. We do not have such an actuator; but if we had one which could set the pendulums horizontal velocity, we could use this to control the position: set the velocity equal to $k_0(r_b - b)$ for some constant k_0, where r_b is the demanded position and b is the current position. We do not have such a velocity actuator, but if we had an actuator that set the bobs acceleration, we could control the velocity $\dot{b}$ to approach a reference value $r_{\dot{b}}$ by applying an acceleration $k_1(r_{\dot{b}} - \dot{b})$. The acceleration is proportional to the pendulum angle, which is proportional to $o = b - c$, where c is the position of the cart. So we can set the acceleration by setting o. We cannot set o directly, but we could control o if we could set the cart's velocity, by setting $\dot{c} = k_2(r_c - c)$, where r_c is the reference cart position. We cannot set $\dot{c}$ directly, but we could control it if we could set the cart's acceleration: $\ddot{c} = k_3(r_{\dot{c}} - \dot{c})$, where $r_{\dot{c}}$ is the demanded cart velocity. Finally, we can set the cart's acceleration by applying a force to the cart, which by hypothesis we are able to do.

The resulting arrangement of four proportional controllers is shown in Figure 6.12. For suitably chosen values of the gain parameters, it is found to work very stably and robustly (although it is not able to swing the pendulum up from the straight down position). Although the construction has been described above on the assumption of linearity, which fails when the pendulum angle departs too far from the vertical, the non-linearities are controlled against in the same way as external disturbances. The physical simulation (from which Figure 6.10 is a screen shot) uses the true differential equations, valid for all pendulum angles (for more technical details, see [Ken99] and the references therein).

6.5 PCT in Psychotherapy: Method of Levels

A PCT-based cognitive approach to psychotherapy is called the *Method of Levels* (MOL). Using MOL, the therapist works with the patient to resolve conflicts by helping the patient shift their awareness to higher levels of perception in order to allow reorganization to take place [Man05, Car06].

In the MOL-domain, PCT contributes with a useful perspective in understanding psychological disorders by first providing a model of satisfactory psychological functioning. Dysfunction is here understood as disruption of successful control, and distress as the experience that results from a person's inability to control important experiences [MCT12]. No attempt is made to treat the symptoms of distress as though they were in themselves the problem. The PCT perspective is that restoring the ability to control eliminates the source of distress. Internal conflict has the effect of denying control to both systems that are in conflict with each other. Conflict is usually transitory. It is when conflict is unresolved and becomes chronic that the symptoms recognized as psychological disorder become apparent.

Within MOL, the core process is to redirect attention to the higher level control systems by recognizing background thoughts, bringing them into the foreground, and then being alert for more background thoughts while the new foreground thoughts are explored. When the level-climbing process reaches an end state without encountering any conflicts, the need for therapy may have ended. When, however, this up-a-level process bogs down, a conflict has

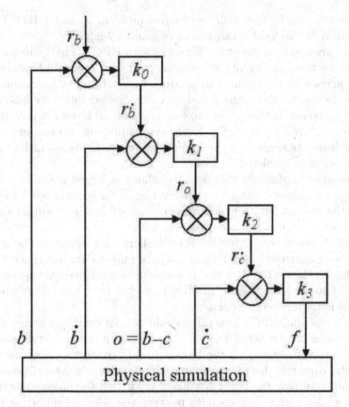

Fig. 6.12. *Proposed control hierarchy for inverted pendulum (adapted from [Ken99]).*

probably surfaced, and the exploration can be turned to finding the systems responsible for generating the conflictand away from a preoccupation with the symptoms and efforts immediately associated with the conflict.

6.6 PCT versus Brooks' Subsumption Architecture

Besides cascade control, described above, there is another approach to the design of robotic systems which bears a superficial resemblance to the present proposal, called the *subsumption architecture* (also known as *behavior-based programming*).[6] This is an architecture originally devised by R. Brooks from

---

[6] Brooks' subsumption architecture [Bro86, Bro90] provides a method for organizing reactive subsystems in a bottom-up fashion, using layered sets of behaviors. Each layer implements a particular goal of the agent, which subsumes that of the underlying layers. For example, the objective of a robots lowest layer could be 'avoid collisions with objects', above it would be the layer tasked to model

MIT [Bro86, Bro90], in which the control problem is, as for HPCT, broken down into a hierarchical arrangement of simpler agents.

There are two fundamental differences with HPCT. Firstly, in a subsumption architecture, the agents are not necessarily conceived of as controllers, that is, agents which attempt to produce a certain input by means of their outputs. Secondly, the main principle of the subsumption architecture, for which it is named, is that all of the controllers at all levels act directly on the actuators, controllers at higher levels suspending the actions of controllers at lower levels as necessary, the lower level resuming its operation when the higher level has completed its task.

Thus some of the actions taken to balance a legged robot in a standing posture are suspended when a higher-level agent for walking needs to lift some legs off the ground; an agent for walking in a straight line will be suspended by an agent for collision avoidance, and so on.

In HPCT, only the bottom-level controllers send signals to the actuators. Higher level controllers send their outputs only to the reference inputs of controllers at the next level down. In subsumption, higher-level agents operate instead of lower level agents; in HPCT, higher-level controllers operate by means of lower level controllers.

In principle, an HPCT controller could act not only by altering the references of lower level controllers, but also, for example, by altering parameters of their output functions, or the linkage matrix connecting them to their descendants. However, there is never any skipping of levels. As mentioned above, we intend to employ the latter scheme of modifying the linkage matrix to implement walking, to switch each leg between the roles of supporting the body and moving the foot to a new position [Ken99].

'wander around', which in turn lies under the layer tasked to 'explore the world'. The upper layer in such a model could represent the ultimate goal of 'creating and following a map'. This way, the lower layers can work as fast-responding mechanisms (i.e., reflexes), while the higher layers control the main direction to be taken in order to achieve a more abstract goal.

6.7 PCT Alternative 1: Lewinian Psycho–Physical Group Dynamics

Kurt Lewin's[7] *topological force–field psychodynamics* [Lew36, Lew46, Lew47, Lew51, Lew97, Gol99] is a study of psycho–physical forces that are either driving or blocking a *goal–directed action* (i.e., helping or hindering forces, respectively), schematically summarized as:[8]

$$\text{Driving Forces} \rightrightarrows \text{Equilibrium} \rightleftharpoons \text{Restraining Forces.}$$

The interplay of Driving and Rrestraining forces creates the stable routine of normal, regular activities, which is described by Lewin as a 'quasi-stationary Equilibrium'. In everyday situations, the driving and restraining forces balance out and equalize to fluctuate around a state of Equilibrium.[9] In this context, achieving *change* involves altering the forces that maintain the Equilibrium. Thus, in the papers on *group dynamics* and *decision-making* [Lew47, Lew48],

---

[7] Kurt Lewin (1890–1947), a German–American psychologist of Jewish origin who left Germany as the Nazis came into power, is universally recognized as the founder of *social psychology* (including organizational development and leadership styles and their effects). He translated *Gestalt shape* ideas into social experience involving *group dynamics*. As a Professor at MIT, in the paper [Lew46], he described the *action research* as "a comparative research on the conditions and effects of various forms of social action and research leading to social action" that uses "a spiral of steps, each of which is composed of a circle of planning, action, and fact–finding about the result of the action." Lewin founded the Society for the Psychological Study of Social Issues, Division 9 of the American Psychological Association.

[8] Three main principles of force–field theory are that: (i) behavior is a function of the existing force–field; (ii) analysis starts from the complete situation and distinguishes its component parts; and (iii) a concrete person in a concrete situation can be mathematically (topologically and geometrically) represented.

Force–field analysis is used extensively for purposes of organisational and human resource development, to help indicate when driving and restraining. Force–field analysis can be used to help distinguish whether factors within a situation or organization are 'driving forces' for change or 'restraining forces' that will work against desired changes. Examples of driving forces might be impulsions such as ambition, goals, needs or fears that drive a person towards or away from something. Restraining forces are viewed by Lewin as different in their nature, in that they act to oppose driving forces rather than comprise independent forces in themselves.

[9] In particular, in group dynamics, two different kinds of Restraining Forces are rooted in the interplay between a group as a whole and the individuals within it, and only Driving Forces that are strong enough to break the habits, challenge the interests or 'unfreeze' the customs of the group will overcome the forces of resistance. As most members will want to stay within the behavioral norms of the group, individual resistance to change will increase as a person is induced to move further away from current group values.

Lewin proposes a general *change model:*[10]

$$\text{Unfreeze} \rightrightarrows \text{Change/Move} \rightrightarrows \text{Freeze},$$

in which the first stage, Unfreeze, involves overcoming inertia and dissolving the existing *mindset:* defense mechanisms need to be bypassed, we are going out of our 'comfort zone'. In the second stage, Change/Move, the change occurs: this is usually a period of *transition and confusion*; we are aware that the old ways are being challenged but we do not have a clear picture as to what we are replacing them with yet. In the third and final stage, Freeze, the *new mindset* is crystallizing and one establishes a new comfort.

As a summary, Lewin suggested that neither *nature* (inborn tendencies) nor *nurture* (how experiences in life shape individuals) alone can account for individuals' behavior and personalities, but rather that both nature and nurture interact to shape each person. Thus, he reduced the *mysteries of human behavior* to the following simple statement: "Behavior is a function of both the Person and their Environment", or formally:[11]

$$B = f(P, E),$$

where B, P, E denote the behavior, person and environment, respectively. This means that one's behavior is related both to one's personal characteristics and to the *social situation* in which one finds oneself.

We emphasize here *Lewinian typology of conflicts*:

approach–approach: we want two different things that we like both (in Lewin's terms, both have 'positive valences');

avoidance–avoidance: we have to pick one or the other alternative, but dislike both (both have 'negative valences');

approach–avoidance: we can either have, or subject ourselves to, one thing that has both positive and negative qualities (valences);

double approach–avoidance: we must choose between two things that each have both positive and negative qualities (valences).

As an application of Lewinian force–field psycho–physics in digital computer era, we can mention the simulation of the approach–avoidance conflict in two–party crowds by [JPS01], in which a linear strength–distance conflict relation was proposed, resembling a kind of Hook's spring.

---

[10] Lewin social psychology deals with the human aspect of *change*. Famous are his words: "If you want to truly understand something, try to change it."

[11] This simple formula, obviously valid from today's perspective, contradicted most popular *psychoanalytic theories* of the time: it gave importance to a person's momentary situation in understanding their behavior, rather than relying entirely on the past.

Lewinian explanatory psychodynamics was recently formalized in [IA07] into a general stochastic quantum–like predictive dynamics[12] within the new concept of 'Life-Space Foam' (LSF), as a natural medium for the *goal–driven human action*.

Within the LSF–formalism, Lewinian individual psychodynamics was formalized hierarchically:

- At the macroscopic level, as a least–action principle, $\delta S = 0$, defined on a smooth psychodynamic manifold with steady force–fields and behavioral paths; and
- At the microscopic level, as wildly fluctuating force–fields, (loco)motion paths and local geometries (and topologies with holes), formally defined

as an adaptive generalization of the Feynman path integral $\oint$ and its associated *quantum probability concept*.

The LSF–approach was then applied:

1. To model the psycho–physical dynamics of the *joint action* of two or more agents[13] [IAY09]; and
2. To formulate an entropic geometric model of general crowd behavior dynamics (see [IRA10, IR10a]).

Furthermore, to avoid computational difficulties associated with numerical solution of the *Feynman path integral*,[14] we have subsequently rewritten the entropic path-integral crowd model in the form of a set of (either weakly or

---

[12] The domain of validity of the 'quantum' is not restricted to the microscopic world [Ume93]. There are macroscopic features of classically behaving systems, which cannot be explained without recourse to the quantum dynamics.

[13] The main result of this paper, obtained by Riemann–Finsler geometric reasoning, is that a *multilateral* joint action of three or more agents (or, groups of agents) is qualitatively more complicated than a *bilateral* co–action of two agents (or, groups). This is in complete agreement with chaos theory of continuous-time systems: there is no chaos in the phase-plane; chaotic behavior requires 3 or more dimensions. This is also in agreement with everyday's common sense ('two of us worked smoothly together until the third one came in'), as well as with global politics and economy. Surprisingly enough, it was a completely new result for social psychology!

[14] As much as various versions of the Feynman path integral represent great conceptual tools for modeling both macro– and micro–phenomena, just a few minutes of crowd dynamics simulated using *path–integral–Monte–Carlo* (PIMC) methods would take weeks on a supercomputer. This inadequacy of digital computers (the von Neumann's concept) for modeling quantum phenomena was the primary reason for Feynman's pioneering initiation of the *quantum–computer concept* in early 1980s [Fey82]. Briefly, 'quantum computer' is a computation device that makes direct use of distinctively quantum phenomena of *superposition* and *entanglement*, to perform operations on data. Whilst in a conventional computer information is stored as bits, in a quantum computer it is stored as quantum binary digits, or *qubits*. The basic principle of quantum computation is that the

strongly) coupled adaptive *nonlinear Schrödinger* (NLS) equations[15] [II09, IR12], suitable for numerical simulation using the powerful *method of lines.*

Finally, turbulence and associated shock waves, solitons and rogue waves in NLS–driven crowd dynamics were analyzed, from both classical and quantum perspective, in [IR12].

6.8 PCT Alternative 2: Model Predictive Control

The so-called *model predictive control* (MPC) is an advanced method of the MIMO process control that has been in use in the process industries (mostly in in chemical plants and oil refineries) for the last three decades. Recently it has also been used in power system balancing models with *uncertainty*. MPC-controllers rely on dynamic models of the process, most often linear empirical models obtained by *system identification*. The main advantage of MPC is the fact that it allows the current timeslot to be optimized, while keeping future timeslots in account. This is achieved by optimizing a finite time-horizon, but only implementing the current timeslot. MPC has the ability to anticipate future events and can take control actions accordingly, while Kalman's LQR controllers (see section 8.2 in the next chapter) do not have this predictive ability. MPC is nearly universally implemented as a digital control, although there is research into achieving faster response times with specially designed analog circuitry (see [Wik16z] and the references therein).

MPC uses iterative optimization of a plant model within the finite horizon τ. At any time instant t the current plant state is sampled and a cost-minimizing control strategy is computed for a relatively short time horizon τ_0 in the future: $[t, t + \tau_0]$. Briefly, an online (or, on-the-fly) calculation is used to explore state trajectories that emanate from the current state and find a cost-minimizing control strategy until time $t + \tau$, by solving the associated *Euler–Lagrangian equations*. Only the first step of the control strategy is implemented, then the plant state is sampled again and the calculations are repeated starting from the new current state, yielding a new control and new predicted state path. The prediction horizon keeps being shifted forward and for this reason MPC is also called receding horizon control. Although this

---

quantum properties can be used to represent and structure data, and that quantum mechanisms can be devised and built to perform operations with these data. For a thorough recent overview, including *topological quantum computers* (which employ 2D quasi-particles called *anyons*, whose *world lines* cross over one another to form *braids*), see [II09].

[15] Briefly, a non-relativistic $n-$body path integral is equivalent to a set of linear quantum-mechanical Schrödinger equations. Once we put the Schrödinger equation into a feedback loop to make it adaptive, we add a *nonlinearity* of either cubic or quintic type. In this way we come to a set of NLS equations, which are both *quantum stochastic filters* and generators of *quantum turbulence* (as well as shock-waves, solitons and rogue-waves).

approach is not optimal, in practice it has given very good results. Most of theoretical research has been done to find fast methods of solution of Euler-Lagrangian equations, to understand the global stability properties of MPC's local optimization, and in general to improve the MPC method (see, e.g. [Nik01] and the references therein).

More formally, MPC is a linear multivariable control algorithm that uses:

(i) an internal dynamic model of the process in the state-space form of (8.4)–(8.5),

(ii) a history of past control moves $\mathbf{u}(t)$, and

(iii) an optimization cost function J over the receding prediction horizon τ, to calculate the optimum control moves $\mathbf{u}_{\mathrm{opt}}(t)$.

The optimization cost function J is given by (with summing over i):

$$J = w_{x_i}(r_i - x_i)^2 + w_{u_i}\Delta u_i{}^2,$$

where x_i is the ith controlled variable (e.g., measured temperature), r_i is the ith reference variable (e.g., required temperature), u_i is the ith manipulated variable (e.g., control valve), w_{x_i} is the weighting coefficient reflecting the relative importance of x_i, w_{u_i} is the weighting coefficient penalizing relative big changes in u_i. Such a linear MPC methodology has been implemented in the $Matlab^{\circledR}$ MPC-Toolbox [BMR15].

Currently under development is the so-called *nonlinear model predictive control* (NMPC), which uses a nonlinear generalization of the state equation (8.4)–(8.5) for the prediction, in the general form: $\dot{x}_i(t) = f_i[X(t)] + u_i(t)$ (see equation (6.14) in the next subsection). The numerical solution of the NMPC optimal control problems is typically based on direct optimal control methods using Newton-type optimization schemes, in one of the variants: direct single shooting, direct multiple shooting methods, or direct collocation (see [HSP14] and the references therein). NMPC algorithms typically exploit the fact that consecutive optimal control problems are similar to each other. Being much harder to effectively solve than linear MPC methods, the NMPC algorithms have yet to be implemented in major software packages.

In addition, there are robust MPC-variants, which are able to account for set bounded disturbance while still ensuring state constraints are met. There are three main approaches to *robust MPC*:

Min-max MPC in which the optimization is performed with respect to all possible evolutions of the disturbance. This is the optimal solution to linear robust control problems, however it carries a high computational cost (see [SM98] and the references therein).

Constraint Tightening MPC in which the state constraints are enlarged by a given margin so that a trajectory can be guaranteed to be found under any evolution of disturbance (see [RH06]).

Tube MPC in which an independent nominal model of the system is used, together with a feedback controller, to ensure the actual state converges to the nominal state (see [LCR04] and the references therein). The amount of separation required from the state constraints is determined by the *robust positively invariant set* (RPIS), which is the set of all possible state deviations that may be introduced by disturbance with the feedback controller.

6.8.1 MPC Application: Control of a Rotational Spacecraft Model

Consider a purely rotational $SO(3)$-model of a spacecraft, defined in its principal body frame fixed to its center of mass. Its kinematics equations represent time evolution of Euler angles, roll $\phi(t)$, pitch $\theta(t)$ and yaw $\psi(t)$, measured in (rad) and their corresponding angular velocities $\omega_i(t)$ (rad/s) for $i = (1, 2, 3)$. Formally, the rotational kinematics of the spacecraft are given by [GKP14]:

$$\begin{bmatrix} \dot{\phi} \\ \dot{\theta} \\ \dot{\psi} \end{bmatrix} = \frac{1}{\cos(\theta)} \begin{bmatrix} \cos(\theta) & \sin(\phi)\sin(\theta) & \cos(\phi)\sin(\theta) \\ 0 & \cos(\phi)\cos(\theta) & -\sin(\phi)\cos(\theta) \\ 0 & \sin(\phi) & \cos(\phi) \end{bmatrix} \begin{bmatrix} \omega_1 \\ \omega_2 \\ \omega_3 \end{bmatrix}, \qquad (6.10)$$

while the corresponding rotational dynamics equations are given by:

$$J_1\dot{\omega}_1 = (J_2 - J_3)\omega_2\omega_3 + T_1 \simeq T_1, \qquad (6.11)$$
$$J_2\dot{\omega}_2 = (J_3 - J_1)\omega_1\omega_3 + T_2 \simeq T_2,$$
$$J_3\dot{\omega}_3 = (J_1 - J_2)\omega_1\omega_2 + T_3 \simeq T_3,$$

where J_i (kgm^2) are the principal moments of inertia and T_i (Nm) are the torques around the Euler angles.

To be able to drive the spacecraft, we would equip it with 3 reaction wheels along each of its body frame axes (considered as perfect discs with moments of inertia $\tilde{J}_i$, for $i = 1, 2, 3$), generating torques about the respective principal axes. In this way, the dynamics equations (6.11) linking the spacecraft torques to the reaction wheels torques are defined as follows:

$$T_1 = -\tilde{J}_1\left(\dot{\omega}_1 + \ddot{\alpha}_1 + \dot{\alpha}_3\omega_2 - \dot{\alpha}_2\omega_3\right) \simeq -\tilde{J}_1(\dot{\omega}_1 + \ddot{\alpha}_1), \qquad (6.12)$$
$$T_2 = -\tilde{J}_2\left(\dot{\omega}_2 + \ddot{\alpha}_2 + \dot{\alpha}_1\omega_3 - \dot{\alpha}_3\omega_1\right) \simeq -\tilde{J}_2(\dot{\omega}_2 + \ddot{\alpha}_2),$$
$$T_3 = -\tilde{J}_3\left(\dot{\omega}_3 + \ddot{\alpha}_3 + \dot{\alpha}_2\omega_1 - \dot{\alpha}_1\omega_2\right) \simeq -\tilde{J}_3(\dot{\omega}_3 + \ddot{\alpha}_3),$$

where $\dot{\alpha}_i$ (rad/s) and $\ddot{\alpha}_i$ (rad/s^2) are angular velocities and accelerations of the wheels, respectively.

Combining kinematics equations (6.10) with dynamics equations (6.12), a 9th-order nonlinear state-space model has been developed in [GKP14], with the 9D-state $x = [\varphi_i \, \omega_i \, \dot{\alpha}_i]^T$, for $i = 1, 2, 3$, where $\varphi_i = (\phi, \theta, \psi)$. In addition, three torques u_i are exerted on the wheels by electric actuators, so that $\ddot{\alpha}_i = u_i/\tilde{J}_i$.

However, the 9D-state model appears to be too complicated for efficient control with the objective to handle a set of constraints on the spacecraft orientation $\varphi_i(t)$, the reaction wheel speeds $\dot{\alpha}_i(t)$ and the control inputs $u_i(t)$.

Therefore, a reduced-order control model has been developed in [GKP14] so that MPC could be affectively applied to it, as follows.

Since the angular momentum is conserved, by neglecting all but linear terms in (6.11)–(6.12), the following linear model is set up (for $i = 1, 2, 3$):

$$\dot{\omega}_i = -\frac{\tilde{J}_i}{J_i}\ddot{\alpha}_i \implies \ddot{\alpha}_i = \frac{J_i}{J_i \tilde{J}_i - \tilde{J}_i^2} u_i = \mathbf{f}\left(J_i, \tilde{J}_i\right) u_i. \tag{6.13}$$

The model (6.13) is then converted into Kalman's state-space form:

$$\dot{x} = Ax + Bu \quad \text{with} \quad \dot{x} = \frac{d}{dt}[\varphi_i \, \omega_i \, \dot{\alpha}_i]^T,$$

so that linear MPC-Toolbox of $Matlab^{\circledR}$ could be applied. The state and control matrices are given by:

$$A = \begin{bmatrix} \mathbf{0}^{3\times3} & \begin{matrix} -\frac{\tilde{J}_1}{J_1} & 0 & 0 \\ 0 & -\frac{\tilde{J}_2}{J_2} & 0 \\ 0 & 0 & -\frac{\tilde{J}_3}{J_3} \end{matrix} \\ \hline \mathbf{0}^{3\times3} & \mathbf{0}^{3\times3} \end{bmatrix}, \quad B = \begin{bmatrix} \mathbf{0}^{3\times3} \\ \hline \mathbf{f}\left(J_1, \tilde{J}_1\right) & 0 & 0 \\ 0 & \mathbf{f}\left(J_2, \tilde{J}_2\right) & 0 \\ 0 & 0 & \mathbf{f}\left(J_3, \tilde{J}_3\right) \end{bmatrix}.$$

This standard linearized control approach enables that: (a) to solve the linearized version of the problem (6.11)–(6.12), taking into account both the spacecraft and reaction wheels dynamics; (b) to minimize the computational impact and memory requirements; (c) can be deployed on fixed-point microcontrollers or as an embedded MPC-on-a-chip device.

For further technical details on linearized MPC for spacecraft control and its Matlab implementation, see [GKP14] and the references therein.

6.8.2 MPC-Based Mean-Field Games for Multi-Agent CPC-Autonomy

The so-called *mean-field games* (MFGs) are differential games with a continuum of players that incorporate the time-dimension through a control-theoretic approach (see, e.g. [DHL14] and the references therein). Simpler approaches relying on the so-called *best reply strategy* (BRP) have been proposed, which assume that the agents navigate their strategies towards their goal by taking the direction of steepest descent of their cost function (i.e. the opposite of the utility function). Recently, the link between MFGs and the BRP approach has been explored in [DHL14], by introducing an MPC framework that consists of setting the mean-field game over a short time interval which recedes as time moves on. The authors have shown that the MPC offers a compromise between a possibly unrealistic MFG approach and the sub-optimal BRP.

Following [DHL14], we consider a set of N particles labeled by $i = 1, \dots, N$ where each particle has a state $x_i \in \mathbb{R}$. We denote by $X = (x_i)_{i=1}^{N}$ the state of all particles and by $X_{-i} = (x_j)_{j=1, j \neq i}^N$ the states of all particles except i. Further, let us assume that each particle's dynamics is governed by a smooth function $f_i : \mathbb{R}^N \to \mathbb{R}$ depending on the state X and we assume that each particle may control its dynamics by a control u_i. The dynamics for the set of particles $i = 1, \ldots, N$ is then given by:

$$\dot{x}_i(t) = f_i\left[X(t)\right] + u_i(t), \quad \text{with initial conditions: } x_i(0) = \bar{x}_i. \tag{6.14}$$

Examples of models of the type (6.14) are *alignment models* in socio–ecological context, microscopic *traffic-flow models*, *production models*, etc. (see, e.g. the recent surveys given in [MT13, NPT10, VZ12]). From the control theoretic perspective, the case of a single control variable $u_i \equiv u$ for all i in equation (6.14) has been considered in [AHP14, APZ14, CF13].

Following [Car10], it is assumed that particle i minimizes its own objective functional and therefore determines the optimal u_i^* by:[16]

$$u_i^*(\cdot) = \text{argmin } _{u_i : [0, \tau] \to \mathbb{R}} \int_0^\tau \left(\frac{\alpha_i(s)}{2} u_i^2(s) + h_i\left[X(s)\right] \right) ds, \tag{6.15}$$

where $X(s)$ is the solution to (6.14) and the optimal control (and the corresponding optimal trajectory) is denoted with superscript $*$.

The problem (6.15) simplifies when each particle i *anticipates* an a priori fixed strategy of all other particles U_{-i}. Then, the problem (6.15) decouples (in i) and the optimal strategy u_i is determined independent of the optimal strategies U_{-i}^*. It has been argued that this is the case for reaction in *pedestrian motions*, where as a substitute for problem (6.14)–(6.15), the following BRS has been proposed (see [DHL14] and the references therein):

$$u_i(t) = -\partial_{x_i} h_i\left[X(s)\right], \quad \text{for } t \in [0, \tau]. \tag{6.16}$$

The BRS (6.16) can be obtained from a MPC approach (see [MM90]) applied to equations (6.14) and (6.15). In order to derive the BRS, the following problem has been considered in [DHL14]: suppose we are given the state $X(t)$ of the system (6.14) at time $t > 0$. Then, we consider a small control horizon of the MPC of $\tau > 0$. It is assumed that the applied control $u_i(s)$ on $(t, t + \tau)$ is constant. For particle each i, the unknown constant is denote by $\tilde{u}_i$. Instead of solving the problem (6.15) now on the full time interval (t, τ) we consider the objective function only on the receding time horizon $(t, t + \tau)$. Further, we discretize the dynamics (6.14) on $(t, t + \tau)$ using an explicit Euler discretization for the initial value $\bar{X} = X_i(t)$. We discretize the objective function by a Riemann sum. A naive discretization leads to a penalization of the control of

---

[16] The minimization is performed on all sufficiently smooth functions $u_i : [0, T] \to \mathbb{R}$ and there is no restriction on the control u_i. The objective $h_i : \mathbb{R}^N \to \mathbb{R}$ related to particle i is supposed to be sufficiently smooth. The weights of the control $\alpha_i(t) > 0$, for all i and $t \geq 0$ and under additional conditions convexity of each optimization problem (6.15) is guaranteed.

the type $\frac{\alpha_i(t+\tau)}{2}\tilde{u}^2$. To obtain a meaningful control in the MPC problem we need to scale the penalization of the control accordingly by τ. This leads to a MPC problem associated with equation (6.15) and given by:

$$x_i(t+\tau) = \bar{x}_i + \tau\left(f_i(\bar{X}) + \tilde{u}_i\right), \qquad (i = 1, \ldots, N), \tag{6.17}$$

$$\tilde{u}_i = \underset{\tilde{u}\in\mathbb{R}}{\text{argmin}} \, \tau\left(h_i\left(X(t+\tau)\right) + \tau\frac{\alpha_i(t+\tau)}{2}\tilde{u}^2\right). \tag{6.18}$$

Solving the minimization problem (6.18) leads to: $\alpha_i(t+\tau)\,\tilde{u}_i = -\partial_{x_i}h_i(\bar{X})$. Now, we obtain a $\tilde{u}_i$ of order $O(1)$ by Taylor expansion of α_i at time t. Within the MPC approach, the control for the time interval $(t, t+\tau)$ is therefore given by equation (6.19):

$$\tilde{u}_i = -\frac{1}{\alpha_i(t)}\partial_{x_i}h_i(\bar{X}). \tag{6.19}$$

Usually, the dynamics (6.17) is then computed with the control computed up to $t + \tau$. Then, the process is repeated using the new state $X(t + \tau)$. Substituting (6.19) into (6.17) and letting $\tau \to 0$ we obtain (for $i = 1, \ldots, N$, $t \in [0, \tau]$):

$$\dot{x}_i(t) = f_i(X(t)) - \frac{1}{\alpha_i(t)}\partial_{x_i}h_i(X(t)), \tag{6.20}$$

This dynamics coincide with the dynamics generated by the best–reply strategy (6.16) provided that $\alpha_i(t) \equiv 1$. Therefore, on a particle level the controlled dynamics (6.20) of the BRS is equivalent to a MPC formulation of the problem (6.15). A particular toy example can be obtained in the form:

$$\dot{x}_i(t) = \frac{1}{N}\sum_{j=1}^{N} P(x_i, x_j)(x_j - x_i) - \frac{1}{(N-1)\alpha_i(t)}\sum_{j=1, j\neq i}^{N} \partial_{x_i}\phi(x_i, x_j). \tag{6.21}$$

For the derivations and more technical details, see [DHL14] and the references therein.

6.9 PCT Alternative 3: Synergetics Approach to CPC-Autonomy

The so-called *synergetics* is an interdisciplinary field of research that was founded by H. Haken in 1969 (see [Hak83, Hak93, Hak96, Hak00]). Synergetics deals with complex systems that are composed of many individual parts (components, elements) that interact with each other and are able to produce spatial, temporal or functional structures by self–organization. In particular, synergetics searches for general principles governing self–organization irrespective of the nature of the individual parts of the systems that may belong to a variety of disciplines such as physics (lasers, fluids, plasmas), meteorology, chemistry (pattern formation by chemical reactions, including flames), biology (morphogenesis, evolution theory) movement science, brain activities, computer sciences (synergetic computer), sociology (e.g., city growth) psychology and psychiatry (including Gestalt psychology).

The aim of synergetics has been to describe processes of *spontaneous self–organization and cooperation* in complex systems built from many subsystems which themselves can be complicated nonlinear objects (like many individual neuro–muscular components of the human motion system, having their own excitation and contraction dynamics, embedded in a synergistic way to produce coordinated human movement). General properties of the subsystems are their own nonlinear/chaotic dynamics as well as mutual nonlinear/chaotic interactions. Furthermore, the systems of synergetics are *open*. The influence from outside is measured by a certain set of *control parameters* $\{\sigma\}$ (like amplitudes, frequencies and time characteristics of neuro–muscular driving forces). Processes of self-organization in synergetics, (like musculo–skeletal coordination in human motion dynamics) are observed as temporal macroscopic patterns. They are described by a small set of *order parameters* $\{o\}$, similar to those in Landau's *phase–transition theory* (named after *Nobel Laureate Lev D. Landau*) of physical systems in *thermal equilibrium* [Hak83].

Now, recall that the *measure for the degree of disorder* in any isolated, or conservative, system (such a system that does not interact with its surrounding, i.e., does neither dissipate nor gain energy) is *entropy*. The *second law of thermodynamics*[17] states that in every conservative irreversible system the entropy ever increases to its maximal value, i.e., to the total disorder of the system (or remains constant for a reversible system).

Example of such a system is conservative Hamiltonian dynamics of human skeleton in the phase–space Γ defined by all joint angles q^i and momenta p_i,[18] defined by ordinary (conservative) Hamilton's equations

$$\dot{q}^i = \partial_{p_i} H, \qquad \dot{p}_i = -\partial_{q^i} H. \tag{6.22}$$

The basic fact of the conservative Hamiltonian system is that its phase–flow, the time evolution of equations (6.22), preserves the phase–space volume (the so-called *Liouville measure*), as proposed by the *Liouville theorem*. This might look fine at first sight, however, the preservation of phase–space volume causes *structural instability* of the conservative Hamiltonian system, i.e., the phase–space spreading effect, by which small phase regions R_t will tend to get distorted from the initial one R_0 during the system evolution. The problem is much more serious in higher dimensions than in lower dimensions, since there are so many 'directions' in which the region can locally spread. Here we see the work of the second law of thermodynamics on an irreversible process: the increase of entropy towards the total disorder/chaos [Pen89]. In this way, the

---

[17] This is the only physical law that implies the arrow of time.

[18] If we neglect joints dissipation and muscular driving forces, we are dealing with pure skeleton conservative dynamics.

conservative Hamiltonian systems of the form (6.22) cover the wide range of dynamics, from completely integrable, to completely ergodic. Biodynamics of human–like movement is probably somewhere in the middle of this range, the more DOF included in the model, the closer to the ergodic case. One can easily imagine that the conservative skeleton–like system with 300 DOF, which means 600–D system of the form (6.22), which is full of trigonometry (coming from its noncommutative rotational matrices), is probably closer to the ergodic than to the completely integrable case.

On the other hand, when we manipulate a system from the outside, by the use of certain *control parameters* $\{\sigma\}$, we can change its *degree of order* (see [Hak83, Hak93]). Consider for example *water vapor*. At elevated temperature its molecules move freely without mutual correlation. When temperature is lowered, a liquid drop is formed, the molecules now keep a mean distance between each other. Their motion is thus highly correlated. Finally, at still lower temperature, at the freezing point, water is transformed into ice crystals. The transitions between the different aggregate states, also called phases, are quite abrupt. Though the same kind of molecules are involved all the time, the macroscopic features of the three phases differ drastically.

Similar type of ordering, but not related to the thermal equilibrium conditions, occurs in *lasers*, mathematically given by Lorenz–like attractor equations. Lasers are certain types of lamps which are capable of emitting coherent light. A typical laser consists of a crystal rod filled with gas, with the following features important from the synergetics point of view: when the atoms the laser material consists of are excited or 'pumped' from the outside, they emit light waves. So, the pump power, or pump rate represents the control parameter σ. At low pump power, the waves are entirely uncorrelated as in a usual lamp. Could we hear light, it would sound like noise to us [Hak83].

When we increase the pump rate to a critical value σ_c, the noise disappears and is replaced by a pure tone. This means that the atoms emit a pure sinusoidal light wave which in turn means that the individual atoms act in a perfectly correlated way — they become self–organized. When the pump rate is increased beyond a second critical value, the laser may periodically emit very intense and short pulses. In this way the following *instability sequence* occurs [Hak83]:

$$\text{noise} \mapsto \{\text{coherent oscillation at frequency}\,\omega_1\} \mapsto$$

periodic pulses at frequency ω_2 which modulate oscillation at frequency ω_1

i.e., no oscillation $\mapsto$ first frequency $\mapsto$ second frequency.

Under different conditions the light emission may become *chaotic* or even *turbulent*. The frequency spectrum becomes broadened.

The laser played a crucial role in the development of synergetics for various reasons [Hak83]. In particular, it allowed detailed theoretical and experimental study of the phenomena occurring within the transition region: *lamp* $\leftrightarrow$ *laser*, where a surprising and far–reaching analogy with phase transitions of systems in thermal equilibrium was discovered. This analogy includes all basic *phase–transition effects*: a *symmetry breaking instability*, *critical slowing down* and *hysteresis effect*.

6.9.1 Nonequilibrium Phase Transitions

Besides water vapor, a typical example is a *ferromagnet* [Hak83]. When a ferromagnet is heated, it suddenly loses its magnetization. When temperature is lowered, the magnet suddenly regains its magnetization. What happens on a microscopic, atomic level, is this: We may visualize the magnet as being composed of many, elementary (atomic) magnets (called spins). At elevated temperature, the elementary magnets point in random directions. Their magnetic moments, when added up, cancel each other and no macroscopic magnetization results. Below a critical value of temperature T_c, the elementary magnets are lined up, giving rise to a macroscopic magnetization. Thus the *order on the microscopic level* is a cause of a *new feature* of the material *on the macroscopic level*. The change of one phase to the other one is called *phase transition*.

A thermodynamical description of ferromagnet is based on analysis of its *free energy potential* (in thermal equilibrium conditions). The free energy $\mathcal{F}$, depends on the *control parameter* $\sigma = T$, the temperature. We seek the minimum of the potential $\mathcal{F}$ for a fixed value of magnetization o, which is called *order parameter* in Landau's theory of phase transitions.

This phenomenon is called a *phase transition of second order* because the second derivative (specific heat) of the free energy potential $\mathcal{F}$ is discontinuous. On the other hand, the entropy S (the first derivative of $\mathcal{F}$) itself is continuous so that this transition is also referred to as a *continuous phase transition*.

In statistical physics one also investigates the temporal change of the order parameter — magnetization o. Usually, in a more or less phenomenological manner, one assumes that o obeys an equation of the form

$$\dot{o} = -\frac{\partial \mathcal{F}}{\partial o} = -\sigma o - \beta o^3. \tag{6.23}$$

For $\sigma \to 0$ we observe a phenomenon called *critical slowing down*, because the 'particle' with coordinate o falls down the slope of the 'potential well' more and more slowly. Simple relation (6.23) is called *order parameter equation*.

We now turn to the case where the free energy potential has the form

$$\mathcal{F}(o, T) = \frac{\sigma}{2}o^2 + \frac{\gamma}{3}o^3 + \frac{\beta}{4}o^4, \tag{6.24}$$

(β and γ — positive but σ may change its sign according to $\sigma = a(T - T_c)$, $(a > 0)$). When we change the control parameter — temperature T, i.e., the parameter σ, we pass through a sequence of deformations of the potential curve.

When lowering temperature, the local minimum first remains at $o_0 = 0$. When lowering temperature, the 'particle' may fall down from o_0 to the new (global) minimum of $\mathcal{F}$ at o_1. The entropies of the two states, o_0 and o_1, differ. This phenomenon is called a *phase transition of first order* because the first derivative of the potential $\mathcal{F}$ with respect to the control parameter T is discontinuous. Since the entropy S is discontinuous this transition is also referred to as a *discontinuous phase transition*. When we now increase the temperature, is apparent that the system stays at o_1 longer than it had been before when lowering the control parameter. This represents *hysteresis effect*.

In the case of the potential (6.24) the order parameter equation gets the form

$$\dot{o} = -\sigma o - \gamma o^2 - \beta o^3.$$

Similar *disorder* $\Rightarrow$ *order* transitions occur also in various non–equilibrium systems of physics, chemistry, biology, psychology, sociology, as well as in human motion dynamics. The analogy is subsumed in Table 6.1.

Table 6.1. *Phase transition analogy.*

System in thermal equilibrium	Non–equilibrium system
Free energy potential $\mathcal{F}$	Generalized potential V
Order parameters o_i	Order parameters o_i
$\dot{o}_i = -\frac{\partial \mathcal{F}}{\partial o_i}$	$\dot{o}_i = -\frac{\partial V}{\partial o_i}$
Temperature T	Control input u
Entropy S	System output y
Specific Heat c	System efficiency e

In the case of human motion dynamics, natural control inputs u_i are muscular torques F_i, natural system outputs y_i are joint coordinates q^i and momenta p_i, while the system efficiencies e_i represent the changes of coordinates and momenta with changes of corresponding muscular torques for the ith joint,

$$e_i^q = \frac{\partial q^i}{\partial F_i}, \qquad e_i^p = \frac{\partial p_i}{\partial F_i}.$$

Order parameters o_i represent certain important qualities of the human motion system, depending on muscular torques as control inputs, similar to *magnetization*, and usually defined by equations similar to (6.23) or

$$\dot{o}_i = -\sigma o - \gamma o^2 - \beta o^3,$$

with nonnegative parameters σ, β, γ, and corresponding to the second and first order phase transitions, respectively. The choice of actual order parameters is a matter of *expert knowledge* and *purpose of macroscopic system modeling* [Hak83].

6.10 A Model-Free PCT Alternative: Adaptive Fuzzy Inference for Human-Like Decision and Control

In this section we propose a brief overview of the model-free PCT alternative: the fuzzy control technology (see, e.g. [PY97] for the technical introduction).

6.10.1 Motivation: Why Adaptive Fuzzy Inference?

Two Approaches to Controlled Complexity

From control-theoretic perspective, there are two standard approaches to controlling complex systems:

- Hard approach of differential or difference equations for modeling *sensors, motions and controllers* (e.g., as implemented in *Control Toolbox* and *Signal Toolbox* of *Matlab/Simulink®*); and
- Soft, model-free, approach of Computational Intelligence.

In this section, we focus on the soft framework of computational-intelligence. The term 'Computational Intelligence' (CI) was coined by IEEE. The IEEE CI-Society publishes three transactions journals:

- IEEE Transactions on Neural Networks;
- IEEE Transactions on Fuzzy Systems; and
- IEEE Transactions on Evolutionary Computation.

Thus, it is implicitly assumed that CI consists of these three areas and their combinations. Two main CI characteristics are: adaptation and knowledge-base.

Here, we focus on *adaptive fuzzy inference system* (AFIS), which is an efficient control technology, already available in a chip (and used e.g. in a dishwasher, camcorder, etc.; see, e.g. [Zim95]). Then, any compatible ANN model would be a nice addition. We remark that, *adaptivity* (or, learning) is not necessarily neural; it can also be of fuzzy own self-organization type (see [LM97] and references therein), or some evolutionary computation type (e.g., GA), or just a simple matrix iteration:

$$New\ Value\,(t+1)\ =\ Old\ Value\,(t)\ +\ Innovation\,(t+1),$$

$$\text{with}\quad Innovation_{\text{Kalman}} = |desired\ output\ -\ achieved\ output|$$

$$\text{or}\quad Innovation_{\text{Suton.Barto}} = |reward - penalty|.$$

Recently, as a part of the Crowd Simulator development (see [IR12] and references therein), a 3D pole-on-a-cart test (with a ball joint, see Figure 6.13) has been performed at DSTO. Performance of the following controllers has been compared:

1. Human controller (with a mouse);

Fig. 6.13. *3D pole-on-a-cart test.*

2. Fuzzy-logic controller (a simple fen controller extended);
3. Kohonen SOM controller (designed for pole-balancing);
4. Boltzmann machine with simulated annealing;
5. Genetic algorithm controller; and
6. Gradient-descent optimizer.

Result: *only fuzzy-logic controller* can hold the pole forever! Fuzzy control is a superior control technology already in a chip (see, e.g. [LT00, PY97]).

An Easy Fuzzy Control Example: Truck Backer-Upper

Let's start with a textbook fuzzy-control example: *truck backer-upper steering control system*. It's basic characteristics are the following:

- Two input linguistic variables: position and direction of the truck, and one output variable: steering angle.
- Invars:
  1. position = {NL,NS,ZR,PS,PL} and
  2. direction = {NL,NM,NS,ZR,PS,PM,PL}
  where NL denotes Negative Large, NM is Negative Medium, NS is Negative Small, etc.
- Outvar: steering angle = {NL,NM,NS,ZR,PS,PM,PL}

Truck backer-upper: defining fuzzy sets/membership functions

Only output fuzzy sets are shown here:

defineSet [NB, -30, 1, -15, 0, -15, 0, -15, 0];
defineSet [NM, -25, 0, -15, 1, -15, 1, -5, 0];
defineSet [NS, -12, 0, -6, 1, -6, 1, 0, 0];
defineSet [ZE, -5, 0, 0, 1, 0, 1, 5, 0];

defineSet [PS, 0, 0, 6, 1, 6, 1, 12, 0];
defineSet [PM, 5, 0, 15, 1, 15, 1, 25, 0];
defineSet [PB, 18, 0, 30, 1, 30, 1, 30, 1];

Fuzzy IF-THEN rules for the truck backer-upper control are:

IF direction is NL & position is NL, THEN steering angle is NL;
IF direction is NL & position is NS, THEN steering angle is NL;
IF direction is NL & position is ZE, THEN steering angle is PL;
IF direction is NL & position is PS, THEN steering angle is PL;
IF direction is NL & position is PL, THEN steering angle is PL;
IF direction is NM & position is NL, THEN steering angle is ZE;
. . . .
IF direction is PL & position is PL, THEN steering angle is PL.

FAM matrix representation

B. Kosko's FAM matrix representation for the fuzzy IF-THEN rules (elegant, but works only for $2 \to 1$ case):

$$\begin{pmatrix} PS(\theta) & PM(\theta) & PM(\theta) & PM(\theta) & PB(\theta) \\ NS(\theta) & PS(\theta) & PM(\theta) & PB(\theta) & PB(\theta) \\ NM(\theta) & NS(\theta) & PS(\theta) & PM(\theta) & PB(\theta) \\ NM(\theta) & NM(\theta) & ZE(\theta) & PM(\theta) & PM(\theta) \\ NB(\theta) & NM(\theta) & NS(\theta) & PS(\theta) & PM(\theta) \\ NB(\theta) & NB(\theta) & NM(\theta) & NS(\theta) & PS(\theta) \\ NB(\theta) & NB(\theta) & NM(\theta) & NM(\theta) & NS(\theta) \end{pmatrix}$$

6.10.2 Standard Fuzzy Control Example: Balancing an Inverted Pendulum

Recall that an *inverted pendulum control problem* is:

- Popular in conventional control theory: there is a demo in *Matlab/ Simulink*®.
- Also popular in PCT: Bill Powers wrote a paper on it;
- Still, it is only a 1DOF dynamical system (the angle θ) which cannot be chaotic ("There cannot be chaos in a phase plane").
- A challenge for neural networks and fuzzy systems in late 1980s was to balance a double and triple pendulum (or, a double pendulum with a glass of water on top).
- Question: Can we learn how to control a system with 50 degrees-of-freedom (DOF) by deep studying a 1DOF system? Answer: No! We need the modern (nonlinear & MIMO) control theory, not the conventional (linear & SISO) control theory.

Inverted Pendulum Control: Mechanics

Both Matlab and Powers try to balance the pendulum using the *force controller* (2nd derivative), which is like pushing the car by a hand. Much more efficient is the *velocity controller* (1st derivative), which is like pressing a pedal in a car (accelerator or brake) and the engine does the control. When a human operator controls a mechanical system, they apply muscular force, but mentally focus on controlling velocity and position. Formally, this means rewriting the Newtonian (or Lagrangian) equation of pendulum's motion that allows only for a force control, as a pair of Hamilton's equations, which allow both force and velocity controllers (see, e.g. [PY97] for technical details).

Possible Problem with Fuzzy Inference: Explosion of Rules

For any control problem with many DOF, there is a possibility for the explosion of the number of fuzzy IF-THEN rules. This problem has been successfully resolved in three ways:

- Classical solution: putting random weights on the rules and, after an off-line training, using only a 'significant' subset of rules;
- Control solution: braking the control system into several, well-defined, subsystems, with limited number of rules;
- Modern solution: rules compression — a modern technique of the fuzzy-space reduction (by removing the redundancy in the fuzzy rule base).

A Harder Control Problem: Truck-and-Trailer Backer-Upper

This is a nontrivial control problem (even for a human operator). Still, a number of efficient nonlinear controllers exist:

- sliding mode controllers;
- extended/unscented Kalman filters;
- fuzzy-logic, ANN, and GA-controllers;
- specially-designed nonlinear controllers (e.g., Lorenz attractor controller for Matlab), etc.

A Very Hard Control Problem: Truck-with-Two (or Several) Trailers Backer-Upper Steering System

To the best of our knowledge, only two solutions exist:

- A *soft control approach* of (adaptive) *fuzzy-logic controller*; and
- A *hard control approach* of (adaptive) *Lie-derivative controller* (together with its exterior-differential dual).
- Unless we want to dig deep into differential geometry, **AFIS** is the only option.

- Besides, many different fuzzy-chips already exist, starting from Motorola's 1996 pioneering one. Current Motorola chip 68HC12 is the standard microcontroller family with a comprehensive fuzzy-logic instruction set and an arbitrary number of inputs and outputs.

6.10.3 History and Basics of Fuzzy Logic

Brief History of Fuzzy Logic

1965 Fuzzy Sets Theory founded by Lotfi Zadeh (UC Berkeley); Zadeh subsequently founded both Fuzzy Logic and Possibility Theory.
1970 Fuzzy-Logic Control founded by E. Mamdani (Queen-Mary College, London) and H. Zimmermann (RWTH Univ. Aachen, Germany);
1975 Introduction of Fuzzy Logic in Japan;
1985 Broad application of Fuzzy Logic in Japan;[19]
1990 Broad application of Fuzzy Logic in Europe;
1995 Broad application of Fuzzy Logic in the US, in spite of two major obstacles: (i) wrong name "fuzzy", and (ii) strong Bayesian probability community, which did not like the possibility-theory competitor.

1996 IEEE Study of Fuzzy-Logic Applications

- Published over 1100 successful fuzzy-logic applications (an estimated 5% of those in existence);
- Almost all applications were MIMO supervisory control, rather than replacement of conventional SISO controllers;
- Applications range from Embedded Control (28%), Industrial Automation (62%) to Process Control (10%);
- In most cases, Fuzzy Logic has slashed Design time by more than half.

Fuzzy Sets

A crisp set X is defined by a binary *characteristic function* $\mu_X(x)$ of its elements x:
$$\mu_X(x) = \begin{cases} 1, & \text{if } x \in X, \\ 0, & \text{if } x \notin X, \end{cases}$$

while a fuzzy set is defined by a continuous characteristic function (which is now called the *membership function*):
$$\mu_X(x) = [0,1] \,,$$

---

[19] Interest in fuzzy systems was sparked by S. Yasunobu and S. Miyamoto of Hitachi, who in 1985 provided simulations that demonstrated the superiority of fuzzy control systems for the Sendai railway.

including all (possible) real values between the two crisp extremes 1 and 0, and including them as special cases.

A fuzzy set X is a collection of ordered pairs

$$X = \{(x, \mu(x))\},$$

where $\mu(x)$ is the *membership function* representing the grade of membership of the element x in the set X.

A single pair is called a fuzzy *singleton* (for technical details, including *possibility theory*, see Zadeh, 1965; 1978).

Fuzzy Inference System (FIS) is a model-free MIMO-system that works as a general function approximator.

FIS *maps* a set of input linguistic variables (IF−part) into a set of output linguistic variables ($THEN$−part).

FIS consists of three sequential modules:

Fuzzification $\Rightarrow$ Inference $\Rightarrow$ Defuzzification

6.10.4 Fuzzy Inference System

The *fuzzy inference system* (FIS) represents the following three-link cascade:

$$InVars \Rightarrow \boxed{\text{Fuzzification}} \Rightarrow \boxed{\text{Inference}} \Rightarrow \boxed{\text{Defuzzification}} \Rightarrow OutVars$$

Fuzzification Module

In the *fuzzification module*, numerical crisp input variables are fuzzified. This is performed as an overlapping partition of their universes of discourse by means of fuzzy membership functions $\mu(x)$, which can have various shapes, including triangular/trapezoidal (shown before), Gaussian:

$$\mu(x) = \exp\left[\frac{-(x-m)^2}{2\sigma^2}\right],$$

(with mean m and standard deviation σ), and sigmoid:

$$\mu(x) = \left[1 + \left(\frac{x-m}{\sigma}\right)^2\right]^{-1}.$$

Inference Module has Two Submodules

The *inference module* has two submodules:

(i) The expert–knowledge base consisting of a set of fuzzy IF-THEN rules relating input and output variables, and

(ii) The inference method, or implication operator, that actually combines the rules to give the fuzzy output. Most common is *Mamdani Min–Max inference*, in which the membership functions for input variables are first combined inside the IF-THEN rules using AND ($\cap$, or Min) operator, and then the output fuzzy sets from different IF-THEN rules are combined using OR ($\cup$, or Max) operator to get the common fuzzy output.

Defuzzification Module

In the *defuzzification module*, fuzzy-linguistic outputs from the inference module are converted to numerical crisp values.

This is achieved by one of the several defuzzification algorithms.

Most common is the *centroid defuzzification*, or Center of Mass (CoM) method, in which the crisp output value is calculated as the abscissa under the center of mass/gravity of the output fuzzy set.

Two Optional Modules

In more complex technical applications of general function approximation, two optional blocks are usually added to the FIS:

- Preprocessor, preceding the fuzzification module, performing various kinds of normalization, scaling, filtering, averaging, differentiation or integration of input data.
- Postprocessor, succeeding the defuzzification module, performing the analog operations on output data.

AFIS: Adaptive Fuzzy Inference System

AFIS makes (some of) the following parameters adjustable:

- Weights on the fuzzy IF-THEN rules;
- Parameters in membership functions (e.g. mean and standard deviation in case of Gaussian fuzzy sets); and
- Centroid (CoM) parameters.

Special Case: Neural AFIS

Although FIS adaptivity can be achieved both by simple matrix iteration:

$$NewVal_{t+1} = OldVal_t + Innov_{t+1},$$

or by GA-evolution, the most common is a *feedforward three-layer perceptron* (for technical details, see [KKK07] and references therein).

6.10.5 Fuzzy Control Basics

There are Four Basics Types of Fuzzy Control:

- Direct Fuzzy Control (rare);
- Supervisory Fuzzy Control (usual);
- Adaptive Fuzzy Control (by design, without NN); and
- Fuzzy Intervention Control.

Direct Fuzzy Control

Here, the FIS-output gives the *command variables* for direct control of an arbitrary plant (see Figure 6.14). In other words, FIS works here like a conventional PID controller ("on steroids").

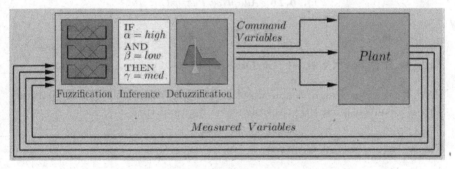

Fig. 6.14. *Direct Fuzzy Control.*

Supervisory Fuzzy Control

Here, FIS sets the values for a cluster of PID controllers (see Figure 6.15). This is (clearly) a more appropriate FIS-application.

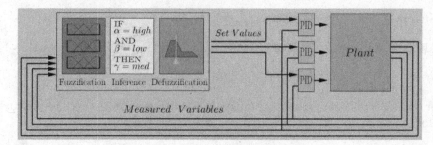

Fig. 6.15. *Supervisory Fuzzy Control.*

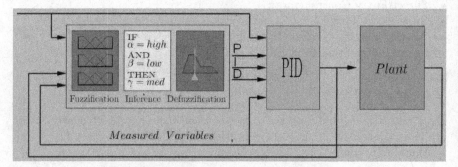

Fig. 6.16. *Adaptive Fuzzy Control.*

Adaptive Fuzzy Control (by Design)

Here, by its own design, a non-adaptive FIS sets/adapts the (P,I,D) parameters of a conventional PID controller (see Figure 6.16).

Fuzzy Intervention Control

Here, FIS-controller and a conventional PID-controller are working in parallel (see Figure 6.17).

6.10.6 Two Detailed Fuzzy Control Examples

Classical Crane Example

As an example of an efficient fuzzy–logic control, consider the standard crane problem: the container (load) is already picked up from the ship. It must be positioned over the truck, so that the container can be released. Crane containers load and unload containers to and from ships in most harbors.

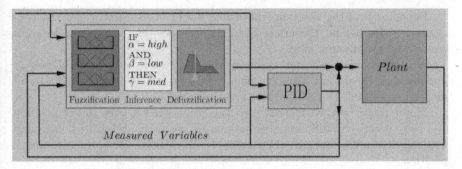

Fig. 6.17. Fuzzy Intervention Control.

They pick up single containers with flexible cables mounted at the crane head. The crane head moves on a horizontal track. When a container is picked up and the crane head starts to move, the container begins to sway. While sway does not affect the transport, a swaying container cannot be released.

There are two trivial solutions to this problem. One is to position the crane head exactly over the target position and wait until the sway dampens to an acceptable level. On a non–windy day, this eventually happens, but it takes far too much time. A container ship has to be loaded and unloaded in minimum time.

The alternative is to move the container so slowly that no sway occurs. Again, this technique works on a non–windy day and takes too much time.

Another solution is to build container cranes where additional cables fix the position of the container during operation. This alternative is very expensive.

Many engineers have attempted to automate this control task via conventional PID, model–based, and fuzzy–logic control strategies.

Conventional PID control was unsuccessful because the control task is inherently nonlinear. For example, sway minimization is important only when the container is close to the target.

Others have tried to derive a mathematical model of the crane to use in a model-based controller. They came up with a fifth-degree differential equation that describes the mechanical behavior. In theory, a controller design based on this model works. In reality, it does not.

One reason for failure is that the weight of the container is unknown. Also, the crane–motor behavior is not as linear as assumed in the model. Its gear box involves slack, its head only moves with friction, and its cables involve elasticity. As well, disturbances such as wind gusts are not included in the model.

On the other hand, a human operator can control a crane without differential equations. An operator does not even use the cable–length sensors that a model–based solution requires. Once the container is picked up, the operator starts the crane with medium motor power to see how the container sways.

Depending on the reaction, the motor power is adjusted to get the container a little behind the crane head. In this position, maximum speed is reached with minimum sway.

In approaching the target position, the operator reduces motor power or applies negative power. The container gets a little ahead of the crane head until the container almost reaches target position.

Motor power is then increased so the crane head is over target position and sway is zero. No differential equations are required, and disturbances and nonlinearities are compensated by the operator's observation of the container's position.

The operator's control strategy can be described by several rules:
(i) start with medium power; (ii) if you're still far away from the target, adjust the motor power so the container gets a little behind the crane head; (iii) if you're closer to the target, reduce speed so the container gets a little ahead of the crane head (iv) when the container is very close to target position, power up the motor; (v) when the container is over the target and the sway is zero, stop the motor [Alt95].

The advantage of fuzzy logic is that it can use the same sort of rules as the human operator.

Table 6.2. *Fuzzy IF–THEN rule–base for the crane controller.*

No.	Angle	Distance	Power
1	PS	0	NS
2	0	0	0
3	PS	Cl	NS
4	0	Cl	0
5	NS	Cl	PS
6	NS	Md	PB
7	NB	MD	PS
8	0	FR	PS
9	NS	FR	PB

To automate control of this crane, sensors are used for the head position (Distance x) and the angle of the container sway (Angle θ). Using these inputs to describe the current condition of the crane, the rules can be translated into the fuzzy IF–THEN statements. Where, the first condition describes the value of Distance, and the second the value of Angle. The conditions are combined by AND since both have to be valid for the respective situation. The full fuzzy–rule base is given in Table 6.2.

In a fuzzy–logic crane controller, all sensor signals have to be translated into linguistic variables. A measured distance of 12m has to be translated to the linguistic value 'still medium, just slightly far'. This step is called fuzzification because it uses fuzzy sets for translating real variables into linguistic variables. Once all input variable values are translated into linguistic variable values, the so-called fuzzy–inference step evaluates the IF–THEN fuzzy rules that define system behavior. This step yields a linguistic value for the linguistic variable. So, the linguistic result for Power could be 'a little less than medium'. Finally, defuzzification translates this linguistic result into a real value that represents the power setting of the motor in kilowatts.

Recall that the development of fuzzy–logic systems involves specific design steps:
(i) Design the inference structure, specify how the output variables connect to the input variables by the rule blocks. (ii) Define the linguistic variables, the variables form the vocabulary used by the fuzzy–logic rules expressing the control strategy. (iii) Create an initial fuzzy–logic rule base using all available knowledge on how the system should perform. (iv) Debug, test, and verify the system off–line for completeness and non–ambiguity, use a software simulation or sample data of the process if it exists in this step. (v) Debug online, connect the fuzzy–logic system to the process under control and analyze its performance in operation. Because fuzzy logic lets you modify the system in a straightforward way from the performance you observe, this step can expedite system design rapidly.

On a standard 12MHz 8051 micro–controller (MCU), small fuzzy–logic systems compute in just one millisecond, and 16–bit MCUs can compute large fuzzy–logic systems in the same amount of time. This speed enables the integration of a fuzzy–logic system with most embedded system designs. However, some embedded system applications require even faster computation (e.g., anti–lock brakes in cars, ignition control, or hard–drive positioning). To expedite the fuzzy–logic algorithm, some semiconductor manufacturers include specific fuzzy–logic instructions with their new–generation MCUs. For example, Motorola's 68HC12 MCU features a complete fuzzy–logic function set in assembly language.

6.10.7 Conclusion: When to Use Adaptive Fuzzy Inference?

Recall that there is a train in Japan (Sendai subway), which is controlled by fuzzy logic. While the ride on this train is so smooth that the passengers do not need to hold straps, train pulls into the station within a few inches of its target and its timing is within a minute.

Comment by E. Cox [Cox92]: Fuzzy control is more accurate, but nevertheless replacing human expert-control.

And this is roughly a recipe when to use AFIS.
   Def: *AFIS is a model-free strategy for human-like control of high-dimensional complex systems with uncertainty.*
So, AFIS should be used in the following 4 cases:

- When the problem is too complex (or, too hard) for one to be able to derive exact system's state/control equations.
- When there is a lot of practical (intuitive) expert knowledge available (e.g. pilot, driver, worker, player).
- When there are many inputs (e.g. 10) and outputs (e.g. 5).
- When the problem scenario is full of uncertainty (or, imprecision).

For more technical details on general model-free fuzzy logic control, see [II07a]; for its human operator modeling application, see [IJM10].

6.10.8 Mathematical Takagi–Sugeno Fuzzy Dynamics

Although fuzzy inference can be used without any formal mathematics, in the form of the so-called *Mamdani Min–Max inference*, fuzzy logic can also complement any standard formal control methods, in the form of the so-called *Takagi–Sugeno inference*.

Basic Takagi–Sugeno Model

As is first proposed in [TS85] a nonlinear system can be described based on fuzzy approach in the following procedure [ZWL02]. First, the system is decomposed into simple linear systems through fuzzy implications (rules) of the following form:

Plant Rule i $(= 1, ..., r)$: IF θ_1 is μ_{i1} and ... θ_p is μ_{ip}
THEN $\dot{x}(t) = A_i x(t) + B_i u(t)$,

where $x(t) \in R^n$ is the vector of state variables, $u(t) \in R^m$ is the vector of control inputs, A_i and B_i are constant matrices of appropriate dimensions, $\theta_j(x)(j = 1, ..., p)$ are the premise variables, which are the functions of state variables, $\mu_{ij}(i = 1, ..., r; j = 1, ..., p)$ are the fuzzy sets, r is the number of the IF–THEN rules, and p is the number of the premise variables. It is assumed that the premise variables are independent of the input variables $u(t)$.

Second, the overall fuzzy model is achieved by fuzzy blending (aggregation) of each individual rule (model) as follows:

$$\dot{x}(t) = \frac{\sum_{i=1}^{r} \omega_i(\theta) \left[A_i x(t) + B_i u(t) \right]}{\sum_{i=1}^{r} \omega_i(\theta)}, \tag{6.25}$$

where $\theta = [\theta_1, ..., \theta_p]$ and $\omega_i : R^p \to [0, 1]$, $i = 1, ..., r$, are the membership function of the systems belonging to plant rule i.

Let us define

$$\alpha_i(\theta) = \frac{\omega_i(\theta)}{\sum_{i=1}^{r} \omega_i(\theta)}.$$

System (6.25) admits the following form:

$$\dot{x}(t) = \sum_{i=1}^{r} \alpha_i(\theta) \left[A_i x(t) + B_i u(t) \right], \tag{6.26}$$

with the constraints

$$\alpha_i(\theta) \geq 0, \qquad \sum_{i=1}^{r} \alpha_i(\theta) = 1.$$

Local and Global Fuzzy Dynamical Models

During the past two decades, many systematic fuzzy controller design methods have been developed based on the *Takagi–Sugeno (TS) fuzzy model* [TS85], or the fuzzy dynamic models. The basic idea of these methods is: (i) to represent the complex nonlinear system in a family of local linear models, each linear model represents the dynamics of the complex system in one local region; (ii) to construct a global nonlinear model by aggregating all the local models through the fuzzy membership functions. The primary advantage of this model is that the controller design can be mainly based on each local model, which is much easier than that for nonlinear systems in the global region, and then the global controller can be constructed from the local controllers.

Many physical systems are very complex in practice so that their rigorous mathematical models can be very difficult to get if not impossible. However, many physical systems can indeed be expressed in some form of mathematical models locally, or those systems can be expressed as an aggregation of a set of mathematical models. Various fuzzy models have been proposed in the last decade [TS85]. Feng [Fen02] considered using the following fuzzy model to represent a complex single–input single–output (SISO) continuous–time system that includes both fuzzy inference rules and local analytic linear models (in the state–space form):

$$R^i : \text{ IF } z_1 \text{ is } F_1^i \text{ AND } \dots z_s \text{ is } F_s^i \qquad (i = 1, ..., m) \tag{6.27}$$
$$\text{THEN } \dot{x}(t) = A_i x(t) + B_i u(t), \qquad y = C_i x(t), \qquad \text{where}$$

$$\begin{bmatrix} 0 & 1 & 0 & \dots & 0 \\ 0 & 0 & 1 & \dots & 0 \\ \vdots & \vdots & \vdots & \ddots & 0 \\ \vdots & \vdots & \vdots & \dots & 1 \\ a_{i1} & a_{i2} & a_{i3} & \dots & a_{in} \end{bmatrix}, \qquad B_i = \begin{bmatrix} 0 \\ 0 \\ \vdots \\ 0 \\ b_i \end{bmatrix}, \qquad C_i = \begin{bmatrix} 1 & 0 & \dots & 0 \end{bmatrix}.$$

The corresponding discrete–time TS–model reads:

$$R^i : \text{ IF } z_1 \text{ is } F_1^i \text{ AND } \dots z_s \text{ is } F_s^i \qquad (i = 1, ..., m)$$
$$\text{THEN } x(t+1) = A_i x(t) + B_i u(t), \qquad y = C_i x(t).$$

Let $\mu(z(t))$ be the normalized membership function of the inferred fuzzy set F^i in (6.27) where

$$F^i = \bigcap_{j=1}^{s} F_s^i \quad \text{and} \quad \sum_{i=1}^{m} = 1.$$

The model (6.27) only represents the properties of the system in a local region and thus is referred to as the *local fuzzy dynamical model*.

Now, by using a standard fuzzy inference method, that is, using a singleton fuzzifier, product fuzzy inference and center–average defuzzifier, the following *global fuzzy dynamical model* can be obtained (in the state–space form) [Fen02]:

$$\dot{x} = \mu_i A_i x + \mu_i B_i u, \qquad y = \mu_i C_i x.$$

Affine Fuzzy System

The continuous *affine fuzzy system* proposed in [KK02] has the following IF–THEN form :

$$R^i : \text{ IF } x_1 \text{ is } M_1^i \text{ AND ... } x_n \text{ is } M_n^i \qquad (6.28)$$
$$\text{THEN } \dot{x} = A_i x + \mu_i,$$

where $x^T = (x_1 x_2 ... x_n)$; R^i $(i = 1, ..., r)$ denotes the ith fuzzy rule and $M_1^i ... M_n^i$ are fuzzy variables. In (6.28), it can be noted that the local subsystem includes a constant affine term. The input–output form of the fuzzy system of (6.28) is represented as

$$\dot{x} = \frac{\omega_i (A_i x + \mu_i)}{\sum_{i=1}^{r} \omega_i} = h_i(x) [A_i x + \mu_i],$$

where

$$\omega_i(x) = \prod_{j=1}^{n} M_j^i(x_j), \qquad h_i(x) = \frac{\omega_i(x)}{\sum_{i=1}^{r} \omega_i(x)},$$

$$h_i(x) \geq 0, \qquad \sum_{i=1}^{r} h_i(x) = 1.$$

Fuzzy Modeling and Control of Chaotic Systems

TS-Modeling of Classical Chaotic Systems

The Takagi–Sugeno fuzzy model is a universal approximator for nonlinear dynamical systems. Following [TW01], we present n the TS modeling framework several typical chaotic systems with the control input term added.

Forced Lorenz Equations

Consider the standard Lorenz equations with the forcing (input) term:

$$\dot{x}_1(t) = -ax_1(t) + ax_2(t) + u(t),$$
$$\dot{x}_2(t) = cx_1(t) - x_2(t) - x_1(t)x_3(t),$$
$$\dot{x}_3(t) = x_1(t)x_2(t) - bx_3(t),$$

where a, b, c are constants and $u(t)$ is the input term. Assume that $x_1(t) \in [-d, d]$ and $d > 0$. Then, we can have the following fuzzy model which exactly represents the nonlinear equation under $x_1(t) \in [-d, d]$:

Rule 1 :   *IF* $x_1(t)$ *is* M_1,

THEN $\dot{x}(t) = A_1 x(t) + Bu(t)$;

Rule 2 :   *IF* $x_1(t)$ *is* M_2,

THEN $\dot{x}(t) = A_2 x(t) + Bu(t)$;

where

$$x(t) = [x_1(t) \quad x_2(t) \quad x_3(t)]^T,$$

$$A_1 = \begin{bmatrix} -a & a & 0 \\ c & -1 & -d \\ 0 & d & -b \end{bmatrix}, \quad A_2 = \begin{bmatrix} -a & a & 0 \\ c & -1 & d \\ 0 & -d & -b \end{bmatrix}, \quad B = \begin{bmatrix} 1 \\ 0 \\ 0 \end{bmatrix},$$

$$M_1(x_1(t)) = \frac{1}{2}\left(1 + \frac{x_1(t)}{d}\right), \quad M_2(x_1(t)) = \frac{1}{2}\left(1 - \frac{x_1(t)}{d}\right).$$

Forced Duffing Oscillator

Consider the forced Duffing oscillator:

$$\dot{x}_1(t) = x_2(t),$$
$$\dot{x}_2(t) = -x_1^3(t) - ax_2(t) + b\cos(t) + u(t).$$

where a, b are constants and $u(t)$ is the input term. Assume that $x_1(t) \in [-d, d]$ and $d > 0$. Then we can have the following fuzzy model (similar to the Lorenz one above):

Rule 1 :   *IF* $x_1(t)$ *is* M_1,

THEN $\dot{x}(t) = A_1 x(t) + Bu^*(t)$;

Rule 2 :   *IF* $x_1(t)$ *is* M_2,

THEN $\dot{x}(t) = A_2 x(t) + Bu^*(t)$;

where

$$x(t) = [x_1(t) \quad x_2(t)]^T, \quad u^*(t) = u(t) + b\cos(t)$$

$$A_1 = \begin{bmatrix} 0 & -1 \\ 0 & a \end{bmatrix}, \quad A_2 = \begin{bmatrix} 0 & 1 \\ -d^2 & a \end{bmatrix}, \quad B = \begin{bmatrix} 0 \\ 1 \end{bmatrix},$$

$$M_1(x_1(t)) = 1 - \frac{x_1^2(t)}{d^2}, \quad M_2(x_1(t)) = \frac{x_1^2(t)}{d^2}.$$

Forced Rossler Equations

Consider the forced Rossler equations:

$$\dot{x}_1(t) = -x_2(t) - x_3(t),$$

$$\dot{x}_2(t) = x_1(t) + ax_2(t),$$

$$\dot{x}_3(t) = bx_1(t) - [c - x_1(t)]x_3(t) + u(t),$$

where a, b, c are constants and $u(t)$ is the input term. Assume that $x_1(t) \in [-d, d]$ and $d > 0$. Then, we can have the following fuzzy model which exactly represents the nonlinear equation under $x_1(t) \in [-d, d]$:

Rule 1 :   IF $x_1(t)$ is M_1,
THEN $\dot{x}(t) = A_1 x(t) + Bu(t);$

Rule 2 :   IF $x_1(t)$ is M_2,
THEN $\dot{x}(t) = A_2 x(t) + Bu(t);$
where
$$x(t) = [x_1(t) \quad x_2(t) \quad x_3(t)]^T,$$

$$A_1 = \begin{bmatrix} 0 & -1 & -1 \\ 1 & a & 0 \\ b & 0 & -d \end{bmatrix}, \quad A_2 = \begin{bmatrix} 0 & -1 & -1 \\ 1 & a & 0 \\ b & 0 & d \end{bmatrix}, \quad B = \begin{bmatrix} 0 \\ 0 \\ 1 \end{bmatrix},$$

$$M_1(x_1(t)) = \frac{1}{2}\left(1 + \frac{c - x_1(t)}{d}\right), \quad M_2(x_1(t)) = \frac{1}{2}\left(1 - \frac{c - x_1(t)}{d}\right).$$

The fuzzy models above have a single input. We can also consider the multi–input case. For instance, we may consider Lorenz equations with multi–inputs:

$$\dot{x}_1(t) = -ax_1(t) + ax_2(t) + u_1(t),$$

$$\dot{x}_2(t) = cx_1(t) - x_2(t) - x_1(t)x_3(t) + u_2(t),$$

$$\dot{x}_3(t) = x_1(t)x_2(t) - bx_3(t) + u_2(t).$$

As before, we can derive the following fuzzy model to exactly represent the nonlinear ODEs under $x_1(t) \in [-d, d]$:

Rule 1 :   *IF* $x_1(t)$ *is* M_1,

THEN $\dot{x}(t) = A_1 x(t) + Bu(t)$;

Rule 2 :   *IF* $x_1(t)$ *is* M_2,

THEN $\dot{x}(t) = A_2 x(t) + Bu(t)$;

where

$$x(t) = [x_1(t) \quad x_2(t) \quad x_3(t)]^T, \qquad u(t) = [u_1(t) \quad u_2(t) \quad u_3(t)]^T,$$

$$A_1 = \begin{bmatrix} -a & a & 0 \\ c & -1 & -d \\ 0 & d & -b \end{bmatrix}, \quad A_2 = \begin{bmatrix} -a & a & 0 \\ c & -1 & d \\ 0 & -d & -b \end{bmatrix}, \quad B = \begin{bmatrix} 1 & 0 & 0 \\ 0 & 1 & 0 \\ 0 & 0 & 1 \end{bmatrix},$$

$$M_1(x_1(t)) = \frac{1}{2}\left(1 + \frac{x_1(t)}{d}\right), \qquad M_2(x_1(t)) = \frac{1}{2}\left(1 - \frac{x_1(t)}{d}\right).$$

CPC-Application: Using Wind Turbulence against a Team of UAVs

In this Chapter[1] we extend the modern theoretical concept of the 2D *quantum turbulence* (see [Tsu06, TKK10, IR12]), experimentally confirmed in *Bose-Einstein condensates* (BEC, see [PS03]), to derive the analytical (closed-form) model of the 3D *turbulent wind flow*, which we call the "wind canon." This *wind canon* is used as a *soft attrition* weapon against a *team of UAVs* flying in an urban environment, in which each UAV has a sophisticated *collision avoidance system* based on a 3D *fuzzy-logic collision-avoidance controller* (described below). In response to the wind turbulence, the team exhibits the behavior called *fuzzy entanglement*.

7.1 Analytical Model of Turbulent Wind Flow

Several years ago a crowd turbulence model was proposed in [IR12], based on the *nonlinear Schrödinger equation* (NLSE, see [Wik16aa] and the references therein), also called the *Gross-Pitaevskii equation* (GPE, see [PS03]). The NLSE determines the complex-valued spatiotemporal *macroscopic wave function* $\psi = \psi(x,t)$, whose absolute square $|\psi(x,t)|^2$ represents the *probability density function* (PDF) of a quantum fluid, or the average density of a compressible macroscopic fluid. The following (cubic, 'defocusing') NLSE form (in natural units) is usually considered:

$$i\partial_t \psi = -\frac{1}{2}\partial_{xx}\psi + V|\psi|^2\psi, \qquad (7.1)$$

where $\partial_u = \frac{\partial}{\partial u}$, $i = \sqrt{-1}$ and $V = V(x)$ represents the potential field of the fluid. The NLSE (7.1) is an integrable solitonic equation (which generates

---

[1] The work presented in this Chapter has been performed in collaboration with Dr. Sharon Boswell, Ag Group Leader Behavior and Control, Decision Sciences, Joint and Operations Analysis Division, Defence Science and Technology Group, Australia.

a variety of nonlinear traveling waves, see Figure 7.1) with the quantum-mechanical origin. It has many physical applications, including description of nonlinear waves and quantum turbulence in BEC, as well as Zakharov's envelope evolution of the (modulated) wave groups in water waves [ZMN80, Per83].

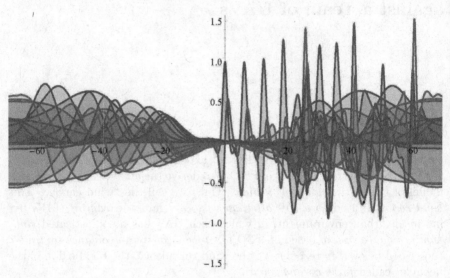

Fig. 7.1. *A variety of nonlinear traveling waves generated by the NLSE (7.1), including solitons, shock-waves and rogue-waves.*

More formally, the NLSE (7.1) determines the dynamics of the macroscopic wave-function:

$$\psi(x,t) = |\psi(x,t)|\,e^{i\phi(x,t)},$$

with the amplitude $|\psi| = |\psi(x,t)|$, whose square $|\psi|^2$ is the average density of a compressible fluid, and the phase $\phi = \phi(x,t)$, whose gradient $v = \partial_x\phi$ is the frictionless-flow velocity vector-field.

The fundamental characteristic of quantum turbulence is that, due to quantization of the circulation, *quantum superfluids* (e.g., BEC) respond to rotation with a 2D *lattice of quantized vortices* (i.e., vortices with quantized circulation: $\Gamma = \oint v \cdot dl$ for an arbitrary closed-loop l in the fluid), rather than with a single vortex. The so-called 'Feynman rule' states that the uniform fluid rotation with angular velocity Ω causes the *curl* of the fluid velocity which is equal to the number density N of a lattice of quantized vortices, given by [Fey55]:

$$N = \text{curl } v = 2\Omega = \int |\psi|^2 dx.$$

Quantum turbulence is comprised of N quantized vortices (see [Tsu06, TKK10, IR12] and the references therein).

Kolmogorov's energy spectra of a compressible fluid dynamics with a lattice of N quantized vortices are determined as follows. The total time-varying fluid energy $E(t)_{\text{tot}}$ is given by the sum of the kinetic energy $E_{\text{kin}}(t)$,[2] the interaction energy $E_{\text{int}}(t)$ and the quantum energy $E_{\text{qu}}(t)$ (see [NAB97a, NAB97b]):

$$E(t)_{\text{tot}} = E_{\text{kin}}(t) + E_{\text{int}}(t) + E_{\text{qu}}(t), \quad \text{where:} \quad (7.2)$$

$$E_{\text{kin}}(t) = \frac{1}{N} \int \left(|\psi| \, \partial_x \phi \right)^2 dx,$$

$$E_{\text{int}}(t) = \frac{V(x)}{2N} \int |\psi|^4 \, dx,$$

$$E_{\text{qu}}(t) = \frac{1}{N} \int \left(\partial_x |\psi| \right)^2 dx.$$

7.1.1 Closed-Form Solutions of the NLSE

The following three categories of analytical (solitonic) solutions of the NLSE (7.1), based on the wave number k and amplitude α, were identified in [Iva10, Iva11, IR12]:

- Using *Jacobi elliptic sine* functions with the *elliptic modulus* $\varepsilon \in [0,1]$, such that $\text{sn}(x,0) = \sin(x)$ and $\text{sn}(x,1) = \tanh(x)$, we obtain the following solutions of (7.1):

$$\psi_1(x,t) = \pm \alpha \varepsilon \sqrt{\frac{1}{V(x)}} \, \text{sn}(x - kt) \, e^{i[kx - \frac{1}{2}t(k^2 - \alpha^2 - 2\varepsilon^2)]}, \quad \varepsilon \in [0,1), \quad (7.3)$$

$$\psi_2(x,t) = \pm \alpha \sqrt{\frac{1}{V(x)}} \, \tanh(x - kt) \, e^{i[kx - \frac{1}{2}t(k^2 - \alpha^2)]}, \quad \varepsilon = 1, \quad (7.4)$$

where (7.3) defines the general sn-solution, while (7.4) defines the *tanh* envelope shock-wave (or, 'dark soliton') solution of the NLSE (7.1).

- Using *Jacobi elliptic cosine* functions, such that $\text{cn}(x,0) = \cos(x)$ and $\text{cn}(x,1) = \text{sech}(x)$, we obtain the following solutions of (7.1):

---

[2] The kinetic energy $E_{\text{kin}}(t)$ is further divided into a compressible part $E_{\text{kin}}^{\text{c}}(t)$, due to compressible excitations, and an incompressible part $E_{\text{kin}}^{\text{i}}(t)$, due to vortices (see [NAB97a, NAB97b] for more technical details).

$$\psi_3(x,t) = \mp\alpha\varepsilon\sqrt{\frac{1}{V(x)}}\,\mathrm{cn}(x-kt)\,\mathrm{e}^{\mathrm{i}[kx-\frac{1}{2}t(k^2-\alpha^2-2\varepsilon^2)]}, \quad \varepsilon \in [0,1), \quad (7.5)$$

$$\psi_4(x,t) = \mp\alpha\sqrt{\frac{1}{V(x)}}\,\mathrm{sech}(x-kt)\,\mathrm{e}^{\mathrm{i}[kx-\frac{1}{2}t(k^2-\alpha^2)]}, \quad \varepsilon = 1, \qquad (7.6)$$

where (7.5) defines the general *cn*-solution, while (7.6) defines the *sech envelope solitary-wave* (or, 'bright soliton') solution of the NLSE (7.1).

- The third type of the NLSE solutions, derived using the Darboux transformation method (see [AAT09]), are the *rogue-waves*:

$$\psi_5(x,t) = \pm\alpha\sqrt{\frac{1}{2V(x)}}\left[1 - \frac{4(1+\alpha^2 t)}{1+2\alpha^2(x-kt)^2+\alpha^4 t^2}\right]\mathrm{e}^{\mathrm{i}[kx-\frac{1}{2}t(k^2-\alpha^2)]}.$$
$$(7.7)$$

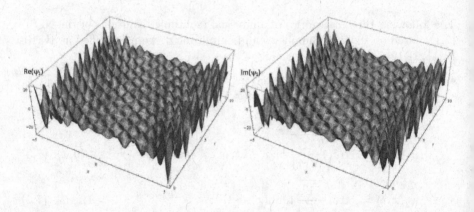

Fig. 7.2. *Real (left) and imaginary (right) components of the Jacobi-sn solution (7.3) of the NLSE (7.1).*

7.1.2 A 10-Component Wind Turbulence Soliton Model

Based on the above three categories of analytical solutions of the NLSE (7.1), we propose the composite wave function $\Psi(x,t) = |\Psi(x,t)|\,\mathrm{e}^{\mathrm{i}\Phi(x,t)}$, with the composite amplitude $|\Psi(x,t)|$ and the composite phase $\Phi(x,t)$, as the sum of the following 10 *NLSE wave components*:

$$\Psi(x,t) = |\Psi(x,t)|\, e^{i\Phi(x,t)} = \sum_{i=1}^{10} \psi_i(x,t,k_i,\alpha_i), \qquad \text{where} \qquad (7.8)$$

$$\psi_1 = \alpha_1 \varepsilon \sqrt{\frac{1}{V(x)}}\, \text{sn}(x - k_1 t)\, e^{i[k_1 x - \frac{1}{2}t(k_1^2 - \alpha_1^2 - 2\varepsilon^2)]},$$

$$\psi_2 = -\alpha_2 \varepsilon \sqrt{\frac{1}{V(x)}}\, \text{sn}(x - k_2 t)\, e^{i[k_2 x - \frac{1}{2}t(k_2^2 - \alpha_2^2 - 2\varepsilon^2)]},$$

$$\psi_3 = -\alpha_3 \varepsilon \sqrt{\frac{1}{V(x)}}\, \text{cn}(x - k_3 t)\, e^{i[k_3 x - \frac{1}{2}t(k_3^2 - \alpha_3^2 - 2\varepsilon^2)]},$$

$$\psi_4 = \alpha_4 \varepsilon \sqrt{\frac{1}{V(x)}}\, \text{cn}(x - k_4 t)\, e^{i[k_4 x - \frac{1}{2}t(k_4^2 - \alpha_4^2 - 2\varepsilon^2)]},$$

$$\psi_5 = \alpha_5 \sqrt{\frac{1}{V(x)}}\, \tanh(x - k_5 t)\, e^{i[k_5 x - \frac{1}{2}t(k_5^2 - \alpha_5^2)]},$$

$$\psi_6 = -\alpha_6 \sqrt{\frac{1}{V(x)}}\, \tanh(x - k_6 t)\, e^{i[k_6 x - \frac{1}{2}t(k_6^2 - \alpha_6^2)]},$$

$$\psi_7 = -\alpha_7 \sqrt{\frac{1}{V(x)}}\, \text{sech}(x - k_7 t)\, e^{i[k_7 x - \frac{1}{2}t(k_7^2 - \alpha_7^2)]},$$

$$\psi_8 = \alpha_8 \sqrt{\frac{1}{V(x)}}\, \text{sech}(x - k_8 t)\, e^{i[k_8 x - \frac{1}{2}t(k_8^2 - \alpha_8^2)]},$$

$$\psi_9 = \alpha_9 \sqrt{\frac{1}{2V(x)}} \left[1 - \frac{4(1 + \alpha_9^2 t)}{1 + 2\alpha_9^2(x - k_9 t)^2 + \alpha_9^4 t^2} \right] e^{i[k_9 x - \frac{1}{2}t(k_9^2 - \alpha_9^2)]},$$

$$\psi_{10} = -\alpha_{10} \sqrt{\frac{1}{2V(x)}} \left[1 - \frac{4(1 + \alpha_{10}^2 t)}{1 + 2\alpha_{10}^2(x - k_{10} t)^2 + \alpha_{10}^4 t^2} \right] e^{i[k_{10} x - \frac{1}{2}t(k_{10}^2 - \alpha_{10}^2)]}.$$

Here, k_i and α_i (for $i = 1, ..., 10$) are the individual wave numbers and amplitudes of the above 10 NLSE wave components, while $\varepsilon \in (0, 1)$ is the Jacobi *elliptic modulus*.

Equation (7.8) has the following three interpretations:

- Quantum probability: the absolute square $|\Psi(x,t)|^2$ defines the probability density function (PDF);
- Quantum turbulence in the complex plane $\mathbb{C} = \mathbb{R}^2$, where the X-axis is given by the real part, $\text{Re}[\Psi(x,t)]$, and the Y-axis is given by the imaginary part, $\text{Im}[\Psi(x,t)]$;
- Kolmogorov's energy spectra can be calculated by making the substitutions: $(\psi \to \Psi, \phi \to \Phi)$ and then applying Eq. (7.2).

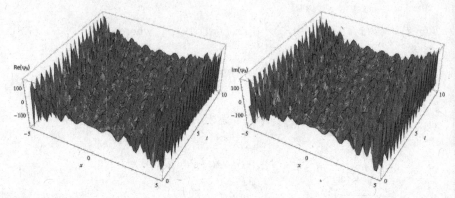

Fig. 7.3. *Real (left) and imaginary (right) components of the tanh solution (7.4) of the NLSE (7.1).*

7.1.3 3D Turbulent Wind Flow Model

From the 10-component soliton model $\Psi(x,t)$ given by Eq. (7.8) we can formulate a 3D turbulent wind flow model as a vector function $\mathcal{F}(x,y,z)$ in Cartesian (X,Y,Z)-axes, if we extend the above 2D turbulence, from the 2D plane $\mathbb{R}^2 = \mathbb{C}$ to the 3D Euclidean space $\mathbb{R}^3$, by defining the Z-axis as the average of the real and imaginary parts of $\Psi(x,t)$. In this way, we obtain the analytical model of the turbulent wind flow with the following Cartesian (X,Y,Z)-components:

1. Turbulent wind flow $\mathcal{F}_x$ along the X-axis, given by: $\mathcal{F}_x = \mathrm{Re}[\Psi(x,t)]$,
2. Turbulent wind flow $\mathcal{F}_y$ along the Y-axis, given by: $\mathcal{F}_y = \mathrm{Im}[\Psi(x,t)]$,
3. Turbulent wind flow $\mathcal{F}_z$ along the Z-axis, given by:
   $\mathcal{F}_z = \frac{1}{2}\left(\mathrm{Re}[\Psi(x,t)] + \mathrm{Im}[\Psi(x,t)]\right)$.

The wind flow model $\mathcal{F}(x,y,z)$ can now be defined as a spatiotemporal 3D vector function with these three (X,Y,Z)-components:

$$\mathcal{F}(x,y,z) = \{\mathcal{F}_x(t), \mathcal{F}_y(t), \mathcal{F}_z(t)\} = \{\mathcal{F}(x,t), \mathcal{F}(y,t), \mathcal{F}(z,t)\} \qquad (7.9)$$

$$= \{\mathrm{Re}[\Psi(x,t)], \mathrm{Im}[\Psi(x,t)], \frac{1}{2}\left(\mathrm{Re}[\Psi(x,t)] + \mathrm{Im}[\Psi(x,t)]\right)\}.$$

For practical wind simulation purposes, we have chosen the *Jacobi-sn* component (7.3), depicted in Figure 7.2, and its particular *tanh*-case (7.4) of the *envelope shock-wave*, depicted in Figure 7.3.

7.2 UAV's Sophisticated 3D Collision Avoidance System

Each UAV in the team has its own sophisticated 3D *collision avoidance system*, based on the set of six sonars (ultrasonic sensors) and six radars (on-a-chip), one sonar + radar on each side of the bounding box of the UAV. All six sonars and radars are controlled, managed and scheduled by a robust, nonlinear 3D *fuzzy-logic collision-avoidance controller*. The controller is developed by a 3D generalization of the Mamdani-type Fuzzy Inference System in the form of FAM-matrices, including trapezoidal In-Out membership functions, Product-Norm conjunctions and Centroid Defuzzifier.

Starting with radars and assuming, for simplicity, that the *speed* of any approaching object from the point-of-view of each individual UAV can be of three kinds: high speed, medium speed and low speed, the following set of 6-side If-Then rules can form the velocity component of the collision avoidance system:

Side 1.
If an object is approaching from Front with high speed
    Then move Backward with high speed.
If an object is approaching from Front with medium speed
    Then move Backward with medium speed.
If an object is approaching from Front with low speed
    Then move Backward with low speed.

Side 2.
If an object is approaching from Back with high speed
    Then move Forward with high speed.
If an object is approaching from Back with medium speed
    Then move Forward with medium speed.
If an object is approaching from Back with low speed
    Then move Forward with low speed.

Side 3.
If an object is approaching from Top with high speed
    Then move Downward with high speed.
If an object is approaching from Top with medium speed
    Then move Downward with medium speed.
If an object is approaching from Top with low speed
    Then move Downward with low speed.

Side 4.
If an object is approaching from Bottom with high speed
    Then move Upward with high speed.
If an object is approaching from Bottom with medium speed
    Then move Upward with medium speed.
If an object is approaching from Bottom with low speed
    Then move Upward with low speed.

Side 5.

```
If an object is approaching from Left with high speed
    Then move Rightward with high speed.
If an object is approaching from Left with medium speed
    Then move Rightward with medium speed.
If an object is approaching from Left with low speed
    Then move Rightward with low speed.

Side 6.
If an object is approaching from Right with high speed
    Then move Leftward with high speed.
If an object is approaching from Right with medium speed
    Then move Leftward with medium speed.
If an object is approaching from Right with low speed
    Then move Leftward with low speed.
```

A completely analogous set of 6-side If-Then rules can be formulated for the six sonar sensors, i.e., distances of the nearby external objects with respect to each individual UAV. Again, for simplicity, we assume only three partitions of the linguistic variable *distance*: very close, close and far. Here is an example rule:

```
If an external object is very close in Front
    Then move Backward with high speed.
```

This set of distance If-Then rules are combined (via conjunctions, realized through Product-Norm operators) with the above set of speed If-Then rules, using six FAM matrices (one per UAV side), each FAM-matrix with two inputs (distance and speed) and one output (UAV-motion). For more details, see section 6.10 from the previous Chapter.

An example of such a 1D FAM-matrix controller, combining distance and speed of an approaching object on one side of a UAV, is the fuzzy-logic controller for the inverted pendulum balance (with two inputs: angle and angular velocity, and a single output: the cart movement; see subsection 6.10.2 in the previous Chapter). Here is a working code for this 1D FAM-matrix controller written in the functional language *Haskell*, using the FuzzyCore code from [MG93]:

```
-- Pendulum.hs : a 2-in => 1-out FAM-matrix controller
-- Author: Michael Pilling, DS, JOAD, DST Group, 2016

module Pendulum where
import Prelude hiding ((&&), (||), not, and, or, any, all)
-- importing the FuzzyCore from Meehan and Joy (1993)
import FuzzyCore

type Angle = Double
type Velocity = Double -- Actually this is angular velocity
```

```
type Motor = Double

nvb_angle, nb_angle, n_angle, z_angle, p_angle,
pb_angle, pvb_angle ::
Fuzzy Angle -- pendulum angle [-40..40] center 0
nvb_angle = down (-40) (-25)
nb_angle  = tri (-40) (-10)
n_angle   = tri (-20) (-0)
z_angle   = tri (-5) 5
p_angle   = tri 0 20
pb_angle  = tri 10 40
pvb_angle = up 25 40

nb_velocity, n_velocity, z_velocity, p_velocity, pb_velocity ::
Fuzzy Velocity -- (angular) [-8..8] dps
nb_velocity = down (-8) (-3)
n_velocity  = tri (-6) (-0)
z_velocity  = tri (-1) 1
p_velocity  = tri 0 6
pb_velocity = up 3 8

nvvb_motor, nvb_motor, nb_motor, n_motor,
z_motor, p_motor, pb_motor, pvb_motor,
pvvb_motor :: Fuzzy Motor -- Actually force: [-32..32] N
nvvb_motor = down (-32) (-24)
nvb_motor  = tri (-32) (-16)
nb_motor   = tri (-24) (-8)
n_motor    = tri (-16) 0
z_motor    = tri (-4) 4
p_motor    = tri 0 16
pb_motor   = tri 8 24
pvb_motor  = tri 16 32
pvvb_motor = up 24 32

scan :: Domain Motor
scan = [-32, -31.75..32]

x_index = [ nvb_angle, nb_angle, n_angle, z_angle,
    p_angle, pb_angle, pvb_angle ]
y_index = [ nb_velocity, n_velocity, z_velocity,
    p_velocity, pb_velocity ]

-- FAM with Angle on the X axis, Velocity on the Y
-- of the Matrix
fam = [
```

```
[nvvb_motor, nvvb_motor, nvb_motor, nb_motor,
   n_motor  , z_motor   , p_motor  ],
[nvvb_motor, nvb_motor , nb_motor , n_motor ,
   z_motor  , p_motor   , pb_motor ],
[nvb_motor , nb_motor  , n_motor  , z_motor ,
   p_motor  , pb_motor  , pvb_motor ],
[nb_motor  , n_motor   , z_motor  , p_motor ,
   pb_motor , pvb_motor , pvvb_motor],
[n_motor   , z_motor   , p_motor  , pb_motor,
   pvb_motor, pvvb_motor, pvvb_motor]
]


-- Returns a list of the degree to which an input
-- activates each fuzzy function
degree :: Double -> [ Fuzzy Double ] -> [ Double ]
degree n f = map ($ n) f


-- Produces a matrix of the combined activation
-- potential of each
degreem :: [ Double ] -> [ Double ] -> [[ Double ]]
degreem _ [] = []
degreem x (y:yas) = map (&& y) x : degreem x yas


non_zero_term :: ( Double, Fuzzy Double ) -> Bool
non_zero_term ( n, _ ) = n /= 0.0


-- imposes a cap on fuzzy function returns set
-- by the limit l
limited_fuzzy :: Double -> Double ->
   Fuzzy Double -> Double
limited_fuzzy l n f = min l (f(n))


-- calculates a single numerator term scaled
-- by the defuzing input
limited_scaled :: Double -> ( Double, Fuzzy Double )
   -> Double
limited_scaled n ( l , f ) = n * (limited_fuzzy l n f)


-- gives the membership value of a fuzzy set held
-- in the second element of a tuple
detuple_fuzzy :: Double -> ( Double, Fuzzy Double )
   -> Double
detuple_fuzzy n ( _ , f ) = f(n)


-- produces a list of capped fuzzy membership
```

```
-- values for the element n
list_capped :: Double -> [( Double, Fuzzy Double )]
    -> [ Double ]
list_capped n ls = map ( limited_scaled n ) ls

-- produces a list of uncapped fuzzy membership values
-- for the element n
list_natural :: Double -> [( Double, Fuzzy Double )]
    -> [ Double ]
list_natural n ls = map ( detuple_fuzzy n ) ls

-- calculates the sum of the numerator sub sum for one input
-- across all the sparse terms
num_subsum :: [( Double, Fuzzy Double )] -> Double -> Double
num_subsum tups n = foldl (+) 0 (list_capped n tups)

-- calculates the sum of the numerator sub sum
-- for one input across all the sparse terms
denom_subsum :: [( Double, Fuzzy Double )] ->
    Double -> Double
denom_subsum tups n = foldl (+) 0 (list_natural n tups)

-- Finally, calculate the centroid
fam_centroid :: [( Double, Fuzzy Double )] ->
    Domain Motor -> Double
fam_centroid tups discrete = if denom == 0 then 0
    else num / denom
    where
num   = foldl (+) 0 (map (num_subsum tups) discrete)
denom = foldl (+) 0 (map (denom_subsum tups) discrete)

-- Calculate the FAM output for particular inputs
fam_output :: Angle -> Velocity -> Motor
fam_output a v = fam_centroid sparse_terms scan
    where
-- lists of the activation of each matrix column/row
x_degree = degree a x_index
y_degree = degree v y_index
-- scalem is a matrix scaling factors scaled by
-- both the x and y indices
scalem = degreem x_degree y_degree
-- scaled_fam is a flattened matrix (list) of tuples
-- of (scaling_factor, fuzzy_set) scaled in both the
-- x and y indices
scaled_fam = zip (concat scalem) (concat fam)
```

```
-- The flattened FAM as a list after we delete any
-- tuples scaling to zero
sparse_terms = filter non_zero_term scaled_fam
```

For the sophisticated collision avoidance system,[3] each of the six sides in the bounding box of each UAV requires its own 1D FAM-matrix controller, to combine distances and velocities of all incoming external objects (from the point-of-view of each individual UAV) and generate the most appropriate UAV-movement. Therefore, the full 3D collision-avoidance controller requires using the above Haskell code six times per UAV.

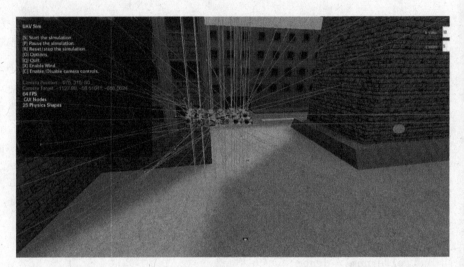

Fig. 7.4. *Start of the simulation: Initial position of the team of UAVs with the red lines representing sonar signals (left) and the blue 'wind canon' (right).*

7.3 Simulating Soft Attrition of a Team of UAVs using the 3D Wind Flow Model

The 3D simulator for the team of UAVs in various urban environments has been developed at B&C group, DS branch, JOAD, DST Group, in C-sharp language, using 3D graphics in the C-sharp wrapper for the Irrlicht 3D engine

---

[3] We remark here that a less sophisticated, yet still working, collision avoidance system can be built by using only either sonars (distance) or radars (speed) — but not both. In this simplistic case, FAM-matrices are not necessary, the direct implementation of the above single-input single-output If-Then rules would do the job correctly. For example, in case of relatively slow-moving quadcopters, the above set of sonar-based speed rules would suffice.

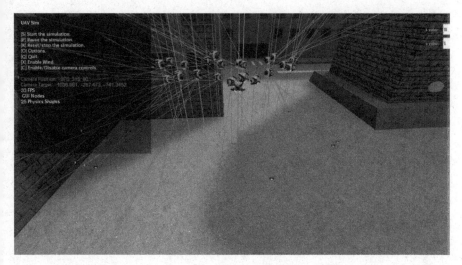

Fig. 7.5. *Team of UAVs navigating around using sonar signals bouncing from the floor and the walls.*

(originally coded in C++) and 3D physics in the C-sharp wrapper for the Bullet physics engine (also originally coded in C++).

The 3D *fuzzy-logic collision-avoidance controller* outlined in the previous section is developed, for each individual UAV, as a 3D-graphics extension of the library of fuzzy computations called AForge.Fuzzy Namespace, from the open source machine-learning software AForge.NET Framework–2.2.5[4] — and its application within a 3D urban environment. Here we provide a brief sketch of the 3D fuzzy sonar controller, based on velocities and distances of approaching objects to each UAV.

As a result of the highly-robust individual 3D fuzzy-logic collision avoidance system (presented above), the team of UAVs expresses a spontaneous behavior called 'fuzzy entanglement'.

The soft attrition scenario goes as follows. The team of UAVs is positioned somewhere in a 3D map of an urban environment; the Blue wind cannon is waiting for them at the entrance of a building or a quart of buildings (see Figure 7.4).

User starts the search mission of the team of UAVs, which goes deeper into the quart/building (see Figure 7.5).

User triggers the blue wind canon. Under the threat to be blown into the walls, the Read Team immediately reacts by exhibiting its fuzzy entanglement: simultaneous landing and the nearest-neighbor grouping/clustering (see Figure 7.6).

User stops the wind and the team of UAVs immediately continues its searching mission (see Figure 7.7).

---

[4] AForge.NET Framework: http://www.aforgenet.com/framework/

Fig. 7.6. *Wind turbulence blowing: the team of UAVs defends itself by fuzzy entanglement: nearest-neighbor clustering and landing on the floor.*

Fig. 7.7. *Wind stops: the team of UAVs resumes its navigation.*

User again triggers the blue wind canon and the team of UAVs immediately responds by its fuzzy entanglement (see Figure 7.8). The scenario continues this way.

Fig. 7.8. *Wind turbulence blowing again: the team of UAVs defends by fuzzy entanglement. Scenario continues this way.*

8

Cognitive Estimation in CPC-Autonomy: Recursive Bayesian Filters and FastSLAM Algorithms

8.1 Bayesian Probability Basics

Recall that for two probabilistic events, A and B, the *Bayes Rule/Inference* gives the fundamental *belief-relation* between the following three basic *conditional probabilities:*[1]

Prior: $P(A)$ is the initial degree-of-belief in event A (i.e., Initial Odds);
Likelihood: $P(B|A)$ is the degree-of-belief in event B, given A (i.e., New Evidence); and
Posterior: $P(A|B)$ is the degree-of-belief in A, given B (i.e., New Odds).

Informally, *Posterior is Prior times Likelihood* (normalized to 1). Formally,

> *Bayes Rule* : provided $P(B) \neq 0$, we have:

$$\underset{\text{Posterior}}{P(A|B)} = \frac{\overset{\text{Prior}}{P(A)} \times \overset{\text{Likelihood}}{P(B|A)}}{P(B)}$$

---

[1] In general, someone's *belief* in an event or statement A will depend on their body of knowledge K. Formally, this is a *belief measure*, or a *degree-of-belief*: $P(A|K)$, where $(\cdot|\cdot)$ means 'given'. When K remains constant, we simply write $P(A)$ instead of $P(A|K)$; however, any statement about $P(A)$ is always *conditioned* on a context K.

The *conditional probability* $P(A|B)$ of an event A given another event B is the probability that the event A will happen given that the event B has already occurred. Also, when we have a *joint event* A and B, we have a *joint probability*: $P(A, B)$, where $(\cdot, \cdot)$ means 'and', $\wedge$, or 'joint'. Conditional probabilities can be defined via joint probabilities and *vice versa*: $P(A|B) = P(A, B)/P(B)$, which implies: $P(A, B) = P(A|B)P(B)$.

Bayes Inference : in particular, $P(B) = $ const gives:

$$\underset{\text{Posterior}}{P(A|B)} \propto \underset{\text{Prior}}{P(A)} \times \underset{\text{Likelihood}}{P(B|A)}, \qquad \text{or}$$

Posterior $\propto$ Prior $\times$ Likelihood,   or

New Odds $\propto$ Initial Odds $\times$ New Evidence.

Statistically speaking, using a hypothesis H and data D, the Bayes rule reads:

$$\underset{\text{Posterior}}{p(H|D)} = \frac{\overset{\text{Prior}}{p(H)} \times \overset{\text{Likelihood}}{p(D|H)}}{p(D)} ,$$

where $p(H)$ is the *prior* probability that the hypothesis is true, $p(D|H)$ is the *likelihood* probability for the data D given a hypothesis H, $p(H|D)$ is the *posterior* probability that the hypothesis is true given the data, and the normalization constant: $p(D) = \sum_H p(D|H)p(H)$ is the probability for the data averaged over all hypotheses.

When the Bayes rule is applied iteratively/recursively over distributions evolving in discrete time steps, so that the old Posterior becomes a new Prior and a New Evidence is added, it becomes the *recursive Bayesian filter*, the 'mother' of all Kalman and particle filters.

8.2 Kalman's State-Space LQR/LQG Control Systems

8.2.1 State-Space Formulation for Linear MIMO Systems

Kalman's modular state-space formulation of [KFA69] (as implemented in *Matlab®*) for *continuous control systems* reads:

$$d\boldsymbol{x}/dt = \boldsymbol{A}(t)\,\boldsymbol{x}(t) + \boldsymbol{B}(t)\,\boldsymbol{u}(t), \qquad (t \in \mathbb{R}) \tag{8.1}$$
$$\boldsymbol{y}(t) = \boldsymbol{C}(t)\,\boldsymbol{x}(t) + \boldsymbol{D}(t)\,\boldsymbol{u}(t),$$

and for *discrete control systems* read:

$$\boldsymbol{x}(n+1) = \boldsymbol{A}(n)\,\boldsymbol{x}(n) + \boldsymbol{B}(n)\,\boldsymbol{u}(n), \qquad (n \in \mathbb{N}) \tag{8.2}$$
$$\boldsymbol{y}(n) = \boldsymbol{C}(n)\,\boldsymbol{x}(n) + \boldsymbol{D}(n)\,\boldsymbol{u}(n).$$

Both in (8.1) and in (8.2) the variables have the following meaning:

$\mathbf{x}(t) \in \mathbb{X}$ is an $n-$vector of *state variables* belonging to the *state space* $\mathbb{X} \subset \mathbb{R}^n$;

$\mathbf{u}(t) \in \mathbb{U}$ is an $m-$vector of *inputs* belonging to the *input space* $\mathbb{U} \subset \mathbb{R}^m$;

$y(t) \in \mathbb{Y}$ is a k−vector of *outputs* belonging to the *output space* $\mathbb{Y} \subset \mathbb{R}^k$;
$A(t) : \mathbb{X} \to \mathbb{X}$ is an $n \times n$ matrix of *state dynamics*;
$B(t) : \mathbb{U} \to \mathbb{X}$ is an $n \times m$ matrix of *input map*;
$C(t) : \mathbb{X} \to \mathbb{Y}$ is an $k \times n$ matrix of *output map*;
$D(t) : \mathbb{U} \to \mathbb{Y}$ is an $k \times m$ matrix of *input−output transform*.

Input $\mathbf{u}(t) \in \mathbb{U}$ can be empirically determined by trial and error; it is properly defined by optimization process called *Kalman regulator* [technically, *linear quadratic regulator* (LQR)]; or more generally (in the presence of noise), by *Kalman filter* [technically, *linear quadratic Gaussian* (LQG)] [Kal60], or even better, *extended Kalman filter* (EKF) — to deal with stochastic nonlinearities.

8.2.2 Linear Stationary Systems and Operators

The most common special case of the general Kalman model, with constant state, input and output matrices (and relaxed boldface vector–matrix notation), is the so-called *stationary linear model*

$$\dot{x} = Ax + Bu, \qquad y = Cx. \tag{8.3}$$

The stationary linear system (8.3) defines a variety of operators, in particular those related to the following problems:

1. regulators,
2. end point controls,
3. servomechanisms, and
4. repetitive modes (see [Bro01]).

The control systems (8.1) and (8.2) become *Kalman filters* (see next section) if Gaussian noises are added to the right-hand sides of all equations.

8.2.3 Kalman's LQR/LQG Controller

To briefly summarize Kalman's LQR/LQG control theory, recall that for a continuous-time linear multi-input multi-output (MIMO) system with a finite final time (or, *horizon*) τ, defined by the vector/matrix state equation:

$$\dot{\mathbf{x}} = A\mathbf{x} + B\mathbf{u}, \qquad (t \in [t_0, t_1]), \tag{8.4}$$

(where x represents the vector of state variables of the system and u is the vector of control inputs), with a *quadratic cost function*:

$$J = \frac{1}{2}\mathbf{x}^T(t_1)F(t_1)\mathbf{x}(t_1) + \int_{t_0}^{t_1} \left(\mathbf{x}^T Q\mathbf{x} + \mathbf{u}^T R\mathbf{u} + 2\mathbf{x}^T N\mathbf{u}\right) dt,$$

where superscript T denotes matrix transpose. The *feedback control law* that minimizes the value of the cost is: $\mathbf{u} = -K\mathbf{x}$, where the *gain matrix* K is given by: $K = R^{-1}(B^T P(t) + N^T)$, while the matrix $P = P(t)$ is found by solving the continuous-time *Riccati ODE*:

$$A^T P(t) + P(t)A - (P(t)B + N)R^{-1}(B^T P(t) + N^T) + Q = -\dot{P}(t)$$

with the boundary condition: $P(t_1) = F(t_1)$.

In particular, the so-called *first-order optimal conditions* for the minimum of the cost function J_{min} are:

State equation: $\dot{\mathbf{x}} = A\mathbf{x} + B\mathbf{u}$;
Co-state equation: $-\dot{\lambda} = Q\mathbf{x} + N\mathbf{u} + A^T\lambda$;
Stationary equation: $0 = R\mathbf{u} + N^T\mathbf{x} + B^T\lambda$;
Boundary conditions: $x(t_0) = \mathbf{x}_0$, $\lambda(t_1) = F(t_1)x(t_1)$.

Furthermore, when such an LQR is combined with a *Kalman filter* (or, *linear-quadratic estimator*), the result represents the so-called *linear-quadratic-Gaussian* (LQG) controller, which concerns *uncertain linear systems* disturbed by additive *Gaussian white noise*, having incomplete state information and undergoing control subject to quadratic costs. The *LQG control problem* is considered to be the most fundamental optimal control problem.

Formally, consider the following continuous-time linear dynamic system that generalizes (8.4):

$$\dot{\mathbf{x}}(t) = A(t)\mathbf{x}(t) + B(t)\mathbf{u}(t) + \mathbf{v}(t), \qquad \mathbf{y}(t) = C(t)\mathbf{x}(t) + \mathbf{w}(t), \qquad (8.5)$$

where x represents the vector of state variables of the system, u the vector of control inputs and $\mathbf{y}$ the vector of measured outputs available for feedback. Both the additive *Gaussian white system noise* $\mathbf{v}(t)$ and the additive *Gaussian white measurement noise* $\mathbf{w}(t)$ affect the system. Given this system, the objective is to find the *control input history* $u(t)$ which at every time t may depend only on the past measurements $\mathbf{y}(t')$, with $(0 \leq t' < t \leq \tau)$ such that the following cost function is minimized:[2]

$$J = E\left[\mathbf{x}^T(t)F\mathbf{x}(T) + \int_0^T \mathbf{x}^T(t)Q(t)\mathbf{x}(t) + \mathbf{u}^T(t)R(t)\mathbf{u}(t)\,dt\right],$$

where E denotes the expected value, while $F \geq 0$, $Q(t) \geq 0$, $R(t) > 0$.

The LQG controller that solves the above LQG control problem is specified by the Kalman filter:

---

[2] Here, the final time, or *horizon*, τ may be either finite or infinite. If the horizon τ tends to infinity, the first term of the cost function, $x^T(t)Fx(T)$, becomes negligible and irrelevant to the problem. Besides, to keep the costs finite, the cost function has to be taken to be J/τ.

$$\dot{\hat{\mathbf{x}}}(t) = A(t)\hat{\mathbf{x}}(t) + B(t)\mathbf{u}(t) + K(t)\left(\mathbf{y}(t) - C(t)\hat{\mathbf{x}}(t)\right), \quad \hat{\mathbf{x}}(0) = E\left(\mathbf{x}(0)\right),$$

with the Kalman gain $K(t)$ and the control input: $u(t) = -L(t)\hat{\mathbf{x}}(t)$.

At each time t this filter generates estimates $\hat{\mathbf{x}}(t)$ of the state $x(t)$ using the past measurements and inputs. The Kalman gain $K(t)$ is computed from the matrices $A(t), C(t)$, the two intensity matrices $V(t), W(t)$ associated to the white Gaussian noises $\mathbf{v}(t)$ and $\mathbf{w}(t)$ and finally $E\left[\mathbf{x}(0)\mathbf{x}^T(0)\right]$. These five matrices determine the Kalman gain through the following associated *matrix Riccati ODE*:

$$\dot{P}(t) = A(t)P(t) + P(t)A^T(t) - P(t)C^T(t)W^{-1}(t)C(t)P(t) + V(t),$$

with $P(0) = E\left(\mathbf{x}(0)\mathbf{x}^T(0)\right)$. For the solution $P(t)$, with $(0 \leq t \leq \tau)$, the Kalman gain matrix is given by:

$$K(t) = P(t)C^T(t)W^{-1}(t).$$

The matrix $L(t)$ is called the *feedback gain matrix*. It is determined by the matrices $A(t), B(t), Q(t), R(t)$ and F through the following associated matrix Riccati ODE:

$$-\dot{S}(t) = A^T(t)S(t) + S(t)A(t) - S(t)B(t)R^{-1}(t)B^T(t)S(t) + Q(t),$$

with $S(T) = F$. For the solution $S(t)$, with $(0 \leq t \leq \tau)$, the feedback gain matrix is given by:

$$L(t) = R^{-1}(t)B^T(t)S(t).$$

8.3 Kalman Filtering Basics

The (discrete) *Kalman filter model* includes two linear vector equations:

1. The *state equation* that assumes that the *posterior state* of a system (at *posterior time* t) evolved from its *prior state* (at *prior time* $t-1$), as:

$$\mathbf{x}_t = \mathbf{A}_t\mathbf{x}_{t-1} + \mathbf{B}_t\mathbf{u}_t + \boldsymbol{\eta}_t, \tag{8.6}$$

where (see, e.g. [Far12] and the references therein):

- $\mathbf{x}_t$ is the *state-vector* containing the terms of interest for the system (e.g., position, velocity, heading) at time t;
- $\mathbf{u}_t$ is the *input vector* containing any control inputs (steering angle, acceleration and deceleration, throttle setting) at time t;
- $\mathbf{A}_t$ is the *state-transition matrix* that applies the effect of each system state at time $t-1$ on the system state at time t (e.g., the position and velocity at prior time $t-1$ affect the position at posterior time t);
- $\mathbf{B}_t$ is the *control input matrix* which applies the effect of each control input in the vector $\mathbf{u}_t$ on the state vector (e.g., applies the effect of the throttle setting on the system velocity and position) at time t;

- $\boldsymbol{\eta}_t$ is the vector containing the *process noise* terms corresponding to each state at time t; and

2. The *measurement equation* that describes the *measurements* of the system (performed at time t), as:

$$\mathbf{y}_t = \mathbf{C}_t \mathbf{x}_t + \mathbf{e}_t, \qquad (8.7)$$

where:

- $\mathbf{y}_t$ is the *measurement vector* at time t;
- $\mathbf{C}_t$ is the *measurement transformation matrix* that maps the system states into the measurement domain at time t;
- $\mathbf{e}_t$ is the vector containing the *measurement noise* terms for each observation in the measurement vector at time t.

Both the process noise $\boldsymbol{\eta}_t$ in (8.6) and the measurement noise $\mathbf{e}_t$ in (8.7) are assumed to be *zero-mean Gaussian white noises* with covariances given by the respective covariance matrices $\mathbf{Q}_t$ and $\mathbf{R}_t$.

8.3.1 Classical (Linear) Kalman Filter

It all started in 1960 with Kalman's seminal paper [Kal60]. Classical *Kalman filter* is an effective (albeit linear) procedure for *combining noisy sensor outputs* to *estimate* the *state* of a *system with uncertain dynamics*. The Kalman filter provides a *recursive solution* to the *linear optimal filtering problem*. It applies to stationary as well as non–stationary environments. The solution is recursive in that each updated estimate of the state is computed from the previous estimate and the new input data, so only the previous estimate requires storage. In addition to eliminating the need for storing the entire past observed data, the Kalman filter is computationally more efficient than computing the estimate directly from the entire past observed data at each step of the filtering process.

Recall from above that Kalman's *linear quadratic regulator* (LQR) represents a *linear state feedback control law*

$$u = -Kx$$

for the linear MIMO–system

$$\dot{x} = Ax + Bu$$

which minimizes a *quadratic cost function*

$$J = \int_0^\infty \left(x(t)^T Q\, x(t) + u(t)^T R\, u(t) \right)\, dt.$$

The control law is called *optimal with respect to the cost function J*.

Now, one might ask whether there is an optimal design technique for a *state estimator*. That is, is there an approach to *observer design* which is equivalent, in some sense, to the linear quadratic regulator?

Given the *observable system*

$$\dot{x} = Ax + Bu, \qquad y = Cx,$$

one may define the *dual system*

$$\dot{\theta} = A^T \theta + C^T \gamma$$

and design an LQR controller to minimize the quadratic cost function

$$J = \int_0^\infty \left(\theta(t)^T Q\, \theta(t) + \gamma(t)^T R\, \gamma(t) \right) dt.$$

However, it is unclear how one should 'penalize' θ and γ in the cost function. Instead, consider the *extended observable system*

$$\dot{x} = Ax + Bu + w, \qquad y = Cx + v,$$

in which the dynamics are subject to random disturbances w and the measurements are subject to random noise v. In parallel with the development of the linear quadratic regulator, Rudolph Kalman examined the following *optimal estimator problem*: Construct a full state observer which minimizes the combined effect of the disturbances and the noise, thus providing a 'most likely' estimate of the system state. Solving this problem requires some information about the random processes. If the processes are zero–mean, Gaussian white noise processes, then the optimal estimator design problem becomes perfectly analogous to the LQR control design problem. In 1960, Kalman published his famous paper describing a recursive solution to the discrete–data linear filtering problem [Kal60]. Since that time, due in large part to advances in digital computing, the Kalman filter has been the subject of extensive particularly in the area of autonomous or GPS-assisted navigation (see, e.g., [Hay01, GWA01]).

The standard Kalman filter is a *discrete–time, two–step process*, the steps of which are usually called *prediction* and *correction*, thus resembling a popular *Adams–Bashforth–Moulton integrator* for ODEs (see, e.g., [WB95]). The *predictor*, or *time update*, projects the current system's state estimate ahead in time. The *corrector*, or *measurement update*, adjusts the projected state estimate by an actual system's measurement at that time. In this way, the correction step makes corrections to an estimate, based on new information obtained from sensor measurements. The continuous–time version is usually referred to as *Kalman–Bucy filter* or *smoother* [KB61, SL03, Asi04].

Consider a generic linear, discrete–time dynamical system. The concept of *discrete state* is fundamental to this description. The *state vector*, denoted by x_k, is defined as the minimal set of data that is sufficient to uniquely describe the unforced dynamical behavior of the system; the subscript k denotes discrete time. In other words, the state is the least amount of data on the past behavior of the system that is needed to predict its future behavior. Typically, the state x_k is unknown. To estimate it, we use a set of observed data, denoted by the *observable* vector y_k.

The state–space model of a generic linear, discrete–time dynamical system includes the *process equation* (9.1) and the *measurement equation* (9.2)

$$x_{k+1} = F_{k+1}, x_k + w_k, \tag{8.8}$$

$$y_k = H_k x_k + v_k, \tag{8.9}$$

where F_{k+1} is the *transition matrix* taking the state x_k from time k to time $k+1$, H_k is the *measurement sensitivity matrix*, while w_k and v_k are independent, additive, zero–mean, white *Gaussian noise* processes, defined below.

The covariance matrix of the *process noise* w_k is defined by

$$E[w_n, w_k^T] = \begin{cases} Q_k, & \text{for } n = k, \\ 0, & \text{for } n = k. \end{cases}$$

Similarly, the covariance matrix of the *measurement noise* v_k is defined by

$$E[v_n, v_k^T] = \begin{cases} R_k, & \text{for } n = k, \\ 0, & \text{for } n = k. \end{cases}$$

The *Kalman filtering problem*, namely, the problem of jointly solving the process and measurement equations for the unknown state in an optimum manner may now be formally stated as follows: Use the entire observed data, consisting of the vectors $y_1, y_2, ..., y_k$, to find for each $k \geq 1$ the minimum mean–square error estimate of the state x_i. The problem is called *filtering* if $i = k$, *prediction* if $i > k$, and *smoothing* if $1 \leq i < k$.

The derivation of the classical Kalman filter is based on the following two theorems (see [Kal60, Hay01]):

- The *conditional mean estimator*. If the stochastic processes $\{x_k\}$ and $\{y_k\}$ are jointly Gaussian, then the optimum estimate $\hat{x}_k$ that minimizes the mean–square error J_k is the conditional mean estimator:

$$\hat{x}_k = E[x_k | y_1, y_2, ..., y_k].$$

- The *principle of orthogonality*. Let the stochastic processes $\{x_k\}$ and $\{y_k\}$ be of zero means; that is,

$$E[x_k] = E[y_k] = 0, \qquad \text{for all } k.$$

Then:
(i) the stochastic process $\{x_k\}$ and $\{y_k\}$ are jointly Gaussian; or
(ii) if the optimal estimate $\hat{x}_k$ is restricted to be a linear function of the observables and the cost function is the mean–square error,
(iii) then the optimum estimate $\hat{x}_k$, given the observables $y_1, y_2, ..., y_k$, is the orthogonal projection of x_k on the space spanned by these observables.

The *Kalman filter design algorithm* consists of (see [Kal60, Hay01]):

1. *Initialization*: For $k = 0$, set

$$\hat{x}_0 = E[x_0], \qquad P_0 = E[(x_0 - E[x_0])(x_0 - E[x_0])^T].$$

and

2. *Computation*: For $k = 1, 2, \ldots$, compute:
   (i) *State estimate propagation*

$$\hat{x}_{\bar{k}} = F_{k,k-1} \hat{x}_{\bar{k}-1};$$

   (ii) *Error covariance propagation*

$$P_{\bar{k}} = F_{k,k-1} P_{k-1} F_{k,k-1}^T + Q_{k-1};$$

   (iii) *Kalman gain matrix*

$$G_k = P_{\bar{k}} H_k^T [H_k P_{\bar{k}} H_k^T + R_k]^{-1};$$

   (iv) *State estimate update*

$$\hat{x}_k = \hat{x}_{\bar{k}} + G_k(y_k - H_k \hat{x}_{\bar{k}});$$

   (v) *Error covariance update*

$$P_k = (I - G_k H_k) P_{\bar{k}}.$$

Therefore, the basic Kalman filter is a linear, discrete–time, finite–dimensional system, which is endowed with a recursive structure that makes a digital computer well suited for its implementation. A key property of the Kalman filter is that it is the minimum mean–square (variance) estimator of the state of a linear dynamical system. The model is stochastic owing to the additive presence of process noise and measurement noise, which are assumed to be Gaussian with zero mean and known covariance matrices.

Steady-State and Time-Varying Kalman Filters

Here we present basic Matlab implementations of both steady-state and time-varying Kalman filters, on the same problem.

A. Problem Description

Given the following discrete plant:

$$x(n + 1) = Ax(n) + Bu(n), \qquad y(n) = Cx(n) + Du(n),$$

we can design a Kalman filter to estimate the output y based on the noisy measurements:

$$yv[n] = Cx[n] + v[n].$$

B. Design of a Steady-State Kalman Filter

Matlab's function `Kalman` determines the optimal *steady-state Kalman filter* gain M based on the process-noise covariance Q and the sensor-noise covariance R.

Firstly, given the following data:

```
A = [1.1269    -0.4940     0.1129,
     1.0000          0        0,
          0     1.0000        0];
```

```
B = [-0.3832
      0.5919
      0.5191];
```

`C = [1 0 0];  D = 0;`

— we need to specify the *plant + noise* model as follows:

```
Plant = ss(A,[B B],C,0,-1,'inputname',{'u' 'w'},'outputname',
       'y');
Q = 2.3;  R = 1; % two positive numbers
```

Then we can design the steady-state Kalman filter with the following equations:

$$\text{Time update}: x[n+1|n] = Ax[n|n-1] + Bu[n] \quad \text{and}$$
$$\text{Measurement update}: x[n|n] = x[n|n-1] + M(yv[n] - Cx[n|n-1]),$$

(where M is the optimal innovation gain), using the `KALMAN` command:

`[kalmf,L,P,M,Z] = kalman(Plant,Q,R);`

The first output of the Kalman filter `KALMF` is the plant output estimate: $y\_e = Cx[n|n]$, while the remaining outputs are the state estimates; we keep only the first output y_e, using the command:

`kalmf = kalmf(1,:);`

To simulate this system, we first build a complete plant model with (u, w, v) as inputs and (y, yv) as outputs, using the following commands:

```
a = A;
b = [B B 0*B];
c = [C;C];
d = [0 0 0;0 0 1];
P = ss(a,b,c,d,-1,'inputname',{'u' 'w' 'v'},'outputname',
    {'y' 'yv'});
```

Next, we connect the plant model and the Kalman filter in parallel by specifying u as a shared input:

```
sys = parallel(P,kalmf,1,1,[],[]);
```

Finally, we connect the plant output yv to the filter input yv:

```
SimModel = feedback(sys,1,4,2,1);
SimModel = SimModel([1 3],[1 2 3]);
```

\We are now ready to simulate the filter behavior. First, we generate a (known) sinusoidal input vector:

```
t = [0:100]';   u = sin(t/5);
```

Next, we generate process noise and sensor noise vectors:

```
randn('seed',0);
w = sqrt(Q)*randn(length(t),1);
v = sqrt(R)*randn(length(t),1);
```

Finally, we simulate the response using the LSIM command:

```
clf;   [out,x] = lsim(SimModel,[w,v,u]);
y = out(:,1);    % true response
ye = out(:,2);   % filtered response
yv = y + v;      % measured response
```

By plotting, we compare the true response with the filtered response:

```
clf; subplot(211), plot(t,y,'b',t,ye,'r--'),
xlabel('No. of samples'), ylabel('Output')
title('Kalman filter response')
subplot(212), plot(t,y-yv,'g',t,y-ye,'r--'),
xlabel('No. of samples'), ylabel('Error')
```

C. Design of a Time-Varying Kalman Filter

The *time-varying Kalman filter* has the following update equations:

Time update :
$$x[n+1|n] = Ax[n|n-1] + Bu[n],$$
$$P[n+1|n] = AP[n|n]A\prime + B*Q*B\prime \qquad \text{and}$$
Measurement update :
$$x[n|n] = x[n|n-1] + M(yv[n] - Cx[n|n-1]),$$
$$M[n] = P[n|n-1]C\prime(CP[n|n-1]C\prime + R)^{-1},$$
$$P[n|n] = (I - M[n]C)P[n|n-1].$$

We will use this filter to perform the same task as before.[3] To implement it, we firstly generate the noisy plant response:

---

[3] A time-varying Kalman filter can perform well even when the noise covariance is not stationary. However for this problem, we will use the same stationary covariance as before.

```
sys = ss(A,B,C,D,-1);
y = lsim(sys,u+w); % w = process noise
yv = y + v; % v = meas. noise
```

Next, we implement the filter recursions in a FOR loop:

```
P=B*Q*B'; % Initial error covariance
x=zeros(3,1); % Initial condition on the state
ye = zeros(length(t),1);
ycov = zeros(length(t),1);

for i=1:length(t)
  % Measurement update
  Mn = P*C'/(C*P*C'+R);
  x = x + Mn*(yv(i)-C*x);   % x[n|n]
  P = (eye(3)-Mn*C)*P;      % P[n|n]

  ye(i) = C*x;
  errcov(i) = C*P*C';

  % Time update
  x = A*x + B*u(i);         % x[n+1|n]
  P = A*P*A' + B*Q*B';      % P[n+1|n]
end
```

Now, we can compare the true response with the filtered response:

```
clf;  subplot(211), plot(t,y,'b',t,ye,'r--'),
xlabel('No. of samples'), ylabel('Output')
title('Response with time-varying Kalman filter')
subplot(212), plot(t,y-yv,'g',t,y-ye,'r--'),
xlabel('No. of samples'), ylabel('Error');
```

The time-varying filter also estimates the output covariance during the estimation. We can plot the output covariance to see if the filter has reached steady state (as we would expect with stationary input noise):

```
subplot(211)
plot(t,errcov), ylabel('Error Covar')
```

Finally, we can compare the covariance errors as:

```
MeasErr = y-yv;
MeasErrCov = sum(MeasErr.*MeasErr)/length(MeasErr);
EstErr = y-ye;
EstErrCov = sum(EstErr.*EstErr)/length(EstErr);
```

Sensor Fusion in Hybrid Systems

Kalman filter can be used to *combine* or *fuse* information from different sensors for hybrid systems, like accelerometers and gyroscopes (see text below). The basic idea is to use the Kalman filter to weight the different mediums most heavily in the circumstances where they each perform best, thus providing more accurate and stable estimates than a system based on any one medium alone (see [Lui02]). In particular, the *indirect feedback Kalman filter* (also called a *complementary* or *error–state Kalman filter*) is often used to combine the two mediums [May79]. In such a configuration, the Kalman filter is used to estimate the difference between the current inertial and optical (or acoustic) outputs, i.e., it continually estimates the error in the inertial estimates by using the optical system as a second (redundant) reference. This error estimate is then used to correct the inertial estimates. The *tuning* of the Kalman filter parameters then adjusts the weight of the correction as a function of frequency. By slightly modifying the Kalman filter, adaptive velocity response can be incorporated also. This can be accomplished by adjusting (in real time) the expected optical measurement error as a function of the magnitude of velocity [WB95].

8.3.2 Extended (Nonlinear) Kalman Filter

The Kalman filtering problem considered so far has addressed the estimation of a state vector in a linear model of a dynamical system. If, however, the model is nonlinear, we may extend the use of Kalman filtering through a linearization procedure. The resulting filter is referred to as the *extended Kalman filter* (EKF) [Hay01]. Such an extension is feasible by virtue of the fact that the Kalman filter is described in terms of difference equations in the case of discrete–time systems. While the ordinary (i.e., linear) Kalman filter is defined in terms of the measurement sensitivity matrix H_k, the extended Kalman filter can be defined in terms of a suitably differentiable vector–valued measurement sensitivity function $h(k, x_k)$.

To set the stage for a development of the extended Kalman filter, consider a nonlinear dynamical system described by the state–space model

$$x_{k+1} = f(k, x_k) + w_k, \qquad y_k = h(k, x_k) + v_k, \qquad (8.10)$$

where, as before, w_k and v_k are independent zero–mean white Gaussian noise processes with covariance matrices R_k and Q_k, respectively. Here, however, the functional $f(k, x_k)$ denotes a nonlinear transition matrix function that is possibly time–variant. Likewise, the functional $h(k, x_k)$ denotes a vector–valued measurement sensitivity function, i.e., a nonlinear measurement matrix that may be time–variant, too [Hay01].

The basic idea of the extended Kalman filter is to linearize the state–space model (8.10) at each time instant around the most recent state estimate, which is taken to be either $\hat{x}_k$ or $\hat{x}_{\bar{k}}$, depending on which particular functional is being considered. Once a linear model is obtained, the standard Kalman filter equations are applied.

The *EKF design algorithm* consists of [Hay01]:

1. The *discrete state–space model* (8.10).
2. *Definitions*

$$F_{k,k} = \left.\frac{\partial f(k,x)}{\partial x}\right|_{x=x_k}, \qquad H_k = \left.\frac{\partial h(k,x)}{\partial x}\right|_{x=x_{\bar{k}}}.$$

3. *Initialization*: For $k = 0$, set

$$\hat{x}_0 = E[x_0], \qquad P_0 = E[(x_0 - E[x_0])(x_0 - E[x_0])^T].$$

4. *Computation*: For $k = 1, 2, ...$, compute:
   (i) *State estimate propagation*

$$\hat{x}_{\bar{k}} = F_{k,k-1}\,\hat{x}_{\bar{k}-1};$$

   (ii) *Error covariance propagation*

$$P_{\bar{k}} = F_{k,k-1}\,P_{k-1}F_k^T{}_{,k-1} + Q_{k-1};$$

   (iii) *Kalman gain matrix*

$$G_k = P_{\bar{k}}H_k^T[H_k P_{\bar{k}}H_k^T + R_k]^{-1};$$

   (iv) *State estimate update*

$$\hat{x}_k = \hat{x}_{\bar{k}} + G_k(y_k - H_k\hat{x}_{\bar{k}});$$

   (v) *Error covariance update*

$$P_k = (I - G_k H_k)P_{\bar{k}}.$$

8.3.3 Unscented Kalman Filter

The *extended Kalman filter* (EKF) represents an efficient recursive update form of the Kalman filter, but still suffers from serious limitations due to linearization and Jacobian matrix calculation. The so-called *unscented transformation* (UT) was developed to address the deficiencies of linearization and the *unscented Kalman filter* (UKF) [JU04] was proposed based on UT.

Still, the state covariance in UKF is propagated in such a way that under some circumstances it cannot maintain the positive semidefiniteness so that its square-root cannot be calculated, which makes UKF numerically unstable under these conditions. Recently, an UKF procedure with guaranteed positive semi-definite state covariance has been proposed in [QS14], thus enhancing the numerical stability of the UKF algorithm. Here is a brief description of this algorithm.

A noisy, discrete-time, MIMO, nonlinear dynamic system can be described (for $k = 1, \ldots, n$) as:

$$\text{System state equation} : \mathbf{x}_k = \mathbf{a}(\mathbf{x}_{k-1}) + \mathbf{q}_{k-1},$$

$$\text{Measurement equation} : \mathbf{y}_k = \mathbf{b}(\mathbf{x}_k) + \mathbf{r}_k,$$

where $\mathbf{x}_k \in \mathbb{R}^n$ are system states (with mean $\mathbf{m}$ and covariance $\mathbf{P}$), $\mathbf{y}_k \in \mathbb{R}^p$ are measurements, $\mathbf{a}$ and $\mathbf{b}$ are nonlinear vector-functions, $\mathbf{q}_{k-1}$ is Gaussian process noise and $\mathbf{r}_k$ is measurement noise.

The unscented transformation calculates a total of $(2n + 1)$ sigma points $\mathbf{X}$ as:

$$\mathbf{X}^{(0)} = \mathbf{m}, \qquad \mathbf{X}^{(i)} = \mathbf{m} + \eta\sqrt{\mathbf{P}}, \qquad (i = 1, \ldots, n),$$

$$\mathbf{X}^{(j)} = \mathbf{m} - \eta\sqrt{\mathbf{P}}, \qquad (j = n + 1, \ldots, 2n),$$

with weights

$$\mathbf{W}_m^{(0)} = \lambda/(n + \lambda), \qquad \mathbf{W}_c^{(0)} = \lambda/(n + \lambda) + (1 - \alpha^2 + \beta),$$

$$\mathbf{W}_m^{(i)} = \mathbf{W}_c^{(i)} = 1/(2(n + \lambda)), \qquad (i = 1, \ldots, 2n),$$

where $\lambda = \alpha^2(n + \kappa) - n$, $\eta = \sqrt{n + \lambda}$ and α, β, κ are positive constants.

Based on the above UT, the Kalman filter algorithm reads [QS14]:

1. The initial state mean and covariance are $\mathbf{m}_0$ and $\mathbf{P}_0$.
2. Prediction Step:

$$\mathbf{X}_{k-1} = \underbrace{[\mathbf{m}_{k-1} \cdots \mathbf{m}_{k-1}]}_{2n+1} + \eta \left[\mathbf{0} \quad \sqrt{\mathbf{P}_{k-1}} \quad -\sqrt{\mathbf{P}_{k-1}} \right],$$

$$\hat{\mathbf{X}}_k = \mathbf{f}(\mathbf{X}_{k-1}), \qquad \mathbf{m}_k^- = \sum_{i=0}^{2n} \mathbf{W}_m^{(i)} \hat{\mathbf{X}}_{i,k},$$

$$\mathbf{P}_k^- = \sum_{i=0}^{2n} \mathbf{W}_m^{(i)} (\hat{\mathbf{X}}_{i,k} - \mathbf{m}_k^-)(\hat{\mathbf{X}}_{i,k} - \mathbf{m}_k^-)^T + \mathbf{Q}_{k-1};$$

3. Update Step:

$$\mathbf{X}_k^- = \underbrace{[\mathbf{m}_k^- \cdots \mathbf{m}_k^-]}_{2n+1} + \eta \left[\mathbf{0} \quad \sqrt{\mathbf{P}_k^-} \quad -\sqrt{\mathbf{P}_k^-} \right],$$

$$\mathbf{Y}_k^- = \mathbf{h}(\mathbf{X}_k^-), \qquad \hat{\mathbf{y}}_k^- = \sum_{i=0}^{2n} \mathbf{W}_m^{(i)} \mathbf{Y}_{i,k}^-,$$

$$\mathbf{P}_{\tilde{\mathbf{y}}_k \tilde{\mathbf{y}}_k} = \sum_{i=0}^{2n} \mathbf{W}_c^{(i)} \left(\mathbf{Y}_{i,k}^- - \hat{\mathbf{y}}_k^- \right) \left(\mathbf{Y}_{i,k}^- - \hat{\mathbf{y}}_k^- \right)^T + \mathbf{R}_k,$$

$$\mathbf{P}_{\mathbf{x}_k \mathbf{y}_k} = \sum_{i=0}^{2n} \mathbf{W}_c^{(i)} \left(\mathbf{X}_{i,k}^- - \mathbf{m}_k^- \right) \left(\mathbf{Y}_{i,k}^- - \hat{\mathbf{y}}_k^- \right)^T,$$

$$\mathbf{K}_k = \mathbf{P}_{\mathbf{x}_k \mathbf{y}_k} \mathbf{P}_{\tilde{\mathbf{y}}_k \tilde{\mathbf{y}}_k}^{-1}, \qquad \mathbf{m}_k = \mathbf{m}_k^- + \mathbf{K}_k \left(\mathbf{y}_k - \hat{\mathbf{y}}_k^- \right),$$

$$\mathbf{P}_k = \mathbf{P}_k^- - \mathbf{K}_k \mathbf{P}_{\tilde{\mathbf{y}}_k \tilde{\mathbf{y}}_k} \mathbf{K}_k^T.$$

For more recent technical details on the unscented Kalman filter, see [QS14] and references therein.

8.3.4 Ensemble Kalman Filter and Nonlinear Estimation

The so-called *Ensemble Kalman Filter* (EnKF, firstly introduced by [Eve94] and later discussed in detail by [EL96, HM98]) is a Monte-Carlo (MC) implementation of the following *Bayesian update problem* [Man09]: Given a PDF of the state of the modeled system (the *prior*; in geophysics, it is usually called the *forecast*) and the data likelihood, the *Bayes theorem* is used to obtain PDF after the data likelihood has been taken into account (the *posterior*). In other words, it is such an MC approach to *Kalman filtering* that estimates the covariances between observed variables and the model state variables through an ensemble of predictive model forecasts. EnKF is a recursive filter suitable for problems with a large number of variables, such as discretizations of PDEs (e.g. in geophysical models).

Here, following [Eve03, GRF12], we briefly outline how the EnKF can be used for *parameter estimation* of a nonlinear dynamical system. Let $\mathbf{p} \in \mathbb{R}^\ell$ be a vector holding the different model parameters, and $\mathbf{x}^f \in \mathbb{R}^n$ be the model state forecast. Let $\left(\mathbf{p}_i, \mathbf{x}_i^f \right)$ for $i = 1, \ldots, N$ be an ensemble of model parameters and state forecasts, and $\mathbf{y}^o \in \mathbb{R}^m$ a vector of m observations, then the estimated parameter values $\mathbf{p}_i^a$ given by the EnKF equations are

$$\mathbf{p}_i^a = \mathbf{p}_i + \tilde{\mathbf{K}} \left(\mathbf{y}_i^o - \mathbf{H} \mathbf{x}_i^f \right), \qquad (i = 1, \ldots, N) \tag{8.11}$$

$$\tilde{\mathbf{K}} = \mathbf{C}^T \mathbf{H}^T \left(\mathbf{H} \mathbf{P}^f \mathbf{H}^T + \mathbf{R} \right)^{-1}, \tag{8.12}$$

where the matrix $\tilde{\mathbf{K}} \in \mathbb{R}^{\ell \times m}$ is a modified *Kalman gain matrix*, $\mathbf{P}^f \in \mathbb{R}^{n \times n}$ is the model forecast covariance matrix, $\mathbf{C} \in \mathbb{R}^{n \times \ell}$ is the cross-correlation matrix between the model forecast and parameters, $\mathbf{R} \in \mathbb{R}^{m \times m}$ is the observations covariance matrix, and $\mathbf{H} \in \mathbb{R}^{m \times n}$ is an observation operator matrix that maps state variables onto observations. In the EnKF, the vector $\mathbf{y}_i^o$ is a *perturbed observation* vector defined as

$$\mathbf{y}_i^o = \mathbf{y}^o + \varepsilon_i, \tag{8.13}$$

where $\varepsilon_i \in \mathbb{R}^m$ is a random vector sampled from a normal distribution with zero mean and a specified standard deviation σ. Usually σ is taken as the variance or error in the observations.

One of the main advantages of the EnKF is that the model forecast covariance matrix is approximated using the ensemble of model forecasts,

$$\mathbf{P}^f \approx \frac{1}{N-1} \sum_{i=1}^{N} \left(\mathbf{x}_i^f - \bar{\mathbf{x}}^f \right) \left(\mathbf{x}_i^f - \bar{\mathbf{x}}^f \right)^T, \tag{8.14}$$

where $\bar{\mathbf{x}}^f \in \mathbb{R}^n$ is the model forecast ensemble average. The use of an ensemble of model forecast to approximate $\mathbf{P}^f$ enables the evolution of this matrix for large non-linear models at a reasonable computational cost. Additionally, the cross-correlation matrix $\mathbf{C}$ is defined as

$$\mathbf{C} = \frac{1}{N-1} \sum_{i=1}^{N} \left(\mathbf{x}_i^f - \bar{\mathbf{x}}^f \right) (\mathbf{p}_i - \bar{\mathbf{p}})^T, \tag{8.15}$$

where $\bar{\mathbf{p}} \in \mathbb{R}^\ell$ is the parameter ensemble average.

The procedure used to estimate the parameters is the following: Let $t_1, \ldots, t_k$ be the time instances where observations are available. For each time instance t_j, $j = 1, \ldots, k$, the EnKF data assimilation provides parameter estimates for the ensemble, $\mathbf{p}_i^a(t_j)$, $i = 1, \ldots, N$. A final parameter estimate is then computed by first taking the ensemble average and then the time average of the parameters:

$$\mathbf{p}^a = \frac{1}{k} \sum_{j=1}^{k} \left[\frac{1}{N} \sum_{i=1}^{N} \mathbf{p}_i^a(t_j) \right] \tag{8.16}$$

This approach avoids the problems of *parameter collapse* and *filter divergence*, since the data assimilation is used to estimate the parameters at each time instance independently. Additionally, since the state is not being updated in the assimilation, and only the parameters are being estimated, localization is not required for the EnKF. For more technical details, see [Eve03, GRF12].

8.4 General Bayesian Filter and Cognitive Control

The whole family of Kalman filters (including particle filters) are special cases of a more general filtering machinery, the so-called *Bayesian filter* (or, *recursive Bayesian estimator*). The Bayesian filter, pioneered by [HL64] (only four years after Kalman's seminal paper [Kal60]), is a general probabilistic model for universal *prediction and control* of noisy time-evolving signals and/or systems (see, e.g. [Jaz70, Sar13]).

8.4.1 Bayesian Filter

Very briefly, the Bayesian filter can be described as follows (compare with, e.g. [Hay09]):

Problem statement: Given a nonlinear dynamical system evolving in a discrete time t, estimate the hidden state x_t of the system in a *recursive manner* by processing a sequence of observations $Y_T = \{y_t\}_{t=1}^{T}$ dependent on the state x_t within a dynamic noise η_t measured as μ_t. The Bayesian filter provides a unifying framework for the optimal solution of this problem, at least in a conceptual sense. Unfortunately, except in a few special cases (mostly the family of Kalman filters), the Bayesian filter is not implementable in practice — hence the need for approximation.

Assumptions: nonlinear state and measurement functions, $a(.)$ and $b(.)$, respectively, are known, while dynamic and measurement noises, η_t μ_t, respectively, are zero-mean Gaussian processes with known covariance matrices.

State-Space Model for a generic Bayesian filter is given by the following data:

1. System state equation:

$$x_{t+1} = a(x_t) + \eta_t; \qquad (8.17)$$

2. Measurement equation:

$$y_t = b(x_t) + \mu_t; \qquad (8.18)$$

3. Time-update equation:

$$p(x_t|Y_{t-1}) = \int_{\mathbb{R}^n} p(x_t|x_{t-1})p(x_{t-1}|Y_{t-1})dx_{t-1}, \qquad (8.19)$$

   where the left-hand side represents the predictive probability distribution, while the two integral terms are the prior distribution and old posterior distribution.

4. Measurement-update equation:

$$p(x_t|Y_t) = Z_t^{(-1)} p(x_t|Y_{t-1})l(y_t|x_t), \qquad (8.20)$$

   where the left-hand side represents the updated posterior probability distribution, the two terms on the right-hand side are the above predictive distribution and the likelihood function l, while Z_t is the normalizing constant, or *partition function* defined by:

$$Z_t = \int_{\mathbb{R}^n} p(x_t|Y_{t-1})l(y_t|x_t)dx_t. \qquad (8.21)$$

The Bayesian filter (8.17)–(8.21) has the following general characteristics:

(i) the posterior fully defines the available information about the state of the environment, given the sequence of observations Y_t;

(ii) the Bayesian filter propagates the posteriori (embodying time and measurement updates for each iteration) across the state-space model; therefore, it is the *maximum a posteriori* (MAP) estimator of the state;

(iii) the classical Kalman filter, applicable to a linear dynamic system in a Gaussian environment, is a special case of the Bayesian filter;

(iv) if the dynamic system is nonlinear and/or the environment is non-Gaussian, then it is no longer feasible to obtain closed-form solutions for the integrals in the time- and measurement-updates,[4] in which case one has to be content with (a number of available) approximate forms of the Bayesian filter (8.17)–(8.21).

Bayesian Filter Applications

There is a number of engineering applications of the Bayesian filter (8.17)–(8.21), including the following (see [Sar13] for technical details):

Global positioning system (GPS) that is a widely used satellite navigation system, in which the EKF-based GPS receiver unit measures arrival times of signals from several GPS satellites and computes its position based on these measurements;

Target tracking methodology (see [CMM11] and references therein), in which a set of sensors (such as active or passive radars, radio frequency sensors, acoustic arrays, infrared sensors, etc.) are used for determining the position and velocity of a remote target (e.g., a robot, a satellite, a car or an airplane);

Multiple target tracking systems (see [RAG04] and references therein), used for remote surveillance in the cases where there are multiple targets moving at the same time in the same geographical area (typically used in remote surveillance for military purposes);

Inertial navigation (see, e.g. [GWA01]) that uses inertial sensors such as accelerometers and gyroscopes for computing the position and velocity of a device such as a car, an airplane, a submarine, or a missile;

Integrated inertial navigation (see, e.g. [GWA01]), which combines the good sides of unbiased but inaccurate sensors, such as altimeters and landmark trackers, and biased but locally accurate inertial sensors;

GPS/INS navigation (see, e.g. [GWA01]), which is a form of integrated inertial navigation where the inertial navigation system (INS) is combined with a GPS receiver unit;

---

[4] At the heart of the Bayesian filter (8.17)–(8.21), we have to compute integrals whose integrands are expressed in the common form: (*Nonlinear function*) $\times$ (*Gaussian function*); the challenge is to numerically approximate the integral so as to completely preserve the 2nd-order information about the state x_t that is contained in the sequence of observations Y_t.

Brain imaging methodology (see, e.g. [LWA06]), including electroencephalography (EEG), magnetoencephalography (MEG), parallel functional magnetic resonance imaging (fMRI) and diffuse optical tomography (DOT), which are all based on reconstruction of the source field in the brain from noisy sensor data by using *minimum norm estimates* (MNE) and its variants;

Spread of infectious diseases (see, e.g. [KR07]) can often be modeled as differential equations for the number of susceptible, infected, and recovered/dead individuals; when uncertainties are introduced into the dynamic equations, and when the measurements are not perfect, the estimation of the spread of the disease can be formulated as an Bayesian filtering problem;

Telecommunications (see, e.g. [Pro01]), including optimal receivers, signal detectors, and phase locked loops, can be interpreted to contain optimal Bayesian filters;

Stochastic optimal control (see, e.g. [SJ72]), which considers control of time-varying stochastic systems, typically found in airplanes, cars, rockets and submarines.

In addition, the Bayesian filter (8.17)–(8.21) has been proposed as a formal basis for *cognitive dynamics and control theory* (see next subsection).

8.4.2 Cognitive Dynamic and Control

According to S. Haykin (see [Hay09, Hay12a, Hay12b, Hay14]) a *cognitive dynamic system* (CDS) is a complex system, capable of emergent behavior, which processes information over the course of time by performing the following three functions: (i) sense (or, perceive) the environment; (i) learn from the environment and adapt to its statistical variations; (iii) build a *predictive model* of prescribed aspects of the environment; — and thereby develop rules of behavior so as to act on (or, control) the environment; for the real-time execution of prescribed tasks, in the face of environmental uncertainties, efficiently and reliably in a cost-effective manner.

At the *core* of any CDS is a *global feedback*, which is responsible for the coordination of its different constituents, mimicking the human brain that has global feedbacks in many of its parts (e.g., visual system, auditory system, or motor control). In particular, the *emergent behavior* of a cognitive dynamic system is due to its global feedback.

The optimal model for a generic CDS is provided by the Bayesian filter (8.17)–(8.21). The major challenge in system design is: *optimality of performance* versus *robustness of behavior* [Hay12]. As in a general case of the Bayesian filter, global optimality of a cognitive dynamic system is not practically feasible, due to: (i) *large-scale nature* of the system, (ii) *infeasible computability*, and (iii) *curse-of-dimensionality*. Hence, the practical requirement of having to settle for a sub-optimal solution of the system design and therefore trade-off global optimality for computational tractability and robust behavior. Criterion for sub-optimality can be stated as: "Do as best as you can, and not more," which is the essence of what the human brain does on a daily basis: "Provide the 'best' solution in the most reliable fashion for the task at hand, given limited resources. The key question here is: How do we define 'best'? The answer is provided by the Bayesian filter (8.17)–(8.21).

The CDS theory is built on Fuster's paradigm of *cognition* [Fus03], which states that a general cognitive system has the following five building blocks: (i) the *perception-action cycle* (PAC[5]), (ii) memory, (iii) attention, (iv) intelligence, and (v) language.[6]

CDSs represent a new way of modeling the environment (world) in information processing terms, without mathematical restrictions imposed on the model [Hay14]. Two among the most prominent examples of cognitive dynamic systems are *cognitive radio*[7] [Hay05] and *cognitive radar*[8] [Hay06].

A particular case of CDS is the so-called *cognitive control* (see [Hay09, Hay12a, Hay12b, Hay14]).

Development of control engineering showed a trend in the evolution of controllers from simple, linear structures, such as open-loop and PID controllers to more and more sophisticated ones, characterized by optimality, robustness, adaptivity, and even some kind of intelligence. As already stated before, design of all these controllers has been based on a trade-off between *optimality*

---

[5] The PAC is the backbone of any closed-loop feedback control system.

[6] A large percentage of the information processing in the brain is performed in the cerebral cortex and it plays a key role in processes attributed to cognition. Regarding the uniform appearance of the cortex, Mountcastle proposed in [Mou98] that all regions of the cerebral cortex may use a basic information processing algorithm to accomplish their tasks, regardless of the nature of the information-bearing sensory input. In other words, all kinds of sensory inputs (i.e., visual, auditory, etc.) are coded in a standard form and fed to this basic processing algorithm. Building on Mountcastle's theory, Fuster proposed the concept of *cognition* for knowledge representation in the cerebral cortex [Fus03].

[7] The *cognitive radio*, built on a software-defined radio, is defined as an intelligent wireless communication system that is aware of its environment and uses the methodology of *understanding-by-building* to learn from the environment and adapt to statistical variations in the input stimuli, with two primary objectives in mind: (i) highly reliable communication whenever and wherever needed; and (ii) efficient utilization of the radio spectrum [Hay05].

[8] The *cognitive radar* is based on the following three components: (i) intelligent signal processing, which builds on learning through interactions of the radar with the surrounding environment; (ii) feedback from the receiver to the transmitter, which is a facilitator of intelligence; and (iii) preservation of the information content of radar returns, which is realized by the Bayesian approach to target detection through tracking. All three of these ingredients feature in the *echo-location system of a bat*, which may be viewed as a physical realization of cognitive radar [Hay06].

and *robustness* (and a sub-optimal approximate solution has frequently been the preferred one [Hay12]).

To respond to the changes and uncertainty of the environment, a new kind of inherently nonlinear, *adaptive controllers* (see [SB89, AW95, IS95, LLS11]) have been formulated in a way that the controller has some adjustable parameters in conjunction with an adaptation mechanism for updating the parameters according to variations in dynamics of the system with which it interacts as well as the nature of disturbances. A particular case of adaptive controllers are neuro-controllers — while adaptive control is mainly based on parameterized mechanistic modeling, neuro-controllers are based on black-box modeling. Hybrid models (i.e., combination of mechanistic modeling and black-box modeling) can also be used, when finding mechanistic models is straightforward for some parts of the system and difficult for other parts [Hay12].

Neural-networks based control systems can be implemented in two ways: (i) the controller itself is a neural network; and (ii) the conventional controller uses a neural-network based model of the plant (see [Hry97, LJY98, NRP00]).

Cognitive Actions

In particular, consider Kalman's LQR-regulator with a *cost function* of the form:

$$J = (\mathbf{x} - \mathbf{x}_d)^T \mathbf{Q}(\mathbf{x} - \mathbf{x}_d) + \mathbf{u}^T \mathbf{R}\mathbf{u} \tag{8.22}$$

to be minimized, where $\mathbf{x}$ and $\mathbf{x}_d$ are the system's state and its corresponding desired-value vectors, $\mathbf{u}$ is the physical control vector, the matrices $\mathbf{Q}$ and $\mathbf{R}$ apply the desired weights for system's state and control, respectively, and the superscript T denotes matrix transposition. To include a cognitive goal, we may add another term to (8.22) to take care of the information gap as well. The resulting cost function may now be formulated as:

$$J = (\mathbf{x} - \mathbf{x}_d)^T \mathbf{Q}(\mathbf{x} - \mathbf{x}_d) + \mathbf{u}^T \mathbf{R}\mathbf{u} + \beta H,$$

where H is the entropy and the scalar β is an importance factor.

8.4.3 Bayesian Programming Framework with Robotic Applications

Bayesian programming (BP) is a generic visual and computational framework for the specification of probabilistic models and solution of a wide class of probabilistic problems with uncertainty and when only a partial/incomplete information is available. Rational reasoning with incomplete and uncertain information is quite a challenge for artificial systems and this is where Bayesian programming comes in. In other words, a *Bayesian program* is a Prolog-like inference engine to automate probabilistic reasoning, having a power of expression equivalent to *probabilistic factor graphs*.[9] In yet another words, a Bayesian program is a unique notation and structure to describe probabilistic knowledge and its use, or more specifically, to specify a family of *joint probability distributions*[10] over a set of variables [Bes03, DBM03, LBD04, BLS08, Wik16m].

Bayesian programming is based on the so-called *subjectivist approach to probability*[11] [Jay03]. The subjectivist approach deals with the ever-present *incompleteness* and *uncertainty* of the real world using a two-step process consisting of *learning* and *inference*. Firstly, learning from experimental data transforms *irreducible incompleteness* into *quantified uncertainty* in the form of *joint probability distributions*. The learning is based on the *maximum entropy principle*.[12] These distributions result from both preliminary knowledge π of the reasoning subject and experimental data δ obtained by observation of the phenomenon. Preliminary knowledge, even when it is imperfect and incomplete, is relevant and provides interesting hints about the observed phenomenon; it is only a *gauge*, with free parameters, waiting to be molded by experimental data (see [CDB10] and references therein).

Secondly, the so-called *Bayesian inference* (BI) is performed over the joint probability distributions (obtained in the first step by learning), using the *Bayes theorem* that relates current to prior belief and/or current to prior evidence. Recall that Bayes' theorem reads:[13]

$$P(X|Y) = P(Y|X)P(X)/P(Y), \qquad (8.23)$$

where the *prior probability* $P(X)$ is the initial degree of belief in X, the *conditional probability*[14] $P(X|Y)$ is the degree of belief in X given Y, and the quotient $P(Y|X)/P(Y)$ represents the support Y provides for X (for further technical details, see [Wik16n] and references therein).

---

[9] Recall that a *factor graph* is a *bipartite graph* (a graph whose vertices can be divided into two disjoint sets U and V such that every edge connects a vertex in U to one in V) representing the factorization of some function.

[10] For example, if we have a model with three variables (X, Y, Z) then their joint probability distribution is calculated as: $P(X \wedge Y \wedge Z) = P(X)P(Y|X)P(Z|Y)$.

[11] The subjectivist approach to probability proposes probability theory as an extension to symbolic logic for rational reasoning in the presence of *incompleteness* and *uncertainty*.

[12] The *maximum entropy principle* states that, subject to precisely stated prior data, the probability distribution which best represents the current state of knowledge is the one with the largest entropy (see [Wik16t] and references therein).

[13] For example in robotics, if we want to infer a robot state x by means of sensory data y, the *Bayes theorem* can be stated as:

$$P(x|y) = P(y|x)P(x)/P(y),$$

to determine the (inverse) probability of data y, assuming x was the case.

[14] The logical dependency between probabilistic variables is specified as a *conditional probability*, i.e., standard logical implication $A \implies B$ is rewritten as: $P(B = true \mid A = true) = 1$.

Using the *Bayes theorem* (8.23), BI is based on the two basic rules (or, postulates) for arbitrary probabilistic propositions[15] (see, e.g. [LBD04] and references therein):

(i) *Normalization*: $P(a|\pi) + P(\neg a|\pi) = 1$, and

(ii) *Conjunction*: $P(a \wedge b|\pi) = P(a|\pi)P(b|a \wedge \pi) = P(b|\pi)P(a|b \wedge \pi)$,

where $P(a|\pi)$ is the probability of each proposition a conditioned by the preliminary knowledge π (i.e., a unique real value from the interval $[0,1]$ assigned to a based on π), $P(\neg a|\pi)$ is the probability of the negation of the proposition a, while $P(a \wedge b|\pi)$ represents the probability of the conjunction of two propositions a and b.[16]

A Generic Template for Bayesian Programming (BP)

The basic components of a generic Bayesian program are:

$$\text{Program-}Pr \begin{cases} \text{Description-}Ds \begin{cases} \text{Specification-}Sp(\pi) \begin{cases} \text{Variables-}Va \\ \text{Decomposition-}Dc \\ \text{Forms-}Fo \end{cases} \\ \text{Identification-}Id \text{ (using data } \delta) \end{cases} \\ \text{Question-}Qu \end{cases}$$

where:

---

[15] To be able to deal with uncertainties, we attach probabilities to propositions. For example, using *ProbLog* (a probabilistic version of the Prolog language) it is easy to express complex probabilistic models as:

0.3::stress(X) : − person(X).

0.2::influences(X,Y) : − person(X), person(Y).

smokes(X) : − stress(X).

0.4::asthma(X) < − smokes(X), etc.

Now, to assign a probability to a proposition, it is necessary to have some preliminary knowledge, summed up by a proposition π. Consequently, the probability of a proposition a is always conditioned by π. Formally, for each different π, $P(a|\pi)$ is an application assigning to each proposition a a unique real value in the interval $[0,1]$ (see [Bes03, DBM03, LBD04]).

[16] As in machine logic, where the *resolution principle* [Rob65, Rob79] is sufficient to solve any inference problem, these two *Bayesian inference rules* are sufficient for any computation with discrete probabilities. Any other rules (e.g., disjunctions and rules for variables) can be derived from these two basic rules (see, e.g. [LBD04] and references therein).

A general form of the *normalization rule*, over the set of variables $Va = \{X\}$, reads: $\sum_X P(X|\pi) = 1$. In addition, for complex calculations over the set of variables Va, the following *marginalization rule* is frequently used: $\sum_X P(X \wedge Y|\pi) = P(Y|\pi)$, which can also be derived from the general form of the two basic postulates (see [Bes03, DBM03, LBD04]).

1. A Program Pr is constructed from a Description Ds (a declarative component that is an effective algorithm of computing a *joint probability distribution*: $P(X_1 \wedge X_2 \wedge \cdots \wedge X_N \mid \delta \wedge \pi)$ over a set of variables: $Va = \{X_1, X_2, \cdots, X_N\}$, given a set of experimental data δ and some preliminary knowledge, or specification π) and a Question Qu (given a description, a question is obtained by partitioning the set of variables Va into three sets: the searched variables, the known variables and the free variables);

2. A Description Ds is constructed using some Specification $Sp(\pi)$ as given by the programmer and an Identification Id, where free parameters are learned from experimental data δ, i.e., learning process for the parameters not completely specified by the Specification $Sp(\pi)$ based on a data set δ;

3. A Specification $Sp(\pi)$ formalizes the modeler's knowledge and is constructed from a set of pertinent Variables Va, a Decomposition Dc [that is, a recursive application of the *Bayes theorem* (8.23)] and a set of Forms Fo;

4. Forms Fo are either parametric forms [i.e., functions $f_\mu(L_k)$], or complete Bayesian programs Pr, or Questions Qu to other Bayesian programs;[17]

5. A Question Qu specifies which probability distribution of the form: P (Searched | Known) has to be computed; answering a Question consists in deciding a value for the variable Searched according to P (Searched | Known), where Searched and Known are conjunctions of variables appearing in disjoint subsets of the set Va; Formally, we have:

$$P \text{ (Searched} \mid \text{Known)}$$
$$= \frac{\sum_{\text{Free}} P \text{ (Searched} \wedge \text{Free} \wedge \text{Known)}}{P \text{ (Known)}}$$
$$= \frac{1}{Z} \sum_{\text{Free}} P \text{ (Searched} \wedge \text{Free} \wedge \text{Known)},$$

where Z denotes the normalization constant (or, more generally a partition function);

6. In general, given the joint probability distribution: $P(X_1 \wedge X_2 \wedge \cdots \wedge X_N \mid \delta \wedge \pi)$, it is always possible to compute any possible question Qu using the following general inference scheme (see [Bes03, LBD04, Wik16m]):

$$P \text{ (Searched} \mid \text{Known} \wedge \delta \wedge \pi)$$
$$= \sum_{\text{Free}} [P \text{ (Searched} \wedge \text{Free} \mid \text{Known} \wedge \delta \wedge \pi)]$$

---

[17] This is similar to calling a subroutine/procedure in classical programming and provides an easy way to build *hierarchical models*.

$$= \frac{\sum_{\text{Free}} [P\,(\text{Searched} \wedge \text{Free} \wedge \text{Known} \mid \delta \wedge \pi)]}{P\,(\text{ Known} \mid \delta \wedge \pi)}$$

$$= \frac{\sum_{\text{Free}} [P\,(\text{Searched} \wedge \text{Free} \wedge \text{Known} \mid \delta \wedge \pi)]}{\sum_{\text{Free} \wedge \text{Searched}} [P\,(\text{Searched} \wedge \text{Free} \wedge \text{Known} \mid \delta \wedge \pi)]}$$

$$= \frac{1}{Z} \sum_{\text{Free}} [P\,(\text{Searched} \wedge \text{ Free} \wedge \text{Known} \mid \delta \wedge \pi)],$$

where the first equality results from the *marginalization rule*, the second results from the *Bayes theorem* and the third corresponds to a second application of the marginalization. There are three possibilities for the simplification of this general expression (which is very important e.g. for the efficient *Bayesian robot programming* [LBD04]): (i) when a term is a uniform distribution it vanishes from the expression and its value will implicitly be taken into account in the normalization constant Z; (ii) when a term is a distribution where all the variables have Known values, then it is simply a constant for this question; (iii) when a term is a distribution where all the variables are either Searched or Known, then it can be factorized out of the sum.

Bayesian Filters via BP

The general *Bayesian filter* (8.17)–(8.21) can be implemented as the following generic Bayesian program (see [DBM03, Wik16m]):

$$Pr \begin{cases} Ds \begin{cases} Sp(\pi) \begin{cases} Va : \{S^0, \cdots, S^T, O^0, \cdots, O^T\} \\ Dc : \begin{cases} P\left(S^0 \wedge \cdots \wedge S^T \wedge O^0 \wedge \cdots \wedge O^T \mid \pi\right) \\ = P\left(S^0 \wedge O^0\right) \times \prod_{t=1}^{T} \left[P\left(S^t \mid S^{t-1}\right) \times P\left(O^t \mid S^t\right)\right] \end{cases} \\ Fo : \begin{cases} P\left(S^0 \wedge O^0\right) \\ P\left(S^t \mid S^{t-1}\right) \\ P\left(O^t \mid S^t\right) \end{cases} \end{cases} \\ Id : \text{any} \end{cases} \\ Qu : \begin{cases} P\left(S^{t+k} \mid O^0 \wedge \cdots \wedge O^t\right) \\ (k = 0) \equiv \text{Filtering} \\ (k > 0) \equiv \text{Prediction} \\ (k < 0) \equiv \text{Smoothing} \end{cases} \end{cases}$$

where $S^0, \ldots, S^T$ and $O^0, \ldots, O^T$ are time series of state and observation variables, while $P(S^t \mid S^{t-1})$ and $P(O^t \mid S^t)$ are Transition and Observation models, respectively, on which the decomposition Dc is based.

In particular, Bayesian Filters $(k = 0)$ have a very interesting *recursive property* which contributes largely to their popularity. Indeed, $P(S^t|O^0 \wedge \cdots \wedge O^t)$ may be simply computed from $P\left(S^{t-1}|O^0 \wedge \cdots \wedge O^{t-1}\right)$ with the following recurrent formula (see [DBM03]):[18]

$$P\left(S^t|O^0 \wedge \cdots \wedge O^t\right) = P(O^t|S^t) \sum_{t=1}^{T} P(S^t|S^{t-1})P\left(S^{t-1}|O^0 \wedge \cdots \wedge O^{t-1}\right)$$

$$(8.24)$$

8.5 Particle Filters: Superior Estimation Models for CPC-Autonomy

In this subsection we give the first, brief encounter with *particle filters*, to be used later within applications in *autonomous robotics*. Briefly, a family of particle filters represent approximate techniques for calculating posteriors in partially observable/controllable *Markov chains*[19] evolving in discrete time.

The particle filter model is based on the notion of a generic *state-space model*,[20] which consists of an unobservable Markov process (X_t), the state of a system or the signal, combined with partial and noisy observations $(Y_i; i \geq 1)$ of the state at discrete times t_i. We denote the initial distribution of X_0 by π_0 and the conditional distribution of X_i given $X_{i-1} = x_{i-1}$ by $P(dx_i|x_{i-1})$.

---

[18] We remark that popular *Particle Filters* may be seen as a specific implementation of Bayesian Filters. The distribution $P\left(S^{t-1}|O^0 \wedge \cdots \wedge O^{t-1}\right)$ is approximated by a set of N particles having weights proportional to their probabilities. The recursive relation (8.24) is then used to inspire a dynamic process that produces an approximation of $P\left(S^t|O^0 \wedge \cdots \wedge O^t\right)$. The principle of this dynamical process is that the particles are first moved according to the Transition model $P(S^t|S^{t-1})$, and then their weights are updated according to the Observation model $P(O^t|S^t)$.

[19] Recall that a *Markov chain* (MC) is a collection of random variables $\{X_t\}$ in discrete time t, having the property that, given the present, the future is conditionally independent of the past. Formally,

$$P(X_t = j|X_0 = i_0, X_1 = i_1, ..., X_{(t-1)} = i_{(t-1)}) = P(X_t = j|X_{(t-1)} = i_{(t-1)}).$$

For technical details on MC, see [Wik16y] and references therein.

A derived class of MC-algorithms (including *random walk Monte Carlo* methods) called *Markov Chain Monte Carlo* (MCMC) are used for sampling from a probability distribution based on constructing a Markov chain that has the desired distribution as its equilibrium distribution. For technical details on MCMC, see [Wik16x] and references therein.

[20] Similar state-space models have a wide range of applications in finance (stochastic volatility, interest rates), engineering (tracking, speech recognition, computer vision), biology (genome sequence analysis, ion channels, stochastic kinetic models), geophysics (meteorology, oceanography, reservoir modeling), analysis of longitudinal data and others.

By the above assumptions on the state and observation models, we have the following joint distributions for $n \geq m$ (see [Kun13] and references therein):

$$(X_{0:n}, Y_{1:m}) \sim \pi_0(dx_0) \prod_{t=1}^{n} P(dx_t|x_{t-1}) \prod_{t=1}^{m} g(y_t|x_t)\nu(dy_t). \qquad (8.25)$$

The information about the state contained in the observations is expressed by the conditional distributions $\pi_{s:t|n}$ of $X_{s:t}$ given $Y_{1:n} = y_{1:n}$. Of particular interest are $\pi_{0:n} := \pi_{0:n|n}$, called here the joint smoothing distribution, and $\pi_n := \pi_{n|n}$, called here the filter distribution (the terminology is not unique). For $n \geq m$, $\pi_{0:n|m}$ follows immediately from (8.25) and *Bayes formula*. Other cases are then obtained (in principle) by *marginalization*. However, we are interested in methods to compute/approximate expectations with respect to these distributions in an explicit and efficient way, using the most useful recursive formulae [Kun13]:

$$\pi_{0:n|n-1}(dx_{0:n}|y_{1:n-1}) = \pi_{0:n-1}(dx_{0:n-1}|y_{1:n-1})P(dx_n|x_{n-1}), \quad (8.26)$$

$$\pi_{0:n}(dx_{0:n}|y_{1:n}) = \pi_{0:n|n-1}(dx_{0:n}|y_{1:n})\frac{g(y_n|x_n)}{p_n(y_n|y_{1:n-1})},$$

$$p_n(y_n|y_{1:n-1}) = \int \pi_{n|n-1}(dx_n|y_{1:n-1})g(y_n|x_n).$$

Marginalization implies the following recursions:

$$\pi_{n|n-1}(dx_n|y_{1:n-1}) = \int \pi_{n-1}(dx_{n-1}|y_{1:n-1})P(dx_n|x_{n-1}), \qquad (8.27)$$

$$\pi_n(dx_n|y_{1:n}) = \pi_{n|n-1}(dx_n|y_{1:n})\frac{g(y_n|x_n)}{p_n(y_n|y_{1:n-1})}.$$

The particle filter recursively computes importance sampling approximations of π_n, as [Kun13]:

$$\pi_n(dx_n|y_{1:n}) \approx \hat{\pi}_n(dx_n|y_{1:n}) = \sum_{i=1}^{N} W_n^i \Delta_{X_n^i}(dx_n).$$

Here the W_n^i are random weights which sum to one, X_n^i are random variables called "particles" and Δ_x is the point mass at x. At time 0, we draw particles from π_0 and set $W_0^i = 1/N$. At time n we start with $\hat{\pi}_{n-1}$ and draw independently new particles X_n^i from $P(\cdot|X_{n-1}^i)$. The particles X_n^i with weights W_{n-1}^i provide an importance sampling approximation of $\pi_{n|n-1}$. If we also update the weights with $W_n^i \propto W_{n-1}^i g(y_n|X_n^i)$, we have closed the recursion by (8.27).

Thus the basic *particle filter*, also called the bootstrap filter or SIR-filter,[21] works as follows:[22]

1. Resample: Draw $(X_{n-1}^{*1}, \ldots, X_{n-1}^{*N})$ from $\hat{\pi}_{n-1}$.
2. Propagate: Draw X_n^i from $P(\cdot | X_{n-1}^{*i})$, independently for different indices i.
3. Reweight: Set $W_n^i \propto g(y_n | X_n^i)$.

For more technical details, see [Kun13] and references therein.

8.5.1 Particle Filtering Basics

Consider a general, discrete-time nonlinear, probabilistic *state-space model* (SSM), which consists of a Markov process $\{x_t\}_{t \geq 1} \subseteq \mathbb{R}^{n_x}$ that is observed indirectly via a measurement process $\{y_t\}_{t \geq 1} \subseteq \mathbb{R}^{n_y}$. The model comprises of the dynamics $f(\cdot)$ and measurement $h(\cdot)$ *probability density functions* (PDFs). Formally, we have a system of nonlinear difference equations, given both in Bayesian probabilistic formulation (left-hand side) and standard state-space formulation (right-hand side):

$$\text{Dynamics}: \quad x_{t+1}|x_t \sim f(x_{t+1}|x_t) \iff x_{t+1} = a(x_t) + \eta_t, \quad (8.28)$$

$$\text{Measurement}: \quad y_t|x_t \sim h(y_t|x_t) \iff y_t = c(x_t) + e_t, \quad (8.29)$$

$$\text{with initial state}: \quad x_1 \sim \mu(x_1),$$

where a and c are the state and output vector-functions, w_t and e_t are process and measurement noise disturbances, respectively, while μ is a given distribution. The *state filtering problem* means to recover information about the current state x_t in (8.28) based on the available measurements $y_{1:t}$ in (8.29). [See, e.g. [SGN05]; for a recent review, see [SLD15] and the references therein.] In case of linear/Gaussian SSMs, the state filtering problems can be analytically solved using the standard Kalman filter [Kal60], obtaining the closed-form solution for the *filter PDF* $p(x_t|y_{1:t})$. However, in general case of nonlinear/non-Gaussian SSMs it is not possible.

A principled solution to the nonlinear/non-Gaussian state filtering problem is provided by the following recursive Bayesian[23] equations:

$$\text{measurement update}: p(x_t|y_{1:t}) = \frac{\overset{\text{measure prediction PDF}}{\overbrace{h(y_t|x_t)} \overbrace{p(x_t|y_{1:t-1})}}}{p(y_t|y_{1:t-1})}, \quad \text{where} \quad (8.30)$$

$$\text{time update}: \overbrace{p(x_t|y_{1:t-1})}^{\text{prediction PDF}} = \int \overbrace{f(x_t|x_{t-1})}^{\text{dynamics}} \overbrace{p(x_{t-1}|y_{1:t-1})}^{\text{prev filter PDF}} dx_{t-1}. \quad (8.31)$$

---

[21] SIR stands for Sampling-Importance-Resampling.

[22] For any function $\varphi : S \to \mathbb{R}$, $N^{-1} \sum_i \varphi(X_{n-1}^{*i})$ always has a larger variance than $\sum_i W_{n-1}^i \varphi(X_{n-1}^i)$. The advantage of resampling is seen only after one or several propagation steps. Because of this, we resample at the beginning and not at the end of a recursion.

[23] Conditional probabilities are often given by the Bayes' rule: $p(a|b) = p(b|a) \, p(a)/p(b)$.

These equations can only be solved in closed form for the linear-Gaussian model, which results in the Kalman filter.

A general state filtering problems associated with the nonlinear/non-Gaussian SSMs (8.30)–(8.31) can be only numerically approximated using the *sequential Monte Carlo* (SMC) methods. The SMC-approximation (denoted by $\widehat{p}$) is an empirical distribution represented as a weighted sum of Dirac-delta functions:

$$\widehat{p}(x_t|y_{1:t}) = \sum_{i=1}^{N} w_t^i \delta_{x_t^i}(x_t), \tag{8.32}$$

where the samples $\{x_t^i\}_{i=1}^N$ are called *particles* (point-masses 'spread out' in the state space); each particle x_t^i represents one possible system state and the corresponding weight w_t^i assigns its probability. In this way defined *particle filter* (PF) plays the role of the Kalman filter for nonlinear/non-Gaussian SSMs. PF approximates the filter PDF $p(x_t|y_{1:t})$ using the SMC approximation (8.32).

Basically, a PF can be interpreted as a sequential application of *importance sampling* (IS, see e.g. [GSS93]). At each time step, the IS is used to approximate the filter PDF $p(x_t|y_{1:t})$ by using the recursive Bayesian equations (8.30)–(8.31) together with the already generated IS approximation of $p(x_{t-1}|y_{1:t-1})$, starting from the initial approximation: $\widehat{p}(x_1|y_1) \propto h(y_1|x_1)\mu(x_1)$. The particles $\{x_1^i\}_{i=1}^N$ are sampled independently from some proposal distribution $r(x_1)$. To account for the discrepancy between the proposal distribution and the target distribution, the particles are assigned importance weights, given by the ratio between the target and the proposal: $w_1^i \propto h(y_1|x_1^i)\mu(x_1^i)/r(x_1^i)$, where the weights are normalized to sum to one.

The IS proceeds in an inductive fashion:

$$\widehat{p}(x_{t-1}|y_{1:t-1}) = \sum_{i=1}^{N} w_{t-1}^i \delta_{x_{t-1}^i}(x_{t-1}),$$

which inserted into (8.31) gives a mixture distribution approximating $p(x_t|y_{1:t-1})$ as:

$$\widehat{p}(x_t|y_{1:t-1}) = \int \overset{\text{dynamics}}{f(x_t|x_{t-1})} \sum_{i=1}^{N} w_{t-1}^i \delta_{x_{t-1}^i}(x_{t-1})dx_{t-1} = \sum_{i=1}^{N} w_{t-1}^i f(x_t|x_{t-1}^i).$$
$$\tag{8.33}$$

Next, inserting (8.33) into (8.30) gives the following approximation of the filter PDF:

$$\overset{\text{filter PDF}}{p(x_t|y_{1:t})} \approx \frac{\overset{\text{measure}}{h(y_t|x_t)}}{p(y_t|y_{1:t-1})} \sum_{i=1}^{N} \overset{\text{weighted dynamics}}{w_{t-1}^i f(x_t|x_{t-1}^i)},$$

which needs to be further approximated using the IS. The *proposal density* is pragmatically chosen as: $r(x_t|y_{1:t}) = \sum_{j=1}^{N} w_{t-1}^j f(x_t|x_{t-1}^j)$. The N ancestor indices $\{a_t^i\}_{i=1}^N$ are *resampled* into a new set of particles $\{a_{t-1}^i\}_{i=1}^N$ that are subsequently used to propagate the particles to time t.

The final step is to assign importance weights to the new particles as:

$$\bar{w}_t^i = \frac{h(y_t|x_t^i) \sum_{j=1}^N w_{t-1}^j f(x_t^i|x_{t-1}^j)}{\sum_{j=1}^N w_{t-1}^j f(x_t|x_{t-1}^j)}.$$

By evaluating $\bar{w}_t^i$ for $i = 1, ..., N$ and normalizing the weights, we obtain a new set of weighted particles $\{x_t^i, w_t^i\}_{i=1}^N$, constituting an empirical approximation of the filter PDF $p(x_t|y_{1:t})$. This completes the algorithm (since these weighted particles can be used to iteratively approximate the filter PDF at future times). The resulting algorithm, with an overall computational complexity of $O(N)$, is called the *bootstrap particle filter* (pioneered by [GSS93]) and is summarized in the following algorithm (see [SLD15]).

Bootstrap PF Algorithm

1. **Initialize the particles** $(t = 1)$:
2.   Sample $x_1^i \sim \mu(x_1)$, $(i = 1, ..., N)$
3.   Compute $\bar{w}_1^i = g(y_1|x_1^i)$ and normalize: $w_1^i = \bar{w}_1^i / \sum_{j=1}^N \bar{w}_1^j$
4. **for** $t = 2$ **to** T **do**
5.   **Resampling:** Sample a_t^i with $P(a_t^i = j) = w_t^j$
6.   **Propagation:** Sample $x_t^i \sim f(x_t|x_{t-1}^{a_t^i})$
7.   **Weighting:** Compute $\bar{w}_t^i = g(y_t|x_t^i)$ and normalize: $w_t^i = \bar{w}_t^i / \sum_{j=1}^N \bar{w}_t^j$
8. **End**

8.6 Low-Dimensional FastSLAM Algorithms

The ability to simultaneously localize a robot and accurately map its surroundings is considered by many to be a key prerequisite of truly autonomous robots. However, few approaches to this problem scale up to handle the very large number of landmarks present in real environments. For instance, Kalman filter-based algorithms require time quadratic in the number of landmarks to incorporate each sensor observation [Thr02]. A far-superior, *particle-filter algorithm* called the *FastSLAM*, presented in [MTK02], recursively estimates the full posterior distribution over robot pose and landmark locations, yet scales logarithmically with the number of landmarks in the map. This algorithm is based on a factorization of the posterior into a product of conditional landmark distributions and a distribution over robot paths. The algorithm has been demonstrated to solve problems with more than 100,000 dimensions in real-time, environments far beyond the reach of any previous approaches (see [MTK02, Thr02]). Similar techniques have been developed for robustly tracking other moving entities, such as people in the proximity of a robot [SBF01, MWT02].

Recall (from subsection 8.5 above) that *particle filters* are approximate techniques for calculating posteriors in partially observable/controllable *Markov chains* evolving in discrete time. Suppose the state of the Markov chain at time t is given by x_t, which itself depends on the previous state x_{t-1} according to the conditional probabilistic law $p(x_t|u_t, x_{t-1})$, where u_t denotes the control asserted in the time interval $(t-1, t]$. As the state in the Markov chain is not observable, one can only measure y_t, which is a random projection of the true state x_t generated via the conditional probabilistic law $p(y_t|x_t)$. Besides, the initial state x_0 is distributed according to some probability distribution $p(x_0)$. In robotics, $p(x_t|u_t, x_{t-1})$ is usually referred to as *actuation model*, while $p(y_t|x_t)$ as *measurement model*, which are both noisy and geometric generalizations of classical robotics notions of kinematics and dynamics [Thr02].

The classical problem in partially observable Markov chains is to recover a posterior distribution over the state x_t at any time t, from all available sensor measurements $Y_t = \{y_0, ..., y_t\}$ and controls $U_t = \{u_0, ..., u_t\}$. A solution to this problem is given by *Bayesian filters* (see, e.g. [Jaz70]), which compute this posterior recursively:

$$p(x_t|Y_t, U_t) = Y \times p(y_t|x_t) \int p(x_t|u_t, x_{t-1}) p(x_{t-1}|Y_{t-1}, U_{t-1}) dx_{t-1} \quad (8.34)$$

under the initial condition $p(x_0|Y_0, U_0) = p(x_0)$. If states, controls, and measurements are all discrete, the Markov chain is equivalent to hidden Markov models (HMM) and equation (8.34) can be implemented exactly. However, in robotics, particle filters are usually applied in continuous state spaces (see [MTK02, Thr02]). For continuous state spaces, closed form solutions for calculating (8.34) are only known for highly specialized cases. If $p(x_0)$ is Gaussian and both $p(x_t|u_t, x_{t-1})$ and $p(y_t|x_t)$ are linear (with added independent Gaussian noise), then (8.34) reduces to the *Kalman filter*. Kalman filters require $O(d^3)$ time for d-dimensional state spaces, although in many robotics problems the locality of sensor data allows for $O(d^2)$ implementations. A common approximation in non-linear non-Gaussian systems is to linearize the actuation and measurements models. If the linearization is obtained via a first-order Taylor series expansion, the result is the *extended Kalman filter* (EKF). The *unscented Kalman filter* often gives a better linear model through (non-random) sampling. However, all these techniques are confined to cases where the Gaussian-linear assumption is a suitable.

This is where particle filters come in — they address the more general case of (nearly) unconstrained Markov chains. The basic idea is to approximate the *posterior* of a set of sample states $\{x_t^{|i|}\}$, or particles, where each $x_t^{|i|}$ represents a concrete state sample of index $i = 1, ..., M =$ the size of the particle filter. The most basic version of particle filters is given by the following algorithm [MTK02, Thr02]:

Initialization: At time $t = 0$, draw M particles according to $p(x_0)$ and label this set of particles X_0; and

Recursion: At time $t > 0$, generate a particle $x_t^{|i|}$ for each particle $x_{t-1}^{|i|} \in X_{t-1}$ by drawing from the actuation model $p(x_t|u_t, x_{t-1}^{|i|})$; label the resulting set $\bar{X}_t$. Subsequently, draw M particles from $\bar{X}_t$, so that each $x_t^{|i|} \in \bar{X}_t$ is drawn (with replacement) with a probability proportional to $p(y_t|x_t^{|i|})$; label the resulting set of particles X_t.

In the limit as $M \to \infty$, this recursive procedure leads to particle sets X_t that converge uniformly to the desired posterior $p(x_t|Y_t, U_t)$, under some mild assumptions on the nature of the Markov chain. Particle filters can be applied to almost any probabilistic robot model that can be formulated as a Markov chain. In addition, particle filters do not require a fixed computation time; instead, their accuracy increases with the available computational resources.

In particular, the common *simultaneous localization and mapping* (SLAM) algorithm (concerned with estimating the locations of some chosen features and the robot's path from the controls u and the measurements y, see e.g. [Wik16dd]), represents a *dynamic Bayesian network* (DBN), reviewed above using *Bayesian Programming*. Suppose that the robot moves from pose x_1 through a sequence of controls, $u_1, u_2, ..., u_t$. As it moves, it observes nearby features $\Phi = \{\varphi_1, \varphi_2\}$: at time $t = 1$, it observes feature φ_1, using the measurement y_1 (range and bearing); at time $t = 2$, it observes the other feature, φ_2, and at time $t = 3$, it observes φ_1 again.

For more technical details on particle filters in robotics and the *FastSLAM algorithm*, see [MTK02, Thr02] and references therein.

8.7 High-Dimensional FastSLAM Algorithms

Notwithstanding the success and popularity of the *FastSLAM/FastSLAM2* algorithms[24] (see [MTK02, MTK03, TMK04]), it is now a well-known fact that only low-dimensional vehicle models can be handled by these algorithms, due to sampling computational constraints on the standard *particle filter* (PF; see, e.g. [GSB07]). This limitation has been overcome by implementing the so-called *Rao-Blackwellized particle filter* (RBPF), also called the *marginalized particle filter* (MPF), which is a special kind of factored PF, where each particle has the optimal linear-Gaussian *Kalman filter* (KF; [Kal60]) associated to it (see [CR96, CL00, DGA00, DGK01, AD02, SGN03, SGN05, KSG05, SKG06]).

Unlike ordinary particle filters (see [AMG02, RAG04]), the RBPF can handle high-dimensional problems, by cleverly avoiding the 'curse of dimensionality'. In RBPF implementation, an extra factorization of the SLAM problem

---

[24] Recall that *simultaneous localization and mapping* (SLAM) is an extension of the *localization/positioning* problem to the case where the environment is unmodeled and has to be mapped on-line (for a SLAM-survey, see [DB06, BD06] and references therein).

has been introduced, by exploiting an existing linear-Gaussian substructure in the model, which makes high-dimensional vehicle models computationally feasible.

The RBPF estimates the behavior of a general discrete-time state-space model with *nonlinear dynamics* f and *nonlinear measurements* h, defined by [KSG05]:

$$x_{t+1} = f(x_t, \eta_t), \qquad y_t = h_t(x_t, e_t), \tag{8.35}$$

where the white-noise processes η_t and e_t are both zero-mean and Gaussian-distributed with covariance matrices Q_t and R_t: $\eta_t \sim \mathcal{N}(0, Q_t)$, $e_t \sim \mathcal{N}(0, R_t)$.

The RBPF exploits any linear and/or Gaussian sub-structure present in the general state-space model (8.35), by partitioning the system's state vector $x_t \in \mathbb{R}^m$ into two parts, as:

$$x_t = \begin{bmatrix} x_t^n \\ x_t^l \end{bmatrix}, \qquad \text{(with } x_t^n \in \mathbb{R}^n, \ x_t^l \in \mathbb{R}^l\text{)}, \tag{8.36}$$

where superscripts 'n' and 'l' denote nonlinear (estimated by PF) and linear (estimated by KF) states, respectively (see [SGN03, SGN05, SKG06]).

Such a linear-Gaussian substructure of (8.35), particularly important for tracking and positioning applications, is usually the standard KF (with the state matrix A_t and the nonlinear measurement function h_t, see [KSG05]):

$$x_{t+1} = A_t x_t + \eta_t, \qquad y_t = h_t(x_t) + e_t,$$

which obeys the *recursive Bayes rule*:

$$\overset{\text{Posterior}}{p(x_t|y_{1:t})} \propto \overset{\text{Prior}}{p(x_t|y_{1:t-1})} \overset{\text{Likelihood}}{p(y_t|x_t)},$$

where $y_{1:t} = \{y_1, ..., y_t\}$ denotes the measurements up to time t.

In essence, the RBPF uses the following factorization of the *posterior distribution* $p(x_t^l, x_{1:t}^n | y_{1:t})$ of the conditionally-linear & Gaussian state-vector x_t (given the measurements $y_{1:t}$), which follows from the Bayes rule[25] [SGN03, SGN05, KSG05, SKG06]:

---

[25] The RBPF represents an efficient solution of the general *Bayesian filter*, which includes the *time-update recursion* for calculating the *prior density*:

$$p(x_t|y_{1:t-1}) = \int_{\mathbb{R}^n} p(x_t|x_{t-1})p(x_{t-1}|y_{1:t-1})dx_{t-1},$$

and the *measurement-update recursion* for calculating the *posterior density*:

$$\overset{\text{Posterior}}{p(x_t|y_{1:t})} = \overset{\text{Prior}}{p(x_t|y_{1:t-1})} \overset{\text{Likelihood}}{p(y_t|x_t)} /Z_t,$$

where Z_t is the normalizing constant (i.e., the *partition function*): $Z_t = \int_{\mathbb{R}^n} p(x_t|y_{1:t-1})p(y_t|x_t)dx_t$.

$$\overset{\text{RBPF}}{p(x_t^l, x_{1:t}^n | y_{1:t})} = \overset{\text{Optimal KF}}{p(x_t^l | x_{1:t}^n, y_{1:t})} \overset{\text{Approx. PF}}{p(x_{1:t}^n | y_{1:t})},$$

where the density $p(x_t^l | x_{1:t}^n, y_{1:t})$ is linear-Gaussian, hence analytically tractable and therefore can be optimally estimated using the KF [Kal60], while the density $p(x_{1:t}^n | y_{1:t})$ can be only approximatively estimated using any standard PF. The RBPF uses a clever combination of parametric and non-parametric probability densities:

$$p(x_t^l, x_{1:t}^n | y_{1:t}) = p(x_t^l | x_{1:t}^n, y_{1:t}) p(x_{1:t}^n | y_{1:t}) = \sum_{i=1}^{N} w_t^i \delta(x_{1:t}^n - x_{1:t}^{n,i}) \mathcal{N}(x_t^l | \hat{x}_{t|t}^{l,i}, P_{t|t}^i),$$

(8.37)

where the estimated density $p(x_t^l, x_{1:t}^n | y_{1:t})$ is given by a weighted sum of Dirac distributions $w_t^i \delta(x_{1:t}^n - x_{1:t}^{n,i})$, while each ith particle has a Gaussian distribution $\mathcal{N}(x_t^l | \hat{x}_{t|t}^{l,i}, P_{t|t}^i)$ attached to it (for technical details on this parametric/non-parametric combination, see [SGN03, SGN05, KSG05, SKG06] and references therein).

The RBPF is applicable to any conditionally linear-Gaussian structure. Formally it includes (i) nonlinear state dynamics (state-PF), (ii) linear state dynamics (state-KF), and (iii) measurement dynamics (measure), combined as the following model 3 in [SGN05]:

$$\text{State-PF}: x_{t+1}^n = f_t^n(x_t^n) + A_t^n(x_t^n)x_t^l + G_t^n(x_t^n)\eta_t^n, \qquad (8.38)$$

$$\text{State-KF}: x_{t+1}^l = f_t^l(x_t^n) + A_t^l(x_t^n)x_t^l + G_t^l(x_t^n)\eta_t^l, \qquad (8.39)$$

$$\text{Measurement}: y_t = h_t(x_t^n) + C_t(x_t^n)x_t^l + e_t. \qquad (8.40)$$

The RBPF model (8.38)–(8.40) was applied in [KG03] to underwater navigation, with the following values of parameters: $G_t^n = G_t^l = I$, $f_t^l = A_t^n = 0$. Also, a somewhat simplified version of this model was applied in [GGB02] to car positioning, terrain navigation, and target tracking problems.

Here is a brief description of the *RBPF-algorithm*.

RBPF–Algorithm

1. **Initialize the particles** $(t = 1)$:
2. **PF time update:**
   a) **Kalman filter measurement update**
   b) **Predict new particles**
   c) **Kalman filter measurement and time update**
3. **PF measurement update**
4. **Resample**
5. **Set** $t := t + 1$ **and repeat from step 2**
6. **End**

The RBPF-algorithm enables estimation of velocity, acceleration, and sensor error models by utilizing any linear Gaussian sub-structure in the model, which is fundamental for performance in applications (see [SKG06]).

Now we apply the above RBPF analysis to the *feature-based SLAM problem*:

$$x_t^v = \begin{bmatrix} x_t^n \\ x_t^l \end{bmatrix} \quad \text{and} \quad m_t = (m_{1:t}, ..., m_{M_t:t}),$$

where the high-dimensional vehicle state-vector x_t^v has been partitioned according to (8.36), while the map-states m_t (landmarks, linearized from 3D/2D feature positions) consist of the entire map at time t, where $m_{i:t}$ denotes the position of the ith map entry and M_t is the number of entries in the map at time t.

To attack this high-dimensional SLAM problem, the RBPF algorithm starts by making the partition of the total (vehicle + map) state-vector x_t [KST08, TS09]:

$$x_t = \begin{bmatrix} x_t^v \\ m_t \end{bmatrix} = \begin{bmatrix} x_t^n \\ x_t^l \\ m_t \end{bmatrix} = \left[(x_t^n)^T \left(x_t^l \right)^T (m_t)^T \right]^T,$$

where the terms are: nonlinear vehicle states x_t^n (to be PF-estimated approximatively), linear vehicle states x_t^l (to be KF-estimated optimally), and linearized map states m_t.

Secondly, the RBPF algorithm estimates the vehicle states $x_t^v = \left[(x_t^n)^T (x_t^l)^T \right]^T$ using a PF-KF combination (8.37) and for each particle, estimate the map m_t using the KF-based Bayes rule [with the Gaussian factorization (8.37)], given by:

$$p(x_{1:t}^v, m_t | y_{1:t}) = p(x_{1:t}^v | y_{1:t}) \, p(m_t | x_{1:t}^v, y_{1:t}),$$

which lowers the complexity from quadratic to linear in the number of map entries. The key factorization to solve this problem successfully is:

$$p(x_{1:t}^n, x_t^l, m_t | y_{1:t}) = \overset{\text{RBPF}}{p(x_{1:t}^n | y_{1:t})} \overset{\text{PF}}{p(x_t^l | x_{1:t}^n, y_{1:t})} \overset{\text{extended KF}}{\prod_{j=1}^{M_t} p(m_{j,t} | x_{1:t}^n, y_{1:t})},$$

where the trajectory $x_{1:t}^n$ is PF-estimated (to make the last factorization possible) and also it is assumed that $m_{j,t}$ is independent of x_t^l.

Finally, in order to devise an estimator for the filtering density $p(x_{1:t}^v, m_t | y_{1:t}) = p(x_{1:t}^n, x_t^l, m_t | y_{1:t})$, the general algorithm has been proposed in [KST08, TS09] as an extension of the RBPF model (8.38)–(8.40), including both a system model (describing the dynamic behavior of the platform) and a measurement model (describing the sensors, using equations relating the measurements y_t to the total state-vector x_t):

$$\text{State-PF} : x_{t+1}^n = f_t^n(x_t^n) + A_t^n(x_t^n)x_t^l + G_t^n(x_t^n)\eta_t^n,$$

$$\text{State-KF} : x_{t+1}^l = f_t^l(x_t^n) + A_t^l(x_t^n)x_t^l + G_t^l(x_t^n)\eta_t^l,$$

$$\text{Map} : m_{j,t+1} = m_{j,t}, \qquad (j = 1, ..., M_t)$$

$$\text{Measure1} : y_{1,t} = h_{1,t}(x_t^n) + C_{1,t}(x_t^n)x_t^l + e_{1,t},$$

$$\text{Measure2} : y_{2,t}^{(j)} = h_{2,t}(x_t^n) + H_{j,t}(x_t^n)m_{j,t} + e_{2,t}^{(j)},$$

where the noise η_t for the platform states is assumed zero-mean and Gaussian-distributed with covariance matrix $Q_t : \eta_t = \left[(\eta_t^n)^T \ (\eta_t^l)^T \right]^T \sim \mathcal{N}(0, Q_t)$.

9

CPC Super-Dynamics for a Universal Large-Scale Autonomous Operation

In this Chapter,[1] a general model is presented for a universal large-scale fleet/swarm of all unmanned vehicles, including Aerial Vehicles (UAVs), Ground Vehicles (UGVs), Sea Vehicles (USVs) and Underwater Vehicles (UUVs), as a Kähler super-dynamics extension of our recent work [IY16]. Based on Newton-Euler dynamics of each vehicle, a control system for the universal autonomous fleet is designed in both Lagrangian and Hamiltonian form, to predict and control all degrees-of-freedom of each individual vehicle in the fleet (regardless of the fleet size). As an application, a 3D simulation is developed, presenting a search-and-rescue operation in an urban environment. The Appendix defines the formalism for the associated continuous system, representing a very large fleet, given in the form of the Kähler–Ricci flow (or, complex Monge–Ampère equation).

9.1 Introduction

As a motivation for the present work, consider a hypothetical city coastline that has been attacked either by some natural disaster or by a terrorist group, leaving many victims both on the ground and in the sea. Fast recovery action is necessary, but the situation is still dangerous for humans. So, the only option for the quick response is to send swarms of many heterogenous robots to perform an *autonomous search-and-rescue operation*. The purpose of this Chapter is to develop a general formal model for such a large-scale multi-robot operation, including swarms of small UGVs (cars) and UAVs (quadcopters), as well as fleets of USVs (boats) and UUVs (submarines). This Chapter is a natural extension of [IY16], where a Hamiltonian control model for swarms of UGVs and UAVs only was developed. The reason for this extension will be

---

[1] The work presented in this chapter has been performed in collaboration with Dr. Martin Oxenham, Decision Sciences Branch, Joint and Operations Analysis Division, Defence Science and Technology Group, Australia.

articulated below. Although there are not many realistic scenarios where such a universal autonomous fleet would be needed, the existence of such a general model would provide a new capability that can be easily specialized to suit a wide range of specific requirements.

To start this ambitious modeling attempt that would cover all possible unmanned vehicles,[2] we first recall a well-known fact from physics that all conservative systems can be described by either Lagrangian or Hamiltonian formalisms, so that each degree-of-freedom (DOF) is governed either by a single second-order Lagrangian equation of motion or by two first-order Hamiltonian equations of motion. More generally, most non-conservative engineering systems (of mechanical, electrical, thermal or hydraulic nature, or their combination) can be described by dissipative and forced Lagrangian or Hamiltonian equations of motion. Even more generally, in modern geometric control theory (see [II13] and the references therein), any nonlinear control system can be formulated as a general Lagrangian or Hamiltonian control system, where appropriate controllers (including, e.g., a linear PID controller, a quadratic Kalman regulator/filter, or higher-order nonlinear Lie-derivative controllers) are added to dissipative and forced Lagrangian or Hamiltonian dynamics, to give the nonlinear generalization of Kalman's state-space control theory. Still, it is possible to generalize this modeling approach and describe any nonlinear high-dimensional system as a union of Lagrangian and Hamiltonian control systems. This is the objective of this Chapter, called the *Kähler super-dynamics*, introduced in [IRS14] and developed in [IR15].

In terms of modern mechanics (see, e.g. [II06b] and the references therein), based on the concept of the configuration n-manifold M (that includes all DOFs coordinated by generalized coordinates $x^i(t)$, $(i = 1, ..., n)$ in the swarm/fleet under consideration; see Figure 1 in [IY16]), the behavior of all vehicles is governed by the velocity vector-field $v^i(t)$, which is formally defined as a cross-section of the tangent bundle TM of the configuration manifold M. Thus, the $2n$-manifold TM, coordinated by $[x^i(t), v^i(t)]$, is called the *velocity phase space;* it is the stage for (dissipative, forced and controlled) Lagrangian dynamics, naturally endowed with Riemannian geometry. Alternatively, the behavior of all vehicles is also governed by the momentum covector-field $p_i(t)$, which is formally defined as a cross-section of the cotangent bundle T^*M of the configuration manifold M. Thus, the $2n$-manifold T^*M, coordinated by $[x^i(t), p_i(t)]$, is called the *momentum phase space;* it is the stage for

---

[2] The universal super-dynamics fleet/swarm model presented in this Chapter can be seen as a superior alternative to a large-scale 3D *agent based modeling* (ABM). Excelling in all the weak points of ABM, our rigorous approach: (i) strictly obeys Newton-Euler mechanics (with coupled 3D rotations and translations for each vehicle represented as a Newtonian rigid body properly defined by its inertia tensor), (ii) uses proven Lagrangian and Hamiltonian control techniques from modern geometric nonlinear control, and (iii) it is designed for *rigorous prediction and control* of all individual degrees-of-freedom in each individual vehicle in the fleet, regardless of the fleet's size.

(dissipative, forced and controlled) Hamiltonian dynamics, naturally endowed with symplectic geometry.[3]

For some engineering systems, like e.g., vehicles moving in the air, the Hamiltonian approach (presented in [IY16]) is stronger, as it allows both force and velocity controllers, while the Lagrangian approach allows only force controllers. However, for other systems like vehicles moving in the water, the Lagrangian (or, more precisely, Kirchhoff-Lagrangian) approach is the only possibility. In general, if we have a large-scale complex system, including four kinds of robots (namely, ground and air vehicles, boats and submarines), in which some components (ground and air vehicles) can be more naturally modeled via the Hamiltonian formalism, while other components (boats and submarines) can be more naturally modeled via the Lagrangian formalism, the union of both approaches, representing "the best of both worlds", would clearly be preferable, naturally leading to the universal autonomous *ground-air-sea-underwater operation model*.

Formally, these two standard formalisms, Lagrangian boats + submarines and Hamiltonian ground + air vehicles, can be unified in the basic definition of the multi-geometric *Kähler manifold* $\mathcal{K}$:

$$\mathcal{K} = TM + i\, T^*M, \qquad (9.1)$$

which states that the joint Kähler $4n$-manifold is defined as the complexified sum (i.e., the sum with the imaginary unit: $i = \sqrt{-1}$) of the Lagrangian $2n$-manifold TM (with Riemannian geometry) and the Hamiltonian $2n$-manifold T^*M (with symplectic geometry). The Kähler super-dynamics are comprised of three mutually compatible geometrical and dynamical structures: (i) Lagrangian dynamics on the Riemannian tangent bundle TM, (ii) Hamiltonian dynamics on the symplectic cotangent bundle T^*M, and (iii) general complex-valued dynamics on their complexified sum manifold $\mathcal{K}$. Put simply, this universal approach can be described as follows: the output from the Lagrangian dynamics/control is a set of real numbers A and the output from the Hamiltonian dynamics/control is another set of real numbers B; their complexified sum: $C = A + iB$ is the set of complex numbers that represents the Kähler super-dynamics.

In this Chapter, using the Kähler super-dynamics formalism, we will develop a general model for the universal unmanned ground-air-sea-underwater operation. Being an extension of the previous purely-Hamiltonian model, in the present paper we will mainly focus on the Lagrangian side of this universal unmanned vehicles problem.

---

[3] In a more rigorous Lagrangian and Hamiltonian analysis, both $2n$D tangent and cotangent bundles, TM coordinated by (x^i, v^i) and T^*M coordinated by (x^i, p_i), respectively, can be *time-extended* to the corresponding $(2n + 1)$D jet manifolds, $JM = \mathbb{R} \times TM$ coordinated by (t, x^i, v^i) and $J^*M = \mathbb{R} \times T^*M$ coordinated by (t, x^i, p_i), respectively, which enable non-autonomous Lagrangian and Hamiltonian formalisms, respectively (see [II06b] and the references therein).

9.2 Lagrangian and Hamiltonian Fleets/Swarms

9.2.1 Basic Newton-Euler Mechanics of Individual Unmanned Vehicles

All unmanned/autonomous vehicles are Newtonian rigid bodies moving in 3D space. Formally, each vehicle is represented by a 6-parameter Euclidean Lie group $SE(3)$ of rigid motions in 3D space $\mathbb{R}^3$, which consists of isometries of $\mathbb{R}^3$ and is defined as a semidirect (noncommutative) product of 3D rotations $SO(3)$ and 3D translations $\mathbb{R}^3$: $SE(3) := SO(3) \triangleright \mathbb{R}^3$. Its main component, rotational subgroup $SO(3)$ is a set of all orthogonal (3×3)-rotational matrices, which can be parameterized in various ways, including quaternions and parameter vectors (see [II13]).

Basic Newton-Euler mechanics for each unmanned $SE(3)$-vehicle are given in vector form (with the overdot representing time derivative) as:

$$\text{Newton}: \quad \dot{p} \equiv M\dot{v} = F + p \times \omega, \tag{9.2}$$
$$\text{Euler}: \quad \dot{\pi} \equiv I\dot{\omega} = T + \pi \times \omega + p \times v,$$

and in tensor form, using *Einstein's summation convention* over repeated indices and the Levi-Civita permutation symbol ε_{ik}^j, as the following system of ordinary differential equations (ODEs):

$$\text{Newton}: \dot{p}_i \equiv M_{ij}\dot{v}^j = F_i + \varepsilon_{ik}^j p_j \omega^k, \quad (i,j,k = 1,2,3) \tag{9.3}$$
$$\text{Euler}: \dot{\pi}_i \equiv I_{ij}\dot{\omega}^j = T_i + \varepsilon_{ik}^j \pi_j \omega^k + \varepsilon_{ik}^j p_j v^k.$$

In Eqs. (9.2) and (9.3) the diagonal mass and inertia matrices (with $i,j = 1,2,3$)[4]

$$\boldsymbol{M} \equiv M_{ij} = \text{diag}\{m_1, m_2, m_3\} \quad \text{and} \quad \boldsymbol{I} \equiv I_{ij} = \text{diag}\{I_1, I_2, I_3\},$$

define the vehicle's mass–inertia distribution. The vehicle's linear and angular velocity vector fields are:

$$\boldsymbol{v} = \dot{\boldsymbol{x}} \equiv v^i = \dot{x}^i \equiv [v_1, v_2, v_3]^T = [\dot{x}_1, \dot{x}_2, \dot{x}_3]^T,$$
$$\boldsymbol{\omega} = \dot{\boldsymbol{\theta}} \equiv \omega^i = \dot{\theta}^i \equiv [\omega_1, \omega_2, \omega_3]^T = [\dot{\theta}_1, \dot{\theta}_2, \dot{\theta}_3]^T,$$

where x^i are Cartesian coordinates of the vehicles center-of mass (CoM) and θ^i are its Euler angles (roll, pitch and yaw). The co-vector fields (or 1-forms)

---

[4] The principal moments of inertia are given in Cartesian (x, y, z)-coordinates by volume integrals:

$$I_1 = \int_{\mathbb{R}^3} \rho(z^2+y^2)dxdydz, \quad I_2 = \int_{\mathbb{R}^3} \rho(x^2+y^2)dxdydz, \quad I_3 = \int_{\mathbb{R}^3} \rho(x^2+y^2)dxdydz,$$

which depend on the vehicle's (average) 3D density function $\rho = \rho(x, y, z)$.

of driving, gravitational and other external forces and torques acting on the vehicle are:

$$\boldsymbol{F} \equiv F_i = [F_1, F_2, F_3] \quad \text{and} \quad \boldsymbol{T} \equiv T_i = [T_1, T_2, T_3],$$

while the corresponding linear and angular momentum co-vector fields are:

$$\boldsymbol{p} = \boldsymbol{M}\boldsymbol{v} \equiv p_i = [p_1, p_2, p_3] = [m_1 v_1, m_2 v_2, m_2 v_2],$$
$$\boldsymbol{\pi} = \boldsymbol{I}\boldsymbol{\omega} \equiv \pi_i = [\pi_1, \pi_2, \pi_3] = [I_1 \omega_1, I_2 \omega_2, I_3 \omega_3].$$

Now we move to a more general, Lagrangian formalism — in this subsection applied to individual vehicles only, to be generalized to the whole fleet in the next subsection. Equations (9.2) and (9.3) can be derived as Lagrangian equations of motion from the *Lagrangian function* $L = L(v = \dot{x}; \omega = \dot{\theta})$ representing (translational + rotational) kinetic energy of each individual vehicle:

$$L = \frac{1}{2}\boldsymbol{v}^T \boldsymbol{M}\boldsymbol{v} + \frac{1}{2}\boldsymbol{\omega}^T \boldsymbol{I}\boldsymbol{\omega} = \frac{1}{2}M_{ij}v^i v^j + \frac{1}{2}I_{ij}\omega^i \omega^j. \tag{9.4}$$

From this Lagrangian function, we can immediately derive conservative (force-free and dissipation-free) Lagrangian equations of motion for translations and rotations, respectively, in both vector and tensor form (using index notation for partial derivatives: $L_z = \frac{\partial L}{\partial z}$):

$$\dot{L}_v = L_x \Leftrightarrow \dot{L}_{v^i} = L_{x^i} \quad \text{and} \quad \dot{L}_\omega = L_\theta \Leftrightarrow \dot{L}_{\omega^i} = L_{\theta^i}, \tag{9.5}$$

(this conservative approach is formally derived and explained in a more general settings in the next subsection).

Standard engineering extensions of conservative Lagrangian dynamics (9.5) include friction forces derived from the Rayleigh dissipative function $R = R(x, v) = \frac{1}{2}\left(v^i x^i\right)^2$, and other external forces and torques, including gradient ones E_{v^i} and E_{ω^i} derived from the vehicle's total potential energy $E(x, \theta)$. In such a way, we obtain the *dissipative and forced Lagrangian dynamics* in vector and tensor form:

Translations : $\dot{L}_v + R_v = L_x + \boldsymbol{F} \Longleftrightarrow \dot{L}_{v^i} + R_{v^i} = L_{x^i} + F_i$, (9.6)

Rotations : $\dot{L}_\omega + R_\omega = L_\theta + \boldsymbol{T} \Longleftrightarrow \dot{L}_{\omega^i} + R_{\omega^i} = L_{\theta^i} + T_i$.

However, for the case of a vehicle immersed in water, Eqs. (9.6) still need to be extended into the so-called *Kirchhoff–Lagrangian equations*, due to the addition of strong water influences which result in several mixed cross-products (see e.g. [Lam32, Leo97] or the original work of Kirchhoff in German), which can be written in vector form:

$$\dot{L}_v + R_v = L_x + \boldsymbol{F} + L_v \times \boldsymbol{\omega}, \tag{9.7}$$
$$\dot{L}_\omega + R_\omega = L_\theta + \boldsymbol{T} + L_\omega \times \boldsymbol{\omega} + L_v \times \boldsymbol{v},$$

and in tensor form:

$$\dot{L}_{v^i} + R_{v^i} = L_{x^i} + F_i + \varepsilon_{ik}^j L_{v^j} \omega^k , \tag{9.8}$$
$$\dot{L}_{\omega^i} + R_{\omega^i} = L_{\theta^i} + T_i + \varepsilon_{ik}^j L_{\omega^j} \omega^k + \varepsilon_{ik}^j L_{v^j} v^k .$$

Using Eqs. (9.4)–(9.8), each vehicle's linear and angular momentum co-vector fields (or, 1-forms) are defined as:

$$\boldsymbol{p} = L_{\boldsymbol{v}} \ \Leftrightarrow \ p_i = L_{v^i}, \qquad \boldsymbol{\pi} = L_{\boldsymbol{\omega}} \ \Leftrightarrow \ \pi_i = L_{\omega^i},$$

with their corresponding time derivatives defining conservative force $\boldsymbol{F}^{\mathrm{con}}$ and torque $\boldsymbol{T}^{\mathrm{con}}$ 1-forms (different from external/dissipative ones, $\boldsymbol{F}$ and $\boldsymbol{T}$):

$$\boldsymbol{F}^{\mathrm{con}} \equiv \dot{\boldsymbol{p}} = \dot{L}_{\boldsymbol{v}} \Leftrightarrow F_i^{\mathrm{con}} \equiv \dot{p}_i = \dot{L}_{v^i},$$
$$\boldsymbol{T}^{\mathrm{con}} \equiv \dot{\boldsymbol{\pi}} = \dot{L}_{\boldsymbol{\omega}} \Leftrightarrow T_i^{\mathrm{con}} \equiv \dot{\pi}_i = \dot{L}_{\omega^i}.$$

9.2.2 Lagrangian Dynamics and Control for a Water (USV + UUV) Fleet

General Lagrangian dynamics for a large unmanned water fleet consisting of m vehicles (boats-USVs and submarines-UUVs, each with 6 DOFs) are defined on the fleet's configuration n-manifold $M_{\mathrm{wat}} = \prod_{k=1}^m SE(3)^k$ (similar to the Figure 1 in [IY16]) with local coordinates $x^i(t)$, (for $i = 1, ..., n = 6m$) and velocity vector-fields defined on its Riemannian tangent bundle TM_{wat} with local coordinates $(x^i; \dot{x}^i = v^i)$. We give a rigorous variational derivation of the water fleet's dynamics and finite control based on its Lagrangian energy function $L(x, \dot{x}) : TM_{\mathrm{wat}} \to \mathbb{R}$, using the formalism of exterior differential systems on the $(2n+1)$-dimensional time-extended tangent bundle, called the jet manifold $JM_{\mathrm{wat}} = j^1(\mathbb{R}, M_{\mathrm{wat}}) \cong \mathbb{R} \times TM_{\mathrm{wat}}$, with local canonical variables $(t; x^i; \dot{x}^i)$ (for technical details, see [Gri83, II06b] and the references therein).

Consider a general variational problem $(I, \omega; \varphi)$ for the water fleet, where (I, ω) represents the Pfaffian exterior differential system on JM_{wat}, given in local coordinates $(t; x^i; \dot{x}^i)$ as:

$$\begin{cases} \theta^i = dx^i - \dot{x}^i \omega = 0 \\ \quad \omega \equiv dt \neq 0 \end{cases},$$

with structure equations

$$d\theta^i = -d\dot{x}^i \wedge \omega,$$

(where the symbols $\wedge$ and d denote exterior product and derivative, respectively). Integral manifolds $N \in j^1(\mathbb{R}, M_{\mathrm{wat}})$ of the Pfaffian system (I, ω) are locally defined by 1-jets $j^1 : t \to [t, x(t), \dot{x}(t)]$ of curves $x(t) : \mathbb{R} \to M_{\mathrm{wat}}$.

Next, we introduce a 1-form $\varphi = L\omega$, where $L = L(t, x, \dot{x})$ is the system's Lagrangian defined on JM_{wat}, having unique coordinate and velocity partial derivatives, denoted by L_{x^i} and $L_{\dot{x}^i}$, respectively. A variational problem

$(I, \omega; \varphi)$ is said to be *strongly non-degenerate*, or *well-posed* [Gri83], if and only if (iff) the determinant of the matrix of mixed velocity partials of the Lagrangian is positive definite: $\det \| L_{\dot{x}^i \dot{x}^j} \| > 0$.

The corresponding extended Pfaffian system:

$$\begin{cases} \theta^i = 0 \\ dL_{\dot{x}^i} - L_{x^i}\, \omega = 0 \\ \omega \equiv dt \neq 0 \end{cases}$$

generates conservative (dissipation-free and force-free) Lagrangian equations for the fleet of water vehicles (a generalization of Eqs. (9.5)):

$$\dot{L}_{\dot{x}^i} = L_{x^i} . \tag{9.9}$$

If an integral manifold N satisfies the Lagrangian equations (9.9) of a well-posed variational problem, then $\frac{d}{dt}\left(\int_{N_t} \varphi \right)_{t=0} = 0$ for any admissible variation $\delta \in N$ with fixed endpoint conditions: $\omega = \theta^i = 0$.

Under the above conditions, the *Griffiths theorem* [Gri83] states that both the (conservative) Lagrangian dynamics with initial conditions:

$$\begin{cases} \dot{L}_{\dot{x}^i} = L_{x^i} \\ x(t_0) = x_0, \quad \dot{x}(t_0) = \dot{x}_0 \end{cases}$$

and the Lagrangian dynamics with endpoint conditions (also called the finite control system):

$$\begin{cases} \dot{L}_{\dot{x}^i} = L_{x^i} \\ x(t_0) = x_0, \quad x(t_1) = x_1 \end{cases}$$

have unique solutions (see [Gri83] for the proof of this theorem).

To generalize this conservative theorem to include both dissipative and driving forces (as we did in the previous section), we use the fact that the tangent bundle TM_{wat} naturally represents a Riemannian $2n$-manifold, with the Riemannian positive-definite metric form:

$$g_R = g_{ij}(x)\, dx^i dx^j, \tag{9.10}$$

which defines both the material metric tensor g_{ij} (given by the smooth symmetric matrix $\| g_{ij}(x) \|$ and representing the mass-inertia distribution of the whole water fleet Ξ) and the kinetic energy $E_{\text{kin}}(x, \dot{x}) = \frac{1}{2} g_R$ of the fleet Ξ. In addition, if the potential energy $E_{\text{pot}}(x)$ of the fleet Ξ is also a smooth function, then the autonomous Lagrangian is defined as: $L(x, \dot{x}) = E_{\text{kin}}(x, \dot{x}) - E_{\text{pot}}(x)$ and automatically satisfies the condition of well-posedness: $\det \| L_{\dot{x}^i \dot{x}^j} \| = \det \| g_{ij}(x) \| > 0$.

In the Riemannian settings, the *covariant Lagrangian equations* (9.9) can be immediately generalized to include both dissipative and driving (gradient) force 1-forms $F_i(x, \dot{x})$ according to Eqs. (9.6), giving:

$$\frac{d}{dt}\left(g_{ij}[x(t)]\,\dot{x}^j(t)\right) = \frac{1}{2}\left(\partial_{x^i}g_{jk}[x(t)]\dot{x}^j(t)\,\dot{x}^k(t)\right) - F_i\left[x(t),\dot{x}(t)\right]. \quad (9.11)$$

Next, letting $\left\|g^{ij}(x)\right\|$ to be the inverse matrix of $\left\|g_{ij}(x)\right\|$ and introducing classical Christoffel symbols:

$$\Gamma^i_{jk} = g^{il}\Gamma_{jkl}, \quad \Gamma_{jkl} = \frac{1}{2}\left(\partial_{x^j}g_{kl} + \partial_{x^k}g_{jl} - \partial_{x^l}g_{jk}\right), \quad (9.12)$$

the equations (9.11) resolve to the classical *contravariant Lagrangian dynamics* (see [II06b])

$$\ddot{x}^i(t) + \Gamma^i_{jk}\dot{x}^j(t)\,\dot{x}^k(t) = F^i\left[x(t),\dot{x}(t)\right]. \quad (9.13)$$

Then the Riemann-generalized Griffiths theorem implies that both the forced and dissipative Lagrangian dynamics with initial conditions:

$$\begin{cases} \ddot{x}^i(t) + \Gamma^i_{jk}\dot{x}^j(t)\,\dot{x}^k(t) = F^i\left[x(t),\dot{x}(t)\right] \\ x(t_0) = x_0, \quad \dot{x}(t_0) = \dot{x}_0 \end{cases} \quad (9.14)$$

and the Lagrangian dynamics with endpoint conditions (the finite control system):

$$\begin{cases} \ddot{x}^i(t) + \Gamma^i_{jk}\dot{x}^j(t)\,\dot{x}^k(t) = F^i\left[x(t),\dot{x}(t)\right] \\ x(t_0) = x_0, \quad x(t_1) = x_1 \end{cases} \quad (9.15)$$

have unique solutions.

. However, to make Lagrangian equations of motion suitable for the sea or underwater fleet dynamics, we need to generalize the external forces from (9.13), to include Kirchhoff-type torques and forces coming from the water medium, an nD analog of Eqs. (9.8). If we denote such generalized torques and forces as $\mathcal{F}^i\left[t, x(t), \dot{x}(t)\right]$, we obtain the general form of the contravariant Lagrangian fleet dynamics:

$$\ddot{x}^i(t) + \Gamma^i_{jk}[x(t)]\,\dot{x}^j(t)\,\dot{x}^k(t) = \mathcal{F}^i\left[t, x(t), \dot{x}(t)\right], \quad (9.16)$$

which can be rewritten in the classical *covariant Lagrangian form* as:

$$\dot{L}_{\dot{x}^i} - L_{x^i} = \mathcal{F}_i, \quad (9.17)$$

with $\mathcal{F}_i = \mathcal{F}_i\left[t, x(t), \dot{x}(t)\right] = F_i\left[x(t), \dot{x}(t)\right] + \mathcal{R}$, where the term $\mathcal{R}$ represents an nD analog of Kirchhoff-type mixed rotational terms: $(\varepsilon^j_{ik}L_{\dot{x}^j}\dot{x}^k, \varepsilon^j_{ik}L_{v^j}\omega^k, \varepsilon^j_{ik}L_{\omega^j}\omega^k)$ of (9.8).

Equation (9.17) is our final Lagrangian dynamics model for the water fleet. However, due to Kirchhoff-type mixed rotational terms $\mathcal{R}$, its existence and uniqueness cannot be demonstrated because it it does not adhere to the conditions imposed by the Griffiths theorem. Therefore, at present, we are unable to formulate a rigorous finite control system for the general Lagrangian dynamics of the water fleet.

So, we move to a stronger alternative, the so-called *affine Lagrangian control system* (see [II13] and the references therein). For this we introduce the *affine Lagrangian control function* $L^a(x, \dot{x}, u) : TM_{\text{wat}} \to \mathbb{R}$, which in local canonical coordinates on TM_{wat} given as:

$$L^a(x, \dot{x}, u) = L^0(x, \dot{x}) - L^j(x, \dot{x})\, u_j(t, x, \dot{x}),$$

where $L^0(x, \dot{x})$ is the above physical Lagrangian, $L^j(x, \dot{x})$, $(j = 1, \dots, m < n)$ are the *coupling Lagrangians* corresponding to the *active* nearest-neighboring vehicles in the fleet, and the control one-forms $u_j = u_j(t, x, \dot{x})$ are defined via the *Lie derivative* control formalism (see Eq. (11) in [IY16]) giving the *control law* for asymptotic tracking of the predefined reference outputs. Then, the affine Lagrangian control system is governed by the following equations on TM_{wat}:[5]

$$\dot{L}_{\dot{x}^i} - L_{x^i} = \mathcal{F}_i + L^j_{x^i}\, u_j. \tag{9.18}$$

9.2.3 Hamiltonian Dynamics and Control for an Air (UGV + UAV) Swarm

As already mentioned, the Hamiltonian dynamics and control model for a joint (UGV + UAV) swarm with the configuration n-manifold $M_{\text{air}} = \prod_{k=1}^{m} SE(3)^k$ consisting of m unmanned air vehicles (each with 6 DOFs) have been presented in detail in [IY16], based on the swarm's Hamiltonian energy function which is defined as a map $H(x, p) : T^* M_{\text{air}} \to \mathbb{R}$ on its symplectic cotangent bundle $T^* M_{\text{air}}$ with the *symplectic form:*

$$\omega_S = dp_i \wedge dx^i \qquad \text{(for } i = 1, \dots, n). \tag{9.19}$$

This Hamiltonian dynamics/control system can be summarized by the following two equations:

Dynamics: The forced and dissipative Hamiltonian dynamics for a joint swarm of land/air vehicles are defined as:

$$\dot{x}^i = H_{p_i} - R_{p_i} \qquad \dot{p}_i = F_i - H_{x^i} + R_{x^i}, \tag{9.20}$$

where x^i are the generalized coordinates associated to all active DOFs within each swarm, p_i are their corresponding momenta (both linear and angular), $F_i = F_i(t, x, p)$ are the generalized driving forces, while $R = R(x, p) = \frac{1}{2} p_i^2 x_i^2$ denotes the Rayleigh dissipative function.

---

[5] If we could neglect the Kirchhoff-type mixed force terms, we could rather apply the standard prescription in geometric nonlinear control (see [II13] and the references therein), based on generic Lagrangian vector-fields $f = (\dot{x}^i, L_{x^i})$ and $g = (-\dot{x}^j, L^a_{x^j})$, to obtain the *affine controller* in the standard nonlinear MIMO-system form: $\dot{x}^i = f(x) + g(x)\, u_j$.

Control: The affine Hamiltonian control system for a swarm of land/air vehicles is derived from the affine Hamiltonian control function $H^a(x, p, u)$: $T^*M_{\text{air}} \to \mathbb{R}$, in local canonical coordinates on T^*M_{air} given as:

$$H^a(x, p, u) = H^0(x, p) - H^j(x, p) u_j(t, x, p), \quad (i = 1, \ldots, n),$$

where $H^0(x, p)$ is the physical Hamiltonian, $H^j(x, p)$, $(j = 1, \ldots, m < n)$ are the affine Hamiltonians corresponding to the *active* nearest-neighboring vehicles in the swarm, while the control 1-forms u_j, defined by the *Lie derivative* control formalism (see Eq. (11) in [IY16]) represent the *control law* for asymptotic tracking of reference swarm outputs. The whole control system includes both contravariant velocity controllers $V^i = V^i(t, x, p)$ and covariant force controllers $F_i = F_i(t, x, p)$, and is governed by the following canonical equations on T^*M_{air}:

$$\dot{x}^i = V^i + H^0_{p_i} - H^j_{p_i} u_j + R_{p_i}, \tag{9.21}$$
$$\dot{p}_i = F_i - H^0_{x^i} + H^j_{x^i} u_j + R_{x^i}.$$

9.3 Super-Dynamics for the Universal (UGV + UAV + USV + UUV) Fleet

9.3.1 Super-Dynamics Formalism on a Kähler 4n-Manifold

A Kähler manifold, $\mathcal{K} \equiv (\mathcal{K}, g) \equiv (\mathcal{K}, \omega)$, is a Hermitian manifold[6] with the real dimension $4n$ (or, complex dimension $2n$) that admits three mutually compatible dynamical structures: (i) Riemannian/Lagrangian, (ii) symplectic/Hamiltonian, and (iii) complex-valued, formally defined as follows.

---

[6] Recall that a complex-valued function $f : \mathbb{C}^n \to \mathbb{C}$ is called *holomorphic* (see e.g., [Wik16ii]) iff $f = f_1 + i f_2$ satisfies the Cauchy–Riemann relations:

$$\partial_{x^j} f_1 = \partial_{y^j} f_2, \qquad \partial_{x^j} f_2 = -\partial_{y^j} f_1, \qquad (\partial_{x^j} \equiv \partial/\partial x^j)$$

for each holomorphic coordinate, $z^j = x^j + i y^j$ (with $i = \sqrt{-1}$). A complex manifold $\mathcal{K}$ is a manifold with an atlas consisting of charts $t_{ij} : U_i \cap U_j \to \mathbb{C}^n$, such that the transition functions $t_{ij}(z)$ are holomorphic and satisfy the *cocycle condition*: $t_{ik}(z) = t_{ij}(z) t_{jk}(z)$ on triple overlaps $U_i \cap U_j \cap U_k$. An almost complex structure J is defined on a complex manifold $\mathcal{K}$ as:

$$J\partial_{z^j} = i\partial_{z^j}, \qquad J\partial_{\bar{z}^j} = -i\partial_{\bar{z}^j}, \qquad J^2 = -1.$$

A *Hermitian manifold* $(\mathcal{K}, g)$ is a complex manifold $\mathcal{K}$ with a Hermitian metric tensor $g_{i\bar{j}} = g_{i\bar{j}}(z^i, z^{\bar{j}})$, such that $\{g_{i\bar{j}}\}$ is a positive-definite Hermitian matrix function, $\{g_{i\bar{j}}\} = \{g_{i\bar{j}}\}^* > 0$ (see [Wik16jj]). A Hermitian manifold $(\mathcal{K}, g)$ becomes a Kähler manifold iff the almost complex structure J on it satisfies the condition: $\nabla_k J = 0$, where ∇_k is the Levi-Civita connection on $(\mathcal{K}, g)$.

We start with a *universal configuration* n-manifold M, including all autonomous unmanned vehicles (UGVs, UAVS, USVs and UUVs, each of them formally defined as an $SE(3)$-group). On the configuration n-manifold M we define two partial bundles, each being a $2n$-manifold: a Riemannian/Lagrangian tangent bundle TM_{wat} which governs the dynamics of water vehicles (USVs and UUVs) and a symplectic/Hamiltonian cotangent bundle T^*M_{air} which governs the dynamics of air vehicles (UGVs and UAVs). The 'water bundle' TM_{wat} is formally defined as a disjoint union of tangent spaces $T_x M_{wat}$ at all water vehicles $x_{wat} \in M$: $TM_{wat} = \sqcup_{x_{wat} \in M} T_x M_{wat}$. Similarly, the 'air bundle' T^*M_{air} is formally defined as a disjoint union of cotangent spaces $T_x^* M_{air}$ at all air vehicles $x_{air} \in M$: $T^*M_{air} = \sqcup_{x_{air} \in M} T_x^* M_{air}$.

Now, the global Kähler $4n$-manifold $\mathcal{K}$, the stage of our super-dynamics, can be constructed in a similar way as a complexified tangent bundle of the configuration manifold M, that is, a disjoint union of complexified tangent spaces $T_x M^{\mathbb{C}}$ at all vehicles $x = x_{wat} + x_{air} \in M$:

$$\mathcal{K} = TM \otimes \mathbb{C} = \sqcup_{x \in M} T_x M^{\mathbb{C}}.$$

It admits a Hermitian metric form g,[7] such that its real part is the Riemannian metric form $g_R \in TM_{wat}$ given by Eq. (9.10) and its imaginary part is a symplectic form $\omega_S \in T^*M_{air}$ given by Eq. (9.19). Thus, we have:

$$(\mathcal{K}, g) = TM_{wat} + i\, T^*M_{air} \quad \text{with}$$
$$g = g_R + i\omega_S = g_{ij}\, dx^i dx^j + i\, dp_i \wedge dx^i.$$

The global Kähler manifold $\mathcal{K}$ has an very rich geometric and dynamical structure, defined as follows.

Any local open chart $U \subset \mathcal{K}$ defines a set of $2n$ holomorphic coordinates, in which x-components come from the Lagrangian water fleet on TM_{wat} and y-components come from the Hamiltonian air fleet on T^*M_{air}. They locally identify $\mathbb{C}^{2n}$ with $\mathbb{R}^{4n}$, as: $\{z^j = x^j + iy^j \mid j = 1, \cdots, 2n\}$, with the corresponding holomorphic differentials:

$$dz^j = dx^j + idy^j \quad \text{and} \quad d\bar{z}^j = dx^j - idy^j,$$

and holomorphic velocities:

$$\dot{z}^j = \dot{x}^j + i\dot{y}^j \quad \text{and} \quad \dot{\bar{z}}^j = \dot{x}^j - i\dot{y}^j.$$

---

[7] All three structures defined on $(\mathcal{K}, g) = TM \otimes \mathbb{C}$, that is, the Hermitian metric g, the Riemannian metric g_R and the symplectic form ω_S, preserve the almost complex structure J. In other words, for any two complex tangent vectors $(\psi, \chi) \in \mathcal{K}$ we have:

$$g(J\psi, J\chi) = g(\psi, \chi), \qquad g_R(J\psi, J\chi) = g_R(\psi, \chi), \qquad \omega_S(J\psi, J\chi) = \omega_S(\psi, \chi).$$

The Hermitian metric tensor $g_{i\bar{j}} = g_{i\bar{j}}(z^i, z^{\bar{j}})$ of the Kähler manifold $\mathcal{K}$ represents the whole mass/inertia-distribution of the universal $(TM_{\text{wat}} + \mathrm{i}\, T^*M_{\text{air}})$ fleet. The metric $g_{i\bar{j}}(z^i, z^{\bar{j}})$ obeys the following *Kähler condition* (independent of the choice of local holomorphic coordinates $z^j \in U$):

$$\partial_j g_{i\bar{k}} = \partial_i g_{j\bar{k}} \quad \text{and} \quad \partial_{\bar{j}} g_{k\bar{i}} = \partial_{\bar{i}} g_{k\bar{j}}, \qquad (\partial_j \equiv \partial/\partial z^j, \ \partial_{\bar{j}} \equiv \partial/\partial z^{\bar{j}})$$
$$(9.22)$$

where $\partial_j \equiv \partial$ and $\partial_{\bar{j}} \equiv \bar{\partial}$ are *Dolbeault's differential operators*, which are the additive components of the standard exterior derivative on $\mathcal{K}$: $d = \partial + \bar{\partial}$.[8]

The *Kähler metric form* $g = g_R + \mathrm{i}\omega_S$ (defined by the Hermitian metric tensor $g_{i\bar{j}}$) is a positive-definite, symmetric $(1, 1)$-form on $\mathcal{K}$ defined in local holomorphic coordinates as:

$$g = g_{i\bar{j}}\, dz^i \otimes d\bar{z}^j > 0, \quad (i, j = 1, \cdots, 2n),$$

which defines the complex kinetic-energy Lagrangian $L^0(\dot{z}, \dot{\bar{z}}) : \mathcal{K} \to \mathbb{C}$ of the universal $(TM_{\text{wat}} + \mathrm{i}\, T^*M_{\text{air}})$ −fleet, in holomorphic coordinates z^i on $\mathcal{K}$ given as:

$$L^0(\dot{z}, \dot{\bar{z}}) = \frac{1}{2}g = \frac{1}{2}g_{i\bar{j}}\,\dot{z}^i \otimes \dot{\bar{z}}^j,$$

so that the complex affine Lagrangian control function $L^a(\dot{z}, \dot{\bar{z}}, u) : \mathcal{K} \to \mathbb{C}$ is given in local coordinates on $\mathcal{K}$ as:

$$L^a(\dot{z}, \dot{\bar{z}}, u) = L^0(\dot{z}, \dot{\bar{z}}) - L^j(\dot{z}, \dot{\bar{z}})\,u_j(t, z, \dot{z}), \quad (j = 1, \ldots, m < n),$$

with coupling Lagrangians $L^j(\dot{z}, \dot{\bar{z}})$ and complex control inputs $u_j(t, z, \bar{z})$. The contravariant Lagrangian equations are now derived from $L^a(\dot{z}, \dot{\bar{z}}, u)$ as:

$$\ddot{z}^i(t) + \Gamma^i_{jk}\,\dot{z}^j(t)\,\dot{\bar{z}}^k(t) = \mathcal{F}^i\left[t, z(t), \dot{z}(t)\right],$$

using the complex Christoffel symbols on $\mathcal{K}$ defined (via the Hermitian metric tensor $g_{i\bar{j}}$) as:

$$\Gamma^k_{ij} = g^{k\bar{l}}\partial_j g_{i\bar{l}} \quad \text{and} \quad \Gamma^{\bar{k}}_{i\bar{j}} = g^{\bar{k}l}\partial_{\bar{j}} g_{l\bar{i}}, \quad (i, j, k = 1, \cdots, 2n).$$

The corresponding covariant Lagrangian equations for the universal $(TM_{\text{wat}} + \mathrm{i}\, T^*M_{\text{air}})$ fleet (complexified and generalized from Eq. (9.18)) are

---

[8] Being components of the exterior derivative d on $\mathcal{K}$, Dolbeault's differential operators are the maps on the space $\Omega^{p,q}(\mathcal{K})$ of exterior forms on $\mathcal{K}$, $\partial : \Omega^{p,q}(\mathcal{K}) \to \Omega^{p+1,q}(\mathcal{K})$ and $\bar{\partial} : \Omega^{p,q}(\mathcal{K}) \to \Omega^{p,q+1}(\mathcal{K})$ (see, e.g. [Wik16kk]).

In a local z^k-coordinate chart $U \subset \mathcal{K}$, for any holomorphic function $f \in U$, ∂ and $\bar{\partial}$ operators are given by:

$$\partial f = \left(\partial_{x^k} f - \mathrm{i}\partial_{y^k} f\right) dz^k, \qquad \bar{\partial} f = \left(\partial_{x^k} f - \mathrm{i}\partial_{y^k} f\right) d\bar{z}^k.$$

$$\dot{L}_{\dot{z}^i} - L_{z^i} = \mathcal{F}_i + L^j_{\dot{z}^i} u_j \,, \tag{9.23}$$

where $\mathcal{F}_i = \mathcal{F}_i\,[t, z(t), \dot{z}(t)]$ represent the general force 1-forms (including dissipation and driving forces as well as Kirchhoff-type mixed rotational terms). The associated *Kähler symplectic form* ω is a positive-definite exterior $(1,1)$-form[9] on $\mathcal{K}$ given in holomorphic coordinates z^i on $\mathcal{K}$ as:

$$\omega = \mathrm{i} g_{i\bar{j}}\, dz^i \wedge d\bar{z}^j > 0, \quad (i, j = 1, \dots, 2n), \tag{9.24}$$

which is the *closed form*: $d\omega = 0$ follows directly from the Kähler condition (9.22). From the Kähler form (9.24) with $\bar{z}^i$ as canonical momenta, the Hamiltonian formalism can be derived from the complex kinetic-energy Hamiltonian $H^0(z, \bar{z}) : \mathcal{K} \to \mathbb{C}$ of the universal $(TM_{\mathrm{wat}} + \mathrm{i}\, T^*M_{\mathrm{air}})$ −fleet, in holomorphic coordinates z^i on $\mathcal{K}$ given as:

$$H^0(z, \bar{z}) = \frac{1}{2} g_{i\bar{j}}\, dz^i \wedge d\bar{z}^j.$$

From the complexified affine Hamiltonian control function $H^a(z, \bar{z}, u) : \mathcal{K} \to \mathbb{C}$, in local canonical coordinates on $\mathcal{K}$ given as:

$$H^a(z, \bar{z}, u) = H^0(z, \bar{z}) - H^j(z, \bar{z})\, u_j(t, z, \bar{z}), \quad (j = 1, \dots, m < n),$$

(with coupling Hamiltonians $H^j(z, \bar{z})$ and complex control inputs $u_j(t, z, \bar{z})$), the *complex affine Hamiltonian control system* (complexified and generalized from Eq. (9.21)) can be defined for the whole $(TM_{\mathrm{wat}} + \mathrm{i}\, T^*M_{\mathrm{air}})$ −fleet as:

$$\dot{z}^i = V^i + H^0_{\bar{z}^i} - H^j_{\bar{z}^i}\, u_j + R_{\bar{z}^i}\,, \tag{9.25}$$
$$\dot{\bar{z}}^i = F_i + \varepsilon^j_{ik} H^k_{z^j} \bar{z} - H^0_{z^i} + H^j_{z^i}\, u_j + R_{z^i}\,,$$

where $V^i = V^i(t, z, \bar{z})$ and $F_i = F_i(t, z, \bar{z})$ are the contravariant velocity controllers and the covariant force controllers, while the term $\varepsilon^j_{ik} H^k_{z^j} \bar{z}$ denotes (somewhat reduced) Kirchhoff-type mixed rotational terms in Hamiltonian form.

Equations (9.23) and (9.25) represent two alternative versions, Lagrangian and Hamiltonian, respectively, of the *discrete super-dynamics* for the universal (UGV, UAV, USV, UUV) −fleet. They are both complexified extensions of our previously defined Lagrangian and Hamiltonian dynamics/control systems for the $(USV + UUV)$ -fleet and $(UGV + UAV)$ -swarm, respectively, each of them covering now the whole universal fleet. These two temporal systems will be generalized in Chapter 10, Appendix 1 to the spatiotemporal system called the complex Monge–Ampère equation.[10] In the next subsection, Eq. (9.25) is applied to perform a 3D simulation in a virtual urban environment.

---

[9] The Kähler form ω is also harmonic ($\delta\omega \equiv *d*\omega = 0$), a result from the *Kähler-Hodge theory* (see, e.g. [Ver11] and the references therein).

[10] This generalization has been moved to Appendix because it is too technical for a non-specialist reader.

9.3.2 Super-Dynamics Application: 3D Simulation in an Urban Environment

Based on the complex affine Hamiltonian control system (9.25), a *3D simulation framework for a universal robotic fleet* has been under development in the Defence Science & Technology Group, Australia (IP of Australian Defence). Currently, it is restricted to a *joint swarm of UAVs and UGVs*,[11] developed in Visual Studio 2015 (a 64 bit compilation in C++ and C# on dot.Net 4.6), using Irrlicht 3D graphics and Bullet physics engines. A search-and-rescue operation in an urban environment is simulated, showing a quick autonomous response to the bomb explosion (see Figures 9.1–9.4). The simulation uses a number of urban maps, as well as a variety of possible initial conditions (i.e., starting placements of UAVs and UGVs) and final conditions (explosion sites). Both driving and navigation of UAVs and UGVs uses simplified Eqs. (9.25), without Kirchhoff-type mixed rotational terms and a possibility to turn-off the nearest-neighbors couplings for the speed-up (but with a small amount of Gaussian noise added to compensate for uncertain environments), numerically solved in complex numbers using the standard Runge-Kutta 4th order (RK4) integrator.[12] The velocity and force controllers, $V^i = V^i(t, z, \bar{z})$ and $F_i = F_i(t, z, \bar{z})$, are reshaped into complex B-spline attractors, using the prescription given in [IY16], now with the phase-plane replaced by the complex plane $\mathbb{C}$. After coming to the building where the explosion happened, the joint swarm switches to the 'indoor navigation mode', in which each vehicle is controlled by its own adaptive fuzzy-logic controller and simulated ultrasonic sensors (developed separately from the present formalism; to be published elsewhere). As soon as the first vehicle, either UAV or UGV, comes to the exact explosion place (a room, or a corridor, or stairs within the building), the whole joint swarm switches back to attractor Hamiltonian Eqs. (9.25), so it is immediately attracted to the explosion place. Converging of both swarms to the bomb completes the simulation.

---

[11] Although both Eqs. (9.23) and (9.25) are capable of simulating the whole universal fleet (or, swarm of UGVs, UAVS, USVs and UUVs), at present it is very difficult to perform a 3D simulation of submarines and boats within a realistically simulated water environment. Hence, our current 3D simulation has been restricted to urban environment, while our near future research will be focused on the underwater 3D domain.

[12] We have also implemented three supposedly superior adaptive integrators: Fehlberg-45, Cash-Karp-45 and Dormand-Prince-45 (see [Wik16ll]), which should be more efficient than the fixed step-size RK4 integrator according to the standard ODE-numerical recipes. However, our experience with this high-dimensional complex-valued fleet is that the step-size in this simulation is necessarily constrained to one millisecond, which simply makes RK4 the fastest integrator, due to the smallest number of arithmetic operations.

Fig. 9.1. *A 3D simulation of a search-and-rescue operation in an urban environment, showing random initial positions of 50 UGVs (left) and 50 UAVs (right).*

Fig. 9.2. *The 3D simulation continued: showing the area of interest: a bomb explosion in another quart (left-up) and immediate deployment of UAVs and UGVs (right and bottom).*

9.4 Continuous Super-Dynamics for a Very Large Fleet

Topology of the Kähler manifold $\mathcal{K}$ is based on the Kähler condition (9.22). Namely, in a local open chart $U \subset \mathcal{K}$, the Kähler symplectic form ω (9.24) can be alternatively defined as:

$$\omega = \mathrm{i}\partial_i\partial_{\bar{j}}\varphi = \mathrm{i}\partial\overline{\partial}\varphi > 0\,, \quad (i,j = 1,\ldots,4n),$$

Fig. 9.3. *The 3D simulation continued: navigation of both swarms using complexified Hamiltonian attractor dynamics, simplified from Eqs. (9.25).*

Fig. 9.4. *The current presentation of the 3D simulation is finished: both swarms arrive at the area of interest. Note that the simulation actually continues indoors (not shown), switching now to the fully autonomous navigation based on fuzzy-logic control and simulated ultrasonic sensors. Once the first vehicle (either UAV or UGV) finds the bomb (or, the target of the search-and-rescue operation), the simulation switches back to the attractor Hamiltonian dynamics so that all the vehicles quickly converge to the target.*

where $\varphi \in U$ is a smooth real-valued function called the *Kähler potential*. This means that Kähler geometry (and therefore, super-dynamics) can be alternatively developed independently of any reference to the prior Lagrangian/Riemannian or Hamiltonian/symplectic geometry. So, although counter-intuitive, we could develop the universal fleet dynamics and control, in either Lagrangian or Hamiltonian form, using Kähler potentials φ instead of coordinates, velocities and momenta. Furthermore, as we can see below, using Kähler potentials φ we can develop a general model of *continuous super-dynamics* for a *very large-scale* universal (UGV, UAV, USV, UUV) –fleet.

In general, any p-form α defined on the Kähler manifold $\mathcal{K}$ is called $\overline{\partial}$-closed iff $\overline{\partial}\alpha = 0$ and $\overline{\partial}$-exact iff $\alpha = \overline{\partial}\eta$ for some $(p$-1)-form η on $\mathcal{K}$. The associated *Dolbeault cohomology* group[13] $H_{\overline{\partial}}^{1,1}(\mathcal{K}, \mathbb{R})$ is a complexification of the standard *de Rham cohomology* group $H_d^2(\mathcal{K}, \mathbb{R})$, defined on $\mathcal{K}$ as the quotient: $H_{\overline{\partial}}^{1,1}(\mathcal{K}, \mathbb{R}) = \frac{\{\overline{\partial}\text{-closed real (1,1)-forms}\}}{\{\overline{\partial}\text{-exact real (1,1)-forms}\}}$. The space $\mathcal{K}_{[\omega]}$ of Kähler forms ω with the same Kähler class $[\omega]$ is given by:

$$\mathcal{K}_{[\omega]} = \{[\omega] \in H^2(\mathcal{K}, \mathbb{R}) \mid V = 0, \quad \omega + i\partial\overline{\partial}\varphi > 0\},$$

i.e., the functional space $\mathcal{P}(\omega)$ of Kähler potentials φ on $(\mathcal{K}, \omega)$ is given by:

$$\mathcal{P}(\omega) = \{\varphi \in C^\infty(\mathcal{K}, \mathbb{R}) \mid \omega_\varphi = \omega + i\partial\overline{\partial}\varphi > 0\}.$$

Next we need to define curvatures on the Kähler manifold $\mathcal{K}$. The mixed and covariant *Riemannian curvature tensors* on $\mathcal{K}$ are:

$$R_{ik\overline{l}}^m = -\partial_{\overline{l}}\Gamma_{ik}^m \quad \text{and} \quad R_{i\overline{j}k\overline{l}} = g_{m\overline{j}}R_{ik\overline{l}}^m.$$

Locally, in an open chart $U \subset \mathcal{K}$, the covariant Riemann tensor[14] reads:

$$R_{i\overline{j}k\overline{l}} = -\partial_i\partial_{\overline{j}}g_{k\overline{l}} + g^{\overline{q}p}(\partial_i g_{k\overline{q}})(\partial_{\overline{j}}g_{p\overline{l}}).$$

Then, the *Ricci curvature* tensor is defined as its contraction:

$$R_{i\overline{j}} = g^{\overline{l}k}R_{i\overline{j}k\overline{l}} = g^{\overline{l}k}R_{k\overline{l}i\overline{j}} = R_{k\ i\overline{j}}^k,$$

---

[13] More specifically, a Kähler form ω on $\mathcal{K}$ defines a nonzero element $[\omega] \in H_{\overline{\partial}}^{1,1}(\mathcal{K}, \mathbb{R})$. If a cohomology class $\alpha \in H_{\overline{\partial}}^{1,1}(\mathcal{K}, \mathbb{R})$ can be written as $\alpha = [\omega]$ for some Kähler form ω on $\mathcal{K}$ then we say that α is a *Kähler class* (and write $\alpha > 0$). Therefore, the Kähler class of ω is its cohomology class $[\omega] \in H_{\overline{\partial}}^{1,1}(\mathcal{K}, \mathbb{R})$. Alternatively, in terms of $H_d^2(\mathcal{K}, \mathbb{R})$, the Kähler class of ω is its cohomology class $[\omega] \in H_d^2(\mathcal{K}, \mathbb{R})$. Usually, all this is simply written: the Kähler class of ω is the cohomology class $[\omega] \in H^2(\mathcal{K}, \mathbb{R})$ represented by ω.

The $\partial\overline{\partial}$-*Lemma* (the holomorphic version of the *Poincaré Lemma*, also follows from the Hodge theory) states: "Let $\mathcal{K}$ be a compact Kähler manifold and suppose that $0 = [\alpha] \in H_{\overline{\partial}}^{1,1}(\mathcal{K}, \mathbb{R})$ for a real smooth $\overline{\partial}$-closed $(1, 1)$-form α. Then there exists a real smooth Kähler potential φ (uniquely determined up to the addition of a constant) with $\alpha = i\partial\overline{\partial}\varphi$." In other words, a real $(1, 1)$-form α is $\overline{\partial}$-exact iff it is $\partial\overline{\partial}$-exact. It is an immediate consequence of the $\partial\overline{\partial}$-Lemma that if ω and ω_φ are Kähler forms in the same Kähler class on $\mathcal{K}$, then $\omega_\varphi = \omega + i\partial\overline{\partial}\varphi$ for smooth Kähler potential function φ.

[14] It has the following three symmetries:
$\overline{R_{i\overline{j}k\overline{l}}} = R_{j\overline{i}l\overline{k}}$ (complex-conjugate);
$R_{i\overline{j}k\overline{l}} = R_{k\overline{j}i\overline{l}} = R_{i\overline{l}k\overline{j}}$ (I Bianchi identity); and
$\nabla_m R_{i\overline{j}k\overline{l}} = \nabla_i R_{m\overline{j}k\overline{l}}$ (II Bianchi identity),
where $\nabla_i \equiv \partial_i + g_{k\overline{q}}g^{\overline{q}j}\Gamma_{ij}^k$ is the complex covariant derivative on $(\mathcal{K}, g)$.

while its trace is the scalar curvature: $R = g^{\bar{j}i}R_{i\bar{j}}$. Locally, in an open chart $U \subset \mathcal{K}$, Ricci tensor is given by:

$$R_{i\bar{j}}(g) = -\partial\bar{\partial}\log[\det(g_{i\bar{j}})], \quad (i, j = 1, \ldots, 4n).$$

The associated *Ricci form* $\mathrm{Ric}(g)$ is the closed $(1,1)$-form on $\mathcal{K}$ given by:

$$\mathrm{Ric}(g) \equiv \mathrm{Ric}(\omega) = iR_{i\bar{j}}(g)\,dz^i \wedge dz^{\bar{j}} = -i\partial\bar{\partial}\log[\det(g_{i\bar{j}})]. \tag{9.26}$$

Now we have all the necessary ingredients to derive the continuous super-dynamics model for a *very large-scale* universal autonomous (UGV, UAV, USV, UUV) fleet. For this, we recall that the *Ricci flow* on a Riemannian n-manifold M (introduced by R. Hamilton [Ham82, Ham86, Ham88] and subsequently used by G. Perelman to prove the 100-year old Poincaré Conjecture), is governed by the nonlinear evolution equation of the Riemannian metric:

$$\partial_t g_{ij}(t) = -2R_{ij}(t), \quad (i, j = 1, ..., n), \tag{9.27}$$

which in local harmonic coordinates on M can be rewritten as:

$$\partial_t g_{ij}(t) = \Delta_M g_{ij} + Q_{ij}(g_{ij}, \partial g_{ij}), \tag{9.28}$$

where Δ_M is the Laplace-Beltrami operator defined locally on M as:

$$\Delta_M \equiv \frac{1}{\sqrt{\det(g_{ij})}}\partial_{x^i}\left(\sqrt{\det(g)}g^{ij}\partial_{x^i}\right),$$

while the tensor function $Q_{ij}(g_{ij}, \partial g_{ij})$ is quadratic in g_{ij} and its first order partial derivatives ∂g_{ij}. Later, in [II11], we proposed Eqs. (9.27)–(9.28) as a general model for all real-valued nonlinear reaction-diffusion systems [with symmetric, positive-definite diffusion matrix $\mathbf{D}$, concentration state vector $\mathbf{u}(\mathbf{x}, t)$ and local reactions $\mathbf{R}(\mathbf{u})$] of the form:

$$\begin{array}{ccccc}
\partial_t \mathbf{u} & = & \mathbf{D}\Delta\mathbf{u} & + & \mathbf{R}(\mathbf{u}) \\
\updownarrow & & \updownarrow & & \updownarrow \\
\partial_t g_{ij} & = & \Delta_M g_{ij} & + & Q_{ij}(g_{ij}, \partial g_{ij})
\end{array}.$$

To make the Kähler super-dynamics model, we need to generalize the Ricci flow (9.27)–(9.28) from the Riemannian n-manifold M to the Kähler $4n$-manifold $\mathcal{K}$, as shown in the previous subsection. To perform this generalization, we first remark that Kähler manifolds are usually classified into the following three subcategories, based on their first Chern class in Dolbeault cohomology.[15] A compact (i.e., closed and bounded) Kähler manifold $(\mathcal{K}, g)$ with positive first Chern class, $c_1(\mathcal{K}) > 0$, is called the *Fano manifold* (the stage for our super-dynamics) in which case, $[\omega] = \pi c_1(\mathcal{K})$. A compact Kähler

---

[15] The first Chern class, denoted by $c_1(\mathcal{K})$, of a Kähler manifold $(\mathcal{K}, g)$, is defined as the cohomology class $[\mathrm{Ric}(g)] \in H^{1,1}_{\bar{\partial}}(\mathcal{K}, \mathbb{R})$.

manifold with vanishing first Chern class, $c_1(\mathcal{K}) = 0$, is called the *Calabi–Yau manifold* (the stage for super-string theory). A compact Kähler manifold with negative first Chern class, $c_1(\mathcal{K}) < 0$, is called the *Kähler–Einstein manifold* (the stage for complex gravity theory), it admits the metric g^{16} defined by: $g = -\text{Ric}(g)$.

A Fano n-manifold $(\mathcal{K}, g)$ admits the (normalized) Kähler–Ricci flow[17] [with the time-dependent Ricci form (9.26)]:

$$\partial_t g_{ij}(t) = g_{ij}(t) - \text{Ric}\,[g(t)], \qquad (9.29)$$

which is locally, in an open chart $U \subset \mathcal{K}$, starting from some smooth initial Kähler metric tensor $g_0 = g_{i\bar{j}}(0)$, given by:

$$\partial_t g_{i\bar{j}}(t) = g_{i\bar{j}}(t) - R_{i\bar{j}}(t), \qquad (i, j = 1, \dots, 4n).$$

In terms of time-dependent Kähler potentials $\varphi = \varphi(t)$, the Kähler–Ricci flow (9.29) can be expressed as:[18]

$$\partial_t \varphi(t) = \varphi(t) + \log \frac{\omega_\varphi^n}{\omega^n} - g(t), \qquad (9.30)$$

where the time-dependent Kähler metric form $g = g(t)$ is defined by:

$$i\partial\bar{\partial}g(t) = \text{Ric}\,[\omega(t)] - \omega(t) \quad \text{and} \quad \int_\mathcal{K} (e^{g(t)} - 1)\omega^n = 0.$$

---

[16] Metric g on $\mathcal{K}$ is called the Kähler–Einstein metric iff:

$$\text{Ric}(\omega) = \lambda\omega, \qquad \text{for a real constant } \lambda = \frac{2\pi}{V}\int_\mathcal{K} c_1(\mathcal{K}) \wedge \omega^{n-1},$$

if $\text{Ric}(g) = 0$ then g is a Ricci–flat metric,

where $c_1(\mathcal{K})$ is the first Chern class of $\mathcal{K}$. If $\mathcal{K}$ admits a Ricci–flat metric [$\text{Ric}(g) = 0$], then its first Chern class must vanish [$c_1(\mathcal{K}) = 0$]. This is the *Calabi conjecture* [Wik16mm], proven by S.-T. Yau [Yau78].

[17] The Kähler–Ricci flow (9.29) preserves the Kähler class $[\omega]$. It has a global solution $g(t) \equiv \omega(t)$ when $g_0 = g_{i\bar{j}}(0)$ has $[\omega] = 2\pi c_1(\mathcal{K})$ as its Kähler class, which is written as $g_0 \in 2\pi c_1(\mathcal{K})$. In particular, by the $\partial\bar{\partial}$-Lemma, there exists a family of real-valued functions $u(t)$, called Ricci potentials of the metric $g(t)$, which are special Kähler potentials. They are determined by:

$$g_{i\bar{j}} - R_{i\bar{j}} = \partial_i\partial_{\bar{j}}u, \qquad \frac{1}{V_R}\int_\mathcal{K} e^{-u(t)}dv_g = 1,$$

where $V_R = \int dv_g$ is the volume of the Kähler–Ricci flow (9.29).

[18] The nth power ω^n of the Kähler symplectic form ω is the volume form on $\mathcal{K}$, given by: $\omega^n = \frac{1}{n!}i^n \det\left(g_{i\bar{j}}\right) dz^1 \wedge d\bar{z}^{\mathsf{T}} \wedge \cdots \wedge dz^n \wedge d\bar{z}^{\overline{n}}$, so that $V = \int_\mathcal{K} \omega^n$ is the standard volume on $\mathcal{K}$.

The corresponding evolutions of the Ricci curvature $R_{i\bar{j}} = R_{i\bar{j}}(t)$ and the scalar curvature $R = R(t)$ on $(\mathcal{K}, g)$ are respectively governed by:

$$\partial_t R_{i\bar{j}} = \triangle R_{i\bar{j}} + R_{i\bar{j}p\bar{q}}R_{q\bar{p}} - R_{i\bar{p}}R_{p\bar{j}}, \qquad \partial_t R = \triangle R + R_{i\bar{j}}R_{j\bar{i}} - R,$$

starting from some smooth initial Ricci and scalar curvatures, $R_{i\bar{j}}(0)$ and $R(0)$.

The existence of the Kähler–Ricci flow in a time interval $t \in [0, t_1)$ can be established as follows: If $\omega(t)$ is a solution of the Kähler–Ricci flow:

$$\partial_t \omega(t) = -\text{Ric}\,[\omega(t)]\,, \qquad \omega(0) = \omega_0, \tag{9.31}$$

then the corresponding cohomology class $[\omega(t)]$ with $[\omega(0)] = [\omega_0]$ evolves on $\mathcal{K}$ as the following ODE:

$$\partial_t[\omega(t)] = -c_1(\mathcal{K}), \qquad \text{with the solution :} \tag{9.32}$$
$$[\omega(t)] = [\omega_0] - t\,c_1(\mathcal{K}) = [i\partial\bar{\partial}\varphi(0)] - t\,c_1(\mathcal{K}) = [ig_0\,dz^i \wedge dz^{\bar{j}}] - t\,c_1(\mathcal{K}).$$

So, the Kähler–Ricci flow (9.31) exists for $t \in [0, t_1)$ iff $[\omega_0] - t\,c_1(\mathcal{K}) > 0$ (see [Cao85]).

Finally, Eq. (9.31) can be rewritten as a *complex parabolic Monge–Ampère equation* (see [Yau78, SPS12]):

$$\partial_t \varphi = \log \frac{(\omega_\varphi + i\partial\bar{\partial}\varphi)^n}{\omega^n}, \qquad \left(\text{with } \omega_\varphi + i\partial\bar{\partial}\varphi > 0\right) \tag{9.33}$$

while, the normalized Kähler–Ricci flow (9.29) can be rewritten as a normalized complex Monge–Ampère equation:

$$\partial_t \varphi = \log \frac{(\omega_0 + i\partial\bar{\partial}\varphi)^n}{\omega^n} - \varphi, \qquad \left(\text{with } \omega_\varphi + i\partial\bar{\partial}\varphi > 0\right). \tag{9.34}$$

For further technical details on Kähler geometry and the Kähler–Ricci flow, see [IR15] and the references therein.

The Kähler–Ricci flow (9.31) with the solution (9.32), equivalently represented by the complex Monge–Ampère equations (9.33)–(9.34), is our continuous super-dynamics model for a very large universal (UGV, UAV, USV, UUV) fleet.

10

Appendix 1: The World of Tensors

Here we present a general computational tensor framework for socio-econo-political sciences. It is based on geometric computational methods validated in theoretical physics, robotics, control theory and various kinds of networks (electrical, neural, biokinetic, 'small worlds', etc.) The basic underlying structure is that of a high-dimensional configuration space, technically called the 'smooth manifold', which is a set of all system's degrees-of-freedom, formalized as a non-linear deformation of a (linear) vector space. Once the configuration manifold of a system under consideration (e.g., any kind of a 'social game', together with its complex decision strategies, or 'tactics') is defined as a 'nonlinear vector space', then a variety of computational tools, the so-called 'tensors', can be defined on it (here we apply the basic computational concept of Wolfram's Mathematica: 'everything is a tensor', including, spinors, twistors, exterior differential systems, chains and cochains). These tensors include a variety of 'socio-economic forces', which can be derived as gradients of 'socio-political energies', upon which the system can be optimized using standard (Euler-Lagrangian) variational techniques, etc. The psycho-social basis for this 'tensors-on-a-manifold' formalism is classical Lewinian 'field theory in social science', in which the collective configuration space is a 'topological product' of individual 'life spaces'.

10.1 Abstract Tensor Algebra and Geometry

Recall that tensors are *geometric objects*,[1] defined locally (at a point) on a chosen smooth manifold.[2] Briefly, tensors are linear computational 'slot machines', designed for computing with high-dimensional nonlinearities, which

---

[1] These are geometric entities (like a point, vector, covector, metric, connection, curvature, torsion, etc.) that exist independently of any coordinate systems or reference frames [MTW73].

[2] The term 'smooth' means C^∞-differentiable. Smooth manifolds are nonlinear/curved vector spaces, which arise as sets of all possible configurations of

take tangent vectors (or, infinitesimal displacements) to numbers. For example, a tensor T_{ab} of type $(0,2)$ takes a pair of vectors[3] (v^a, w^a) into a single real number $T_{ab}v^a w^b$, where *Einstein's summation convention* over repeated indices is assumed (as always in this section).

One of important characteristics of tensors is their symmetry: e.g., tensor T_{ab} is symmetric if $T_{ab} = T_{ba}$; its symmetric $T_{(ab)}$ and antisymmetric parts $T_{[ab]}$ are:

$$T_{(ab)} = \frac{1}{2}(T_{ab} + T_{ba}), \qquad T_{[ab]} = \frac{1}{2}(T_{ab} - T_{ba}).$$

More generally, we have, e.g.:

$$T_{[de]}^{(ab)c} = \frac{1}{4}(T_{de}^{abc} + T_{de}^{bac} - T_{ed}^{abc} - T_{ed}^{bac}).$$

In this section we present the basics of abstract tensor geometry, mainly following the 'physical mathematics' developed in [Wal84] and [Pen07].[4]

10.2 Tensors on Smooth Manifolds

10.2.1 Vector-Fields and Commutators on Configuration Manifolds

More formally, given a point p on a smooth manifold M, consider a tangent space T_p at p (for a more formal treatment, see subsection 10.4.1 below). A tangent vector-field v^a on M is an assignment of a tangent vector $v^a|_p \in T_p$

---

complex dynamical systems (called configuration manifolds, like the relativistic spacetime, or a set of all degrees-of-freedom of a humanoid robot, etc.) and in which we can perform all advanced calculus operations as in the space $\mathbb{R}^n$ of real numbers. A smooth map between two smooth manifolds is called a *diffeomorphism* if it is 'one-to-one' and 'onto' and also has a smooth inverse.

[3] Whenever we use the terms 'vectors' or 'tensors', we are actually dealing with 'vector-fields' and 'tensor-fields', respectively, which are vectors and tensors, respectively, defined as functions of space and time.

[4] Our abstract tensor geometry is formulated using *abstract index notation* of R. Penrose (see [Pen72, PR84, Wal84, Pen07, Wik16k]) as a combination of classical Ricci's index component notation (framed into Einstein's summation convention and widely used by physicists) and abstract index-free geometric-object notation (denoted by bold letters and widely used by mathematicians). Penrose's notation is in our view 'the best of both worlds' (including both the computational power of indices and the coordinate-independence of index-free notation), so that e.g., we may view the geometric object T_{de}^{abc} as consisting of the tensor T and the elements $\{a, b, c, d, e\}$ of a labeling set which mark the 'slots' of this tensor (see description of the metric tensor, below). The corresponding component labels (in the component notation) are always denoted with Greek letters as $T_{\delta\varepsilon}^{\alpha\beta\gamma}$. In this way, any valid tensor equation expressed in the abstract index notation will have the corresponding component notation in the chosen coordinate basis, and vice versa.

at each point $p \in M$.[5] Given a smooth scalar function f and two (tangent) vector-fields, $\mathbf{v} = v^a$ and $\mathbf{w} = w^a$, on a manifold M, their *commutator* is another vector-field on M defined by:

$$[\mathbf{v}, \mathbf{w}](f) = \mathbf{v}[\mathbf{w}(f)] - \mathbf{w}[\mathbf{v}(f)]. \qquad (10.1)$$

For any three smooth vector-fields $(\mathbf{v}, \mathbf{w}, \mathbf{u})$ on M, their commutator (10.1) satisfies the *Jacobi identity*:

$$[[\mathbf{v}, \mathbf{w}], \mathbf{u}] + [[\mathbf{w}, \mathbf{u}], \mathbf{v}] + [[\mathbf{u}, \mathbf{v}], \mathbf{w}] = 0.$$

A new set of vector-fields on a manifold M can be generated by repeated Lie brackets of $\mathbf{u}, \mathbf{v}, \mathbf{w} \in M$.

10.2.2 Metric Tensor

A fundamental geometric object on any Riemannian manifold is the *metric tensor* $\mathbf{g} = g_{ab}$, a machine for computing vector lengths and scalar products [MTW73], with two input slots for the insertion of two vectors: $\mathbf{g}(slot_1, slot_2)$. Inserting the same vector $\mathbf{v}$ into both slots gives the square of it's length: $\mathbf{g}(\mathbf{v}, \mathbf{v}) = \mathbf{v}^2$. Inserting (in either order) two different vectors, $\mathbf{v} = v^a$ and $\mathbf{w} = w^a$, gives a single number $\mathbf{v} \cdot \mathbf{w}$, the scalar product of $\mathbf{v}$ and $\mathbf{w}$: $\mathbf{g}(\mathbf{v}, \mathbf{w}) = \mathbf{g}(\mathbf{w}, \mathbf{v}) = \mathbf{v} \cdot \mathbf{w} = \mathbf{w} \cdot \mathbf{v} = g_{ab} v^a w^b$.

More formally, a Riemannian metric $\mathbf{g}$ on a smooth manifold M is a symmetric, positive-definite (or, at least non-degenerate) tensor-field g_{ab} of type $(0, 2)$ with components (given in the coordinate basis $\{x^\mu\}$ at a point $m \in M$):

$$\mathbf{g} = g_{\mu\nu} dx^\mu dx^\nu.$$

Applied to a vector v^a, the metric tensor g_{ab} gives the dual vector: $v_a = g_{ab} v^b$, which shows the isomorphism: $T_m M \simeq T_m^* M$ between the tangent space $T_m M$ and the cotangent space $T_m^* M$ at the point $m \in M$.

The length L of a smooth curve $\gamma = \gamma(s)$ with the parameter s and tangent vector t^a on a manifold M with Riemannian metric g_{ab} is defined by:

---

[5] More precisely, a *one-parameter group of diffeomorphisms* ϕ_t (in physics, ϕ_t is called the *one-parameter group of transformations*, while in mathematics ϕ_t is called the *flow*) on a smooth manifold M is a smooth map from $\mathbb{R} \times M \to M$ such that for fixed $t \in \mathbb{R}$, $\phi_t : M \to M$ is a diffeomorphism and for all $t, s \in \mathbb{R}$, we have $\phi_t \circ \phi_s = \phi_{t+s}$. We can associate to ϕ_t a vector-field v^a as follows: for fixed $p \in M$, $\phi_t(p) : \mathbb{R} \to M$ is a curve (called an *orbit* of ϕ_t) that passes through p at $t = 0$. If we define $v^a|_p$ to be the tangent to this curve at $t = 0$, then to a one-parameter group of transformations of M there is associated a tangent vector-field v^a which is the infinitesimal generator of these transformations. In other words, ϕ is flow of a vector-field v^a. For each smooth vector-field, the existence and uniqueness of its flow, consisting of integral curves of the vector-field v^a, is determined by the corresponding *existence and uniqueness theorem* for a system of first-order (nonlinear) ordinary differential equations.

$$L = \int_\gamma \sqrt{g_{ab} t^a t^b} \, ds.$$

The inverse of g_{ab} s the (2,0)-tensor $g^{ab} = (g_{ab})^{-1}$ that exists due to the non-degeneracy of g_{ab}. By definition, $g^{ab} g_{bc} = \delta^a_c$ is the identity map $(T_m M \to T^*_m M)$, called the Kronecker delta tensor. Applied to a dual vector w_a, the inverse metric g^{ab} gives the vector: $w^a = g^{ab} w_b$. More generally, the so-called 'index gymnastics' of raising and lowering tensor indices denotes application of the metric g_{ab} and its inverse g^{ab} to that slot; e.g., if T^{abc}_{de} is a tensor of type (3,2), then $T^{acde}_b = g_{bf} g^{dh} g^{ej} T^{afc}_{hj}$.

10.2.3 Tensor Derivative ∇-Operator (Connection)

Our core differential operation defined on any smooth manifold (with a Riemannian metric g_{ab}) is the *tensor derivative* ∇-operator (also called the covariant derivative, or the torsion-free connection on a manifold; it is most often used as the covector ∇_a with the associated vector $\nabla^a = g^{ab}\nabla_b$), a generalized, coordinate-independent gradient operator ($\nabla \equiv$ grad), which is an invariant, metric-dependent, generalization of the partial derivative ∂-operator (most often used as ∂_a and $\partial^a = g^{ab}\partial_b$): $\nabla_a = \partial_a + A_a$, for some gauge-covector A_a.[6] In addition, ∇-operator is anticommutative:

$$\nabla_a \nabla_b - \nabla_b \nabla_a = 2\nabla_{[a}\nabla_{b]}.$$

Finally, ∇-operator is a map defined on a manifold M which takes each smooth tensor-field of type (m, n) to a smooth tensor-field of type $(m, n+1)$, and has the following properties [Wal84, Pen07]:

1. ∇-operator is linear (i.e., for any two mixed tensors A^a_b, B^a_b and any two constants k_1, k_2):

$$\nabla_c(k_1 A^a_b + k_2 B^a_b) = k_1 \nabla_c A^a_b + k_2 \nabla_c B^a_b.$$

2. Leibnitz rule for ∇_a:

$$\nabla_c(A^a_b B^c_d) = (\nabla_c A^a_b) B^c_d + A^a_b (\nabla_c B^c_d).$$

3. Commutativity of ∇_a with contraction:

$$\nabla_d(A^{ac}_{bc}) = \nabla_d A^{ac}_{bc}.$$

4. ∇_a is a directional derivative (for any tangent vector $\mathbf{t} = t^a$ and any smooth scalar function f on M):

$$\mathbf{t}(f) = t^a \nabla_a f, \qquad \text{or} \qquad \nabla_a f = \partial_a f.$$

---

[6] While an ordinary partial derivative $\partial \equiv \partial/\partial x$ is in prefix notation applied as ∂_a and in postfix notation by the comma '$,a$' subscript (e.g., $\partial_a f \equiv f_{,a}$), the tensor (or, covariant) derivative ∇-operator is in prefix notation applied by ∇_a and in postfix notation by the semicolon '$;a$' subscript (e.g., $\nabla_a f \equiv f_{;a}$, or $\nabla_a T^{bc} = T^{bc}_{;a}$).

5. As postulated, ∇-operator is torsion free (for any smooth scalar function f on M):

$$\nabla_a \nabla_b f = \nabla_b \nabla_a f.$$

Otherwise, there would exist a *torsion tensor* T^c_{ab} of type (1,2), defined by:

$$(\nabla_a \nabla_b - \nabla_b \nabla_a) f = -T^c_{ab} \nabla_c f.$$

6. For any two smooth vector-fields v^a, w^a we have the following ∇-torsion relation:

$$T^c_{ab} v^a w^b = v^a \nabla_a w^c - w^a \nabla_a v^c - [v, w]^c.$$

7. Commutator $[v^a, w^a] = [v, w]^a$ is expressed via ∇_a as:

$$[v, w]^b = v^a \nabla_a w^b - w^a \nabla_a v^b.$$

8. If v^a and w^a commute and satisfy: $\nabla_a v^a = \nabla_a w^a$ then $\nabla_a(v^{[a} w^{b]}) = 0$.
9. $\nabla \mathbf{g} = 0$ is zero: $\nabla_a g_{bc} \equiv g_{ab;c} = 0$, which uniquely determines ∇_a.
10. In case of a covector field ω_a we have:

$$\nabla_{[b} \nabla_c \omega_{a]} = 0 \iff d^2 \omega_a = 0.$$

11. Laplacian is defined on M as: $\nabla^2 = g^{ab} \nabla_a \nabla_b$.
12. ∇-operator is usually defined in terms of the *Christoffel symbol* Γ^c_{ab} given by:

$$\Gamma^c_{ab} = \frac{1}{2} g^{cd} (\partial_a g_{bd} + \partial_b g_{ad} - \partial_d g_{ab}).$$

13. ∇-operator acts on vectors and covectors (via Christoffel symbols) as:

$$\nabla_b v^a \equiv v^a_{;b} = \partial_b v^a + \Gamma^a_{bc} v^c \qquad \text{and} \qquad \nabla_b \omega_a \equiv \omega_{a;b} = \partial_b \omega_a - \Gamma^c_{ba} \omega_c.$$

14. ∇-operator acts on second-order tensors (T^{ab}, T_{ab}, T^a_b) as:

$$\nabla_c T^{ab} \equiv T^{ab}_{;c} = \partial_c T^{ab} + \Gamma^a_{cd} T^{db} + \Gamma^b_{cd} T^{ad},$$

$$\nabla_c T_{ab} \equiv T_{ab;c} = \partial_c T_{ab} - \Gamma^d_{ca} T_{db} - \Gamma^d_{cb} T_{ad},$$

$$\nabla_c T^a_b \equiv T^a_{b;c} = \partial_c T^a_b + \Gamma^a_{cd} T^d_b - \Gamma^d_{cb} T^a_d.$$

15. ∇-operator defines a *parallel transport* along a curve γ with the tangent vector t^a:
(i) of a vector v^a:

$$t^a \nabla_a v^b = 0 \qquad \text{or} \qquad t^a \partial_a v^b + t^a \Gamma^b_{ac} v^c = 0.$$

(ii) of a covector ω_a:

$$t^a \nabla_a \omega_b = 0 \qquad \text{or} \qquad t^a \partial_a \omega_b - t^a \Gamma^c_{ab} \omega_c = 0.$$

(iii) of a mixed second-order tensor T^b_a:

$$0 = t^a \nabla_a T^b_c \qquad \text{or}$$

$$0 = t^a \partial_a T^b_c + t^a \Gamma^b_{ad} T^d_c - t^a \Gamma^d_{ac} T^b_d.$$

16. In local coordinates $\{x^\mu\}$ on the manifold M, the natural volume element induced by the metric $\mathbf{g} = g_{ab}$ is $V = \sqrt{|g|}dx^1...dx^n$ and also, $\Gamma^a_{a\mu} = \frac{1}{2g}\partial_\mu g = \partial_\mu \ln\sqrt{|g|}$, (where $g = \det(g_{\mu\nu})$, so that the *divergence* $\nabla_a T^a$ of an arbitrary vector-field T^a is in components given by:

$$\nabla_a T^a \equiv T^a_{;a} = \partial_a T^a + \Gamma^a_{ab}T^b = \left(\sqrt{|g|}\right)^{-1}\partial_\mu\left(\sqrt{|g|}T^\mu\right).$$

10.2.4 Riemann and Ricci Curvature Tensors

Given a vector v^a and a covector ω_a on M, the Riemann curvature tensor R^d_{abc} is (in the torsion-free case) defined by the *Ricci identities*:

$$(\nabla_a\nabla_b - \nabla_b\nabla_a)\omega_c = R^d_{abc}\omega_d \quad \text{and} \quad (\nabla_a\nabla_b - \nabla_b\nabla_a)v^c = -R^c_{abd}v^d.$$
$$(10.2)$$

In components (in the local coordinate basis on M), the Riemann tensor is given by:
$$R^\sigma_{\mu\nu\rho} = \partial_\nu\Gamma^\sigma_{\mu\rho} - \partial_\mu\Gamma^\sigma_{\nu\rho} + (\Gamma^\alpha_{\mu\rho}\Gamma^\sigma_{\alpha\nu} - \Gamma^\alpha_{\nu\rho}\Gamma^\sigma_{\alpha\mu}).$$

Given a mixed second-order tensor T^b_a and the metric g_{ab} we have:

$$(\nabla_a\nabla_b - \nabla_b\nabla_a)T^d_c = R^e_{abc}T^d_e - R^d_{abd}T^d_c \quad \text{and}$$
$$(\nabla_a\nabla_b - \nabla_b\nabla_a)g_{cd} = R^e_{abc}g_{cd} + R^e_{abd}g_{ce} = R_{abcd} + R_{abdc}.$$

The Riemann curvature tensor has the following properties [Wal84, Pen07]:

1. Antisymmetry: $R^d_{abc} = -R^d_{bac}$, which follows from (10.2);
2. *Bianchi symmetry:* $R^d_{[abc]} = 0 \iff R^d_{abc} + R^d_{bca} + R^d_{cab} = 0$, which follows from:
   $$\nabla_{[a}\nabla_b\omega_{c]} = 0 \iff d^2\boldsymbol{\omega} = 0, \text{ as: } 0 = 2\nabla_{[a}\nabla_b\omega_{c]} = \nabla_{[a}\nabla_b\omega_{c]} - \nabla_{[b}\nabla_a\omega_{c]} = R^d_{[abc]}\omega_d;$$
3. The covariant curvature tensor $R_{abcd} = R^e_{abc}g_{ed}$ is also antisymmetric: $R_{abcd} = -R_{abdc}$, which follows from: $0 = (\nabla_a\nabla_b - \nabla_b\nabla_a)g_{cd} = R_{abcd} + R_{abdc}$.
4. *Bianchi identity:* $\nabla_{[a}R^e_{bc]d} = 0 \iff \nabla_a R^e_{bcd} + \nabla_b R^e_{cad} + \nabla_c R^e_{abd} = 0$, which follows from: $\omega_e\nabla_{[a}R^e_{bc]d} = 0$;
5. *Ricci tensor*[7] R_{ac} is the symmetric trace of Riemann: $R_{ac} = R^b_{abc}$;
6. Scalar curvature R is the trace of Ricci: $R = R^a_a$;
7. The 'trace free part' of Riemann is the conformal Weyl tensor C_{abcd} defined
   (for manifolds of dimension $n \geq 3$, with $c_1 = \frac{2}{n-2}$, $c_2 = \frac{2}{(n-1)(n-2)}$) by:
   $$C_{abcd} = R_{abcd} - c_1(g_{a[c}R_{d]b} - g_{b[c}R_{d]a}) + c_2 Rg_{a[c}g_{d]b};$$

---

[7] Note that a hot topic in contemporary mathematics (the main tool for proving the 100-year old Poincaré conjecture) is the *Ricci flow*, a generic geometric form of a nonlinear reaction-diffusion system (see [II11] and references therein).

8. Contraction of the Bianchi identity ($\nabla_{[a} R^e_{bc]d} = 0$) gives:

$$\nabla_a R^a_{bcd} + \nabla_b R_{cd} - \nabla_c R_{bd} = 0 \Leftrightarrow \nabla_a R^a_c + \nabla_b R^b_c - \nabla_c R = 0,$$

or, $\nabla^a G_{ab} = 0$, where $G_{ab} = R_{ab} - \frac{1}{2} R g_{ab}$ is the Einstein tensor.

10.2.5 Geodesics and Geodesic Deviation

A geodesic γ is a 'straightest possible' curve on the manifold M whose tangent vector t^a is parallel-propagated along itself [Wal84]:

$$t^a \nabla_a t^b = 0 \iff t^a \partial_a t^b + t^a \Gamma^b_{ac} t^c = 0.$$

In components (with $\dot{x}^\mu \equiv dx^\mu/dt$),

$$t^\mu = \dot{x}^\mu, \qquad \text{so we have:} \qquad \ddot{x}^\mu + \Gamma^\mu_{\sigma\nu} \dot{x}^\sigma \dot{x}^\nu = 0.$$

Given a point p on the manifold M, and any tangent vector $t^a \in T_p \subset M$, there always exists a unique geodesic through p with the tangent t^a (this is similar to the equations of motion in ordinary mechanics: given an initial position and velocity, a unique solution exists).

Jacobi's *geodesic deviation equation* relates the tendency of geodesics to accelerate toward or away from each other to the curvature of the manifold. A family of geodesics Σ_γ depends on two parameters/coordinates (t, s) and is described by two vectors: (i) tangent vector: $t^a = (\partial/\partial t)^a$ and (ii) its orthogonal deviation vector: $s^a = (\partial/\partial s)^a$, which respectively satisfy:

$$t^a \nabla_a t^b = 0 \qquad \text{and} \qquad t^b \nabla_b s^a = s^b \nabla_b t^a \Rightarrow s^a t_a = 0.$$

The quantity $v^a = t^b \nabla_b s^a$, that gives the rate of change along a geodesic of the displacement to an infinitesimally nearby geodesic in the family Σ_γ, can be interpreted as the relative velocity of an infinitesimally nearby geodesic. Similarly, the quantity

$$w^a = t^c \nabla_c v^a = t^c \nabla_c (t^b \nabla_b s^a)$$

can be interpreted as the relative acceleration of an infinitesimally nearby geodesic in the family Σ_γ. The fundamental equation that relates the acceleration vector w^a to the Riemann curvature tensor of the manifold M is the *Jacobi equation of geodesic deviation*. It is given by:

$$w^a = -R^a_{cbd} s^b t^c t^d, \tag{10.3}$$

which is derived as:

$$\begin{aligned}
w^a &= t^c \nabla_c (t^b \nabla_b s^a) = t^c \nabla_c (s^b \nabla_b t^a) \\
&= (t^c \nabla_c s^b)(\nabla_b t^a) + s^b t^c \nabla_c \nabla_b t^a \\
&= (s^c \nabla_c t^b)(\nabla_b t^a) + s^b t^c \nabla_b \nabla_c t^a - R^a_{cbd} s^b t^c t^d \\
&= s^c \nabla_c (t^b \nabla_b t^a) - R^a_{cbd} s^b t^c t^d \\
&= -R^a_{cbd} s^b t^c t^d.
\end{aligned}$$

Thus, $w^a = 0$ for all families Σ_γ iff $R^a_{cbd} = 0$. Some initially parallel geodesics, with $v^a = t^b \nabla_b s^a = 0$ initially, will diverge eventually iff $R^a_{cbd} \neq 0$.

In (t^μ, s^μ)-components, defined in the local coordinate $\{x^\mu, y^\mu\} \in \Sigma_\gamma$ basis on M, we have:

$$t^\mu = \dot{x}^\mu, \quad s^\mu = \dot{y}^\mu, \quad w^\mu = \ddot{x}^\mu,$$

so the geodesic deviation equation (10.3) reads:

$$\ddot{x}^\sigma = -R^\sigma_{\mu\nu\rho} \dot{y}^\nu \dot{x}^\mu \dot{x}^\rho.$$

Solutions $x^\mu = x^\mu(t^\mu, s^\mu)$ of this equation, called *Jacobi fields*, define the infinitesimal separations of nearby geodesics.

10.3 Basic Lie Groups and Lie Derivatives

10.3.1 Lie Groups and Their Lie Algebras

The notion of a Lie group generalizes to 'm parameters' the notion of a 1-parameter group of transformations (or, diffeomorphisms) explained before.

Firstly, recall that a *group* G is a set together with a map $G \times G \to G$ (called *multiplication*) and a preferred element e (called the *identity element*) such that:

(i) the multiplication law is associative, $g_1(g_2 g_3) = (g_1 g_2) g_3$;

(ii) for all $g \in G$, we have $eg = ge = g$; and

(iii) for every $g \in G$ there is an element of $g^{-1} \in G$, called the inverse of g, such that $gg^{-1}l = g^{-1}g = e$.

Many sets consisting of a finite number of elements provide examples of groups. A good example of a group with infinitely many elements is the collection of diffeomorphisms $\phi_t \in Diffeo(M)$ of a manifold M with 'multiplication' given by composition: $\phi_t \circ \phi_s$, and e taken as the identity map, $e(p) = p$ for all $p \in M$. Similarly, the collection of isometries $Iso(M) \subset Diffeo(M)$ of a manifold M with metric g_{ab} also forms a group, since the composition of two isometries is an isometry, and the inverse of any isometry is an isometry.

A special (and very rich) case of a group is a Lie group G of dimension m, which is also an m-manifold, such that the *inverse map* $i(g) = g^{-1}$ and the *multiplication map* $\mu(g_1, g_2) = g_1 g_2$ are both C^∞-smooth maps (see, e.g. [IR12] and Lie-algebra related references therein). Thus, the elements of a Lie group can be characterized locally by m parameters, and the multiplication and inverse operations depend smoothly on these parameters. The *group of diffeomorphisms $Diffeo(M)$* does not yield a (finite-dimensional) Lie group, since this group is 'too big' to be characterized by m parameters. However, the *group of isometries $Iso(M)$* always yields a (possibly 0-dimensional or disconnected) Lie group.

Let G be a Lie group of dimension m. It follows from the smoothness of i and μ that for all $h \in G$ the map: $\phi_h(g) = hg$, called the *left translation* by

h, is a diffeomorphism. Let ϕ_h^* denote the map on tensors induced by ϕ_h. If a vector-field v^a on G satisfies:

$$\phi_h^* v^a = v^a, \qquad \text{(for all } h \in G),$$

then v^a is called *left invariant*; it is determined by its value at $T_e \in G$, the tangent space at the identity element e. More generally, a tensor field invariant under ϕ_h^* for all $h \in G$ is said to be left invariant. All left invariant vector-fields form an mD vector space, since sums and scalar multiples of left invariant vector-fields are also left invariant.

If ϕ is any diffeomorphism on any manifold and v^a and w^a are any two vector-fields, we have the following commutator relation:

$$\phi^*[v, w]^a = [\phi^*(v), \phi^*(w)]^a.$$

Thus, if v^a and w^a are left invariant vector-fields on a Lie group, the commutator $[v, w]^a$ also will be a left invariant vector-field. Since the commutator depends linearly on v^a and w^a, this implies that there exists a left invariant tensor field c_{bc}^a, called the structure constant tensor of the Lie group, such that:

$$[v, w]^a = c_{bc}^a v^b w^c. \tag{10.4}$$

It follows immediately from its definition that:

$$c_{bc}^a = -c_{cb}^a. \tag{10.5}$$

Furthermore, from the Jacobi identity we have:

$$[u, [v, w]]^a + [v, [w, u]]^a + [w, [u, v]]^a = 0 \implies c_{d[a}^e c_{bc]}^d = 0. \tag{10.6}$$

A finite-dimensional vector space with a structure constant tensor c_{bc}^a of type $(1,2)$ satisfying Eqs. (10.5)–(10.6) is called a *Lie algebra*. We have shown above that the left invariant vector-fields of a Lie group comprise a Lie algebra. Thus, every Lie group gives rise to a Lie algebra. Conversely, it is possible to show that every Lie algebra gives rise to a Lie group in a unique way up to global topological structure. More precisely, given any Lie algebra, there exists a unique connected, simply connected Lie group whose Lie algebra coincides with the given Lie algebra. This fact significantly simplifies the analysis of Lie groups, since Lie algebras are much simpler objects to work with than Lie groups.

Let α_a be a left invariant covector-field on a Lie group G. If v^a is a left invariant vector-field on G, then their inner product $\alpha_a v^a$ is constant, so we have [Wal84]:

$$0 = \nabla_b(\alpha_a v^a) = v^a \nabla_b \alpha_a + \alpha_a \nabla_b v^a,$$

where ∇_a is any derivative operator on G. If w^a is another left invariant vector-field on G, we have:

$$2v^a w^b \nabla_{[a} \alpha_{b]} = (v^a w^b - v^b w^a) \nabla_a \alpha_b \qquad (10.7)$$
$$= -v^a \alpha_b \nabla_a w^b + \alpha_b w^a \nabla_a v^b$$
$$= -\alpha_b [v, w]^b$$
$$= -\alpha_b c^b_{cd} v^c w^d,$$

from which it follows that every left invariant covector-field α_b satisfies:

$$2\nabla_{[a} \alpha_{b]} = -\alpha_c c^c_{ab}. \qquad (10.8)$$

The right translation map χ_h defined by $\chi_h(g) = gh$, also is a diffeomorphism. We define right invariant tensor fields analogously to left invariant tensor fields. If x^a is a right invariant vector-field on a Lie group G and v^a is a left invariant vector-field on G, we have:

$$[x, v]^a = 0.$$

Similarly, if x^a is a right invariant vector-field and α_a is a left invariant covector-field on G, we have:

$$x^a \nabla_a \alpha_b + \alpha_a \nabla_b x^a = 0,$$

where ∇_a is any derivative operator on G. Consequently, if x^a and y^a are both right invariant but α_b is left invariant, we find, by a calculation similar to (10.7):

$$2x^a y^b \nabla_{[a} \alpha_{b]} = y^b x^a \nabla_a \alpha_b - x^b y^a \nabla_a \alpha_b$$
$$= \alpha_a [x, y]^a.$$

On the other hand, by Eq. (10.8) we have:

$$2x^a y^b \nabla_{[a} \alpha_{b]} = x^a y^b (-\alpha_c c^c_{ab}),$$

so that we find:

$$[x, v]^c = -c^c_{ab} x^a y^b, \qquad (10.9)$$

that is, except for a change in sign, the right invariant vector-fields satisfy the same commutation relations as the left invariant vector-fields. Besides, Eq. (10.9) shows that the structure constant tensor c^a_{bc} is also right invariant. More precisely, the tensor $c^c_{da} c^d_{cb}$ is symmetric in a and b; for *semisimple Lie groups* it also is nondegenerate. Thus, semisimple Lie groups possess a natural bi-invariant (i.e., left and right invariant) metric:

$$g_{ab} = c^c_{da} c^d_{cb}.$$

10.3.2 Lie Derivative and Killing Vector-Fields

Another tensor derivative on a smooth manifold is the *Lie derivative* $\mathfrak{L}_v$ that does not depend on the metric g_{ab} and does not increase the tensor rank (unlike the ∇-derivative). $\mathfrak{L}_v$ is another generalization of a directional derivative ∂_v along a vector v^a, which has the following particular cases:

1. The commutator (or, Lie bracket) of two vector-fields, v^a and u^a,

$$[v^a, u^a] = \mathfrak{L}_v u^a = v^a \nabla_a u^b - u^a \nabla_a v^b,$$

   is the Lie derivative of the vector-field u^a with respect to (or, along) the vector-field v^a.

2. The Lie derivative of a covector-field w_a (along the same vector-field v^a) is:

$$\mathfrak{L}_v w_a = v^b \nabla_b w_a + w_b \nabla_a v^b.$$

3. The Lie derivative of a scalar field ϕ (along v^a) is given by:

$$\mathfrak{L}_v \phi = v^a \nabla_a \phi = v^a \partial_a \phi.$$

4. The Lie derivative of a $(0, 2)$-tensor T_{ab} (along v^a) is:

$$\mathfrak{L}_v T_{ab} = v^c \nabla_c T_{ab} + (\nabla_a v^c) T_{cb} + (\nabla_b v^c) T_{ac}.$$

5. The Lie derivative of a closed 2-form F_{ab} (along v^a) is:

$$\mathfrak{L}_v F_{ab} = -2\nabla_{[a}(F_{b]c} v^c).$$

A *Killing vector-field* on a Riemannian manifold is a vector-field ξ^a which has the property that Lie differentiation with respect to it annihilates the metric:

$$\mathfrak{L}_\xi g_{ab} = 0 \iff \nabla_a \xi_b + \nabla_b \xi_a \equiv \nabla_{(a} \xi_{b)} = 0, \qquad (\text{with } \xi_a = g_{ab}\xi^b).$$

If $\phi_t : M \to M$ is one-parameter group of isometries on a smooth manifold M, $\phi_t^* g_{ab} = g_{ab}$, the vector-field ξ^a which generates ϕ_t, is a Killing vector-field. The necessary and sufficient condition for ϕ_t to be a group of isometries is: $\mathfrak{L}_\xi g_{ab} = 0$. Consequently, the necessary and sufficient condition that ξ^a be a Killing vector-field is that it satisfies *Killing's equation*:

$$\nabla^a \xi^b + \nabla^b \xi^a = 0.$$

More generally, for any Killing field ξ^a and any conserved, symmetric tensor-field T_{ab} on a smooth manifold M, we have:

$$\nabla^a (T_{ab}\xi^b) = T_{ab}\nabla^a \xi^b = 0.$$

10.4 Basic Applications to General Nonlinear Dynamics

10.4.1 The Phase-Space Formalism of (Co)tangent Bundles

In general nonlinear dynamics (see [Iva04, II08, II06b, II07b] and references therein),[8] to any system's configuration n-manifold M there is associated its velocity phase-space $2n$-manifold TM, called the tangent bundle of M. The original smooth manifold M is called the base of TM. There is an onto map $\pi : TM \to M$, called the projection. Above each point $x \in M$ there is a tangent space $T_x M = \pi^{-1}(x)$ to M at x, which is called a fibre. The fibre $T_x M \subset TM$ is the subset of TM, such that the total tangent bundle TM is a disjoint union of tangent spaces $T_x M$ to M for all points $x \in M$. From dynamical perspective, the most important quantity in the tangent bundle concept is the smooth map $v : M \to TM$, which is an inverse to the projection π, i.e, $\pi \circ v = \mathrm{Id}_M$, $\pi(v(x)) = x$. It is called the velocity vector-field. Its graph $(x, v(x))$ represents the cross-section of the tangent bundle TM. This explains the dynamical term velocity phase-space, given to the tangent bundle TM of the manifold M. The tangent bundle is where tangent vectors live, and is itself a smooth manifold. Vector-fields are cross-sections of the tangent bundle TM. System's *Lagrangian* (energy function) is a natural energy function on the tangent bundle.[9]

A dual notion to the tangent space $T_x M$ to a smooth n-manifold M at a point x is its cotangent space $T_x^* M$ at the same point x. Similarly to the

---

[8] Note that in this subsection we are not restricted to abstract tensor notation, but we use a general tensor formalism in the smooth charts of the configuration manifold, which can be, however, computationally implemented as an abstract tensor calculus, due to a one-to-one correspondence between the two formalisms.

[9] For example in robotics, the velocity phase-space TM has the Riemannian geometry with the *local metric form*:

$$\langle g \rangle \equiv ds^2 = g_{ij} dx^i dx^j, \tag{10.10}$$

where $g_{ij} = g_{ij}(m, x)$ is the material metric tensor defined by the robotics system's *mass-inertia matrix* and dx^i are differentials of the local joint coordinates x^i on M. Besides giving the local distances between the points on the manifold M, the Riemannian metric form $\langle g \rangle$ defines the system's kinetic energy:

$$T = \frac{1}{2} g_{ij} \dot{x}^i \dot{x}^j,$$

giving the *Lagrangian equations* of the conservative skeleton motion with Lagrangian $L = T - V$, with the corresponding *geodesic form* of the free motion (with $\partial_t = \frac{d}{dt}$):

$$\partial_t L_{\dot{x}^i} - L_{x^i} = 0, \quad \text{or} \quad \ddot{x}^i + \Gamma_{jk}^i \dot{x}^j \dot{x}^k = 0, \tag{10.11}$$

where subscripts denote partial derivatives, while Γ_{jk}^i are the Christoffel symbols of the affine Levi-Civita connection of the robotics manifold M (see [Iva10, II05, II06b] and references therein).

tangent bundle, for a smooth manifold M of dimension n, its cotangent bundle T^*M is a momentum phase-space $2n$-manifold, which is the disjoint union of all the cotangent spaces T_m^*M at all points $x \in M$. Therefore, the cotangent bundle of a M is the vector bundle $T^*M = (TM)^*$, the dual of the tangent bundle TM. The cotangent bundle is where 1-forms live, and is itself a smooth $2n$-manifold. Covector-fields (or, 1-forms) are cross-sections of the cotangent bundle T^*M. System's *Hamiltonian* is a natural energy function on the cotangent bundle.[10]

---

[10] Again, in robotics, the momentum phase-space $P = T^*M$ provides a natural *symplectic structure* that can be defined as follows. As the robotics configuration space M is a smooth $n-$manifold, we can pick local coordinates $\{dx^1, ..., dx^n\} \in M$. Then $\{dx^1, ..., dx^n\}$ defines a basis of the cotangent space T_x^*M, and by writing $\theta \in T_x^*M$ as $\theta = p_i dx^i$, we get local coordinates $\{x^1, ..., x^n, p_1, ..., p_n\}$ on T^*M. We cannow define the canonical symplectic form ω on $P = T^*M$ as:

$$\omega = dp_i \wedge dx^i,$$

where '$\wedge$' denotes the wedge or exterior product of exterior differential forms. This 2$-$form ω is obviously independent of the choice of coordinates $\{x^1, ..., x^n\}$ and independent of the base point $\{x^1, ..., x^n, p_1, ..., p_n\} \in T_x^*M$. Therefore, it is locally constant, and so $d\omega = 0$.

If (P, ω) is a $2n$D symplectic manifold then about each point $x \in P$ there are local coordinates $\{x^1, ..., x^n, p_1, ..., p_n\}$ such that $\omega = dp_i \wedge dx^i$. These coordinates are called canonical or symplectic. By the Darboux theorem, ω is constant in this local chart, i.e., $d\omega = 0$.

Let the smooth real$-$valued *Hamiltonian function* $H : P \to \mathbb{R}$, representing the total robotics energy $H(x, p) = T(p) + V(x)$ (T and V denote kinetic and potential energy of the system, respectively), be given in local canonical coordinates $x^i, p_i \in U$, U open in P. The *Hamiltonian vector-field* X_H, condition by $i_{X_H}\omega = dH$, is actually defined via symplectic matrix J, in a local chart U, as

$$X_H = J\nabla H = (\partial_{p_i}H, -\partial_{x^i}H), \qquad J = \begin{pmatrix} 0 & I \\ -I & 0 \end{pmatrix}, \tag{10.12}$$

where I denotes the $n \times n$ identity matrix and ∇ is the gradient operator.

Let (P, ω) be a symplectic phase$-$space manifold and $X_H = J\nabla H$ a Hamiltonian vector-field corresponding to a smooth real$-$valued Hamiltonian function $H : P \to \mathbb{R}$, on it. If a unique one$-$parameter group of diffeomorphisms $\phi_t : P \to P$ exists so that $\partial_t|_{t=0}\phi_t x = J\nabla H(x)$, it is called the *Hamiltonian phase$-$flow*.

A smooth curve $t \mapsto \left(x^i(t), p_i(t)\right)$ on (P, ω) represents an *integral curve* of the Hamiltonian vector-field $X_H = J\nabla H$, if in the local canonical coordinates $x^i, p_i \in U$, U open in P, *Hamiltonian canonical equations* hold:

$$\dot{q}^i = \partial_{p_i}H, \qquad \dot{p}_i = -\partial_{q^i}H. \tag{10.13}$$

An integral curve is said to be *maximal* if it is not a restriction of an integral curve defined on a larger interval of $\mathbb{R}$. It follows from the standard theorem on the *existence* and *uniqueness* of the solution of a system of ODEs with smooth r.h.s, that if the manifold (P, ω) is Hausdorff, then for any point $x = (x^i, p_i) \in U$,

10.4.2 A Generic Tensor Model for a 'Social-Game Situation'

Given an arbitrary 'social-game situation', we can develop its general nonlinear model using the following tensor formalism:

1. Firstly, we associate with this 'social-game' (e.g., a soccer game in the FIFA World Cup) *two* independent coordinate systems, constituting two independent smooth Riemannian manifolds. Let us denote these two coordinate systems and their respective manifolds as:[11]

- Internal coordinates: $x^i = x^i(t)$, $(i = 1, ..., m)$, constituting the mD internal configuration manifold: $M^m \equiv \{x^i\}$; and
- External coordinates: $y^e = y^e(t)$, $(e = 1, ..., n)$, constituting the nD external configuration manifold: $N^n \equiv \{y^e\}$.
  Therefore, in this first, engineering step (I) of our tensor modeling, we associate to the given socio-political-game system, not one but two different and independent smooth configuration manifolds, somewhat like viewing from two different satellites a certain place on Earth with a soccer game playing in it.

1. Once that we have precisely defined two smooth manifolds, as two independent views on the given social-game situation, we can apply our differential–geometric modeling to it and give it a natural social-game interpretation. More precisely, once we have two smooth Riemannian manifolds, $M^m \equiv \{x^i\}$ and $N^n \equiv \{y^e\}$, we can formulate two smooth maps between them:[12]

$$f : N \to M, \text{ given by coordinate transformation: } x^i = f^i(y^e), \quad (10.14)$$

and

$$g : M \to N, \text{ given by coordinate transformation: } y^e = g^e(x^i). \quad (10.15)$$

U open in P, there exists a maximal integral curve of $X_H = J\nabla H$, passing for $t = 0$, through point x. In case X_H is complete, i.e., X_H is C^p and (P, ω) is compact, the maximal integral curve of X_H is the Hamiltonian phase–flow $\phi_t : U \to U$.

The phase–flow ϕ_t is *symplectic* if ω is constant along ϕ_t, i.e., $\phi_t^* \omega = \omega$ ($\phi_t^* \omega$ denotes the *pull–back* of ω by ϕ_t),

if and only if ('iff' for short) $\mathcal{L}_{X_H} \omega = 0$

($\mathcal{L}_{X_H} \omega$ denotes the *Lie derivative* of ω upon X_H).

Symplectic phase–flow ϕ_t consists of canonical transformations on (P, ω), i.e., diffeomorphisms in canonical coordinates $x^i, p_i \in U$, U open on all (P, ω) which leave ω invariant. In this case the *Liouville theorem* is valid: ϕ_t *preserves* the *phase volume* on (P, ω). Also, the system's total energy H is conserved along ϕ_t, i.e., $H \circ \phi_t = H$.

[11] For example, in a standard robotic system, x^i denote internal joint coordinates, while y^e denote external Cartesian coordinates of individual segmental masses.

[12] This means that we are working in the category of smooth manifolds.

If the Jacobian matrices of these two maps are nonsingular (regular), that is if their Jacobian determinants are nonzero, then these two maps are mutually inverse, $f = g^{-1}$, and they represent the standard *forward and inverse kinematics*.

2. Although, maps f and g define some completely general nonlinear coordinate (functional) transformations, which are even unknown at the moment, there is something linear and simple that we know about them (from calculus). Namely, the corresponding infinitesimal transformations are linear and homogenous: from (10.14) we have (applying everywhere Einstein's summation convention over repeated indices)

$$dx^i = \frac{\partial f^i}{\partial y^e}\, dy^e, \tag{10.16}$$

while from (10.15) we have

$$dy^e = \frac{\partial g^e}{\partial x^i}\, dx^i. \tag{10.17}$$

Furthermore, (10.16) implies the linear and homogenous transformation of internal velocities,

$$v^i \equiv \dot{x}^i = \frac{\partial f^i}{\partial y^e}\, \dot{y}^e, \tag{10.18}$$

while (10.17) implies the linear and homogenous transformation of external velocities,

$$u^e \equiv \dot{y}^e = \frac{\partial g^e}{\partial x^i}\, \dot{x}^i. \tag{10.19}$$

In this way, we have defined two velocity vector–fields, the internal one: $v^i = v^i(x^i, t)$ and the external one: $u^e = u^e(y^e, t)$, given respectively by the two nonlinear systems of ODEs, (10.18) and (10.19).[13]

3. The next step in our tensor modelling/analysis is to define second derivatives of the manifold maps f and g, that is the two acceleration vector–fields, which we will denote by $a^i = a^i(x^i, \dot{x}^i, t)$ and $w^e = w^e(y^e, \dot{y}^e, t)$, respectively. However, unlike simple physics in linear Euclidean spaces, these two acceleration vector–fields on manifolds M and N are not the simple time derivatives of the corresponding velocity vector–fields ($a^i \neq \dot{v}^i$ and $w^e \neq \dot{u}^e$), due to the existence of the *Levi–Civita connections* ∇_M and ∇_N on both M and N. Properly defined, these two acceleration vector–fields respectively read:

$$a^i = \dot{v}^i + \Gamma^i_{jk} v^j v^k = \ddot{x}^i + \Gamma^i_{jk} \dot{x}^j \dot{x}^k, \quad \text{and} \tag{10.20}$$

$$w^e = \dot{u}^e + \Gamma^e_{hl} u^h u^l = \ddot{y}^e + \Gamma^e_{hl} \dot{y}^h \dot{y}^l, \tag{10.21}$$

---

[13] Although transformations of differentials and associated velocities are linear and homogeneous, the systems of ODE's define nonlinear vector–fields, as they include Jacobian (functional) matrices.

where Γ^i_{jk} and Γ^e_{hl} denote the (second–order) Christoffel symbols of the connections ∇_M and ∇_N.

Therefore, in the previous step we gave the first–level model of our social-game situation in the form of two ordinary vector–fields, the first–order vector–fields (10.18) and (10.19). For some simple situations (e.g., modeling ecological systems), we could stop at this modeling level. Using social-game terminology we call them velocity vector–fields. Following this, in the step (IV) we have defined the two second–order vector–fields (10.20) and (10.21), as a connection–base derivations of the previously defined first–order vector–fields. Using social-game terminology, we call them 'acceleration vector–fields'.

4. Finally, following our generic social-game terminology, as a natural next step we would expect to define some kind of generic Newton–Maxwell force–fields. And we can actually do this, with a little surprise that individual forces involved in the two force–fields will not be vectors, but rather the dual objects called 1–forms (or, 1D differential forms). Formally, we define the two covariant force–fields as

$$F_i = \mathfrak{m}g_{ij}a^j = \mathfrak{m}g_{ij}(\dot{v}^j + \Gamma^j_{ik}v^iv^k) = \mathfrak{m}g_{ij}(\ddot{x}^j + \Gamma^j_{ik}\dot{x}^i\dot{x}^k), \quad (10.22)$$

$$G_e = \mathfrak{m}g_{eh}w^h = \mathfrak{m}g_{eh}(\dot{u}^h + \Gamma^h_{el}u^eu^l) = \mathfrak{m}g_{eh}(\ddot{y}^h + \Gamma^h_{el}\dot{y}^e\dot{y}^l), \quad (10.23)$$

where $\mathfrak{m}$ is the mass of each single segment (unique, for simplicity), while $g_{ij} = g^M_{ij}$ and $g_{eh} = g^N_{eh}$ are the two Riemannian metric tensors corresponding to the manifolds M and N. The two force–fields, F_i defined by (10.22) and G_e defined by (10.23), are generic force–fields corresponding to the manifolds M and N, which represent the material cause for the given social-game situation. Technically, they are the *generators* of the corresponding dynamics and kinematics.

10.5 Exterior Differential Forms

A totally antisymmetric covariant tensor field $\omega_{a_1...a_p}$ on a smooth manifold M is a differential p-form: $\omega = \omega_{a_1...a_p} = \omega_{[a_1...a_p]} \in \Omega^p(M)$. In particular, smooth functions (or, scalar fields) on M are 0-forms. Given a derivative ∇–operator, a map $d : \Omega^p(M) \to \Omega^{p+1}(M)$, from smooth p-forms to $(p+1)$-forms, called the exterior derivative, is defined by (see, e.g. [II06b, II07b]):

$$\omega_{a_1...a_p} \mapsto \nabla_{[b}\omega_{a_1...a_p]} \quad \text{or} \quad (d\omega)_{a_1...a_p} = \nabla_{[b}\omega_{a_1...a_p]}.$$

In particular, for a scalar smooth function f on M, $df = \nabla f = \partial f$.

The main property of the map d is the *Poincaré lemma*: $d \circ d = d^2 = 0$. That is, $d^2\omega = 0$, for any p-form $\omega = \omega_{a_1...a_p} = \omega_{[a_1...a_p]}$. It can be proved as follows:

$$(d^2\omega)_{bca_1...a_p} = \nabla_{[b}\nabla_c\omega_{a_1...a_p]} = \partial_{[b}\partial_c\omega_{a_1...a_p]} = 0,$$

because of the equality of mixed partial derivatives in $\mathbb{R}^n$.

Conversely, given a *closed* p-form ω (i.e., satisfying $d\omega = 0$), then locally only (i.e., in any open region diffeomorphic to $\mathbb{R}^n$) this form is *exact*, that is, there exists a $(p-1)$-form θ such that $\omega = d\theta$.[14]

A solution of the equation $\nabla_a \nabla^a \omega = 0$ is called a *harmonic function*.

10.5.1 The Closure Principle: 'Boundary of a Boundary is Zero'

Given a smooth n-manifold M (for $n \geq 4$) with the tangent bundle TM and the cotangent bundle T^*M, there is a local *frame* $\{\partial_i = \partial/\partial x^i\}_{i=1}^n \in TM$, that is, an orthonormal basis of vector-fields (or, cross-sections of TM), as well as a local *coframe* $\{dx^i\}_{i=1}^n \in T^*M$, that is, a dual orthonormal basis of 1-forms (or, cross-sections of T^*M).

In the coframe $\{dx^i\}$, using the exterior derivative $d = \partial_i dx^i$[15] and the exterior product $\wedge$, the following exterior differential forms can be defined:

1-form: $A = A_i dx^i$.

2-form: $B = dA$;
$B = \frac{1}{2} B_{ij} dx^i \wedge dx^j$;
$B = (\partial_j A_i - \partial_i A_j) dx^j \wedge dx^i \implies B_{ij} = \partial_i A_j - \partial_j A_i = -2\partial_j A_i = -B_{ji}$.

3-form: $C = dB = ddA = 0$ (BBZ);
$C = \frac{1}{3!} C_{ijk} dx^i \wedge dx^j \wedge dx^k$;
$C = \partial_k B_{[ij]} dx^k \wedge dx^i \wedge dx^j \implies C_{ijk} = -3! \partial_k B_{[ij]}$.

4-form: $D = dC = ddB = 0$ (BBZ, provided $A = 0$);
$D = \frac{1}{4!} D_{ijkl} dx^i \wedge dx^j \wedge dx^k \wedge dx^l$;
$D = \partial_l C_{[ijk]} dx^l \wedge dx^i \wedge dx^j \wedge dx^k \implies D_{ijk} = -4! \partial_l C_{[ijk]}$.

$(n+1)$-form $= 0$ on n-manifold M.

In general, the exterior derivative and the exterior product are defined by the relation:
$$d(\theta \wedge \omega) = d\theta \wedge \omega + (-1)^p \theta \wedge d\omega.$$

---

[14] However, in general this result is not valid globally. The celebrated *de Rham's theorem* in algebraic topology establishes that the dimension of the vector space of closed p-forms modulo the exact p-forms equals a topological invariant: the pth *Betti number* of the manifold.

[15] The exterior derivative d is a generalization of ordinary vector differential operators (*grad*, *div* and *curl*) that transforms p-forms ω into $(p+1)$-forms $d\omega$, with the *BBZ-closure property*: $d \circ d = d^2 = 0$.

For any *cocycle* $\omega \in \Omega^p(M)$, which is a closed p-form, or a p-cochain such that $d\omega = 0$, and any *cycle* $C \in \mathcal{C}_p(M)$, which is a closed p-chain, or a p-chain with zero boundary: $\partial C = 0$, on a smooth n-manifold M, the following is valid:

— the *de Rham period*:

$$\int_C \omega \iff \langle C, \omega \rangle \,,$$

where $\langle C, \omega \rangle = \omega(C)$ is their inner product $\langle C, \omega \rangle : \Omega^p(M) \times \mathcal{C}_p(M) \to \mathbb{R}$. From the following *Poincaré lemma*, a closed p-form ω is exact iff

$$\langle C, \omega \rangle = 0.$$

— the *Poincaré lemma*:   *All (co)boundaries are (co)cycles*   (or, all exact forms are closed):

$$\text{boundaries} : \omega = d\theta \implies d\omega = 0 : \text{cycles}$$
$$(\text{for any } (p-1) - \text{form } \theta \in M);$$
$$\text{coboundaries} : C = \partial B \implies \partial C = 0 : \text{cocycles}$$
$$(\text{for any } (p-1) - \text{chain } B \in M).$$

The converse is true only for smooth contractible manifolds (including $\mathbb{R}^n$ or star-like nD sets). In general, it is only partially true (by the *Poincaré lemma*): every closed form is only *locally exact*. Here are two particular cases from vector calculus in $\mathbb{R}^3$:

1. If $\text{curl}\, F = 0$, then locally $F = \text{grad}\, f$;   and
2. If $\text{div}\, F = 0$, then locally $F = \text{curl}\, G$ (see de Rham complex in $\mathbb{R}^3$ given below).

— the *Stokes theorem*:

$$\int_{\partial C} \omega = \int_C d\omega \iff \langle \partial C, \omega \rangle = \langle C, d\omega \rangle \,.$$

— the *BBZ-closure property*: $\partial^2 = 0 \iff d^2 = 0$.
   Proof:

$$0 = \langle \partial^2 C, \omega \rangle = \langle \partial C, d\omega \rangle = \langle C, d^2\omega \rangle = 0, \qquad \text{or}$$

$$0 = \int_{\partial^2 C} \omega = \int_{\partial C} d\omega = \int_C d^2\omega = 0.$$

— the *de Rham cochain complex* in $\mathbb{R}^3$:

$$0 \to \Omega^0(\mathbb{R}^3) \xrightarrow[\text{grad}]{d} \Omega^1(\mathbb{R}^3) \xrightarrow[\text{curl}]{d} \Omega^2(\mathbb{R}^3) \xrightarrow[\text{div}]{d} \Omega^3(\mathbb{R}^3) \to 0.$$

From $d^2 = 0$ we have the following vector-calculus identities:

$$\text{curl} \cdot \text{grad} = 0 \qquad \text{and} \qquad \text{div} \cdot \text{curl} = 0.$$

— the *de Rham cochain complex* on an n-manifold M:

$$0 \to \Omega^0(M) \xrightarrow{d} \Omega^1(M) \xrightarrow{d} \Omega^2(M) \xrightarrow{d} \Omega^3(M) \xrightarrow{d} \cdots \xrightarrow{d} \Omega^n(M) \to 0, \tag{10.24}$$

satisfying the closure property on M, $d \circ d \equiv d^2 = 0$.

The functional space of closed p-forms (or cocycles ω, such that $d\omega = 0$) modulo exact $(p-1)$-forms (or coboundaries θ, such that $\omega = d\theta$) on a smooth n-manifold M is called the *de Rham cohomology*.[16]

10.5.2 Hodge's and Maxwell's Theories

The *Hodge duality operator* $\star : \Omega^p(M) \to \Omega^{n-p}(M)$, which maps any p-form α into its *dual* $(n-p)$-form $\star\alpha$ on a smooth n-manifold M, depends on the Riemannian metric $g = g_{ij}$ on M and also on the orientation (reversing orientation will change the sign). The *volume form* μ is defined in local coordinates on M as:

$$\mu = \text{vol} = \star(1) = \sqrt{\det(g_{ij})}\, dx^1 \wedge \ldots \wedge dx^n, \tag{10.26}$$

and the total volume on M is given by:

$$\text{vol}(M) = \int_M \star(1).$$

For any two p-forms $\alpha, \beta \in \Omega^p(M)$ with compact support on M, we define bilinear and positive–definite Hodge L^2-inner product as:

$$(\alpha, \beta) = \int_M \langle \alpha, \beta \rangle \star(1) = \int_M \alpha \wedge \star\beta, \tag{10.27}$$

---

[16] More precisely, the set of all cocycles, or closed p-forms on M, denoted by $Z^p(M) \subset \Omega^p(M)$, is the kernel $\text{Ker}(d)$ of the de Rham d-homomorphism. The set of all coboundaries, or exact $(p-1)$-forms on M, denoted by $B^p(M) \subset Z^p(M)$, is the image $\text{Im}(d)$ of the d-homomorphism. Their *quotient space* is a topological invariant of a manifold M called the pth *de Rham cohomology group*, defined as:

$$H^p(M) := \frac{Z^p(M)}{B^p M} = \frac{\text{Ker}\left(d : \Omega^p(M) \to \Omega^{p+1}(M)\right)}{\text{Im}\left(d : \Omega^{p-1}(M) \to \Omega^p(M)\right)}. \tag{10.25}$$

Two p-cocycles $\alpha, \beta \in \Omega^p(M)$ are *cohomologous*, or belong to the same *cohomology class* $[\alpha] \in H^p(M)$, if they differ by a $(p-1)$-coboundary: $\alpha - \beta = d\theta \in \Omega^{p-1}(M)$. The dimension $b_p = \dim H^p(M)$ of the pth de Rham cohomology group is called the Betti number. Betti numbers defined the *Euler–Poincaré characteristic* of the manifold M as:

$$\chi(M) = \sum_{p=1}^{n} (-1)^p b_p.$$

where $\alpha \wedge \star \beta$ is an n-form. The inner product (10.27) is linear in each variable and symmetric, $(\alpha, \beta) = (\beta, \alpha)$. We have: $(\alpha, \alpha) \geq 0$ and $(\alpha, \alpha) = 0$ iff $\alpha = 0$. Also, $(\star \alpha, \star \beta) = (\alpha, \beta)$.

From (10.27) it follows that for every p–form $\alpha \in \Omega^p(M)$ we can define the *norm functional*

$$\|\alpha\|^2 = (\alpha, \alpha) \doteq \int_M \langle \alpha, \alpha \rangle \star (1) = \int_M \alpha \wedge \star \alpha,$$

for which the *Euler–Lagrangian equation* becomes the Laplace equation:

$$\Delta \alpha = 0.$$

For example, the standard *Lagrangian* $\mathcal{L}$ for the free *Maxwell electromagnetic field*: $F = dA$ (where $A = A_i dx^i$ is the potential 1-form), is given by:

$$\mathcal{L}(A) = \frac{1}{2}(F \wedge \star F),$$

with the corresponding action:

$$S(A) = \frac{1}{2} \int F \wedge \star F.$$

Using the Hodge L^2-inner product (10.27), we can rewrite this electrodynamic action as

$$S(A) = \frac{1}{2}(F, F). \tag{10.28}$$

The Hodge dual (or, formal adjoint) to the exterior derivative $d : \Omega^p(M) \to \Omega^{p+1}(M)$ on a smooth n-manifold M is the *Hodge codifferential* δ, a linear map $\delta : \Omega^p(M) \to \Omega^{p-1}(M)$, which is a generalization of the divergence, defined by:

$$\delta = (-1)^{n(p+1)+1} \star d\star, \qquad \text{so that} \qquad d = (-1)^{np} \star \delta \star.$$

That is, for even-dimensional manifolds: $\delta = -\star d\star$, while for odd-dimensional manifolds: $\delta = \star d\star$.

Applied to any p-form $\omega \in \Omega^p(M)$, the codifferential δ gives:

$$\delta\omega = (-1)^{n(p+1)+1} \star d \star \omega, \qquad \delta d\omega = (-1)^{np+1} \star d \star d\omega.$$

If $\omega = f$ is a 0–form, or a scalar function, then $\delta f = 0$. If a p-form α is a codifferential of a $(p+1)$-form β, that is $\alpha = \delta\beta$, then β is called the *coexact* form. A p-form α is *coclosed* if $\delta\alpha = 0$; then $\star\alpha$ is closed (i.e., $d \star \alpha = 0$) and conversely.

A standard example is classical electrodynamics, in which the *gauge field* is an electromagnetic potential 1-form (a *connection* on a $U(1)$–bundle),

$$A = A_\mu dx^\mu = A_\mu dx^\mu + df, \qquad (f = \text{arbitrary scalar field}),$$

with the corresponding electromagnetic field 2-form (the *curvature* of the connection A):

$$F = dA, \quad \text{in components given by:}$$

$$F = \frac{1}{2} F_{\mu\nu}\, dx^{\mu} \wedge dx^{\nu}, \quad \text{with} \quad F_{\mu\nu} = \partial_{\nu} A_{\mu} - \partial_{\mu} A_{\nu}.$$

Electrodynamics is governed by the *Maxwell equations,* which in exterior formulation read[17]

$$dF = 0, \quad \delta F = -4\pi J, \quad \text{or in components,}$$
$$F_{[\mu\nu,\eta]} = 0, \quad F_{\mu\nu},^{\mu} = -4\pi J_{\mu},$$

where comma denotes the partial derivative and the 1-form of electric current $J = J_{\mu} dx^{\mu}$ is conserved, by the electrical *continuity equation,*

$$\delta J = 0, \quad \text{or in components,} \quad J_{\mu},^{\mu} = 0.$$

The codifferential δ can be coupled with the exterior derivative d to construct the *Hodge Laplacian* $\Delta : \Omega^{p}(M) \to \Omega^{p}(M)$, a harmonic generalization of the *Laplace-Beltrami differential operator*, given by:

$$\Delta = \delta d + d\delta = (d + \delta)^{2}.$$

A p-form α is called *harmonic form* iff

$$\Delta\alpha = 0 \iff (d\alpha = 0, \ \delta\alpha = 0).$$

Thus, α is harmonic in a compact domain $D \subset M^{18}$ iff it is both closed and coclosed in D. Informally, every harmonic form is both closed and coclosed. As a proof, we have:

$$0 = (\alpha, \ \Delta\alpha) = (\alpha, d\delta\alpha) + (\alpha, \delta d\alpha) = (\delta\alpha, \delta\alpha) + (d\alpha, d\alpha).$$

---

[17] The first, sourceless Maxwell equation, $dF = 0$, gives vector magnetostatics and magnetodynamics,

$$\text{Magnetic Gauss' law}: \operatorname{div} \mathbf{B} = 0,$$
$$\text{Faraday's law}: \partial_{t}\mathbf{B} + \operatorname{curl}\mathbf{E} = 0.$$

The second Maxwell equation with source, $\delta F = J$ (or, $d \star F = - \star J$), gives vector electrostatics and electrodynamics,

$$\text{Electric Gauss' law}: \operatorname{div} \mathbf{E} = 4\pi\rho,$$
$$\text{Ampère's law}: \partial_{t}\mathbf{E} - \operatorname{curl}\mathbf{B} = -4\pi\mathbf{j}.$$

[18] A domain D is *compact* (i.e., *closed and bounded*) if every open cover of D has a finite subcover.

Since $(\beta,\ \beta) \geq 0$ for any form β, $(\delta\alpha, \delta\alpha)$ and $(d\alpha, d\alpha)$ must vanish separately. Thus, $d\alpha = 0$ and $\delta\alpha = 0$.

All harmonic p-forms on a smooth manifold M form the vector space $H^p_\Delta(M)$.

For example, to translate notions from vector calculus, we first identify scalar functions with 0-forms, field intensity vectors with 1-forms, flux vectors with 1-forms and scalar densities with 1-forms. We then have the following correspondence:

grad $\longrightarrow d$: on 0–forms;   curl $\longrightarrow \star d$: on 1–forms;

div $\longrightarrow \delta$: on 1–forms;   div grad $\longrightarrow \Delta$: on 0–forms;

curl curl $-$ grad div $\longrightarrow \Delta$: on 1–forms.

We remark that exact and coexact p-forms ($\alpha = d\beta$ and $\omega = \delta\beta$, respectively) are mutually orthogonal with respect to the L^2-inner product (10.27). The orthogonal complement consists of forms that are both closed and co-closed: that is, of harmonic forms ($\Delta\gamma = 0$).

If α is a p-form and β is a $(p+1)$-form then we have:

$$(d\alpha, \beta) = (\alpha, \delta\beta) \qquad \text{and} \qquad (\delta\alpha, \beta) = (\alpha, d\beta). \tag{10.29}$$

This relation is usually interpreted as saying that the two exterior differentials, d and δ, are *adjoint* (or, dual) to each other. Relation (10.29) implies that the Hodge Laplacian Δ is *self-adjoint* (or, self-dual) elliptic operator:

$$(\Delta\alpha, \beta) = (\alpha, \Delta\beta).$$

The celebrated *Hodge decomposition theorem* (HDT) states that, on a compact orientable smooth n-manifold M (with $n \geq p$), any exterior p-form can be written as a unique sum of an *exact form*, a *coexact form*, and a *harmonic form*. More precisely, for any p-form $\omega \in \Omega^p(M)$ there are three unique forms: a $(p-1)$-form $\alpha \in \Omega^{p-1}(M)$, a $(p+1)$-form $\beta \in \Omega^{p+1}(M)$ and a harmonic p-form $\gamma \in \Omega^p(M)$, such that the following identity holds:

$$\underset{\omega}{\underset{\text{any form}}{}} = \underset{d\alpha}{\underset{\text{exact}}{}} + \underset{\delta\beta}{\underset{\text{coexact}}{}} + \underset{\gamma}{\underset{\text{harmonic}}{}}.$$

In physics community, the exact form $d\alpha$ is called *longitudinal form*, while the coexact form $\delta\beta$ is called *transversal form*, so that they are mutually orthogonal. Thus, any form can be orthogonally decomposed into a harmonic, a longitudinal and transversal form. For example, in *fluid dynamics*, any vector-field v can be decomposed into a sum of two vector-fields, one of which is divergence–free, and the other is curl–free.

Since γ is harmonic, $d\gamma = 0$. Also, by Poincaré lemma, $d(d\alpha) = 0$. In case ω is a closed p–form, $d\omega = 0$, then the term $\delta\beta$ in HDT is absent, so we have the *short Hodge decomposition*:

$$\omega = d\alpha + \gamma, \tag{10.30}$$

thus ω and γ differ by $d\alpha$. In topological terminology, ω and γ belong to the same *cohomology class* $[\omega] \in H^p(M)$. Now, by the de Rham theorems it follows that if C is any p–cycle, then

$$\int_C \omega = \int_C \gamma,$$

that is, γ and ω have the same periods. More precisely, if ω is any closed p–form, then there exists a unique harmonic p–form γ with the same periods as those of ω (see [Rha84, Fla63]).

The *Hodge–Weyl theorem* [Voi02, Rha84] states that every de Rham cohomology class has a unique harmonic representative. In other words, the space $H_\Delta^p(M)$ of harmonic p–forms on a smooth manifold M is isomorphic to the de Rham cohomology group (10.25), or $H_\Delta^p(M) \cong H_{DR}^p(M)$. That is, the harmonic part γ of HDT depends only on the global structure, i.e., the topology of M.

For example, in $(2+1)$D electrodynamics (in the complex plane $\mathbb{C}$), p-form Maxwell equations in the Fourier domain $\Sigma \subset \mathbb{C}$ are written as [TC99]:

$$dE = \mathrm{i}wB, \qquad dB = 0,$$
$$dH = -\mathrm{i}wD + J, \qquad dD = Q,$$

where H is a 0–form (magnetizing field), D (electric displacement field), J (electric current density) and E (electric field) are 1–forms, while B (magnetic field) and Q (electric charge density) are 2–forms. From $d^2 = 0$ it follows that the J and the Q satisfy the *continuity equation*

$$dJ = \mathrm{i}wQ,$$

where $\mathrm{i} = \sqrt{-1}$ and w is the field frequency. Constitutive equations, which include all metric information in this framework, are written in terms of the Hodge star operator:

$$D = \star E, \qquad B = \star H.$$

Applying HDT to the electric field intensity 1–form E, we get [HT05]

$$E = d\phi + \delta A + \chi,$$

where ϕ is a 0–form (a scalar field) and A is a 2–form; $d\phi$ represents the static field and δA represents the dynamic field, and χ represents the harmonic field component. If domain Σ is contractible, χ is identically zero and we have the short Hodge decomposition,

$$E = d\phi + \delta A.$$

10.5.3 Cartan Calculus

Basic Cartan calculus consists of the following data:

Main exterior forms

1. Basis 1-form (coframe): θ^a
2. Connection 1-form: ω_a^b
3. Curvature 2-form: Ω_a^b
4. Torsion 2-form: Θ^a

Structure equations

Curvature (or, second) structure equation:

$$\Omega_a^b = d\omega_a^b + \omega_a^c \wedge \omega_c^b$$

Torsion (or, first) structure equation:

$$\Theta^a = d\theta^a - \theta^b \wedge \omega_b^a$$

Bianchi identities

Taking the exterior derivative of the curvature structure equation gives:

$$d\Omega_a^b - \omega_a^c \wedge d\omega_c^b + \omega_c^b \wedge d\omega_a^c = 0,$$

and subsequently applying both structure equations, we obtain the second Bianchi identity:

$$d\Omega_a^b + \omega_p^b \wedge \Omega_a^p - \omega_a^p \wedge \Omega_p^b = 0.$$

Taking the exterior derivative of the torsion structure equation gives:

$$d\Theta^a - \theta^b \wedge d\omega_b^a + \omega_b^a \wedge d\theta^b = 0,$$

and subsequently applying both structure equations, we obtain the first Bianchi identity:

$$d\Theta^a - \theta^p \wedge \Omega_p^a + \omega_p^a \wedge \Theta^p = 0.$$

10.5.4 Gauge Potential, Field Strength and Cartan's Equations

Let G be a Lie group with its Lie algebra $\mathfrak{g}$. The so-called *gauge potential* is a $\mathfrak{g}$-valued 1-form $\omega \in G$, governed by the *Maurer-Cartan structure equation* (see, e.g. [II06b, II07b]):

$$d\omega + \frac{1}{2}[\omega, \omega] = O, \qquad \text{or} \qquad d\omega + \omega \wedge \omega = 0. \tag{10.31}$$

The corresponding *field strength* is its exterior-covariant derivative: $D\omega \in G$, which is a $\mathfrak{g}$-valued 2-form Ω given by:

$$\Omega = D\omega = d\omega + \frac{1}{2}[\omega, \omega] = d\omega + \omega \wedge \omega. \tag{10.32}$$

Equation (10.32) means that the 2–form Ω measures the extent to which the 1–form ω fails to satisfy the Maurer-Cartan equation (10.31). In the language of *principal bundles*, the gauge potential ω corresponds to *connection*, while the field strength Ω corresponds to *curvature*.

The most important special case is when the group G is a Riemannian manifold with the tangent bundle TG and the cotangent bundle T^*G, with the *Levi–Civita connection* $\Gamma = \Gamma_{ij}^k(e)$ given by the *Christoffel symbols* $\Gamma_{ij}^k(e)$ (with $i, j, k = 1, 2, ..., \dim G$). In the *local frame* $e = \{e_i\} \subset TG$, the connection Γ is defined by the covariant derivative $\nabla = \nabla_{e_i}$ as:

$$\nabla e = \Gamma e, \qquad \text{in components:} \qquad \nabla_{e_i} e_j = \Gamma_{ij}^k e_k.$$

If $\theta = \{\theta^i\} \subset T^*G$ denotes the *local coframe*, i.e., the dual basis on T^*G, such that $\theta^i(e_j) = \delta_j^i$, then the connection 1-form $\omega = \omega_i^j(e)$ is defined in θ by:

$$\omega = \Gamma\theta, \qquad \text{in components:} \qquad \omega_i^j(e) = \Gamma_{ki}^j \theta^k(e).$$

The *curvature* 2–form $\Omega = \Omega_i^j(e)$, corresponding to the Levi-Civita connection Γ, still defined as the exterior-covariant derivative $\Omega = D\omega$ in (10.32), is in the local coframe θ given by:

$$\Omega = d\omega + \omega \wedge \omega, \qquad \text{in components:} \qquad \Omega_i^j(e) = d\omega_i^j(e) + \omega_k^j(e) \wedge \omega_i^k(e).$$

10.6 Basic Physical Applications: From Einstein to Quantum

For historical reasons only, we provide here a quick overview of abstract tensor methods in the 20th Century physics.[19] We emphasize that these geometric tools originated from pure Riemann-Ricci-Civita mathematics, while its first application was given in the work of A. Einstein. However, these computational tools have been subsequently applied (in late 20th Century) to many different fields, including rigid-body mechanics (where the configuration manifold is simply the set of all degrees of freedom, while time is an independent parameter, like in Hamiltonian dynamics (see [II06b, II07b] and references therein), robotics/biomechanics (see [II05, Iva10] and references therein), nonlinear dynamics and complexity theory (see [II08] and references therein), crowd dynamics (see [IR10b] and references therein), nonlinear control theory (see[II13], electrical networks, neural networks, (bio)kinetic networks, etc. A tensor is simply a generalization of a vector, matrix and graph; so tensor methods have been highly-beneficial in a wide of fields.

---

[19] In this subsection, we again restrict ourselves to the abstract tensor notation only.

10.6.1 Special Relativity

The metric η_{ab} of spacetime is in any global inertial coordinate system $\{x^\mu\}$ defined by:

$$\eta_{ab} = \eta_{\mu\nu}(dx^\mu)_a(dx^\nu)_b \quad \text{with} \quad \eta_{\mu\nu} = \text{diag}(-1,1,1,1) \quad \text{and} \quad \partial_c\eta_{ab} = 0.$$

Since ordinary derivatives commute, the curvature of η_{ab} vanishes. The geodesics of η_{ab} are those curves which are straight lines when expressed in global inertial coordinates. Spacetime is the manifold $\mathbb{R}^4$ with a flat metric η_{ab} of Lorentz signature $(-1,1,1,1)$ defined on it.

Curves are classified as timelike, null, or spacelike according to whether the norm $\eta_{ab}t^a t^b$ of their tangent t^a, is respectively, negative, zero, or positive. Special relativity asserts that the paths in spacetime of material particles are always timelike curves. We may parameterize a timelike curve $\gamma = \gamma(s)$ by the proper time τ (on a clock carried along the given curve) defined by: $\tau = \int \sqrt{-\eta_{ab}t^a t^b}\,ds$, with increasing s corresponding to 'forward in time' [Wal84].

The tangent vector u^a to a timelike world line parameterized by τ is called the 4-velocity of a particle, sitting on curve of unit length: $u^a u_a = -1$. A particle subject to no external forces will travel on a geodesic, i.e., its 4-velocity will satisfy the equation of motion: $u^a \partial_a u^b = 0$, where ∂_a is the ordinary derivative operator of a global inertial coordinate system associated with η_{ab}.

The energy-momentum 4-vector, p^a, of a particle of mass m is defined by: $p^a = mu^a$. The energy of a particle as measured by an observer (present at the site of the particle) whose 4-velocity is v^a is defined by: $E = -p_a v^a$.

Continuous matter distributions in special relativity are described by a symmetric $(0,2)$-tensor T_{ab} called the stress-energy-momentum tensor. For an observer with 4-velocity v^a, the nonnegative component $T_{ab}v^a v^b \geq 0$ is interpreted as the energy density, i.e., the mass-energy per unit volume, as measured by this observer. If x^a is orthogonal to v^a, the component $-T_{ab}v^a x^b$ is interpreted as the momentum density of the matter in the x^a-redirection. If y^a also is orthogonal to v^a, then $T_{ab}x^a y^b$ represents the $x^a - y^a$ component of the stress tensor of the material.

A perfect fluid is defined to be a continuous distribution of matter with stress-energy tensor T_{ab} of the form:

$$T_{ab} = \rho u_a u_b + P(\eta_{ab} + u_a u_b),$$

where u_a is a unit timelike vector-field representing the 4-velocity of the fluid, while the functions ρ and P are, respectively, the mass-energy density and pressure of the fluid as measured in its rest frame. The fluid is called 'perfect' because of the absence of heat conduction terms and stress terms corresponding to viscosity.

The equation of motion of a perfect fluid subject to no external forces is simply:

$$\partial^a T_{ab} = 0. \tag{10.33}$$

In terms of ρ, P, and u^a, and projecting the resulting equation parallel and perpendicular to u^a, Eq. (10.33) becomes:

$$u^a \partial_a \rho + (\rho + P)\partial^a u_a = 0,$$
$$(P + \rho)u^a \partial_a u_b + (\eta_{ab} + u_a u_b)\partial^a P = 0.$$

Equation (10.33) implies:

$$\partial^a J_a = 0, \qquad \text{where} \qquad J_a = -T_{ab}v^b$$

represents the conserved mass-energy current density 4-vector of the fluid.

In special relativity, electric field **E** and magnetic field **B** are combined into a single antisymmetric spacetime tensor-field: $F_{ab} = -F_{ba}$ with six independent components. For an observer moving with 4-velocity v^a, the quantity: $E_a = F_{ab}v^b$, is interpreted as the electric field measured by that observer, while $B_a = -\frac{1}{2}\epsilon_{ab}{}^{cd}F_{cd}v^b$ is interpreted as the magnetic field, where ϵ_{abcd} is the totally antisymmetric tensor of positive orientation with norm $\epsilon_{abcd}\epsilon^{abcd} = -24$ so that in a right-handed orthonormal basis we have $\epsilon_{0123} = 1$.

In terms of F_{ab}, Maxwell's equations take the simple and elegant form:

$$\partial^a F_{ab} = -4\pi j_b, \qquad \partial_{[a}F_{bc]} = 0,$$

where j_a is the current density 4-vector of electric charge. Note that the antisymmetry of F_{ab} implies that

$$0 = \partial^b \partial^a F_{ab} = -4\pi \partial^a j_a.$$

Thus, Maxwell's equations imply $\partial^a j_a = 0$, which, by the same argument as given above for J_a, states that electric charge is conserved. The equation of motion of a particle of charge q moving in the electromagnetic field F_{ab} is given by the Lorentz force law:

$$u^a \partial_a u_b = \frac{q}{m} F_{bc} u^c.$$

The stress-energy tensor of the electromagnetic field is:

$$T_{ab} = \frac{1}{4\pi}\left[F_{ac}F_b{}^c - \frac{1}{4}\eta_{ab}F_{de}F^{de} \right].$$

Again, T_{ab} satisfies the energy condition: $T_{ab}v^a v^b \geq 0$ and if $j_a = 0$, we have Eq. (10.33) by virtue of Maxwell's equations. If $j_a \neq 0$, then the stress-energy T_{ab} of the electromagnetic field alone is not conserved, but the total stress-energy of the field and the charged matter is still conserved.

By the converse of the Poincaré lemma, the second Maxwell equation, $\partial_{[c}F_{ab]} = 0$, implies that there exists a covector-field A_a, called the vector potential, such that:

$$F_{ab} = \partial_a A_b - \partial_b A_a$$

so that the first Maxwell equation reads:

$$\partial^a \left(\partial_a A_b - \partial_b A_a \right) = -4\pi j_b \iff \partial^a \partial_a A_b = -4\pi j_b,$$

using the Lorentz gauge condition: $\partial^a A_a = 0$.

10.6.2 General Relativity

Space-time is a manifold M on which is defined a Lorentz metric g_{ab}. The laws of physics in general relativity are governed by two basic principles: (i) the principle of general covariance, which states that the metric g_{ab} and quantities derivable from it are the only spacetime quantities that can appear in the equations of physics; and (ii) the requirement that equations must reduce to the equations satisfied in special relativity in the case where the metric is flat, $g_{ab} \to \eta_{ab}$. These two principles suggest the following simple rule: In the equations holding in special relativity, replace everywhere the metric η_{ab} of special relativity by g_{ab} and correspondingly replace the ordinary partial derivative operator ∂_a (associated with η_{ab}) by the tensor derivative operator ∇_a (associated with g_{ab}). This is called the 'minimal substitution' rule: $\eta_{ab} \to g_{ab}$, $\partial_a \to \nabla_a$.

Again, a free particle satisfies the geodesic equation of motion: $u^a \nabla_a u^b = 0$. If the acceleration of the particle, $a^b = u^a \nabla_a u^b$, is non-vanishing, we say that a force: $f^b = m a^b$ acts on the particle, where m is its (rest) mass. For example, if the particle has (rest) mass m and charge q and is placed in an electromagnetic field F_{ab}, it satisfies the Lorentz force equation [Wal84]:

$$u^a \nabla_a u^b = \frac{q}{m} F_c^b u^c, \qquad \text{where} \qquad F_c^b = g^{bd} F_{dc}.$$

The stress tensor of a perfect fluid is given by:

$$T_{ab} = \rho u_a u_b + P(g_{ab} + u_a u_b),$$

and it satisfies the (zero divergence) equations of motion:

$$\nabla^a T_{ab} = 0, \qquad \text{which yield:}$$
$$u^a \nabla_a \rho + (\rho + P) \nabla^a u_a = 0,$$
$$(P + \rho) u^a \nabla_a u_b + (g_{ab} + u_a u_b) \nabla^a P = 0.$$

Maxwell's equations in curved spacetime become:

$$\nabla^a F_{ab} = -4\pi j_b, \qquad \nabla_{[a} F_{bc]} = 0,$$

while the electromagnetic stress-energy tensor becomes:

$$T_{ab} = \frac{1}{4\pi} \left[F_{ac} F_b^c - \frac{1}{4} g_{ab} F_{de} F^{de} \right].$$

However, Maxwell's equations for the vector potential A_a in the Lorentz gauge contains an explicit Ricci curvature term R_b^a resulting from the commutation of derivatives:

$$\nabla^a \nabla_a A_b - R_b^d A_d = -4\pi j_b \Longrightarrow \nabla^a j_a = 0.$$

Taking the trace of the Einstein equation:

$$G_{ab} \equiv R_{ab} - \frac{1}{2} R g_{ab} = 8\pi T_{ab} \quad \text{gives:} \tag{10.34}$$

$$R = -8\pi T \Longrightarrow R_{ab} = 8\pi \left(T_{ab} - \frac{1}{2} g_{ab} T \right).$$

The entire content of general relativity may be summarized as follows: Spacetime is a manifold M on which there is defined a Lorentz metric g_{ab}; the curvature of g_{ab} is related to the matter distribution in spacetime by Einstein's equation (10.34).

Given the massless Klein-Gordon scalar field ϕ, the Einstein-Klein-Gordon system is defined by:

$$\nabla^a \nabla_a \phi = 0, \quad T_{ab} = \nabla_a \phi \nabla_b \phi, \quad T = \nabla_a \phi \nabla^a \phi,$$

$$G_{ab} = 8\pi \left(T_{ab} - \frac{1}{2} g_{ab} T \right).$$

10.6.3 Homogeneous Cosmological Models

In a spatially homogeneous spacetime (M, g_{ab}), there exists a family of spacelike hypersurfaces Σ_t such that for any two points $p, q \in \Sigma_t$ there exists an element $g : M \to M$ of the *Lie group of isometries* G such that $g(p) = q$. (G is said to *act transitively* on each Σ_t) We will restrict attention to the case where for all Σ_t and for all $p, q \in \Sigma_t$ there is a unique element $g \in G$ such that $g(p) = q$, in which case G is said to *act simply transitively* on each Σ_t. This implies $\dim(G) = \dim(\Sigma_t) = 3$ [Wal84].

The advantage of considering simply transitive action is that if we (arbitrarily) choose a point $p \in \Sigma_t$ then we can put the elements of G into correspondence with the points of Σ_t by the association $g \to g(p)$. (A simply transitive action is needed to ensure that this correspondence is one-to-one.) Under this identification of G and Σ_t the *action of the isometry g on Σ_t* corresponds to left multiplication by g on G. Thus, the tensor fields on Σ_t which are preserved under the isometries (in particular, the spatial metric h_{ab} on Σ_t) correspond precisely to the left invariant tensor fields on G. In particular, this means that the vector-fields on Σ_t which are preserved under the isometries satisfy the commutation relations (10.4), and similarly, the invariant dual vectors satisfy Eq. (10.8). Furthermore, the Killing vector-fields of Σ_t, which are infinitesimal generators of the isometries on Σ_t, correspond to the right invariant vector-fields of G. Thus, the Killing vector-fields of Σ_t satisfy the commutation relations (10.9).

For a spatially homogeneous spacetime on which the spatial isometry group G acts in a simply transitive manner, the manifold structure is $M = \mathbb{R} \times G$. By defining the function t and the left invariant covector-fields $(\sigma^k)_a$, $(k = 1, 2, 3)$ on M, which satisfy:

$$\nabla_{[a}(\sigma^k)_{b]} = -\frac{1}{2} c^c_{ab}(\sigma^k)_c,$$

we can express the spacetime metric g_{ab} in the form:

$$g_{ab} = -\nabla_a t \nabla_b t + h_{km}(t)(\sigma^k)_a(\sigma^m)_b, \qquad (k, m = 1, 2, 3). \tag{10.35}$$

Thus, to construct spatially homogeneous cosmological models, we simply choose a 3D Lie group G, choose a basis $(\sigma^k)_a$, $(k = 1, 2, 3)$ of left invariant covector-fields on G, and choose a time-dependent left invariant metric $h_{km}(t)$ on G. We then define the spacetime metric g_{ab} on $M = \mathbb{R} \times G$ by Eq. (10.35). All homogeneous cosmologies with simply transitive action can be constructed in this manner [Wal84].

10.6.4 Canonical Quantization

Recall that in classical Hamiltonian mechanics, the state of an nDOF system is (at any time-instant t) described by a representative point in its phase space M with local canonical coordinates $(q^\mu, p_\mu) \in M$, $(\mu = 1, ..., n)$. Technically, given the system's smooth nD configuration manifold Q, the corresponding $2n$D symplectic manifold M, called the *phase space*, is defined by a non-degenerate, closed symplectic two-form $\omega = \omega_{ab}$, given at a point $m \in M$ as a local tensor-field $\omega : T_m M \times T_m M \to \mathbb{R}$ by [Wal94]:

$$\omega_{ab} = dq^\mu \wedge dp_\mu = 2\nabla_{[a} p_{|\mu|} \nabla_{b]} q^\mu. \tag{10.36}$$

Also recall that the state of any quantum-mechanical system is (at any time-instant t) described by a ket-vector in an infinite-dimensional Hilbert space $\mathcal{H}$, while the corresponding quantum *observable* is a Hermitian (self-adjoint) operator in $\mathcal{H}$.

In the classical nDOF system, defined by specifying the Hamiltonian function $H = H(q, p)$, the time rate of change of any observable f (a real smooth function defined on M) is given in terms of the Poisson bracket $\{,\}$, as:

$$\partial_t f = \{f, H\}, \qquad \text{with} \qquad \{f, g\} = \omega^{ab} \nabla_a f \nabla_b g, \qquad [\omega^{ab} = (\omega_{ab})^{-1}]. \tag{10.37}$$

In the corresponding quantum-mechanical system, defined by specifying the Hamiltonian operator $\hat{H}$, the time rate of change of an observable $\hat{f}$ is (in the Heisenberg picture) given in terms of the corresponding quantum commutator $[,]$, as:

$$\partial_t \hat{f} = -\mathrm{i}[\hat{f}, \hat{H}], \qquad (\mathrm{i} = \sqrt{-1}), \tag{10.38}$$

following Dirac's canonical quantization rule: 'Poisson bracket goes to commutator times imaginary unit',

$$[\hat{f}, \hat{g}] = i\widehat{\{f, g\}}. \tag{10.39}$$

Although it is well-known that Dirac's quantization (10.39) has some operator domain problems (technically, the relation (10.39) is not functorial), it is valid when implemented on a restricted class of linear observables $\hat{f}, \hat{g}, ... \in \mathcal{H}$, which arises when the classical configuration space Q has the vector-space structure, in which case the symplectic two-form ω_{ab} is not a local tensor-field ω : $T_m M \times T_m M \to \mathbb{R}$, but rather a global bilinear map $\omega : M \times M \to \mathbb{R}$ (see [Wal94] for technical details).

10.6.5 Hodge Decomposition and Gauge Path Integral

Feynman Path Integral

The 'driving engine' of quantum field theory is the Feynman path integral. Very briefly, there are three basic forms of the path integral (see, e.g., [II08b, II09]):

1. *Sum–over–histories*, developed in Feynman's version of quantum mechanics (QM)[20] [Fey65];

2. *Sum–over–fields*, started in Feynman's version of quantum electrodynamics (QED) [Fey49] and later improved by Fadeev–Popov [FP67];

3. *Sum–over–geometries/topologies* in quantum gravity (QG), initiated by S. Hawking and properly developed in the form of causal dynamical triangulations (see [ALW08]; for a 'softer' review, see [Lol08]).

In all three versions, Feynman's *action–amplitude formalism* includes two components:

1. A real–valued, classical, *Hamilton's action functional*,

$$S[\Phi] := \int_{t_{ini}}^{t_{fin}} L[\Phi] \, dt,$$

with the Lagrangian energy function L defined over the Lagrangian density $\mathcal{L}$,

$$L[\Phi] = \int d^n x \, \mathcal{L}(\Phi, \partial_\mu \Phi), \qquad (\partial_\mu \equiv \partial/\partial x^\mu),$$

---

[20] Feynman's *amplitude* is a space-time equivalent to the Schrödinger *wave-function* ψ, which describes how the quantum state of a (non-relativistic) physical system changes in space and time, i.e.:

$$\langle \text{Out}_{t_{fin}} | \text{In}_{t_{ini}} \rangle = \psi(\mathbf{x}, t), \qquad (\text{for } \mathbf{x} \in [\text{In}, \text{Out}], \ t \in [t_{ini}, t_{fin}]).$$

while Φ is a common symbol denoting all three things to be summed upon (histories, fields and geometries). The action functional $S[\Phi]$ obeys the *Hamilton's least action principle*, $\delta S[\Phi] = 0$, and gives, using standard variational methods,[21] the Euler–Lagrangian equations, which define the shortest path, the extreme field, and the geometry of minimal curvature (and without holes).

---

[21] In Lagrangian field theory, the fundamental quantity is the action

$$S[\Phi] = \int_{t_{in}}^{t_{out}} L\, dt = \int_{\mathbb{R}^4} d^n x\, \mathcal{L}(\Phi, \partial_\mu \Phi),$$

so that the least action principle, $\delta S[\Phi] = 0$, gives

$$0 = \int_{\mathbb{R}^4} d^n x \left\{ \frac{\partial \mathcal{L}}{\partial \Phi} \delta \Phi + \frac{\partial \mathcal{L}}{\partial(\partial_\mu \Phi)} \delta(\partial_\mu \Phi) \right\}$$
$$= \int_{\mathbb{R}^4} d^n x \left\{ \frac{\partial \mathcal{L}}{\partial \Phi} \delta \Phi - \partial_\mu \left(\frac{\partial \mathcal{L}}{\partial(\partial_\mu \Phi)} \right) \delta \Phi + \partial_\mu \left(\frac{\partial \mathcal{L}}{\partial(\partial_\mu \Phi)} \delta \Phi \right) \right\}.$$

The last term can be turned into a surface integral over the boundary of the $\mathbb{R}^4$ (4D space-time region of integration). Since the initial and final field configurations are assumed given, $\delta \Phi = 0$ at the temporal beginning t_{in} and end t_{out} of this region, which implies that the surface term is zero. Factoring out the $\delta \Phi$ from the first two terms, and since the integral must vanish for arbitrary $\delta \Phi$, we arrive at the Euler-lagrange equation of motion for a field,

$$\partial_\mu \left(\frac{\partial \mathcal{L}}{\partial(\partial_\mu \Phi)} \right) - \frac{\partial \mathcal{L}}{\partial \Phi} = 0.$$

If the Lagrangian (density) $\mathcal{L}$ contains more fields, there is one such equation for each. The momentum density $\pi(x)$ of a field, conjugate to $\Phi(x)$ is defined as: $\pi(x) = \frac{\partial \mathcal{L}}{\partial_\mu \Phi(x)}$.

For example, the standard electromagnetic action

$$S = -\frac{1}{4} \int_{\mathbb{R}^4} d^4 x\, F_{\mu\nu} F^{\mu\nu}, \qquad \text{where} \qquad F_{\mu\nu} = \partial_\mu A_\nu - \partial_\nu A_\mu,$$

gives the sourceless Maxwell's equations:

$$\partial_\mu F^{\mu\nu} = 0, \qquad \epsilon^{\mu\nu\sigma\eta} \partial_\nu F_{\sigma\eta} = 0,$$

where the field strength tensor $F_{\mu\nu}$ and the Maxwell equations are invariant under the *gauge transformations*,

$$A_\mu \longrightarrow A_\mu + \partial_\mu \epsilon.$$

The equations of motion of charged particles are given by the Lorentz–force equation,

$$m \frac{du^\mu}{d\tau} = e F^{\mu\nu} u_\nu,$$

where e is the charge of the particle and $u^\mu(\tau)$ its four-velocity as a function of the proper time.

2. A complex–valued, quantum *transition amplitude*,[22]

---

[22] The transition amplitude is closely related to *partition function* Z, which is a quantity that encodes the statistical properties of a system in thermodynamic equilibrium. It is a function of temperature and other parameters, such as the volume enclosing a gas. Other thermodynamic variables of the system, such as the total energy, free energy, entropy, and pressure, can be expressed in terms of the partition function or its derivatives. In particular, the partition function of a *canonical ensemble* is defined as a sum $Z(\beta) = \sum_j e^{-\beta E_j}$, where $\beta = 1/(k_B T)$ is the 'inverse temperature', where T is an ordinary temperature and k_B is the Boltzmann's constant. However, as the position x^i and momentum p_i variables of an ith particle in a system can vary continuously, the set of microstates is actually uncountable. In this case, some form of *coarse–graining* procedure must be carried out, which essentially amounts to treating two mechanical states as the same microstate if the differences in their position and momentum variables are 'small enough'. The partition function then takes the form of an integral. For instance, the partition function of a gas consisting of N molecules is proportional to the $6N$–dimensional phase–space integral,

$$Z(\beta) \sim \int_{\mathbb{R}^{6N}} d^3 p_i \, d^3 x^i \exp[-\beta H(p_i, x^i)],$$

where $H = H(p_i, x^i)$, $(i = 1, ..., N)$ is the classical Hamiltonian (total energy) function.

Given a set of random variables X_i taking on values x^i, and purely potential Hamiltonian function $H(x^i)$, the partition function is defined as

$$Z(\beta) = \sum_{x^i} \exp\left[-\beta H(x^i)\right].$$

The function H is understood to be a real-valued function on the space of states $\{X_1, X_2, ...\}$ while β is a real-valued free parameter (conventionally, the inverse temperature). The sum over the x^i is understood to be a sum over all possible values that the random variable X_i may take. Thus, the sum is to be replaced by an integral when the X_i are continuous, rather than discrete. Thus, one writes

$$Z(\beta) = \int dx^i \exp\left[-\beta H(x^i)\right],$$

for the case of continuously-varying random variables X_i.

Now, the number of variables X_i need not be countable, in which case the set of coordinates $\{x^i\}$ becomes a field $\phi = \phi(x)$, so the sum is to be replaced by the *Euclidean path integral* (that is a Wick–rotated Feynman transition amplitude (10.43) in imaginary time), as

$$Z(\phi) = \int \mathcal{D}[\phi] \exp\left[-H(\phi)\right].$$

More generally, in quantum field theory, instead of the field Hamiltonian $H(\phi)$ we have the action $S(\phi)$ of the theory. Both Euclidean path integral,

$$Z(\phi) = \int \mathcal{D}[\phi] \exp\left[-S(\phi)\right], \qquad \text{real path integral in imaginary time,} \quad (10.40)$$

$$\langle \text{Out}_{t_{fin}} | \text{In}_{t_{ini}} \rangle := \int_\Omega \mathcal{D}[\Phi]\, e^{iS[\Phi]}, \qquad (10.42)$$

where $\mathcal{D}[\Phi]$ is 'an appropriate' Lebesgue–type measure,

$$\mathcal{D}[\Phi] = \lim_{N\to\infty} \prod_{s=1}^{N} \Phi_s^i, \qquad (i=1,...,n),$$

so that we can 'safely integrate over a continuous spectrum and sum over a discrete spectrum of our problem domain Ω', of which the absolute square is the real–valued probability density function,

$$P := |\langle \text{Out}_{t_{fin}} | \text{In}_{t_{ini}} \rangle|^2.$$

This procedure can be redefined in a mathematically cleaner way if we Wick–rotate the time variable t to imaginary values, $t \mapsto \tau = t$, thereby making all integrals real:

$$\int \mathcal{D}[\Phi]\, e^{iS[\Phi]} \xrightarrow{\ Wick\ } \int \mathcal{D}[\Phi]\, e^{-S[\Phi]}. \qquad (10.43)$$

For example, in non-relativistic quantum mechanics (see Appendix), the propagation amplitude from x_a to x_b is given by the *configuration path integral*[23]

---

and Lorentzian one,

$$Z(\phi) = \int \mathcal{D}[\phi] \exp\left[iS(\phi)\right], \qquad \text{complex path integral in real time,} \qquad (10.41)$$

are usually called 'partition functions'. While the Lorentzian path integral (10.41) represents a quantum-field theory-generalization of the Schrödinger equation, the Euclidean path integral (10.40) represents a statistical-field-theory generalization of the Fokker–Planck equation.

[23] On the other hand, the *phase–space path integral* (without peculiar constants in the functional measure) reads

$$U(q_a, q_b; T) = \left(\prod_i \int \mathcal{D}[q(t)] \mathcal{D}[p(t)] \right) \exp\left[i \int_0^T \left(p_i \dot{q}^i - H(q,p) \right) dt \right],$$

where the functions $q(t)$ (space coordinates) are constrained at the endpoints, but the functions $p(t)$ (canonically–conjugated momenta) are not. The functional measure is just the product of the standard integral over phase space at each point in time

$$\mathcal{D}[q(t)] \mathcal{D}[p(t)] = \prod_i \frac{1}{2\pi} \int dq^i dp_i.$$

Applied to a non-relativistic real scalar field $\phi(x,t)$, this path integral becomes

$$\left\langle \phi_b(x,t) | e^{-iHT} | \phi_a(x,t) \right\rangle = \int \mathcal{D}[\phi] \exp\left[i \int_0^T \mathcal{L}(\phi)\, d^4x \right], \quad \text{with } \mathcal{L}(\phi) = \frac{1}{2}(\partial_\mu \phi)^2 - V(\phi).$$

$$U(x_a, x_b; T) = \langle x_b | x_a \rangle = \langle x_b | e^{-iHT} | x_a \rangle = \int \mathcal{D}[x(t)] \, e^{iS[x(t)]},$$

which satisfies the Schrödinger equation (in natural units)

$$i\frac{\partial}{\partial T} U(x_a, x_b; T) = \hat{H} U(x_a, x_b; T), \quad \text{where} \quad \hat{H} = -\frac{1}{2}\frac{\partial^2}{\partial x_b^2} + V(x_b).$$

Functional measure on the space of differential forms

The Hodge inner product (10.27) leads to a natural (metric–dependent) functional measure $\mathcal{D}\mu[\omega]$ on $\Omega^p(M)$, which normalizes the *Gaussian functional integral*

$$\int \mathcal{D}\mu[\omega] \, e^{i\langle \omega | \omega \rangle} = 1. \tag{10.44}$$

One can use the invariance of (10.44) to determine how the functional measure transforms under the Hodge decomposition. Using HDT and its orthogonality with respect to the inner product (10.27), it was shown in [GK94] that

$$\langle \omega, \omega \rangle = \langle \gamma, \gamma \rangle + \langle d\alpha, d\alpha \rangle + \langle \delta\beta, \delta\beta \rangle = \langle \gamma, \gamma \rangle + \langle \alpha, \delta d\alpha \rangle + \langle \beta, d\delta\beta \rangle, \tag{10.45}$$

where the following differential/conferential identities were used [CD82]

$$\langle d\alpha, d\alpha \rangle = \langle \alpha, \delta d\alpha \rangle \quad \text{and} \quad \langle \delta\beta, \delta\beta \rangle = \langle \beta, d\delta\beta \rangle.$$

Since, for any linear operator O, one has

$$\int \mathcal{D}\mu[\omega] \exp i\langle \omega | O\omega \rangle = \det^{-1/2}(O),$$

(10.44) and (10.45) imply that

$$\mathcal{D}\mu[\omega] = \mathcal{D}\mu[\gamma]\mathcal{D}\mu[\alpha]\mathcal{D}\mu[\beta] \det^{1/2}(\delta d)\det^{1/2}(d\delta).$$

Abelian Chern–Simons theory

Recall that the classical action for an Abelian Chern–Simons theory,

$$S = \int_M A \wedge dA,$$

is invariant (up to a total divergence) under the gauge transformation:

$$A \longmapsto A + d\varphi. \tag{10.46}$$

We wish to compute the *partition function* for the theory

$$Z := \int \frac{1}{V_G} \mathcal{D}\mu[A] \, e^{iS[A]},$$

where V_G denotes the volume of the group of gauge transformations in (10.46), which must be factored out of the partition function in order to guarantee that the integration is performed only over physically distinct gauge fields. We can handle this by using the Hodge decomposition to parametrize the potential A in terms of its gauge invariant, and gauge dependent parts, so that the volume of the group of gauge transformations can be explicitly factored out, leaving a functional integral over·gauge invariant modes only [GK94].

We now transform the integration variables:

$$A \longmapsto \alpha, \beta, \gamma,$$

where α, β, γ parameterize respectively the exact, coexact, and harmonic parts of the connection A. Using the Jacobian (10.45) as well as the following identity on 0–forms $\Delta = \delta d$, we get [GK94]

$$Z = \int \frac{1}{V_G} \mathcal{D}\mu[\alpha] \mathcal{D}\mu[\beta] \mathcal{D}\mu[\gamma] \det^{1/2}(\Delta) \det^{1/2}(d\delta) \, e^{iS},$$

from which it follows that

$$V_G = \int \mathcal{D}\mu[\alpha], \tag{10.47}$$

while the classical action functional becomes, after integrating by parts, using the harmonic properties of γ and the nilpotency of the exterior derivative operators, and dropping surface terms:

$$S = -\langle \beta, \star \delta d \delta \beta \rangle \ .$$

Note that S depends only the coexact (transverse) part of A. Using (10.47) and integrating over β yields:

$$Z = \int \mathcal{D}\mu[\gamma] \det^{-1/2}(\star \delta d \delta) \det^{1/2}(\Delta) \det^{1/2}(d\delta) \ .$$

Also, it was proven in [GK94] that

$$\det(\star \delta d \delta) = \det^{1/2}((d\delta d)(\delta d \delta)) = \det^{\frac{3}{2}}(d\delta).$$

As a consequence of Hodge duality we have the identity

$$\det(\delta d) = \det(d\delta),$$

from which it follows that

$$Z = \int \mathcal{D}\mu[\gamma] \det^{-3/4}\left(\Delta_{(1)}^T\right) \det^{1/2}(\Delta) \det^{1/2}\left(\Delta_{(1)}^T\right) \ .$$

The operator $\Delta_{(1)}^T$ is the transverse part of the Hodge Laplacian acting on 1−forms:
$$\Delta_{(1)}^T := (\delta d)_{(1)}.$$
Applying identity for the Hodge Laplacian $\Delta_{(p)}$ [GK94]

$$\det\left(\Delta_{(p)}\right) = \det\left((\delta d)_{(p)}\right)\det\left((\delta d)_{(p-1)}\right),$$

we get

$$\det\left(\Delta_{(1)}^T\right) = \det\left(\Delta_{(1)}\right)/\det\left(\Delta\right)$$

and hence

$$Z = \int \mathcal{D}\mu[\gamma]\det^{-1/4}\left(\Delta_{(1)}\right)\det^{3/4}\left(\Delta\right).$$

The space of harmonic forms γ (of any order) is a finite set. Hence, the integration over harmonic forms (10.47) is a simple sum.

10.7 Computational Tensor Framework in *Mathematica*®

In this section we develop a unique computational framework for socio-econo-political sciences, based on *Mathematica* suite of tensor packages *xAct*.

10.7.1 Computing with Abstract and Riemannian Tensors

In this section we give a brief review of both abstract and Riemannian geometric calculations with *xAct'xTensor.m* performed on a hypothetical dynamical system with a 9-dimensional configuration manifold M^9. Note that the computational basis of all *xAct* packages (written for both *Mathematica* and *Maple*) is the fast *canonicalization*, performed using an external executable written in C-code. The inputs to *Mathematica* are denoted by 'in :', while the outputs are presented as centered displayed expressions.

Load the package:
in : <<xAct'xTensor'

Define the manifold M^9, together with the set of abstract index slots $\{a, b, c, d, e, f\}$:
in : DefManifold[M9,9,{a,b,c,d,e,f}]

Abstract tensor calculations

Define two tensors: a vector $\mathbf{v} = v^a$ and a 2-form $\mathbf{F} = F_{ab}$, using negative bracketed indices to denote subscripts and positive ones to denote super-scripts:

in : DefTensor[v[a],M9];

in : DefTensor[F[-a,-b],M9,Antisymmetric[{-a,-b}]]]

We start the computations by calculating the ordinary (tensor) product of $\mathbf{v}$ and $\mathbf{F}$, defined by their simple juxtaposition:

in : F[-a,-b]v[b]

$$F_{ab}v^b$$

Next, to make a scalar quadratic form out of this product, we again multiply the current memory content (%) by the vector $\mathbf{v}$:

in : % v[a]

$$F_{ab}v^av^b$$

To check out if this expression is really a scalar (i.e., 0-tensor), we need to perform the Simplification, which includes: fast canonicalization (using an external executable written in C-code), followed by *Mathematica*'s ordinary Simplify command:

in : %//Simplification

$$0$$

Our abstract tensor ∇-derivative is defined as 'Cd[-a]' (without any metric, by default with curvature, but without torsion – which can be changed using the options) and denoted by '∇_a':

in : DefCovD[Cd[-a]]

The Leibnitz rule is automatic in ∇_a, as can be seen from:

in : Cd[-a][F[-b,-c]v[c]]

$$v^c\nabla_aF_{bc} + F_{bc}\nabla_av^c$$

which simplifies into:

in : % v[b]//Simplification

$$F_{bc}v^b\nabla_av^c$$

As soon as ∇-derivative is defined, the abstract Riemann curvature tensor $R[\nabla]_{abc}{}^d$ is also defined (together with its Christoffel symbol $\Gamma[\nabla]^a{}_{bc}$):

in : RiemannCd[-a,-b,-c,d]+RiemannCd[-b,-a,-c,d]

$$R[\nabla]_{abc}{}^d + R[\nabla]_{bac}{}^d$$

which simplifies into:

in : %//Simplification

$$0$$

Here is a sample calculation with Riemann in terms of Christoffel symbols:

in : RiemannCd[-a,-b,-c,d]+RiemannCd[-b,-c,-a,d]+
RiemannCd[-c,-a,-b,d]//RiemannToChristoffel

$$-\Gamma[\nabla]^{d}{}_{ce}\Gamma[\nabla]^{e}{}_{ab} + \Gamma[\nabla]^{d}{}_{be}\Gamma[\nabla]^{e}{}_{ac} + \Gamma[\nabla]^{d}{}_{ce}\Gamma[\nabla]^{e}{}_{ba} - \Gamma[\nabla]^{d}{}_{ae}\Gamma[\nabla]^{e}{}_{bc}$$

$$-\Gamma[\nabla]^{d}{}_{be}\Gamma[\nabla]^{e}{}_{ca} + \Gamma[\nabla]^{d}{}_{ae}\Gamma[\nabla]^{e}{}_{cb} - \partial_{a}\Gamma[\nabla]^{d}{}_{bc} + \partial_{a}\Gamma[\nabla]^{d}{}_{cb}$$

$$+ \partial_{b}\Gamma[\nabla]^{d}{}_{ac} - \partial_{b}\Gamma[\nabla]^{d}{}_{ca} - \partial_{c}\Gamma[\nabla]^{d}{}_{ab} + \partial_{c}\Gamma[\nabla]^{d}{}_{ba}$$

Here is the check of the second Bianchi identity:

in : Antisymmetrize[Cd[-e][RiemannCd[-c,-d,-b,a]],{-c,-d,-e}]

$$\tfrac{1}{6}(\nabla_{c}R[\nabla]_{deb}{}^{a} - \nabla_{c}R[\nabla]_{edb}{}^{a} - \nabla_{d}R[\nabla]_{ceb}{}^{a} + \nabla_{d}R[\nabla]_{ecb}{}^{a}$$

$$+\nabla_{e}R[\nabla]_{cdb}{}^{a} - \nabla_{e}R[\nabla]_{dcb}{}^{a})$$

This simplifies into:

in : %//Simplification

$$\nabla_{c}R[\nabla]_{deb}{}^{a} - \nabla_{d}R[\nabla]_{ceb}{}^{a} + \nabla_{e}R[\nabla]_{cdb}{}^{a}$$

We can expand it in terms of Christoffel symbols as:

in : %//CovDToChristoffel

$$\Gamma[\nabla]^{a}{}_{ef}R[\nabla]_{cdb}{}^{f} - \Gamma[\nabla]^{f}{}_{eb}R[\nabla]_{cdf}{}^{a} - \Gamma[\nabla]^{a}{}_{df}R[\nabla]_{ceb}{}^{f} + \Gamma[\nabla]^{f}{}_{db}R[\nabla]_{cef}{}^{a} +$$

$$\Gamma[\nabla]^{f}{}_{de}R[\nabla]_{cfb}{}^{a} - \Gamma[\nabla]^{f}{}_{ed}R[\nabla]_{cfb}{}^{a} + \Gamma[\nabla]^{a}{}_{cf}R[\nabla]_{deb}{}^{f} - \Gamma[\nabla]^{f}{}_{cb}R[\nabla]_{def}{}^{a} -$$

$$\Gamma[\nabla]^{f}{}_{ce}R[\nabla]_{dfb}{}^{a} - \Gamma[\nabla]^{f}{}_{ec}R[\nabla]_{fdb}{}^{a} - \Gamma[\nabla]^{f}{}_{cd}R[\nabla]_{feb}{}^{a} + \Gamma[\nabla]^{f}{}_{dc}R[\nabla]_{feb}{}^{a} +$$

$$\partial_{c}R[\nabla]_{deb}{}^{a} - \partial_{d}R[\nabla]_{ceb}{}^{a} + \partial_{e}R[\nabla]_{cdb}{}^{a}$$

Upon simplification, this gives:

in : %//Simplification

$$\Gamma[\nabla]^{a}{}_{ef}R[\nabla]_{cdb}{}^{f} - \Gamma[\nabla]^{f}{}_{be}R[\nabla]_{cdf}{}^{a} - \Gamma[\nabla]^{a}{}_{df}R[\nabla]_{ceb}{}^{f} + \Gamma[\nabla]^{f}{}_{bd}R[\nabla]_{cef}{}^{a} +$$

$$\Gamma[\nabla]^{a}{}_{cf}R[\nabla]_{deb}{}^{f} - \Gamma[\nabla]^{f}{}_{bc}R[\nabla]_{def}{}^{a} + \partial_{c}R[\nabla]_{deb}{}^{a} - \partial_{d}R[\nabla]_{ceb}{}^{a} + \partial_{e}R[\nabla]_{cdb}{}^{a}$$

Commutation of ∇-derivatives is shown by their composition:

in : Cd[-a]@Cd[-b]@v[c]

$$\nabla_{a}\nabla_{b}v^{c}$$

followed by forcing their commutation:

in : CommuteCovDs[%, Cd, -b, -a]

$$R[\nabla]_{bad}{}^{c}v^{d} + \nabla_{b}\nabla_{a}v^{c}$$

Lie derivative calculations

Here we give some basic tensor calculations with Lie derivative.

We start by defining two new tensors on our manifold M^{9}, the vector w^{a} and the (1,1)-tensor S^{b}_{a}:

in : DefTensor[w[a], M9]

in : DefTensor[S[-a, b], M9]

Lie derivative of S_a^b:
in : LieD[v[a]][S[-b, c]]

$$\mathcal{L}_v S_b{}^c$$

A sample Lie-derivative calculation:
in : LieD[3 v[a]][F[-a, -b] v[b]]

$$3v^b \mathcal{L}_v F_{ab}$$

Expressions with Lie-derivatives can be expanded:
either in terms of partial derivatives:
in : LieDToCovD[LieD[w[a]][S[-b, c]], PD]

$$w^a \partial_a S_b{}^c - S_b{}^a \partial_a w^c + S_a{}^c \partial_b w^a$$

or, in terms of ∇-derivatives indirectly:
in : LieDToCovD[LieD[w[a]][S[-b, c]], Cd]

$$w^a \nabla_a S_b{}^c - S_b{}^a \nabla_a w^c + S_a{}^c \nabla_b w^a$$

or, directly:
in : LieD[w[a], Cd][S[-b, c]]

$$w^a \nabla_a S_b{}^c - S_b{}^a \nabla {}_a w^c + S_a{}^c \nabla_b w^a$$

The Leibnitz rule is automatic in LieD, as can be seen from:
in : LieD[w[a]][S[a] T[-a]]

$$T_a \mathcal{L}_w S^a + S^a \mathcal{L}_w T_a$$

Using abstract indices, commutator (Lie-bracket) can be expressed as:
in : Bracket[v[b], w[b]][a]

$$[v^b, w^b]^a$$

Here is a sample commutator calculation:
in : Bracket[v[a], F[a, -b] v[b]][a]

$$[v^a, F^a{}_b v^b]^a$$

and a more complicated one:
in : Bracket[v[b] + w[b], 3 w[b] + r[] v[b]][a]

$$3[v^b, w^b]^a - r[v^b, w^b]^a + +v^a \partial_v r + v^a \partial_w r$$

(pseudo-)Riemannian tensor calculations

So far, all calculations have been abstract, independent of any metric and
not related to any kind of Riemannian geometry. Now we make our manifold

M^9 pseudo-Riemannian (suitable for Lorentzian, pseudo-Riemannian geometry, as used by the general relativity theory), by introducing the metric tensor $\mathbf{g} = g_{ab}$ on it with negative determinant. This automatically defines its covariant derivative (or, Levi-Civita connection, torsion-free by default, defined by 'CD' and displayed by 'D' – to distinguish it from the abstract ∇-derivative), together with the covariant Riemann tensor, as well as the three derived tensors of Riemannian geometry: Ricci, Einstein, and conformal Weyl tensor.

We define the metric as:

in : DefMetric[-1, g[-a, -b], CD, SymbolOfCovD → {"—", "D"}]

Then various tensors from Riemannian geometry are called as follows:

in : RiemannCD[-a, -b, -c, -d]

$$R[D]_{abcd}$$

in : RicciCD[-a, -b]

$$R[D]_{ab}$$

in : RicciScalarCD[]

$$R[D]$$

in : EinsteinCD[-a, -b]

$$G[D]_{ab}$$

in : WeylCD[-a, -b, -c, -d]

$$W[D]_{abcd}$$

We can show that these tensors have standard properties. Covariant derivative of the metric g_{ab} is zero:

in : CD[-a][g[-b, -c]]

$$0$$

Covariant derivative of the Einstein tensor $G[D]_{ab}$ is also zero:

in : CD[-a][EinsteinCD[a, b]]

$$0$$

Trace of the metric equals the dimension of the manifold:

in : g[a, -a]

$$9$$

Inner product (contraction) of the metric g_{ab} with the inverse metric g^{ab} gives the Kronecker delta tensor $\delta_b{}^a$:

in : g[a, b] g[-b, -c]

$$\delta_c{}^a$$

As we have properly introduced the covariant Riemann curvature tensor $R[D]_{abcd}$, we can now check the antisymmetry of its second pair of indices; in other words, the following expression should be zero:

in : RiemannCD[-a, -b, -c, -d] + RiemannCD[-a, -b, -d, -c]

$$R[D]_{abcd} + R[D]_{abdc}$$

To show that this expression is zero, we firstly expand it in derivatives of Christoffel symbols and then canonicalize:

in : % // RiemannToChristoffel

$$g_{de}(\Gamma[D]^e{}_{bf}\Gamma[D]^f{}_{ac} - \Gamma[D]^e{}_{af}\Gamma[D]^f{}_{bc} - \partial_a\Gamma[D]^e{}_{bc} + \partial_b\Gamma[D]^e{}_{ac}) +$$
$$g_{ce}(\Gamma[D]^e{}_{bf}\Gamma[D]^f{}_{ad} + -\Gamma[D]^e{}_{af}\Gamma[D]^f{}_{bd} - \partial_a\Gamma[D]^e{}_{bd} + \partial_b\Gamma[D]^e{}_{ad})$$

This expression is zero only for the metric connection (not for an arbitrary one), so we need to expand it further into partial derivatives (gradients) of the metric as:

in : % // ChristoffelToGradMetric // Expand

$$-\tfrac{1}{2}\partial_a\partial_b g_{cd} - \tfrac{1}{2}\,\partial_a\partial_b g_{dc} + \tfrac{1}{2}g^{ef}\partial_a g_{df}\partial_b g_{ce} - \tfrac{1}{4}g^{fe}\partial_a g_{fd}\partial_b g_{ce} -$$
$$\tfrac{1}{2}g^{ef}\partial_a g_{de}\partial_b g_{cf} + \tfrac{1}{2}g^{ef}\partial_a g_{cf}\partial_b g_{de} - \tfrac{1}{4}g^{fe}\partial_a g_{fc}\partial_b g_{de} -$$
$$\tfrac{1}{2}g^{ef}\partial_a g_{ce}\partial_b g_{df} + \tfrac{1}{4}g^{fe}\partial_a g_{de}\partial_b g_{fc} + \tfrac{1}{4}g^{fe}\partial_a g_{ce}\partial_b g_{fd} +$$
$$\tfrac{1}{2}\partial_b\partial_a g_{cd} + \tfrac{1}{2}\partial_b\partial_a g_{dc} - \tfrac{1}{2}g^{ef}\partial_b g_{df}\partial_c g_{ae} + \tfrac{1}{4}g^{fe}\partial_b g_{fd}\partial_c g_{ae} +$$
$$\tfrac{1}{4}g^{fe}\partial_b g_{de}\partial_c g_{af} + \tfrac{1}{2}g^{ef}\partial_a g_{df}\partial_c g_{be} - \tfrac{1}{4}g^{fe}\partial_a g_{fd}\partial_c g_{be} -$$
$$\tfrac{1}{4}g^{fe}\partial_a g_{de}\partial_c g_{bf} - \tfrac{1}{2}g^{ef}\partial_b g_{cf}\partial_d g_{ae} + \tfrac{1}{4}g^{fe}\partial_b g_{fc}\partial_d g_{ae} -$$
$$\tfrac{1}{4}g^{fe}\partial_c g_{bf}\partial_d g_{ae} + \tfrac{1}{4}g^{fe}\partial_b g_{ce}\partial_d g_{af} + \tfrac{1}{4}g^{fe}\partial_c g_{be}\partial_d g_{af} +$$
$$\tfrac{1}{2}g^{ef}\partial_a g_{cf}\partial_d g_{be} - \tfrac{1}{4}g^{fe}\partial_a g_{fc}\partial_d g_{be} + \tfrac{1}{4}g^{fe}\partial_c g_{af}\partial_d g_{be} -$$
$$\tfrac{1}{4}g^{fe}\partial_a g_{ce}\partial_d g_{bf} - \tfrac{1}{4}g^{fe}\partial_c g_{ae}\partial_d g_{bf} + \tfrac{1}{2}g^{ef}\partial_b g_{df}\partial_e g_{ac} -$$
$$\tfrac{1}{4}g^{fe}\partial_b g_{fd}\partial_e g_{ac} + \tfrac{1}{4}g^{fe}\partial_d g_{bf}\partial_e g_{ac} + \tfrac{1}{2}g^{ef}\partial_b g_{cf}\partial_e g_{ad} -$$
$$\tfrac{1}{4}g^{fe}\partial_b g_{fc}\partial_e g_{ad} + \tfrac{1}{4}g^{fe}\partial_c g_{bf}\partial_e g_{ad} - \tfrac{1}{2}g^{ef}\partial_a g_{df}\partial_e g_{bc} +$$
$$\tfrac{1}{4}g^{fe}\partial_a g_{fd}\partial_e g_{bc} - \tfrac{1}{4}g^{fe}\partial_d g_{af}\partial_e g_{bc} - \tfrac{1}{2}g^{ef}\partial_a g_{cf}\partial_e g_{bd} +$$
$$\tfrac{1}{4}g^{fe}\partial_a g_{fc}\partial_e g_{bd} - \tfrac{1}{4}g^{fe}\partial_c g_{af}\partial_e g_{bd} - \tfrac{1}{4}g^{fe}\partial_b g_{de}\partial_f g_{ac} -$$
$$\tfrac{1}{4}g^{fe}\partial_d g_{be}\partial_f g_{ac} + \tfrac{1}{4}g^{fe}\partial_e g_{bd}\partial_f g_{ac} - \tfrac{1}{4}g^{fe}\partial_b g_{ce}\partial_f g_{ad} -$$
$$\tfrac{1}{4}g^{fe}\partial_c g_{be}\partial_f g_{ad} + \tfrac{1}{4}g^{fe}\partial_e g_{bc}\partial_f g_{ad} + \tfrac{1}{4}g^{fe}\partial_a g_{de}\partial_f g_{bc} +$$
$$\tfrac{1}{4}g^{fe}\partial_d g_{ae}\partial_f g_{bc} - \tfrac{1}{4}g^{fe}\partial_e g_{ad}\partial_f g_{bc} + \tfrac{1}{4}g^{fe}\partial_a g_{ce}\partial_f g_{bd} +$$
$$\tfrac{1}{4}g^{fe}\partial_c g_{ae}\partial_f g_{bd} - \tfrac{1}{4}g^{fe}\partial_e g_{ac}\partial_f g_{bd}$$

which finally reduces to zero by canonicalization:

in : % // Simplification

$$0$$

Here is an expansioin of the Ricci scalar curvature in terms of partial derivatives:

in :   RicciScalarCD[]//RiemannToChristoffel//ChristoffelToGradMetric// Expand

$$(g^{ab}(\tfrac{1}{4}g^{ce}g^{df}(\partial_c g_{de} + \partial_d g_{ce} - \partial_e g_{cd})(\partial_a g_{bf} + \partial_b g_{af} - \partial_f g_{ab}) -$$

$$\tfrac{1}{4}g^{cf1}g^{df2}(\partial_a g_{df1} + \partial_d g_{af1} - \partial_{f1} g_{ad})(\partial_b g_{cf2} + \partial_c g_{bf2} - \partial_{f2} g_{cb})$$

$$+\tfrac{1}{2}(-g^{cf3}(\partial_a \partial_b g_{cf3} + \partial_a \partial_c g_{bf3} - \partial_a \partial_{f3} g_{cb}) +$$

$$g^{cf4}g^{f3f5}\partial_a g_{f4f5}(\partial_b g_{cf3} + \partial_c g_{bf3} - \partial_{f3} g_{cb}))$$

$$+\tfrac{1}{2}(g^{cf6}(\partial_c \partial_a g_{bf6} + \partial_c \partial_b g_{af6} - \partial_c \partial_{f6} g_{ab}) -$$

$$g^{cf7}g^{f6f8}\partial_c g_{f7f8}(\partial_a g_{bf6} + \partial_b g_{af6} - \partial_{f6} g_{ab}))))$$

which is simplified to:
in : % // Simplification

$$-\tfrac{1}{4}(g^{ab}g^{cd}g^{ef}\partial_c g_{ab}\partial_d g_{ef}) + (g^{ab}g^{cd}\partial_d \partial_b g_{ac}) - (g^{ab}g^{cd}\partial_d \partial_c g_{ab})$$

$$-\tfrac{1}{2}(g^{ab}g^{cd}g^{ef}\partial_d g_{bf}\partial_e g_{ac}) + \tfrac{3}{4}(g^{ab}g^{cd}g^{ef}\partial_e g_{ac}\partial_f g_{bd})$$

$$-(g^{ab}g^{cd}g^{ef}\partial_b g_{ac}\partial_f g_{de}) + (g^{ab}g^{cd}g^{ef}\partial_c g_{ab}\partial_f g_{de})$$

The proposed Computational Framework is based on $Mathematica^{®}$'s universal tensor package $xAct$.

10.7.2 Computing with Exterior Differential Forms

In this section we demonstrate computing with differential forms, using the xAct'xTensor.m package.

Exterior (wedge) product ∧

Load the package:
in : <<xAct'xTensor.m

Firstly, we define a smooth manifold M of symbolic dimension dim:
in : DefConstantSymbol[dim, PrintAs → "D"]
in : DefManifold[M, dim, {a, b, c, d, e, f, g, h}]

and introduce on M some differential forms (of degree Deg, as the third argument):
in : DefDiffForm[A0[], M, 0, PrintAs → "A^0"]
in : DefDiffForm[A1[], M, 1, PrintAs → "A^1"]
in : DefDiffForm[A2[], M, 2, PrintAs → "A^2"]
in : DefDiffForm[A3[], M, 3, PrintAs → "A^3"]

Now, we are ready to perform some basic calculations:
in : Wedge[A1[],A2[],A3[]] or A1[]∧A2[]∧A3[]

$$A^1 \wedge A^2 \wedge A^3$$

in : % ∧ A0[]

$$A^0 A^1 \wedge A^2 \wedge A^3,$$

as a 0-form corresponds to a scalar field (and thus the wedge product ∧ reduces to the standard × product). Deg can be used to check the degree of any expression with differential forms:

in : Deg@%

$$6$$

in : Deg /@ {A2[]∧A3[], A3[]∧A3[] + A2[]∧A2[]∧A2[]}

$$\{5, 6\}$$

Command ToCanonical calls for the canonicalizer, as follows:
in : A1[]∧A2[] + A2[]∧A1[]

$$A^1 \wedge A^2 + A^2 \wedge A^1$$

in : ToCanonical@%

$$2A^1 \wedge A^2$$

in : A1[]∧A2[]// ToCanonical

$$0$$

in : A1[]∧A2[]∧A1[]// ToCanonical

$$0$$

in : A2[]∧A1[]∧A2[]// ToCanonical

$$A^1 \wedge A^2 \wedge A^2,$$

where the automatic sorting of factors is shown.
in : A3[]∧A2[]∧A1[]∧A2[]// ToCanonical

$$-(A^1 \wedge A^2 \wedge A^2 \wedge A^3)$$

in : A1[]∧A3[]∧A3[]∧A2[]

$$A^1 \wedge A^3 \wedge A^3 \wedge A^2$$

in : % // ToCanonical

$$0$$

Tensor-valued forms

Tensor-valued forms can be defined with arbitrary symmetries, as follows:
in : DefDiffForm[ω1[a], M, 1, PrintAs → "$^1\omega$"]
in : DefDiffForm[ω2[a, b], M, 2, Symmetric[{1, 2}], PrintAs → "$^2\omega$"]
in : DefDiffForm[ω3[a, b], M, 3, PrintAs → "$^3\omega$"]
    Now we can canonicalize expressions involving tensor-valued forms, as:
in : ω1[b]∧ω1[a]

$$^1\omega^b \wedge {}^1\omega^a$$

in : % // ToCanonical

$$- \left({}^{1}\omega^{a} \wedge^{1} \omega^{b}\right)$$

The priority is to sort the forms (with less symmetric tensors first), not the indices, as can be seen here:

in : $\omega 3[a, b] \wedge \omega 2[c, d] \wedge \omega 1[e]$ // ToCanonical

$$-\left({}^{1}\omega^{e} \wedge^{3} \omega^{ab} \wedge^{2} \omega^{cd}\right).$$

Exterior derivative d

The exterior derivative d of a differential form is defined by Diff and it is a graded derivation (so that all the standard d-properties are implemented), as can be ssen from the following computations:

in : Diff[A0[] $\omega 1[a]$]

$$A^{0} d[{}^{1}\omega^{a}] + d[A^{0}] \wedge^{1} \omega^{a}$$

in : Diff[$\omega 1[a] \wedge \omega 2[b, c]$]

$$d[{}^{1}\omega^{a}] \wedge^{2} \omega^{bc} -^{1} \omega^{a} \wedge d[{}^{2}\omega^{bc}]$$

in : Diff[$\omega 1[b] \wedge \omega 1[a]$]

$$d[{}^{1}\omega^{b}] \wedge^{1} \omega^{a} -^{1} \omega^{b} \wedge d[{}^{1}\omega^{a}]$$

in : % // ToCanonical

$$^{1}\omega^{a} \wedge d[{}^{1}\omega^{b}] -^{1} \omega^{b} \wedge d[{}^{1}\omega^{a}]$$

in : Diff@%

$$d[{}^{1}\omega^{a}] \wedge d[{}^{1}\omega^{b}] - d[{}^{1}\omega^{b}] \wedge d[{}^{1}\omega^{a}]$$

in : % // ToCanonical

$$0$$

Canonical form

Canonical form θ^{a} is defined by:
in : {Coframe[M][a], dx[M][a]}

$$\{\theta^{a}, dx^{a}\},$$

where the first element of the list is the generic canonical 1-form θ^{a} and the second element of the list is the holonomic canonical 1-form dx^{a}. Degree of the list is:
in : Deg /@ %

$$\{1, 1\}$$

in : Coframe[M][b] $\wedge$ Coframe[M][a] // ToCanonical

$$- \left(\theta^a \wedge \theta^b \right)$$

in : Diff@%

$$- \left(d[\theta^a] \wedge \theta^b \right) + \theta^a \wedge d[\theta^b]$$

in : % // ToCanonical

$$- \left(d[\theta^a] \wedge \theta^b \right) + d[\theta^b] \wedge \theta^a$$

in : Diff@%

$$- \left(d[\theta^a] \wedge d[\theta^b] \right) + d[\theta^b] \wedge d[\theta^a]$$

in : % // ToCanonical

$$0$$

Cartan's forms and structure equations

Here we derive, expand and validate integrability conditions of Cartan's structure equations, including the Christoffel, Riemann and Torsion 2-forms.

To start with, we define the abstract covariant derivative ∇ (with Torsion, metric-independent) on the previously defined manifold M:

in : DefCovD[CD[-a], {";", "∇"}, Torsion $\to$ True], which automatically defines the Christoffel symbol and Riemann, Ricci and Torsion tensors.

Now, we can work with ∇-related differential forms, as follows:

in : ChristoffelForm[CD][a, -b]

$$\Gamma[\nabla]^a{}_b$$

in : % // Deg

$$1$$

in : RiemannForm[CD][a, -b]

$$R[\nabla]^a{}_b$$

in : % // Deg

$$2$$

in : TorsionForm[CD][a]

$$\tau[\nabla]^a$$

in : % // Deg

$$2$$

These forms are related by the following *Cartan's structure equations*, which can be obtained with the UseCartan command, as follows:

in : CartanStructureEqs = {
    Diff@Coframe[M][a] ==UseCartan[Diff[Coframe[M][a]], CD],
    Diff@Γ[CD][a, -b] ==UseCartan[Diff[Γ[CD][a, -b]], CD],

Diff@τ[CD][a] == UseCartan[Diff[τ[CD][a]], CD],
Diff@R[CD][a, -b] ==UseCartan[Diff[R[CD][a, -b]], CD] }[24]

$$d(\theta^a) = \tau(\nabla)^a - \Gamma(\nabla)^a_b \wedge \theta^b,$$

$$d(\Gamma(\nabla)^a_b) = R(\nabla)^a_b - \Gamma(\nabla)^a_c \wedge \Gamma(\nabla)^c_b,$$

$$d(\tau(\nabla)^a) = \theta^b \wedge R(\nabla)^a_b - \Gamma(\nabla)^a_b \wedge \tau(\nabla)^b,$$

$$d(R(\nabla)^a_b) = \Gamma(\nabla)^c_b \wedge R(\nabla)^a_c - R(\nabla)^c_b \wedge \Gamma(\nabla)^a_c$$

The complete integrability conditions for the Cartan system can be checked by taking the exterior derivative d of the above structure equations:
in : Diff@%

$$0 = d(\tau(\nabla)^a) - d(\Gamma(\nabla)^a_b) \wedge \theta^b + \Gamma(\nabla)^a_b \wedge d(\theta^b),$$

$$0 = d(R(\nabla)^a_b) - d(\Gamma(\nabla)^a_c) \wedge \Gamma(\nabla)^c_b + \Gamma(\nabla)^a_c \wedge d(\Gamma(\nabla)^c_b),$$

$$0 = d(\theta^b) \wedge R(\nabla)^a_b - d(\Gamma(\nabla)^a_b) \wedge \tau(\nabla)^b + \Gamma(\nabla)^a_b \wedge d(\tau(\nabla)^b) - \theta^b \wedge d(R(\nabla)^a_b),$$

$$0 = d(\Gamma(\nabla)^c_b) \wedge R(\nabla)^a_c - d(R(\nabla)^c_b) \wedge \Gamma(\nabla)^a_c - \Gamma(\nabla)^c_b \wedge d(R(\nabla)^a_c) - R(\nabla)^c_b \wedge d(\Gamma(\nabla)^a_c)$$

followed by:
in : UseCartan[%, CD]

$$0 = \theta^b \wedge R(\nabla)^a_b - R(\nabla)^a_b \wedge \theta^b - \Gamma(\nabla)^a_b \wedge \Gamma(\nabla)^b_c \wedge \theta^c + \Gamma(\nabla)^a_c \wedge \Gamma(\nabla)^c_b \wedge \theta^b,$$

$$0 = \Gamma(\nabla)^a_c \wedge R(\nabla)^c_b + \Gamma(\nabla)^c_b \wedge R(\nabla)^a_c - R(\nabla)^a_c \wedge \Gamma(\nabla)^c_b - R(\nabla)^c_b \wedge \Gamma(\nabla)^a_c - \Gamma(\nabla)^a_c \wedge \Gamma(\nabla)^c_d \wedge \Gamma(\nabla)^d_b + \Gamma(\nabla)^a_d \wedge \Gamma(\nabla)^d_c \wedge \Gamma(\nabla)^c_b,$$

$$0 = -(R(\nabla)^a_b \wedge \tau(\nabla)^b) + \tau(\nabla)^b \wedge R(\nabla)^a_b$$
$$-\Gamma(\nabla)^a_b \wedge \Gamma(\nabla)^b_c \wedge \tau(\nabla)^c + \Gamma(\nabla)^a_b \wedge \theta^c \wedge R(\nabla)^b_c$$
$$+\Gamma(\nabla)^a_c \wedge \Gamma(\nabla)^c_b \wedge \tau(\nabla)^b - \Gamma(\nabla)^b_c \wedge \theta^c \wedge R(\nabla)^a_b$$
$$-\theta^b \wedge \Gamma(\nabla)^c_b \wedge R(\nabla)^a_c + \theta^b \wedge R(\nabla)^c_b \wedge \Gamma(\nabla)^a_c,$$

$$0 = -(\Gamma(\nabla)^c_b \wedge \Gamma(\nabla)^d_c \wedge R(\nabla)^a_d) + \Gamma(\nabla)^c_b \wedge R(\nabla)^d_c \wedge \Gamma(\nabla)^a_d$$
$$-\Gamma(\nabla)^c_d \wedge \Gamma(\nabla)^d_b \wedge R(\nabla)^a_c - \Gamma(\nabla)^d_b \wedge R(\nabla)^c_d \wedge \Gamma(\nabla)^a_c$$
$$+R(\nabla)^c_b \wedge \Gamma(\nabla)^a_d \wedge \Gamma(\nabla)^d_c + R(\nabla)^d_b \wedge \Gamma(\nabla)^c_d \wedge \Gamma(\nabla)^a_c,$$

in : ToCanonical[%]

$$\{True, True, True, True\}$$

---

[24] For simplicity/readability, in the following output we have replaced $Mathematica$'s equation operator '==' with the assignment one '='.

11

Appendix 2: Classical Neural Networks and AI

11.1 Classical Artificial Neural Networks as Simplistic Brain Models

Recall that *artificial neural networks* (ANNs) are *nonlinear dynamical systems* that act as *functional approximators* [Kos92]. The ANN builds *discriminant functions* from its processing elements (PE)s. The ANN topology determines the *number* and *shape* of the discriminant functions. The shapes of the discriminant functions change with the topology, so ANNs are considered *semi–parametric classifiers*. One of the central advantages of ANNs is that they are sufficiently powerful to create arbitrary discriminant functions so ANNs can achieve optimal classification.

The placement of the discriminant functions is controlled by the network weights. Following the ideas of non–parametric training, the weights are adjusted directly from the training data without any assumptions about the data's statistical distribution. Hence one of the central issues in neural network design is to utilize systematic procedures, the so-called *training algorithm*, to modify the weights so that as accurate a classification as possible is achieved. The accuracy is quantified by an error criterion [PEL00].

The training is usually performed in the following way. First, data is presented, and an output is computed. An error is obtained by comparing the output $\{y\}$ with a desired response $\{d\}$ and it is used to modify the weights with a training algorithm. This procedure is repeated using all the data in the training set until a convergence criterion is met. Thus, in ANNs (and in adaptive systems in general) the designer does not have to specify the *parameters* of the system. They are automatically extracted from the input data and the desired response by means of the training algorithm. The two central issues in neural network design (semi–parametric classifiers) are the selection of the shape and number of the discriminant functions and their placement in pattern space such that the classification error is minimized [PEL00].

11.1.1 Biological Versus Artificial Neural Nets (ANNs)

In biological neural networks, signals are transmitted between neurons by electrical pulses (action potentials or spike trains) traveling along the axon. These pulses impinge on the afferent neuron at terminals called synapses. These are found principally on a set of branching processes emerging from the cell body (soma) known as dendrites. Each pulse occurring at a synapse initiates the release of a small amount of chemical substance or neurotransmitter which travels across the synaptic cleft and which is then received at postsynaptic receptor sites on the dendritic side of the synapse. The neurotransmitter becomes bound to molecular sites here which, in turn, initiates a change in the dendritic membrane potential. This postsynaptic potential (PSP) change may serve to increase (hyperpolarize) or decrease (depolarize) the polarization of the postsynaptic membrane. In the former case, the PSP tends to inhibit generation of pulses in the afferent neuron, while in the latter, it tends to excite the generation of pulses. The size and type of PSP produced will depend on factors such as the geometry of the synapse and the type of neurotransmitter. Each PSP will travel along its dendrite and spread over the soma, eventually reaching the base of the axon (axon-hillock). The afferent neuron sums or integrates the effects of thousands of such PSPs over its dendritic tree and over time. If the integrated potential at the axon-hillock exceeds a threshold, the cell fires and generates an action potential or spike which starts to travel along its axon. This then initiates the whole sequence of events again in neurons contained in the efferent pathway.

ANNs are very loosely based on these ideas. In the most general terms, a ANN consists of large numbers of simple processors linked by weighted connections. By analogy, the processing nodes may be called artificial neurons. Each node output depends only on information that is locally available at the node, either stored internally or arriving via the weighted connections. Each unit receives inputs from many other nodes and transmits its output to yet other nodes. By itself, a single processing element is not very powerful; it generates a scalar output, a single numerical value, which is a simple nonlinear function of its inputs. The power of the system emerges from the combination of many units in an appropriate way [FS92].

ANN is specialized to implement different functions by varying the connection topology and the values of the connecting weights. Complex functions can be implemented by connecting units together with appropriate weights. In fact, it has been shown that a sufficiently large network with an appropriate structure and property chosen weights can approximate with arbitrary accuracy any function satisfying certain broad constraints. In ANNs, the design motivation is what distinguishes them from other mathematical techniques: an ANN is a processing device, either an algorithm, or actual hardware, whose design was motivated by the design and functioning of animal brains and components thereof.

There are many different types of ANNs, each of which has different strengths particular to their applications. The abilities of different networks can be related to their structure, dynamics and learning methods.

11.1.2 Most Popular Classical Discrete ANNs

Multilayer Perceptrons

The most common ANN model is the *feedforward neural network* with one input layer, one output layer, and one or more hidden layers, called *multilayer perceptron* (MLP). This type of neural network is known as a *supervised network* because it requires a desired output in order to learn. The goal of this type of network is to *create a model* $f : x \to y$ that correctly maps the input x to the output y using historical data so that the model can then be used to produce the output when the desired output is unknown [Kos92].

In MLP the inputs are fed into the input layer and get multiplied by interconnection weights as they are passed from the input layer to the first hidden layer. Within the first hidden layer, they get summed then processed by a nonlinear function (usually the hyperbolic tangent). As the processed data leaves the first hidden layer, again it gets multiplied by interconnection weights, then summed and processed by the second hidden layer. Finally the data is multiplied by interconnection weights then processed one last time within the output layer to produce the neural network output.

MLPs are typically trained with *static backpropagation*. These networks have found their way into countless applications requiring static pattern classification. Their main advantage is that they are easy to use, and that they can approximate any input/output map. The key disadvantages are that they train slowly, and require lots of training data (typically three times more training samples than the number of network weights).

McCulloch–Pitts Processing Element

MLPs are typically composed of *McCulloch–Pitts neurons* (see [MP43]). This processing element (PE) is simply a sum–of–products followed by a threshold nonlinearity. Its input–output equation is

$$y = f(\text{net}) = f\left(w_i x^i + b\right), \qquad (i = 1, ..., D),$$

where D is the number of inputs, x^i are the inputs to the PE, w_i are the weights and b is a bias term (see e.g., [MP69]). The activation function is a *hard threshold* defined by *signum* function,

$$f(\text{net}) = \begin{cases} 1, & \text{for} \quad \text{net} \geq 0, \\ -1, & \text{for} \quad \text{net} < 0. \end{cases}$$

Therefore, McCulloch–Pitts PE is composed of an adaptive linear element (*Adaline*, the weighted sum of inputs), followed by a signum nonlinearity [PEL00].

Sigmoidal Nonlinearities

Besides the hard threshold defined by signum function, other nonlinearities can be utilized in conjunction with the McCulloch–Pitts PE. Let us now smooth out the threshold, yielding a sigmoid shape for the nonlinearity. The most common nonlinearities are the *logistic* and the *hyperbolic tangent threshold activation functions*,

$$\text{hyperbolic}: \qquad f(\text{net}) = \tanh(\alpha \, \text{net}),$$

$$\text{logistic}: \qquad f(\text{net}) = \frac{1}{1 + \exp(-\alpha \, \text{net})},$$

where α is a *slope parameter* and normally is set to 1. The major difference between the two sigmoidal nonlinearities is the range of their output values. The logistic function produces values in the interval $[0, 1]$, while the hyperbolic tangent produces values in the interval $[-1, 1]$. An alternate interpretation of this PE substitution is to think that the discriminant function has been generalized to

$$g(x) = f(w_i x^i + b), \qquad (i = 1, ..., D),$$

which is sometimes called a *ridge* function. The combination of the synapse and the tanh axon (or the sigmoid axon) is usually referred to as the modified McCulloch–Pitts PE, because they all respond to the full input space in basically the same functional form (a sum of products followed by a global nonlinearity). The output of the logistic function varies from 0 to 1. Under some conditions, the logistic function allows a very powerful interpretation of the output of the PE as a'posteriori probabilities for Gaussian–distributed input classes. The tanh is closely related to the logistic function by a linear transformation in the input and output spaces, so neural networks that use either of these can be made equivalent by changing weights and biases [PEL00].

Gradient Descent on the Net's Performance Surface

The *search* for the weights to meet a *desired response* or internal constraint is the essence of any *connectionist* computation. The central problem to be solved on the road to machine–based classifiers is how to automate the process of *minimizing the error* so that the machine can independently make these weight changes, without need for hidden agents, or external observers. The optimality criterion to be minimized is usually the *mean square error* (MSE)

$$J = \frac{1}{2N} \sum_{i=1}^{N} \varepsilon_i^2,$$

where ε_i is the instantaneous error that is added to the output y_i (the linearly fitted value), and N is the number of observations. The function $J(w)$ is called the *performance surface* (the total error surface plotted in the space of weights w).

The search for the minimum of a function can be done efficiently using a broad class of methods based on *gradient information*. The gradient has two main advantages for the search:

1. It can be computed locally, and
2. It always points in the direction of maximum change.

The *gradient of the performance surface*, $\nabla J = \nabla_w J$, is a vector (with the dimension of w) that always points toward the direction of maximum J−change and with a magnitude equal to the slope of the tangent of the performance surface. The minimum value of the error J_{min} depends on both the input signal x^i and the desired signal d_i,

$$J_{min} = \frac{1}{2N} \left[\sum_i d_i^2 - \frac{\left(d_i x^i\right)}{\sum_i x^i} \right], \qquad (i = 1, ..., D).$$

The location in coefficient space where the minimum w^* occurs also depends on both x^i and d_i. The performance surface shape depends only on the input signal x^i [PEL00].

Now, if the goal is to reach the minimum, the search must be in the direction opposite to the gradient. The overall method of gradient searching can be stated in the following way: Start the search with an arbitrary initial weight $w(0)$, where the iteration number is denoted by the index in parentheses. Then compute the gradient of the performance surface at $w(0)$, and modify the initial weight proportionally to the negative of the gradient at $w(0)$. This changes the operating point to $w(1)$. Then compute the gradient at the new position $w(1)$, and apply the same procedure again, that is,

$$w(n + 1) = w(n) - \eta \nabla J(n),$$

where η is a small constant and $\nabla J(n)$ denotes the gradient of the performance surface at the nth iteration. The constant η is used to maintain stability in the search by ensuring that the operating point does not move too far along the performance surface. This search procedure is called the *steepest descent method*.

In the late 1960s, Widrow proposed an extremely elegant algorithm to estimate the gradient that revolutionized the application of gradient descent procedures. His idea is very simple: Use the instantaneous value as the estimator for the true quantity:

$$\nabla J(n) = \frac{\partial}{\partial w(n)} J \approx \frac{1}{2} \frac{\partial}{\partial w(n)} \left(\varepsilon^2(n)\right) = -\varepsilon(n)\, x(n),$$

i.e., instantaneous estimate of the gradient at iteration n is simply the product of the current input $x(n)$ to the weight $w(n)$ times the current error $\varepsilon(n)$. The amazing thing is that the gradient can be estimated with one multiplication per weight. This is the gradient estimate that led to the celebrated *least means square algorithm* (LMS):

$$w(n+1) \ = \ w(n) + \eta \varepsilon(n) \, x(n), \tag{11.1}$$

where the small constant η is called the *step size*, or the *learning rate*. The estimate will be noisy, however, since the algorithm uses the error from a single sample instead of summing the error for each point in the data set (e.g., the MSE is estimated by the error for the current sample).

Now, for fast convergence to the neighborhood of the minimum a large step size is desired. However, the solution with a large step size suffers from rattling. One attractive solution is to use a large learning rate in the beginning of training to move quickly toward the location of the optimal weights, but then the learning rate should be decreased to get good accuracy on the final weight values. This is called *learning rate scheduling*. This simple idea can be implemented with a variable step size controlled by

$$\eta(n+1) \ = \ \eta(n) - \beta,$$

where $\eta(0) = \eta_0$ is the initial step size, and β is a small constant [PEL00].

Perceptron and Its Learning Algorithm

Rosenblatt perceptron (see [Ros58, MP69]) is a *pattern–recognition* machine that was invented in the 1950s for optical character recognition. The perceptron has an input layer fully connected to an output layer with multiple McCulloch–Pitts PEs,

$$y_i = f(\underset{i}{\mathrm{net}}) = f(w_i x^i + b_i), \qquad (i = 1, ..., D),$$

where b_i is the bias for each PE. The number of outputs y_i is normally determined by the number of classes in the data. These PEs add the individual scaled contributions and respond to the entire input space.

F. Rosenblatt proposed the following procedure to directly minimize the error by changing the weights of the McCulloch–Pitts PE: Apply an input example to the network. If the output is correct do nothing. If the response is incorrect, tweak the weights and bias until the response becomes correct. Get the next example and repeat the procedure, until all the patterns are correctly classified. This procedure is called the *perceptron learning algorithm*, which can be put into the following form:

$$w(n+1) = w(n) + \eta(d(n) - y(n)) \, x(n),$$

where η is the step size, y is the network output, and d is the desired response.

Clearly, the functional form is the same as in the LMS algorithm (11.1), that is, the old weights are incrementally modified proportionally to the product of the error and the input, but there is a significant difference. We cannot say that this corresponds to gradient descent since the system has a discontinuous nonlinearity. In the perceptron learning algorithm, $y(n)$ is the output of the nonlinear system. The algorithm is directly minimizing the difference between the response of the McCulloch–Pitts PE and the desired response, instead of minimizing the difference between the Adaline output and the desired response [PEL00].

This subtle modification has tremendous impact on the performance of the system. For one thing, the McCulloch–Pitts PE learns only when its output is wrong. In fact, when $y(n) = d(n)$, the weights remain the same. The net effect is that the final values of the weights are no longer equal to the linear regression result, because the nonlinearity is brought into the weight update rule. Another way of phrasing this is to say that the weight update became much more selective, effectively gated by the system performance. Notice that the LMS update is also a function of the error to a certain degree. Larger errors have more effect on the weight update than small errors, but all patterns affect the final weights implementing a 'smooth gate'. In the perceptron the net effect is that the placement of the discriminant function is no longer controlled smoothly by all the input samples as in the Adaline, only by the ones that are important for placing the discriminant function in a way that explicitly minimizes the output error.

The Delta Learning Rule

One can show that the LMS rule is equivalent to the chain rule in the computation of the *sensitivity* of the cost function J with respect to the unknowns. Interpreting the LMS equation (11.1) with respect to the sensitivity concept, we see that the gradient measures the sensitivity. LMS is therefore updating the weights proportionally to how much they affect the performance, i.e., proportionally to their sensitivity.

The LMS concept can be extended to the McCulloch–Pitts PE, which is a nonlinear system. The main question here is how can we compute the sensitivity through a nonlinearity? [PEL00] The so-called $\delta-rule$ represents a direct extension of the LMS rule to nonlinear systems with smooth nonlinearities. In case of the McCulloch–Pitts PE, *delta–rule* reads:

$$w_i(n + 1) = w_i(n) + \eta\, \varepsilon_p(n)\, x_p^i(n)\, f'(\underset{p}{\text{net}}(n)),$$

where $f'(\text{net})$ is the partial derivative of the static nonlinearity, such that the *chain rule* is applied to the network topology, i.e.,

$$f'(\text{net})\, x^i = \frac{\partial y}{\partial w_i} = \frac{\partial y}{\partial \text{net}}\frac{\partial}{\partial w_i}. \tag{11.2}$$

As long as the PE nonlinearity is smooth we can compute how much a change in the weight δw_i affects the output y, or from the point of view of the sensitivity, how sensitive the output y is to a change in a particular weight δw_i.

Note that we compute this output sensitivity by a product of partial derivatives through intermediate points in the topology. For the nonlinear PE there is only one intermediate point, net, but we really do not care how many of these intermediate points there are. The chain rule can be applied as many times as necessary. In practice, we have an error at the output (the difference between the desired response and the actual output), and we want to adjust all the PE weights so that the error is minimized in a statistical sense. The obvious idea is to distribute the adjustments according to the sensitivity of the output to each weight.

To modify the weight, we actually *propagate back the output error* to intermediate points in the network topology and scale it along the way as prescribed by (11.2) according to the element transfer functions:

$$\text{forward path} : \quad x^i \longmapsto w_i \longmapsto \text{net} \longmapsto y$$

$$\text{backward path 1} : \quad w_i \overset{\partial \text{net}/\partial w}{\longleftarrow} \text{net} \overset{\partial y/\partial \text{net}}{\longleftarrow} y$$

$$\text{backward path 2} : \quad w_i \overset{\partial y/\partial w}{\longleftarrow} y.$$

This methodology is very powerful, because we do not need to know explicitly the error at intermediate places, such as net. The chain rule automatically derives the error contribution for us. This observation is going to be crucial for adapting more complicated topologies and will result in the *backpropagation* algorithm, discovered in 1988 by Werbos [Wer74].

Now, several key aspects have changed in the performance surface (which describes how the cost changes with the weights) with the introduction of the nonlinearity. The nice, parabolic performance surface of the linear least squares problem is lost. The performance depends on the topology of the network through the output error, so when nonlinear processing elements are used to solve a given problem the 'performance – weights' relationship becomes nonlinear, and there is no guarantee of a single minimum. The performance surface may have several minima. The minimum that produces the smallest error in the search space is called the *global minimum*. The others are called *local* minima. Alternatively, we say that the performance surface is *nonconvex*. This affects the search scheme because gradient descent uses local information to search the performance surface. In the immediate neighborhood, local minima are indistinguishable from the global minimum, so the gradient search algorithm may be caught in these suboptimal performance points, 'thinking' it has reached the global minimum [PEL00].

δ−rule extended to perceptron reads:

$$w_{ij}(n + 1) = w_{ij}(n) - \eta \frac{\partial J}{\partial w_{ij}} = w_{ij}(n) + \eta\, \delta_{ip}\, x_p^j,$$

which are local quantities available at the weight, that is, the activation x_p^j that reaches the weight w_{ij} from the input and the local error δ_{ip} propagated from the cost function J. This algorithm is local to the weight. Only the local error δ_i and the local activation x^j are needed to update a particular weight. This means that it is immaterial how many PEs the net has and how complex their interconnection is. The training algorithm can concentrate on each PE individually and work only with the local error and local activation [PEL00].

Backpropagation

The multilayer perceptron constructs input–output mappings that are a nested composition of nonlinearities, that is, they are of the form

$$y = f\left(\sum f\left(\sum (\cdot)\right)\right),$$

where the number of function compositions is given by the number of network layers. The resulting map is very flexible and powerful, but it is also hard to analyze [PEL00].

MLPs are usually trained by generalized δ–rule, the so-called *backpropagation* (BP). The weight update using backpropagation is

$$w_{ij}(n+1) = w_{ij}(n) + \eta f'(\underset{i}{\text{net}}(n))\left(\varepsilon^k(n)\, f'(\underset{k}{\text{net}}(n))\, w_{ki}(n)\right) y_j(n). \quad (11.3)$$

The summation in (11.3) is a sum of local errors δ_k at each network output PE, scaled by the weights connecting the output PEs to the ith PE. Thus the term in parenthesis in (11.3) effectively computes the total error reaching the ith PE from the output layer (which can be thought of as the ith PE's contribution to the output error). When we pass it through the ith PE nonlinearity, we have its local error, which can be written as

$$\delta_i(n) = f'(\underset{i}{\text{net}}(n))\, \delta^k w_{ki}(n).$$

Thus there is a unifying link in all the gradient–descent algorithms. All the weights in gradient descent learning are updated by multiplying the local error $\delta_i(n)$ by the local activation $x^j(n)$ according to Widrow's estimation of the instantaneous gradient first shown in the LMS rule:

$$\Delta w_{ij}(n) = \eta\, \delta_i(n)\, y_j(n).$$

What differs is the calculation of the local error, depending on whether the PE is linear or nonlinear and if the weight is attached to an output PE or a hidden–layer PE [PEL00].

Momentum Learning

Momentum learning is an improvement to the straight gradient–descent search in the sense that a memory term (the past increment to the weight) is used to speed up and stabilize convergence. In *momentum learning* the equation to update the weights becomes

$$w_{ij}(n+1) = w_{ij}(n) + \eta\,\delta_i(n)\,x_j(n) + \alpha\left(w_{ij}(\overline{n}) - w_{ij}(n-1)\right),$$

where α is the momentum constant, usually set between 0.5 and 0.9. This is called momentum learning due to the form of the last term, which resembles the momentum in mechanics. Note that the weights are changed proportionally to how much they were updated in the last iteration. Thus if the search is going down the hill and finds a flat region, the weights are still changed, not because of the gradient (which is practically zero in a flat spot), but because of the rate of change in the weights. Likewise, in a narrow valley, where the gradient tends to bounce back and forth between hillsides, the momentum stabilizes the search because it tends to make the weights follow a smoother path. Imagine a ball (weight vector position) rolling down a hill (performance surface). If the ball reaches a small flat part of the hill, it will continue past this local minimum because of its momentum. A ball without momentum, however, will get stuck in this valley. Momentum learning is a robust method to speed up learning, and is usually recommended as the default search rule for networks with nonlinearities.

Advanced Search Methods

The popularity of *gradient descent method* is based more on its simplicity (it can be computed locally with two multiplications and one addition per weight) than on its search power. There are many other search procedures more powerful than backpropagation. For example, *Newtonian method* is a second–order method because it uses the information on the curvature to adapt the weights. However Newtonian method is computationally much more costly to implement and requires information not available at the PE, so it has been used little in neurocomputing. Although more powerful, Newtonian method is still a local search method and so may be caught in local minima or diverge due to the difficult neural network performance landscapes. Other techniques such as *simulated annealing*[1] and *genetic algorithms* (GA)[2] are global search procedures, that is, they can avoid local minima. The issue is that they are more costly to implement in a distributed system like a neural network, either because they are inherently slow or because they require nonlocal quantities [PEL00].

---

[1] Simulated annealing is a global search criterion by which the space is searched with a random rule. In the beginning the variance of the random jumps is very large. Every so often the variance is decreased, and a more local search is undertaken. It has been shown that if the decrease of the variance is set appropriately, the global optimum can be found with probability one. The method is called simulated annealing because it is similar to the annealing process of creating crystals from a hot liquid.

[2] Genetic algorithms are global search procedures proposed by J. Holland that search the performance surface, concentrating on the areas that provide better solutions. They use 'generations' of search points computed from the previous search points using the operators of crossover and mutation (hence the name).

The problem of search with local information can be formulated as an approximation to the functional form of the *matrix cost function* $J(\mathbf{w})$ at the operating point $\mathbf{w}_0$. This immediately points to the Taylor series expansion of J around $\mathbf{w}_0$,

$$J(\mathbf{w} - \mathbf{w}_0) = J_0 + (\mathbf{w} - \mathbf{w}_0)\nabla J_0 + \frac{1}{2}(\mathbf{w} - \mathbf{w}_0)\mathbf{H}_0(\mathbf{w} - \mathbf{w}_0)^T + ...,$$

where ∇J is our familiar gradient, and $\mathbf{H}$ is the Hessian matrix, that is, the matrix of second derivatives with entries

$$H_{ij}(\mathbf{w}_0) = \left.\frac{\partial^2 J(w)}{\partial w_i \partial w_j}\right|_{w=w_0},$$

evaluated at the operating point. We can immediately see that the Hessian cannot be computed with the information available at a given PE, since it uses information from two different weights. If we differentiate J with respect to the weights, we get

$$\nabla J(\mathbf{w}) = \nabla J_0 + \mathbf{H}_0(\mathbf{w} - \mathbf{w}_0) + ... \tag{11.4}$$

so we can see that to compute the full gradient at $\mathbf{w}$ we need all the higher terms of the derivatives of J. This is impossible. Since the performance surface tends to be bowl shaped (quadratic) near the minimum, we are normally interested only in the first and second terms of the expansion [PEL00].

If the expansion of (11.4) is restricted to the first term, we get the gradient–search methods (hence they are called *first–order–search methods*), where the gradient is estimated with its value at $\mathbf{w}_0$. If we expand to use the second–order term, we get *Newton method* (hence the name second–order method). If we equate the truncated relation (11.4) to 0 we immediately get

$$w = w_0 - \mathbf{H}_0^{-1}\nabla J_0,$$

which is the equation for the Newton method, which has the nice property of quadratic termination (it is guaranteed to find the exact minimum in a finite number of steps for quadratic performance surfaces). For most quadratic performance surfaces it can converge in one iteration.

The real difficulty is the memory and the computational cost (and precision) to estimate the Hessian. Neural networks can have thousands of weights, which means that the Hessian will have millions of entries. This is why methods of approximating the Hessian have been extensively researched. There are two basic classes of approximations [PEL00]:

1. Line search methods, and
2. Pseudo–Newton methods.

The information in the first type is restricted to the gradient, together with line searches along certain directions, while the second seeks approximations to the Hessian matrix. Among the line search methods probably the most effective is the *conjugate gradient method*. For quadratic performance surfaces the conjugate gradient algorithm preserves quadratic termination and can reach the minimum in D steps, where D is the dimension of the weight space. Among the Pseudo–Newton methods probably the most effective is the *Levenberg–Marquardt algorithm* (LM), which uses the Gauss–Newton method to approximate the Hessian. LM is the most interesting for neural networks, since it is formulated as a sum of quadratic terms just like the cost functions in neural networks.

The *extended Kalman filter* (EKF) forms the basis of a second–order neural network training method that is a practical and effective alternative to the batch–oriented, second–order methods mentioned above. The essence of the recursive EKF procedure is that, during training, in addition to evolving the weights of a network architecture in a sequential (as opposed to batch) fashion, an approximate error covariance matrix that encodes second–order information about the training problem is also maintained and evolved.

Homotopy Methods

The most popular method for solving nonlinear equations in general is the *Newton–Raphson method*. Unfortunately, this method sometimes fails, especially in cases when nonlinear equations possess multiple solutions (zeros). An emerging family of methods that can be used in such cases are homotopy (continuation) methods. These methods are robust and have good convergence properties.

Homotopy methods or *continuation methods* have increasingly been used for solving variety of nonlinear problems in fluid dynamics, structural mechanics, systems identifications, and integrated circuits (see [Wat90]). These methods, popular in mathematical programming, are globally convergent provided that certain coercivity and continuity conditions are satisfied by the equations that need to be solved [Wat90]. Moreover, they often yield all the solutions to the nonlinear system of equations.

The idea behind a homotopy or continuation method is to embed a parameter λ in the nonlinear equations to be solved. This is why they are sometimes referred to as *embedding methods*. Initially, parameter λ is set to zero, in which case the problem is reduced to an easy problem with a known or easily–found solution. The set of equations is then gradually deformed into the originally posed difficult problem by varying the parameter λ. The original problem is obtained for $\lambda = 1$. Homotopies are a class of continuation methods, in which parameter λ is a function of a path arc length and may actually increase or decrease as the path is traversed. Provided that certain coercivity conditions imposed on the nonlinear function to be solved are satisfied, the homotopy path does not branch (bifurcate) and passes through all the solutions of the nonlinear equations to be solved.

The zero curve of the homotopy map can be tracked by various techniques: an *ODE–algorithm*, a *normal flow algorithm*, and an *augmented Jacobian matrix algorithm*, among others [Wat90].

As a typical example, homotopy techniques can be applied to find the zeros of the gradient function $F : \mathbb{R}^N \to \mathbb{R}^N$, such that

$$F(\theta) = \frac{\partial E(\theta)}{\partial \theta_k}, \qquad 1 \le k \le N,$$

where $E = (\theta)$ is the certain error function dependent on N parameters θ_k. In other words, we need to solve a system of nonlinear equations

$$F(\theta) = 0. \tag{11.5}$$

In order to solve equation (11.5), we can create a linear homotopy function

$$H(\theta, \lambda) = (1 - \lambda)(\theta - a) + \lambda F(\theta),$$

where a is an arbitrary starting point. Function $H(\theta, \lambda)$ has properties that equation $H(\theta, 0) = 0$ is easy to solve, and that $H(\theta, 1) \equiv F(\theta)$.

ANNs as Functional Approximators

The *universal approximation theorem* of Kolmogorov states [Hay94]:
Let $\phi(\cdot)$ be a nonconstant, bounded, and monotone–increasing continuous (C^0) function. Let I^N denote ND unit hypercube $[0, 1]^N$. The space of C^0–functions on I^N is denoted by $C(I^N)$. Then, given any function $f \in C(I^N)$ and $\epsilon > 0$, there exist an integer M and sets of real constants $\alpha_i, \theta_i, \omega_{ij}, i = 1, \ldots, M; j = 1, \ldots, N$ such that we may define

$$F(x_1, \ldots, x_N) = \alpha_i \phi(\omega_{ij} x_j - \theta_i),$$

as an approximate realization of the function $f(\cdot)$; that is

$$|F(x_1, \ldots, x_N) - f(x_1, \ldots, x_N)| < \epsilon \qquad \text{for all} \quad \{x_1, \ldots, x_N\} \in I^N.$$

This theorem is directly applicable to *multilayer perceptrons*. First, the logistic function $1/[1 + \exp(-v)]$ used as the sigmoidal nonlinearity in a neuron model for the construction of a multilayer perceptron is indeed a nonconstant, bounded, and monotone–increasing function; it therefore satisfies the conditions imposed on the function $\phi(\cdot)$. Second, the upper equation represents the output of a multilayer perceptron described as follows:

1. The network has n input nodes and a single hidden layer consisting of M neurons; the inputs are denoted by $x_1, \ldots, x_N$.
2. ith hidden neuron has synaptic weights $\omega_{i1}, \ldots, \omega_{iN}$ and threshold θ_i.
3. The network output y_j is a linear combination of the outputs of the hidden neurons, with $\alpha_i, \ldots, \alpha_M$ defining the coefficients of this combination.

The theorem actually states that a single hidden layer is sufficient for a multilayer perceptron to compute a uniform ϵ approximation to a given training set represented by the set of inputs $x_1, \ldots, x_N$ and desired (target) output $f(x_1, \ldots, x_N)$. However, the theorem does not say that a single layer is *optimum* in the sense of learning time or ease of implementation.

Recall that training of multilayer perceptrons is usually performed using a certain clone of the BP algorithm (11.3). In this forward–pass/backward–pass gradient–descending algorithm, the adjusting of synaptic weights is defined by the extended $\delta-rule$, given by equation

$$\Delta\omega_{ji}(N) = \eta \cdot \delta_j(N) \cdot y_i(N), \tag{11.6}$$

where $\Delta\omega_{ji}(N)$ corresponds to the *weight correction*, η is the *learning–rate parameter*, $\delta_j(N)$ denotes the *local gradient* and $y_i(N)$ — the *input signal of neuron* j; while the *cost function* E is defined as the instantaneous sum of squared errors e_j^2

$$E(n) = \frac{1}{2}\sum_j e_j^2(N) = \frac{1}{2}\sum_j [d_j(N) - y_j(N)]^2, \tag{11.7}$$

where $y_j(N)$ is the output of jth neuron, and $d_j(N)$ is the desired (target) response for that neuron. The slow BP convergence rate (11.6)–(11.7) can be accelerated using the faster LM algorithm (see subsection 11.1.2 above), while its robustness can be achieved using an appropriate fuzzy controller.

Summary of Supervised Learning Methods

Gradient Descent Method

Given the $(D+1)$D weights vector $\mathbf{w}(n) = [w_0(n), ..., w_D(n)]^T$ (with $w_0 =$ *bias*), and the correspondent MSE–gradient (including partials of MSE w.r.t. weights)

$$\nabla\mathbf{e} = \left[\frac{\partial e}{\partial w_0}, ..., \frac{\partial e}{\partial w_D}\right]^T,$$

and the learning rate (step size) η, we have the vector learning equation

$$\mathbf{w}(n+1) = \mathbf{w}(n) - \eta\nabla\mathbf{e}(n),$$

which in index form reads

$$w_i(n+1) = w_i(n) - \eta\nabla e_i(n).$$

LMS Algorithm

$$\mathbf{w}(n+1) = \mathbf{w}(n) + \eta\varepsilon(n)\,x(n),$$

where x is an input (measurement) vector, and ε is a zero–mean Gaussian noise vector uncorrelated with input, or

$$w_i(n+1) = w_i(n) + \eta\varepsilon(n)\,x^i(n).$$

Newton's Method

$$\mathbf{w}(n+1) = \mathbf{w}(n) - \eta\,\mathbf{R}^{-1}\mathbf{e}(n),$$

where $\mathbf{R}$ is input (auto)correlation matrix, or

$$\mathbf{w}(n+1) = \mathbf{w}(n) + \eta\,\mathbf{R}^{-1}\varepsilon(n)\,x(n),$$

Conjugate Gradient Method

$$\mathbf{w}(n+1) = \mathbf{w}(n) + \eta\,\mathbf{p}(n),$$
$$\mathbf{p}(n) = -\nabla\mathbf{e}(n) + \beta(n)\mathbf{p}(n-1),$$
$$\beta(n) = \frac{\nabla\mathbf{e}(n)^T\nabla\mathbf{e}(n)}{\nabla\mathbf{e}(n-1)^T\nabla\mathbf{e}(n-1)}.$$

Levenberg–Marquardt Algorithm

Putting
$$\nabla\mathbf{e} = \mathbf{J}^T\mathbf{e},$$
where $\mathbf{J}$ is the Jacobian matrix, which contains first derivatives of the network errors with respect to the weights and biases, and $\mathbf{e}$ is a vector of network errors, LM algorithm reads

$$\mathbf{w}(n+1) = \mathbf{w}(n) - [\mathbf{J}^T\mathbf{J} + \mu\mathbf{I}]^{-1}\mathbf{J}^T\mathbf{e}. \tag{11.8}$$

Other Standard ANNs

Generalized Feedforward Nets

The *generalized feedforward network* (GFN) is a generalization of MLP, such that connections can jump over one or more layers, which in practice, often solves the problem much more efficiently than standard MLPs. A classic example of this is the two–spiral problem, for which standard MLP requires hundreds of times more training epochs than the generalized feedforward network containing the same number of processing elements. Both MLPs and GFNs are usually trained using a variety of backpropagation techniques and their enhancements like the nonlinear LM algorithm (11.8). During training in the spatial processing, the weights of the GFN converge iteratively to the analytical solution of the 2D Laplace equation.

Modular Feedforward Nets

The *modular feedforward networks* are a special class of MLP. These networks process their input using several parallel MLPs, and then recombine the results. This tends to create some structure within the topology, which will foster specialization of function in each submodule. In contrast to the MLP, modular networks do not have full inter–connectivity between their layers. Therefore, a smaller number of weights are required for the same size network (i.e., the same number of PEs). This tends to speed up training times and reduce the number of required training exemplars. There are many ways to segment a MLP into modules. It is unclear how to best design the modular topology based on the data. There are no guarantees that each module is specializing its training on a unique portion of the data.

Jordan and Elman Nets

Jordan and Elman networks (see [Elm90]) extend the multilayer perceptron with context units, which are processing elements (PEs) that remember past activity. Context units provide the network with the ability to extract temporal information from the data. In the Elman network, the activity of the first hidden PEs are copied to the context units, while the Jordan network copies the output of the network. Networks which feed the input and the last hidden layer to the context units are also available.

Kohonen Self–Organizing Map

Kohonen self–organizing map (SOM) is widely used for image pre–processing as well as a pre–processing unit for various hybrid architectures. SOM is a winner–take–all neural architecture that quantizes the input space, using a distance metric, into a discrete feature output space, where neighboring regions in the input space are neighbors in the discrete output space. SOM is usually applied to neighborhood clustering of random points along a circle using a variety of distance metrics: Euclidean, L^1, L^2, and L^n, Machalanobis, etc. The basic SOM architecture consists of a layer of Kohonen synapses of three basic forms: line, diamond and box, followed by a layer of winner–take–all axons. It usually uses added Gaussian and uniform noise, with control of both the mean and variance. Also, SOM usually requires choosing the proper initial neighborhood width as well as annealing of the neighborhood width during training to ensure that the map globally represents the input space.

The Kohonen SOM algorithm is defined as follows: Every stimulus $\mathbf{v}$ of an Euclidian input space V is mapped to the neuron with the position $\mathbf{s}$ in the neural layer R with the highest neural activity, the 'center of excitation' or 'winner', given by the condition

$$|\mathbf{w_s} - \mathbf{v}| = \min_{r \in R} |\mathbf{w_r} - \mathbf{v}|,$$

where $|.|$ denotes the Euclidian distance in input space. In the Kohonen model the learning rule for each synaptic weight vector $\mathbf{w_r}$ is given by

$$\mathbf{w_r^{new}} = \mathbf{w_r^{old}} + \eta \cdot g_{rs} \cdot (\mathbf{v} - \mathbf{w_r^{old}}), \qquad (11.9)$$

with g_{rs} as a gaussian function of Euclidian distance $|\mathbf{r} - \mathbf{s}|$ in the neural layer. Topology preservation is enforced by the common update of all weight vectors whose neuron $\mathbf{r}$ is adjacent to the center of excitation $\mathbf{s}$. The function g_{rs} describes the topology in the neural layer. The parameter η determines the speed of learning and can be adjusted during the learning process.

Radial Basis Function Nets

The *radial basis function network* (RBF) provides a powerful alternative to MLP for function approximation or classification. It differs from MLP in that the overall input–output map is constructed from local contributions of a layer of Gaussian axons. It trains faster and requires fewer training samples than MLP, using the hybrid supervised/unsupervised method. The unsupervised part of an RBF network consists of a competitive synapse followed by a layer of Gaussian axons. The means of the Gaussian axons are found through competitive clustering and are, in fact, the weights of the Conscience synapse. Once the means converge the variances are calculated based on the separation of the means and are associated with the Gaussian layer. Having trained the unsupervised part, we now add the supervised part, which consists of a single–layer MLP with a soft–max output.

Principal Component Analysis Nets

The *principal component analysis networks* (PCAs) combine unsupervised and supervised learning in the same topology. Principal component analysis is an unsupervised procedure that finds a set of uncorrelated features, principal components, from the input. A MLP is supervised to perform the nonlinear classification from these components. More sophisticated are the *independent component analysis networks* (ICAs).

Co-active Neuro–Fuzzy Inference Systems

The *co-active neuro–fuzzy inference system* (CANFIS), which integrates adaptable fuzzy inputs with a modular neural network to rapidly and accurately approximate complex functions. Fuzzy–logic inference systems (see next section) are also valuable as they combine the explanatory nature of rules (membership functions) with the power of 'black box' neural networks.

Support Vector Machines

The *support vector machine* (SVM), implementing the statistical learning theory, is used as the most powerful nonlinear (e.g., spiral) classification system.

SVMs are a radically different type of classifier that has attracted a great deal of attention lately due to the novelty of the concepts that they bring to pattern recognition, their strong mathematical foundation, and their excellent results in practical problems. SVM represents the coupling of the following two concepts: the idea that transforming the data into a high–dimensional space makes linear discriminant functions practical, and the idea of large margin classifiers to train the MLP or RBF. It is another type of a kernel classifier: it places Gaussian kernels over the data and linearly weights their outputs to create the system output. To implement the SVM–methodology, we can use the Adatron–kernel algorithm, a sophisticated nonlinear generalization of the RBF networks, which maps inputs to a high–dimensional feature space, and then optimally separates data into their respective classes by isolating those inputs, which fall close to the data boundaries. Therefore, the Adatron–kernel is especially effective in separating sets of data, which share complex boundaries, as well as for the training for nonlinearly separable patterns. The support vectors allow the network to rapidly converge on the data boundaries and consequently classify the inputs.

The main advantage of SVMs over MLPs is that the learning task is a *convex optimization problem* which can be reliably solved even when the example data require the fitting of a very complicated function [Vap95, Vap98]. A common argument in computational learning theory suggests that it is dangerous to utilize the full flexibility of the SVM to learn the training data perfectly when these contain an amount of noise. By fitting more and more noisy data, the machine may implement a rapidly oscillating function rather than the smooth mapping which characterizes most practical learning tasks. Its prediction ability could be no better than random guessing in that case. Hence, modifications of SVM training [CS00] that allow for training errors were suggested to be necessary for realistic noisy scenarios. This has the drawback of introducing extra model parameters and spoils much of the original elegance of SVMs.

Mathematics of SVMs is based on real *Hilbert space* methods.

Genetic ANN–Optimization

Genetic optimization, added to ensure and speed–up the convergence of all other ANN–components, is a powerful tool for enhancing the efficiency and effectiveness of a neural network. Genetic optimization can fine–tune network parameters so that network performance is greatly enhanced. Genetic control applies a *genetic algorithm* (GA, see next section), a part of broader *evolutionary computation*, see MIT journal with the same name) to any network parameters that are specified. Also through the *genetic control*, GA parameters such as mutation probability, crossover type and probability, and selection type can be modified.

11.1.3 Most Popular Classical Continuous ANNs

Virtually all computer–implemented ANNs (mainly listed above) are discrete dynamical systems, mainly using supervised training (except Kohonen SOM) in one of gradient–descent searching forms. They are good as problem–solving tools, but they fail as models of animal nervous system. The other category of ANNs are continuous neural systems that can be considered as models of animal nervous system. However, *as models of the human brain, all current ANNs are simply trivial.*

Neurons as Functions

According to B. Kosko, neurons behave as functions [Kos92]; they transduce an unbounded input *activation* $x(t)$ into output *signal* $S(x(t))$. Usually a sigmoidal (S–shaped, bounded, monotone-nondecreasing: $S' \geq 0$) function describes the transduction, as well as the input–output behavior of many operational amplifiers. For example, the *logistic signal* (or, the *maximum–entropy*) function

$$S(x) = \frac{1}{1 + e^{-cx}}$$

is sigmoidal and strictly increases for positive scaling constant $c > 0$. Strict monotonicity implies that the *activation derivative* of S is positive:

$$S' = \frac{dS}{dx} = cS(1 - S) > 0.$$

An infinitely steep logistic signal function gives rise to a threshold signal function

$$S(x^{n+1}) = \begin{cases} 1, & \text{if} \quad x^{n+1} > T, \\ S(x^n), & \text{if} \quad x^{n+1} = T, \\ 0, & \text{if} \quad x^{n+1} < T, \end{cases}$$

for an arbitrary real–valued threshold T. The index n indicates the discrete time step.

In practice signal values are usually binary or bipolar. *Binary signals*, like logistic, take values in the unit interval $[0, 1]$. *Bipolar signals* are signed; they take values in the bipolar interval $[-1, 1]$. Binary and bipolar signals transform into each other by simple scaling and translation. For example, the bipolar logistic signal function takes the form

$$S(x) = \frac{2}{1 + e^{-cx}} - 1.$$

Neurons with bipolar threshold signal functions are called *McCulloch–Pitts neurons.*

A naturally occurring bipolar signal function is the *hyperbolic–tangent* signal function

$$S(x) = \tanh(cx) = \frac{e^{cx} - e^{-cx}}{e^{cx} + e^{-cx}},$$

with activation derivative

$$S' = c(1 - S^2) > 0.$$

The *threshold linear* function is a binary signal function often used to approximate neuronal firing behavior:

$$S(x) = \begin{cases} 1, & \text{if} \quad cx \geq 1, \\ 0, & \text{if} \quad cx < 0, \\ cx, & \text{else,} \end{cases}$$

which we can rewrite as

$$S(x) = \min(1, \max(0, cx)).$$

Between its upper and lower bounds the threshold linear signal function is trivially monotone increasing, since $S' = c > 0$.

Gaussian, or bell–shaped, signal function of the form $S(x) = e^{-cx^2}$, for $c > 0$, represents an important exception to signal monotonicity. Its activation derivative $S' = -2cxe^{-cx^2}$ has the sign opposite the sign of the activation x.

Generalized Gaussian signal functions define potential or radial basis functions $S_i(x^i)$ given by

$$S_i(x) = \exp[-\frac{1}{2\sigma_i^2} \sum_{j=1}^{n} (x_j - \mu_j^i)^2],$$

for input activation vector $x = (x^i) \in \mathbb{R}^n$, variance σ_i^2, and mean vector $\mu_i = (\mu_j^i)$. Each radial basis function S_i defines a spherical *receptive field* in $\mathbb{R}^n$. The ith neuron emits unity, or near-unity, signals for sample activation vectors x that fall in its receptive field. The mean vector μ centers the receptive field in $\mathbb{R}^n$. The variance σ_i^2 localizes it. The radius of the Gaussian spherical receptive field shrinks as the variance σ_i^2 decreases. The receptive field approaches $\mathbb{R}^n$ as σ_i^2 approaches ∞.

The *signal velocity* $\dot{S} \equiv dS/dt$ is the *signal time derivative*, related to the activation derivative by

$$\dot{S} = S'\dot{x},$$

so it depends explicitly on *activation velocity*. This is used in unsupervised learning laws that adapt with *locally available information*.

The signal $S(x)$ induced by the activation x represents the neuron's firing frequency of action potentials, or pulses, in a sampling interval. The firing frequency equals the average number of pulses emitted in a sampling interval.

Short–term memory is modeled by *activation dynamics*, and *long–term memory* is modeled by *learning dynamics*. The overall neural network behaves as an *adaptive filter* (see [Hay91]).

In the simplest and most common case, neurons are not topologically ordered. They are related only by the synaptic connections between them. Kohonen calls this *lack of topological structure* in a *field of neurons* the *zeroth–order topology*. This suggests that ANN–models are *abstractions*, not *descriptions* of the brain neural networks, in which order does matter.

Basic Activation and Learning Dynamics

One of the oldest continuous training methods, based on Hebb's biological synaptic learning [Heb49], is *Oja–Hebb learning rule* [Oja82], which calculates the weight update according to the ODE

$$\dot{\omega}_i(t) = O(t)\left[I_i(t) - O(t)\,\omega_i(t)\right],$$

where $O(t)$ is the output of a simple, linear processing element; $I_i(t)$ are the inputs; and $\omega_i(t)$ are the synaptic weights.

Related to the Oja–Hebb rule is a special matrix of synaptic weights called *Karhunen–Loeve covariance matrix* $\mathbf{W}$ (KL), with entries

$$W_{ij} = \frac{1}{N}\omega_i^\mu\,\omega_j^\mu, \qquad \text{(summing over } \mu\text{)}$$

where N is the number of vectors, and ω_i^μ is the ith component of the μth vector. The KL matrix extracts the principal components, or directions of maximum information (correlation) from a dataset.

In general, continuous ANNs are *temporal dynamical systems*. They have two coupled dynamics: activation and learning. First, a general system of coupled ODEs for the output of the ith *processing element* (PE) x^i, called the *activation dynamics*, can be written as

$$\dot{x}^i = g_i(x^i, \underset{i}{\text{net}}), \tag{11.10}$$

with the *net input* to the ith PE x^i given by $\text{net}_i = \omega_{ij}x^j$.

For example,

$$\dot{x}^i = -x^i + f_i(\underset{i}{\text{net}}),$$

where f_i is called *output*, or *activation, function*. We apply some input values to the PE so that $\text{net}_i > 0$. If the inputs remain for a sufficiently long time, the output value will reach an equilibrium value, when $\dot{x}^i = 0$, given by $x^i = f_i(\text{net}_i)$. Once the unit has a nonzero output value, removal of the inputs will cause the output to return to zero. If $\text{net}_i = 0$, then $\dot{x}^i = -x^i$, which means that $x \to 0$.

Second, a general system of coupled ODEs for the *update* of the synaptic weights ω_{ij}, i.e, *learning dynamics*, can be written as a generalization of the Oja–Hebb rule, i.e.,

$$\dot{\omega}_{ij} = G_i(\omega_{ij}, x^i, x^i),$$

where G_i represents the *learning law*; the learning process consists of finding weights that encode the knowledge that we want the system to learn. For most realistic systems, it is not easy to determine a closed–form solution for this system of equations, so the approximative solutions are usually enough.

Standard Models of Continuous Nets

Hopfield Continuous Net

One of the first physically–based ANNs was developed by J. Hopfield. He first made a discrete, Ising–spin based network in [Hop82], and later generalized it to the continuous, graded–response network in [Hop84], which we briefly describe here. Later we will give full description of Hopfield models. Let $\text{net}_i = u_i$ — the net input to the ith PE, biologically representing the summed action potentials at the axon hillock of a neuron. The PE *output function* is

$$v_i = g_i(\lambda u_i) = \frac{1}{2}(1 + \tanh(\lambda u_i)),$$

where λ is a constant called the *gain parameter*. The network is described as a transient RC circuit

$$C_i \dot{u}_i = T_{ij} v_j - \frac{u_i}{R_i} + I_i, \qquad (11.11)$$

where I_i, R_i and C_i are inputs (currents), resistances and capacitances, and T_{ij} are synaptic weights.

The Hamiltonian energy function corresponding to (11.11) is given as

$$H = -\frac{1}{2} T_{ij} v_i v_j + \frac{1}{\lambda} \frac{1}{R_i} \int_0^{v_i} g_i^{-1}(v)\, dv - I_i v_i, \qquad (j \neq i) \qquad (11.12)$$

which is a generalization of a discrete, *Ising–spin Hopfield network* with energy function

$$E = -\frac{1}{2} \omega_{ij} x^i x^j, \qquad (j \neq i).$$

where $g_i^{-1}(v) = u$ is the inverse of the function $v = g(u)$. To show that (11.12) is an appropriate *Lyapunov function* for the system, we shall take its time derivative assuming T_{ij} are symmetric:

$$\dot{H} = -\dot{v}_i(T_{ij} v_j - \frac{u_i}{R_i} + I_i) = -C_i \dot{v}_i \dot{u}_i = -C_i \dot{v}_i^2 \frac{\partial g_i^{-1}(v_i)}{\partial v_i}. \qquad (11.13)$$

All the factors in the summation (11.13) are positive, so $\dot{H}$ must decrease as the system evolves, until it eventually reaches the stable configuration, where $\dot{H} = \dot{v}_i = 0$. For further development on Hopfield nets, see section 11.1.6 below.

Hecht–Nielsen Counterpropagation Net

Hecht–Nielsen counterpropagation network (CPN) is a full–connectivity, graded–response generalization of the standard BP algorithm (see [NC02, Hec90]).
The outputs of the PEs in CPN are governed by the set of ODEs

$$\dot{x}^i = -Ax_i + (B - x^i)I_i - x^i \sum_{j \neq i} I_j,$$

where $0 < x^i(0) < B$, and $A, B > 0$. Each PE receives a net excitation (on–
center) of $(B - x^i)I_i$ from its corresponding input value, I. The addition of
inhibitory connections (off–surround), $-x^i I_j$, from other units is responsible
for preventing the activity of the processing element from rising in proportion
to the absolute pattern intensity, I_i. Once an input pattern is applied, the
PEs quickly reach an equilibrium state ($\dot{x}^i = 0$) with

$$x^i = \Theta_i \frac{BI_i}{A + I_i},$$

with the normalized *reflectance pattern* $\Theta_i = I_i \left(\sum_i I_i \right)^{-1}$, such that
$\sum_i \Theta_i = 1$.

Competitive Net

Activation dynamics is governed by the ODEs

$$\dot{x}^i = -Ax_i + (B - x^i)[f(x^i) + \underset{i}{\text{net}}] - x^i \left[\sum_{j \neq i} f(x_j) + \sum_{j \neq i} \text{net}_j \right],$$

where $A, B > 0$ and $f(x^i)$ is an output function.

Kohonen's Continuous SOM and Adaptive Robotics Control

Kohonen continuous self organizing map (SOM) is actually the original Kohonen model of the biological neural process (see [Koh88]). SOM activation
dynamics is governed by

$$\dot{x}^i = -r_i(x^i) + \underset{i}{\text{net}} + z_{ij}x_j, \tag{11.14}$$

where the function $r_i(x^i)$ is a general form of a loss term, while the final term
models the lateral interactions between units (the sum extends over all units
in the system). If z_{ij} takes the form of the Mexican–hat function, then the
network will exhibit a bubble of activity around the unit with the largest value
of net input.

   SOM learning dynamics is governed by

$$\dot{\omega}_{ij} = \alpha(t)(I_i - \omega_{ij})U(x^i),$$

where $\alpha(t)$ is the learning momentum, while the function $U(x^i) = 0$ unless $x^i > 0$ in which case $U(x^i) = 1$, ensuring that only those units with positive activity participate in the learning process.

Kohonen's continuous SOM (11.14) is widely used in adaptive robotics control. Having an n–segment robot arm with n chained $SO(2)$– joints, for a particular initial position x and desired velocity $\dot{x}^j_{desir}$ of the end–effector, the required torques T_i in the joints can be found as

$$T_i = a_{ij}\,\dot{x}^j_{desir},$$

where the inertia matrix $a_{ij} = a_{ij}(x)$ is learned using SOM.

11.1.4 Recurrent Neural Nets (RNNs)

Time–Lagged Recurrent Nets

The *time–lagged recurrent networks* (TLRNs) are MLPs extended with short term memory structures [Wer89]. Most real–world data contains information in its time structure, i.e., how the data changes with time. Yet, most neural networks are purely static classifiers. TLRNs are the state of the art in nonlinear time series prediction, system identification and temporal pattern classification. Time–lagged recurrent nets usually use memory Axons, consisting of IIR filters with local adaptable feedback that act as a variable memory depth. The time–delay neural network (TDNN) can be considered a special case of these networks, examples of which include the Gamma and Laguerre structures. The Laguerre axon uses locally recurrent all–pass IIR filters to store the recent past. They have a single adaptable parameter that controls the memory depth. Notice that in addition to providing memory for the input, we have also used a Laguerre axon after the hidden Tanh axon. This further increases the overall memory depth by providing memory for that layer's recent activations.

Fully Recurrent ANNs

The *fully recurrent networks* feed back the hidden layer to itself. Partially recurrent networks start with a fully recurrent net and add a feedforward connection that bypasses the recurrency, effectively treating the recurrent part as a state memory. These recurrent networks can have an infinite memory depth and thus find relationships through time as well as through the instantaneous input space. Most real–world data contains information in its time structure. Recurrent networks are the state of the art in nonlinear time series prediction, system identification, and temporal pattern classification. In case of large number of neurons, here the firing states of the neurons or their membrane potentials are the microscopic stochastic dynamical variables, and one is mostly interested in quantities such as average state correlations and global information processing quality, which are indeed measured by macroscopic observables. In contrast to layered networks, one cannot simply write down the values of successive neuron states for models of recurrent ANNs; here they must be solved from (mostly stochastic) coupled dynamic equations. For nonsymmetric networks, where the asymptotic (stationary) statistics are not known, dynamical techniques from non–equilibrium statistical mechanics are the only tools available for analysis. The natural set of macroscopic quantities (or order parameters) to be calculated can be defined in practice as the smallest set which will obey closed deterministic equations in the limit of an infinitely large network.

Being high–dimensional nonlinear systems with extensive feedback, the dynamics of recurrent ANNs are generally dominated by a wealth of attractors (fixed–point attractors, limit–cycles, or even more exotic types), and the practical use of recurrent ANNs (in both biology and engineering) lies in the potential for creation and manipulation of these attractors through adaptation of the network parameters (synapses and thresholds) (see [Hop82, Hop84]). Input fed into a recurrent ANN usually serves to induce a specific initial configuration (or firing pattern) of the neurons, which serves as a cue, and the output is given by the (static or dynamic) attractor which has been triggered by this cue. The most familiar types of recurrent ANN models, where the idea of creating and manipulating attractors has been worked out and applied explicitly, are the so-called attractor, associative memory ANNs, designed to store and retrieve information in the form of neuronal firing patterns and/or sequences of neuronal firing patterns. Each pattern to be stored is represented as a microscopic state vector. One then constructs synapses and thresholds such that the dominant attractors of the network are precisely the pattern vectors (in the case of static recall), or where, alternatively, they are trajectories in which the patterns are successively generated microscopic system states. From an initial configuration (the cue, or input pattern to be recognized) the system is allowed to evolve in time autonomously, and the final state (or trajectory) reached can be interpreted as the pattern (or pattern sequence) recognized by network from the input. For such programmes to work one clearly needs recurrent ANNs with extensive ergodicity breaking: the state vector will during the course of the dynamics (at least on finite time–scales) have to be confined to a restricted region of state–space (an ergodic component), the location of which is to depend strongly on the initial conditions. Hence our interest will mainly be in systems with many attractors. This, in turn, has implications at a theoretical/mathematical level: solving models of recurrent ANNs with extensively many attractors requires advanced tools from disordered systems theory, such as replica theory (i.e., statics) and generating functional analysis (i.e., dynamics).

Dynamical Games and Recurrent ANNs

IPD Games

Recall that *Prisoners' Dilemma* (PD) *game*[3] gets its name from the scenario where two people are arrested for some crime and are questioned separately. Each is given the opportunity to either cooperate with his/her accomplice and not give any information to the police, or defect against his/her partner by ratting to the police in exchange for some kind of immunity. The PD game is constructed to mimic this situation by providing payoffs to the players based on how they both respond. A typical payoff is to give 3 points to each if they both cooperate (police have no case against criminals and can only get them for a very light crime). If one cooperates, and the other defects, the defector gets 5 points, while his partner receives none. If both players defect, they each only receive 1 point (police get them for a moderate crime, but not as severe as if only one person had taken the blame). The total payoff to both players is greatest for mutual cooperation (6 points), while a cooperate–defect play results in 5 points, and mutual defection only hands out 2 points. So, clearly, it is best for the collective system if all players cooperate, but here is the interesting paradox. Each player individually is better off by defecting in any given situation. If your partner cooperates, you can get 3 points by cooperating back, but you can get 5 by defecting. Similarly, if your partner defects, you get nothing if you cooperate, but you can still salvage 1 point by defecting back.

The extension of the PD game to permit repeated PD game play between players is known as the *Iterated Prisoner's Dilemma* (IPD) game. In 1979, R. Axelrod hosted a tournament at the University of Michigan to see what

---

[3] Recall that *game theory*, first formulated by John von Neumann and Oskar Morgenstern first formalized the subject in 1944 [NM44] is a branch of applied mathematics that uses models to study interactions with formalized incentive structures ('games'). It has applications in a variety of fields, including economics, international relations, evolutionary biology, political science, and military strategy. Game theorists study the predicted and actual behavior of individuals in games, as well as optimal strategies. Seemingly different types of interactions can exhibit similar incentive structures, thus all exemplifying one particular game. The Prisoner's Dilemma game, as popularized by mathematician A. Tucker, furnishes an example of the application of game theory to real life; it has many implications for the nature of human co–operation. Another important concept in game theory is the *Nash equilibrium*, formulated by *Nobel Laureate John Nash* in his dissertation on Non–Cooperative Games in 1950. Nash showed that the various solutions for games that had been given earlier all yield Nash equilibria. For example, the Prisoner's dilemma has one Nash equilibrium: when both players defect. However, 'both defect' is inferior to 'both cooperate', in the sense that the total jail time served by the two prisoners is greater if both defect. The strategy 'both cooperate' is unstable, as a player could do better by defecting while their opponent still cooperates. Thus, 'both cooperate' is not an equilibrium.

kinds of strategies would perform best over the long haul in the IPD game [Axe76]. Various game theorists were solicited for IPD strategies in the form of computer algorithms, and the submitted strategies were then pitted against each other in repeated round–robin PD game play. The strategy that received the highest total payoff from this repeated PD game play was declared the winner of the tournament.

Recurrent ANN Model for a Two–Player IPD Game

A two–player IPD game was modeled using a *recurrent ANN* in [TI99]. The authors created two *internal models* of game players. The first one was 'pure reductionist Bob', who made the opponent's model by a recurrent ANN. He thought that the opponent might behave with simple algorithms like finite automata, which could be expressed by the recurrent nets. The second one was 'clever Alice', who assumed that the opponent behaved like 'pure reductionist Bob'. She knew that the opponent made her model by recurrent nets and she decided the next action based on that model of herself. In other words, she builded the internal model of herself and treated that model as her image in the opponent.

Building the model of a player's behavior may involve many methods such as finite automata, Markov chain, etc. In [TI99] the authors used *dynamical recognizers*, simple and powerful tools for studying dynamical behavior from the view points of cognitive studies. Dynamical recognizers were first discussed by Pollack [Pol91], who showed that some automata could be learned very well by dynamical recognizers. When it could not learn automata, fractal–like patterns were generated in context spaces.

The so-called *cascaded recurrent ANN* consists of a function and a context net [Pol91]. It is quite similar to a two–layer linear perceptron, though the recurrent outputs are feedbacked not to the input nodes but to the weights of the function network. The recurrent outputs memorize the opponent's current status, and the context network converts the recurrent outputs to the weights of the function network which predicts the next action. The space constructed by the outputs from the function network (including both recurrent and network outputs) was called the *context space*. The output was taken from a node of the function network. In [TI99], only one input and one output node were necessary since the IPD game had only two actions, cooperation and defection. The authors defined cooperation as 0 and defection as 1 in the network. The output was rounded off to 0 (cooperation) and 1 (defection). The network is described by the following equations,

$$z_i(n) = g(w_i y(n) + w_i^0), \quad w_i = u_{ij} z_j(n-1) + u_i^b, \quad w_i^0 = u_{ij}^0 z_j(n-1) + u_i^{0b},$$

where symbols have the following meanings: $g(x) = (e^{-x}+1)^{-1}$ is the sigmoid function, $y(n)$ is the input, $z_0(n)$ is the output, $z_i(n)$, $(i = 1 \cdots N)$ are the recurrent outputs, w_i is the weight of function network, w_i^0 is the bias of function network, u_{ij}, u_{ij}^0 is the weight of context network and u_i^b, u_i^{0b} is the bias of context network.

This recurrent ANN was trained by a form of the back–propagation method. In the game, the player knew only his or her own past actions and those of the opponent. In the case of 'pure reductionist Bob', the model of the opponent was built by the recurrent ANN. This means that the recurrent ANN takes the player's last action as an input and outputs the opponent's next action. Thus, the target for training is a series of the opponent's action when the inputs are the player's actions. However, since the number of training targets becomes too large as a game proceeds, the weights for learning are varied for each action so that far actions in the distant past are forgotten. Thus, the error $E(n)$ after the nth game is

$$E(n) = \sum_{k=1}^{n} \lambda^{n-k} (z_0(k) - d(k))^2,$$

where $d(k)$ is a target (i.e., the actual opponent's action in the kth game), $z_0(k)$ is the predicted action by the recurrent ANN, and λ (= 0.9 for most simulations) is a parameter which controls the memory retention of the past actions.

To determine the player's next action, the authors of [TI99] used the prediction of the opponent's future action based on the recurrent ANN. First, the algorithm for pure reductionist Bob was explained. Bob chose his forward actions up to M games. Then, he could predict the opponent's actions from his forward actions, and the expected score could be evaluated. The process was repeated for all possible strings of actions of length M and Bob chose the action with the highest score as the best action.

Clever Alice considered the opponent was a pure reductionist Bob, so she chose her forward M actions. She predicted the opponent's actions assuming that he behaved like pure reductionist Bob. Again the process was repeated for all strings of the length M and she chose the action string with the highest score as the best one. In other words, she predicted her image in the other person and tried to educate him to have a favorable image through her actions.

11.1.5 Grossberg's Adaptive Resonance Theory

Principles derived from an analysis of experimental literatures in vision, speech, cortical development, and reinforcement learning, including attentional blocking and cognitive–emotional interactions, led to the introduction of S. Grossberg's *adaptive resonance theory* (ART) as a theory of human *cognitive information processing* (see [CG03]). The theory has evolved as a series of real–time neural network models that perform unsupervised and supervised learning, pattern recognition, and prediction. Models of unsupervised learning include ART1, for binary input patterns, and fuzzy–ART and ART2, for analog input patterns [Gro82, CG03]. ARTMAP models combine two un-supervised modules to carry out supervised learning. Many variations of the basic supervised and unsupervised networks have since been adapted for tech-nological applications and biological analyzes.

A central feature of all ART systems is a *pattern matching process* that compares an external input with the internal memory of an active code. ART matching leads either to a resonant state, which persists long enough to permit learning, or to a parallel memory search. If the search ends at an established code, the memory representation may either remain the same or incorporate new information from matched portions of the current input. If the search ends at a new code, the memory representation learns the current input. This match–based learning process is the foundation of ART *code stability*. Match–based learning allows memories to change only when input from the external world is close enough to internal expectations, or when something completely new occurs. This feature makes ART systems well suited to problems that require on–line learning of large and evolving databases (see [CG03]).

Many ART applications use fast learning, whereby adaptive weights con-verge to equilibrium in response to each input pattern. Fast learning enables a system to adapt quickly to inputs that occur rarely but that may require im-mediate accurate recall. Remembering details of an exciting movie is a typical example of learning on one trial. Fast learning creates memories that depend upon the order of input presentation. Many ART applications exploit this feature to improve accuracy by voting across several trained networks, with voters providing a measure of confidence in each prediction.

The so-called is complementary to *error–based learning*, which responds to a mismatch by changing memories so as to reduce the difference between a tar-get output and an actual output, rather than by searching for a better match. Error–based learning is naturally suited to problems such as adaptive control and the learning of *sensory–motor maps*, which require ongoing adaptation to present statistics. Neural networks that employ error–based learning include backpropagation and other multilayer perceptrons (MLPs).

Activation dynamics of ART2 is governed by the ODEs [Gro82, CG03]

$$\epsilon \dot{x}_i = -Ax_i + (1 - Bx_i)I_i^+ - (C + Dx_i)I_i^-,$$

where ϵ is the 'small parameter', I_i^+ and I_i^- are excitatory and inhibitory inputs to the ith unit, respectively, and $A, B, C, D > 0$ are parameters.

General *Cohen–Grossberg activation equations* have the form:

$$\dot{v}_j = -a_j(v_j)[b_j(v_j) - f_k(v_k)m_{jk}], \qquad (j = 1, ..., N), \qquad (11.15)$$

and the *Cohen–Grossberg theorem* ensures the global stability of the system (11.15). If

$$a_j = 1/C_j, b_j = v_j/R_j - I_j, f_j(v_j) = u_j,$$

and constant $m_{ij} = m_{ji} = T_{ji}$, the system (11.15) reduces to the Hopfield circuit model (11.11).

ART and distributed ART (dART) systems are part of a growing family of self–organizing network models that feature attentional feedback and stable code learning. Areas of technological application include industrial design and manufacturing, the control of mobile robots, face recognition, remote sensing land cover classification, target recognition, medical diagnosis, electrocardiogram analysis, signature verification, tool failure monitoring, chemical analysis, circuit design, protein/DNA analysis, 3D visual object recognition, musical analysis, and seismic, sonar, and radar recognition. ART principles have further helped explain parametric behavioral and brain data in the areas of visual perception, object recognition, auditory source identification, variable–rate speech and word recognition, and *adaptive sensory–motor control* (see [CG03]).

Spatiotemporal Networks

In *spatiotemporal networks*, activation dynamics is governed by the ODEs

$$\dot{x}^i = A(-ax_i + b[I_i - \Gamma]^+),$$
$$\dot{\Gamma} = \alpha(S - T) + \beta \dot{S}, \quad \text{with}$$

$$[u]^+ = \begin{cases} u & \text{if} \quad u > 0 \\ 0 & \text{if} \quad u \le 0 \end{cases},$$

$$A(u) = \begin{cases} u & \text{if} \quad u > 0 \\ cu & \text{if} \quad u \le 0 \end{cases}.$$

where $a, b, \alpha, \beta > 0$ are parameters, $T > 0$ is the *power–level target*, $S = \sum_i x^i$, and $A(u)$ is called the *attack function*.

Learning dynamics is given by *differential Hebbian law*

$$\dot{\omega}_{ij} = (-c\omega_{ij} + dx_i x_j)U(\dot{x}^i)U(-\dot{x}_j), \quad \text{with}$$

$$U(s) = \begin{cases} 1 & \text{if} \quad s > 0 \\ 0 & \text{if} \quad s \le 0 \end{cases} \quad \text{where } c, d > 0 \text{ are constants.}$$

11.1.6 Hopfield's Associative RNNs

Ising–Spin Neurons

The paradigm for the unsupervised, self–organizing, associative, and recurrent ANN is the discrete Hopfield network (see [Hop82]). Hopfield gives a collection of simple threshold automata, called *formal neurons* by McCulloch and Pitts (see [Hay94]): two–state, 'all–or–none', firing or non–firing units that can be modeled by *Ising spins* (uniaxial magnets) $\{S_i\}$ such that $S_i = \pm 1$ (where $1 = |\uparrow\rangle = $ 'spin up' and $-1 = |\downarrow\rangle = $ 'spin down'; the label of the neuron is i and ranges between 1 and the size of the network N). The neurons are connected by synapses J_{ij}.

Firing *patterns* $\{\xi_i^\mu\}$ represent specific S_i-spin *configurations*, where the label of the pattern is μ and ranges between 1 and q.

Using random patterns $\xi_i^\mu = \pm 1$ with equal probability $1/2$, we have the *synaptic efficacy* J_{ij} of jth neuron operating on ith neuron given by

$$J_{ij} = N^{-1}\xi_i^\mu\xi_j^\mu \equiv N^{-1}\boldsymbol{\xi_i} \cdot \boldsymbol{\xi_j}. \tag{11.16}$$

Postsynaptic potential (PSP) represents an *internal local field*

$$h_i(t) = J_{ij}S_j(t). \tag{11.17}$$

Now, the *sequential (threshold) dynamics* is defined in the form of discrete equation

$$S_i(t + \Delta t) = \text{sgn}[h_i(t)]. \tag{11.18}$$

Dynamics (11.18) is equivalent to the rule that the state of a neuron is changed, or a spin is flipped iff the total network *energy*, given by *Ising Hamiltonian*

$$H_N = -\frac{1}{2}J_{ij}S_iS_j, \tag{11.19}$$

is lowered [Hop82, HT85]. Therefore, the Ising Hamiltonian H_N represents the monotonically decreasing *Lyapunov function* for the sequential dynamics (11.18), which converges to a local minimum or ground state of H_N. This holds for any *symmetric coupling* $J_{ij} = J_{ji}$ with $J_{ii} = 0$ and if spin–updating in (11.18) is asynchronous. In this case the patterns $\{\xi_i^\mu\}$ after convergence become identical, or very near to, ground states of H_N, each of them at the bottom of the valley.

Data are *stored* in the neural net if, by a suitable choice of the J_{ij}, several specific patterns $\{\xi_i^\mu\}$ are made local minima of H_N. If this can be achieved, the neural net will function as *content–addressable* or (auto)*associative memory*. A network state which 'somehow resembles' one of the stored prototypes corresponds to a location in the energy landscape which is close enough to the minimum representing that prototype to lie in its *basin of attraction*. By spontaneously moving downhill, or relaxing to the energy minimum, the network *recalls* the data or reconstructs the prototype.

Suppose that we have somehow stored several (stationary) patterns $\{\xi_i^\mu\}$ in the J_{ij} and that the system is offered a noisy version of one of them. If the noise was not too strong, the system remains in the valley associated with that pattern and under its natural dynamics it will relax to the energy minimum were the stored patterns live. That is, the system has recalled the pattern.

In statistical mechanics, one is usually given the synapses J_{ij} and one of the first tasks consists in finding the minima of the Ising Hamiltonian H_N (11.19). In the theory of neural networks, however, one is given the patterns $\{\xi_i^\mu\}$ and one is asked to solve the *inverse problem*: finding synapses J_{ij} such that the patterns $\{\xi_i^\mu\}$ are minima of the Hamiltonian H_N.

To see why the Hopfield model with synapses given by (11.16) has patterns $\{\xi_i^\mu\}$ as *attractors* of the dynamics (11.18), note that the sequential dynamical law embodies a two–step process, the evolution of the local field (PSP) (11.17), which is a *linear* operation, and a *nonlinear* decision process (11.18).

Graded–Response Neurons

Graded–response neurons have continuous input–output relation (like nonlinear operational amplifiers) of the form $V_i = g_i(\lambda u_i)$, where u_i denotes the input at i, a constant λ is called the gain parameter, and V_i is the output [Hop84]. Usually, g_i are taken to be sigmoid functions, odd, and monotonically increasing (e.g., $g(\cdot) = \frac{1}{2}(1 + \tanh(\cdot))$), while discrete Ising spins have $g_i(u_i) = \text{sgn}_i(u_i)$. The behavior of the *continuous Hopfield network* is usually described by a set of coupled RC–transient equations

$$C_i \dot{u}_i = I_i + J_{ij} V_j - \frac{u_i}{R_i}, \tag{11.20}$$

where $u_i = g^{-1}(V_i)$, R_i and C_i denote input capacitance and resistance, and I_i represents an external source.

The Hamiltonian of the continuous system (11.20) is given by

$$H = -\frac{1}{2} J_{ij} V_i V_j + \sum_{i=1}^{N} R_i^{-1} \int_0^{V_i} dV g^{-1}(V) - I_i V_i. \tag{11.21}$$

However, according to Hopfield [Hop84] the synapses J_{ij} retain the form (11.16) with random patterns $\xi_i^\mu = \pm 1$ with equal probability $1/2$, and the synaptic symmetry $J_{ij} = J_{ji}$ implies that the continuous Hamiltonian (11.21) represents a *Lyapunov function* of the system (11.20), i.e., H decreases under the continual neuro–dynamics governed by equation (11.20) as time proceeds.

More general form of synapses is

$$J_{ij} = N^{-1} Q(\boldsymbol{\xi_i}; \boldsymbol{\xi_j}),$$

for some synaptic kernel Q on $\mathbb{R}'' \times \mathbb{R}''$. The vector $\boldsymbol{\xi_i}$ varies as i travels from 1 to N, but remains on a corner of the *Hamming hypercube* $[-1, 1]^q$.

Hopfield's Overlaps

Assuming that the number q of stored patterns is small compared to the number of neurons, i.e., $q/N \to 0$, we find that the synapses (11.16) give rise to a local field of the form

$$h_i = \xi_i^\mu m_\mu, \qquad \text{where} \tag{11.22}$$

$$m_\mu = N^{-1} \xi_i^\mu S_i \tag{11.23}$$

is the *auto–overlap* (or simply *overlap*)[4] of the network state $\{S_i\}$ with the pattern $\{\xi_i^\mu\}$, measuring the proximity between them. We can see that

---

[4] Resembling the auto–correlation function of a time–series, where distinct peaks indicate that the series at the certain time t is similar to the series at time $t + \Delta t$.

$m_\mu = 1$ (like peak–up in auto–correlation) if $\{S_i\}$ and $\{\xi_i^\mu\}$ are identical patterns, $m_\mu = -1$ (like peak–down in autocorrelation) if they are each other's complement, and $m_\mu = O(1/\sqrt{N})$ if they are uncorrelated (like no–peak in auto–correlation) with each other. Overlaps m_μ are related to the Hamming distance d_μ between the patterns (the fraction of spins which differ) by $d_\mu = \frac{1}{2}(1 - m_\mu)$.

As a pattern ξ_i^μ represents (in the simplest case) a specific Ising–spin S_i–configuration, then $(\xi_i^\mu)^2 = 1$. If $S_i = \xi_i^\mu$ for all i, then $m_\mu = 1$. Conversely, if $m_\mu = 1$, then $S_i = \xi_i^\mu$. In all other cases $m_\mu < 1$, by the Cauchy–Schwartz inequality. If ξ_i^μ and S_i are uncorrelated, we may expect m_μ to be of the order of $N^{-1/2}$, since the sum consists of N terms, each containing a ξ_i^μ. On the other hand, if the S_i are positively correlated with ξ_i^μ, then m_μ is of the order of unity. So the overlaps give the global information about the network and hence are good order parameters. Also, according to Hopfield [Hop84], the extension to the continual network is straightforward.

Using overlaps, the *Ising Hamiltonian* becomes

$$H_N = -\frac{1}{2}N \sum_{\mu=1}^{q} m_\mu^2 . \tag{11.24}$$

The similarity between two different patterns ξ_i^μ and ξ_i^ν is measured by their *mutual overlap* or *cross–overlap* $m_{\mu\nu}$ (in other parlance it is called *Karhunen–Loeve covariance matrix* (see [FS92]), which extracts the principal components from a data set),[5] equal

$$m_{\mu\nu} = N^{-1}\xi_i^\mu \xi_i^\nu . \tag{11.25}$$

For similar patterns the cross–overlap is close to unity whereas for uncorrelated patterns it is random variable with zero mean and small $(1/\sqrt{N})$ variance.

The symmetric *Hopfield synaptic matrix* J_{ij} can be expressed in terms of the cross–overlaps $m_{\mu\nu}$ as

$$J_{ij} = N^{-1}\xi_i^\mu (m_{\mu\nu})^{-1}\xi_j^\nu = J_{ji} , \tag{11.26}$$

where $(m_{\mu\nu})^{-1}$ denotes the *Moore–Penrose pseudoinverse* of the cross–overlap matrix $m_{\mu\nu}$.

Besides the Hopfield model, the proposed pattern–overlap picture can be extended to cover some more sophisticated kinds of associative memory, among them (see, e.g., [DHS91]):

1. Forgetful memories, characterized by iterative synaptic prescription

---

[5] Resembling the cross–correlation function of two time–series, with several distinct peaks, indicating that the two series are very similar at each point in time where the peaks occur.

$$J_{ij}^{(\mu)} = \phi(\epsilon \xi_i^\mu \xi_j^\mu + J_{ij}^{(\mu-1)}),$$

for some small parameter ϵ and some odd function ϕ. If $\phi(\cdot)$ saturates as $|\cdot| \to \infty$, the memory creates storage capacity for new patterns by forgetting the old ones.

2. Temporal associative memories, which can store and retrieve a sequence of patterns, through synapses

$$NJ_{ij} = \xi_i^\mu \xi_j^\mu + \epsilon \sum_{\mu=1}^q \xi_i^{(\mu+1)} \xi_j^\mu, \tag{11.27}$$

where the second term on the right is associated with a temporal delay, so that one can imagine that the second term 'pushes' the neural system through an energy landscape created by the first term.

Overlap Dynamics

According to Hopfield [Hop84], the extension of the sequential dynamics $S_i = \mathrm{sgn}(\sum_\mu m_\mu \xi_i^\mu)$ of the network made of the simplest Ising–spin–neurons to the network made of continual graded–response amplifier–neurons, is straightforward using the probabilistic *Glauber dynamics*

$$\mathrm{Prob}\{S_i \mapsto -S_i\} = \frac{1}{2}[1 - \tanh(\beta h_i S_i)], \qquad i = 1, \ldots, N, \tag{11.28}$$

where β represents the universal temperature ($\beta = \frac{1}{k_B T}$, k_B is the normalized Boltzmann's constant and $k_B T$ has dimension of energy).

Under the Glauber's dynamics (11.28), and as $N \to \infty$ (transition from the single neurons to the neural field), for time–dependent patterns $\xi^\mu(t) = \xi_\mu(t)$, vector auto–overlaps $m_\mu(t)$, and tensor cross–overlaps $m_{\mu\nu}(t)$, we present the dynamics of overlaps governed by the following nonlinear differential equations (generalized from [DHS91], pp. 23), respectively in the vector form

$$\dot{m}_\mu(t) = -m_\mu(t) + \langle \xi_\mu(t) \tanh[\beta m_\mu(t)\xi^\mu(t)] \rangle, \tag{11.29}$$

and in the tensor form

$$\dot{m}_{\mu\nu}(t) = -m_{\mu\nu}(t) + \langle \xi_\mu(t)\xi_\nu(t) \tanh[\beta m_{\mu\nu}(t)\xi^\mu(t)\xi^\nu(t)] \rangle, \tag{11.30}$$

where the angular brackets denote an average over the q patterns $\xi^\mu(t)$.

The stationary solutions (for any fixed instant of time $t = \tau$) of equations (11.29) and (11.30) are given by corresponding fixed–point vector and tensor equations

$$m_\mu = \langle \xi_\mu \tanh[\beta m_\mu \xi^\mu] \rangle, \qquad \text{and} \tag{11.31}$$

$$m_{\mu\nu} = \langle \xi_\mu \xi_\nu \tanh[\beta m_{\mu\nu} \xi^\mu \xi^\nu] \rangle, \tag{11.32}$$

respectively.

Hebbian Learning Dynamics

In terms of stochastic feed–forward multi–layer neural networks, the tensorial equation (11.30) corresponds to the average, general, self–organizing Hebbian neural learning scheme (see [Heb49, Kos92])

$$\dot{m}_{\mu\nu}(t) = -m_{\mu\nu}(t) + \langle \mathcal{I}_{\mu\nu} \rangle, \tag{11.33}$$

with random signal *Hebbian innovation*

$$\mathcal{I}_{\mu\nu} = f_\mu[\xi^\mu(t)] f_\nu[\xi^\nu(t)] + \sigma_{\mu\nu}(t), \tag{11.34}$$

where $\sigma_{\mu\nu}$, denotes the tensorial, additive, zero–mean, Gaussian white–noise, independent of the main innovation function $I_{\mu\nu}$, while $f_{\mu,\nu}[\cdot]$ represent the hyperbolic tangent (sigmoid) neural activation functions. A single–layer Hebbian learning scheme, corresponding to the tensor equation (11.33), gives

$$\dot{m}_\mu(t) = -m_\mu(t) + \langle \mathcal{I}_\mu \rangle, \tag{11.35}$$

with the vector innovation

$$\mathcal{I}_\mu = f_\mu[\xi^\mu(t)] + \sigma_\mu(t),$$

where σ_μ, denotes the vector additive zero–mean Gaussian white–noise, also independent of the main innovation function I_μ, while $f_\mu[\cdot]$ represents the hyperbolic tangent (sigmoid) neural activation function.

If we assume the small absolute value of the average (stochastic) terms, the nonlinear overlap–dynamics equations (11.29) and (11.30) can be presented in the form of *weakly–connected neural networks* (see [HI97]), respectively, as a single–layer network

$$\dot{m}_\mu(t) = -m_\mu(t) + \varepsilon g_\mu(m_\mu, \varepsilon), \qquad \varepsilon \ll 1, \tag{11.36}$$

and a multi–layer network

$$\dot{m}_{\mu\nu}(t) = -m_{\mu\nu}(t) + \varepsilon g_{\mu\nu}(m_{\mu\nu}, \varepsilon), \qquad \varepsilon \ll 1, \tag{11.37}$$

where, g_μ and $g_{\mu\nu}$, corresponding to the average (bracket) terms in (11.29) and (11.30), describe (vector and tensor, respectively) synaptic connections and the 'small' parameter ε describes their (dimensionless) strength. These weakly–connected neural systems represent ε–perturbations of the corresponding linear systems

$$\dot{m}_\mu(t) = -m_\mu(t) \qquad \text{and} \qquad \dot{m}_{\mu\nu}(t) = -m_{\mu\nu}(t),$$

with exponential maps as solutions

$$m_\mu(t) = m_\mu \, e^{-t} \qquad \text{and} \qquad m_{\mu\nu}(t) = m_{\mu\nu} \, e^{-t},$$

using the stationary (fixed–point) solutions (11.31), (11.32) as initial conditions m_μ and $m_{\mu\nu}$. According to the *Hartman–Grobman theorem* from dynamical systems theory, the weakly–connected systems (11.36), (11.37) are topologically equivalent (homeomorphic) to the corresponding linear systems. Therefore the whole analysis for the linear vector and matrix flows can be applied here, with only difference that instead of increasing transients e^t here we have decreasing (i.e., asymptotically–stable) transients e^{-t}.

On the other hand, in terms of *synergetics* [Hak83], both nonlinear overlap–dynamics equations (11.29)–(11.30) and Hebbian learning equations (11.33)–(11.34), represent (covariant) *order parameter equations*.

By introducing the scalar quadratic potential fields, dependent on vector and tensor order parameters (overlaps), respectively

$$V(m_\mu) = -\frac{1}{2} \sum_{\mu=1}^{q} m_\mu^2 \quad \text{and} \quad V(m_{\mu\nu}) = -\frac{1}{2} m_{\mu\nu}^2,$$

we can generalize the overlap–dynamics equations (11.29)–(11.30) to the *stochastic–gradient order parameter equations*, in vector and tensor form, respectively

$$\dot{m}_\mu(t) = -\frac{\partial V(m_\mu)}{\partial m_\mu(t)} + F_\mu(t), \tag{11.38}$$

and

$$\dot{m}_{\mu\nu}(t) = -\frac{\partial V(m_{\mu\nu})}{\partial m_{\mu\nu}(t)} + F_{\mu\nu}(t). \tag{11.39}$$

$F_\mu(t)$ in (11.38) represents a vector fluctuating force, with average (over the stochastic process which produces the fluctuating force $F_\mu(t)$)

$$\langle F_\mu(t) \rangle = \langle \xi_\mu(t) \tanh[\beta m_\mu(t) \xi^\mu(t)] \rangle,$$

and variation

$$\langle F_\mu(t) F_\mu(t') \rangle = Q_\mu \delta(t - t'), \tag{11.40}$$

while $F_{\mu\nu}(t)$ in (11.39) represents a tensor fluctuating force, with average (over the stochastic process which produces the fluctuating force $F_{\mu\nu}(t)$)

$$\langle F_{\mu\nu}(t) \rangle = \langle \xi_\mu(t) \xi_\nu(t) \tanh[\beta m_{\mu\nu}(t) \xi^\mu(t) \xi^\nu(t)] \rangle,$$

and variation

$$\langle F_{\mu\nu}(t) F_{\mu\nu}(t') \rangle = Q_{\mu\nu} \delta(t - t'). \tag{11.41}$$

Coefficients Q_μ in (11.40) and $Q_{\mu\nu}$ in (11.41) represent strengths of the corresponding stochastic processes, while Dirac δ–functions $\delta(t - t')$ express their short–term memories.

Recall that standard interpretation of synergetics (see [Hak83]) describes the stochastic gradient systems (11.38)–(11.39) as the overdamped motion of (vector and tensor, respectively) representative particles in scalar potential fields $V(m_\mu)$ and $V(m_{\mu\nu})$, subject to fluctuating forces $F_\mu(t)$ and $F_{\mu\nu}(t)$.

These particles undergo *non–equilibrium phase transitions* (in the similar way as the magnet undergoes transition from its unmagnetized state into a magnetized state, or a superconductor goes from its normal state into the superconducting state, only occurring now in systems far from thermal equilibrium), and associated phenomena, including a *symmetry breaking instability* and *critical slowing down* (see [Hak83]).

The non–equilibrium phase transitions of vector and tensor order parameters (overlaps) $m_\mu(t)$ and $m_{\mu\nu}(t)$, are in synergetics described in terms of probability distributions $p(m_\mu, t)$ and $p(m_{\mu\nu}, t)$, respectively, defined by corresponding *Fokker–Planck equations*

$$\dot{p}(m_\mu, t) = p(m_\mu, t) + \frac{1}{2} Q_\mu \frac{\partial^2 p(m_\mu, t)}{\partial m_\mu^2},$$

and

$$\dot{p}(m_{\mu\nu}, t) = p(m_{\mu\nu}, t) + \frac{1}{2} Q_{\mu\nu} \frac{\partial^2 p(m_{\mu\nu}, t)}{\partial m_{\mu\nu}^2}.$$

11.1.7 Kosko's Bidirectional Competitive RNNs

Hopfield recurrent associative memory network can be generalized to get a *bidirectional associative memory* network, the so-called BAM model of Kosko [Kos92]. Here we derive an alternative self–organizing neural net model with competitive *Lotka-Volterra ensemble dynamics*[6] (see [Vol31, II06a]).

We start from $(n + m)$D linear ODEs, describing two competitive neural ensembles participating in a two–party game,

$$\dot{R}^i = -\alpha_B^j B_j, \qquad R^i(0) = R_0^i, \tag{11.44}$$

$$\dot{B}_j = -\beta_i^R R^i, \qquad B_j(0) = B_j^0, \qquad (i = 1, \ldots, n; \; j = 1, \ldots, m),$$

where $R^i = R^i(t)$ and $B_j = B_j(t)$ respectively represent the numerical strengths of the two neural ensembles at time t, R_0^i, B_j^0 are their initial conditions, and α_B and β^R represent the effective spiking rates (which are either constant, or Poisson random process). In this way, we generate a $(n + m)$D smooth manifold M, a *neural state–space*, and two dynamical objects acting

---

[6] The competitive Lotka-Volterra equations are a simple model of the population dynamics of two species competing for some common resource. It is the pair of coupled logistic ODEs for two competing populations with sizes x_1, x_2,

$$\dot{x}_1 = r_1 x_1 \left(\frac{K_1 - x_1 - \alpha_{12} x_2}{K_1} \right) \tag{11.42}$$

$$\dot{x}_2 = r_2 x_2 \left(\frac{K_2 - x_2 - \alpha_{21} x_1}{K_2} \right), \tag{11.43}$$

where $r_{1,2}$ are their growth rates, $K_{1,2}$ are their respective carrying capacities, while $\alpha_{1,2}, \alpha_{2,1}$ are the mutual (coupling) effects of one species onto another.

on it: an nD smooth *vector–field* $\dot{R}^i$, and an mD differential $1-form$ $\dot{B}_j$. Their dot product $\dot{R}^i \cdot \dot{B}_j$, represents a hypothetical *neural outcome*. This is a linear system, with the passive–decay couplings $\alpha_B^j B_j$ and $\beta_i^R R^i$, fully predictable but giving only equilibrium solutions.

Secondly, to incorporate competitive dynamics of Lotka–Volterra style as commonly used in ecological modeling and known to produce a global chaotic attractor (see [Wik16a] and references therein), we include to each of the neural ensembles a nonlinear competing term depending only on its own units,

$$\dot{R}^i = a^i R^i (1 - b^i R^i) - \alpha_B^j B_j, \tag{11.45}$$
$$\dot{B}_j = c_j B_j (1 - d_j B_j) - \beta_i^R R^i.$$

Now we have a *competition between the two chaotic attractors*, one for the R^i and one for the B_j ensemble, i.e., the two self–organization patterns emerging far–from–equilibrium.

Thirdly, to make this even more realistic, we include the ever–present *noise* in the form of Langevin–type random forces $F^i = F^i(t)$, and $G_j = G_j(t)$, thus adding the 'neural heating', i.e., noise induced entropy growth, to the competitive dynamics

$$\dot{R}^i = a^i R^i (1 - b^i R^i) - \alpha_B^j B_j + F^i, \tag{11.46}$$
$$\dot{B}_j = c_j B_j (1 - d_j B_j) - \beta_i^R R^i + G_j.$$

Finally, to overcome the deterministic chaos and stochastic noise with an adaptive *brain–like dynamics*, we introduce the *field competition potential* V, in the scalar form

$$V = -\tfrac{1}{2}(\omega_i^j R^i B_j + \varepsilon_i^j B_j R^i), \tag{11.47}$$

where ω_i^j and ε_i^j represent *synaptic associative–memory* matrices for the R^i and B_j ensemble, respectively. From the negative potential V, we get a *Lyapunov–stable gradient system* $\dot{R}^i = -\frac{\partial V}{\partial B_j}$, $\dot{B}_j = -\frac{\partial V}{\partial R^i}$. This robust system, together with the *sigmoidal activation functions* $S(\cdot) = \tanh(\cdot)$, and *control inputs* $u_{OLN}^i = u_{OLN}^i(t)$ and $v_j^{OLN} = v_j^{OLN}(t)$, we incorporate into (11.46) to get the *full neural competitive–associative dynamics* (see [II07a])

$$\dot{R}^i = u_{OLN}^i - \alpha_B^j B_j + a^i R^i (1 - b^i R^i) + \omega_i^j S_j(B_j) + F^i, \tag{11.48}$$
$$\dot{B}_j = v_j^{OLN} - \beta_i^R R^i + c_j B_j (1 - d_j B_j) + \varepsilon_i^j S^i(R^i) + G_j,$$
$$\text{with initial conditions}$$
$$R^i(0) = R_0^i, \qquad B_j(0) = B_j^0.$$

Now, each ensemble learns by trial–and–error from the opposite side. In a standard ANN–fashion, we model this learning on the spot by initially setting the random values to the synaptic matrices ω_i^j and ε_i^j, and subsequently adjust

these values using the standard *Hebbian learning scheme*:
New Value = Old Value + Innovation. In our case it reads:

$$\dot{\omega}_i^j = -\omega_i^j + \Phi_i^j(R^i, B_j), \qquad (11.49)$$
$$\dot{\varepsilon}_i^j = -\varepsilon_i^j + \Psi_i^j(B_j, R^i),$$

with *innovation* given in tensor signal form (generalized from [Kos92])

$$\Phi_i^j = S_j(R^i)\, S_j(B_j) + \dot{S}_j(R^i)\, \dot{S}_j(B_j), \qquad (11.50)$$
$$\Psi_i^j = S^i(R^i)\, S^i(B_j) + \dot{S}^i(R^i)\, \dot{S}^i(B_j),$$

where terms with overdots, equal $\dot{S}(\cdot) = 1 - \tanh(\cdot)$, denote the *signal velocities*.

11.1.8 Support Vector Machines (SVMs)

Recall that *support vector machines* (SVMs) are a set of related *supervised learning* methods used for *classification* and *regression* (see [Vap95, Vap98, SS01, CS00]). Their common factor is the use of a technique known as the '*kernel trick*' to apply *linear classification* techniques to *nonlinear classification* problems.

Linear Classification Problem

Suppose we want to classify some data points into two classes. Often we are interested in classifying data as part of a machine–learning process. These data points may not necessarily be points in $\mathbb{R}^2$ but may be multidimensional $\mathbb{R}^p$ (statistics notation) or $\mathbb{R}^n$ (computer science notation) points. We are interested in whether we can separate them by a *hyperplane*. As we examine a hyperplane, this form of classification is known as linear classification. We also want to choose a hyperplane that separates the data points 'neatly', with maximum distance to the closest data point from both classes — this distance is called the *margin*. We desire this property since if we add another data point to the points we already have, we can more accurately classify the new point since the separation between the two classes is greater. Now, if such a hyperplane exists, the hyperplane is clearly of interest and is known as the *maximum–margin hyperplane* or the *optimal hyperplane*, as are the vectors that are closest to this hyperplane, which are called the *support vectors*.

Formalization

Consider data points of the form

$$\{(\mathbf{x}_1, c_1), (\mathbf{x}_2, c_2), \ldots, (\mathbf{x}_n, c_n)\},$$

where the c_i is either 1 or -1; this constant denotes the class to which the point $\mathbf{x}_i$ belongs. Each $\mathbf{x}_i$ is a pD (statistics notation), or nD (computer science notation) vector of scaled $[0, 1]$ or $[-1, 1]$ values. The scaling is important to guard against variables (attributes) with larger variance that might otherwise dominate the classification. We can view this as *training data*, which denotes the correct classification which we would like the SVM to eventually distinguish, by means of the dividing hyperplane, which takes the form:

$$\mathbf{w} \cdot \mathbf{x} - b = 0.$$

As we are interested in the maximum margin, we are interested in the support vectors and the parallel hyperplanes (to the optimal hyperplane) closest to these support vectors in either class. It can be shown that these parallel hyperplanes can be described by equations

$$\mathbf{w} \cdot \mathbf{x} - b = 1, \tag{11.51}$$
$$\mathbf{w} \cdot \mathbf{x} - b = -1. \tag{11.52}$$

We would like these hyperplanes to maximize the distance from the dividing hyperplane and to have no data points between them. By using geometry, we find the distance between the hyperplanes being $2/|\mathbf{w}|$, so we want to minimize $|\mathbf{w}|$. To exclude data points, we need to ensure that for all i either

$$\mathbf{w} \cdot \mathbf{x}_i - b \geq 1, \qquad \text{or}$$
$$\mathbf{w} \cdot \mathbf{x}_i - b \leq -1.$$

This can be rewritten as

$$c_i(\mathbf{w} \cdot \mathbf{x}_i - b) \geq 1, \qquad (1 \leq i \leq n). \tag{11.53}$$

The problem now is to minimize $|w|$ subject to the constraint (11.53). This is a *quadratic programming optimization* (QP) problem.

After the SVM has been trained, it can be used to classify unseen 'test' data. This is achieved using the following decision rule,

$$\hat{c} = \begin{cases} 1 & \text{if} \quad \mathbf{w} \cdot \mathbf{x} + b \geq 0, \\ -1 & \text{if} \quad \mathbf{w} \cdot \mathbf{x} + b \leq 0. \end{cases}$$

Writing the classification rule in its dual form reveals that classification is only a function of the support vectors, i.e., the training data that lie on the margin.

Vapnik–Chervonenkis SVM Theory

The use of the maximum–margin hyperplane is motivated by *Vapnik–Chervonenkis SVM theory*, which provides a probabilistic test *error bound* that is minimized when the margin is maximized. However the utility of this theoretical analysis is sometimes questioned given the large slack associated with these bounds: the bounds often predict more than 100% error rates.

The parameters of the maximum–margin hyperplane are derived by solving the optimization. There exist several specialized algorithms for quickly solving the QP problem that arises from SVMs. The most common method for solving the QP problem is Platt's *SMO algorithm*.

Nonlinear Classification

The original optimal hyperplane algorithm proposed by Vladimir Vapnik in 1963 was a *linear classifier*. However, in 1992, B. Boser, I. Guyon and Vapnik suggested a way to create nonlinear classifiers by applying the *kernel trick* (originally proposed by Aizerman) to maximum–margin hyperplanes. The resulting algorithm is formally similar, except that every *dot product* is replaced by a nonlinear *kernel* function. This allows the algorithm to fit the maximum–margin hyperplane in the transformed feature *space*. The transformation may be nonlinear and the transformed space high dimensional; thus though the classifier is a hyperplane in the high–dimensional feature space it may be nonlinear in the original input space.

If the kernel used is a Gaussian *radial basis function*, the corresponding feature space is a *Hilbert space* of infinite dimension. Maximum margin classifiers are well *regularized*, so the infinite dimension does not spoil the results. Some common kernels include:

1. *Polynomial (homogeneous)*:

$$k(\mathbf{x}, \mathbf{x}') = (\mathbf{x} \cdot \mathbf{x}')^d;$$

2. *Polynomial (inhomogeneous)*:

$$k(\mathbf{x}, \mathbf{x}') = (\mathbf{x} \cdot \mathbf{x}' + 1)^d;$$

3. *Radial Basis Function*:

$$k(\mathbf{x}, \mathbf{x}') = \exp(-\gamma \|\mathbf{x} - \mathbf{x}'\|^2), \qquad \text{for} \qquad \gamma > 0;$$

4. *Gaussian radial basis function*:

$$k(\mathbf{x}, \mathbf{x}') = \exp(-\frac{\|\mathbf{x} - \mathbf{x}'\|^2}{2\sigma^2}); \qquad \text{and}$$

5. *Sigmoid:*

$$k(\mathbf{x}, \mathbf{x}') = \tanh(\kappa \mathbf{x} \cdot \mathbf{x}' + c),$$

for some (not every) $\kappa > 0$ and $c < 0$.

Soft Margin

In 1995, Vapnik suggested a modified maximum margin idea that allows for mislabeled examples. If there exists no hyperplane that can split the 'yes' and 'no' examples, the so-called *soft margin method* will choose a hyperplane that splits the examples as cleanly as possible, while still maximizing the distance to the nearest cleanly split examples. This work popularized the expression *support vector machine* or *SVM*. This method introduces slack variables and the equation (11.53) now transforms to:

$$c_i(\mathbf{w} \cdot \mathbf{x_i} - b) \geq 1 - \xi_i, \qquad (1 \leq i \leq n), \tag{11.54}$$

and the optimization problem becomes:

$$\min \|w\|^2 + C \sum_i \xi_i \qquad \text{such that} \qquad c_i(\mathbf{w} \cdot \mathbf{x_i} - b) \geq 1 - \xi_i, \qquad (1 \leq i \leq n).$$

This constraint in (11.54) along with the objective of minimizing $|w|$ can be solved using *Lagrange multipliers* or setting up a dual optimization problem to eliminate the slack variable.

SVM Regression

A version of a SVM for regression was proposed in 1995 by Vapnik, S. Golowich, and A. Smola (see [Vap98, SS01]). This method is called *support vector regression* (SVR). The model produced by support vector classification (as described above) only depends on a subset of the training data, because the cost function for building the model does not care about training points that lie beyond the margin. Analogously, the model produced by SVR only depends on a subset of the training data, because the cost function for building the model ignores any training data that is close (within a threshold ε) to the model prediction.

11.1.9 Spiking Neural Nets as Axonal Brain Models

In the last decades, much studies have been made for the stochastic resonance (SR), in which weak input signals are enhanced by background noises (see [GHJ98]). This paradoxical SR phenomenon was first discovered in the context of climate dynamics, and it is now reported in many nonlinear systems such as electric circuits, ring lasers, semiconductor devices and neurons.

For single neurons, SR has been studied by using various theoretical models such as the *integrate–and–fire model* (IF) [BED96, SPS99], the *FitzHough–Nagumo model* (FN) [Lon93, LC94] and the *Hodgkin–Huxley model* (HH) [LK99]. In these studies, a weak periodic (sinusoidal) signal is applied to the neuron, and it has been reported that the peak height of the *inter–spike–interval* (ISI) distribution [BED96, Lon93] or the *signal–to–noise ratio* (SNR) of output signals [WPP94, LK99] shows the maximum when the noise intensity is changed.

SR studies mentioned above are motivated from the fact that peripheral sensory neurons play a role of transducers, receiving analog stimuli and emitting spikes. In central neural systems, however, cortical neurons play a role of data–processors, receiving and transmitting spike trains. The possibility of SR in the spike transmission has been reported [CGC96, Mat98]. The response to periodic coherent spike–train inputs has been shown to be enhanced by an addition of weak spike–train noises whose inter–spike intervals (ISIs) have the Poison or gamma distribution.

The limitation of the *Fourier transform* (FT) analysis in this domain[7] can be partly resolved by using the *short–time Fourier transform* (STFT). Assuming that the signal is quasi–stationary in the narrow time period, the FT is applied with time–evolving narrow windows. Then STFT yields the time evolution of the frequency spectrum. The STFT, however, has a critical limitation violating the *uncertainty principle*, which asserts that if the window is too narrow, the frequency resolution will be poor whereas if the window is too wide, the time resolution will be less precise. This limitation becomes serious for signals with much transient components, like spike signals.

The disadvantage of the STFT is overcome in the *wavelet transform* (WT), which appears to be an ideal tool for analyzing signals of a non–stationary nature. In contrast to the FT, the WT offers the 2D expansion for a time–dependent signal with the scale and translation parameters which are interpreted physically as the inverse of frequency and time, respectively. As a basis of the WT, we employ the *mother wavelet* which is localized in both frequency and time domains. The WT expansion is carried out in terms of a family of wavelets which is made by dilation and translation of the mother wavelet. The time evolution of frequency pattern can be followed with an optimal time–frequency resolution.

11.2 Current Research in AI and Supercomputing

Artificial Intelligence (AI) is the science and engineering of making intelligent machines and systems. This is an important multi-disciplinary field which is now an essential part of technology industry, providing the 'heavy lifting' for many of the most challenging problems in computer science. For example,

---

[7] The FT requires that a signal to be examined is stationary, not giving the time evolution of the frequency pattern. Actual biological signals are, however, not necessarily stationary. It has been reported that neurons in different regions have different firing activities. In thalamus, which is the major gateway for the flow of information toward the cerebral cortex, *gamma oscillations* (30–70 Hz), mainly 40 Hz, are reported in arousal, whereas spindle oscillations (7–14 Hz) and slow oscillations (1–7 Hz) are found in early sleeping and deepen sleeping states, respectively [BM93].

The 2015 International Conference on Artificial Intelligence includes (but is not limited to) the following areas:
- Brain models, Brain mapping, Cognitive science
- Natural language processing
- Fuzzy logic and soft computing
- Software tools for AI
- Expert systems
- Decision support systems
- Automated problem solving
- Knowledge discovery, representation, acquisition
- Knowledge-intensive problem solving techniques
- Intelligent information systems
- Intelligent web-based business
- Intelligent agents
- Intelligent networks
- Intelligent databases
- AI and evolutionary algorithms
- Intelligent tutoring systems
- Distributed AI systems and architectures
- Neural networks and applications
- Heuristic searching methods
- Constraint-based reasoning and constraint programming
- Learning and adaptive sensor fusion
- Search and meta-heuristics
- Evaluation of AI tools
- Social intelligence (markets and computational societies)
- Emerging technologies
- Applications (including: computer vision, signal processing, military, surveillance, robotics, medicine, pattern recognition, face recognition, finger print recognition, finance and marketing, stock market, education, emerging applications, ...)

Closely associated field of *Machine Learning* (ML) includes (but is not limited to) the following areas:
- Statistical learning theory
- Unsupervised and Supervised Learning
- Multivariate analysis
- Hierarchical learning models
- Bayesian methods
- Stochastic optimization
- Simulated annealing
- Heuristic optimization techniques
- Neural networks
- Multi-criteria reinforcement learning
- Markov chain Monte Carlo (MCMC) methods
- Non-parametric methods

- Bayesian networks
- Cross-Entropy method
- Ant colony optimization
- Fuzzy logic and learning
- Graph kernel and graph distance methods
- Graph-based semi-supervised learning
- Graph clustering
- Graph learning based on graph grammars
- Graph learning based on graph matching
- Aspects of knowledge structures
- Computational Intelligence
- Knowledge acquisition and discovery techniques
- Latent semantic analysis
- Intelligent linguistic
- Biostatistics
- High-throughput data analysis
- General Structure-based approaches in information retrieval, web authoring, information extraction, and web content mining, ...

Another related field is the so-called *Supercomputing*, which includes (but is not limited to) the following areas:
- Big Data and High-Performance Computing (including: novel computational methodologies, HPC and scalable algorithms for enhancing data quality, models and frameworks for Big Data, graph algorithms, computational science, computational intelligence, Scalable systems and architectures for Big Data, ...)
- Parallel/Distributed Applications (including: numerical computations/ methods, neural networks and fuzzy logic, medicine, remote sensing, computer vision, computer graphics and virtual reality, parallel/distributed databases, banking, financial markets, high-performance computational biology, ...)
- Parallel/Distributed Architectures (including: clusters and parallel systems of various topologies, supercomputers, shared memory, distributed memory, general- and special-purpose architectures, instructional level parallelism, ...)
- Networks and Interconnection Networks (including: scalable networks, re-configurable networks, routing issues, general-purpose network performance for distributed applications, network protocols, internet technology, optical interconnections and computing, novel network topologies, ...)
- Energy/power-aware Computing (including: energy-aware resource management, green computing, energy efficiency planning, energy-aware technologies, low power virtualization and software techniques, low power logic/circuit/ process technology design, methods and tools for forecasting, estimating, and validating power use, ...)
- Reliability and Fault-tolerance (including: software and hardware fault-tolerance [system- and application-level], fault diagnosis, fault-tolerance measurement)
- Building Block Processors (including: applications of processors that can be

used as basic building blocks for multicomputer systems)
- Real-time and Embedded Systems (including: small-scale parallel systems for high-performance control, data acquisition, and analysis; configuration, routing, scheduling, performance guarantees, ...)
- Parallel/Distributed Algorithms (including: algorithms exploiting clusters and general-purpose distributed and parallel systems, new vector/pipeline issues, shared memory, distributed memory, virtual memory, ...)
- Multimedia Communications, Systems, and Applications (including: high-speed networking, multimedia architectures and protocols, multimedia applications, quality of service support, operating system and networking support, internet tools and applications, audio/video delivery over the internet, ...)
- Software Tools and Environments for Parallel and Distributed Platforms (including: operating systems, compilers, languages, debuggers, monitoring tools, software engineering on parallel/distributed systems, ...)
- High-performance Computing in Computational Science (including: Intra-disciplinary and multi-disciplinary research programs and applications)
...

11.2.1 Strong AI vs. Weak AI

In general AI-research is usually divided into three categories (see, e.g. [Cop00]):

- The so-called *strong AI*,[8] which aims to build machines whose overall intellectual ability is indistinguishable from that of a human being. This is defined by the so-called *Turing test: a computer is intelligent if and only if the test fails to distinguish it from a human being.* However, A. Turing himself pointed out that his test cannot provide a definition of intelligence. He said: 'It is possible that a computer which ought to be described as intelligent might nevertheless fail the test because it is not capable of successfully imitating a human being'. For example, why should an intelligent robot designed to oversee mining on the moon necessarily be able to pass itself off in conversation as a human being? If an intelligent entity can fail the test, then the test cannot function as a definition of intelligence. It is even questionable whether a computer's passing the test would show that the computer is intelligent. In 1956 C. Shannon and J. McCarthy raised the objection to the test that it is possible in principle to design a program containing a complete set of 'canned' responses to all the questions that an interrogator could possibly ask during the fixed time-span of the test. M. Minsky's response to the problem of defining intelligence is to maintain

---

[8] Strong AI is a term coined in 1980 by the philosopher J. Searle of the University of California at Berkeley, currently used to describe a certain mindset of artificial intelligence development. Strong AI's goal is to develop artificial intelligence to the point where the machine's intellectual capability is functionally equal to a human's.

that 'intelligence' is simply our name for whichever problem-solving mental processes we do not yet understand. He likens intelligence to the concept 'unexplored regions of Africa': it disappears as soon as we discover it. Turing himself made a similar point earlier, saying 'One might be tempted to define thinking as consisting of those mental processes that we don't understand'. However, the important problem remains of giving a clear criterion of what would count as success in strong artificial intelligence research.

- The so-called *applied AI*, also known as *advanced information processing*, aims to produce commercially viable 'smart' systems, such as e.g. a security system that is able to recognize the faces of people who are permitted to enter a particular building. The general Bayesian filter (described before) is an important example from this category.
- The so-called *cognitive simulation* (CS), in which computers are used to test theories about how the human mind works, e.g., theories about how we recognize faces and other objects, or about how we solve abstract problems. The theory that is to be tested is expressed in the form of a computer program and the program's performance at the task (e.g., face recognition) is compared to that of a human being. Computer simulations of networks of neurons have contributed both to psychology and to neurophysiology.

11.2.2 IBM's Watson and TrueNorth vs. Top Supercomputers

IBM's Watson computer is an AI system capable of answering questions posed in natural language,[9] developed in IBM's DeepQA project by a research team led by principal investigator David Ferrucci. In particular, IBM Watson Health is working to create a more complete picture of healthcare and life sciences. In 2011, Watson competed on Jeopardy! and won the first place, by having access to 200 million pages of structured and unstructured content consuming four terabytes of disk storage including the full text of Wikipedia (but was not connected to the Internet during the game). For each clue, Watson's three most probable responses were displayed on the television screen. Watson consistently outperformed its human opponents on the game's signaling device, but had trouble responding to a few categories, notably those having short clues containing only a few words.

Watson is a *question answering* (QA) computing system that IBM built to apply advanced *natural language processing, information retrieval, knowledge representation, automated reasoning,* and *machine learning* technologies to the field of *open domain question answering*.[10] According to IBM, 'more than 100 different techniques (including deep learning) are used to analyze

---

[9] Watson is a computer system like no other ever built. It analyzes natural language questions and content well enough and fast enough to compete and win against champion players at Jeopardy!

[10] The key difference between QA technology and document search is that document search takes a keyword query and returns a list of documents, ranked in order of

natural language, identify sources, find and generate hypotheses, find and score evidence, and merge and rank hypotheses'. Watson uses IBM's DeepQA software and the Apache UIMA (Unstructured Information Management Architecture) framework. The system was written in various languages, including Java, C++, and Prolog. The system is workload optimized, integrating massively parallel POWER7 processors and being built on IBM's DeepQA technology, which it uses to generate hypotheses, gather massive evidence, and analyze data. Watson is composed of a cluster of ninety IBM Power 750 servers, each of which uses a 3.5 GHz POWER7 eight core processor, with four threads per core. In total, the system has 2,880 POWER7 processor cores and has 16 terabytes of RAM. According to Rennie, Watson can process 500 gigabytes, the equivalent of a million books, per second (see [Wik16hh] and the references therein).

However, Watson's performance stands at 80 TeraFLOPs, which is not enough to place it at *Top 500 Supercomputers* list (see Figure 11.1).[11] According to [Wik16ff], since 1993, the following computer systems have been ranked Number 1:

- NUDT Tianhe-2A (National Supercomputing Center of Guangzhou China, June 2013–present)
- Cray Titan (Oak Ridge National Laboratory United States, November 2012–June 2013)
- IBM Sequoia Blue Gene/Q (Los Alamos National Laboratory United States, June 2012–November 2012)
- Fujitsu K computer (RIKEN Advanced Institute for Computational Science Japan, June 2011–June 2012)
- NUDT Tianhe-1A (National Supercomputing Center of Tianjin China, November 2010–June 2011)
- Cray Jaguar (Oak Ridge National Laboratory United States, November 2009–November 2010)
- IBM Roadrunner (Los Alamos National Laboratory United States, June 2008–November 2009)
- IBM Blue Gene/L (Lawrence Livermore National Laboratory United States, November 2004–June 2008)

---

relevance to the query (often based on popularity and page ranking), while QA technology takes a question expressed in natural language, seeks to understand it in much greater detail, and returns a precise answer to the question.

[11] The TOP500 project ranks and details the 500 most powerful (non-distributed) computer systems in the world. The project was started in 1993 and publishes an updated list of the supercomputers twice a year. The first of these updates always coincides with the International Supercomputing Conference in June, and the second one is presented in November at the ACM/IEEE Supercomputing Conference. The project aims to provide a reliable basis for tracking and detecting trends in high-performance computing and bases rankings on HPL,[1] a portable implementation of the high-performance LINPACK benchmark written in Fortran for distributed-memory computers (see [Wik16ff]).

Top 10 positions of the 44th TOP500 on November, 2014

Rank	Rmax Rpeak (PFLOPS)	Name	Computer design Processor type, interconnect	Vendor	Site Country, year	Operating system
1	33.863 54.902	Tianhe-2	NUDT Xeon E5-2692 + Xeon Phi 31S1P, TH Express-2	NUDT	National Supercomputing Center in Guangzhou China, 2013	Linux (Kylin)
2	17.590 27.113	Titan	Cray XK7 Opteron 6274 + Tesla K20X, Cray Gemini Interconnect	Cray Inc.	Oak Ridge National Laboratory United States, 2012	Linux (CLE, SLES based)
3	17.173 20.133	Sequoia	Blue Gene/Q PowerPC A2, Custom	IBM	Lawrence Livermore National Laboratory United States, 2013	Linux (RHEL and CNK)
4	10.510 11.280	K computer	RIKEN SPARC64 VIIIfx, Tofu	Fujitsu	RIKEN Japan, 2011	Linux
5	8.586 10.066	Mira	Blue Gene/Q PowerPC A2, Custom	IBM	Argonne National Laboratory United States, 2013	Linux (RHEL and CNK)
6	6.271 7.779	Piz Daint	Cray XC30 Xeon E5-2670 + Tesla K20X, Aries	Cray Inc.	Swiss National Supercomputing Centre Switzerland, 2013	Linux (CLE)
7	5.168 8.520	Stampede	PowerEdge C8220 Xeon E5-2680 + Xeon Phi, Infiniband	Dell	Texas Advanced Computing Center United States, 2013	Linux (CentOS)[11]
8	5.008 5.872	JUQUEEN	Blue Gene/Q PowerPC A2, Custom	IBM	Forschungszentrum Jülich Germany, 2013	Linux (RHEL and CNK)
9	4.293 5.033	Vulcan	Blue Gene/Q PowerPC A2, Custom	IBM	Lawrence Livermore National Laboratory United States, 2013	Linux (RHEL and CNK)
10	3.577 6.132		Cray CS Xeon E5-2660v2 10C and Nvidia K40, Infiniband	Cray Inc.	United States, 2014	Linux

Fig. 11.1. The list of 10 fastest supercomputers in the world (adapted from [Wik16ff].

- NEC Earth Simulator (Earth Simulator Center Japan, June 2002–November 2004)
- IBM ASCI White (Lawrence Livermore National Laboratory United States, November 2000–June 2002)
- Intel ASCI Red (Sandia National Laboratories United States, June 1997–November 2000)
- Hitachi CP-PACS (University of Tsukuba Japan, November 1996–June 1997)
- Hitachi SR2201 (University of Tokyo Japan, June 1996–November 1996)
- Fujitsu Numerical Wind Tunnel (National Aerospace Laboratory of Japan Japan, November 1994–June 1996)
- Intel Paragon XP/S140 (Sandia National Laboratories United States, June 1994–November 1994)
- Fujitsu Numerical Wind Tunnel (National Aerospace Laboratory of Japan Japan, November 1993–June 1994)
- TMC CM-5 (Los Alamos National Laboratory United States, June 1993–November 1993).

On the other hand, IBM's TrueNorth chip (see [Ser14] and the references therein) is a neuromorphic CMOS chip that consists of 4096 hardware cores, each one simulating 256 programmable silicon 'neurons' for a total of just over a million neurons. In turn, each neuron has 256 programmable 'synapses' which convey the signals between them. Hence, the total number of programmable synapses is just over 268 million (2^{28}). In terms of basic building blocks, the chip hosts 5.4 billion transistors. Since memory, computation, and communication are handled in each one of the 4096 neurosynaptic cores, TrueNorth circumvents the von-Neumann-architecture bottlenecks and is very energy-efficient, boasting a power consumption of 70 milliwatts, about 1/10,000th the power density of conventional microprocessors.

According to IBM Research, TrueNorth is the first single, self-contained chip to achieve: (i) One million individually programmable neurons–sixteen times more than the current largest neuromorphic chip; (ii) 256 million individually programmable synapses on chip which is a new paradigm; (iii) 5.4B transistors. By device count, largest IBM chip ever fabricated, second largest (CMOS) chip in the world; (iv) 4,096 parallel and distributed cores, interconnected in an on-chip mesh network; and (v) Over 400 million bits of local on-chip memory (100 Kb per core) to store synapses and neuron parameters. TrueNorth is the first to support: (i) Breaks path with 70 years old von-Neumann architecture underlying today's computers; (ii) Hierarchical communication, with on-chip message spike-routing network followed by a local fanout crossbar, greatly reducing network traffic; (iii) Tileable two-dimensional on-chip network of cores (4,096 cores in 28nm); (iv) Tileable and Scalable two-dimensional network of chips, with no need for additional interface circuits; and (v) Flexible architecture that naturally supports advances in packaging, 3D, and novel devices.

Bibliography

AAM76.   Anderson, B.D., Arbib, M.A., Manes, E.G.: Foundations of System Theory: Finitary and Infinitary Conditions. Lecture Notes in Economics and Mathematical Systems Theory, Springer, New York, (1976)

AAT09.   Akhmediev, N., Ankiewicz, A., Taki, M.: Waves That Appear from Nowhere and Disappear without a Trace, Phys. Lett. A **373**(6), 675-678, (2009); Akhmediev, N., Ankiewicz, Soto-Crespo, J.M.: Rogue Waves and Rational Solutions of the Nonlinear Schrödinger Equation, Phys. Rev. E **80**(2), 026601, (2009)

ABG13.   A'imeur, E., Brassard, G., Gambs, S.: Quantum speed-up for unsupervised learning, Mach. Learn. **90**, 261-287, (2013)

ALR16.   Al-Rfou, R. *et al.*: Theano: A Python framework for fast computation of mathematical expressions, arXiv:1605.02688, (2016)

AC86.   Arvind, Culler, D.E.: Annual review of computer science vol. 1, 1986. chapter Dataflow Architectures, 225-253. (1986); http://www.dtic.mil/cgi-bin/GetTRDoc?Location=U2&doc=GetTRDoc.pdf&AD=ADA166235

ACL12.   Augusiak, R., Cucchietti, F.M., Lewenstein, M.: Modern Theories of Many-Particle Systems in Condensed Matter Physics, Lect. Not. Phys. **843**, 245-294, (2012)

AD02.   Andrieu, C., Doucet, A.: Particle filtering for partially observed Gaussian state space models, J. Roy. Stat. Soc. **64**(4), 827-836, (2002)

AEP08.   Argyriou, A., Evgeniou, T., Pontil, M.: Convex multi-task feature learning, Mach. Learn. **73**(3), 243-272, (2008)

AG04.   Aaronson, S., Gottesman, D.: Improved Simulation of Stabilizer Circuits, Phys. Rev. A **70**, 052328, (2004)

AG15.   Alruwaili, F., Gulliver T.A.: SecSDLC: A practical life cycle approach for cloud-based information security. International Journal of Research in Computer and Communication Technology, **4**(2), (2015)

AHP14.   Albi, G., Herty, M., Pareschi, L.: Kinetic description of optimal control problems and applications to opinion consensus, Comm. Math. Sci., (2014)

AKV15.   Angelova, A., Krizhevsky, A., Vanhoucke, V.: Pedestrian detection with a large-field-of-view deep network. In Robotics and Automation (ICRA), 2015 IEEE International Conference on,

704-711. IEEE, (2015); `http://www.vision.caltech.edu/anelia/publications/Angelova15LFOV.pdf`

ALM16.　Abbass, H.A., Leu, G., Merrick, K.: A review of theoretical and practical challenges of trusted autonomy in big data. IEEE Access, **4**, 2808-2830, (2016)

ALW08.　Ambjorn, J., Loll, R., Watabiki, Y., Westra, W., Zohren, S.: A matrix model for 2D quantum gravity defined by Causal Dynamical Triangulations, Phys. Lett. B **665**, 252-256, 2008.; *Ibid.* Topology change in causal quantum gravity, Proc. JGRG 17, Nagoya, Japan, December 2007; *Ibid.* A string field theory based on Causal Dynamical

AM78.　Abraham, R., Marsden, J.: Foundations of Mechanics. Benjamin, Reading, (1978)

AMG02.　Arulampalam, S., Maskell, S., Gordon, N., Clapp, T.: A Tutorial on Particle Filters for Online Nonlinear/Non-Gaussian Bayesian Tracking, IEEE Trans. Sig. Proc. **50**(2), 174-188, (2002)

APM16.　Abbass, H.A., Petraki, E., Merrick, K., Harvey, J., Barlow, M.: Trusted autonomy and cognitive cyber symbiosis: Open challenges. Cognitive Computation, **8**(3), 385-408, (2016)

APZ14.　Albi, G., Pareschi, L., Zanella, M.: Boltzmann type control of opinion consensus through leaders, arXiv:1405.0736, (2014)

ARH00.　Abdul-Rahman, A., Hailes, S.: Supporting trust in virtual communities. In Proc. 33rd Annual Hawaii International Conference on System Sciences, Jan (2000)

AT14.　Aref, A., Tran, T.: Using fuzzy logic and q-learning for trust modeling in multi-agent systems. In 2014 Federated Conference on Computer Science and Information Systems, 59-66, Sept (2014)

AW95.　Aström, K.J., Wittenmark, B.: Adaptive Control, Prentice-Hall, Englewood Cliffs, NJ, (1995)

Aba16a.　Abadi, M. *et al.*: TensorFlow: Large-Scale Machine Learning on Heterogeneous Distributed Systems, arXiv:1603.04467, (2016); Software available from `http://tensorflow.org`.

Aba16b.　Abadi, M. *et al.*: TensorFlow: A system for large-scale machine learning, arXiv:1605.08695, (2016)

Abr02.　Abramsky, S.: Categories, Proofs and Processes. Course at Oxford University Computing Laboratory. Documentation and lecture notes are available at web.comlab.ox.ac.uk/oucl/courses/topics05-06/cpp/, (2002 → ..)

Abr93.　Abramsky, S.: Computational Interpretations of linear logic, Theor. Comp. Sc. **111**, 3-57, (1993)

Alt95.　von Altrock, C.: Fuzzy Logic and Neuro-Fuzzy Applications Explained. Prentice Hall, Englewood Cliffs, NJ, (1995)

Arb98.　Arbib, M. (ed.): Handbook of Brain Theory and Neural Networks (2nd ed.). MIT Press, Cambridge, MA, (1998)

Arn78.　Arnold, V.I.: Mathematical Methods of Classical Mechanics, Springer, New York, (1978)

Ash57.　Ashby, W.R.: An Introduction to Cybernetics, Chapman & Hall, London, (1957)

Asi04.　Asif, A.: Fast implementations of the Kalman-Bucy filter for satellite data assimilation. IEEE Sig. Proc. Let., **11**(2), 235-238, (2004)

Axe76.   Axelrod, R.: Structure of Decision, The Cognitive Maps of Political Elites. Princeton Univ. Press, Princeton, NJ, (1976)

BAF69.   Blatt, S.J., Allison, J., Feirstein, A.: The capacity to cope with cognitive complexity, **37**(2), 269-88, (1969)

BB14.   Bergstra, J.A., Burgess, M.: Promise Theory: Principles and Applications. χtAxis Press, Oslo, Norway, (2014)

BBC93.   Bennett, C.H., Brassard, G., Crépeau, C. *et al.*: Teleporting an unknown quantum state via dual classical and Einstein-Podolsky-Rosen channels, Phys. Rev. Lett. **70**, 1895-1899, (1993)

BBO07.   Burgess, N., Barry, C., O'Keefe, J.: An oscillatory interference model of grid cell firing. Hippocampus **17**, 801-12, (2007)

BCN12.   Byrd, R.H., Chin, G.M., Nocedal, J., Wu, Y.: Sample size selection in optimization methods for machine learning, Mathematical Programming, **134**(1):127-155, (2012); http://dx.doi.org/10.1007/s10107-012-0572-5

BD06.   Bailey, T., Durrant-Whyte, H.: Simultaneous localization and mapping (SLAM): Part II, IEEE Rob. Aut. Mag. **13**(3), 108-117, (2006)

BD98.   Baez, J., Dolan, J.: Higher-Dimensional Algebra III: $n-$categories and the Algebra of Opetopes. Adv. Math. **135**(2), 145-206, (1998)

BDS89.   Buhmann, J., Divko, R., Schulten, K.: Associative memory with high information content. Phys. Rev. A **39**, 2689-2692, (1989)

BDS96.   Bennett, C.H., DiVincenzo, D.P., Smolin, J.A., Wootters, W.K.: Mixed State Entanglement and Quantum Error Correction, Phys. Rev. A **54**, 3824 (1996)

BDV03.   Bengio, Y., Ducharme, R., Vincent, P., Jauvin, C.: A neural probabilistic language model. J. Machine Learning Research, 3:1137-1155, (2003); http://www.iro.umontreal.ca/~lisa/pointeurs/BengioDucharmeVincentJauvin_jmlr.pdf

BED96.   Bulsara, A.R., Elston, T.C., Doering, C.R., Lindenberg, K.: Cooperative behavior in periodically driven noisy integrate-fire models of neuronal dynamics. Phys. Rev. E **53**, 3958-3969, (1996)

BF06.   Brants, T., Franz, A.: Web 1T 5-gram version 1, (2006); https://catalog.ldc.upenn.edu/LDC2006T13

BF71.   Bransford, J.D., Franks, J.J.: The Abstraction of Linguistic Ideas. Cogn. Psych., **2**, 331-350, (1971)

BHB07.   Barry, C., Hayman, R., Burgess, N., Jeffery, K.J.: Experience-dependent rescaling of entorhinal grids. Nat. Neurosci. **10**, 682-84, (2007)

BHJ12.   Brockt, C., Haegeman, J., Jennings, D., Osborne, T.J., Verstraete, F.: The continuum limit of a tensor network: a path integral representation, arXiv:1210.5401, (2012)

BHV09.   Bañuls, M.C., Hastings, M.B., Verstraete, F., Cirac, J.I.: Matrix Product States for Dynamical Simulation of Infinite Chains, Phys. Rev. Lett. **102**, 240603, (2009)

BKH13.   Blanco, D.D., Casini, H., Hung, L.-Y., Myers, R.C.: Relative Entropy and Holography, JHEP **1308**, 060, (2013)

BLS08.   Bessière, P., Laugier, C., Siegwart, R. (eds.): Probabilistic Reasoning and Decision Making in Sensory-Motor Systems, Springer, Tracts in Advanced Robotics **46**, Berlin, (2008)

BM93.   Bal, T., McCormick, D.A.: Cellular mechanisms of a synchronized oscillation in the thalamus. Science **261**, 361-364, (1993)

356   Bibliography

BMK14.   Ba, J., Mnih, V., Kavukcuoglu, K.: Multiple object recognition with
           visual attention, arXiv:1412.7755, (2014)
BMK91.   Bostock, E., Muller, R.U., Kubie, J.L.: Experience-dependent modifica-
           tions of hippocampal place cell firing. Hippocampus **1**, 193-205, (1991)
BMM90.   Barnes, C.A., McNaughton, B.L., Mizumori, S.J., Leonard, B.W., Lin,
           L.H.: Comparison of spatial and temporal characteristics of neuronal
           activity in sequential stages of hippocampal processing. Prog. Brain
           Res. **83**, 287-300, (1990)
BMR15.   Bemporad, A., Morari, M., Ricker, N.L.: Model Predictive Control Tool-
           box, *Matlab*® R2015a, MathWorks, (2015)
BNS11.   Burnett, C., Norman, T.J., Sycara, K.: Trust decision-making in multi-
           agent systems. In Proc. 22nd Int. Joint Conference on Artificial Intelli-
           gence, 115-120, (2011)
BRN96.   van den Bogert, A.J., Read, L., Nigg, B.M.: A method for inverse dy-
           namic analysis using accelerometry. J. Biomech., **29**(7), 949-954, (1996)
BS74.   Balbes, R., Dwinger, P.: Distributive Lattices. Univ. Missouri Press,
           Columbia, (1974)
BS98.   Braun, O.M., Kivshar, Yu.S.: Nonlinear dynamics of the Frenkel-
           Kontorova model, Phys. Rep. **306**, 1-108, (1998)
BSP04.   Bellot, D., Siegwart, R., Bessière, P., Tapus, A., Coué, C., Diard,
           J.: Bayesian modeling and reasoning for real world robotics: Basics
           and examples. A chapter in Embodied Artificial Intelligence (F. Iida,
           R. Pfeifer, L. Steels, Y. Kuniyoshi, eds.) vol. 3139 of Lecture Notes in
           Computer Science, pp. 186-201, Springer, (2004)
BW05.   Barr, M., Wells, C.: Toposes, Triples and Theories, Reprints in The.
           Appl. Cat. **1**, 1-289, (2005)
BWZ07.   Blair, H.T., Welday, A.C., Zhang, K.: Scale-invariant memory repre-
           sentations emerge from moire interference between grid fields that pro-
           duce theta oscillations: a computational model. J. Neurosci. **27**, 3211-29,
           (2007)
BY97.   Bar-Yam, Y.: Dynamics of Complex Systems. Perseus Books, Reading,
           (1997)
Bén67.   Bénabou, J.: Introduction to bicategories. In: Lecture Notes in Mathe-
           matics. Springer, New York, (1967)
Bae02.   Baez, J.: Categorified gauge theory. Lecture in the Joint Spring Meet-
           ing of the Pacific Northwest Geometry Seminar and Cascade Topology
           Seminar, (2002)
Bae97.   Baez, J.: An introduction to n−categories. *7th* Conference on Category
           Theory and Computer Science, E. Moggi and G. Rosolini (eds.), Lecture
           Notes in Computer Science, Springer, Berlin, (1997)
Bal87.   Ballard, D.H.: Modular learning in neural networks. In AAAI, 279-284,
           (1987)
Bar94.   Barendrecht, H.P.: The Lambda Calculus - Its Syntax and Semantics.
           North-Holland, Amsterdam, (1994)
Bel64.   Bell, J.S.: On the Einstein-Podolsky-Rosen Paradox, Physics **1**, 195-200,
           (1964)
Bel88.   Bell, J.L.: Toposes and Local Set Theories. Clarendon Press, Oxford,
           (1988)
Ben67.   Bénabou, J.: Introduction to bicategories, Series: Lecture Notes in
           Mathematics, Springer, New York, (1967)

BBC95.   Barenco, A., Bennett, C.H., Cleve, R. *et al.*: Elementary gates for quantum computation, Phys. Rev. **A52**, 3457, (1995)

Ber47.   Bernstein, N.A.: On the Construction of Human Movement (in Russian: O Postroenii Dvizhenii), Med. Pub., Moscow, (1947); Libraries Australia ID 48358485.

Ber67.   Bernstein, N.A.: The co-ordination and regulation of movements. Pergamon Press, Oxford, (1967)

Ber96.   Bernstein's traditions in motor control: International Conference, Pennsylvania State Univ. (August 22-25, 1996)

Bes03.   Bessière, P.: Survey: Probabilistic Methodology and Techniques for Artefact Conception and Development, Tec. Report RR-4730, INRIA Rhone-Alpes, Montbonnot, France, (2003)

Beu16.   Beurer GmbH: FT90 coreal-time temperature sensor. Viewed Dec. (2016); http://www.beurer.com/web/en/products/body_temperature/body_temperature/FT-90

Bor94.   Borceux, F.: Handbook of Categorical Algebra 3, In Encyclopedia of Mathematics and its Applications, Vol. 53, Cambridge Univ. Press, (1994)

Bro01.   Brockett, R.: New Issues in the Mathematics of Control. In Mathematics Unlimited - 2001 and Beyond, Springer, New York, (2001)

Bro86.   Brooks, R.: A robust layered control system for a mobile robot. IEEE JRA **2**(1), 14-23, (1986)

Bro90.   Brooks, R.: Elephants Don't Play Chess, Robotics and Autonomous Systems **6**(1), 3-15, (1990)

Bur06.   Burrows, M.: The Chubby lock service for loosely-coupled distributed systems. In Proc. 7th Symposium on Operating Systems Design and Implementation, OSDI '06, USENIX Association, 335-350, Berkeley, CA, USA, (2006); https://www.usenix.org/legacy/event/osdi06/tech/full_papers/burrows/burrows.pdf

CB09.   Coecke, B., Oliver, E.: Categories for the practising physicist. arXiv:physics.quant-ph. arXiv:0905.3010, (2009)

CBG15.   Crankshaw, D., Bailis, P., Gonzalez, J.E. *et al.*: The missing piece in complex analytics: Low latency, scalable model management and serving with Velox. In CIDR 2015, Seventh Biennial Conference on Innovative Data Systems Research, Asilomar, CA, USA, January 4-7, 2015, Online Proceedings, (2015) arXiv:1409.3809, (2014)

CBM02.   Collobert, R., Bengio, S., Mariéthoz, J.: Torch: A modular machine learning software library. Technical report, IDIAP, (2002) http://infoscience.epfl.ch/record/82802/files/rr02-46.pdf

CD82.   Choquet-Bruhat, Y., DeWitt-Morete, C.: Analysis, Manifolds and Physics (2nd ed). North-Holland, Amsterdam, (1982)

CDB10.   Colas, F., Diard, J., Bessière, P.: Common Bayesian Models for Common Cognitive Issues, Acta Biotheor. **58**, 191-216, (2010)

CDL13.   Chung, E.S., Davis, J.D., Lee, J.: LINQits: Big data on little clients. In Proc. 40th Annual International Symposium on Computer Architecture, ISCA '13, 261-272, New York, NY, USA, (2013); http://doi.acm.org/10.1145/2485922.2485945

CF13.   Caponigro, M., Fornasier, M., Piccoli, B., Trélat, E.: Sparse stabilization and optimal control of the Cucker-Smale model, Math. Control Relat. Fields, **3**, 447-466, (2013)

CG03.   Carpenter, G.A., Grossberg, S.: Adaptive Resonance Theory. In M.A. Arbib (Ed.), The Handbook of Brain Theory and Neural Networks, Second Edition, Cambridge, MA: MIT Press, 87-90, (2003)

CG83.   Cohen, M.A., Grossberg, S.: Absolute stability of global pattern formation and parallel memory storage by competitive neural networks. IEEE Trans. Syst., Man, Cybern., **13**(5), 815-826, (1983)

CGC96.   Chapeau-Blondeau, F., Godivier, X., Chambet, N.: Stochastic resonance in a neuron model that transmits spike trains. Phys. Rev. E **53**, 1273-1275, (1996)

CGH99.   Castilho, M. A., Gasquet, O., Herzig, A.: Formalizing action and change in modal Logic 1: the frame problem, J. Logic Comp. **9**(5), 701-735, (1999)

CGS03.   Cahill, V., Gray, E., Seigneur, J.M. *et al.*: Using trust for secure collaboration in uncertain environments. IEEE Pervasive Computing, **2**(3), 52-61, July (2003)

CGT00.   Conn, A.R., Gould, N.I.M., Toint, P.L.: Trust region methods, Mathematical Programming Society, Philadelphia, PA, USA: SIAM, (2000)

CHM11.   Casini, H., Huerta, M., Myers, R.C.: Towards a derivation of holographic entanglement entropy, JHEP **1105**, 036, (2011)

CHV02.   Castilho, M.A., Herzig, A., Varzinczak, I.: It depends on the context! A decidable logic of actions and plans based on a ternary dependence relation, in NMR'02, 343-348, (2002).

CK90.   Cash, J.R., Karp, A.H.: A variable order Runge-Kutta method for initial value problems with rapidly varying right-hand sides, ACM Trans. Math. Software **16**, 201-222, (1990)

CKL07.   Chu, C., Kim, S.K., Lin, Y. *et al.*: Map-reduce for machine learning on multicore. In B. Schölkopf, J. C. Platt, and T. Hoffman, editors, Advances in Neural Information Processing Systems 19, 281-288. MIT Press, (2007); http://papers.nips.cc/paper/3150-map-reduce-for-machine-learning-on-multicore.pdf

CL00.   Chen, R., Liu, J.S.: Mixture Kalman filters, J. Roy. Stat. Soc. **62**(3), 493-508, (2000)

CLL15.   Chen, T., Li, M., Li, Y. *et al.*: MXNet: A flexible and efficient machine learning library for heterogeneous distributed systems. In Proc. Workshop on Machine Learning Systems at Neural Information Processing Systems (LearningSys), Dec. (2015); https://www.cs.cmu.edu/~muli/file/mxnet-learning-sys.pdf.

CMB16.   Chen, J., Monga, R., Bengio, S., Jozefowicz, R.: Revisiting distributed synchronous SGD. In Int. Conf. Learning Representations Workshop Track, 2016. arXiv:1604.00981, (2016)

CMM11.   Challa, S., Morelande, M.R., Musicki, D., Evans, R.J.: Fundamentals of Object Tracking. Cambridge Univ Press, Cambridge, UK, (2011)

CMS12.   Ciresan, D.C., Meier, J., Schmidhuber, J.: Multicolumn deep neural networks for image classification. In CVPR, (2012)

CMS13.   Chelba, C., Mikolov, T., Schuster, M., Ge, Q., Brants, T., Koehn, P.: One billion word benchmark for measuring progress in statistical language modeling. CoRR, arXiv:1312.3005, (2013)

CP09.   Coecke, B., Paquette, E.O.: Categories for the practising physicist. In: New Structures for Physics, B. Coecke (ed.), Springer Lecture Notes in Physics, (2009)

CPS11.   Cirac, J.I., Poilblanc, D., Schuch, N., Verstraete, F.: Entanglement spec-
            trum and boundary theories with projected entangled-pair states, Phys.
            Rev. B **83**, 245134, (2011)
CR96.   Casella, G., Robert, C.P.: Rao-Blackwellisation of sampling schemes,
            Biometrika, **83**(1), 81-94, (1996)
CS00.   Cristianini, N., Shawe-Taylor, J.: Support Vector Machines. Cambridge
            Univ. Press, Cambridge, (2000)
CS07.   Cervera, J., van der Schaft, A.J., Baños, A.: Interconnection of port-
            Hamiltonian systems and composition of Dirac structures. Automatica
            43, 212-225, (2007)
CS14.   Clark, S., Storkey, A.: Teaching deep convolutional neural networks to
            play go, arXiv:1412.3409, (2014)
CS16a.   Cohen, N., Shashua, A.: Inductive Bias of Deep Convolutional Networks
            through Pooling Geometry, arXiv:1605.06743, (2016)
CS16b.   Cohen, N., Shashua, A.: Convolutional Rectifier Networks as General-
            ized Tensor Decompositions, arXiv:arXiv:1603.00162, (2016)
CSA14.   Chilimbi, T., Suzue, Y., Apacible, J., Kalyanaraman, K.: Project Adam:
            Building an efficient and scalable deep learning training system. In 11th
            USENIX Symposium on Operating Systems Design and Implementation
            (OSDI 14), 571-582, (2014)
CSB07.   Cervera, J., van der Schaft, A.J., Baños, A.: Interconnection of port-
            Hamiltonian systems and composition of Dirac structures, Automatica
            43, 212-225, (2007)
CSS15.   Cohen, N., Sharir, O., Shashua, A.: On the expressive power of deep
            learning: a tensor analysis, arXiv:1509.05009, (2015)
CW95.   Ciufolini, I., Wheeler, J.A.: Gravitation and Inertia, Princeton Series in
            Physics, Princeton Univ. Press, Princeton, New Jersey, (1995)
CWV14.   Chetlur, S., Woolley, C., Vandermersch, P. *et al.*: cuDNN: Efficient prim-
            itives for deep learning, arXiv:1410.0759, (2014)
CZG16.   Cui, H., Zhang, H., Ganger, G.R., Gibbons, P.B., Xing, E.P.: GeePS:
            Scalable deep learning on distributed GPUs with a GPU-specialized
            parameter server. In Proc. 11th European Conference on Computer
            Systems, EuroSys '16, (2016); `http://www.pdl.cmu.edu/PDL-FTP/`
            `CloudComputing/GeePS-cui-eurosys16.pdf`
Cao85.   Cao, H.-D.: Deformation of Kähler metrics to Kähler-Einstein metrics
            on compact Kähler manifolds, Invent. Math. **81**(2), 359-372, (1985)
Car06.   Carey, T.: The method of levels: how to do psychotherapy without get-
            ting in the way. Hayward, CA: Living Control Systems Publishing. ISBN
            9780974015545, (2006)
Car10.   Cardaliaguet, P.: Notes on mean field games, from P.-L. Lions' lectures
            at College de France, (2010)
Car97.   Caruana, R.: Multitask learning, Mach. Learn. **28**, 41-75, (1997)
Cep13.   Ceperley, D.M.: An Overview of Quantum Monte Carlo Meth-
            ods, PHY, 411-506, (2013); `http://www.physics.buffalo.edu/`
            `phy411-506/topic5/index.html`
Che03.   Chen, Z.: Bayesian Filtering: From Kalman Filters to Particle Fil-
            ters, and Beyond, Tec. Report, McMaser University, Hamilton, Canada,
            (2003)
Chi16.   Chintala, S.: convnet-benchmarks, (2016); `https://github.com/`
            `soumith/convnet-benchmarks`.

Coe04.   Coecke, B.: The Logic of Entanglement, arXiv:quant-ph/0402014, (2004)

Coe06.   Coecke, B.: Introducing categories to the practicing physicist. In: What is Category Theory? Advanced Studies in Mathematics and Logic **30**, Polimetrica Publishing, (2006)

Coe08.   Coecke, B.: Introducing categories to the practicing physicist. arXiv:physics.quant-ph.0808.1032, (2008)

Coe09.   Coecke, B.: Quantum picturalism. Contemp. Phys. **51**, 59-83, (2009)

Com16.   Compumedics Limited: Grael 4K EEG Amplifier. Viewed Dec. (2016); http://compumedicsneuroscan.com/product/grael-4k-eeg-amplifier

Com16.   Compumedics Limited: SynAmps RT EEG/ERP/EP Amplifier. Viewed Dec. (2016); http://compumedicsneuroscan.com/synamps-rt-eegerpep-amplifier

Cop00.   Copeland, J.: What is Artificial Intelligence? AlanTuring.net, (2000)

Cow15.   Cowen, R.: The quantum source of space-time, Nature **527**(7578), 290-3, (2015)

Cox92.   Cox, E.: Fuzzy Fundamentals, IEEE Spectrum, 58-61, (1992)

Cox94.   Cox, E.: The Fuzzy Systems Handbook. AP Professional, (1994)

D-W16.   D-Wave: Quantum Computing (How D-Wave Systems Work), (2016); http://www.dwavesys.com/quantum-computing
The D-Wave $2X^{TM}$ System (The most advanced quantum computer in the world), (2015); http://www.dwavesys.com/d-wave-two-system

Dav10.   Davidson, P.: Black Swans and Knight's Epistemological Uncertainty: Are These Concepts also Underlying Behavioural and Post-Walrasian Theory?, J. Post-Keynesian Economics, **32**(4), 567-570, (2010)

Dav12.   Davidson, P.: Is Economics a Science? Should Economics be Rigorous?, Real-World Economics Review, **59**, 58-66, (2012)

DB06.   Durrant-Whyte, H., Bailey, T.: Simultaneous localization and mapping (SLAM): Part I, IEEE Rob. Aut. Mag. **13**(2), 99-110, (2006)

DB07.   Dorigo, M., Birattari, M.: Swarm intelligence, Scholarpedia, **2**(9), 1462, (2007); http://www.scholarpedia.org/article/Swarm_intelligence

DB08.   Diard, J., Bessière, P.: Bayesian maps: probabilistic and hierarchical models for mobile robot navigation, a chapter in [BLS08], pp. 153-176, (2008)

DBM03.   Diard, J., Bessière, P., Mazer, E.: A survey of probabilistic models, using the bayesian programming methodology as a unifying framework. Proc. 2nd Int. Conf. Comput. Intel., Rob. Autonom. Sys. (CIRAS 2003), Singapore, (2003)

DCM12.   Dean, J., Corrado, G.S., Monga, R. *et al.*: Large scale distributed deep networks. In NIPS, (2012); http://research.google.com/archive/large_deep_networks_nips2012.pdf

DFP05.   Delgado, M.R., Frank, R.H., Phelps, E.A.: Perceptions of moral character modulate the neural systems of reward during the trust game. Nature Neuroscience, **8**(11), 1611-1618, (2005)

DG04.   Dean, J., Ghemawat, S.: Mapreduce: Simplified data processing on large clusters. In Proc. 6th Conference on Symposium on Opearting Systems Design & Implementation - Volume 6, USENIX Association. OSDI'04, Berkeley, CA, USA, (2004); http://research.google.com/archive/mapreduce-osdi04.pdf

DGA00.   Doucet, A., Godsill, S.J., Andrieu, C.: On sequential Monte Carlo sampling methods for Bayesian filtering, Stat. Comp. **10**(3), 197-208, (2000)

DGK01.   Doucet, A., Gordon, N., Krishnamurthy, V.: Particle filters for state estimation of jump Markov linear systems, IEEE Trans. Sig. Proc. **49**(3), 613-624, (2001)

DHL14.   Degond, P., Herty, M., Liu, J.-G.: Meanfield games and model predictive control, arXiv[math.OC]:1412.7517, (2014)

DHS91.   Domany, E., van Hemmen, J.L., Schulten, K. (eds.): Models of Neural Networks. Springer, Berlin, (1991)

DI08a.   Döring, A., Isham, C.J.: A topos foundation for theories of physics: I. Formal Languages for Physics. J. Math. Phys. **49**, 053515, (2008)

DI08b.   Döring, A., Isham, C.J.: A topos foundation for theories of physics: II. Daseinisation and the liberation of quantum theory. J. Math. Phys. **49**, 053516, (2008)

DI08c.   Döring, A., Isham, C.J.: A topos foundation for theories of physics: III. Quantum theory and the representation of physical quantities with arrows. J. Math. Phys. **49**, 053517, (2008)

DI08d.   Döring, A., Isham, C.J.: A topos foundation for theories of physics: IV. Categories of systems. J. Math. Phys. **49**, 053518, (2008)

DIS11.   Das, A., Islam, M.M., Sorwar, G.: Dynamic trust model for reliable transactions in multi-agent systems. In 13th International Conference on Advanced Communication Technology (ICACT2011), 1101-1106, Feb (2011)

DK87.   Dress, W.B., Knisley, J.R.: A Darwinian approach to artificial neural systems. Proc IEEE Conf. Sys., Man Cybern., (1987)

DK89.   Dean, T., Kanazawa, K.: A model for reasoning about persistence and causation. Comput. Intel. **5**(3), 142-150, (1989)

DKU04.   Daley, A.J., Kollath, C., Schollwöck, U., Vidal, G.: Time-dependent density-matrix renormalization-group using adaptive effective Hilbert spaces, J. Stat. Mech.: Theor. Exp. P04005, (2004)

DM03.   Dorogovtsev, S.N., Mendes, J.F.F.: Evolution of Networks. Oxford Univ. Press, (2003)

DM15.   Dean, J., Monga, R.: TensorFlow - Googles latest machine learning system, open sourced for everyone, Research at Google, (Nov 2015); http://googleresearch.blogspot.com.au/2015/11/tensorflow-googles-latest-machine_9.html

DMS09.   Duindam, V., Macchelli, A., Stramigioli, S., Bruyninckx, H. (Eds.): Modeling and Control of Complex Physical Systems: The Port-Hamiltonian Approach. Springer, Berlin, (2009)

DOL15.   Dai, A., Olah, C., Le, Q.V.: Document embedding with paragraph vectors, arXiv:1507.07998, (2015)

DP01.   Dosen, K., Petric, Z.: The Maximality of Cartesian Categories. Math. Logic Quart. **47**, 137-144, (2001)

DP04.   Dosen, K., Petric, Z.: Proof-Theoretical Coherence. Studies in Logic **1**, King's College Publ. London, (2004)

DP80.   Dubois, D., Prade, H.: Fuzzy Sets and Systems. Academic Press, New York, (1980)

DS99.   Dalsmo, M., van der Schaft, A.J.: On representations and integrability of mathematical structures in energy-conserving physical systems, SIAM J. Con. Opt. **37**(1), 54-91, (1999)

DSB10.   Diard, J., Gilet, E., Simonin, E., Bessière, P.: Incremental learning of Bayesian sensorimotor models: from low-level behaviours to large-scale structure of the environment. Connect. Sci. **22**(4), 291-312, (2010)

Deu62.   Deutsch, M.: Cooperation and Trust: Some theoretical notes. In Nebraska Symposium on Motivation, 275-320, Univer. Nebraska Press, (1962)

Deu77.   Deutsch, M.: The resolution of conflict: Constructive and destructive processes. Yale University Press, (1977)

Deu85.   Deutsch, D.: Quantum theory, the Church-Turing principle and the universal quantum computer, Proc. Roy. Soc. A **400** (1818), 97-117, (1985)

Die88.   Dieudonne, J.A.: A History of Algebraic and Differential Topology 1900-1960. Birkháuser, Basel, (1988)

Dir30.   Dirac, P.A.M.: The Principles of Quantum Mechanics, Oxford Univ. Press, (1930)

Dor09.   Döring, A.: Topos Theory and 'Neo-Realist' Quantum Theory. In B. Fauser et al. (Eds.) Quantum Field Theory. Birkhauser Verlag, Basel, (2009)

Dos01.   Dosen, K.:   Abstraction   and   Application   in   Adjunction, arXiv:math.CT/0111061, (2001)

Dp02.   Dosen, K., Petric, Z.: Bicartesiaan Coherence. Studia Logica **71**, 331-353, (2002)

EL96.   Evensen, G., van Leeuwen, P.: Assimilation of Geosat altimeter data for the Agulhas Current using the ensemble Kalman filter with a quasi-geostrophic model, Mon. Wea. Rev. **124**, 85-96, (1996)

EM45.   Eilenberg, S., Mac Lane, S.: General theory of natural equivalences. Transactions of the American Mathematical Society, **58**, 231-294, (1945)

EP04.   Evgeniou, T., Pontil, M.: Regularized multi-task learning. Proc. 10th Int. Conf. Knowledge Discovery and Data Mining (KDD), 109-117, (2004)

EPR35.   Einstein, A., Podolsky, B., Rosen, N.: Can Quantum-Mechanical Description of Physical Reality Be Considered Complete?. Phys. Rev. **47**(10), 777-780, (1935)

ER35.   Einstein, A., Rosen, N.: The Particle Problem in the General Theory of Relativity, Phys. Rev. **48**(1), 73-77, (1935)

EV14a.   Evenbly, G., Vidal, G.: Class of Highly Entangled Many-Body States that can be Efficiently Simulated, Phys. Rev. Lett. **112**, 240502, (2014)

EV14b.   Evenbly, G., Vidal, G.: Scaling of entanglement entropy in the (branching) multiscale entanglement renormalization ansatz, Phys. Rev. B **89**, 235113, (2014)

Elm90.   Elman, J.: Finding structure in time. Cogn. Sci. **14**, 179-211, (1990)

Emo16a.   Emotive Inc.: Epoc+ a revolutionary neuroheadset and scientific contextual eeg offering high resolution and full spatial resolution. Viewed Dec. (2016); https://www.emotiv.com/epoc.php

Emo16b.   Emotive Inc.: INSIGHT Brainwear that allows you to monitor your cognitive health and wellbeing and optimize your performance. Viewed Dec. (2016); https://www.emotiv.com/insight.php

Eve03.   Evensen, G.: The ensemble Kalman filter: Theoretical formulation and practical implementation, Ocean dynamics, **53**, 343-367, (2003)

Eve94.   Evensen, G.: Sequential data assimilation with a nonlinear quasi-
            geostrophic model using Monte Carlo methods to forecast error statis-
            tics, J. Geophys. Res. **99 (C5)**, 10,143-10 162, (1994)

FB12.   di Franco, C., Ballester, D.: Optimal path for a quantum teleportation
            protocol in entangled networks. Phys. Rev. A **85**, 010303(R), (2012)

FCN13.   Farabet, C., Couprie, C.C., Najman, L., LeCun, Y.: Learning Hierarchi-
            cal Features for Scene Labeling, IEEE Trans. Patt. Anal. Mach. Intel.
            (Special Issue on Deep Learning), (2013)

FCS13.   Frome, A., Corrado, G.S., Shlens *et al.*: DeVISE: A deep visual-
            semantic embedding model. In Advances in Neural Information Process-
            ing Systems, 2121-2129, (2013); http://research.google.com/pubs/
            archive/41473.pdf

FHK94.   Fukuma, M., Hosono, S., Kawai, H.: Lattice Topological Field Theory
            in Two Dimensions, Commun. Math. Phys. **161**, 157-176, (1994)

FKM05.   Fullam, K.K., Klos, T.B., Muller, G. *et al.*: A specification of the agent
            reputation and trust (ART) testbed: Experimentation and competition
            for trust in agent societies. In Proc. 4th Int. joint Conf. Autonomous
            Agents and Multiagent systems, 645-651, ACM, (2005)

FL79.   Fisher, M.J., Ladner, R.E.: Propositional dynamic logic of regular pro-
            grams, Journal of Computer and System Sciences, **18**, 194-211, (1979)

FMW04.   Fyhn, M., Molden, S., Witter, M.P., Moser, E.I., Moser, M.-B.: Spatial
            representation in the entorhinal cortex. Science **305**, 1258-1264, (2004)

FNW93.   Fannes, M., Nachtergaele, B., Werner, R.F.: Finitely correlated states
            on quantum spin chains, Commun. Math. Phys. **144**, 443-490, (1992)

FOM08.   Fan, X., Oh, S., McNeese, M. *et al.*: The influence of agent reliability on
            trust in human-agent collaboration. In ECCE'08 Proc. 15th European
            conference on Cognitive Ergonomics: The Ergonomics of Cool Interac-
            tion, ACM, New York, NY, USA, (2008)

FP67.   Faddeev, L.D., Popov, V.N.: Feynman diagrams for the Yang-Mills field.
            Phys. Lett. B **25**, 29, (1967)

FS92.   Freeman, J.A., Skapura, D.M.: Neural Networks: Algorithms, Appli-
            cations, and Programming Techniques. Addison-Wesley, Reading, MA,
            (1992)

FSB05.   Finnie, G., Sun, Z., Barker, J.: Trust and Deception in Multi-Agent
            Trading Systems: A Logical Viewpoint. In Proc. 11th Americas Confer-
            ence on Information Systems (AMCIS), 1020-1026, (2005)

FT06.   Fuhs, M.C., Touretzky, D.S.: A spin glass model of path integration in
            rat medial entorhinal cortex, J. Neurosci. **26**, 4266-76, (2006)

Far12.   Faragher, R.: Understanding the Basis of the Kalman Filter Via a Sim-
            ple and Intuitive Derivation, IEEE Sig. Proc. Mag. 128-132, (2012)

Fen02.   Feng, G.: An Approach to Adaptive Control of Fuzzy Dynamic Systems.
            IEEE Trans. Fuzzy Systt. **10**(2), 268-275, (2002)

Fey65.   Feynman, R.P.: Space-time approach to non-relativistic quantum me-
            chanics, Rev. Mod. Phys. **20**, 367-387, 1948; Feynman, R.P., Hibbs,
            A.R.: Quantum Mechanics and Path Integrals, McGraw-Hill, New York,
            (1965)

Fey49.   Feynman, R.P.: Space-time approach to quantum electrodynamics,
            Phys. Rev. **76**, 769-789, (1949); *Ibid.* Mathematical formulation of the
            quantum theory of electromagnetic interaction, Phys. Rev. **80**, 440-457,
            (1950)

Fey51.   Feynman, R.P.: An Operator Calculus Having Applications in Quantum Electrodynamics. Phys. Rev. **84**, 108-128, (1951)

Fey55.   Feynman, R.P.: Application of quantum mechanics to liquid helium. Progress in Low Temperature Physics Vol. 1 (Gorter, C. J. ed.), North-Holland, Amsterdam, 17-53, (1955)

Fey82.   Feynman, R.P.: Simulating physics with computers, Int. J. The. Physics, **21**, 467-488, (1982)

Fla63.   Flanders, H.: Differential Forms: with Applications to the Physical Sciences. Acad. Press, (1963)

Fra04.   Francois, C.: International Encyclopedia of Systems and Cybernetics (2nd Ed.), Walter de Gruyter, (2004)

Fuk79.   Fukushima, K.: Neural network model for a mechanism of pattern recognition unaffected by shift in position - neocognitron. In Trans. IECE, (1979)

Fus03.   Fuster, J.M.: Cortex and Mind: Unifying Cognition. Oxford Univ. Press, Oxford, U.K., (2003)

GBC16.   Goodfellow, I., Bengio, Y., Courville, A.: Deep learning. Book in preparation for MIT Press, (2016); http://goodfeli.github.io/dlbook/.

GC09.   Garratt, M., Cheung, A.: Obstacle Avoidance in Cluttered Environments using Optic Flow, Australasian Conf. Rob. Autom. Sydney, Australia, (2009)

GGB02.   Gustafsson, F., Gunnarsson, F., Bergman, N., Forssell, U., Jansson, J., Karlsson, R., Nordlund, P-J.: Particle filters for positioning, navigation and tracking. IEEE Trans. Sig. Proc. **50**(2), 425-437, (2002)

GHJ98.   Gammaitoni, L., Hännggi, P., Jung, P., Marchesoni, F.: Stochastic resonance. Rev. Mod. Phys. **70**, 223-287, (1998)

GHK59.   Gardner, R.W., Holzman, P.S., Klein, G.S., Linton, H.P., Spence, D.P.: Cognitive Control: A study of individual consistencies in cognitive behavior. Psych. Issues, **1**(4, Whole No. 4), Int. Univ. Press, New York, (1959)

GJM60.   Gardner, R.W., Jackson, D.N., Messick, S.J.: Personality organization in cognitive controls and intellectual abilities. Psych. Issues, **2**(8), Int. Univ. Press, New York, (1960)

GK94.   Gegenberg, J., Kunstatter, G.: The Partition Function for Topological Field Theories, Ann. Phys. **231**, 270-289, (1994)

GKP14.   Guiggiani, A., Kolmanovsky, I., Patrinos, P., Bemporad, A.: Fixed-Point Constrained Model Predictive Control of Spacecraft Attitude, arXiv[OC]:1411.0479, (2014)

GL62a.   Gardner, R.W., Long, R.I.: Cognitive controls of attention and inhibition: A study of individual consistencies. Brit. J. Psych. **53**, 381-388, (1962)

GL62b.   Gardner, R.W., Long, R.I.: Control, defence, and centration effect: A study of scanning behaviour. Brit. J. Psych. **53**, 129-140, (1962)

GL99.   Griffiths, N., Luck, M.: Cooperative plan selection through trust. In Proc. 9th European Workshop on Modelling Autonomous Agents in a Multi-Agent World: MultiAgent System Engineering, MAAMAW '99, 162-174, Springer-Verlag, London, UK, (1999)

GLM15.   Gonzalez-Dominguez, J., Lopez-Moreno, I., Moreno, P.J., Gonzalez-Rodriguez, J.: Frame-by-frame language identification in short utterances using deep neural networks. Neural Networks, **64**, 49-58, (2015); http://research.google.com/en//pubs/archive/42929.pdf

GLW08.   Gu, Z.-C., Levin, M., Wen, X.-G.: Tensor-entanglement renormaliza-
          tion group approach as a unified method for symmetry breaking and
          topological phase transitions, Phys. Rev. B **78**, 205116, (2008)
GM11.   Gomez-Munoz, J.L.: Quantum - Mathematica Add-On, v.2.3.0, (2011);
          http://homepage.cem.itesm.mx/lgomez/quantum/
GMH.   Graves, A., Mohamed, A-R., Hinton, G.: Speech Recognition with Deep
          Recurrent Neural Networks, arXiv:1303.5778, (2013)
GPM14.   Goodfellow, I.J., Pouget-Abadie, J., Mirza, M. *et al.*: Generative ad-
          versarial nets. In Advances in Neural Information Processing Systems
          27: Annual Conference on Neural Information Processing Systems 2014,
          December 8-13 2014, Montreal, Quebec, Canada, 2672-2680,
GRF12.   Godinez, H.C., Reisner, J.M., Fierro, A.O., Guimond, S.R., Kao, J.:
          Determining Key Model Parameters of Rapidly Intensifying Hurricane
          Guillermo (1997) Using the Ensemble Kalman Filter, J. Atmos. Sci.,
          69, 3147-3171, (2012)
GS13.   Giles, B., Selinger, P.: Exact synthesis of multiqubit Clifford+T circuits,
          Phys. Rev. **A87**, 032332, (2013)
GS62.   Gardner, R.W., Schoen, R.A.: Differentiation and abstraction in concept
          formation. Psych. Monogr., **76** (41, Whole No. 560), (1962)
GSB07.   Grisetti, G., Stachniss, C., Burgard, W.: Improved techniques for grid
          mapping with Rao-Blackwellized particle filters, IEEE Trans. Robotics,
          23(1), 34-46, (2007)
GSS93.   Gordon, N.J., Salmond, D.J., Smith, A.F.M.: Novel approach to
          nonlinear/non-Gaussian Bayesian state estimation. In IEE Proc. on
          Radar and Sig. Proc. **140**, 107-113, (1993)
GWA01.   Grewal, M.S., Weill, L.R., Andrews, A.P.: Global Positioning Systems,
          Inertial Navigation, and Integration. Wiley, New York, (2001)
Gar53.   Gardner, R.: Cognitive style in categorizing behaviour, Perceptual and
          Motor Skills **22**, 21433, (1953)
Gar61.   Gardner, R.W.: Cognitive controls of attention deployment as determi-
          nants of visual illusions. J. Abnorm. Soc. Psych. **62**, 120-127, (1961)
Gar62.   Gardner, R.: Cognitive controls in adaptation: Research and measure-
          ment. A chapter in Measurement in personality and cognition (Eds.
          S.J. Messick, J. Ross), Wiley, New York, (1962)
Gar64.   Gardner, R.: The development of cognitive structures. A chapter in
          Cognition (Ed. C. Scheerer), Harper & Row, New York (1964)
GPS04.   Gilboa I., Postlewaite A., Schmeidler, D.: Rationality of Be-
          lief. Or: Why Bayesianism is Neither Necessary nor Sufficient
          for Rationality, Cowles Foundation Discussion Papers1484,
          Cowles Foundation for Research in Economics, Yale Univ.,
          https://ideas.repec.org/p/cwl/cwldpp/1484.html, (2004)
God92.   Gödel, K.: On Formally Undecidable Propositions of Principia Mathe-
          matica and Related Systems, Dover, New York, (1992)
Gra09.   Gray, R.M.: Probability, Random Processes, and Ergodic Properties
          (2nd Ed.), Springer, New York, (2009)
Gim15.   Gimlett, J.: Quantum-Assisted Sensing and Read-
          out, DARPA, (2015); http://www.darpa.mil/program/
          quantum-assisted-sensing-and-readout
Gol84.   Goldblatt, R.: Topoi: The Categorial Analysis of Logic. North-Holland,
          London, (1984)

Gol99.   Gold, M., A Kurt Lewin Reader, the Complete Social Scientist, Am. Psych. Assoc., Washington, (1999)

Gou15.   Gough, M.: Researchers design architecture for a quantum computer in silicon, Newsroom, UNSW Australia, (2015)

Gri06.   Griffiths, N.: A Fuzzy Approach to Reasoning with Trust, Distrust and Insufficient Trust, In Cooperative Information Agents X: 10th International Workshop, CIA 2006 Proceedings, 360-374, Springer, Berlin, Heidelberg, (2006)

Gri83.   Griffiths, P.A.: Exterior Differential Systems and the Calculus of Variations, Birkhauser, Boston, (1983)

Gro05.   Gros, C.: Self-Sustained Thought Processes in a Dense Associative Network. Springer Lecture Notes in AI **3698**, 375-388, (2005)

Gro69.   Grossberg, S.: Embedding fields: A theory of learning with physiological implications. J. Math. Psych. **6**, 209-239, (1969)

Gro82.   Grossberg, S.: Studies of Mind and Brain. Dordrecht, Holland, (1982)

Gro88.   Grossberg, S.: Neural Networks and Natural Intelligence. MIT Press, Cambridge, MA, (1988)

Gro99.   Grossberg, S.: How does the cerebral cortex work? Learning, attention and grouping by the laminar circuits of visual cortex. Spatial Vision **12**, 163-186, (1999)

HC10.   Haegeman, J., Cirac, J.I., Osborne, T.J., Verschelde, H., Verstraete, F.: Applying the Variational Principle to (1+1)-Dimensional Quantum Field Theories, Phys. Rev. Lett. **105**, 251601, (2010)

HC96.   Hughes, G.E., Cresswell, M.J.: A new introduction to modal logic, Routledge, (1996)

HCH12.   Hinchman, J., Clark, M., Hoffman, J., Hulbert, B., Snyder, C.: Towards safety assurance of trusted autonomy in air force flight critical systems. In Computer Security Applications Conference, Layered Assurance Workshop, (2012)

HCO11.   Haegeman, J., Cirac, J.I., Osborne, T.J., Pizorn, I., Verschelde, H., Verstraete, F.: Time-Dependent Variational Principle for Quantum Lattices, Phys. Rev. Lett. **107**, 070601, (2011)

HDLT13.   Huang, W.M., Deng, Z., Li, R.H., Tang, X.X.: Trust-based particle swarm optimization for grid task scheduling. Applied Mechanics and Materials, **239-240**, 1331-1335, (2013)

HDY12.   Hinton, G.E., Deng, L., Yu, D. *et al.*: Deep neural networks for acoustic modeling in speech recognition: The shared views of four research groups. IEEE Signal Process. Mag., **29**(6), 82-97, (2012); http://www. cs.toronto.edu/~gdahl/papers/deepSpeechReviewSPM2012.pdf

HFM05.   Hafting, T., Fyhn, M., Molden, S., Moser, M.-B., Moser, E.I.: Microstructure of a spatial map in the entorhinal cortex. Nature **436**, 801-806, (2005)

HFM06.   Hafting, T., Fyhn, M., Moser, M.-B., Moser, E.I.: Phase precession and phase locking in entorhinal grid cells. Soc. Neurosci. Abstr. **32**, 68-80, (2006)

HH95.   Hopfield, J.J., Hertz, A.V.M.: Rapid local synchronization of action potentials: Toward computation with coupled integrate-and-fire neurons. Proc. Natl. Acad. Sci. USA, **92**, 6655-6662, (1995)

HH97.   Harmon, M.E., Harmon, S.S.: Reinforcement learning: A tutorial. Tec. Rep. Wright Laboratory and Wright State University, (1997)

HHP95.   Herrmann, M., Hertz, J., Prügel-Bennett, A.: Analysis of synfire chains. Network: Computat. Neural Syst. **6**, 403-414, (1995)

HI97.   Hoppensteadt, F.C., Izhikevich, E.M.: Weakly Connected Neural Networks. Springer, New York, (1997)

HJM06.   Hofstede, G.J., Jonker, C.M., Meijer, S., Verwaart, T.: Modelling trade and trust across cultures. In 4th International Conference on Trust Management, 120-134, Springer, (2006)

HJV09.   Hofstede, G.J., Jonker, C.M., Verwaart, T.: A Multi-agent Model of Deceit and Trust in Intercultural Trade. In Proc. Computational Collective Intelligence. Semantic Web, Social Networks and Multiagent Systems: First International Conference, ICCCI 2009, 205-216, Springer, Berlin, Heidelberg, (2009)

HK09.   Hackbusch, W., Kühn, S.: A New Scheme for the Tensor Representation. J. Fourier Analysis and Applications, **15**(5), 706-722, (2009)

HK99.   Hanm, S.-H., Koh, I.G.: Stability of neural networks and solitons of field theory. Phys. Rev. E **60**, 7608-7611, (1999)

HKH09.   Hübener, R., Kruszynska, C., Hartmann, L., Dür, W.: Renormalization algorithm with graph enhancement, Phys. Rev. A **79**, 022317, (2009)

HKJ10.   Hunt, P., Konar, M., Junqueira, F.P., Reed, B.: ZooKeeper: Wait-free coordination for internet-scale systems. In Proc. 2010 USENIX Conf. USENIX Annual Technical Conference, USENIXATC'10, 11-11, Berkeley, CA, USA, USENIX Association, (2010); https://www.usenix.org/legacy/event/atc10/tech/full_papers/Hunt.pdf

HKZ11.   Hindman, B., Konwinski, A., Zaharia, M. et al.: Mesos: A platform for fine-grained resource sharing in the data center. In Proc. 8th USENIX Conference on Networked Systems Design and Implementation, NSDI'11, 295-308, Berkeley, CA, USA, USENIX Association, (2011); https://www.cs.berkeley.edu/~alig/papers/mesos.pdf

HL64.   Ho, Y.C., Lee, R.C.K.: A Bayesian approach to problems in stochastic estimation and control, IEEE Trans. Aut. Control **9**, 333-339, (1964)

HM98.   Houtekamer, P., Mitchell, H.: Data assimilation using an ensemble Kalman filter technique, Mon. Wea. Rev. **126**, 796-811, (1998)

HOT06.   Hinton, G.E., Osindero, S., The, Y.: A fast learning algorithm for deep belief nets. Neural Computation, **18**, 1527-1554, (2006)

HOV13.   Haegeman, J., Osborne, T.J., Verschelde, H., Verstraete, F.: Entanglement Renormalization for Quantum Fields in Real Space, Phys. Rev. Lett. **110**, 100402, (2013)

HS06.   Hinton, G.E., Salakhutdinov, R.R.: Reducing the dimensionality of data with neural networks. Science **313**, 504-507, (2006)

Hal13.   Halmos, P.: Lectures on Ergodic Theory, Martino Fine Books, ISBN: 9781614274612, (2013)

HS94.   Haelterman, M., Sheppard, A.P.: Bifurcation phenomena and multiple soliton bound states in isotropic Kerr media. Phys. Rev. E **49**, 3376-3381, (1994)

HS97.   Hochreiter, S., Schmidhuber, J.: Long short-term memory. Neural Computation, **9**(8), 1735-1780, (1997)

HSK12.   Hinton, G.E., Srivastave, N., Krizhevsky, A., Sutskever, I., Salakhutdinov, R.R.: Improving neural networks by preventing co-adaptation of feature detectors. arXiv:1207.0580, (2012)

368   Bibliography

HSP14.   Hedengren, J.D., Shishavan, R.A., Powell, K.M., Edgar, T.F.: Nonlinear
          modeling, estimation and predictive control in APMonitor, Comput. &
          Chem. Eng. **70**(5), 133-148, (2014)
HT05.   He, B., Teixeira, F.L.: On the degrees of freedom of lattice electrody-
          namics. Phys. Let. A **336**, 1-7, (2005)
HT85.   Hopfield, J.J., Tank, D.W.: Neural computation of decisions in optimi-
          sation problems. Biol. Cybern., **52**, 114-152, (1985)
HVS13.   Heigold, G., Vanhoucke, V., Senior, A. *et al.*: Multilingual acoustic
          models using distributed deep neural networks. In Acoustics, Speech
          and Signal Processing (ICASSP), 2013 IEEE International Conference
          on, 8619-8623. IEEE, (2013); https://research.google.com/pubs/
          archive/40807.pdf.
HW08.   Hamann, H., Wörn, H.: A framework of space-time continuous models
          for algorithm design in swarm robotics, Swarm Intel. **2**(2), 209-239,
          (2008)
HW62.   Hubel, D.H., Wiesel, T.: Receptive fields, binocular interaction, and
          functional architecture in the cat's visual cortex. J. Physiology (London)
          160, 106-154, (1962)
HW65.   Hubel, D., Wiesel, T.: Receptive fields and functional architecture in
          two nonstriate visual areas (18 and 19) in the cat. J. Neurophysiol. **28**,
          229-289, (1965)
HWZ08.   Hu, J., Wu, Q., Zhou, B.: FCTrust: A Robust and Efficient Feedback
          Credibility-Based Distributed P2P Trust Model. In 2008 The 9th In-
          ternational Conference for Young Computer Scientists, 1963-1968, Nov
          (2008)
HZR15.   He, K., Zhang, X., Ren, S., Sun, J.: Deep residual learning for image
          recognition. CoRR, arXiv:1512.03385, (2015)
Hac12.   Hackbusch, W.: Tensor Spaces and Numerical Tensor Calculus, vol-
          ume 42 of Springer Series in Computational Mathematics. Springer Sci-
          ence & Business Media, Berlin, Heidelberg, (2012)
Hak00.   Haken, H.: Information and Self-Organization: A Macroscopic Approach
          to Complex Systems. Springer, Berlin, (2000)
Hak02.   Haken, H.: Brain Dynamics, Synchronization and Activity Patterns in
          Pulse-Coupled Neural Nets with Delays and Noise, Springer, New York,
          (2002)
Hak83.   Haken, H.: Synergetics: An Introduction (3rd ed). Springer, Berlin,
          (1983)
Hak91.   Haken, H.: Synergetic Computers and Cognition. Springer-Verlag,
          Berlin, (1991)
Hak93.   Haken, H.: Advanced Synergetics: Instability Hierarchies of Self-
          Organizing Systems and Devices (3nd ed). Springer, Berlin, (1993)
Hak96.   Haken, H.: Principles of Brain Functioning: A Synergetic Approach to
          Brain Activity, Behavior and Cognition, Springer, Berlin, (1996)
Ham82.   Hamilton, R.S.: Three-manifolds with positive Ricci curvature, J. Diff.
          Geom. **17**, 255-306, (1982)
Ham86.   Hamilton, R.S.: Four-manifolds with positive curvature operator, J. Dif.
          Geom. **24**, 153-179, (1986)
Ham88.   Hamilton, R.S.: The Ricci flow on surfaces, Cont. Math. **71**, 237-261,
          (1988)

Har09.   Harrison, J.: Handbook of Practical Logic and Automated Reasoning. Cambridge Univ. Press, (2009)
Hay01.   Haykin, S. (Ed.): Kalman Filtering and Neural Networks. Wiley, New York, (2001)
Hay05.   Haykin, S.: Cognitive Radio: Brain-Empowered Wireless Communications, IEEE J. Selec. Areas in Commun. 23(2), 201-220, (2005)
Hay06.   Haykin, S.: Cognitive Radar: A way of the future, IEEE Sig. Proc. Mag. 31, 30-40, (2006)
Hay09.   Haykin, S.: Foundations of Cognitive Dynamic Systems, IEEE Lecture, Queens Univ., Kingston, Ontario, Canada, (2009)
Hay12.   Haykin, S., Fatemi, M., Setoodeh, P., Xue, Y.: Cognitive Control, Proc. IEEE, 100(12), 3156-3169, (2012)
Hay12a.   Haykin, S.: Cognitive dynamic systems: Radar, control, and radio, Proc. IEEE, 100(7), 2095-2103, (2012)
Hay12b.   Haykin, S.: Cognitive Dynamic Systems. Cambridge Univ. Press, Cambridge, U.K. (2012)
Hay14.   Haykin, S. (Guest Editor): Cognitive Dynamic Systems (special issue), Proceedings of the IEEE, 102(4), April (2014)
Hay91.   Haykin, S.: Adaptive Filter Theory. Prentice-Hall, Englewood Cliffs, (1991)
Hay94.   Haykin, S.: Neural Networks: A Comprehensive Foundation. Macmillan, (1994)
Heb49.   Hebb, D.O.: The Organization of Behavior, Wiley, New York, (1949)
Hec87.   Hecht-Nielsen, R.: Counterpropagation networks. Applied Optics, 26(23), 4979-4984, (1987)
Hec90.   Hecht-Nielsen, R.: NeuroComputing. Addison-Wesley, Reading, (1990)
Hei73.   Heinlein, R.A.: Time Enough For Love. G.P. Putnam's Sons, New York, NY, USA (1973)
Hey13.   Christof Heyns. Report of the special rapporteur on extrajudicial, summary or arbitrary executions, Christof Heyns. Report A/HRC/23/47, Office of the United Nations High Commissioner for Human Rights, Palais des Nations,CH-1211 Geneva 10, Switzerland, April (2013)
Hin07.   Hinton, G.: Boltzmann machine, Scholarpedia, 2(5), 1668, (2007)
Hin09.   Hinton, G.: Deep belief networks, Scholarpedia, 4(5), 5947, (2009)
Hin10.   Hinton, G.: A Practical Guide to Training Restricted Boltzmann Machines, UTML TR 2010003, Univ. Toronto, (2010)
Hin86.   Hinton, G.E.: Learning distributed representations of concepts. In Proceedings of the Eighth Annual Conference of the Cognitive Science Society, 1-12. Hillsdale, NJ: Erlbaum, (1986); http://www.cogsci.ucsd.edu/~ajyu/Teaching/Cogs202_sp13/Readings/hinton86.pdf
Hop82.   Hopfield, J.J.: Neural networks and physical systems with emergent collective computational abilities. Proc. Natl. Acad. Sci. USA 79, 2554, (1982)
Hop84.   Hopfield, J.J.: Neurons with graded response have collective computational properties like those of two-state neurons. Proc. Natl. Acad. Sci. USA, 81, 3088-3092, (1984)
Hor01.   Horn, P.: Autonomic computing: IBM's Perspective on the State of Information Technology. IBM Corporation, New York, NY, USA (2001); https://web.archive.org/web/20110916160342/http://www.research.ibm.com/autonomic/manifesto/autonomic_computing.pdf

Hry97.   Hrycej, T.: Neurocontrol: Towards an Industrial Control Methodology, Wiley-Interscience, New York (1997)

IA07.   Ivancevic, V.G., Aidman, E.V.: Life-space foam: A medium for motivational and cognitive dynamics, Physica A: Statistical Mechanics and its Applications, **382**, 616-630, (2007)

IAY09.   Ivancevic, V.G., Aidman, E.V., Yen, L.: Extending feynman's formalisms for modeling human joint action coordination, International Journal of Biomathematics, **2**(1), 1-7, (2009)

IFB08.   Yu, Y., Isard, M., Fetterly, D. *et al.*: DryadLINQ: A system for general-purpose distributed data-parallel computing using a high-level language. In Proc. 8th USENIX Conf. Operating Systems Design and Implementation, OSDI'08, 1-14, USENIX Association, Berkeley, CA

IGG14.   Ivancevic, T., Greenberg, H., Greenberg, R.: Enhancing Performance and Reducing Stress in Sports: Technological Advances. Springer Series Cognitive Systems Monographs, Berlin, (2014)

II05.   Ivancevic, V., Ivancevic, T.: Human-Like Biomechanics. Springer, Series: Microprocessor-Based and Intelligent Systems Engineering, Vol. 28, (2005)

II06a.   Ivancevic, V., Ivancevic, T.: Natural Biodynamics. World Scientific, Series: Mathematical Biology, (2006)

II06b.   Ivancevic, V., Ivancevic, T.: Geometrical Dynamics of Complex Systems. Springer, Series: Microprocessor-Based and Intelligent Systems Engineering, Vol. 31, (2006)

II07a.   Ivancevic, V., Ivancevic, T.: Neuro-Fuzzy Associative Machinery for Comprehensive Brain and Cognition Modelling. Springer, Berlin, (2007)

II07b.   Ivancevic, V., Ivancevic, T.: Applied Differential Geometry: A Modern Introduction. World Scientific, Singapore, (2007)

II08.   Ivancevic, V., Ivancevic, T.: Complex Nonlinearity: Chaos, Phase Transitions, Topology Change and Path Integrals, Springer, Berlin, (2008)

II08b.   Ivancevic, V., Ivancevic, T.: Quantum Leap: From Dirac and Feynman, Across the Universe, to Human Body and Mind. World Scientific, Singapore, (2008)

II09.   Ivancevic, V., Ivancevic, T.: Quantum Neural Computation, Springer, Berlin, (2009)

II11.   Ivancevic, V., Ivancevic, T.: Ricci flow and nonlinear reaction-diffusion systems in biology, chemistry, and physics, Nonl. Dyn. **65**(1-2), 35-54, (2011)

II13.   Ivancevic, V., Ivancevic, T.: New Trends in Control Theory. World Scientific, Singapore, (2013)

II13.   Ivancevic, V., Ivancevic, T.: Sine-Gordon Solitons, Kinks and Breathers as Physical Models of Nonlinear Excitations in Living Cellular Structures, J. Geo. Sym. Phys. **31**, 1-56, (2013)

IJM10.   Ivancevic, T., Jovanovic, B., Markovic, S.: Fuzzy control strategies in human operator and sport modeling, Fuz. Inf. Eng. (Springer), **2**(2), 157-186, (2010)

IR10a.   Ivancevic, V., Reid, D.: Entropic geometry of crowd dynamics. A Chapter in Nonlear Dynamics (T. Evancs, Ed.), Intech, Vienna, (2010)

IR10b.   Ivancevic, V., Reid, D.: Geometrical and Topological Duality in Crowd Dynamics. Int. J. Biomath. **3**(4), 493-507, (2010)

IR11.   Ivancevic, V.G., Reid, D.J.: Formal-Language-Oriented Foundation of Dynamics of Human Crowds Using Topos-Theory. In Innovations in Defence Support Systems Vol. 2, Studies in Computational Intelligence Vol. 338, 21-113, (2011)

IR12.   Ivancevic, V., Reid, D.: Turbulence and Shock-Waves in Crowd Dynamics, Nonlin. Dyn. **68**, 285-304, (2012)

IR14.   Ivancevic, V., Reid, D.: Controlled Complexity in Pulse Conduction: Traveling Solitons from Neural to Optical Fibers, Math. Eng., Sci. Aerospace, **5**(1), 17-32, (2014)

IR15.   Ivancevic, V., Reid, D.: Complexity and Control: Towards a Rigorous Behavioral Theory of Complex Dynamical Systems, World Scientific, Singapore, (2015)

IRA10.   Ivancevic, V., Reid, D., Aidman, E.: Crowd behavior dynamics: entropic path-integral model. Nonl. Dyn. **59**, 351-373, (2010)

IRS14.   Ivancevic, V., Reid, D., Scholz, J.: Action-Amplitude Approach to Controlled Entropic Self-Organization, Entropy **16**, 2699-2712, (2014)

IS15.   Ioffe, S., Szegedy, C.: Batch normalization: Accelerating deep network training by reducing internal covariate shift. CoRR, arXiv:1502.03167, (2015)

IS95.   Ioannou, P., Sun, J.: Robust Adaptive Control, Prentice-Hall, Englewood Cliffs, NJ, (1995)

IY16.   Ivancevic, V., Yue, Y.: Hamiltonian Dynamics and Control of a Joint Autonomous Land-Air Operation, Nonlinear Dynamics, **84**(4), 1853-1865, (2016)

Ill04.   Illusie, L.: What is a Topos, Notices of AMS, **51**(9), 1060-1061, (2004)

Isi89.   Isidori, A.: Nonlinear Control Systems. An Introduction, (2nd ed.) Springer, Berlin, (1989)

Iva04.   Ivancevic, V.: Symplectic rotational geometry in human biomechanics, SIAM Rev., **46**(3), 455-474, (2004)

Iva10.   Ivancevic, V.: Adaptive-Wave Alternative for the Black-Scholes Option Pricing Model, Cogn. Comput. **2**(1), 17-30, (2010)

Iva10.   Ivancevic, V.G.: Nonlinear complexity of human biodynamics engine, Nonlin. Dynamics, **61**(1-2), 123-139, (2010)

Iva11.   Ivancevic, V.: Adaptive Wave Models for Sophisticated Option Pricing, J. Math. Finance, **1**(3), 41-49, (2011)

JCM15.   Jean, S., Cho, K., Memisevic, R., Bengio, Y.: On using very large target vocabulary for neural machine translation. In Proc. of the 53rd Annual Meeting of the Association for Computational Linguistics and the 7th International Joint Conference on Natural Language Processing (Volume 1: Long Papers), 1-10, Beijing, China, July (2015)

JG15.   Jacob, B., Guennebaud, G. *et al.*: Eigen library for linear algebra, (2015); http://eigen.tuxfamily.org

JIB07.   Jsang, A., Ismail, R., Boyd, C.: A survey of trust and reputation systems for online service provision. Decision Support Systems, **43**(2), 618-644, (2007)

JJ06.   Jarvis, B., Jain, L.: Trust in LORA: Towards a Formal Definition of Trust in BDI Agents. In Knowledge-Based Intelligent Information and Engineering Systems: 10th International Conference, KES 2006 Proceedings, Part II, 458-463. Springer, Berlin, Heidelberg, (2006)

JMT05.   Jonker, C.M., Meijer, S., Tykhonov, D., Verwaart, T.: Modelling and simulation of selling and deceit for the trust and tracing game. In Proc. Trust in Agent Societies Workshop, 78-90, (2005)

JPS01.   Jager, W., Popping, R., van de Sande, H.: Clustering and fighting in two-party crowds: Simulating the approach-avoidance conflict, J. Artificial Societies and Social Simulation, 4(3), 7, (2001)

JSD14.   Jia, Y., Shelhamer, E., Donahue, J. *et al.*: Caffe: Convolutional architecture for fast feature embedding. In Proc. ACM International Conference on Multimedia, 675-678. ACM, (2014); arXiv:1408.5093, (2014)

JT99.   Jonker, C.M., Treur, J.: Formal analysis of models for the dynamics of trust based on experiences. Lecture Notes in Computer Science (including subseries Lecture Notes in Artificial Intelligence and Lecture Notes in Bioinformatics), **1647**, 221-231, (1999)

JU04.   Julier, S.J., Uhlmann, J.K.: Unscented filtering and nonlinear estimation, Proc. IEEE, **92**(3), 401-422, (2004)

JVS16.   Józefowicz, R., Vinyals, O., Schuster, M., Shazeer, N., Wu, Y.: Exploring the limits of language modeling. CoRR, arXiv:1602.02410, (2016)

Jac15.   Jacob, B. *et al.*: Gemmlowp: a small self-contained low-precision GEMM library, (2015); https://github.com/google/gemmlowp

Jay03.   Jaynes, E.T.: Probability theory: the logic of science. Cambridge Univ. Press, Cambridge, UK, (2003)

Jaz70.   Jazwinsky, A.M.: Stochastic Processes and Filtering Theory. Academic Press, New York, (1970)

Joa00.   Joao, M.L.: An Extended Kalman Filter for Quaternion-Based Attitude Estimation. Master thesis, Computer Science Department, Naval Postgraduate School, Monterey, CA, (2000)

Jor86.   Jordan, M.I.: Serial order: A parallel distributed processing approach. ICS report 8608, Institute for Cognitive Science, UCSD, La Jolla, (1986); http://cseweb.ucsd.edu/~gary/PAPER-SUGGESTIONS/Jordan-TR-8604.pdf

Jos99.   Josang, A.: Trust-based decision making for electronic transactions. In Proc. 4th Nordic Workshop on Secure Computer Systems (NORDSEC99), 496-502, (1999)

Jou16.   Jouppi, N.: Google supercharges machine learning tasks with TPU custom chip, (2016); https://cloudplatform.googleblog.com/2016/05/Google-supercharges-machine-learning-tasks-with-custom-chip.html

KB09.   Kolda, T.G., Bader, B.W.: Tensor Decompositions and Applications. SIAM Review, **51**(3), 455-500, (2009)

KB09.   Kolda, T.G., Bader, B.W.: Tensor decompositions and applications, SIAM Rev. **51**(3), 455-500, (2009)

KB61.   Kalman, R.E., Bucy, R.S.: New Results in Linear Filtering and Prediction Theory, J. Basic Eng. **96**, 95-108, (1961)

KD01.   van der Kooij, H., Jacobs, R., van der Helm, F.: An adaptive model of sensory integration in a dynamic environment applied to human stance control. Biol. Cybern **84**, 103-115, (2001)

KD03.   van der Kooij, H., Donker, S.: Use of Adaptive Model of Balance Control in the Identification of Postural Dynamics. Proc. ISB'03, Univ. Otago, Dunedin, NZ, (2003)

KD12.   Kumar, A., Daumé III, H.: Learning task grouping and overlap in multi-
            task learning. Proc. 29th Int. Conf. Machine Learning (ICML), (2012)
KFA69.   Kalman, R.E., Falb, P., Arbib, M.A.: Topics in Mathematical System
            Theory. McGraw Hill, New York, (1969)
KG03.   Karlsson, R., Gustafsson, F.: Particle filter and Cramer-Rao lower
            bound for underwater navigation. In Proc. IEEE Int. Conf. Acoustics,
            Speech, Signal Proc. (ICASSP), Hong Kong, (2003)
KK02.   Kim, E., Kim, S.: Stability analysis and synthesis for an affine fuzzy
            control system via LMI and ILMI: Continuous case, IEEE Trans. Fuzzy
            Syst. 10(3), 391-400, (2002)
KKK07.   Kurnaz, S., Kaynak, O., Konakoğlu, E.: Adaptive Neuro-Fuzzy Infer-
            ence System Based Autonomous Flight Control of Unmanned Air Ve-
            hicles. A chapter in Advances in Neural Networks (ed. D. Liu et al.),
            Lecture Notes in Computer Science, 4491, 14-21, Springer, (2007)
KR07.   Keeling, M., Rohani, P.: Modeling Infectious Diseases in Humans and
            Animals. Princeton Univ. Press, Princeton, NJ, (2007)
KS80.   Kindermann, R., Snell, J.L.: Markov Random Fields and Their Appli-
            cations. American Mathematical Society, New York, (1980)
KSG05.   Karlsson, R., Schön, T., Gustafsson, F.: Complexity analysis of the
            marginalized particle filter, IEEE Trans. Sig. Proc, 53(11), 4408-4411,
            (2005)
KSH12.   Krizhevsky, A., Sutskever, I., Hinton, G.E.: ImageNet classification
            with deep convolutional neural networks. In Advances in Neural Infor-
            mation Processing Systems, (2012); https://papers.nips.cc/paper/4824-
            imagenet-classification-with-deep-convolutional-neural-networks.pdf
KSM13.   Koster, A., Sabater-Mir, J., Schorlemmer, M.: Argumentation and
            Trust. In Ossowski, S. (ed), Agreement Technologies, chapter 25, 441-
            451, Springer Netherlands, Dordrecht, (2013)
KSS13.   Koster, A., Schorlemmer, M., Sabater-Mir, J.: Opening the black box
            of trust: reasoning about trust models in a bdi agent. Journal of Logic
            and Computation, 23(1), 25-58, (2013)
KST08.   Karlsson, R., Schön, T., Törnqvist, D., Conte, G., Gustafsson, F.: Uti-
            lizing model structure for efficient simultaneous localization and map-
            ping for a UAV application, Proc. IEEE Aerospace Conf. Big Sky, MT,
            (2008)
KTS14.   Karpathy, A., Toderici, G., Shetty, S. et al.: Large-scale video classifica-
            tion with convolutional neural networks. In Computer Vision and Pat-
            tern Recognition (CVPR), 2014 IEEE Conference on, 1725-1732. IEEE,
            (2014); https://research.google.com/pubs/archive/42455.pdf.
KZ95.   Kwon, T.M., Zervakis, M.: KWTA networks and their application. Mul-
            tidim. Syst. and Sig. Proccessing 6, 333-346, (1995)
Kal60.   Kalman, R.E.: A new approach to linear filtering and prediction prob-
            lems. Trans. ASME, Ser. D, J. Bas. Eng., 82, 34-45, (1960)
Kan58.   Kan, D.M.: Adjoint Functors. Trans. Am. Math. Soc. 89, 294-329,
            (1958)
Ken99.   Kennaway, J.R.: Control of a multi-legged robot based on hierarchical
            perceptual control theory. J. PCT 1(1), (1999)
Kip95.   Kipnis, D.: Trust and Technology. In Kramer, R.M., Tyler, T.R. (eds),
            Trust in organizations: Frontiers of theory and research. Sage Publica-
            tions, (1995)

Key73.   Keynes, J.M.: The General Theory of Employment, Interest and Money, Macmillan, London, (1973)

Koh82.   Kohonen, T.: Self-Organized Formation of Toplogically Correct Feature Maps. Biological Cybernetics **43**, 59-69, (1982)

Koh88.   Kohonen, T.: Self Organization and Associative Memory. Springer, (1988)

Koh91.   Kohonen, T.: Self-Organizing Maps: Optimization Approaches. In: Artificial Neural Networks, ed. T. Kohonen *et al.* North-Holland, Amsterdam, (1991)

Koh.   NIHON KOHDEN Corp.: Mobile long-term EEG. Viewed Dec. (2016);   http://www.nihonkohden.de/products/neurology/eeg/mobile-long-term-eeg.html?L=1

Kos86.   Kosko, B.: Fuzzy Cognitive Maps. Int. J. Man-Mach. Stud. **24**, 65-75, (1986)

Kos88.   Kosko, B.: Bidirectional Associative Memory. IEEE Trans. Sys. Man Cyb. **18**, 49-60, (1988)

Kos92.   Kosko, B.: Neural Networks and Fuzzy Systems, A Dynamical Systems Approach to Machine Intelligence. Prentice-Hall, New York, (1992)

Kos93.   Kosko, B.: Fuzzy Thinking. Disney Books, Hyperion, (1993)

Kos96.   Kosko, B.: Fuzzy Engineering. Prentice Hall, New York, (1996)

Kos99.   Kosko, B.: The Fuzzy Future: From Society and Science to Heaven in a Chip. Random House, Harmony, (1999)

Kri14.   Krizhevsky, A.: One weird trick for parallelizing convolutional neural networks, arXiv:1404.5997, (2014)

Kum15.   Kumar, P.: Quantum effects in Biological Environments (QuBE), DARPA, (2015); http://www.darpa.mil/program/quantum-effects-in-biological-environments

Kun13.   Künsch, H.R.: Particle filters, Bernoulli, **19**(4), 1391-1403, (2013)

LA16.   Leu, G., Abbass, H.: A multi-disciplinary review of knowledge acquisition methods: From human to autonomous eliciting agents. Knowledge-Based Systems, **105**, 1-22, (2016)

LAP14.   Li, M., Andersen, D.G., Park, J. *et al.*: Scaling distributed machine learning with the Parameter Server. In 11th USENIX Symposium on Operating Systems Design and Implementation (OSDI 14), 583-598, (2014); https://www.usenix.org/system/files/conference/osdi14/osdi14-paper-chilimbi.pdf

LBD04.   Lebeltel, O., Bessière, P., Diard, J., Mazer, E.: Bayesian robot programming. Aut. Robots, **16**(1), 49-79, (2004)

LBD89.   LeCun, Y., Boser, B., Denker, J.S., Henderson, D., Howard, R.E., Hubbard, W., Jackel, L.D.: Backpropagation applied to handwritten zip code recognition. Neural Comput. **1**(4), 541-551, (1989)

LBH15.   LeCun, Y., Bengio, Y., Hinton, G.: Deep learning, Nature **521**, 436-444, (2015)

LBL09.   Larochelle, H., Bengio, Y., Louradour, J., Lamblin, P.: Exploring strategies for training deep neural networks. Journal of Machine Learning Research, **10**, 1-40, (2009); http://deeplearning.cs.cmu.edu/pdfs/1111/jmlr10_larochelle.pdf

LC94.   Longtin, A., Chialvo, D.R.: Stochastic and Deterministic Resonances for Excitable Systems. Phys. Rev. Lett. **81**, 4012-4015, (1994)

LCR04.   Langson, W., Chryssochoos, I., Rakovic, S.V., Mayne, D.Q.: Robust
            model predictive control using tubes. Automatica **40**(1), 125-133, (2004)

LH08.   Li, H., Haldane, F.D.M.: Entanglement Spectrum as a Generalization
            of Entanglement Entropy: Identification of Topological Order in Non-
            Abelian Fractional Quantum Hall Effect States, Phys. Rev. Lett. **101**,
            010504, (2008)

LHD84.   Luhmann, N., Davis, H., Raffan, J., Rooney, K.: Trust and power. Mod-
            ern Law Review, **47**(5), 603, (1984)

LJM92.   Lozano-Pérez, T., Jones, J., Mazer, E., O'Donnell, P.: HANDEY, A
            Robot Task Planner. MIT Press, Cambridge, MA, (1992)

LJY98.   Lewis, F.W., Jagannathan, S., Yesildirak, A.: Neural Network Control of
            Robot Manipulators and Non-Linear Systems. CRC Press, Boca Raton,
            FL (1998)

LK99.   Lee, S., Kim, S.: Parameter dependence of stochastic resonance in the
            stochastic Hodgkin-Huxley neuron. Phys. Rev. E **60**, 826-830, (1999)

LLB05.   Leutgeb, S., Leutgeb, J.K., Barnes, C.A., Moser, E.I., McNaughton,
            B.L., Moser, M.-B.: Independent codes for spatial and episodic memory
            in hippocampal neuronal ensembles. Science **309**, 619-23, (2005)

LLS11.   Landau, I.D., Lozano, R., M'Saad, M., Karimi, A.: Adaptive Control:
            Algorithms, Analysis and Applications (2nd ed.), Springer, New York,
            (2011)

LM97.   Lin, C-M., Maa, J-H.: Flight Control System Design by Self-Organizing
            Fuzzy Logic Controller, J. Guidance, Control, and Dynamics, **20**(1),
            189-190, (1997)

LMV00.   Lathauwer, L.D., Moor, B.D., Vandewalle, J.: A multilinear singular
            value decomposition, SIAM. J. Matrix Anal. & Appl. **21**(4), 1253-1278,
            (2000)

LN07.   Levin, M., Nave, C.P.: Tensor Renormalization Group Approach to
            Two-Dimensional Classical Lattice Models, Phys. Rev. Lett. **99**, 120601,
            (2007)

LR08.   Latorre, J.I., Riera, A.: A short review on entanglement in quantum spin
            systems, J. Phys. A: Math. Theor. **42**, 504002 (2009); Amico, L., Fazio,
            R., Osterloh, A., Vedral, V.: Entanglement in Many-Body Systems, Rev.
            Mod. Phys. **80**, 517-576, (2008)

LRM12.   Le, Q., Ranzato, M., Monga, R. *et al.*: Building high-level features
            using large scale unsupervised learning. In ICML'2012, (2012); http:
            //research.google.com/archive/unsupervised_icml2012.pdf

LS15.   Lavin, A., Gray, S.: Fast algorithms for convolutional neural networks.
            CoRR, arXiv:1509.09308, (2015)

LS86.   Lambek, J., Scott, P.J.: Introduction to higher order categorical logic.
            Cambridge University Press, Cambridge, (1986)

LS97.   Lawvere, W., Schanuel, S.: Conceptual Mathematics: A First Introduc-
            tion to Categories. Cambridge Univ. Press, Cambridge, (1997)

LT00.   Lee, C.-H., Teng, C.-C.: Identification and control of dynamic systems
            using recurrent fuzzy neural networks. IEEE Trans. Fuz. Sys. **8**(4), 349-
            366, (2000)

LTG03.   Lamon, P., Tapus, A., Glauser, E., Tomatis, N., Siegwart, R.: Envi-
            ronmental modeling with fingerprint sequences for topological global
            localization, in Proc. Int. Conf. Intel. Rob. Sys. **4**, pp. 3781-3786, Las
            Vegas, (2003)

LWA06.   Lin, F.-H., Wald, L.L., Ahlfors, S.P., Hämäläinen, M. S., Kwong, K.K.,
          Belliveau, J.W.: Dynamic magnetic resonance inverse imaging of human
          brain function. Magnetic Resonance in Medicine, **56**(4), 787-802, (2006)
LZC14.   Li, M., Zhang, T., Chen, Y., Smola, A.J.: Efficient mini-batch training
          for stochastic optimization. In Proc. of the 20th ACM SIGKDD Int.
          Conf. Knowledge Discovery and Data Mining, KDD '14, 661-670, New
          York, NY, USA, ACM, (2014); `https://www.cs.cmu.edu/~muli/file/`
          `minibatch_sgd.pdf`
Lam32.   Lamb, H.: Hydrodynamics (6th ed). Dover, New York, (1932)
Lam68.   Lambek, J.: Deductive systems and categories I: Syntactic calculus and
          residuated categories, Mathematical Systems Theory **2**, 287-318, (1968)
Lam69.   Lambek, J.: Deductive systems and categories II: Standard construc-
          tions and closed categories, in: Category Theory, Homology Theory and
          their Applications I, Lecture Notes in Mathematics 86, Springer, Berlin,
          76-122, (1969)
Lam72.   Lambek, J.: Deductive systems and categories III: Cartesian closed cat-
          egories, intuitionist propositional calculus, and combinatory logic, in:
          F. W. Lawvere ed., Toposes, Algebraic Geometry and Logic, Lecture
          Notes in Mathematics 274, Springer, Berlin, 57-82, (1972)
Lan14.   Lanting, T. *et al.*: Entanglement in a Quantum Annealing Processor,
          Phys. Rev. X **4**, 021041, (2014)
Law75.   Lawvere, F.W.: Continuously variable sets: algebraic geometry = geo-
          metric logic. In Proc. Logic Colloquium Bristol 1973, North-Holland,
          Amsterdam, (1975)
Lax68.   Lax, P.: Integrals of nonlinear equations of evolution and solitary waves.
          Comm. Pure Appl. Math. **21**, 467-490, (1968)
LB95.   LeCun, Y., Bengio, Y.: Convolutional networks for images, speech, and
          time series. In The handbook of brain theory and neural networks, 3361,
          (1995)
LBH15.   LeCun, Y., Bengio, Y., Hinton, G.: Deep learning. Nature, 521(7553),
          436-444, (2015)
Lei02.   Leinster, T.: A survey of definitions of n-category. Theor. Appl. Categ.
          10, 1-70, (2002)
Lei03.   Leinster, T.: Higher Operads, Higher Categories, London Mathematical
          Society Lecture Notes Series, Cambridge Univ. Press, (2003)
Lei04.   Leinster, T.: Operads in higher-dimensional category theory. Theor.
          Appl. Categ. **12**, 73-194, (2004)
LM05.   Lane, D., Maxfield, R.: Ontological Uncertainty and Innovation, J. Evol.
          Economics, **15**(1), (2005)
LV08.   Li, M, Vitnyi, P.: An Introduction to Kolmogorov Complexity and its
          Applications (2008 Ed.), Springer, New York, (2008)
Leo97.   Leonard, N.E.: Stability of a bottom-heavy underwater vehicle. Auto-
          matica, **33**(3), 331-346, (1997)
Leu05.   Leutgeb, J.K. *et al.*: Progressive transformation of hippocampal neu-
          ronal representations in "morphed" environments. Neuron 48, 345-58,
          (2005)
Lev09.   Levien, R.: Attack-Resistant Trust Metrics. In Golbeck, J. (ed.) Com-
          puting with Social Trust, chapter5, 121-132, Springer, London, (2009)
Lew36.   Lewin, K.: Principles of Topological Psychology, McGraw-Hill, New
          York, (1936)

Lew46.   Lewin, K.: Action research and minority problems. J. Soc. Issues 2(4), 34-46, (1946)

Lew47.   Lewin, K.: Frontiers in Group Dynamics I: Concept, method, and reality in social science, Human Relations **1**, 5-41; II: Channels of group life; social planning and action research, ibid, 143-153, (1947)

Lew47.   Lewin, K.: Frontiers in Group Dynamics I: Concept, method, and reality in social science, Human Relations **1**, 5-41; II: Channels of group life; social planning and action research, ibid, 143-153, (1947)

Lew48.   Lewin, K.: Resolving Social Conflicts: Selected Papers on Group Dynamics. Harper and Row, New York, (1948)

Lew51.   Lewin, K.: Field Theory in Social Science. Univ. Chicago Press, (1951)

Lew97.   Lewin, K.: Resolving Social Conflicts and Field Theory in Social Science. Am. Psych. Assoc. Washington, (1997)

Lol08.   Loll, R.: The emergence of spacetime or quantum gravity on your desktop, Class. Quantum Grav. **25**, 114006, (2008); Loll, R., Ambjorn, J., Jurkiewicz, J.: The Universe from scratch, Contemp. Phys. **47**, 103-117, (2006); Ambjorn, J., Jurkiewicz, J., Loll, R.: Reconstructing the Universe, Phys. Rev. D **72**, 064014, (2005)

Lon93.   Longtin, A.: Stochastic Resonance in Neuron Models. J. Stat. Phys. **70**, 309, (1993)

Lor63.   Lorenz, E.N.: Deterministic Nonperiodic Flow. J. Atmos. Sci., **20**, 130-141, (1963)

Lov11.   Lovric, M.: International Encyclopedia of Statistical Science, Springer, Berlin, (2011)

Lug02.   Luger, G.F.: Artificial Intelligence: Structures and Strategies for Complex Problem Solving. Pearson Educ (4th ed.) Ltd, Harlow, UK, (2002)

Lui02.   Luinge, H.J.: Inertial Sensing of Human Movement. Ph.D. thesis Univ. Twente, Twente Univ. Press, (2002)

MBJ06.   McNaughton, B.L., Battaglia, F.P., Jensen, O., Moser, E.I., Moser, M.-B.: Path integration and the neural basis of the 'cognitive map', Nat. Rev. Neurosci. **7**, 663-678, (2006)

MCC13.   Mikolov, T., Chen, K., Corrado, G., Dean, J.: Efficient estimation of word representations in vector space. In Int. Conf. Learning Representations: Workshops Track, arXiv:1301.3781, (2013)

MCC98.   McKnight, D.H., Cummings, L.L., Chervany, N.L.: Initial trust formation in new organizational relationships. Academy of Management review, **23**(3), 473-490, (1998)

MCM91.   McNaughton, B.L., Chen, L.L., Markus, E.J.: 'Dead reckoning', landmark learning, and the sense of direction: a neurophysiological and computational hypothesis. J. Cog. Neurosci. **3**, 190-202, (1991)

MCT12.   Mansell, W., Carey, T., Tai, S.: A transdiagnostic approach to CBT using method of levels therapy: distinctive features. The CBT distinctive features series. Milton Park, Abingdon, Oxon; New York: Routledge, (2012)

MF00.   Mel, B., Fiser, J.: Minimizing Binding Errors Using Learned Conjunctive Features. Neural Comp. **12**, 731-762, (2000)

MG77.   Mackey, M.C., Glass, L.: Oscillation and chaos in physiological control systems. Science **197**, 287-295, (1977)

MG93.   Meehan, G., Joy, M.: Animated Fuzzy Logic, J. Func. Prog. (Cambridge) **1**(1), 1-23, (1993)

MGM06.   Marti, S., Garcia-Molina, H.: Taxonomy of trust: Categorizing P2P rep-
          utation systems. Computer Networks, **50**(4), 472-484, (2006)
MGh96.   McGhee, R.B.: Research Notes: A Quaternion Attitude Filter Using An-
          gular Rate Sensors, Accelerometers, and a 3-Axis Magnetometer, Com-
          puter Science Department, Naval Postgraduate School, Monterey, CA,
          (1996)
MHS14.   Maddison, C.J., Huang, A., Sutskever, I., Silver, D.: Move evaluation in
          Go using deep convolutional neural networks, arXiv:1412.6564, (2014)
MIM15.   McSherry, F., Isard, M., Murray, D.G.: Scalability! But at what
          COST? In Proc. 15th USENIX Conf. Hot Topics in Operat-
          ing Systems, HOTOS'15, Berkeley, CA, USA, USENIX Associ-
          ation, (2015); https://www.usenix.org/system/files/conference/
          hotos15/hotos15-paper-mcsherry.pdf
MKM08.   Moser, E.I., Kropff, E., Moser, M.-B.: Place Cells, Grid Cells, and the
          Brain's Spatial Representation System, Annu. Rev. Neurosci. **31**, 69-89,
          (2008)
MKS15.   Mnih, V., Kavukcuoglu, K., Silver, D. *et al.*: Human-level control
          through deep reinforcement learning. Nature, **518**(7540), 529-533,
          (2015)
Mac87.   Machina, M.: Choice Under Uncertainty: Problems Solved and Un-
          solved, J. Economic Persp., **1**(1), 121-154, (1987)
Mir02.   Mirowski, P.: Machine Dreams: Economics Becomes a Cyborg Science,
          Cambridge Univ. Press, (2002)
McD76.   McDermott, D.: Artificial Intelligence Meets Natural Stupidity,
          SIGART Newsletter, **57**, (1976)
MLI16.   MLI: Machine Learning and Inference Laboratory, (2016); http://www.
          mli.gmu.edu/mission
MLN10.   Murg, V., Legeza, Ö., Noack, R.M., Verstraete, F.: Simulating strongly
          correlated quantum systems with tree tensor networks, Phys. Rev. B
          82, 205105, (2010)
MLS94.   Murray, R.M., Li, X., Sastry, S.: Robotic Manipulation, CRC Press,
          Boco Raton, Fl, (1994)
MM02.   Mougin, G., Magnaudet, J.: The generalized Kirchhoff equations and
          their application to the interaction between a rigid body and an ar-
          bitrary time-dependent viscous flow, Int. J. Multiphase Flow, **28**(11),
          1837-1851, (2002)
MM09.   Merrick, K.E., Maher, M.L,: Motivated reinforcement learning. [elec-
          tronic resource] : curious characters for multiuser games. Springer,
          Berlin, London, (2009)
MM80.   Mittelstaedt, M.L., Mittelstaedt, H.: Homing by path integration in a
          mammal (in German), Naturwissenschaften **67**, 566-567, (1980)
MM90.   Mayne, D.Q., Michalska, H.: Receding horizon control of nonlinear sys-
          tems, IEEE Trans. Automat. Control, **35**, 814-824, (1990)
MM92.   MacLane, S., Moerdijk, I.: Sheaves in Geometry and Logic: A First
          Introduction to Topos Theory. Springer-Verlag, London, (1992)
MMS05.   Mahoney, G., Myrvold, W.J., Shoja, G.C.: Generic reliability trust
          model. In Proc. 3rd Annual Conference on Privacy, Security and Trust,
          5, 113-120, (2005)
MNS16.   Moritz, P., Nishihara, R., Stoica, I., Jordan, M.I.: SparkNet: Training
          deep networks in Spark. In Int. Conf. Learning Representations, (2016)

MP43. McCulloch, W., Pitts, W.: A logical calculus of the ideas imminent in the nervous activity. Bull. Math. Biophys. **5**, 115-133, 1943

MP69. Minsky, M., Papert, S.: Perceptrons. MIT Press, Cambridge, MA, (1969)

MPR98. McLeod, P., Plunkett, K., Rolls, E.T.: Introduction to connectionist modelling of cognitive processes. Oxford Univ. Press, Oxford, (1998)

MRS95. Müller, B., Reinhardt, J., Strickland, M.T.: Neural Networks, An Introduction. Springer, (1995)

MSB09. Mezzacapo, F., Schuch, N., Boninsegni, M., Cirac, J.I.: Ground-state properties of quantum many-body systems: entangled-plaquette states and variational Monte Carlo, New J. Phys. **11**, 083026, (2009)

MSB92. Maschke, B., van der Schaft, A.J., Breedveld, P.: An intrinsic Hamiltonian formulation of network dynamics: non-standard poisson structures and gyrators, J. of the Franklin Inst. **329**, 923-966, (1992)

MSI13. Murray, D.G., McSherry, F., Isaacs, R., Isard, M., Barham, P., Abadi, M.: Naiad: a timely dataflow system. In Proc. 24 ACM Symposium on Operating Systems Principles, 439-455. ACM, (2013); http://research.microsoft.com:8082/pubs/201100/naiad_sosp2013.pdf

MSR12. Mars, R.B., Sallet, J., Rushworth, M.F.S., Yeung, N.: Neural Basis of Motivational and Cognitive Control. Cambridge, MA: MIT Press, (2012)

MT13. Motsch, S., Tadmor, E.: Heterophilious dynamics enhances consensus, arXiv:1301.4123, (2013)

MTK02. Montemerlo, M., Thrun, S., Koller, D., Wegbreit, B.: FastSLAM: A factored solution to the simultaneous localization and mapping problem. Proc. AAAI-02, (2002)

MTK03. Montemerlo, M., Thrun, S., Koller, D., Wegbreit, B.: FastSLAM 2.0: An improved particle filtering algorithm for simultaneous localization and mapping that provably converges. Proc. IJCAI, 1151-1156, (2003)

MTW73. Misner, C.W., Thorne, K.S., Wheeler, J.A.: Gravitation, W.H. Freeman and Company, New York, (1973)

MVB04. Monteiro, S., Vaz, M., Bicho, E.: Attractor dynamics generates robot formation: from theory to implementation. In Proc. 2004 IEEE Int. Conf. ICRA'04 (Robotics and Automation, 2004), **3**, 2582-2586, (2004)

MW09. Murphy, R.R., Woods, D.D.: Beyond Asimov: The Three Laws of Responsible Robotics. Intelligent Systems, IEEE, **24**(4), 14-20, (2009)

MWT02. Montemerlo, M., Whittaker, W., Thrun, S.: Conditional particle filters for simultaneous mobile robot localization and people-tracking. Proc. ICRA-02, (2002)

Mac63. MacLane, S.: Natural associativity and commutativity. Rice University Studies, Papers in Mathematics **49**, 28-46, (1963)

Mac98. MacLane, S.: Categories for the Working Mathematician (2nd edition), Springer, New York, (1998)

Man05. Mansell, W.: Control theory and psychopathology: an integrative approach. Psychology and Psychotherapy: Theory, Research and Practice **78**(2), 141-178, (2005)

Man09. Mandel, J.: A Brief Tutorial on the Ensemble Kalman Filter, arXiv[physics.ao-ph]:0901.3725, (2009)

Man74. Manakov, S.V.: On the theory of two-dimensional stationary self-focusing of electromagnetic waves. (in Russian) Zh. Eksp. Teor. Fiz. **65**,

(1973), 505-516; (transleted into English) Sov. Phys. JETP **38**, 248-253, (1974)

Mar01.   Marken, R.S.: Controlled Variables: Psychology as the Center Fielder Views It, AJP **114**(2), 259-281, (2001)

Mar12a.   Markoff, J.: Scientists See Promise in Deep-Learning Programs, The New York Times, November 23, (2012)

Mar12b.   Marcus, G.: Is Deep Learning a Revolution in Artificial Intelligence? The New Yorker, November 25, (2012)

Mar14.   Marken, R.S.: Control of Perception and other Java Demos, (2008); http://mindreadings.com/demos.htm

Mar90.   Marken, R.S.: A science of purpose. Am. Beh. Sci. **34**, 6-13, (1990)

Mar94a.   Marsh, S.: Optimism and pessimism in trust. In Proc. Ibero-American Conference on Artificial Intelligence (IBERAMIA), 1-12, (1994)

Mar94b.   Marsh, S.P.: Formalising Trust as a Computational Concept. PhD thesis, Dept. Computer Science and Mathematics, University of Stirling, Stirling, Scotland, (1994)

Mat98.   Mato, G.: Stochastic resonance in neural systems: Effect of temporal correlation in the spike trains. Phys. Rev. E **58**, 876-880, (1998)

May79.   Maybeck, P.S.: Stochastic Models, Estimation, and Control, Volume 1, Academic Press, New York, (1979)

McN96.   McNaughton, B.L. *et al.*: Deciphering the hippocampal polyglot: the hippocampus as a path integration system. J. Exp. Biol. **199**, 173-185, (1996)

MoD11.   United Kingdom Ministry of Defence: The UK approach to Unmanned Aircraft Systems. Joint Doctorine Note 2/11, March (2011); https://www.gov.uk/government/publications/jdn-2-11-the-uk-approach-to-unmanned-aircraft-systems

Mou98.   Mountcastle, V.B.: Perceptual Neuroscience: The Cerebral Cortex. Harvard Univ. Press, Cambridge, MA, (1998)

Mov16.   Movidius Ltd. Movidius announces Deep Learning Accelerator and Fathom software framework, (2016); http://www.movidius.com/news/movidius-announces-deep-learning-accelerator-and-fathom-software-framework

Mui87.   Muir, B.M.: Trust between humans and machines, and the design of decision aids. Int. J. Man-Machine Studies, **27**(5), 527-539, (1987)

Mur04.   Murch, R.: Autonomic Computing, IBM Press, (2004)

Mur15.   Muradian, R.: Quantum Fourier Transform Circuit, from the Wolfram Demonstrations Project, (2015)

NAB97a.   Nore, C., Abid, M., Brachet, M.E.: Kolmogorov turbulence in low-temperature superflows, Phys. Rev. Lett. **78**, 3296-3299, (1997)

NAB97b.   Nore, C., Abid, M., Brachet, M.E.: Decaying Kolmogorov turbulence in a model of superflow, Phys. Fluids **9**, 2644-2669, (1997)

NC02.   Nielsen, M.A., Chuang, I.L.: Quantum Computation and Quantum Information. Cambridge Univ. Press, (2002)

NH10.   Nair, V., Hinton, G.: Rectified linear units improve restricted boltzmann machines. In Proc. 27th Int. Conf. Machine Learning (ICML-10), 807-814, (2010)

NHO01.   Nishino, T., Hieida, Y., Okunishi, K. *et al.*: Two-dimensional tensor product variational formulation, Prog. Theor. Phys. **105**, No. 3, 409-417, (2001)

NM44.   von Neumann, J., Morgenstern, O.: Theory of Games and Economic Behavior. Princeton Univ. Press, Princeton, NJ, (1944)

NNM00.   Nagao, N., Nishimura, H., Matsui, N.: A Neural Chaos Model of Multistable Perception. Neural Processing Letters **12**(3): 267-276, (2000)

NPT10.   Naldi, G., Pareschi, L., Toscani, G.: Mathematical Modeling of Collective Behavior in Socio-Economic and Life Sciences, Series: Modeling and Simulation in Science, Engineering and Technology, Birkhauser, Boston, (2010)

NRP00.   Nørgaard, M., Ravn, O., Poulsen, N.K., Hansen, L.K.: Neural Networks for Modelling and Control of Dynamic Systems: A Practitioner's Handbook. Springer, New York, (2000)

NS16.   Nervana   Systems.   neon,   (2016);   https://github.com/NervanaSystems/neon.

NS83.   Nash, C., Sen, S.: Topology and Geometry for Physicists. Academic Press, London, (1983)

Nie12.   Neis, A.: Computability and Randomness, Oxford Univ. Press, (2012)

NS90.   Nijmeijer, H., van der Schaft, A.J.: Nonlinear Dynamical Control Systems, Springer, Dordrecht, (1990)

NS90.   Nijmeijer, H., Van der Schaft, A.J.: Nonlinear Dynamical Control Systems. Springer, New York, (1990)

NSB15.   Nair, A., Srinivasan, P., Blackwell, S. *et al.*: Massively parallel methods for deep reinforcement learning, arXiv:1507.04296, (2015)

NV16.   NVIDIA Corporation. NCCL: Optimized primitives for collective multi-gpu communication, (2016); https://github.com/NVIDIA/nccl

Nik01.   Nikolaou, M.: Model predictive controllers: A critical synthesis of theory and industrial needs, Chapter in Advances in Chemical Engineering, Vol. **26**, 131-204, Academic Press, New York, (2001)

Nit16.   Nithyananda Ed. Team: Avatar Shastra, Nithyananda Univ. Press, Montclair, CA, (2016)

Nit97.   Nitta, T.: An extension of the back-propagation algorithm to complex numbers. Neural Net. **10**(8), 1392-1415, (1997)

OBD98.   O'Keefe, J., Burgess, N., Donnett, J.G., Jeffery, K.J., Maguire, E.A.: Place cells, navigational accuracy, and the human hippocampus, Phil. Trans. R. Soc. Lond. **B 353**, 1333-1340, (1998)

O'Ke76.   O'Keefe, J.: Place units in the hippocampus of the freely moving rat, Exp. Neurol. **51**, 78-109, (1976)

O'Ke99.   O'Keefe, J.: Do hippocampal pyramidal cells signal non-spatial as well as spatial information? Hippocampus **9**, 352-364, (1999)

OB05.   O'Keefe, J., Burgess, N.: Dual phase and rate coding in hippocampal place cells: theoretical significance and relationship to entorhinal grid cells. Hippocampus **15**, 853-66, (2005)

OB05.   O'Keefe, J., Burgess, N.: Dual phase and rate coding in hippocampal place cells: theoretical significance and relationship to entorhinal grid cells. Hippocampus **15**, 853-66, (2005)

OB07.   Oxtoby, O.F., Barashenkov, I.V.: Moving solitons in the discrete nonlinear Schrödinger equation, Phys. Rev. E **76**, 036603, (2007)

OD71.   O'Keefe, J., Dostrovsky, J.: The hippocampus as a spatial map: preliminary evidence from unit activity in the freely moving rat. Brain Res. **34**, 171-175, (1971)

OG08.   Orús, R., Vidal, G.: Infinite time-evolving block decimation algorithm beyond unitary evolution, Phys. Rev. B **78**, 155117, (2008)

ON78.   O'Keefe, J., Nadel, L.: The Hippocampus as a Cognitive Map. Clarendon Press, Oxford, (1978)

OR93.   O'Keefe, J., Recce, M.L.: Phase relationship between hippocampal place units and the EEG theta rhythm, Hippocampus **3**, 317-30, (1993)

ORK15.   Ovtcharov, K., Ruwase, O., Kim, J.-Y. *et al.*: Toward accelerating deep learning at scale using specialized logic. In Hot Chips: A Symposium on High Performance Chips. HOTCHIPS, August (2015); http://research.microsoft.com/apps/pubs/default.aspx?id=246506

Oja82.   Oja, E.: A simplified neuron modeled as a principal component analyzer. J. Math. Biol. **15**, 267-273, (1982)

Oru14.   Orús, R.: Advances on Tensor Network Theory: Symmetries, Fermions, Entanglement, and Holography, Eur. Phys. J. **B87**, 280, (2014)

Oru13.   Orús, R.: A Practical Introduction to Tensor Networks: Matrix Product States and Projected Entangled Pair States, Ann. Phys. **349**, 117-158, (2014)

Ose11.   Oseledets, I.V.: Tensor-train decomposition, SIAM J. Sci. Comput. **33**(5), 2295-2317, (2011)

Oue15.   Ouellette, J.: The Quantum Fabric of Space-Time, Quanta Magazine, (2015); https://www.quantamagazine.org/20150428-how-quantum-pairs-stitch-space-time/

PEL00.   Principe, J., Euliano, N., Lefebvre, C.: Neural and Adaptive Systems: Fundamentals Through Simulations. Wiley, New York, (2000)

PKB07.   Poli, R., Kennedy, J., Blackwell, T.: Particle swarm optimization: An overview, Swarm Intel. **1**(1), 33-57, (2007)

PMB13.   Pascanu, R., Mikolov, T., Bengio, Y.: On the difficulty of training recurrent neural networks. In ICML (3), volume 28 of JMLR Proceedings, 1310-1318. JMLR.org, (2013); http://www.jmlr.org/proceedings/papers/v28/pascanu13.pdf

PR84.   Penrose, R., Rindler, W.: Spinors and space-time, Vol. I, Two-spinor calculus and relativistic fields, Cambridge Univ. Press, (1984)

PS03.   Pitaevskii, L., Stringari, S.: Bose-Einstein Condensation, Oxford University Press, Oxford, (2003)

PSM08.   Pinyol, I., Sabater-Mir, J.: Arguing about Reputation: The LRep Language. In International Workshop on Engineering Societies in the Agents World, 284-299, Springer, Berlin, Heidelberg, (2008)

PSM13.   Pinyol, I., Sabater-Mir, J.: Computational trust and reputation models for open multi-agent systems: a review. Artificial Intelligence Review, ISSN: 0269-2821, Online ISSN: 1573-7462, **40**(1), 1-25, Jun. (2013)

PVC04.   Porras, D., Verstraete, F., Cirac, J.I.: Density matrix renormalization group and periodic boundary conditions: a quantum information perspective, Phys. Rev. Lett. **93**, 227205, (2004)

PY97.   Passino, K.M., Yurkovich, S.: Fuzzy Control, Addison-Wesley, Reading, MA, (1998)

Pea88.   Pearl, J.: Probabilistic Reasoning in Intelligent Systems: Networks of Plausible Inference. Morgan Kaufmann, San Mateo, CA, (1988)

Pei00.   Peinado, A.: Traveling slow waves of neural activity: a novel form of network activity in developing neocortex. J. Neurosci. **20**, RC54(1-6), (2000)

Pen07.   Penrose, R.: The Road to Reality: A Complete Guide to the Laws of the Universe, Vintage Books, (2007)

Pen72.   Penrose, R.: Techniques of differential topology in relativity, SIAM, (1972)

Pen89.   Penrose, R.: The Emperor's New Mind, Oxford Univ. Press, Oxford, (1989)

Pen94.   Penrose, R.: Shadows of the Mind. Oxford Univ. Press, Oxford, (1994)

Per83.   Peregrine, D.H.: Water Waves, Nonlinear Schrödinger Equations and Their Solutions, J. Austral. Math. Soc. Ser. B **25**, 16-43, (1983)

Per84.   Peretto, P.: Collective properties of neural networks: a statistical physics approach. Biol. Cybern. **50**, 51, (1984)

Per92.   Peretto, P.: An Introduction to the Theory of Neural Computation. Cambridge Univ. Press, Cambridge, (1992)

Pet02.   Peterka, R.J.: Sensorimotor Integration in Human Postural Control. J. Neurophysiol. **88**, 1097-1118, (2002)

Pol91.   Pollack, J.B.: The induction of dynamical recognizers. Mach. Learn., **7**, 227-252, (1991)

Pow04.   Powers, W.T.: File inverted_pendulum.pdf, from www. livingcontrolsystems.com, (2004)

Pow05.   Powers, W.T.: Behavior: the control of perception, Benchmark Publications Inc., New Canaan, (2005)

Pow11.   Powers, W.T.: The neglected phenomenon of negative feedback control, in: D. Forssell (Ed.), Perceptual Control Theory, Science and Applications, (2011)

Pow15.   Powell, K.: Nvidia devtech blog post, (2015); `https://blogs.nvidia.com/blog/2015/03/17/digits-devbox/`

Pow73a.   Powers, W.T.: Feedback: beyond behaviorism, Science **179**, 351-356, (1973)

Pow73b.   Powers, W.T.: Behaviorism and feedback control, Science **181**, 1118-1120, (1973)

Pro01.   Proakis, J.G.: Digital Communications (4th edn.) McGraw-Hill, New York, (2001)

QS14.   Qi, J., Sun, K.: Power system dynamic state estimation by unscented Kalman filter with guaranteed positive semidefinite state covariance, arXiv:[cs.IT]1405.6426, (2014)

Que12.   QUEST: QUantum Electron Simulation Toolbox (a FORTRAN 90/95 package), (2012), including: Elementary Introduction to the Hubbard Model by R. Scalettar *et al.* UCD, (2012); Numerical methods for Quantum Monte Carlo Simulations of the Hubbard Model by Z. Bai *et al.*; and QUEST User's Manual.

RAG04.   Ristic, B., Arulampalam, S., Gordon, N.: Beyond the Kalman Filter. Artech House, (2004)

RBA13.   Ragan-Kelley, J., Barnes, C., Adams, A. *et al.*: Halide: A language and compiler for optimizing parallelism, locality, and recomputation in image processing pipelines. ACM SIGPLAN Notices, **48**(6), 519-530, (2013); `http://people.csail.mit.edu/fredo/tmp/Halide-5min.pdf`

RDS15.   Russakovsky, O., Deng, J., Su, H. *et al.*: ImageNet Large Scale Visual Recognition Challenge, Int. J. Computer Vision (IJCV), **115**(3), 211-252, (2015)

RE12.   Rakitianskaia, A.S., Engelbrecht, A.P.: Training feedforward neural networks with dynamic particle swarm optimisation, Swarm Intel. **6**(3), 233-270, (2012)

RH06.   Richards A., How, J.: Robust stable model predictive control with constraint tightening. In Proc. 2006 Amer. Control Conf., (2006)

RHW86. Rumelhart, D.E., Hinton, G.E., Williams, R.J.: Learning representations by back-propagating errors. Nature **323**(6088), 533-536, (1986)

RHW88. Rumelhart, D.E., Hinton, G.E., Williams, R.J.: Learning representations by back-propagating errors. Cognitive modeling, **5**, 3, (1988); http://www.cs.toronto.edu/~hinton/absps/naturebp.pdf

RHZ85. Rempel, J.K., Holmes, J.G., Zanna, M.P.: Trust in close relationships. Journal of Personality and Social Psychology, **49**(1), 95-112, (1985)

RP99.   Riesenhuber, M., Poggio, T.: Are cortical models really bound by the 'Binding Problem'? Neuron, **24**, 87-93, (1999)

RPC06. Ranzato, M., Poultney, C., Chopra, S., LeCun, Y.: Efficient learning of sparse representations with an energy-based model. In Advances in Neural Information Processing Systems (NIPS 2006). MIT Press, (2006)

RRW11. Recht, B., Re, C., Wright, S., Niu, F.: Hogwild: A lock-free approach to parallelizing stochastic gradient descent. In Advances in Neural Information Processing Systems, 693-701, (2011); http://papers.nips.cc/paper/4390-hogwild-a-lock-free-approach-to-parallelizing-stochastic-gradient-descent

RSE06. Rolls, E.T., Stringer, S.M., Elliot, T.: Entorhinal cortex grid cells can map to hippocampal place cells by competitive learning, Network **17**, 447-65, (2006)

RYC13. Rossbach, C.J., Yu, Y., Currey, J., Martin, J.-P., Fetterly, D.: Dandelion: a compiler and runtime for heterogeneous systems. In Proc. 24th ACM Symposium on Operating Systems Principles, 49-68. ACM, (2013); http://research-srv.microsoft.com/pubs/201110/sosp13-dandelion-final.pdf

Ran85. Ranck, J.B.: Electrical Activity of the Archicortex (eds. Buzsaki, G. & Vanderwolf, C. H.) 217-220, Akademiai Kiado, Budapest, (1985)

Rei98. O'Reilly, R.C.: Six principles for biologically based computational models of cortical cognition. Trends Cog. Sci. **2**, 455-462, (1998)

Rey03. Reyes, A.: Synchrony-dependent propagation of firing rate in iteratively constructed networks in vitro. Nature Neurosci. **6**, 593-599, (2003)

Rha84. de Rham, G.: Differentiable Manifolds. Springer, Berlin, (1984)

Rob65. Robinson, J.A.: A Machine Oriented Logic Based on the Resolution Principle. J. Assoc. Comput. **12**(1), 23-41, (1965)

Rob79. Robinson, J.A.: Logic: Form and Function. North-Holland, New York, (1979)

Ros58. Rosenblatt, F.: The Perceptron: a probabilistic model for information storage and organization in the brain. Psych. Review, **65**(6), 386-408, (1958)

SA09.   Steiner, N., Athanas, P.: Hardware autonomy and space systems. In Aerospace conference, 2009 IEEE, 1-13, (2009)

SB89.   Sastry, S., Bodson, M.: Adaptive Control: Stability, Convergence and Robustness, Prentice-Hall, Englewood Cliffs, NJ, (1989)

SB98.   Sutton, R.S., Barto, A.G.: Reinforcement Learning: An Introduction. MIT Press, Cambridge, MA, (1998)

SBF01.   Schulz, D., Burgard, W., Fox, D., Cremers, A.: Tracking multiple mov-
          ing targets with a mobile robot using particles filters and statistical data
          association. Proc. ICRA-01, (2001)
SCS11.   Scholz, J.B., Calbert, G.J., Smith, G.A.: Unravelling Bueno De
          Mesquita's group decision model, J. Theor. Politics, **23**(4), 510-531,
          (2011)
SD12.   Syme, D., Granicz, A. Cisternino, A.: Expert F# 3.0 (3rd Ed.), Apress
          Pub. (2012)
SDV06.   Shi, Y., Duan, L., Vidal, G.: Classical simulation of quantum many-
          body systems with a tree tensor network, Phys. Rev. A **74**, 022320,
          (2006)
SFG15.   Stachniss, C., Frese, U., Grisetti, G.: OpenSLAM, (2015); https://
          openslam.org/
SGN03.   Schön, T., Gustafsson, F., Nordlund, P.-J.: Marginalized Particle Fil-
          ters for Nonlinear State-space Models, Tec. Report LiTH-ISY-R-2548,
          Linköping Univ. (2003)
SGN05.   Schön, T., Gustafsson, F., Nordlund, P.-J.: Marginalized particle filters
          for mixed linear/nonlinear state-space models, IEEE Trans. Sig. Proc,
          53(7), 2279-2289, (2005)
SGN05.   Schön, T.B., Gustafsson, F., Nordlund, P.-J.: Marginalized Particle Fil-
          ters for Mixed Linear/Nonlinear State-Space Models, IEEE Trans. Sig.
          Proc. **53**(7), 2279-2289, (2005)
SHG14.   Shen, Y., He, X., Gao, J., Deng, L., Mesnil, G.: Learning semantic
          representations using convolutional neural networks for web search. In
          Proc. 23rd international conference on World wide web companion, 373-
          374. Int. World Wide Web Conf. Steering Committee, (2014)
SHO14.   Sartoretti, G., Hongler, M.-O., de Oliveira, M.-E., Mondada, F.: De-
          centralized self-selection of swarm trajectories: from dynamical systems
          theory to robotic implementation, Swarm Intel. **8**(4), 329-351, (2014)
SI89.   Sastri, S.S., Isidori, A.: Adaptive control of linearizable systems, IEEE
          Trans. Aut. Con. **34**(11), 1123-1131, (1989)
SJ04.   Spector, M.D., Jones, G.E.: Trust in the workplace: Factors affecting
          trust formation between team members. Journal of Social Psychology,
          144(3), 311-321, (2004)
SJ72.   Stengel, R.F.: Optimal Control and Estimation. Dover, London, (1994)
SJ72.   Sussmann, H., Jurdjevic, V.: Controllability of nonlinear systems. J.
          Diff. 12, 95-116, (1972)
SKG06.   Schön, T., Karlsson, R., Gustafsson, F.: The marginalized particle filter
          in practice, Proc. IEEE Aerospace Conf. Big Sky, MT, (2006)
SL03.   Stevens, B.L., Lewis, F.L.: Aircraft Control and Simulation (2nd ed.).
          Wiley, Hoboken, NJ, (2003)
SLD15.   Schön, T.B., Lindsten, F., Dahlin, J. et al.: Sequential Monte Carlo
          methods for system identification, In Proc. 17th IFAC Symp. Sys. Ident.
          SYSID, (2015)
SLJ14.   Szegedy, C., Liu, W., Jia, Y. et al.: Going deeper with convolutions. In
          CVPR'2015, 2015; arXiv:1409.4842, (2014)
SLJ15.   Szegedy, C., Liu, W., Jia, Y. et al.: Going Deeper with Convolutions,
          CVPR, (2015)
SM13.   van der Schaft, A.J., Maschke, B.M.: Port-Hamiltonian systems on
          graphs, SIAM J. Con. Opt. **51**(2), 906-937, (2013)

SM97.   Samsonovich, A., McNaughton, B.L.: Path integration and cognitive mapping in a continuous attractor neural network model, J. Neurosci. **17**, 5900-5920, (1997)

SM98.   Scokaert, P.O., Mayne, D.Q.: Min-max feedback model predictive control for constrained linear systems. IEEE Transactions on Automatic Control **43**(8), 1136-1142, (1998)

SMD13.   Sutskever, I., Martens, J., Dahl, G.E., Hinton, G.E.: On the importance of initialization and momentum in deep learning. In Proc. 30th Int. Conf. Machine Learning (ICML-13), 1139-1147. JMLR Workshop and Conference Proceedings, (2013); http://jmlr.org/proceedings/papers/v28/sutskever13.pdf

SME06.   Solstad, T., Moser, E.I., Einevoll, G.T.: From grid cells to place cells: a mathematical model, Hippocampus **16**, 1026-31, (2006)

SMO02.   Spooner, J.T., Maggiore, M., Ordonez, R., Passino, K.M.: Stable Adaptive Control and Estimation for Nonlinear Systems: Neural and Fuzzy Approximator Techniques. Wiley, New York, (2002)

SN10.   Smola, A., Narayanamurthy, S.: An architecture for parallel topic models. Proc. VLDB Endow., **3**(1-2), 703-710, (2010); http://vldb.org/pvldb/vldb2010/papers/R63.pdf

SPS12.   Song, J., Phong, D.H., Sturm, J.: Complex Monge-Ampere equations, Surv. Dif. Geo. 17, 327-411, (2012)

SPS99.   Shimokawa, T., Pakdaman, K., Sato, S.: Time-scale matching in the response of a leaky integrate-and-fire neuron model to periodic stimulus with additive noise. Phys. Rev. E **59**, 3427-3443, (1999)

SR14.   Swingle, B., van Raamsdonk, M.: Universality of Gravity from Entanglement, arXiv:1405.2933, (2014)

SRK98.   Schäfer, C., Rosenblum, M.G., Kurths, J., Abel, H.-H.: Heartbeat Synchronized with Ventilation. Nature **392**, 239-240, (1998)

SS01.   Scholkopf, B., Smola, A.: Leaning with Kernels. MIT Press, Cambridge, MA, (2001)

SS05.   Sabater, J., Sierra, C.: Review on computational trust and reputation models. Artificial Intelligence Review, **24**(1), 33-60, (2005)

SV07.   Sandvik, A.W., Vidal, G.: Variational Quantum Monte Carlo Simulations with Tensor-Network States, Phys. Rev. Lett. **99**, 220602, (2007)

SV09.   Selinger, P., Valiron, B.: Quantum lambda calculus. In: Semantic Techniques in Quantum Computation, (Eds. S. Gay, I. Mackie), Cambridge Univ. Press, pp. 135-172, (2009)

SVI15.   Szegedy, C., Vanhoucke, V., Ioffe, S., Shlens, J., Wojna, Z.: Rethinking the inception architecture for computer vision. CoRR, abs/1512.00567, (2015)

SVL14.   Sutskever, I., Vinyals, O., Le, Q.V.: Sequence to sequence learning with neural networks. In NIPS, (2014); http://papers.nips.cc/paper/5346-sequence-to-sequence-learning-with-neural

SVM10.   Silvi, P., Giovannetti, V., Montangero, S., Rizzi, M., Cirac, J.I., Fazio, R.: Homogeneous binary trees as ground states of quantum critical Hamiltonians, Phys. Rev. A **81**, 062335, (2010)

SW49.   Shannon, C.E., Weaver, W.: The Mathematical Theory of Communication. Univ. Illinois Press, Chicago, IL, (1949)

SWV08. Schuch, N., Wolf, M.M., Verstraete, F., Cirac, J.I.: Simulation of Quantum Many-Body Systems with Strings of Operators and Monte Carlo Tensor Contractions, Phys. Rev. Lett. **100**, 040501, (2008)

SZ14. Simonyan, K., Zisserman, A.: Very deep convolutional networks for large-scale image recognition, arXiv:1409.1556, (2014)

Sab03. Sabry, A.: Modeling quantum computing in Haskell, in Proc. Haskell '03, ACM SIGPLAN Haskell, (2003)

Sar06. Sargolini, F. *et al.*: Conjunctive representation of position, direction and velocity in the medial entorhinal cortex. Science **312**, 758-762, (2006)

Sar13. Särkkä, S.: Bayesian Filtering and Smoothing. Cambridge Univ. Press, Cambridge, UK, (2013)

Sat09. Simon, H.: Guru, all latest updates. The Economist, March (2009); http://www.economist.com/node/13350892

Sat14. Wikipedia: Satisficing, viewed Nov. (2014); https://en.wikipedia.org/wiki/Satisficing

Sch00. van der Schaft, A.J.: L_2-Gain and Passivity Techniques in Nonlinear Control. Springer Communications and Control Engineering series. Springer-Verlag, London, 2nd revised and enlarged edition, (2000)

Sch01. Schuster, H.G.: Complex Adaptive Systems: An Introduction. Scator, (2001)

Sch06. van der Schaft, A.J.: Port-Hamiltonian systems: an introductory survey. In Proc. Inte. Congress of Mathematicians, **3**, 1339-1365, Madrid, (2006)

Sch06. van der Schaft, A.J.: Port-Hamiltonian systems: an introductory survey, in: Proc. Int. Con. Math., Madrid, Spain, (2006)

ST99. Scalettar, R.T., Trivedi, N., Huscroft, C.: Quantum Monte Carlo Study of the Disordered Attractive Hubbard Model, Phys. Rev. B **59**, 4364-4375 (1999)

Sch13. Schmidhuber, J.: My First Deep Learning System of 1991 + Deep Learning Timeline 1962-2013, arXiv:1312.5548, (2013)

Sch14. Schmidhuber, J.: Deep Learning in Neural Networks: An Overview, Technical Report IDSIA-03-14 / arXiv:1404.7828, (2014)

Sch91. Schmidhuber, J.: Neural sequence chunkers. Tec. Report FKI-148-91, Institut für Informatik, Technische Universität München, (1991)

Sch95. Schumacher, B.: Quantum coding, Phys. Rev. **A51**(4), 2738-2747, (1995)

Sch99. van der Schaft, A.J.: The Mathematics of Systems and Control, From Intelligent Control to Behavioral Systems, chapter Interconnection and Geometry, 203-218. eds. J.W. Polderman, H.L. Trentelman. Uny. Groningen, Netherlands, (1999)

Sel13. Selinger, P.: Quantum circuits of T-depth one, Phys. Rev. **A87**, 042302, (2013)

Sel15. Selinger, P.: Generators and relations for n-qubit Clifford operators, Log. Meth. Comp. Sci. **11**(2:10), 1-17, (2015)

Ser14. Service, R.F.: The brain chip, Science **345**(619), 614-668, (Aug. 2014)

Sha48. Shannon, C.E.: A mathematical theory of communication, Bell Syst. Tec. J. **27**, 379-423, (1948)

Sil64. Silverman, J.: Scanning-control mechanism and 'cognitive filtering' in paranoid and non-paranoid schizophrenia, J. Consult. Psych. (APS) **28**(5), 385-393, (1964)

Smi16.   Smith, R.E.: Idealisations of Uncertainty, and Lessons from Artificial In-
            telligence, Economics: The Open-Access, Open-Assessment E-Journal,
            10, 20017-7, (2016)

Soa16.   Soare, R.I.: Turing Computability: Theory and Applications, Springer,
            New York, (2016)

Sin09a.   Singer, P.W.: Attack of the Military Drones. The Brookings In-
            titute, Jun. (2009); `http://www.brookings.edu/research/opinions/`
            `2009/06/27-drones-singer`

Sin09b.   Singer, P.W.: Wired for War: The robotics revolution and conflict in
            the twenty-first century. Penguin.com, (2009)

Smo86.   Smolensky, P.: Information processing in dynamical systems: Founda-
            tions of harmony theory. In Rumelhart, D. E. and McClelland, J. L.,
            editors, Parallel Distributed Processing: Volume 1: Foundations,
            pp. 194-281. MIT Press, Cambridge, MA, (1986)

Sod94.   Soderkvist, J.: Micromachined gyroscopes. Sensors and Actuators A,
            43, 65-71, (1994)

Son99.   Sontag, E.D.: Mathematical Control Theory: Deterministic Finite Di-
            mensional Systems (2nd ed.) Springer, (1999)

Spo09.   Sporns, O.: From complex networks to intelligent systems. In Send-
            hoff, B., Krner, E., Sporns, O, Ritter, H., Doya, K. (eds), Creating
            Brain-Like Intelligence, Lecture Notes in Computer Science **5436**, 15-
            30. Springer, Berlin, Heidelberg, (2009); `http://dx.doi.org/10.1007/`
            `978-3-642-00616-6_2`

Sre93.   Srednicki, M.: Entropy and area, Phys. Rev. Lett. **71**, 666 (1993); Riera,
            A., Latorre, J.I.: Area law and vacuum reordering in harmonic networks,
            Phys. Rev. A **74**, 052326, (2006)

Sta09.   Stanford: Intuitionistic Logic, Stanford Encyclopedia of Phylosophy.
            Stanford Univ, (2009)

Sta15.   Starr, M.: Physicists prove Einstein's 'spooky' quantum entanglement,
            CNET Sci-Tech, November 19, (2015)

Sto36.   Stone, M.H.: The theory of representations for Boolean algebras, Trans.
            Amer. Math. Soc. **40**, 37-111, (1936)

Stu99.   Stuart, J.: Calculus (4th ed.). Brooks/Cole Publ. Pacific Grove, CA,
            (1999)

Swi75.   Switzer, R.K.: Algebraic Topology - Homology and Homotopy. Springer,
            New York, (1975)

TBF98.   Thrun, S., Burgard, W., Fox, D: A probabilistic approach to concurrent
            mapping and localization for mobile robots. Mach. Learn. Auton. Rob.
            (joint issue), **31**(5), 1-25, (1998)

TC99.   Teixeira, F.L., Chew, W.C.: Lattice electromagnetic theory from a topo-
            logical viewpoint, J. Math. Phys. **40**, 169-187, (1999)

TEV09.   Tagliacozzo, L., Evenbly, G., Vidal, G.: Simulation of two-dimensional
            quantum systems using a tree tensor network that exploits the entropic
            area law, Phys. Rev. B **80**, 235127, (2009)

TFB00.   Thrun, S., Fox, D., Burgard, W., Dellaert, F.: Robust monte carlo lo-
            calization for mobile robots. Art. Intel. Mag. **128** (1-2), (2000)

TI99.   Taiji, M., Ikegami, T.: Dynamics of internal models in game players.
            Physica D, **134**, 253-266, (1999)

TKK00.   Tanaka, T., Kakiya, S., Kabashima, Y.: Capacity Analysis of Bidirectional Associative Memory. In Proc. Seventh Int. Conf. Neural Information Processing, Vol. 2, 779-784, Taejon, Korea, (2000)

TKK10.   Tsubota, M., Kasamatsu, K, Kobayashi, M.: Quantized vortices in superfluid helium and atomic Bose-Einstein condensates, arXiv: cond-mat.quant-gas 1004.5458v2, (2010)

TLO97.   Tanaka, H.A., Lichtenberg, A.J., Oishi, S.: Self-synchronization of coupled oscillators with hysteretic response. Physica D $\mathbf{100}$, 279, (1997)

TMK04.   Thrun, S., Montemerlo, M., Koller, D., Wegbreit, B. Nieto, J., Nebot, E.: FastSLAM: An efficient solution to the simultaneous localization and mapping problem with unknown data association, JMLR, (2004)

TNT14.   TNTgo!: Tensor Network Theory library, Oxford Univ., (2014)

TPJ06.   Teacy, W.T.L., Patel, J., Jennings, N.R., Luck, M.: Travos: Trust and Reputation in the Context of Inaccurate Information Sources. Autonomous Agents & Multi-Agent Systems, $\mathbf{12}(2)$, 183-198, (2006)

TS09.   Törnqvist, D., Schön, T., Karlsson, R., Gustafsson, F.: Particle Filter SLAM with High Dimensional Vehicle Model, J. Intel. Rob. Sys. $\mathbf{55}$(4-5), 249-266, (2009)

TS85.   Takagi, T., Sugeno, M.: Fuzzy identifcation of systems and its applications to modeling and control, IEEE Trans. Sys. Man. Cyber. $\mathbf{15}(1)$, 116-132, (1985)

Ter10.   Terzi, A.: Keynes's Uncertainty is Not About White or Black Swans, J. Post-Keynesian Economics, $\mathbf{42}(4)$, 559-566, (2010)

TS95.   Tsodyks, M., Sejnowski, T.: Associative memory and hippocampal place cells, Int. J. Neural Syst. $\mathbf{6}$, S81-S86, (1995)

TSL00.   Tenenbaum, J.B., de Silva, V., Langford, J.C.: A global geometric framework for nonlinear dimensionality reduction. Science $\mathbf{290}$, 2319-2323, (2000)

TW01.   Tanaka, K., Wang, H.O.: Fuzzy Control Systems Design and Analysis. Wiley, New York, (2001)

TYR14.   Taigman, Y., Yang, M., Ranzato, M.A., Wolf, L.: DeepFace: Closing the Gap to Human-Level Performance in Face Verification. In CVPR '14: Proc. 2014 IEEE Conf. Computer Vision and Pattern Recognition. IEEE Computer Society, (2014)

Tai10.   Taibi, T.: Incorporating trust into the BDI architecture. International Journal of Artificial Intelligence and Soft Computing, $\mathbf{2}(3)$, 223-230, (2010)

Ter05.   Terrazas, A. et al.: Self-motion and the hippocampal spatial metric. J. Neurosci. $\mathbf{25}$, 8085-8096, (2005)

Tha05.   Thaller, B.: Visual Quantum Mechanics, Springer, 1999; Ibid. Advanced Visual Quantum Mechanics, Springer, (2005)

Thr00.   Thrun, S.: Probabilistic algorithms in robotics. AI Magazine, $\mathbf{21}(4)$, 93-109, (2000)

Thr02.   Thrun, S.: Particle Filters in Robotics, Invited talk, Proc. UAI-02, 511-518, (2002)

Thr02.   Thrun, S.: Robotic mapping: A survey. Tech. Report CMU-CS-02-111, Carnegie Mellon Univ. (2002)

Tim93.   Timmermann, A.: How Learning in Financial Markets Generates Excess Volatility and Predictability in Stock Stock Prices, Quarterly J. of Economics, $\mathbf{108}$, (1993)

Tod89.   Toda, M.: Theory of Nonlinear Lattices (2nd ed.), Springer Berlin, (1989)

Tol48.   Tolman, E.C.: Cognitive maps in rats and men. Psychol. Rev. **55**, 189-208, (1948)

Ton04.   van Tonder, A.: A Lambda Calculus for Quantum Computation, SIAM J.Comput. **33**, 1109-1135, (2004)

Tsu06.   Tsubota, M.: Quantized vortices in superfluid helium and Bose-Einstein condensates, J. Physics: Conf. Ser. **31**, 88-94, (2006)

Tur53.   Turing A.M.: The chemical basis of morphogenesis. Phil. Trans. R. Soc. B **237**, 37-72 (1953); reprinted in Bull. Math. Biol. **52**, 153-197, (1990)

Twe12.   Tweedale, J.W.: Using Mutli-Agent Systems to Improve the Level of Autonomy for Operators Controlling Unmanned Vehicles. In Frontiers in Artificial Intelligence and Applications, Advances in Knowledge-Based and Intelligent Information and Engineering Systems **243**, 1666-1675. IOS Press, (2012)

Ume93.   Umezawa, H.: Advanced Field Theory: Micro, Macro, and Thermal Physics. American Institue of Physics, (1993)

VC04.   Verstraete, F., Cirac, J.I.: Renormalization algorithms for Quantum-Many Body Systems in two and higher dimensions, arXiv:cond-mat/0407066, (2004)

VC10.   Verstraete, F., Cirac, J.I.: Continuous Matrix Product States for Quantum Fields, Phys. Rev. Lett. **104**, 190405, (2010)

VKK14.   Vinyals, O., Kaiser, L., Koo, T. *et al.*: Grammar as a foreign language. Tech. report, arXiv:1412.7449, (2014)

VPK15.   Verma, A., Pedrosa, L., Korupolu, M. *et al.*: Large-scale cluster management at Google with Borg. In Proc 10 European Conf. Computer Systems, p. 18. ACM, (2015); `http://research.google.com/pubs/archive/43438.pdf`

VZ12.   Vicsek, T., Zafeiris, A.: Collective motion, Phys. Rep. **517**, 71-140, (2012)

Vap95.   Vapnik, V.: The Nature of Statistical Learning Theory. Springer, New York, (1995)

Vap98.   Vapnik, V.: Statistical Learning Theory. Wiley, New York, (1998)

Ver11.   Verbitsky, M.: Hodge theory on nearly Kähler manifolds, arXiv:math/0510618 [math.DG], (2011)

Vid03.   Vidal, G.: Efficient Classical Simulation of Slightly Entangled Quantum Computations, Phys. Rev. Lett. **91**, 147902, (2003)

Vid04.   Vidal, G.: Efficient Simulation of One-Dimensional Quantum Many-Body Systems, Phys. Rev. Lett. **939**, 040502, (2004)

Vid07a.   Vidal, G.: Classical Simulation of Infinite-Size Quantum Lattice Systems in One Spatial Dimension, Phys. Rev. Lett. **98**, 070201 (2007); R. Orús, G. Vidal, Infinite time-evolving block decimation algorithm beyond unitary evolution, Phys. Rev. B **78**, 155117, (2008)

Vid07b.   Vidal, G.: Entanglement Renormalization, Phys. Rev. Lett. **99**, 220405 (2007)

Vid10.   Vidal, G.: Entanglement Renormalization: An Introduction, In the book Understanding Quantum Phase Transitions, edited by Lincoln D. Carr, Taylor & Francis, Boca Raton, (2010)

Voi02.   Voisin, C.: Hodge Theory and Complex Algebraic Geometry I. Cambridge Univ. Press, Cambridge, (2002)

Vol31.   Volterra, V.: Variations and fluctuations of the number of individuals in animal species living together, in Animal Ecology. McGraw-Hill, New York, (1931)

WB95.   Welch, G., Bishop, G.: An Introduction to the Kalman Filter. Univ. North Carolina, Dep. Comp. Sci., TR 95-041, (1995)

WBK98.   Whitener, E.M., Brodt, S.E., Korsgaard, M.A., Werner, J.M.: Managers as Initiators of Trust: An exchange relationship framework for understanding managerial trustworthy behavior. Academy of Management Review, **23**(3), 513-530, (1998)

WDH15.   Wallach, I., Dzamba, M., Heifets, A.: Atomnet: A deep convolutional neural network for bioactivity prediction in structure-based drug discovery. arXiv:1510.02855, (2015)

WK01.   Wells, C.V., Kipnis, D.: Trust, dependency, and control in the contemporary organization. Journal of Business and Psychology, **15**(4), 593-603, (2001)

WM06.   Witter, M.P., Moser, E.I.: Spatial representation and the architecture of the entorhinal cortex, Trends Neurosci. **29**, 671-78, (2006)

WM93.   Wilson, M.A., McNaughton, B.L.: Dynamics of the hippocampal ensemble code for space, Science **261**, 1055-1058, (1993)

WPP94.   Wiesenfeld, K., Pierson, D., Pantazelou, E., Dames, C., Moss, F: Stochastic resonance on a circle. Phys. Rev. Lett. **72**, 2125-2129, (1994)

Wal84.   Wald, R.M.: General Relativity, Univ. Chicago Press, (1984)

Wal94.   Wald, R.M.: Quantum Field Theory in Curved Spacetime and Black Hole Thermodynamics. Univ. Chicago Press, (1994)

Wan96.   Wang, Z.: A Bidirectional Associative Memory Based on Optimal Linear Associative Memory. IEEE Trans. Comp. **45**(10), 1171-1179, (1996)

Wat90.   Watson, L.T.: Globally convergent homotopy algorithms for nonlinear systems of equations. Nonlinear Dynamics, **1**, 143-191, (1990)

Wat99.   Watts, D.J.: Small Worlds: The Dynamics of Networks Between Order and Randomness. Princeton Univ. Press, Princeton, NY, (1999)

Wel01.   Wells, C.V.: Trust, gender, and race in the workplace. Journal of Social Behavior and Personality, **16**(1), 115-126, (2001)

Wer74.   Werbos, P.J.: Beyond Regression: New Tools for Prediction and Analysis in the Behavioral Sciences. PhD thesis, Harvard University, (1974)

Wer89.   Werbos, P.J.: Backpropagation and neurocontrol: A review and prospectus. In IEEE/INNS Int. Joint Conf. Neu. Net., Washington, D.C., vol. 1, 209-216, (1989)

Wer90.   Werbos, P.: Backpropagation through time: what it does and how to do it. Proc. IEEE, **78** (10), (1990)

Whi92a.   White, S.R.: Density matrix formulation for quantum renormalization groups, Phys. Rev. Lett. **69**, 2863-2866, (1992)

Whi92b.   White, S.R.: Density-matrix algorithms for quantum renormalization groups, Phys. Rev. B **48**, 10345, (1992)

Wie48.   Wiener, N.: Cybernetics, or Control and Communication in the Animal and the Machine. MIT Press, Cambridge, MA, (1948)

Wer09.   Werndl, C.: What Are the New Implications of Chaos for Unpredictability?, British J. Phil. Sci. **60**(1), (2009)

Wik16a.   Wikipedia: Competitive LotkaVolterra equations, (2016)
            http://en.wikipedia.org/wiki/Competitive_Lotka%E2%80%
            93Volterra_equations

Wik16b.   Wikipedia: BRST quantization, (2016); https://en.wikipedia.org/
           wiki/BRST_quantization
Wik16c.   Wikipedia: Big data, (2016); https://en.wikipedia.org/wiki/Big_
           data
Wik16d.   Wikipedia: Quantum entanglement, (2016); https://en.wikipedia.
           org/wiki/Quantum_entanglement
Wik16e.   Wikipedia: Classical Heisenberg model, (2016); https://en.
           wikipedia.org/wiki/Classical_Heisenberg_model
Wik16f.   Wikipedia: Internet of things, (2016); https://en.wikipedia.org/
           wiki/Internet_of_things
Wik16g.   Wikipedia: Ising model, (2016); https://en.wikipedia.org/wiki/
           Ising_model
Wik16h.   Wikipedia: Perceptual control theory, (2016)
           http://en.wikipedia.org/wiki/Perceptual_control_theory
Wik16i.   Wikipedia: Cybernetics, (2016)
           http://en.wikipedia.org/wiki/Cybernetics
Wik16j.   Wikipedia: Inverted pendulum, (2016)
           http://en.wikipedia.org/wiki/Inverted_pendulum
Wik16k.   Wikipedia: Abstract index notation, (2016)
Wik16l.   Wikipedia: Bayesian network, (2016); http://en.wikipedia.org/
           wiki/Bayesian_network
Wik16m.   Wikipedia: Bayesian programming, (2016); http://en.wikipedia.org/
           wiki/Bayesian_programming
Wik16n.   Wikipedia: Bayes' theorem, (2016); http://http://en.wikipedia.
           org/wiki/Bayes'_theorem
Wik16o.   Wikipedia: Cyber-physical system, (2016); https://en.wikipedia.
           org/wiki/Cyber-physical_system
Wik16p.   Wikipedia: Deep Learning, (2016); http://en.wikipedia.org/wiki/
           Deep_learning
Wik16r.   Wikipedia: Embodied cognition, (2016); https://en.wikipedia.org/
           wiki/Embodied_cognition
Wik16s.   Wikipedia: Quantum entanglement, (2016); https://en.wikipedia.
           org/wiki/Quantum_entanglement
Wik16t.   Wikipedia: Principle of maximum entropy, (2016); http://http://en.
           wikipedia.org/wiki/Principle_of_maximum_entropy
Wik16u.   Wikipedia: Hidden Markov model, (2016); http://en.wikipedia.org/
           wiki/Hidden_Markov_model
Wik16v.   Wikipedia, Hadamard transform, (2016); https://en.wikipedia.org/
           wiki/Hadamard_transform
Wik16w.   Wikipedia: Hilbert space, (2016); https://en.wikipedia.org/wiki/
           Hilbert_space
Wik16x.   Wikipedia: Markov chain Monte Carlo, (2016); http://en.wikipedia.
           org/wiki/Markov_chain_Monte_Carlo
Wik16y.   Wikipedia: Markov chain, (2016); http:en.wikipedia.org/wiki/
           Markov_chain
Wik16z.   Wikipedia: Model predictive control, (2016); http://en.wikipedia.
           org/wiki/Model_predictive_control
Wik16aa.   Wikipedia: Nonlinear Schrödinger equation, (2016)
Wik16bb.   Wikipedia: Quantum computing, (2016); https://en.wikipedia.org/
           wiki/Quantum_computing

Wik16cc.   Wikipedia: Qubit, (2016); https://en.wikipedia.org/wiki/Qubit
Wik16dd.   Wikipedia: Simultaneous localization and mapping, (2016); http://en.
            wikipedia.org/wiki/Simultaneous_localization_and_mapping
Wik16ee.   Wikipedia: Tensor product, (2016); https://en.wikipedia.org/wiki/
            Tensor_product
Wik16ff.   Wikipedia: TOP500, (2016)
            http://en.wikipedia.org/wiki/TOP500
Wik16gg.   Wikipedia: Viterbi algorithm, (2016); http://en.wikipedia.org/
            wiki/Viterbi_algorithm
Wik16hh.   Wikipedia: Watson (computer), (2016); http://en.wikipedia.org/
            wiki/Watson_(computer)
Wik16ii.   Wikipedia: Holomorphic function, (2016)
Wik16jj.   Wikipedia: Hermitian manifold, (2016)
Wik16kk.   Wikipedia: Dolbeault cohomology, (2016)
Wik16ll.   Wikipedia: Runge-Kutta methods, (2016)
Wik16mm.   Wikipedia: Calabi conjecture, (2016)
Wis06.   Wise, D.K.: Lattice p-form electromagnetism and chain field theory,
            Class. Quantum Grav. **23**, 5129-5176, (2006)
XCQ12.   Xie, Z.Y., Chen, J., Qin, M.P., Zhu, J.W., Yang, L.P., Xiang, T.: Coarse-
            graining renormalization by higher-order singular value decomposition,
            Phys. Rev. B **86**, 045139, (2012)
XCY14.   Xie, Z.Y., Chen, J., Yu, J.F., Kong, X., Normand, B., Xiang, T.: Ten-
            sor Renormalization of Quantum Many-Body Systems Using Projected
            Entangled Simplex States, Phys. Rev. X **4**, 011025, (2014)
XJC09.   Xie, Z.Y., Jiang, H.C., Chen, Q.N., Weng, Z.Y., Xiang, T.: Sec-
            ond Renormalization of Tensor-Network States, Phys. Rev. Lett. **103**,
            160601, (2009)
XL04.   Xiong, L., Liu, L.: PeerTrust: Supporting reputation-based trust for
            peer-to-peer electronic communities. IEEE transactions on Knowledge
            and Data Engineering, **16**(7), 843-857, (2004)
XLS01.   Xiang, T., Lou, J., Su, Z.: Two-dimensional algorithm of the density-
            matrix renormalization group, Phys. Rev. B **64**, 104414 (2001); Plenio,
            M., Eisert, J., Dreißig, J., Cramer, M.: Entropy, Entanglement, and
            Area: Analytical Results for Harmonic Lattice Systems, Phys. Rev. Lett.
            94, 060503 (2005)
XXT12.   Xu, G., Xu, C., Tian, X., Zhang, L, Li, X., Li, W.: PSO-TPS: An optimal
            trust path selection algorithm based on particle swarm optimization in
            small world network. In Proceedings of the 2012 Second International
            Conference on Cloud and Green Computing CGC'12, 594-600, IEEE
            Computer Society, Washington, DC, USA, (2012)
YH16.   Yang, Y., Hospedales, T.: Deep Multi-task Representation Learning: A
            Tensor Factorisation Approach, arXiv:1605.06391, (2016)
YSL13.   Yu, H., Shen, Z., Leung, C., Miao, C., Lesser, V.R.: A survey of multi-
            agent trust management systems. IEEE Access, **1**, 35-50, (2013)
YU13.   Yartsev, M.M., Ulanovsky, N.: Representation of Three-Dimensional
            Space in the Hippocampus of Flying Bats, Science **340**(6130), 367-372,
            (April 2013)
Yan97.   Yang, J.: Classification of the solitary wave in coupled nonlinear
            Schrödinger equations. Physica D **108**, 92-112, (1997)

Yar13.   Yartsev, M.M.: Space Bats: Multidimensional Spatial Representation in the Bat, Science **342**(6158), 573-574, (November 2013)

Yau78.   Yau, S.T.: On the Ricci curvature of a compact Kähler manifold and the complex Monge-Ampere equation. Comm. Pure Appl. Math. **31**, 339-441, (1978)

Yua15.   Yuan, Y.: Recent advances in trust region algorithms. Mathematical Programming, **151**(1), 249-281, (2015)

ZCD12.   Zaharia, M., Chowdhury, M., Das, T. *et al.*: Resilient distributed datasets: A fault-tolerant abstraction for in-memory cluster computing. In Proceedings of the 9th USENIX conference on Networked Systems Design and Implementation. USENIX Association

ZCY09.   Zhang, Y., Chen, S., Yang, G.: SFTrust: A double trust metric based trust model in unstructured P2P system. In 2009 IEEE International Symposium on Parallel Distributed Processing, 1-7, May (2009)

ZF01.   Zhang, D., Foo, N.Y.: EPDL: a logic for causal reasoning, in Proceedings of the IJCAI 2001, 131-138, (2001)

ZF13.   Zeiler, M.D., Fergus, R.: Visualizing and Understanding Convolutional Networks. arXiv:1311.2901, (2013)

ZL04.   Ziegler, C.N., Lausen, G.: Spreading activation models for trust propagation. In IEEE International Conference on e-Technology, e-Commerce and e-Service, 2004. EEE'04, 83-97, (2004)

ZMN80.   Zakharov, V.E., Manakov, S.V., Novikov, S.P., Pitaevskii, L.P.: Soliton theory: inverse scattering method, Science, Moscow, (1980)

ZRM13.   Zeiler, M.D., Ranzato, M., Monga, R. *et al.*: On rectified linear units for speech processing. In ICASSP, (2013); `http://research.google.com/pubs/archive/40811.pdf`

ZWL02.   Zheng, F., Wang, Q-G., Lee, T.H.: Output tracking control of MIMO fuzzy nonlinear systems using variable structure control approach. IEEE Trans. Fuzzy Syst. **10**(6), 686-697, (2002)

ZXC10.   Zhao, H.H., Xie, Z.Y., Chen, Q.N., Wei, Z.C., Cai, J.W., Xiang, T.: Renormalization of tensor-network states, Phys. Rev. B **81**, 174411, (2010)

ZYZ13.   Zha, X., Yuan, C., Zhang, Y.: Generalized Criterion of Maximally Multi-Qubit Entanglement, Laser Phys. Lett. **10**, 045201, (2013)

Zac99.   Zacharia, G.: Collaborative reputation mechanisms for online communities. Master's thesis, Massachusetts Institute of Technology, (1999)

Zee03.   Zee, A.: Quantum Field Theory in a Nutshell, Princeton Univ. Press, (2003)

Zha96.   Zhang, K.: Representation of spatial orientation by the intrinsic dynamics of the head-direction cell ensemble: a theory, J. Neurosci. **16**, 2112-2126, (1996)

Zim95.   Zimmermann, H.-J. (Ed.): Fuzzy Logic and Intelligent Systems, Int. Series in Intelligent Technologies Vol. 3, Springer, (1995)

Index

Printed in the United States
By Bookmasters